Selected Currencies and Symbols

Country	Currency	Symbol	Country	Currency	Symbol
Afghanistan	Afghani	Af	Dominican Republic	peso	RD$
Albania	lek	lek	Ecuador	sucre	S/.
Algeria	dinar	DA	Egypt	pound	LE
Antigua and Barbuda	E.C. dollar	E.C.$	El Salvador	colon	C
Argentina	peso	Arg$	Fiji	dollar	F$
Australia	dollar	$A	Finland	markka	Fmk
Austria	schilling	S	France	franc	FF
Bahamas	dollar	B$	Germany	deutsche mark	DM
Bahrain	dinar	BD			
Barbados	dollar	BDS$	Greece	drachma	Dr
Belgium	franc	BF	Guatemala	quetzal	Q
Belize	dollar	BZ$	Honduras	lempira	L
Bermuda	dollar	Ber$	Hong Kong	dollar	HK$
Bolivia	boliviano	Bs	Hungary	forint	Ft
Botswana	pula	P	India	rupee	Rs
Brazil*	cruzeiro	Cr$	Indonesia	rupiah	Rp
Cambodia	riel	CR	Iran, Islamic Republic of	rial	Rls
Canada	dollar	$ or Can$	Ireland	pound	£ or £
Cayman Islands	dollar	C$	Israel	new sheqel	NIS
Chile	peso	Ch$	Italy	lira	Lit
China, People's Republic of**	yuan	Y	Jamaica	dollar	J$
			Japan	yen	¥
Colombia	peso	Col$	Kenya	shilling	K Sh
Costa Rica	colón	C	Korea, Republic of	won	W
Cyprus	pound	£ or C£	Kuwait	dinar	KD
Denmark	krone	DKr	Liberia	dollar	$

* Prior to 1989 Brazil's currency was the cruzado, Cz$.
**The currency is the renminbi, while the currency unit is the yuan.

Foundations of Multinational Financial Management

SECOND EDITION

Foundations of Multinational Financial Management

ALAN C. SHAPIRO, *University of Southern California*

ALLYN AND BACON

Boston London Toronto Sydney Tokyo Singapore

Editor-in-Chief, Business and Economics: *Rich Wohl*
Editorial Assistant: *Jennifer Strada*
Cover Administrator: *Linda Dickinson*
Manufacturing Buyer: *Megan Cochran*
Text Designer: *Sylvia Dovner, Technical Texts*
Editorial-Production Service: *Betty O'Bryant*
Cover Designer: *Susan Paradise*

Copyright © 1994, 1991 by Allyn and Bacon
A Division of Paramount Publishing
160 Gould Street
Needham Heights, Massachusetts 02194

Library of Congress Cataloging-in-Publication Data

Shapiro, Alan C.
   Foundations of multinational financial management / Alan C. Shapiro. — 2nd ed.
      p. cm.
   Includes bibliographical references and index.
   ISBN 0-205-15665-7
   1. International business enterprises—Finance. 2. Decision making. I. Title.
HG4027.5.S44 1993
658.15'99—dc20   93-5509
                                                                          CIP

Printed in the United States of America

10 9 8 7 6 5 4 3 2 1   98 97 96 95 94 93

To my brothers—Fred, Dan, and Robert—
for their love and friendship

Preface

APPROACH

The basic thrust of this second edition of *Foundations of Multinational Financial Management* is to provide a conceptual framework within which the key financial decisions of the multinational firm can be analyzed. As in the fourth edition of *Multinational Financial Management*, my more comprehensive book on this topic, the approach is to treat international financial management as a natural and logical extension of the principles learned in the foundations course in financial management. Thus, it builds on and extends the valuation framework provided by domestic corporate finance to account for dimensions unique to international finance.

Foundations focuses on decision making in an international context. Analytical techniques help translate the often vague rules of thumb used by international financial executives into specific decision criteria. The book offers a variety of real-life examples, both numerical and institutional, that demonstrate the use of financial analysis and reasoning in solving international financial problems. These examples have been culled from the thousands of illustrations of corporate practice that I have collected over the years from business periodicals and from my consulting experience. By scattering the best of these examples throughout the text, students can see the value of examining decision problems with the aid of a solid theoretical foundation. Seemingly disparate facts and events can then be interpreted as specific manifestations of more general financial principles.

All the traditional areas of corporate finance are explored, including working capital management, capital budgeting, cost of capital, and financial structure. However, this is done from the perspective of a multinational corporation, concentrating on those decision elements that are rarely, if ever, encountered by purely domestic firms. These elements include multiple currencies with frequent exchange rate changes and varying rates of inflation, differing tax systems, multiple money markets, exchange controls, segmented capital markets, and political risks such as nationalization or expropriation. Throughout the book, I have tried to demystify and simplify multinational financial management by showing that its basic principles rest on the same foundation as does corporate finance.

The emphasis throughout this book is on taking advantage of being multinational. Too often companies focus on the threats and risks inherent in venturing abroad rather than on the opportunities that are available to multinational firms. These opportunities include the ability to obtain a greater degree of international diversification than security purchases alone can provide as well as the ability to arbitrage between imperfect capital markets, thereby obtaining funds at a lower cost than could a purely domestic firm.

AUDIENCE

Foundations of Multinational Management is a briefer version of my other text, *Multinational Financial Management* (MFM). It emphasizes broad concepts and practices rather than extensive quantitative material. Compared to MFM, *Foundations* reduces the range and complexity of the subject matter covered. Although *Foundations* is intended primarily for an undergraduate audience, it is suitable for use in masters level courses where there is not enough time to cover the full range of topics dealt with in MFM or where the students do not have the necessary preparation for using MFM. It is also suitable for use in bank management and other executive development programs.

FEATURES

Foundations of Multinational Financial Management presumes a knowledge of basic corporate finance, economics, and algebra. However, it assumes no prior knowledge of international economics or international finance and is, therefore, self-contained in that respect. For those who are not familiar with *Multinational Financial Management,* here are some of the distinctive features that have led to its widespread adoption. These features have been incorporated and enhanced in *Foundations.*

Distinctive topic coverage includes the following:

— Role of expectations in determining exchange rates (Chapter 2)
— Use of the balance-of-payments framework to assess the economic links among nations (Chapter 4)
— Understanding of currency futures and options contracts (Chapter 6) and their use in exchange risk management (Chapter 9)
— Use of currency risk sharing in international contracts (Chapter 9)
— Identification of the economic, as opposed to accounting, aspects of foreign exchange risk (Chapter 10)
— Development of marketing and production strategies to cope with exchange risk (Chapter 11)
— Evaluation of foreign currency denominated debt (Chapter 12)
— Role of countertrade in financing international trade (Chapter 13)
— Costs and benefits of managing interaffiliate fund flows on a global basis (Chapter 15)
— Integration of tax management with financial management based on the Tax Reform Act of 1986 (Chapters 15 and 23)
— Understanding of the nature and consequences of international portfolio investment (Chapter 16)
— Development of global strategies of MNCs (Chapter 17)
— Assessment of the true profitability of a foreign operation (Chapter 18)
— Valuation of the growth options often associated with foreign investments (Chapter 18)
— Assessment of the cost of capital for foreign investments (Chapter 19)

— Understanding of political risk measurement and management (Chapter 20)
— Use of interest rate and currency swaps and LDC debt-equity swaps (Chapter 22)
— Design of a global financing strategy (Chapter 23)
— Discussion of new perspectives on the international debt crisis and country risk analysis (Chapter 25)
— Analysis of the August 1993 European currency crisis (Appendix A at the back of the book)

CHANGES TO THE SECOND EDITION

Changes that have been made to the second edition include the following:

— Extensive discussion of the September 1992 and August 1993 currency crises in the European Monetary System
— Extensive discussion of the changes in Mexico, including the North American Free Trade Agreement, and Latin America in recent years
— Addition of several cases including a comprehensive case on the financing and analysis of Euro Disneyland
— Update on Japanese banking and international risk-based capital standards
— Additional discussion of currency swaps
— Deletion of Chapter 20 on international tax planning
— Comparison of the cost of capital in Japan and the United States
— Discussion of how the Japanese financial system helps to reduce the costs of financial distress

The book also contains many new charts and illustrations of corporate practice that are designed to highlight specific techniques or teaching points. Again, the emphasis is on reinforcing and making more relevant the concepts developed in the body of each chapter. To make the text more suitable as a teaching vehicle, I have added numerous questions and problems at the ends of the chapters, most of which are based on up-to-date information and real-life situations.

PEDAGOGY

The pedagogical thrust of the book is greatly enhanced by including the following learning and teaching aids:

1. *Focus on Corporate Practice.* Throughout the text, there are numerous real-world examples and vignettes that provide actual applications of financial concepts and theories. They show how the issues, tools, and techniques discussed in the book are being applied to day-to-day financial decision making.

2. *Extensive Use of Examples and Illustrations.* Numerous short illustrations and examples of specific concepts and techniques are scattered throughout the body of most chapters.

3. *Lengthier Illustrations of Corporate Practice.* There are seven, longer illustrations of actual company practices, at the end of key chapters, that are designed to demonstrate different aspects of international financial management.

4. *Problems and Discussion Questions.* There are hundreds of realistic end-of-chapter questions and problems that offer practice in applying the concepts and theories being taught. Many of these questions and problems relate to actual situations and companies.

5. *Learning Objectives.* Each chapter opens with a statement of its action-oriented learning objectives. This statement enhances learning by previewing and guiding the reader's understanding of the materials that will be encountered in the chapter.

6. *Key Terms.* The introduction to each chapter also contains a list of key terms. Placing these terms at the beginning of the chapter gives readers added preparation for what is to come.

7. *Key Concepts.* Most pages contain one or two key ideas in the margins next to the point where these ideas appear in the text. Highlighting these key ideas serves as an effective study and review tool for students.

8. *Glossary.* The back of the book contains a Glossary that defines all the key terms appearing in the text.

9. *Supplements.* A complete set of ancillary materials is available for adopters of *Foundations* to supplement the text. These include the following:

— An *Instructor's Manual* with *Testbank* contains detailed solutions to the end-of-chapter questions and problems and tips for teaching each chapter. The *Testbank* contains over 160 additional questions and problems suitable for use in multiple choice exams. The *Testbank* is also available in computerized form as *The A & B Test Manager.*
— The *Lotus 1-2-3 Templates* are designed to solve a wide variety of international financial management problems. Problems in the text that can be solved using these templates are noted in the *Instructor's Manual.*
— A *Study Guide* written by Andrea L. DeMaskey, Villanova University, is available. The *Study Guide* contains detailed chapter outlines and a number of solved questions and problems.

THANKS

I have been greatly aided in developing *Foundations of Multinational Financial Management* by the helpful suggestions of the following reviewers: Robert Aubey, University of Wisconsin, Madison; James Baker, Kent State University; Donald T. Buck, Southern Connecticut State University; C. Edward Chang, Southwest Missouri State University; Jay Choi, Temple University; Robert C. Duvic, University of Texas at Austin; Janice Wickstead Jadlow, Oklahoma State University; Steve Johnson, University of Texas at El Paso; Boyden C. Lee, New Mexico State University; Marc Lars Lipson, Boston University; Dileep Mehta, Georgia State University; Margaret Moore, Franklin University; William Pugh, Auburn University; Bruce Seifert, Old Dominion University; Jay Sultan, Bentley College; Paul J. Swanson, Jr., University of Cincinnati; and Steve Wyatt, University of Cincinnati.

My family, especially my wife, Diane, as well as my mother and three brothers, has provided me (once again) with continual support and encouragement during the writing of this book. I appreciate the (usual) cheerfulness with which Diane and my children, Thomas and Kathryn, endured the many hours I spent writing the second edition of this text.

A.C.S.

Environment of International Financial Management

Introduction: Multinational Enterprise and Multinational Financial Management

1

> What is prudence in the conduct of every private family can scarce be folly in that of a great kingdom. If a foreign country can supply us with a commodity cheaper than we ourselves can make it, better buy it of them with some part of the produce of our own industry employed in a way in which we have some advantage.
>
> Adam Smith (1776)

CHAPTER LEARNING OBJECTIVES

- To explain why multinational corporations are the key players in international economic competition today
- To classify the three historical types of multinational corporation (MNC) and explain their motivations for international expansion
- To identify the stages of corporate expansion overseas by which companies gradually become MNCs
- To explain why managers of MNCs need to exploit rapidly changing global economic conditions and why political policymakers must also be concerned with the same changing conditions
- To describe the areas of financial flexibility and opportunity available to financial managers of MNCs for moving money and profits among their affiliated units to maximize overall corporate value and explain why these financial decisions may conflict with national objectives
- To identify the advantages of being multinational, including the benefits of international diversification
- To describe the general importance of financial economics to multinational financial management and the particular importance of the concepts of arbitrage, market efficiency, capital asset pricing, and total risk

■ To characterize the global financial marketplace and explain why MNC managers must be alert to capital market imperfections and asymmetries in tax regulations

The rise of the multina-
tional corporation was
not anticipated by the
classical theory of international trade.

International business activity is not new. The transfer of goods and services across national borders has been taking place for thousands of years, antedating even Joseph's advice to the rulers of Egypt to establish that nation as the granary of the Middle East. Since the end of World War II, however, international business has undergone a revolution out of which has emerged what is probably the most important economic phenomenon of the latter half of the twentieth century: the multinational corporation (MNC).

1.1 THE RISE OF THE MULTINATIONAL CORPORATION

The *multinational corporation* is a company engaged in producing and selling goods or services in more than one country. It ordinarily consists of a parent company located in the home country and at least five or six foreign subsidiaries, typically with a high degree of strategic interaction among the units. Some MNCs have upwards of 100 foreign subsidiaries scattered around the world.

Based in part on the development of modern communications and transportation technologies, the rise of the multinational corporation was unanticipated by the classical theory of international trade as first developed by Adam Smith and David Ricardo. According to this theory, which rests on the *doctrine of comparative advantage*, each nation should specialize in the production and export of those goods that it can produce with highest relative efficiency and import those goods that other nations can produce relatively more efficiently.

Underlying this theory is the assumption that goods and services can move internationally, but that factors of production such as capital, labor, and land are relatively immobile. Furthermore, the theory deals only with trade in commodities—that is, undifferentiated products; it ignores the roles of uncertainty, economies of scale, and technology in international trade and is static rather than dynamic. For all these defects, however, it is a valuable theory and still provides a well-reasoned theoretical foundation for free-trade arguments. But the growth of the MNC can be understood only by relaxing the traditional assumptions of classical trade theory.

Classical trade theory implicitly assumes that countries differ enough from one another in terms of resource endowments and economic skills for these differences to be at the center of any analysis of corporate competitiveness. Differences among individual corporate strategies are considered to be of only secondary importance; a company's citizenship is the key determinant of international success in the world of Adam Smith and David Ricardo.

However, this theory is increasingly irrelevant to the analysis of the countries presently at the core of the world economy—the United States, Japan, Western Europe, and, to an increasing extent, the most successful East Asian countries. Within this advanced and highly integrated core economy, differences among corporations are becoming more important than aggregate differences among countries. Furthermore, the increasing capacity of even small companies to operate in a global perspective makes the old analytical framework even more obsolete.

> The multinational corporation acquires and allocates resources on a globally coordinated basis to maximize group performance.

Not only are the "core nations" more homogeneous than before in terms of living standards, lifestyles, and economic organization, but their factors of production tend to move more rapidly in search of higher returns. Natural resources have lost much of their previous role in national specialization as advanced, knowledge-intensive societies move rapidly into the age of artificial materials and genetic engineering. Capital moves around the world in massive amounts at the speed of light; increasingly, corporations raise capital simultaneously in several major markets. Labor skills and labor wages in these countries can no longer be considered fundamentally different; many of the students enrolled in American graduate schools are foreign, while training has become a key dimension of many joint ventures between international corporations. Technology and "know-how" are also close to becoming a global pool. Trends in protection of intellectual property and export controls clearly have less impact than the massive development of the means to communicate, duplicate, store, and reproduce information.

Against this background, the ability of corporations of all sizes to use these globally available factors of production is a far bigger factor in international competitiveness than broad macroeconomic differences among countries. Contrary to the postulates of Smith and Ricardo, the very existence of the multinational enterprise is based on the international mobility of certain factors of production. Capital raised in London on the Eurodollar market may be used by a Swiss-based pharmaceutical firm to finance the acquisition of German equipment by a subsidiary in Brazil. A single Barbie doll is made in 10 countries—designed in the United States, with parts and clothing from Japan, Korea, Italy, and Taiwan, and assembled in Mexico.

It is the globally coordinated allocation of resources by a single centralized management that differentiates the multinational enterprise from other firms engaged in international business. MNCs make decisions about market-entry strategy; ownership of foreign operations; and production, marketing, and financial activities with an eye to what is best for the corporation as a whole. The true multinational corporation emphasizes group performance rather than the performance of its individual parts.

ILLUSTRATION: General Electric Globalizes Its Medical Systems Business

A critical element of General Electric's global strategy is to be first or second in the world in a business or to get out. For example, in 1987, GE swapped its RCA consumer electronics division for Thomson CGR, the medical equipment business of Thomson SA of France, to strengthen its own medical unit. Together with GE Medical Systems Asia (GEMSA) in Japan, CGR makes GE No. 1 in the world market for X-ray, CAT scan, magnetic resonance, ultrasound, and other diagnostic imaging devices, ahead of Siemens (Germany), Philips (Netherlands), and Toshiba (Japan).

GE's production is also globalized, with each unit exclusively responsible for equipment in which it is the volume leader. Hence, GE Medical Systems now makes the high end of its CAT scanners and magnetic resonance equipment near Milwaukee (its headquarters) and the low end in Japan. The middle market is supplied by General Electric CGR S.A. in France. Engineering skills pass horizontally from the United States to Japan to France and back again. Each subsidiary supplies the marketing skills to its own home market.

Evolution of the Multinational Corporation

International business is of great importance to a growing number of companies, many of which are household names.

Every year, *Fortune* publishes a list of the ten most-admired U.S. corporations. Year in and year out, most of these firms are largely multinational in philosophy and operations. In contrast, the least-admired tend to be national firms with much smaller proportions of assets, sales, or profits derived from foreign operations. Although multinationality and economic efficiency do not necessarily go hand in hand, international business is clearly of great importance to a growing number of U.S. and non-U.S. firms. The list of large American firms that receive 50% or more of their revenues and profits from abroad and have a sizable fraction of their assets abroad as well reads like a Who's Who: IBM, Gillette, NCR, Dow Chemical, Colgate-Palmolive, Xerox, and Hewlett-Packard. Coca-Cola earns more money selling soda in Japan than it does in the United States.

Industries differ greatly in the extent to which foreign operations are of importance to them. For example, the oil companies and banks are far more heavily involved overseas than are packaged food companies and automakers. Even within industries, companies differ markedly in their commitment to international business. For example, in 1989 Exxon had about 56% of its assets, 73% of its sales, and 97% of its profits abroad. The corresponding figures for Atlantic Richfield are 19%, 18%, and 6%.

Appendix 1A provides further evidence of the growing *internationalization* of American business. It presents data on the size and scope of overseas investment by U.S. firms and U.S. investment by foreign firms. The numbers involved are in the hundreds of billions of dollars. Moreover, these investments have grown steadily over time. A brief taxonomy of the MNC and its evolution is given in the sections that follow.

Raw-Materials Seekers. Raw-materials seekers were the earliest multinationals, the villains of international business. They are the firms—the British, Dutch, and French East India Companies, the Hudson's Bay Trading Company, and the Union Miniere Haut-Katanga—that first grew under the protective mantle of the British, Dutch, French, and Belgian colonial empires. Their aim was to exploit the raw materials that could be found overseas. The modern-day counterparts of these firms, the multinational oil and mining companies, were the first to make large foreign investments, beginning during the early years of the twentieth century. Hence, large oil companies such as British Petroleum and Standard Oil were among the first true multinationals; hard-mineral companies such as International Nickel, Anaconda Copper, and Kennecott Copper were also early investors abroad.

Market Seekers.   The market seeker is the archetype of the modern multinational firm that goes overseas to produce and sell in foreign markets. Examples include IBM, Volkswagen, and Unilever. Although there are some early examples of market-seeking MNCs (for example, Colt Firearms, Singer, Coca-Cola, N.V. Philips, and Imperial Chemicals), the bulk of *foreign direct investment*, which is the acquisition abroad of physical assets such as plant and equipment, took place after World War II. This investment was primarily a one-way flow—from the United States to Western Europe—until the early 1960s. At that point, the phenomenon of *reverse foreign investment* began, primarily with West European firms acquiring American firms. More recently, Japanese firms have begun investing in the United States and Western Europe, largely in response to perceived or actual restrictions on their exports to these markets.

> The three basic types of multinational firms are raw materials seekers, market seekers, and cost minimizers.

Cost Minimizers.   Cost minimizers is a fairly recent category of firms doing business internationally. These firms seek out and invest in lower-cost production sites overseas (for example, Hong Kong, Taiwan, and Ireland) to remain cost competitive both at home and abroad. Many of these firms are in the electronics industry. Examples include Texas Instruments, Atari, and Zenith.

1.2 THE PROCESS OF OVERSEAS EXPANSION

Studies of corporate expansion overseas indicate that firms become multinational by degree, with foreign direct investment being a late step in a process that begins with exports. For most companies, the *globalization process* does not occur through conscious design, at least in the early stages. It is the unplanned result of a series of corporate responses to a variety of threats and opportunities appearing at random abroad. From a broader perspective, however, the globalization of firms is the inevitable outcome of the competitive strivings of members of oligopolistic industries. Each member tries to both create and exploit monopolistic product and factor advantages internationally while simultaneously attempting to reduce the competitive threats posed by other industry members.

To meet these challenges, companies gradually increase their commitment to international business, developing strategies that are progressively more elaborate and sophisticated. The sequence normally involves exporting, setting up a foreign sales subsidiary, securing licensing agreements, and eventually establishing foreign production. This evolutionary approach to overseas expansion

The process of international expansion ordinarily evolves from a low risk-low return strategy to a higher risk-higher return strategy.

is a risk-minimizing response to operating in a highly uncertain foreign environment. By internationalizing in phases, a firm can gradually move from a relatively low risk-low return, export-oriented strategy to a higher risk-higher return strategy emphasizing international production. In effect, the firm is investing in information, learning enough at each stage to significantly improve its chances for success at the next stage. Exhibit 1.1 depicts the usual sequence of overseas expansion.

Exporting

Exporting provides the opportunity to learn about a foreign market.

Firms facing highly uncertain demand abroad will typically begin by exporting to a foreign market. The advantages of exporting are significant: Capital requirements and start-up costs are minimal, risk is low, and profits are immediate. Furthermore, this initial step provides the opportunity to learn about present and future supply and demand conditions, competition, channels of distribution, payment conventions, financial institutions, and financial techniques. Building on prior successes, companies then expand their marketing organizations abroad, switching from using export agents and other intermediaries to dealing directly with foreign agents and distributors. As increased communication with customers reduces uncertainty, the firm might set up its own sales subsidiary and new service facilities, such as a warehouse, with these marketing activities culminating in the control of its own distribution system.

Overseas Production

A major drawback to exporting is the inability to realize the full sales potential of a product. By manufacturing abroad, a company can more easily keep abreast of market developments, adapt its products and production schedules to changing local tastes and conditions, fill orders faster, and provide more comprehensive after-sales service. Many companies also set up R&D facilities along with their foreign operations; they aim to pick the best brains, wherever they are. The results help companies to keep track of the competition and to design new products. For example, the Japanese subsidiary of Loctite, a U.S. maker of

Exhibit 1.1 Typical Foreign Expansion Sequence

engineering adhesives, came up with several new applications for sealants in the electronics industry.

Setting up local production facilities also shows a greater commitment to the local market, which typically brings added sales, and provides increased assurance of supply stability. Certainty of supply is particularly important for firms that produce intermediate goods for sale to other companies. A case in point is SKF, the Swedish ball bearing manufacturer. SKF was forced to manufacture in the United States to guarantee that its product, a crucial component in military equipment, would be available when needed. The Pentagon would not permit its suppliers of military hardware to be dependent on imported ball bearings, because imports could be halted in wartime and are always subject to the vagaries of ocean shipping.

Foreign production helps companies boost sales abroad.

Thus, most firms selling in foreign markets eventually find themselves forced to manufacture abroad. Foreign production covers a wide spectrum of activities from repairing, packaging, and finishing to processing, assembly, and full manufacture. Firms typically begin with the simpler stages—for example, packaging and assembly—and progressively integrate their manufacturing activities backward—for example, production of components and subassemblies.

Because the optimal entry strategy can change over time, a firm must continually monitor and evaluate the factors that bear on the effectiveness of its current entry strategy. New information and market perceptions change the risk-return trade-off for a given entry strategy, leading to a sequence of preferred entry modes, each adapted on the basis of prior experience to sustain and strengthen the firm's market position over time.

Associated with a firm's decision to produce abroad is the question of whether to *create* its own affiliates or *acquire* going concerns. A major advantage of an acquisition is the capacity to effect a speedy transfer overseas of highly developed but underutilized parent skills, such as a novel production technology. Often the local firm also provides a ready-made marketing network. This is especially important if the parent is a late entrant to the market. Many firms have used the acquisition approach to gain knowledge about the local market or a particular technology. The disadvantage, of course, is the cost of buying an ongoing company. In general, the larger and more experienced a firm becomes the less frequently it uses acquisitions to expand overseas. Smaller and relatively less experienced firms often turn to acquisitions.

Companies can expand overseas more quickly by acquiring local firms.

Regardless of its preferences, a firm interested in expanding overseas may not have the option of acquiring a local operation. Michelin, the French manufacturer of radial tires, set up its own facilities in the United States because its tires are built on specially designed equipment; taking over an existing operation would have been out of the question.[1] Similarly, companies moving into developing countries often find they are forced to begin from the ground up because their line of business has no local counterpart.

---

[1]Once that equipment became widespread in the industry, Michelin was able to expand through acquisition (which it did, in 1989, when it acquired Uniroyal-Goodrich).

Licensing

An alternative, and at times a precursor, to setting up production facilities abroad is to *license* a local firm to manufacture the company's products in return for royalties and other forms of payment. The principal advantages of licensing are the minimal investment required, faster market-entry time, and fewer financial and legal risks involved. But the corresponding cash flow is also relatively low, and there may be problems in maintaining product quality standards. The licensor may also face difficulty controlling exports by the foreign licensee, particularly when, as in Japan, the host government refuses to sanction restrictive clauses on sales to foreign markets. Thus, a licensing agreement may lead to the establishment of a competitor in third-country markets, with a consequent loss of future revenues to the licensing firm. The foreign licensee may also become such a strong competitor that the licensing firm will have difficulty entering the market when the agreement expires, leading to a further loss of potential profits.

For some firms, licensing alone is the preferred method of penetrating foreign markets. Other firms with diversified innovative product lines prefer to follow a strategy of trading technology for both equity in foreign joint ventures and royalty payments.

A Behavioral Definition of the Multinational Corporation

Regardless of the foreign entry or global expansion strategy pursued, the true multinational corporation is characterized more by its state of mind than by the size and worldwide dispersion of its assets. Rather than confine its search to domestic plant sites, the multinational firm asks, Where in the world should we build that plant? Similarly, multinational marketing management seeks global, not domestic, market segments to penetrate, while multinational financial management does not limit its search for capital or investment opportunities to any single national financial market. Hence, the essential element that distinguishes the true multinational is its commitment to seeking out, undertaking, and integrating manufacturing, marketing, R&D, and financing opportunities on a global, not domestic, basis. For example, IBM's superconductivity project was pioneered in Switzerland by a German scientist and a Swiss scientist, both of whom recently shared a Nobel Prize in Physics for their work on this project.

A necessary complement to the integration of worldwide operations is flexibility, adaptability, and quickness. Indeed, speed has become one of the critical competitive weapons in the fight for world market share. The ability to develop, make, and distribute products or services quickly enables companies to capture customers who demand constant innovation and rapid, flexible response. Exhibit 1.2 illustrates the combination of globally integrated activities and rapid response times of The Limited, a 3,200-store clothing chain headquartered in Columbus, Ohio.

Another critical aspect of competitiveness in this new world is focus. *Focus* means figuring out, and building on, what a company does best. This typically

Exhibit 1.2 How The Limited Cuts the Fashion Cycle to 60 Days

From point-of-sale computers, daily reports on what is selling well flow into headquarters of The Limited in Colubus, Ohio.

To restock, the company sends orders by satellite to plants in the U.S., Hong Kong, South Korea, Singapore, and Sri Lanka.

The goods are hustled back to Columbus from Hong Kong aboard a chartered Boeing 747 that makes four flights a week.

At a highly automated distribution center in Columbus, apparel is sorted, priced, and prepared for shipment—all within 48 hours.

By truck and plane, the apparel moves out to The Limited's 3,200 stores, including Express and Victoria's Secret outlets.

Within 60 days of the order, the apparel goes on sale. Most competitors still place orders six months or more in advance.

SOURCE: *FORTUNE*, September 26, 1988, p. 56. Chart by Renee Klein. *FORTUNE*, © 1988 Time, Inc. All rights reserved.

involves divesting unrelated business activities and seeking attractive investment opportunities in the core business.

Successful multinationals focus on their key value-creating skills.

ILLUSTRATION: ARCO Chemical Develops a Worldwide Strategy

In the 1980s, ARCO Chemical shed its less successful product lines. At one point, revenue shrank from $3.5 billion annually to $1.5 billion. But by stripping down to its most competitive lines of business, ARCO could better respond to the world political and economic events it is constantly buffeted by. Around the world it can take advantage of its technological edge within its narrow niche—mostly intermediate chemicals and fuel additives. This strategy has paid off: In 1992, ARCO had over 40% of its $3 billion in sales from abroad, and it now makes about half of its new investment outside the United States. And it claims half the global market for the chemicals it sells.

ARCO Chemical went global because it had to. The company's engineering resins are sold to the auto industry. In the past, that meant selling exclusively to Detroit's Big Three in the U.S. market. Today, ARCO Chemical sells to Nissan, Toyota, Honda, Peugeot, Renault, and Volkswagen in Japan, the United States, and Europe. And it deals with Ford and General Motors in the United States and

Europe. ARCO must be able to deliver a product anywhere in the world or else lose the business.

Global operations have also meant, however, that ARCO Chemical faces increasingly stiff competition from abroad, in addition to its traditional U.S. competitors such as Dow Chemical. European companies have been expanding operations in America and Japanese competitors also began to attack ARCO Chemical's business lines. For example, in 1990 Japan's Asahi Glass began a fierce price-cutting campaign in both Asia and Europe on products in which ARCO Chemical is strong.

In response, ARCO set up production facilities around the world and entered into joint ventures and strategic alliances. It counterattacked Asahi Glass by trying to steal one of Asahi's biggest customers in Japan. ARCO's joint-venture partner, Sumitomo Chemical, supplied competitive intelligence, and its knowledge of the Japanese market was instrumental in launching the counterattack.

In this world-oriented corporation, a person's passport is not the criterion for promotion. Nor is a firm's citizenship a critical determinant of its success. Success depends on a new breed of businessperson: the *global manager*.

The Global Manager

Today's managers must think globally and be able to anticipate and respond quickly to constant change.

In a world in which change is the rule and not the exception, the key to international competitiveness is the ability of management to adjust to change and volatility at an ever faster rate. In the words of General Electric Chairman Jack Welch, "I'm not here to predict the world. I'm here to be sure I've got a company that is strong enough to respond to whatever happens."[2]

The rapid pace of change means that the new global manager needs detailed knowledge of his or her own operation. The global manager must know how to make the product, where the raw materials and parts come from, how they get there, the alternatives, where the funds come from, and what their changing relative value does to his or her bottom line. He or she must also understand the political and economic choices facing key nations and how these choices will affect the outcomes of his or her decisions.

In making decisions for the global company, managers search their array of plants in various nations for the most cost-effective mix of supplies, components, transport, and funds. All this is done with the constant awareness that the choices change and have to be made again and again.

The problem of constant change disturbs some managers. It always has. But today's global managers have to anticipate it, understand it, deal with it, and turn it to their company's advantage. The payoff to thinking globally is a quality of decision making that enhances the firm's prospects for survival, growth, and profitability in the evolving world economy.

[2]Quoted in Ronald Henkoff, "How to Plan for 1995," *Fortune*, December 31, 1990, p. 70.

Political and Labor Union Concerns About Global Competition

Politicians and labor leaders, unlike corporate leaders, usually take a more parochial view of global investment flows. Many instinctively denounce local corporations that invest abroad as job "exporters," even though most welcome foreign investors in their own countries as job creators. However, a growing number of U.S. citizens today view the current tide of American asset sales to foreign companies as a dangerous assault on U.S. sovereignty. They are unaware, for example, that foreign-owned companies account for more than 20% of industrial production in Germany and more than 50% in Canada without either of these countries appearing to have experienced the slightest loss of sovereignty.

Global competition leads to winners and losers.

Indeed, in an ever more integrated *global economy*, the ability of any nation's industries to gain or protect world market share—the ultimate gauge of their ability to produce jobs—will increasingly be determined by the efficiency with which companies manage their overseas expansion. Ford and IBM, for example, would be generating less U.S.-based employment today had they not been able earlier to invest abroad—both by "outsourcing" the production of parts to low-wage countries such as Mexico and by establishing assembly plants and R&D centers in Europe and Japan.

The growing irrelevance of borders for corporations will force policymakers to rethink old approaches to regulation. For example, corporate mergers that would once have been barred as anticompetitive might make sense if the true measure of a company's market share is global rather than national.

International economic integration also reduces the freedom of governments to determine their own economic policy. If a government tries to raise tax rates on business, for example, it is increasingly easy for business to shift production abroad. Similarly, nations that fail to invest in their physical and intellectual infrastructure—roads, bridges, R&D, education—will likely lose entrepreneurs and jobs to those that do. In short, economic integration is forcing governments, as well as companies, to compete.

Politicians must accept the reality of a global economy or watch their nations fall behind.

The stresses caused by global competition have stirred up protectionists and given rise to new concerns about the consequences of free trade. For example, the recent U.S.-Canada trade agreement, which ends tariff barriers by the year 2000, has caused major disruption to Canada's manufacturing industry. Plants are closing, mergers are proliferating, and both domestic and multinational companies are adjusting their operations to the new continental market. As the following illustration of the U.S. auto industry indicates, companies and unions are quite rational in fearing the effects of foreign competition. It disrupts established industry patterns and limits the wages and benefits of workers. Similarly, the North American Free Trade Agreement (NAFTA) that will create a giant free trade area, from the Yukon to the Yucatan, has stirred spirited opposition among the affected parties.

So it is all the more encouraging that political leaders keep trying to stretch borders. The world's long march toward a global economy should accelerate considerably in the next few years if the U.S.-Canada-Mexico free-trade pact and the European Community's drive to create a truly common market proceed as planned. The greater integration of national economies is likely to continue despite the stresses it causes as politicians worldwide increasingly come to realize that they either accept this integration or watch their nation fall behind.

ILLUSTRATION: Japanese Competition Affects the
American Auto Industry

Japanese competition has steadily eroded the influence of the Big Three U.S. automakers in the auto industry. During the 1980s, Japanese auto companies raised their U.S. market share 8 points, to 28%, versus 65% for Detroit and 5% for Europe. The future looks even bleaker for Detroit: Japanese car companies now win some 46% of buyers under age 45. If these buyers stay loyal to the Japanese as they age, Japan's market share will rise much further.

The tough Japanese competition is a big factor in the sales and profit crunch that has hit the Big Three. GM, Ford, and Chrysler have responded by shutting down U.S. plants and acting to curb labor costs. Thus, Japanese competition limits the wages and benefits that United Auto Workers union members can earn, as well as the prices that U.S. companies can charge for their cars. One solution, which allows both the Big Three and the UAW to avoid making hard choices—sales volume versus profit margin, and jobs versus wages—is political: Limit Japanese competition through quotas, tariffs, and other protectionist devices, and thereby limit its effects on the U.S. auto industry. Unfortunately, American consumers get stuck with the tab for this apparent free lunch in the form of higher car prices and less choice.

1.3 MULTINATIONAL FINANCIAL MANAGEMENT: THEORY AND PRACTICE

The objective of multinational financial management is to maximize shareholder wealth.

Although all functional areas can benefit from a global perspective, this book concentrates on developing financial policies that are appropriate for the multinational firm. The main objective of multinational financial management is to maximize shareholder wealth as measured by share price. Although an institution as complex as the multinational corporation cannot be said to have a single, unambiguous will, the principle of shareholder wealth maximization provides a rational guide to financial decision making. However, other financial goals that reflect the relative autonomy of management and external pressures will also be examined here.

The Multinational Financial System

From a financial management standpoint, one of the distinguishing characteristics of the multinational corporation, in contrast to a collection of independent national firms dealing at arm's length with one another, is its ability to move money and profits among its affiliated companies through internal transfer mechanisms. These mechanisms include transfer prices on goods and services traded internally, intercompany loans, dividend payments, leading (speeding up) and lagging (slowing down) intercompany payments, and fee and royalty charges. They lead to patterns of profits and movements of funds that would be impossible in the world of Adam Smith.

Financial transactions within the MNC result from the internal transfer of goods, services, technology, and capital. These product and factor flows range from intermediate and finished goods to less tangible items such as management skills, trademarks, and patents. Those transactions not liquidated immediately give rise to some type of financial claim, such as royalties for the use of a patent or accounts receivable for goods sold on credit. In addition, capital investments lead to future flows of dividends and interest and principal repayments. Exhibit 1.3 depicts some of the myriad financial linkages possible in the MNC.

Although all of the links portrayed in Exhibit 1.3 can and do exist among independent firms, the MNC has greater control over the mode and timing of these financial transfers.[3]

Mode of Transfer. The MNC has considerable freedom in selecting the *financial channels* through which funds, allocated profits, or both are moved. For example, patents and trademarks can be sold outright or transferred in return for a contractual stream of royalty payments. Similarly, the MNC can move profits and cash from one unit to another by adjusting *transfer prices* on intercompany sales and purchases of goods and services. With regard to *investment flows*, capital can be sent overseas as debt with at least some choice of interest rate, currency of denomination, and repayment schedule, or as equity with returns in the form of dividends. Multinational firms can use these various channels, singly or in combination, to transfer funds internationally, depending on the specific circumstances encountered. Furthermore, within the limits of various national laws and with regard to the relations between a foreign affiliate and its host government, these flows may be more advantageous than those that would result from dealings with independent firms.

Timing Flexibility. Some of the internally generated financial claims require a fixed payment schedule; others can be accelerated or delayed. This *leading and lagging* is most often applied to *interaffiliate trade credit* where a change in open account terms, say from 90 to 180 days, can involve massive shifts in liquidity. (Some nations have regulations about the repatriation of the proceeds of export sales. Thus, there is typically not complete freedom to move funds by leading and

The multinational firm can control the mode and timing of internal financial transfers and thereby maximize global profits.

---

[3]See Donald R. Lessard, "Transfer Prices, Taxes, and Financial Markets; Implications of Internal Financial transfers Within the Multinational Firm," in *The Economic Effects of Multinational Corporations*, Robert G. Hawkins, ed. (Greenwich, Conn.: JAI Press, 1979); and David P. Rutenberg, "Maneuvering Liquid Assets in a Multinational Company," *Management Science*, June 1970, pp. B–671–684. This section draws extensively from Lessard's article.

Exhibit 1.3 The Multinational Corporate Financial System

SOURCE: Adapted from Figure 1 in Donald R. Lessard, "Transfer Prices, Taxes, and Financial Markets: Implications of Internal Financial Transfers Within the Multinational Firm," in Robert G. Hawkins, ed., *The Economic Effects of Multinational Corporations* (Greenwich, Conn.: JAI Press, 1979), by permission of the author and the publisher.

lagging.) In addition, the timing of fee and royalty payments may be modified when all parties to the agreement are related. Even if the contract cannot be altered once the parties have agreed, the MNC generally has latitude when the terms are initially established.

In the absence of *exchange controls*—government regulations that restrict the transfer of funds to nonresidents—firms have the greatest amount of flexibility in the timing of equity claims. The earnings of a foreign affiliate can be retained or used to pay dividends that in turn can be deferred or paid in advance.

Despite the frequent presence of governmental regulations or limiting contractual arrangements, most MNCs have some flexibility as to the timing of fund flows. This latitude is enhanced by the MNC's ability to control the timing of many of the underlying real transactions. For instance, shipping schedules can be altered so that one unit carries additional inventory for a sister affiliate.

Value. By shifting profits from high-tax to lower-tax nations, the MNC can reduce its global tax payments. Similarly, the MNC's ability to transfer funds among its several units may allow it to circumvent currency controls and other regulations and to tap previously inaccessible investment and financing opportunities. However, since most of the gains derive from the MNC's skill at taking advantage of openings in tax laws or regulatory barriers, governments do not always appreciate the MNC's capabilities and global profit-maximizing behavior. Thus, controversy has accompanied the international orientation of the multinational corporation.

Criticisms of the Multinational Corporation

Critics of the MNC liken its behavior to that of an octopus with tentacles extended, squeezing the nations of the world to satisfy the apparently insatiable appetite of its center. Its defenders claim that only by linking activities globally can world output be maximized. According to this view, greater profits from overseas activities are the just reward for providing the world with new products, technologies, and know-how.

The ability of MNCs to avoid taxes and regulatory barriers by shifting money and profits among their various units has led to conflicts with nation-states.

Because its focus is on multinational financial management, this book does not deal directly with this controversy. It concentrates instead on the development of analytical approaches to deal with the major environmental problems and decisions involving overseas investment and financing. In carrying out these financial policies, though, conflicts with nation-states will inevitably arise.

A classic case is that of General Motors-Holden's Ltd. The General Motors wholly owned Australian affiliate was founded in 1926 with an initial equity investment of A$3.5 million. The earnings were reinvested until 1954, at which time the first dividend, for A$9.2 million, was paid to the parent company in Detroit. This amount seemed reasonable to GM management, considering the 28 years of foregoing dividends, but the Australian press and politicians denounced a dividend equal to over 260% of GM's original equity investment as economic exploitation and imperialism.[4]

More recently, Brazil, facing one of its periodic balance-of-payments crisis, chose to impose stringent controls on the removal of profits by MNCs, thereby affecting the financial operations of such firms as Volkswagen and Scott Paper. In

[4]Reported in, among other places, Sidney M. Robbins and Robert B. Stobaugh, *Money in the Multinational Enterprise* (New York: Basic Books, 1973), p. 59.

addition, companies operating in countries as diverse as Canada and Chile, Italy and India, and the United States and Uruguay have faced various political risks, including price controls and confiscation of local operations. This book will examine the modification of financial policies in line with national objectives in an effort to reduce such risks and minimize the costs of the adjustments.

This text also considers the links between financial management and other functional areas. After all, the analysis of investment projects is dependent on sales forecasts and cost estimates, and the dispersal of production and marketing activities affects a firm's ability to flow funds internationally as well as its vulnerability to expropriation.

Functions of Financial Management

Financial management is traditionally separated into two basic functions: the acquisition of funds and the investment of these funds. The first function, also known as the *financing decision*, involves generating funds from internal sources or from sources external to the firm at the lowest long-run cost possible. The *investment decision* is concerned with the allocation of funds over time in such a way that shareholder wealth is maximized. Many of the concerns and activities of multinational financial management, however, cannot be categorized so neatly.

Internal corporate fund flows such as loan repayments are often undertaken to access funds that are already owned, at least in theory, by the MNC. Other flows such as dividend payments may take place to reduce taxes or currency risk. Capital structure and other financing decisions are frequently motivated by a desire to reduce investment risks as well as financing costs. Furthermore, exchange risk management involves both the financing decision and the investment decision. Throughout this book, therefore, the interaction between financing and investment decisions will be stressed because it is the right combination of these decisions that will maximize the value of the firm to its shareholders.

Theme

Financial executives of MNCs face added political and economic risks, as well as more complex tax laws and multiple money markets.

Financial executives in multinational corporations face many factors that have no domestic counterparts. These factors include exchange and inflation risks; international differences in tax rates; multiple money markets, often with limited access; currency controls; and political risks, such as sudden and creeping expropriation.

When examining the unique characteristics of multinational financial management, it is understandable that companies normally emphasize the additional political and economic risks faced when going abroad. However, a broader perspective is necessary if firms are to take advantage of being multinational.

The ability to move people, money, and material on a global basis enables the multinational corporation to be more than the sum of its parts. By having operations in different countries, the MNC can access segmented capital markets to lower its overall cost of capital, shift profits to lower its taxes, and take advantage of *international diversification* of markets and production sites to reduce the riskiness of its earnings. Multinationals have taken the old adage of "don't put all your eggs in one basket" to its logical conclusion.

Operating globally confers other advantages as well: It increases the bargaining power of multinational firms when they negotiate investment agreements and operating conditions with foreign governments and labor unions; it gives MNCs continuous access to information on the newest process technologies available overseas and the latest research and development activities of their foreign competitors; and it helps them to diversify their funding sources by giving them expanded access to the world's capital markets.

Benefits of global operations include international diversification, access to new information, and enhanced bargaining power with unions and governments.

In summary, this book emphasizes the many opportunities associated with being multinational without neglecting the corresponding risks. To properly analyze and balance these international risks and rewards, we must use the lessons to be learned from domestic corporate finance.

Relationship to Domestic Financial Management

In recent years there has been an abundance of new research in the area of international corporate finance. The major thrust of this work has been to apply the methodology and logic of financial economics to the study of key international financial decisions. Critical problem areas, such as foreign exchange risk management and foreign investment analysis, have benefited from the insights provided by *financial economics*—a discipline that emphasizes the use of economic analysis to understand the basic workings of financial markets, particularly the measurement and pricing of risk and the intertemporal allocation of funds.

By focusing on the behavior of financial markets and their participants, rather than on how to solve specific problems, we can derive fundamental principles of valuation and develop from them superior approaches to financial management—much as a better understanding of the basic laws of physics leads to better-designed and functioning products. We can also better gauge the validity of existing approaches to financial decision making by seeing whether their underlying assumptions are consistent with our knowledge of financial markets and valuation principles.

Financial economics, which focuses on the behavior of financial markets, contains valuable insights for international financial managers.

Three concepts arising in financial economics have proved to be of particular importance in developing a theoretical foundation for international corporate finance: arbitrage, market efficiency, and capital asset pricing. We will be relying on these concepts throughout the remainder of this book. Brief descriptions follow.

Three basic concepts provide the foundation for the study of international finance: arbitrage, market efficiency, and capital asset pricing.

Arbitrage.   *Arbitrage* has traditionally been defined as the purchase of securities or commodities on one market for immediate resale on another in order to profit from a price discrepancy. However, in recent years arbitrage has been used to describe a broader range of activities. *Tax arbitrage*, for example, involves the shifting of gains or losses from one tax jurisdiction to another in order to profit from differences in tax rates. In a broader context, *risk arbitrage*, or speculation, describes the process that leads to equality of risk-adjusted returns on different securities, unless market imperfections that hinder this adjustment process exist. In fact, it is the process of arbitrage that ensures market efficiency.

Market Efficiency.   An *efficient market* is one in which the prices of traded securities readily incorporate new information. Numerous studies of U.S. and foreign capital markets have shown that traded securities are correctly priced in that trading rules based on past prices or publicly available information cannot consistently lead to profits (after adjusting for transactions costs) in excess of those due solely to risk taking.

The predictive power of markets lies in their ability to collect in one place a mass of individual judgments from around the world. These judgments are based on current information. If the trend of future policies changes, people will revise their expectations, and prices will change to incorporate the new information.

Capital Asset Pricing.   *Capital asset pricing* refers to the way in which securities are valued in line with their anticipated risks and returns. Because risk is such an integral element of international financial decisions, this book briefly summarizes the results of over two decades of study on the pricing of risk in capital markets. The outcome of this research has been to posit a specific relationship between risk (measured by return variability) and required asset returns, now formalized in the *capital asset pricing model* (CAPM).

The CAPM assumes that the total variability of an asset's returns can be attributed to two sources: (1) market-wide influences that affect all assets to some extent, such as the state of the economy, and (2) other risks that are specific to a given firm, such as a strike. The former type of risk is usually termed *systematic* or *nondiversifiable risk*, and the latter, *unsystematic* or *diversifiable risk*. It can be shown that unsystematic risk is largely irrelevant to the highly diversified holder of securities because the effects of such disturbances cancel out, on average, in the portfolio. On the other hand, no matter how well diversified a stock portfolio is, systematic risk, by definition, cannot be eliminated, and thus the investor must be compensated for bearing this risk. This distinction between systematic risk and unsystematic risk provides the theoretical foundation for the study of risk in the multinational corporation and is referred to throughout the book.

The Importance of Total Risk

Total risk can adversely affect a company's value by leading to higher costs and lower sales.

Although the message of the CAPM is that only the systematic component of risk will be rewarded with a risk premium, this does not mean that *total risk*—the combination of systematic and unsystematic risk—is unimportant to the value of the firm. In addition to the effect of systematic risk on the appropriate discount rate, total risk may have a negative impact on the firm's *expected* cash flows. [5]

The inverse relation between risk and expected cash flows arises because financial distress, which is more likely to occur for firms with high total risk, can impose costs on customers, suppliers, and employees and thereby affect their willingness to commit themselves to relationships with the firm. For example, potential customers will be nervous about purchasing a product that they might

[5]The effect of total risk is discussed in Alan C. Shapiro and Sheridan Titman, "An Integrated Approach to Corporate Risk Management," *Midland Corporate Finance Journal,* Summer 1985, pp. 41–56.

have difficulty getting serviced if the firm goes out of business. Similarly, a firm struggling to survive is unlikely to find suppliers willing to provide it with specially developed products or services, except at a higher-than-usual price. The uncertainty created by volatile earnings and cash flows may also hinder management's ability to take a long view of the firm's prospects and make the most of its opportunities.

To summarize, total risk is likely to adversely affect a firm's value by leading to lower sales and higher costs. Consequently, any action taken by a firm that decreases its total risk will improve its sales and cost outlooks, thereby increasing its expected cash flows.

These considerations justify the range of corporate hedging activities that multinational firms engage in to reduce total risk. This text will focus on those risks that appear to be more international in nature, including inflation risk, exchange risk, and political risk. As we will see, however, appearances can be deceiving because these risks also affect firms that do business in only one country. Moreover, international diversification may actually allow firms to reduce the total risk they face. Much of the general market risk facing a company is related to the cyclical nature of the domestic economy of the home country. Operating in several nations whose economic cycles are not perfectly in phase should reduce the variability of the firm's earnings. Thus, even though the riskiness of operating in any one foreign country may be greater than the risk of operating in the United States (or other home country), diversification can eliminate much of that risk.

The Global Financial Marketplace

Market efficiency has been greatly facilitated by the marriage of computers and telecommunications. The resulting electronic infrastructure melds the world into one global market for ideas, data, and capital, all moving at almost the speed of light to any part of the planet. Today there are more than 200,000 terminals in hundreds of trading rooms, in dozens of nations, that light up to display an unending flow of news. It takes about two minutes between the time a president, a prime minister, or a central banker makes a statement and the time traders buy or sell currency, stocks, and bonds according to their evaluation of that policy's effect on the market.

The result is a continuing global referendum on a nation's economic policies, which is the final determinant of the value of its currency. Just as we learn from TV the winner of a presidential election weeks before the electoral college even assembles, so also we learn instantly from the foreign exchange market what the world thinks of our announced economic policies even before they are implemented. In a way, the financial market is a form of economic free speech. Although many politicians don't like what it is saying, the market presents judgments that are clear-eyed and hard-nosed. It knows that there are no miracle drugs that can replace sound fiscal and monetary policies. Thus, cosmetic political fixes will exacerbate, not alleviate, a falling currency.

Financial markets continually judge each nation's economic policies.

The Role of the Financial Executive in an Efficient Market

Financial managers can create value by taking advantage of capital market imperfections and tax asymmetries.

The basic insight into financial management we can gain from recent empirical research in financial economics is the following: *Attempts to increase the value of a firm by purely financial measures or accounting manipulations are unlikely to succeed unless there are capital market imperfections or asymmetries in tax regulations.*

Rather than downgrading the role of the financial executive, the net result of these research findings has been to focus attention on those areas and circumstances in which financial decisions can have a measurable impact. The key areas are capital budgeting, working capital management, and tax management. The circumstances to be aware of include *capital market imperfections,* primarily caused by government regulations, and asymmetries in the tax treatment of different types and sources of revenues and costs.

The value of good financial management is enhanced in the international arena because of the much greater likelihood of market imperfections and multiple tax rates. In addition, the greater complexity of international operations is likely to increase the payoffs from a knowledgeable and sophisticated approach to internationalizing the traditional areas of financial management.

1.4 OUTLINE OF THIS BOOK

This book is divided into six parts. These parts are

— Part I: Environment of International Financial Management
— Part II: Foreign Exchange Risk Management
— Part III: Multinational Working Capital Management
— Part IV: Foreign Investment Analysis
— Part V: Financing Foreign Operations
— Part VI: International Banking

The following sections briefly discuss these parts and their chapters.

Environment of International Financial Management

Part I examines the environment in which international financial decisions are made. Chapter 2 discusses the basic factors that affect currency values. It also explains the basics of central bank intervention in foreign exchange markets, including the economic and political motivations for such intervention. Chapter 3 describes the international monetary system and shows how the choice of system affects the determination of exchange rates. Chapter 4 analyzes the balance of payments and the links between national economies, while Chapter 5 describes the foreign exchange market and how it functions. Foreign currency futures and options contracts are discussed in Chapter 6. Chapter 7 is a crucial chapter because it introduces the five key equilibrium relationships—between inflation rates, interest rates, and exchange rates—in international finance that form the basis for much of the analysis in the remainder of the text.

Foreign Exchange Risk Management

Part II discusses foreign exchange risk management, a traditional area of concern that is receiving even more attention today. Chapter 8 discusses the likely impact of an exchange rate change on a firm (its exposure) from an accounting perspective, while Chapter 9 analyzes the costs and benefits of alternative financial techniques to hedge against these exchange risks. Chapter 10 examines exposure from an economic perspective. As part of the analysis of economic exposure, the relationship between inflation and currency changes and its implications for corporate cash flows is recognized. Chapter 11 develops marketing, logistic, and financial policies to cope with the competitive consequences of currency changes.

Multinational Working Capital Management

Part III examines working capital management in the multinational corporation. Chapter 12 deals with current liability management, presenting the alternative short-term financing techniques available and showing how to evaluate their relative costs. The subject of trade financing is covered in Chapter 13. Chapter 14 discusses current asset management in the MNC, including the management of cash, inventory, and receivables. Chapter 15 describes the mechanisms available to the MNC to shift funds and profits among its various units, while considering the tax and other consequences of these maneuvers. The aim of these maneuvers is to create an integrated global financial planning system.

Foreign Investment Analysis

Part IV analyzes the foreign investment decision process. Chapter 16 begins by discussing the nature and consequences of international portfolio investing—the purchase of foreign stocks and bonds. In Chapter 17 the strategy of foreign direct investment is discussed, including an analysis of the motivations for going abroad and those factors that have contributed to business success overseas. Chapter 18 presents techniques for evaluating foreign investment proposals, emphasizing how to adjust cash flows for the various political and economic risks encountered abroad, such as inflation, currency fluctuations, and expropriations. Chapter 19 seeks to determine the cost-of-capital figure(s) that MNCs should use in evaluating foreign investments. Chapter 20 discusses the measurement and management of political risks. It identifies political risk and then shows how companies can control these risks by appropriately structuring the initial investment and by making suitable modifications to subsequent operating decisions.

Financing Foreign Operations

Part V focuses on laying out and evaluating the medium- and long-term financing options facing the multinational firm, then developing a financial package that is tailored to the firm's specific operating environment. Chapter 21 describes the alternative external medium- and long-term debt financing options available to the multinational corporation. These options include an outline of the international capital markets; namely, the Eurocurrency and Eurobond markets. Chapter 22 discusses special financing vehicles available to the MNC, including interest rate and currency swaps and debt-equity swaps. In conclusion, Chapter 23 presents a three-stage framework for designing a global financing strategy.

International Banking

Part VI contains two chapters dealing with international banking. Chapter 24 discusses the development and expansion of international banking activities and the international debt crisis. Finally, Chapter 25 shows how to analyze country risk—the credit risk on loans to a foreign nation—a topic of great concern these days.

QUESTIONS

1. **a.** What are the various categories of multinational firms?
   b. What is the motivation for international expansion of firms within each category?

2. **a.** How does foreign competition limit the prices that domestic companies can charge and the wages and benefits that workers can demand?
   b. What political solutions can help companies and unions avoid the limitations imposed by foreign competition?
   c. Who pays for these political solutions? Explain.

3. **a.** What is the internal financial transfer system of the multinational firm?
   b. What are its distinguishing characteristics?
   c. What are the different modes of internal fund transfers available to the MNC?

4. How does the internal financial transfer system add value to the multinational firm?

5. **a.** Why do companies generally follow a sequential strategy in moving overseas?
   b. What are the pluses and minuses of exporting? Licensing? Foreign production?

6. What is an efficient market?

7. In seeking to predict tomorrow's exchange rate, are you better off knowing today's exchange rate or the exchange rates for the past 100 days?

8. **a.** What is the capital asset pricing model?
   b. What is the basic message of the CAPM?
   c. How might a multinational firm use the CAPM?

9. Why might setting up production facilities abroad lead to expanded sales in the local market?

10. **a.** Are multinational firms riskier than purely domestic firms?
    b. What data would you need to address this question?
    c. Is there any reason to believe that MNCs may be less risky than purely domestic firms? Explain.

11. In what ways do financial markets grade government economic policies?

12. **a.** How might total risk affect a firm's production costs and its ability to sell? Give some examples of firms in financial distress that saw their sales drop.
    b. What is the relation between the effects of total risk on a firm's sales and costs and its desire to hedge foreign exchange risk?

SIZE AND SCOPE OF MULTINATIONAL CORPORATIONS ABROAD

This appendix presents data on direct foreign investment by U.S. firms and on the U.S. investment position of foreign firms. It also discusses some recent changes in the overall U.S. foreign investment position.

1A.1 U.S. DIRECT INVESTMENT ABROAD

Exhibit 1A.1 shows the foreign direct investment positions of U.S. firms, broken down by major areas of the world, for the (alternating) years 1977–1991. The *foreign direct investment position* is defined as the book value of the equity in, and net loans outstanding to, foreign businesses in which Americans own or control, directly or indirectly, at least 10% of the voting securities. The data reveal the strong preference exhibited by U.S. firms for investment in developed countries; the fraction of U.S. direct investment going to developed countries has remained at a stable 73%–75% of the total. Canada alone accounts for just under 20% of total U.S. direct investments abroad. Slightly less than 25% of U.S. foreign direct investment goes to the *less-developed countries* (LDCs) of Latin America, Africa, the Middle East, Asia, and the Pacific, with the remainder being investments in foreign affiliates with operations spanning more than one country.

Despite the overall stability of the investment breakdowns, the regional shares have varied over time. Most noticeably, direct investment in Latin America declined substantially in absolute and percentage terms beginning in 1982. This decline coincided with the Latin American debt crisis and reflects both the poorer economic prospects of these countries and the additional constraints imposed on MNCs' ability to repatriate profits from their Latin American units. As Latin American prospects have improved in recent years so has the flow of direct investment, both in absolute and percentage terms.

The basic generalization we can draw from the data is that American investment flows to those nations with the largest economies and best economic prospects. The most striking departure from this generalization is Japan. Although the Japanese economy is the second largest in the non-Communist world, and one of the most dynamic, U.S. direct investment in Japan is now about 5%. This is less even than U.S. direct investment in the Netherlands and about one-fourth of such investment in Great Britain. This is strong evidence of the strong barriers, both formal and informal, to American direct investment in Japan.

The pattern of U.S. foreign direct investment is also noteworthy for what it doesn't indicate. Despite claims by U.S. labor unions, overseas investment by American multinationals does not appear to be driven solely by the search for low-cost manufacture; U.S. investment in Mexico fell 17% between 1980 and 1987, despite the growth of low-cost, labor-intensive maquiladora factories on the American border.

Exhibit 1A.2 shows the U.S. direct foreign investment position cross-classified by industrial sector and region of the world at the end of 1991. The industrial sectors are petroleum, manufacturing, and other (mining, trade, banking and finance, and other industries).

Manufacturing is the most important sector, accounting for 39% of total foreign direct investment by U.S. companies. Far behind is petroleum, at 13%. Although the data

Exhibit 1A.1 U.S. Direct Investment Abroad by Major Regions, 1977–1991

	Billions of U.S. Dollars							
	1977	*1979*	*1981*	*1983*	*1985*	*1987*	*1989*	*1991*
Developed Countries								
Canada	35	41	47	48	47	58	67	69
Ten Common Market countries	49	66	81	79	81	120	150	225
Other Europe	13	17	21	24	24	26	27	36
Japan	5	6	7	8	9	15	19	23
Australia, New Zealand, and South Africa	8	10	12	12	10	13	16	19
Total	110	139	167	170	172	232	279	335
Developing Countries								
Latin America	28	35	39	30	28	45	61	77
Africa	2	3	4	5	4	5	4	4
Middle East	−3	−1	2	3	5	5	4	5
Asia and Pacific	6	7	11	13	15	17	21	25
Total	32	45	56	51	53	72	91	112
International	4	4	5	6	5	5	4	3
All Countries	146	188	228	226	230	309	373	450
	Percent of Total							
	1977	*1979*	*1981*	*1983*	*1985*	*1987*	*1989*	*1991*
Developed Countries								
Canada	24	22	21	22	20	19	18	15
Ten Common Market countries	34	35	36	35	35	39	40	42
Other Europe	9	9	9	11	10	8	7	8
Japan	3	3	3	4	4	5	5	5
Australia, New Zealand, and South Africa	6	5	5	5	4	4	4	4
Total	75	74	73	75	75	75	75	75
Developing Countries								
Latin America	19	19	17	13	12	15	16	17
Africa	1	2	2	2	2	2	1	1
Middle East	−2	−1	1	1	2	2	1	1
Asia and Pacific	4	4	5	6	7	6	6	6
Total	22	24	25	23	23	23	24	25
International	3	2	2	3	2	2	1	1
All Countries	100	100	100	100	100	100	100	100

NOTE: The numbers may not sum exactly because of rounding errors.

SOURCE: *Survey of Current Business*, U.S. Department of Commerce, various issues.

Exhibit 1A.2 U.S. Direct Investment Abroad by Industrial Sector and Region, 1991 (U.S. $ Billions)

	Petroleum		Manufacturing		Other		Total	
	Amount	Percent	Amount	Percent	Amount	Percent	Amount	Percent
Developed Countries								
Canada	11	16	32	47	25	37	69	100
Europe	23	10	89	40	113	50	225	100
Other	8	18	18	42	17	41	42	100
Total	41	12	139	41	155	46	335	100
Developing Countries								
Latin America	4	6	26	33	47	61	77	100
Other	11	33	11	31	12	36	34	100
Total	16	14	36	33	60	54	112	100
International	2	78	0	0	1	22	3	100
All Countries	59	13	175	39	216	48	450	100

NOTE: Numbers may not sum exactly because of rounding.

SOURCE: *Survey of Current Business,* U.S. Department of Commerce, August 1992, p. 117.

are not presented here, the three most important manufacturing industries in terms of foreign direct investment are chemicals, nonelectrical equipment, and transportation equipment.

1A.2 FOREIGN DIRECT INVESTMENT IN THE UNITED STATES

The United States itself is an increasingly attractive source of foreign direct investment prospects. Foreigners now own Firestone Tire & Rubber, Rockefeller Center, Columbia Pictures, MCA/Universal, TV Guide, A&P, 20th Century Fox, Brooks Brothers, CBS Records, RCA, Pillsbury, MGM/UA, and about 30% of all office space in downtown Los Angeles. However, recession and slow growth has led to a decline in capital flowing into the United States. Exhibit 1A.3 shows that the foreign direct investment position in the United States grew by less than 3% in 1991—to $408 billion—compared with 8% in 1990, 21% in both 1989 and 1988, and 23% in 1987. From 1983 through 1986, growth in foreign direct investment in the United States averaged 15% annually. In the four years before 1982, the average annual growth rate was 30%. The pickup in foreign direct investment in the United States, after the slowdown during the mid-1980s, coincided with a lower dollar, leading to the charge that foreigners have been buying American assets on the cheap. Of course, the foreigners also get a dollar earnings stream that is worth less in their currencies.

The importance of foreign investment in the United States is indicated by a few facts: Four of America's six major record concerns are now foreign-owned; Goodyear is the last major American-owned tire manufacturer; as of 1993, Japanese auto companies were able to build more than two million cars a year in their U.S. plants, over 25% of the total in a typical sales year; four of Hollywood's largest film companies are now foreign-owned; and

Exhibit 1A.3 Foreign Direct Investment in the United States, 1991 (U.S. $ Billions)

By Country	Total End 1990	1991 Inflow	Increase (%)	Total End 1991	Percent of Total FDI
United Kingdom	$1032	$ 3	3%	$106	26%
Japan	82	5	6	87	217
Netherlands	64	0	0	64	16
Canada	30	0	0	30	7
West Germany	284	0	0	28	7
Switzerland	19	4	21	23	6
France	18	0	−1	18	4
Netherlands Antilles	131	−5	−37	8	2
Other	41	4	9	45	11
Total	$397	$11	3%	$408	100%

By Industry	Amount	Percent of Total FDI
Manufacturing	$163	40%
Wholesale trade	53	13
Petroleum	40	10
Real estate	34	8
Insurance	33	8
Banking	21	5
Retail trade	9	2
Mining	7	2
Other	48	12
Total	$408	100%

of the 21 companies manufacturing televisions in the United States, Zenith is the only American-owned one.

European corporate parents accounted for 63% of the year-end 1991 foreign investment position. Canadian and Japanese parents accounted for another 7% and 21%, respectively. By industry of the U.S. affiliates, 40% of the position was in manufacturing, 13% in wholesale trade, 10% in petroleum, and 37% in other industries, mainly real estate, banking, and insurance.

Two countries—the United Kingdom and Japan—account for over 47% of the foreign direct investment in the United States. Busy as the Japanese are, the data reveal that they are by no means the biggest U.S. shoppers. That prize goes to the British, whose companies had invested $106 billion by the end of 1991, primarily in manufacturing and wholesale trade. Japanese parents had a 1991 U.S. direct investment position of $87 billion, largely in manufacturing and real estate. The Dutch, who were bypassed in 1987 by the Japanese as the second largest foreign direct investors in the United States, had invested $64 billion by the end of 1991. Although not displayed here, a striking aspect of the returns on U.S. investments earned by foreign companies is how low they are, an average return on equity of 0.63% (−2.4% for the Japanese) for the years 1989–1991. Apparently, foreign firms are willing to invest large sums in the United States, earning only marginal returns compared with what could be earned in Treasury bills or other riskless instruments.

Motives for Foreign Direct Investment in the United States

Investment by foreign multinationals in the United States can be attributed to many of the same factors that propelled U.S. firms abroad: the size and growth potential of the market, the fear of future protectionism (especially true for Japanese firms), the desire to compete with and learn from rivals on their home ground, and lower relative production costs in some industries. Foreign firms may also seek access to new technology and operations that complement existing product lines in order to improve their global market positions. The positive aspects of foreign direct investment in the United States are that it often brings technology, spurs competition, and provides access to foreign markets.

1A.3 THE NET INTERNATIONAL WEALTH OF THE UNITED STATES

The preceding sections concentrated on direct investment abroad. However, direct investment is only one part of capital flows. Even more important is the flow of portfolio investment and bank lending overseas. The net of U.S. investment abroad and foreign investment domestically makes up the net international wealth of the United States. In 1981, the net U.S. international wealth peaked at $141 billion. Beginning in 1982, net U.S. international wealth began a long-term decline. Sometime during 1985, the continued decline in net international wealth turned negative. Exhibit 1A.4 depicts the changing net

Exhibit 1A.4 International Investment Position of the United States, 1970–1992

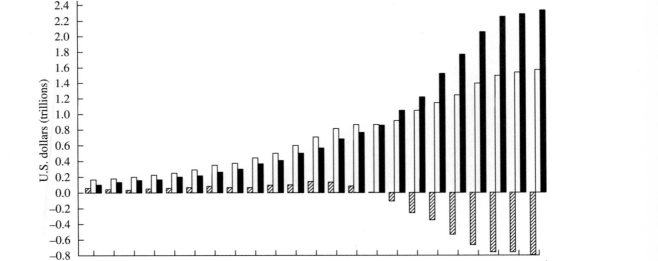

* 1992 data through third quarter

▨ Net U.S. international investment position

☐ U.S. assets abroad   ■ Foreign assets in United States

SOURCE: Based on data from *Survey of Current Business*, U.S. Department of Commerce, various issues; and *Economic Report of the President* (Washington, D.C.: U.S. Government Printing Office, January 1993).

international wealth position of the United States from 1970 through 1992. The negative net international wealth position of the United States reached –$785 billion by the end of 1992.

It should be noted that these figures are expressed on an historical cost basis. Since the average age of U.S. investments abroad exceeds the average age of foreign investments in the United States, historical cost figures will tend to significantly understate the true U.S. net international wealth position. Calculated on a current cost basis, the U.S. net international wealth position is much less negative, –$362 billion at the end of 1991, about half the historical cost figure of –$726 billion in that year.

Historical Perspective

The United States was a net debtor to the rest of the world until World War I. In the early stages of its industrial development, the United States depended heavily on foreign capital; in building up its industries, it "mortgaged" part of its wealth to foreigners. In 1900, for example, when the total wealth of the United States, including land and reproducible assets, was an estimated $88 billion, net liabilities to foreigners were $2.5 billion; these liabilities far exceeded U.S. claims on foreigners. On the eve of World War I, total foreign investment in the United States amounted to $7.2 billion—nearly twice the $3.7 billion Americans had invested abroad. The effects of the war reversed this situation: By the end of 1919, U.S. claims on foreigners exceeded foreign claims on the United States by $3.7 billion.

Net U.S. international wealth continued to increase throughout the 1920s, and by 1930, it reached a peak of about $9 billion. During the depression-ridden 1930s, the value of U.S. assets abroad declined, while the flight of capital from war-threatened Europe to the United States increased total foreign claims on the United States. These factors contributed to a slightly negative net U.S. foreign investment position.

The Post–World War II Period

Following the end of World War II, U.S. wealth abroad increased dramatically, first as a result of the vast flow of aid-related credits provided by the U.S. government to war-devastated countries; then later as U.S. companies sharply expanded their investment in foreign countries. By 1970 the U.S. international investment position showed a surplus of some $60 billion.

During the 1970s, the basic trend in the net U.S. international investment position was sharply upward. Between 1971 and 1979, U.S. foreign assets rose from about $165 billion to $510 billion, and foreign assets in the U.S. rose from $107 billion to $416 billion. These capital flows boosted the net U.S. international wealth position to $94 billion by 1980, as shown in Exhibit 1A.4.

The 1980s

From 1980 through 1986, U.S. foreign assets rose at an average annual rate of 11%, bringing total U.S. assets abroad to $1.068 trillion. At the same time, however, U.S. liabilities to foreigners were rising at an annual rate of 18%. In 1985, the inevitable consequence of these trends finally occurred: The United States became a net international debtor, reverting to the position it was in at the turn of the century. This decline in net international wealth reflects the large trade deficits the United States has been running in recent years. The trade deficits in turn result from basic shifts in savings and investment behavior in the United States and abroad. Chapter 4 discusses these factors at length.

The Consequences

The consequences of a reduction in a nation's net international wealth depend on the nature of the foreign capital inflows that cause the erosion. If the capital inflows finance new investments that enhance the nation's productive capacity, they are self-financing in that they will eventually generate the necessary resources for their repayment. But if the investment flows finance current consumption, their repayment will eventually reduce the nation's standard of living below where it would have been in the absence of such inflows. The need to reduce future living standards to pay back foreign debts is the problem facing many of the debtor Latin American nations.

In the case of the United States, a good portion of the inflows seem to have been of the "productive" variety. But a growing share of capital inflows, particularly since 1982, might be classified as "consumption" in nature. If so, the erosion of net U.S. international wealth, traceable to the U.S. federal budget deficits (see Chapter 4), will inflict new burdens on the U.S. economy in the future.

BIBLIOGRAPHY

Eaker, Mark R. "Teaching International Finance: An Economist's Perspective." *Journal of Financial and Quantitative Analysis*, November 1977, pp. 607–608.

Folks, William R., Jr. "Integrating International Finance into a Unified Business Program." *Journal of Financial and Quantitative Analysis*, November 1977, pp. 599–600.

Lessard, Donald R. "Transfer Prices, Taxes, and Financial Markets: Implications of International Financial Transfers within the Multinational Firm." In *The Economic Effects of Multinational Corporations*, Robert G. Hawkins, ed. Greenwich, Conn.: JAI Press, 1979.

2 The Determination of Exchange Rates

> Experience shows that neither a state nor a bank ever have had the unrestricted power of issuing paper money without abusing that power.
>
> David Ricardo (1817)

CHAPTER LEARNING OBJECTIVES

- To explain the concept of an equilibrium exchange rate
- To identify the basic factors affecting exchange rates in a floating exchange rate system
- To calculate the amount of currency appreciation or depreciation associated with a given exchange rate change
- To describe the motives and different forms and consequences of central bank intervention in the foreign exchange market
- To explain how and why expectations affect exchange rates

Economic activity is globally unified today to an unprecedented degree. Changes in one nation's economy are rapidly transmitted to that nation's trading partners. These fluctuations in economic activity are reflected, almost immediately, in fluctuations in currency values. Consequently, multinational corporations, with their integrated cross-border production and marketing operations, continually face devaluation or revaluation worries somewhere in the world. The purpose of this chapter and the next one is to provide an understanding of what an exchange rate is and why it might change. Such an understanding is basic to dealing with currency risk.

This chapter first describes what an exchange rate is and how it is determined in a *freely floating exchange rate* regime—that is, in the absence of government intervention. The chapter next discusses the role of expectations in exchange rate determination. It also examines the different forms and consequences of central bank intervention in the foreign exchange market. Chapter 3 describes the political aspects of currency determination under alternative exchange rate systems and presents a brief history of the international monetary system.

Before proceeding further, here are definitions of several terms commonly used to describe currency changes. Technically, a *devaluation* refers to a decrease in the stated par value of a *pegged currency*, one whose value is set by the government; an increase in par value is known as a *revaluation*. By contrast, a *floating currency*—one whose value is set primarily by market forces—is said to *depreciate* if it loses value and to *appreciate* if it gains value. However, discussions in this book will use the terms devaluation and depreciation and revaluation and appreciation interchangeably.

2.1 SETTING THE EQUILIBRIUM SPOT EXCHANGE RATE

On the most fundamental level, *exchange rates* are market-clearing prices that equilibrate supplies and demands in foreign exchange markets. The determinants of currency supplies and demands are first discussed with the aid of a two-country model featuring the United States and Germany. Later, the various currency influences will be studied more closely.

The demand for the Deutsche mark (DM), Germany's currency, in the foreign exchange market (which in this two-country world is equivalent to the supply of dollars) derives from the American demand for German goods and services and DM-denominated financial assets. Since German prices are set in DM, in order for Americans to pay for their German purchases they must first exchange their dollars for DM. That is, they will demand DM.

> The demand for a foreign currency derives from the demand for that country's goods, services, and assets.

An increase in the DM's dollar value is equivalent to an increase in the dollar price of German products. This higher dollar price will normally reduce the U.S. demand for German goods, services, and assets. Conversely, as the dollar value of the DM falls, Americans will demand more DM to buy the less-expensive German products, resulting in a downward sloping demand curve for Deutsche marks. As the dollar cost of the DM (the exchange rate) falls, Americans will tend to buy more German goods and so will demand more DM.

Similarly, the supply of Deutsche marks (which is equivalent to the demand for dollars) is based on German demand for U.S. goods and services and dollar-denominated financial assets. In order for Germans to pay for their U.S. purchases, they must first acquire dollars. As the dollar value of the Deutsche mark increases, which lowers the DM cost of U.S. goods, the increased German demand for U.S. goods will cause an increase in the German demand for dollars and, hence, an increase in the amount of Deutsche marks supplied.[1]

In Exhibit 2.1, e is the spot exchange rate (dollar value of one DM), and Q is the quantity of Deutsche marks supplied and demanded. The DM supply (S) and demand (D) curves intersect at e_0, the *equilibrium exchange rate*. The foreign

---

[1]This statement holds provided the price elasticity of German demand, E, is greater than 1. In general, $E = -(\Delta Q/Q)/(\Delta P/P)$, where Q is the quantity of goods demanded, P is the price, and ΔQ is the change in quantity demanded for a change in price, ΔP. If $E > 1$, then total spending goes up when price declines.

Exhibit 2.1 Equilibrium Exchange Rate

Quantity of Deutsche marks

An equilibrium exchange rate is the price that just balances currency supply and demand in the foreign exchange market.

exchange market is said to be in equilibrium at e_0 since both the demand for DM and the supply of DM at this price is Q_0.

Suppose that the supply of dollars increases relative to its demand. This excess growth in the money supply will cause inflation in the United States, which means that U.S. prices begin to rise relative to prices of German goods and services. German consumers are likely to buy fewer U.S. products and begin switching to German substitutes, leading to a decrease in the amount of Deutsche marks supplied at every exchange rate. The result is a leftward shift in the DM supply curve to S' in Exhibit 2.2. Similarly, higher prices in the United States will lead American consumers to substitute German imports for U.S. products, resulting in an increase in the demand for Deutsche marks as depicted by D'. In effect, both Germans and Americans are searching for the best deals worldwide and will switch their purchases accordingly. Hence, a higher rate of inflation in the United States than in Germany will simultaneously increase German exports to the United States and reduce U.S. exports to Germany.

Inflation causes a nation's currency to depreciate.

A new equilibrium rate $e_1 > e_0$ results. In other words, a higher rate of inflation in the United States than in Germany will lead to a depreciation of the dollar relative to the Deutsche mark or, equivalently, to an appreciation of the mark relative to the dollar. In general, a nation running a relatively high rate of inflation will find its currency declining in value relative to the currencies of countries with lower inflation rates. This relationship will be formalized in Chapter 7 as purchasing power parity (PPP).

Depending on the current value of the Deutsche mark relative to the dollar, the amount of DM appreciation or depreciation is computed as the fractional increase or decrease in the dollar value of the DM:

$$\text{Amount of DM appreciation (depreciation)} = \frac{\text{New dollar value of DM} - \text{Old dollar value of DM}}{\text{Old dollar value of DM}}$$

$$= \frac{e_1 - e_0}{e_0} \qquad\qquad \textbf{(2.1)}$$

Exhibit 2.2 Impact of U.S. Inflation on the Equilibrium Exchange Rate

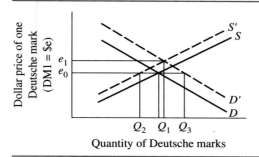

Alternatively, the dollar is said to have depreciated (appreciated) by the fractional decrease (increase) in the DM value of the dollar:

$$\begin{matrix} \text{Amount of dollar} \\ \text{depreciation} \\ \text{(appreciation)} \end{matrix} = \frac{\begin{matrix}\text{New DM value} \\ \text{of dollar} \end{matrix} - \begin{matrix}\text{Old DM value} \\ \text{of dollar}\end{matrix}}{\text{Old DM value of dollar}} \quad \text{(2.2)}$$

$$= \frac{1/e_1 - 1/e_0}{1/e_0} = \frac{e_0 - e_1}{e_1}$$

For example, an increase in the exchange rate from \$0.64 to \$0.68 is equivalent to a DM appreciation of 6.25% [(0.68 − 0.64)/0.64 = 0.0625] or a dollar depreciation of 5.88% [(0.64 − 0.68)/0.68 = −0.0588]. (Why don't the two exchange rate changes equal each other?)[2]

ILLUSTRATION: *Calculating Dollar Appreciation Against the Italian Lira*

On July 19, 1985, the Italian lira devalued by 17% against the U.S. dollar. By how much has the dollar appreciated against the lira?

Solution. If e_0 is the initial dollar value of the lira and e_1 is the post-devaluation exchange rate, then we know from Equation 2.1 that $(e_1 - e_0)/e_0 = -17\%$. Solving for e_1 in terms of e_0 yields $e_1 = 0.83e_0$. From Equation 2.2, we know that the dollar's appreciation against the lira equals $(e_0 - e_1)/e_1$ or $(e_0 - 0.83e_0)/0.83e_0 = 0.17/0.83 = 20.48\%$.

Interest rate differentials will also affect the equilibrium exchange rate. A rise in U.S. interest rates relative to German rates, all else being equal, will cause investors in both nations to switch from DM- to dollar-denominated securities to

Higher interest rates cause a nation's currency to appreciate.

[2]The reason the DM appreciation is unequal to the amount of dollar depreciation depends on the fact that the value of one currency is the inverse of the value of the other one. Hence, the percentage change in currency value differs because the base off which the change is measured differs.

take advantage of the higher dollar rates. The net result will be depreciation of the DM in the absence of government intervention. Similarly, because a stronger economy attracts capital, economic growth should lead to a stronger currency. Empirical evidence supports this hypothesis.

Low-risk currencies are more highly valued than high-risk currencies.

Other factors that can influence exchange rates include political and economic risks. Investors prefer to hold lesser amounts of riskier assets; thus, low-risk currencies—those associated with more politically and economically stable nations—are more highly valued than high-risk currencies.

ILLUSTRATION: East-West Politics Affect the Deutsche Mark

Following the reform movement that swept Eastern Europe in late 1989, West Germany's stock market soared. The rise in the West German stock market reflected the general belief among investors that West German industry stood to benefit significantly from the opening of Eastern Europe. For example, economists estimated that the modernization of East Germany's economy alone would cost up to $300 billion over the coming decade, with much of the reconstruction to be performed by West German industry.

As foreign capital flowed into West Germany, attracted by its strong growth prospects in Eastern Europe, the demand for Deutsche marks in the foreign exchange market led to a steady increase in the DM's value. On January 30, 1990, however, the DM fell about 3% as panicked traders and investors dumped Deutsche marks and other foreign currencies and bought dollars following an unconfirmed report on Cable News Network that Mikhail Gorbachev, the architect of the Soviet Union's reform policies, might resign as head of the Soviet Communist Party. The dollar has traditionally been considered a safe haven for investors during periods of international turmoil.

The foreign exchange consequences of the CNN report, which was televised just after 2 p.m. EST and raised the specter of an unraveling of the reform movement in the Soviet Union and Eastern Europe, are vividly illustrated in Exhibit 2.3. By later in the day, the dollar retreated after the White House said that it had no information to support the CNN report. Over the next two days, the DM rose another 1.4% when Mr. Gorbachev denied the report. These currency fluctuations illustrate the importance of political factors in the foreign exchange market.

2.2 EXPECTATIONS AND THE ASSET MARKET MODEL OF EXCHANGE RATES

Athough currency values are affected by current events and current supply and demand flows in the foreign exchange market, they also depend on expectations about future exchange rate movements. And exchange rate expectations are influenced by every conceivable economic, political, and social factor.

Exhibit 2.3 How Political Factors Affect Exchange Rates

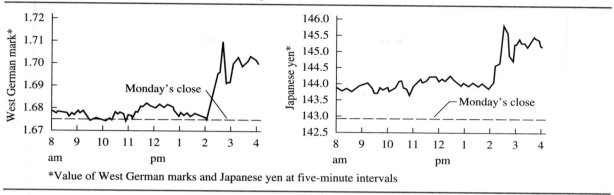

*Value of West German marks and Japanese yen at five-minute intervals

The role of expectations in determining exchange rates depends on the fact that currencies are financial assets and that an exchange rate is simply the relative price of two financial assets—one country's currency in terms of another's. Thus, currency prices are determined in the same manner that the prices of assets such as stocks, bonds, gold, or real estate are determined. Unlike the prices of services or products with short storage lives, asset prices are influenced comparatively little by current events. Rather, they are determined by people's willingness to hold the existing quantities of assets, which in turn depends on their expectations of the future worth of these assets. Thus, for example, frost in Florida can bump up the price of oranges, but it should have little impact on the price of the citrus groves producing the oranges; instead, longer- term expectations of the demand and supply of oranges governs the values of these groves.

Since currencies are long-lived assets, foreign exchange rates are strongly influenced by expectations of future economic, political, and social factors.

Similarly, the value today of a given currency, say, the dollar, depends on whether or not—and how strongly—people still want the amount of dollars and dollar-denominated assets they held yesterday. According to this view—known as the *asset market model* of exchange rate determination—the exchange rate between two currencies represents the price that just balances the relative supplies of, and demands for, assets denominated in those currencies. Consequently, shifts in preferences can lead to massive shifts in currency values.

A brief examination of the dollar's ups and downs, using some stylized facts, provides further insight into the relation of exchange rate movements to the asset-like character of money. In the early 1960s, the United States was clearly the dominant nation in the world. The U.S. political system was stable and its economic health was good: U.S. inflation averaged about 1% annually; economic growth averaged almost 5% annually. Not surprisingly, the world was willing to hold a large fraction of its wealth in the form of dollars and dollar-denominated assets.

In the late 1960s and 1970s, problems appeared. The Vietnam War was sharply divisive, and the U.S. political system was shaken. One president was driven from office, another was forced to resign, and two others lost the confidence of the American people. Monetary growth accelerated, leading to double-digit inflation and sharply higher effective tax rates as inflation forced everyone into higher tax brackets. Economic growth slowed to about 3% annually, compared to about 4% in other developed nations. These factors, combined with increased government regulation, lowered the attractiveness of holding dollars and U.S. assets relative to foreign assets; the world decided to hold a much smaller fraction of its wealth in the form of dollars and dollar-denominated assets. This massive portfolio shift caused a sharp decline in the value of the dollar.

The changing fortunes of the U.S. dollar can be attributed largely to changes in the desire of investors to hold U.S. assets.

Then, in the early 1980s, Americans elected a new president who was committed to cutting inflation, taxes, and government regulation. The authority of the presidency was restored, taxes and inflation were sharply reduced, and after a brief recession, economic growth accelerated and reached 6.5% in 1984, compared to average growth of 0.9% in other developed countries. Capital was attracted to the United States by the strength of its economy, the high after-tax real (inflation-adjusted) rate of return, and the favorable political climate—conditions superior to those attainable elsewhere. Foreigners once again found the United States to be a safer and more rewarding place in which to invest, so they added substantially more U.S. assets to their portfolios. The dollar rose sharply.

As U.S. growth slowed down in 1985 and foreign growth accelerated, foreign assets became attractive again. At the same time, foreigners fled U.S. assets when they perceived that the U.S. government itself wanted the dollar to decline. The world's decreased willingness to hold U.S. assets led to another massive portfolio rebalancing; this time, investors substituted foreign assets for U.S. assets. The dollar declined once again.

Since the desire to hold a currency today depends critically on expectations of the factors that can affect the currency's future value, what matters is not only what is happening today but what markets expect will happen in the future. Thus, currency values are forward looking; they are set by investor expectations of their issuing countries' future economic prospects rather than by contemporaneous events alone.

The Nature of Money and Currency Values

To understand the factors that affect currency values, it helps to examine the special character of money. To begin, money has value because people are willing to accept it in exchange for goods and services. The value of money, therefore, depends on its purchasing power. Money also provides *liquidity*—that is, you can readily exchange it for goods or other assets, thereby facilitating economic transactions. Thus, money represents both a *store of value* and a *store of liquidity*. The demand for money, therefore, depends on money's ability to maintain its value and on the level of economic activity. Hence, the lower the expected inflation rate, the more money people will demand. Similarly, higher economic growth means more transactions and a greater demand for money to pay bills.

The demand for money is also affected by the demand for assets denominated in that currency. The higher the expected real return and the lower the riskiness of a country's assets, the greater is the demand for its currency to buy those assets. In addition, as people who prefer assets denominated in that currency (usually residents of the country) accumulate wealth, the value of the currency rises.

Because the exchange rate reflects the relative demands for two moneys, factors that increase the demand for the home currency should also increase the price of home currency on the foreign exchange market. In summary, the economic factors that affect a currency's value include its usefulness as a store of value, determined by its expected rate of inflation; the demand for liquidity, determined by the volume of transactions in that currency; and the demand for assets denominated in that currency, determined by the risk-return pattern on investment in that nation's economy and by the wealth of its residents. The first factor depends primarily on the country's future monetary policy, while the latter two factors depend largely on expected economic growth and political and economic stability. All three factors ultimately depend on the soundness of the nation's economic policies. The sounder these policies, the more valuable the nation's currency will be; conversely, the more uncertain a nation's future economic and political course, the riskier its assets will be, and the more depressed and volatile its currency's value.

> The demand for money depends on its usefulness as a store of value, as well as on the demand for assets denominated in that currency.

ILLUSTRATION: An Earthquake Hits the Mexican Peso

After the devastating Mexico City earthquake in September 1985, the Mexican government expropriated private property in what was called "a bold gesture to speed the rebuilding of the capital." But the abrupt, carelessly executed expropriation shredded private-sector confidence in the government. People rushed to sell Mexican assets and the peso plunged 30%.

The asset market view that sound economic policies strengthen a currency is challenged by critics who point to the links between the huge U.S. budget deficits, high real interest rates, and the strong dollar in the early 1980s. But others find this argument unconvincing, especially now that the dollar has fallen while the deficit has risen further. If the big deficits were responsible for high real U.S. interest rates, there would be more evidence that private borrowing was being crowded out in interest-sensitive areas, such as fixed business investment and residential construction. Yet the rise in real interest rates coincided with rapid growth in capital spending.

> Sound economic policies strengthen a nation's currency.

An alternative explanation for high real interest rates is that a vigorous U.S. economy, combined with a major cut in business taxes in 1981, raised the after-tax profitability of business investments. The result was a capital spending boom and a strong dollar.

Indeed, if large government deficits and excessive government borrowing cause currencies to strengthen, then the Russian ruble and Brazilian cruzeiro should be among the strongest currencies in the world. Instead, they are among the weakest currencies since their flawed economic policies scare off potential investors.

Central Bank Reputations and Currency Values

Expectations of central bank behavior affect currency values.

Another critical determinant of currency values is central bank behavior. A *central bank* is the nation's official monetary authority; its job is to use the instruments of monetary policy, including the sole power to create money, so as to achieve one or more of the following objectives: price stability, low interest rates, or a target currency value. As such, the central bank affects the risk associated with holding money. This risk is inextricably linked to the nature of a *fiat money*, which is non-convertible paper money. Until 1971, every major currency was linked to a commodity. Today no major currency is linked to a commodity. With a commodity base, usually gold, there was a stable, long-term anchor to the price level. Prices varied a great deal in the short term, but they eventually returned to where they had been.

With a fiat money, there is no anchor to the price level—that is, there is no standard of value that investors can use to find out what the currency's future value might be. Instead, a currency's value is largely determined by the central bank through its control of the money supply. If the central bank creates too much money, inflation will occur and the value of money will fall. *Expectations* of central bank behavior will also affect exchange rates today; a currency will decline if people *think* the central bank will expand the money supply in the future.

Viewed this way, money becomes a brand name product whose value is backed by the reputation of the central bank that issues it. And just as reputations among automobiles vary—from Mercedes Benz to Yugo—so currencies come backed by a range of quality reputations—from the Deutsche mark, Swiss franc, and Japanese yen on the high side to the Mexican peso, Brazilian cruzeiro, and Russian ruble on the low side. Underlying these reputations is trust in the willingness of the central bank to maintain price stability.

The high-quality currencies are those expected to maintain their purchasing power because they are issued by reputable central banks. A reputable central bank is one that the markets trust to do the right thing, and not merely the politically expedient thing, when it comes to monetary policy. This trust, in turn, comes from past history: Reputable banks, like the Bundesbank, have developed their credibility by having done hard, cruel, and painful things for years in order to fight inflation. In contrast, the low-quality currencies are those that bear little assurance their purchasing power will be maintained. And as in the car market, high-quality currencies sell at a premium, and low-quality currencies sell at a discount (relative to their values based on economic fundamentals alone). That is, investors demand a risk premium to hold a riskier currency, whereas safer currencies will be worth more than their economic fundamentals would indicate.

Because good reputations are slow to build and quick to disappear, many economists recommend that central banks adopt rules for price stability that are verifiable, unambiguous, and enforceable—along with the independence and accountability necessary to realize this goal.[3] For example, the Bundesbank has managed to maintain such a low rate of German inflation because of its statutory commitment to price stability, a legacy of Germany's hyperinflation in the 1920s (which peaked at 200 billion percent in 1923). Absent such rules, the natural accountability of central banks to government becomes an avenue for political influence. The greater scope for political influence will, in turn, add to the perception of inflation risk.

This perception stems from the fact that government officials and other critics routinely exhort the central bank to follow "easier" monetary policies, by which they mean boosting the money supply to lower interest rates. These exhortations arise because many people believe (1) that the central bank can "trade off" a higher rate of inflation for more economic growth and (2) that the central bank determines the rate of interest independently of the rate of inflation and other economic conditions. Despite the questionable merits of these beliefs, central banks—particularly those that are not independent—often respond to these demands by expanding the money supply. The inevitable result is more inflation and a devalued currency.

The link between central bank independence and sound monetary policies is borne out by the empirical evidence.[4] Exhibit 2.4a shows that countries whose central banks are less subject to government intervention tend to have lower inflation rates and vice versa. The central banks of Germany, Switzerland, and the United States, identified as the most independent in the post-World War II era, also showed the lowest inflation rates from 1951 to 1988. Least independent were the central banks of Italy, New Zealand, and Spain, countries wracked by the highest inflation rates in the industrial world. Moreover, Exhibit 2.4b indicates that this lower inflation rate is not achieved at the expense of economic growth; rather central bank independence and economic growth seem to go together.

Independent central banks tend to follow sound money policies.

The idea that central bank independence can help in establishing a credible monetary policy is being put into practice today, as countries that have been plagued with high inflation rates are enacting legislation to reshape their conduct of monetary policy. For example, New Zealand, Canada, and Chile all have passed laws that mandate an explicit inflation goal or that give their central banks more independence.

Some countries, like Argentina, have gone even further and established what is in effect a currency board. Under a *currency board* system, there is no central bank. Instead, the currency board issues notes and coins that are convertible on demand and at a fixed rate into a foreign reserve currency. As reserves, the currency board holds high-quality, interest-bearing securities denominated in the

[3]See, for example, W. Lee Hoskins, "A European System of Central Banks: Observations from Abroad," *Economic Commentary,* Federal Reserve Bank of Cleveland, November 15, 1990.

[4]See, for example, Alberto Alesina, "Macroeconomics and Politics," in *NBER Macroeconomic Annual, 1988* (Cambridge, Mass.: MIT Press, 1988).

Exhibit 2.4 Central Bank Independence, Inflation, and Economic Growth

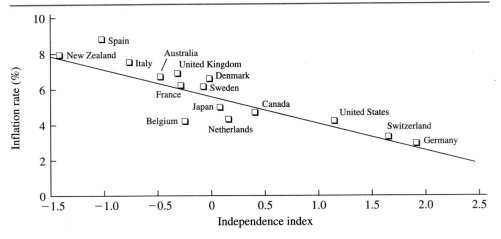

(a) Central Bank Independence Versus Inflation

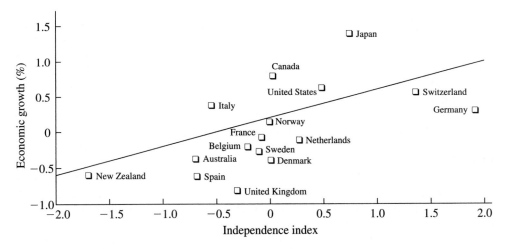

(b) Central Bank Independence Versus Economic Growth

SOURCE: Adapted from J. Bradford DeLong and Lawrence H. Summers, "Macroeconomic Policy and Long-Run Growth," *Economic Review*, Federal Reserve Bank of Kansas City, Fourth Quarter 1992, pp. 14 and 16.

reserve currency. Its reserves are equal to 100%, or slightly more, of its notes and coins in circulation. The board has no discretionary monetary policy. Instead, market forces alone determine the money supply.

Historically, more than 60 countries (mainly former British colonies) had currency boards. So long as they kept their boards, all of those countries had the same rate of inflation as the country issuing the reserve currency and successfully maintained convertibility at a fixed exchange rate into the reserve currency. Currency boards still exist in Hong Kong, Singapore, and Brunei, where they continue to operate successfully.

Currency boards promote sound money policies.

ILLUSTRATION: *Argentina Reforms Its Currency*

Argentina has long been considered one of Latin America's worst basket cases, with rampant inflation (averaging 450% annually during the 1980s), chronic budget deficits, and an over-regulated, arthritic economy. The direct cause of all that inflation has been the Argentine central bank. To buy votes, Argentine politicians have allowed government ministries and its state-owned companies to operate with huge budget deficits. The central bank filled the void by printing money. But in 1991, President Carlos Menem and his fourth Minister of Economy Domingo Cavallo launched the Convertibility Act. (The first Minister of Economy, Miguel Roig, took one look at the economy and died of a heart attack six days into the job.) This act made the austral (the Argentine currency) fully convertible at a fixed rate of 10,000 australs to the dollar, and by law the monetary supply must now be 100% backed by gold and foreign currency reserves, mostly dollars. This link to gold and the dollar imposes a straitjacket on monetary policy. If, for example, the central bank has to sell dollars to support the currency, the money supply automatically shrinks. Better still, the government can no longer print money to finance a budget deficit. In January 1992, the government knocked four zeros off the austral and renamed it the peso, worth exactly $1.

By effectively locking Argentina into the U.S. monetary system, the Convertibility Act has had remarkable success in restoring confidence in the peso and providing an anchor for inflation expectations. Inflation fell from over 2,300% in 1990 to 170% in 1991 and below 20% in 1992 (see Exhibit 2.5). Argentine capital transferred overseas to escape Argentina's hyperinflation has started to come home. It has spurred rapid economic growth and led to a rock-solid currency. In response to the good economic news, stock prices quintupled, in dollar terms, during the first year of the plan. And the price of Argentina's foreign debt rose from 13% of its face value in 1990 to 45% in 1992.

The likelihood that the Convertibility Act marks a permanent change in Argentina and will not be revoked at a later date—an important consideration for investors—is increased by the other economic actions the Argentine government has taken to reinforce its commitment to price stability and economic growth: It has deregulated its economy, sold off money-losing state-owned businesses to the private sector, cut taxes, opened its capital markets, lowered barriers to trade, and cut red tape.

Exhibit 2.5 Argentina's Inflation History, 1980–1992

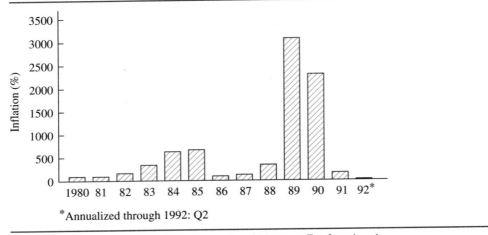

*Annualized through 1992: Q2

SOURCE: *International Financial Statistics*, International Monetary Fund, various issues.

Uncertainty over a nation's monetary policy can depress the value of its currency.

The importance of expectations and central bank reputations in determining currency values was dramatically illustrated on June 2, 1987, when the financial markets learned that Paul Volcker was resigning as chairman of the Federal Reserve Board. Within seconds after this news appeared on the ubiquitous video screens used by traders to watch the world, both the price of the dollar on foreign exchange markets and the prices of bonds began a steep decline. By day's end, the dollar had fallen 2.6% against the Japanese yen, and the price of Treasury bonds declined 2.3%—one of the largest one-day declines ever. The price of corporate bonds fell by a similar amount. All told, the value of U.S. bonds fell by more than $100 billion.

The response by the financial markets reveals the real forces that are setting the value of the dollar and interest rates under our current monetary system. On that day, there was no other economic news of note. There was no news about American competitiveness. There was no change in Federal Reserve (Fed) policy or inflation statistics; nor was there any change in the size of the budget deficit, the trade deficit, or the growth rate of the U.S. economy.

What actually happened on that announcement day? Foreign exchange traders and investors simply became less certain of the path U.S. monetary policy would take in the days and years ahead. Volcker was a known inflation fighter. Alan Greenspan, the incoming Fed chairman, was an unknown quantity. The possibility that he would emphasize growth over price stability raised the specter of a more expansive monetary policy. Because the natural response to risk is to hold less of the asset whose risk has risen, investors tried to reduce their holdings of dollars and dollar-denominated bonds, driving down their prices in the process.

The import of what happened on June 2, 1987, is that prices of the dollar and those billions of dollars in bonds were changed by nothing more or less than investors changing their collective assessment of what actions the Fed would or wouldn't take. A critical lesson for business people and policymakers alike surfaces: A shift in the trust that people have for a currency can change its value now by changing its expected value in the future. The level of interest rates is also affected by trust in the future value of money. All else being equal, the greater the trust in the promise that money will maintain its purchasing power, the lower interest rates will be. This theory will be formalized in Chapter 7 as the Fisher effect.

2.3 THE FUNDAMENTALS OF CENTRAL BANK INTERVENTION

The exchange rate is one of the most important prices in a country because it links the domestic economy and the rest-of-world economy. As such, it affects relative national competitiveness.

We have already seen the link between exchange rate changes and relative inflation rates. The important point for now is that an appreciation of the exchange rate beyond that necessary to offset the inflation differential between two countries raises the price of domestic goods relative to the price of foreign goods. This rise in the *real* or *inflation-adjusted exchange rate*—measured as the nominal exchange rate adjusted for changes in relative price levels—proves to be a mixed blessing. For example, the rise in the value of the U.S. dollar from 1980 to 1985 translated directly into a reduction in the dollar prices of imported goods and raw materials. As a result, prices of imports and of products that compete with imports began to ease. This development contributed significantly to the slowing of U.S. inflation in the early 1980s.

> A rise in the real or inflation-adjusted exchange rate causes the price of foreign goods to fall relative to the price of domestic goods.

Yet the rising dollar had some distinctly negative consequences for the U.S. economy as well. Declining dollar prices of imports had their counterpart in the increasing foreign currency prices of U.S. products sold abroad. As a result, American exports became less competitive in world markets, and American-made import substitutes became less competitive in the United States. Sales of domestic traded goods declined, generating unemployment in the traded-goods sector and inducing a shift in resources from the traded- to the nontraded-goods sector of the economy.

> A strong dollar hurts U.S. exports, while giving consumers access to cheaper foreign products; a weak dollar helps U.S. exports but hurts American consumers.

Alternatively, home currency depreciation results in a more competitive traded-goods sector, stimulating domestic employment and inducing a shift in resources from the nontraded- to the traded-goods sector. The bad part is that currency weakness also results in higher prices for imported goods and services, eroding living standards and worsening domestic inflation.

From its peak in mid-1985, the U.S. dollar fell by more than 50% over the next few years, enabling Americans to experience the joys and sorrows of both a strong and a weak currency in less than a decade. The weak dollar made U.S. companies more competitive worldwide; at the same time, it lowered the living standards of Americans who enjoyed consuming foreign goods and services. Exhibit 2.6 charts the real value of the U.S. dollar from 1970 to 1992. Despite recent ups and downs, the dollar is still well below its level back in 1970.

Exhibit 2.6   Real Value of the U.S. Dollar, 1970–1992

SOURCE: *World Financial Markets,* Morgan Guaranty Trust Company, various issues.

Depending on their economic goals, some governments will prefer an over-valued domestic currency, whereas others will prefer an undervalued currency. Still others just want a correctly valued currency, but economic policymakers may feel that the rate set by the market is irrational; that is, they feel they can better judge the correct exchange rate than the marketplace can.

No matter what category they fall in, most governments will be tempted to intervene in the foreign exchange market to move the exchange rate to the level consistent with their goals or beliefs. *Foreign exchange market intervention* refers to official purchases and sales of foreign exchange that nations undertake through their central banks to influence their currencies.

For example, looking back at Section 2.1, suppose the U.S. and German governments decide to maintain the old exchange rate e_0 in the face of the new equilibrium rate e_1. According to Exhibit 2.2, the result will be an excess demand for Deutsche marks equal to $Q_3 - Q_2$; this DM shortage is the same as an excess supply of $(Q_3 - Q_2)e_0$ dollars. Either the Federal Reserve (the American central bank), or the Bundesbank (the German central bank), or both will then have to intervene in the market to supply this additional quantity of Deutsche marks (to buy up the excess supply of dollars). Absent some change, the United States will face a perpetual balance-of-payments deficit equal to $(Q_3 - Q_2)e_0$ dollars, which is the dollar value of the German balance-of-payments surplus of $(Q_3 - Q_2)$ Deutsche marks.

Most governments are tempted to intervene in the foreign exchange market to pursue their economic goals.

Foreign Exchange Market Intervention

Although the mechanics of central bank intervention vary, the general purpose of each variant is basically the same: to increase the market demand for one currency by increasing the market supply of another. To see how this purpose can be accomplished, suppose in the previous example that the Bundesbank wants to reduce the value of the DM from e_1 to its previous equilibrium value of e_0. To do so, the Bundesbank must sell an additional $(Q_3 - Q_2)$ DM in the foreign exchange market, thereby eliminating the shortage of DM that would otherwise exist at e_0. This sale of DM (which involves the purchase of an equivalent amount of dollars) will also eliminate the excess supply of $(Q_3 - Q_2)e_0$ dollars that now exists at e_0. The simultaneous sale of DM and purchase of dollars will balance the supply and demand for DM (and dollars) at e_0.

Central banks intervene in the foreign exchange market by buying or selling foreign currencies.

If the Fed also wants to raise the value of the dollar, it will buy dollars with Deutsche marks. Regardless of whether the Fed or the Bundesbank initiates this foreign exchange operation, the net result is the same: The U.S. money supply will fall, and Germany's money supply will rise.

The Effects of Foreign Exchange Market Intervention

The basic problem with central bank intervention is that it is likely to be either ineffectual or irresponsible. This conclusion is consistent with the experiences of the United States and other industrial nations in their intervention policies. Between March 1973 and April 1983, industrial nations bought and sold a staggering $772 billion of foreign currencies to influence exchange rates. Foreign central banks bought over $100 billion in 1987 alone to support the dollar. More recently, the U.S. government bought over $36 billion of foreign currencies between July 1988 and July 1990 to stem the rise in the value of the dollar. Despite these large interventions, exchange rates appear to have been moved largely by basic market forces.

Foreign exchange intervention to control currency values tends to be either ineffectual or irresponsible.

On the other hand, intervention can have a lasting effect on exchange rates, but insidiously—by creating inflation in some nations and deflation in others. In the example presented above, Germany would wind up with a permanent (and inflationary) increase in its money supply, and the United States would end up with a deflationary decrease in its money supply. If the resulting increase in German inflation and decrease in U.S. inflation were sufficiently large, the exchange rate would remain at e_0 without the need for further government intervention. But it is the money supply changes, and not the intervention by itself, that affect the exchange rate. Moreover, moving the *nominal* (or *actual*) *exchange rate* from e_1 to e_0 should not affect the real exchange rate because the change in inflation rates offsets the nominal exchange rate change.

If forcing a currency below its equilibrium level causes inflation, it follows that devaluation cannot be much use as a means of restoring competitiveness. A devaluation improves competitiveness only to the extent that it does not cause higher inflation. If the devaluation causes domestic wages and prices to rise, any gain in competitiveness is quickly eroded.

ILLUSTRATION: Britain Pegs the Pound to the Mark

In early 1987, Nigel Lawson, Britain's Chancellor of the Exchequer, began pegging the pound sterling against the Deutsche mark. Unfortunately, his exchange rate target greatly undervalued the pound. In order to prevent sterling from rising against the DM he had to massively intervene in the foreign exchange market. The resulting explosion in the British money supply reignited the inflation that Prime Minister Margaret Thatcher had spent so long subduing. With high inflation, the pound fell against the mark and British interest rates surged. The combination of high inflation and high interest rates led first to Mr. Lawson's resignation in October 1989 and then to Mrs. Thatcher's resignation a year later, in November 1990.

Of course, when the world's central banks execute a coordinated surprise attack, the impact on the market can be dramatic—for a short period. Early in the morning on February 27, 1985, for example, Western European central bankers began telephoning banks and investment firms in London, Frankfurt, Milan, and other financial centers to order the sale of hundreds of millions of dollars; the action—joined a few hours later by the Federal Reserve in New York—panicked the markets and drove the dollar down by 5% that day.

But keeping the market off balance requires credible repetitions. Shortly after the February 27 blitzkrieg, the dollar was back on the rise. The Fed intervened again, but it wasn't until clear signs of a U.S. economic slowdown emerged that the dollar turned down in March.

Real exchange rates are primarily determined by real economic variables.

To summarize the empirical evidence, *real* exchange rates are primarily determined by real economic variables, such as relative national incomes and interest rates between countries; real exchange rates, in turn, determine the magnitudes and the direction of flows of goods, services, and capital among countries. A change in the supply-demand relationship in the foreign exchange market that was brought about by intervention may temporarily influence the movement of the real exchange rate. However, unless the underlying economic variables that typically give rise to broadly based, market-generated supply-and-demand forces change, these forces will eventually swamp the impact of the intervention. Thus, nations intent on fixing their exchange rate in defiance of market forces must ultimately bow to those forces or else resort to currency controls.

2.4 SUMMARY AND CONCLUSIONS

This chapter studied the process of determining exchange rates under a floating exchange rate system. We saw that in the absence of government intervention, exchange rates respond to the forces of supply and demand, that in turn are dependent on relative inflation rates, interest rates, and GNP growth rates. Monetary policy is crucial here. If the central bank expands the money supply at a faster rate than the growth in money demand, the purchasing power of money declines both at home (inflation) and abroad (currency depreciation). In addition, the healthier the economy is, the stronger the currency is likely to be. Exchange rates are also crucially affected by expectations of future exchange rate changes, which depend on forecasts of future economic and political conditions.

In order to achieve certain economic or political objectives, governments often intervene in the currency markets to affect the exchange rate. Although the mechanics of such intervention vary, the general purpose of each variant is basically the same: to increase the market demand for one currency by increasing the market supply of another. Alternatively, the government can control the exchange rate directly by setting a price for its currency and then restricting access to the foreign exchange market.

A critical factor that helps explain the volatility of exchange rates is that with a fiat money there is no anchor to a currency's value, nothing around which beliefs can coalesce. In this situation, where people are unsure of what to expect, any new piece of information can dramatically alter their beliefs. Thus, if the underlying domestic economic policies are unstable, exchange rates will be volatile as traders react to new information.

QUESTIONS

1. Suppose prices start rising in the United States relative to prices in Japan. What would we expect to see happen to the dollar:yen exchange rate? Explain.

2. If a foreigner purchases a U.S. government security, what happens to the supply of, and demand for, dollars?

3. Describe how these three typical transactions should affect present and future exchange rates.

   a. Seagram imports a year's supply of French champagne. Payment in French francs is due immediately.

   b. American Motors sells a new stock issue to Renault, the French car manufacturer. Payment in dollars is due immediately.

   c. Korean Airlines buys five Boeing 747s. As part of the deal, Boeing arranges a loan to KAL for the purchase amount from the U.S. Export-Import Bank. The loan is to be paid back over the next seven years with a two-year grace period.

4. In 1987, the British government cut taxes significantly, raising the after-tax return on investments in Great Britain. What would be the likely consequence of this tax cut on the equilibrium value of the British pound?

5. Some economists have argued that a lower government deficit could cause the dollar to drop by reducing high real interest rates in the United States. What does the asset view of exchange rates predict will happen if the United States lowers its budget deficit? What is the evidence from countries such as Mexico and Brazil?

6. The maintenance of money's value is said to depend on the monetary authorities. What might the monetary authorities do to a currency that would cause its value to drop?

7. For each of the following six scenarios, say whether the value of the dollar will appreciate, depreciate, or remain the same relative to the Japanese yen. Explain each answer. Assume that exchange rates are free to vary and that other factors are held constant.

    a. The growth rate of national income is higher in the United States than in Japan.

    b. Inflation is higher in the United States than in Japan.

    c. Prices in Japan and the United States are rising at the same rate.

    d. Real interest rates are higher in the United States than in Japan.

    e. The United States imposes new restrictions on the ability of foreigners to buy American companies and real estate.

    f. U.S. wages rise relative to Japanese wages, while American productivity falls behind Japanese productivity.

8. The Fed adopts an easier monetary policy. How is this likely to affect the value of the dollar and U.S. interest rates?

9. What is there about a fiat money that makes its exchange rate especially volatile?

10. Comment on the following headlines in *The Wall Street Journal*.

    a. "Sterling Drops Sharply Despite Good Health of British Economy: Oil Price Slump Is Blamed" (January 17, 1985).

    b. "Dollar Surges as Coup in Soviet Union Revives Unit's Appeal as a Safe Haven" (August 20, 1991).

    c. "Dollar Plummets on Soviet Coup Failure" (August 22, 1991).

    d. "Dollar Falls Across the Board as Fed Cuts Discount Rate to 6.5% From 7%" (December 19, 1990).

    e. "Canadian Dollar Likely to Fall Further On Recession and Constitutional Crisis" (September 28, 1992).

    f. "Dollar Soars on U.S. and Iraqi Tension, Hints of Possible Lower German Rates" (December 12, 1992).

    g. "Inflation, Slow Growth Seen Spurring Latin America to Devaluate Currencies" (January 22, 1990).

11. Suppose a new Russian government makes threatening moves against Western Europe. How is this threat likely to affect the dollar's value? Why?

12. Comment on the following statement: "One of the puzzling aspects of central bank intervention is how those who manage our economic affairs think they know what is the 'right' price for a dollar in terms of francs, pounds, yen, or Deutsche marks. And if they do know, why do they keep changing their minds?"

13. In a widely anticipated move, on August 30, 1990, the Bank of Japan raised the discount rate (the rate it charges on loans to financial institutions) to 6% from 5.25% in a move to reduce inflationary pressures in Japan. Many currency traders had expected the Japanese central bank to raise its rate by more than 0.75%. What was the likely consequence of this interest rate rise on the yen:dollar exchange rate?

14. On November 28, 1990, Federal Reserve Chairman Alan Greenspan told the House Banking Committee that despite possible benefits to the U.S. trade balance, "a weaker dollar also is a cause for concern." This statement departed from what appeared to be an attitude of benign neglect by U.S. monetary officials toward the dollar's depreciation. He also rejected the notion that the Fed should aggressively ease monetary policy, as some Treasury officials had been urging. At the same time, Mr. Greenspan didn't mention foreign exchange market intervention to support the dollar's value.

    a. What was the likely reaction of the foreign exchange market to Mr. Greenspan's statements. Explain.

b. Can Mr. Greenspan support the value of the U.S. dollar without intervening in the foreign exchange market? If so, how?

15. In the late 1980s, the Bank of Japan bought billions of dollars in the foreign exchange market to prop up the dollar's value against the yen. What were the likely consequences of this foreign exchange market intervention for the Japanese economy?

16. Countries with high inflation need to keep devaluing their currencies to maintain competitiveness. But countries that try to maintain their competitiveness by devaluing their currencies only end up with even higher inflation. Discuss.

17. The Russian government is trying to figure out how to stabilize the value of its currency. What advice would you offer to it?

18. As the year 1992 began, the Russian government and the central bank tightened credit in an attempt to slow the growth in the supply of rubles. However, the moves weren't popular with the country's giant state-run industrial enterprises, which are still dependent on official subsidies and cheap credit. In July 1992, the Russian Parliament appointed Viktor Gerashchenko head of the central bank. One of his first acts was to say that he didn't think the time was right to make the ruble convertible. Then he said that he would continue to extend credits to bankrupt and inefficient state enterprises.

    a. How independent is the Russian central bank likely to be? What political pressures is it facing?

    b. What is the likely effect of Mr. Gerashchenko's statements on inflationary expectations in Russia?

    c. How do you think the ruble:dollar exchange rate was affected by these statements?

19. In January 1991, President Mikhail Gorbachev banned all 50-ruble and 100-ruble bills, while permitting Soviet citizens to change only 1,000 rubles in these large bills into smaller denominations. In addition, savings-bank accounts were frozen for six months. The object of these measures was to strip the country's powerful black marketeers of their operating capital, driving as many as possible out of business, and to reduce inflation, which has been running at about 80% a year. The official Russian news agency Tass reported that the government had "clearly decided that the confiscation version of monetary reform was the most efficient and least expensive version at its disposal."

    a. Were these measures likely to achieve President Gorbachev's objectives?

    b. How do you think the ruble's exchange rate responded to President Gorbachev's initiative? Explain.

20. Under the Convertibility Act, Argentina's central bank is allowed to count dollar-denominated bonds issued by the Argentine government as part of its "foreign" reserve assets. What potential problem do you see with this rule?

PROBLEMS

  1. Suppose the Mexican peso devalues by 75% against the dollar. What is the percentage appreciation of the dollar against the peso?

  2. Suppose the dollar appreciates by 500% against the Brazilian cruzeiro. How much has the cruzeiro devalued against the dollar?

  3. Between 1988 and 1991, the price of a room at the Milan Hilton rose from Lit 346,400 to Lit 475,000. At the same time, the exchange rate went from Lit 1,302:$1 in 1988 to Lit 1,075:$1 in 1991.

a. By how much has the dollar cost of a room at the Milan Hilton changed over this three-year period?

b. What has happened to the lira's dollar value during this period?

BIBLIOGRAPHY

Batten, Dallas S., and Mack Ott. "What Can Central Banks Do About the Value of the Dollar?" *Federal Reserve Bank of St. Louis Review*, May 1984, pp. 16-26.

Dornbusch, Rudiger. "Expectations and Exchange Rate Dynamics." *Journal of Political Economy*, December 1976, pp. 1161-1176.

Frenkel, Jacob A., and Harry G. Johnson, eds. *The Economics of Exchange Rates*. Reading, Mass.: Addison-Wesley, 1978.

Levich, Richard M. "Empirical Studies of Exchange Rates: Price Behavior, Rate Determination and Market Efficiency." In *Handbook of International Economics*, vol. II. Ronald W. Jones and Peter B. Kenen, eds. Netherlands: Elsevier B.V., 1985, pp. 980-1040.

Marrinan, Jane. "Exchange Rate Determination: Sorting Out Theory and Evidence." *New England Economic Review*, November/December 1989, pp. 39-51.

Stockman, Alan C. "The Equilibrium Approach to Exchange Rates." *Economic Review*, Federal Reserve Bank of Richmond, March/April 1987, pp. 12-30.

The International Monetary System

3

The monetary and economic disorders of the past fifteen years . . . are a reaction to a world monetary system that has no historical precedent. We have been sailing on uncharted waters and it has been taking time to learn the safest routes.

Milton Friedman
Winner of Nobel Prize in Economics

CHAPTER LEARNING OBJECTIVES

- To distinguish between a free float, a managed float, a target-zone arrangement, and a fixed-rate system of exchange rate determination
- To describe how equilibrium in the foreign exchange market is achieved under alternative exchange rate systems, including a gold standard
- To identify the three categories of central bank intervention under a managed float
- To describe the purposes, operation, and consequences of the European Monetary System
- To identify the four alternatives to devaluation under a system of fixed exchange rates
- To explain the political realities that underlie government intervention in the foreign exchange market
- To describe the history and consequences of the gold standard
- To explain why the postwar international monetary system broke down

The currency problems faced by firms today have been exacerbated by the breakdown of the postwar international monetary system established at the Bretton Woods Conference in 1944. The main features of the *Bretton Woods system* were the relatively fixed exchange rates of individual currencies in terms of the U.S. dollar and the convertibility of the dollar into gold for foreign official institutions. These fixed exchange rates were supposed to reduce the riskiness of international transactions, thus promoting growth in world trade.

Yet in 1971, the Bretton Woods system fell victim to the international monetary turmoil it was designed to avoid. It was replaced by the present regime of rapidly fluctuating exchange rates, resulting in major problems and opportunities for multinational corporations. The purpose of this chapter is to help managers, both financial and nonfinancial, understand what the international monetary system is and how the choice of system affects currency values. It also provides a historical background of the international monetary system to enable managers to gain perspective when trying to interpret the likely consequences of new policy moves in the area of international finance. After all, although the types of government foreign exchange policies may at times appear to be limitless, they are all variations on a common theme.

3.1 ALTERNATIVE EXCHANGE RATE SYSTEMS

The basic market mechanisms for establishing exchange rates include the free float, managed float, target-zone arrangement, and fixed-rate system.

The *international monetary system* refers primarily to the set of policies, institutions, practices, regulations, and mechanisms that determine the rate at which one currency is exchanged for another. This section considers five different market mechanisms for establishing exchange rates: free float, managed float, target-zone arrangement, fixed-rate system, and the current hybrid system.

Free Float

We have already seen that free market exchange rates are determined by the interaction of currency supplies and demands. The supply-and-demand schedules, in turn, are influenced by price level changes, interest differentials, and economic growth. In a *free float*, as these economic parameters change—for example, due to new government policies or acts of nature—market participants will adjust their current, and expected, future currency needs. In the two-country example of Germany and the United States, the shifts in the Deutsche mark supply-and-demand schedules will, in turn, lead to new equilibrium positions. Over time, the exchange rate will fluctuate randomly as market participants assess and react to new information, much as security and commodity prices in other financial markets respond to news. These shifts and oscillations are illustrated in Exhibits 3.1 and 3.2; D_t and S_t are the hypothetical DM demand-and-supply curves, respectively, for period t. Such a system of freely floating exchange rates is usually referred to as a *clean float*.

A free float relies solely on market forces to determine exchange rates.

Managed Float

Not surprisingly, few countries have been able to resist for long the temptation to actively intervene in the foreign exchange market in order to reduce the economic uncertainty associated with a clean float. Too abrupt a change in the value of its currency, it is feared, could imperil a nation's export industries (if the currency appreciates) or lead to a higher rate of inflation (if the currency depreciates). Moreover, the experience with floating rates in the 1980s has not been encouraging. Instead of reducing economic volatility, as they were supposed to do, floating exchange rates appear to have increased it. Exchange rate uncertainty also reduces economic efficiency by acting as a tax on trade and foreign investment.

Exhibit 3.1 Supply-and-Demand Curve Shifts

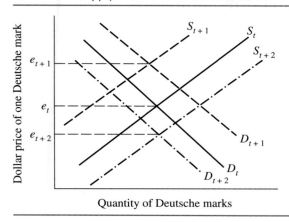

Therefore, most countries with floating currencies have attempted, via central bank intervention, to smooth out exchange rate fluctuations. Such a system of managed exchange rates, called a *managed float*, is also known as a *dirty float*.

Managed floats fall into three distinct categories of central bank intervention. The approaches, which vary in their reliance on market forces, are as follows:

Managed floats vary in their reliance on market forces.

1. *Smoothing out daily fluctuations*: Governments following this route attempt only to preserve an orderly pattern of exchange rate changes. They occasionally enter the market on the buy or sell side to ease the transition from one rate to another, rather than resist fundamental market forces, tending to bring about longer-term currency appreciation or depreciation.

2. *"Leaning against the wind:"* This approach is an intermediate policy designed to moderate or prevent abrupt short- and medium-term fluctuations

Exhibit 3.2 Fluctuating Exchange Rate

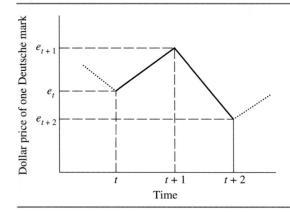

brought about by random events whose effects are expected to be only temporary. The rationale for this policy—which is primarily aimed at delaying, rather than resisting, fundamental exchange rate adjustments—is that government intervention can reduce for exporters and importers the uncertainty caused by disruptive exchange rate changes. It is questionable, though, whether governments are more capable than private forecasters of distinguishing between fundamental and temporary (irrational) values.

3. *Unofficial pegging*: This strategy evokes memories of a fixed-rate system. It involves resisting fundamental upward or downward exchange rate movements for reasons clearly unrelated to exchange market forces. Thus, Japan has historically resisted revaluation of the yen for fear of its consequences for Japanese exports. With unofficial pegging, however, there is no publicly announced government commitment to a given exchange rate level.

Target-Zone Arrangement

A target-zone arrangement allows exchange rates for member currencies to vary within a narrow band.

Many economists and policy makers have argued that the industrialized countries could minimize exchange rate volatility and enhance economic stability if the United States, Germany, and Japan linked their currencies in a target-zone system. Under a *target-zone arrangement*, countries adjust their national economic policies to maintain their exchange rates within a specific margin around agreed-upon, fixed central exchange rates. Such a system already exists for the major European currencies participating in the European Monetary System.

The *European Monetary System* (EMS) began operating in March 1979. Its purpose is to foster monetary stability in the *European Community* (EC, or the *Common Market*). As part of this system, the members have established the European Currency Unit, which plays a central role in the functioning of the EMS. The *European Currency Unit* or ECU is a composite currency that consists of fixed amounts of ten European currencies. The quantity of each country's currency in the ECU reflects that country's relative economic strength in the European Community. The ECU functions as a unit of account, as a means of settlement, and as a reserve asset for the members of the EMS.

The European Monetary System uses a target-zone arrangement to foster currency stability.

At the heart of the system is an *exchange-rate mechanism* (ERM), which provides for each member to determine a mutually agreed upon central exchange rate for its currency; each rate is denominated in currency units per ECU. These central rates attempt to establish equilibrium exchange values, but members can seek adjustments to the central rates. With the last realignment on January 12, 1987, the ECU central rates were the following: 42.4582 Belgian francs, 7.85212 Danish kroner, 2.05853 Deutsche marks, 6.90403 French francs, 2.31943 Dutch guilders, 0.798411 Irish pounds, and 1483.58 Italian lire. Other nations, including Norway, Sweden, and Finland, though not members of the ERM, also tied their currencies to the ECU.

Central rates establish a grid of bilateral cross-exchange rates between the currencies. For example, 2.05853 Deutsche marks per ECU, divided by 7.85212 Danish kroner per ECU, equals 0.26216 DM per krone, which also implies 3.81443 kroner per DM. Nations (except Spain and Britain) participating in the ERM pledged to keep their currencies within a 2.25% margin on either side of these central cross-exchange rates. (Spain and Britain had 6% margins.) Thus, if the Danish krone should strengthen against the Deutsche mark and reach the upper intervention limit, the Bundesbank will sell kroner to commercial banks at 3.73 kroner per DM, and Denmark's National Bank will buy DM at 0.26810 kroner per DM.

In September 1992, however, the ERM came unglued as speculators knocked sterling and the lira out of the ERM and obliged the peseta and Finnish markka to devalue. In round 2, beginning in November 1992, the Norwegian krone, Swedish krona, Irish punt, Portuguese escudo, and, once again, the peseta were forced to devalue. The final blow to the system was landed in round 3, which culminated in August 1993. In August, the EC agreed that currencies should henceforth trade within bands of 15% above or below their central rates (although Germany and the Netherlands pledged to voluntarily hold to the old 2.25% fluctuation range between the DM and the guilder). Such wide bands, of course, mock the intent of the ERM. Appendix A, at the back of the book, discusses the events of August 1993 in more detail.

Fixed-Rate System

Under a *fixed-rate system*, such as Bretton Woods, governments are committed to maintaining target exchange rates. Each central bank actively buys or sells its currency in the foreign exchange market whenever its exchange rate threatens to deviate from its stated par value by more than an agreed-upon percentage. The resulting coordination of monetary policy ensures that each member nation has the same inflation rate. Put another way, in order for a fixed-rate system to work, each member must accept the group's joint inflation rate as its own.

A fixed-rate system requires its members to coordinate their monetary policies so as to maintain target exchange rates.

Under the Bretton Woods system, whenever the commitment to the official rate became untenable, it was abruptly changed and a new rate was announced publicly. Currency devaluation or revaluation, however, was usually the last in a string of temporizing alternatives for solving a persistent balance-of-payments deficit or surplus.

Four policy alternatives to devaluation have been employed. What follows is a discussion of the efficacy of each policy. In general, these policies and their effects would be reversed in the case of revaluation.

1. *Foreign borrowing*: As we saw in Chapter 2, an overvalued currency will lead to a balance-of-payments deficit. Governments typically try to finance these payments deficits by borrowing abroad. However, foreign borrowing is only a temporary solution to a persistent payments deficit. Foreign money can be withdrawn as easily as it was brought in. If capital controls are imposed to counter this possibility, few additional funds will be forthcoming. Even the threat of controls is likely to lead to large capital outflows and further worsen a country's deficit.

Government access to foreign capital markets can be maintained only as long as investors have a reasonable expectation of being repaid. For example, Mexico financed large payments deficits during the late 1970s with increasingly heavy foreign borrowing. However, by early 1982, investors began withholding additional funds from Mexico when they perceived a decrease in the country's ability to pay its debts. The peso was devalued shortly thereafter.

2. *Austerity*: Austerity brought about by a combination of reduced government expenditures and increased taxes can be a permanent substitute for devaluation. If austerity works as intended, national income will be reduced, bringing about a decline in imports; the greater the decline in imports, the more effective austerity will be at reducing a trade deficit. But if a fall in imports were the only consequence of the decline in national income, austerity would not boost the value of the currency. As we saw previously, a decline in national income is likely to lower, not raise, a currency's value.

Thus, to work properly, the primary effect of austerity must be to bring about a lower rate of domestic inflation (disinflation). Disinflation will strengthen the currency's value, lessening the need for a devaluation. However, disinflation often leads to a short-run increase in unemployment, a cost of austerity that politicians today generally consider to be unacceptable.

3. *Wage and price controls*: An alternative to austerity is the imposition of wage and price controls. Although varying in its popularity, this alternative is perhaps more politically palatable. However, the historical evidence on these controls emphasizes the futility of attacking symptoms rather than the problem itself. Moreover, the policy is likely to increase pressure on the currency because it clearly indicates that the government doesn't possess the political will to deal with fundamental causes.

4. *Exchange controls*. In addition to other measures, many governments attempt to achieve a balance-of-payments equilibrium by imposing exchange controls. Exchange controls have become a way of life in most developing countries. Nations with overvalued currencies ration foreign exchange, while countries facing revaluation, such as South Korea and Switzerland, may restrict capital inflows.

In effect, government controls supersede the allocative function of the foreign exchange market. The most drastic situation is when all foreign exchange earnings must be surrendered to the central bank which, in turn, apportions these funds to users on the basis of government priorities. The buying and selling rates need not be equal, nor need they be uniform across all transaction categories. Exhibit 3.3 lists the most frequently used currency control measures. These controls are a major source of market imperfection, providing opportunities as well as risks for multinational corporations.

Some countries, such as Italy and France, have established (and abandoned) *two-tier foreign exchange markets*. This arrangement involves an official market (at the official rate) for current account transactions and a free market for capital account transactions. The incentive for arbitrage between these two markets increases as the rate spread widens; arbitrage, however, is illegal.

The Current System of Exchange Rate Determination

The current international monetary system is a hybrid, with major currencies floating on a managed basis, some currencies freely floating, and other currencies

Currency controls are an important alternative to devaluation in a fixed-rate system.

Exhibit 3.3 Typical Currency Control Measures

— Restriction or prohibition of certain remittance categories such as dividends or royalties.
— Ceilings on direct foreign investment outflows (e.g., the elaborate U.S. Office of Foreign Direct Investment controls in effect 1968–1975)
— Controls on overseas portfolio investments
— Import restrictions
— Required surrender of hard-currency export receipts to central bank
— Limitations on prepayments for imports
— Requirements to deposit in interest-free accounts with central bank, for a specified time, some percentage of the value of imports and/or remittances
— Foreign borrowings restricted to a minimum or maximum maturity
— Ceilings on granting of credit to foreign firms
— Imposition of taxes and limitations on foreign-owned bank deposits
— Multiple exchange rates for buying and selling foreign currencies, depending on category of goods or services each transaction falls into

moving in and out of various types of pegged exchange rate relationships. Exhibit 3.4 presents a currency map that describes the various zones and blocs linking the world's currencies as of December 31, 1992.

3.2 A BRIEF HISTORY OF THE INTERNATIONAL MONETARY SYSTEM

Almost from the dawn of history, gold has been used as a medium of exchange because of its desirable properties. It is durable, storable, portable, easily recognized, divisible, and easily standardized. Another valuable attribute of gold is that short-run changes in its stock are limited by high production costs, making it costly for governments to manipulate. Most importantly, because gold is a commodity money, it ensures a long-run tendency toward price stability. The reason is that the purchasing power of an ounce of gold, or what it will buy in terms of all other goods and services, will tend toward equality with its long-run cost of production.

> The desirable properties of gold have led it to play an important role historically in the international monetary system.

For these reasons, most major currencies, until recently, were on a gold standard, which defined their relative values or exchange rates. The *gold standard* essentially involved a commitment by the participating countries to fix the prices of their domestic currencies in terms of a specified amount of gold. The countries maintained these prices by being willing to buy or sell gold to anyone at that price. For example, from 1821 to 1914, Great Britain maintained a fixed price of gold at £3, 17s, 10½d per ounce; the United States, over the 1834–1933 period, maintained the price of gold at $20.67 per ounce (with the exception of the Greenback period from 1861–1878). Thus, over the period 1834–1914 (with the exception of 1861–1878), the dollar/pound sterling exchange rate was perfectly

Exhibit 3.4   Exchange Rate Arrangements, December 31, 1992

Currency Pegged to				Flexibility Limited	More Flexible	
U.S. Dollar	French Franc	Other Currency	Other Composite[1]	Single Currency[2]	Managed Floating	Independently Floating
Angola	Benin	Bhutan	Algeria	Bahrain	China, P.R.	Afghanistan
Antigua &	Burkina Faso	(Indian Rs.)	Austria	Qatar	Ecuador	Albania
Barbuda	Cameroon	Estonia (DM)	Bangladesh	Saudi Arabia	Egypt	Australia
Argentina	C. African	Kiribati (A$)	Botswana	United Arab	Greece	Bolivia
Bahamas, The	Rep.	Lesotho	Cape Verde	Emirates	Guinea	Brazil
Barbados	Chad	(So. African R)	Cyprus		Guinea-	Bulgaria
Belize	Comoros	Nambia	Czechoslovakia	*Cooperative*	Bissau	Canada
Djibouti	Congo	(So. African R)	Fiji	*Arrangements*[3]	India	Costa Rica
Dominica	Côte d'Ivoire	Swaziland	Hungary	Belgium	Indonesia	Dominican
Ethiopia	Equatorial	(So. African R)	Iceland	Denmark	Israel	Rep.
Grenada	Guinea		Jordan	France	Korea	El Salvador
Iraq	Gabon	*SDR*	Kenya	Germany	Lao P.D.	Finland
Liberia	Mali		Kuwait	Ireland	Rep.	Gambia, The
Marshall Islands	Niger	Iran, I. R. of	Malawi	Luxembourg	Maldives	Ghana
Mongolia	Senegal	Libya	Malaysia	Netherlands	Mexico	Guatemala
Oman	Togo	Myanmar	Malta	Portugal	Pakistan	Guyana
Panama		Rwanda	Mauritania	Spain	Poland	Haiti
St. Kitts & Nevis	*Russian Ruble*	Seychelles	Mauritius		Sao Tome &	Honduras
St. Lucia			Morocco		Principe	Italy
St. Vincent &	Armenia		Nepal		Singapore	Jamaica
the Grenadines	Azerbaijan		Papua New		Somalia	Japan
Suriname	Belarus		Guinea		Sri Lanka	Latvia
Syrian Arab Rep.	Georgia		Solomon Islands		Tunisia	Lebanon
Trinidad &	Kyrgyzstan		Tanzania		Turkey	Mozambique
Tobago	Moldova		Thailand		Viet Nam	New Zealand
Yemen, Republic of			Tonga			Nigeria
			Vanuatu		*Adjusted*[4]	Norway
			Western Samoa			Paraguay
			Zimbabwe		Chile	Peru
					Colombia	Philippines
					Madagascar	Romania
						Russia
						Sierra Leone
						South Africa
						Sudan
						Sweden
						Switzerland
						Uganda
						Ukraine
						United
						Kingdom
						United States
						Venezuela
						Zaïre
						Zambia

NOTE: For members with dual or multiple exchange markets, the arrangement shown is that in the major market.
[1]Comprises currencies which are pegged to various "baskets" of currencies of the members' own choice, as distinct from the SDR basket.
[2]Exchange rates of all currencies have shown limited flexibility in terms of the U.S. dollar.
[3]Refers to the cooperative arrangement maintained under the European Monetary System.
[4]Includes exchange arrangements under which the exchange rate is adjusted at relatively frequent intervals, on the basis of indicators determined by the respective member countries.

SOURCE: *International Financial Statistics,* International Monetary Fund, March 1993, p. 6.

determined. The fixed exchange rate of $4.867 per pound was referred to as the *par exchange rate.*

Since the value of gold relative to other goods and services does not change much over long periods of time, the monetary discipline imposed by a gold standard should ensure long-run price stability for both individual countries and groups of countries. Indeed, there was remarkable long-run price stability in the period before World War I when most countries were on a gold standard. As Exhibit 3.5 shows, price levels at the start of World War I were roughly the same as they had been in the late 1700s before the Napoleonic Wars began.

Exhibit 3.5 Wholesale Price Indices, Pre–World War I

Year	Belgium	Britain	France	Germany	United States
1776	na	101	na	na	84
1793	na	120	na	98	100
1800	na	186	155	135	127
1825	na	139	126	76	101
1850	83	91	96	71	82
1875	100	121	111	100	80
1900	87	86	85	90	80
1913	100	100	100	100	100

SOURCE: Data from B. R. Mitchell, *European Historical Statistics;* Bureau of the Census, *Historical Statistics of the United States.*

This record is all the more remarkable when contrasted with the post–World War II inflationary experience of the industrialized nations of Europe and North America. As shown in Exhibit 3.6, 1985 price levels in all these nations were several times as high as they were in 1950. Even in Germany the value of the currency in 1985 was less than one-third of its 1950 level, while the comparable magnitude was less than one-tenth for France, Italy, and the United Kingdom. Although there were no episodes of extremely rapid inflation, price levels rose steadily and substantially.

The gold standard created a remarkable record of price stability.

How the Gold Standard Worked in Theory

A gold standard is often considered an anachronism in our modern, high-tech world because of its needless expense; on the most basic level, it means digging up gold in one corner of the globe for burial in another corner. John Maynard Keynes, the famous British economist, labeled gold a "barbarous metal." Nikolai Lenin predicted that socialism would eventually reduce the value of gold to

Exhibit 3.6 Consumer Price Indices, Post–World War II

Nation	CPI, 1950	CPI, 1985	Loss of Purchasing Power During Period (%)
Belgium	100	466.8	76.8
France	100	1012.2	90.1
Germany	100	308.7	67.6
Italy	100	1369.1	92.7
Netherlands	100	513.4	80.5
United Kingdom	100	1056.0	90.5
United States	100	446.9	77.6

SOURCE: *International Financial Statistics,* International Monetary Fund, various issues.

where it would be used to "coat the walls and floors of public lavatories." The data in Exhibit 3.6 indicate that even under the gold standard, there were substantial fluctuations in the price level. The long-run stability of the price level includes alternating periods of inflation and deflation. Nonetheless, discontent with the current monetary system, which has produced over two decades of worldwide inflation and widely fluctuating exchange rates, has prompted interest in a return to some form of a gold standard.

To put it bluntly, calls for a new gold standard reflect a fundamental distrust of government's willingness to maintain the integrity of fiat money. *Fiat money* is nonconvertible paper money backed only by faith in the monetary authorities that they will not cheat (by issuing more money). This faith has been tempered by hard experience; the 100% profit margin on issuing new fiat money has proved to be an irresistible temptation for most governments.

By contrast, the net profit margin on issuing more money under a gold standard is zero. The government must acquire more gold before it can issue more money, and the government's cost of acquiring the extra gold equals the value of the money it issues. Thus, expansion of the money supply is constrained by the available supply of gold. This fact is crucial in understanding how a gold standard works.

Under the classical gold standard, disturbances in the price level in one country would be wholly or partly offset by an automatic balance-of-payments adjustment mechanism called the *price-specie-flow mechanism*. (Specie refers to gold coins.) To see how this adjustment mechanism worked to equalize prices across countries and automatically bring international payments back in balance, consider the following example.

Suppose that a technological advance increases productivity in the nongold-producing sector of the U.S. economy. This productivity will lower the price of other goods and services relative to the price of gold, and the U.S. price level will decline. The fall in U.S. prices will result in lower prices of U.S. exports; export prices will decline relative to import prices (determined largely by supply and demand in the rest of the world). Consequently, foreigners will demand more U.S. exports, and Americans will buy fewer imports.

Starting from a position of equilibrium in its international payments, the United States will now run a balance-of-payments surplus. The difference will be made up by a flow of gold into the United States. The gold inflow will increase the U.S. money supply (under a gold standard, more gold means more money in circulation), reversing the initial decline in prices. At the same time, the other countries will experience gold outflows, reducing their money supplies (less gold, less money in circulation) and, thus, their price levels. In final equilibrium, price levels in all countries will be slightly lower than they were before, due to the increase in the worldwide supply of other goods and services relative to the supply of gold. Exchange rates will remain fixed.

Thus, the operation of the price-specie-flow mechanism tended to keep prices in line for those countries that were on the gold standard. As long as the world was on a gold standard, all adjustments were automatic, and although there were many undesirable things that might have happened under a gold standard, enduring inflation was not one of them.

How the Classical Gold Standard Worked in Practice: 1821–1914

In 1821, following the Napoleonic Wars and their associated inflation, England returned to the gold standard. From 1821 to 1880, more and more countries joined the gold standard. By 1880, the majority of the nations of the world were on some form of gold standard. The period from 1880 to 1914, during which the classical gold standard prevailed in its most pristine form, was a remarkable period in world economic history. The period was characterized by a rapid expansion of virtually free international trade, stable exchange rates and prices, a free flow of labor and capital across political borders, rapid economic growth, and, in general, world peace. Advocates of the gold standard harken back to this period.

The period during which the classical gold standard prevailed was a remarkable period in world economic history.

Opponents of a rigid gold standard, in contrast, point to some less-than-idyllic economic conditions during this period: a major depression during the 1890s, a severe economic contraction in 1907, and repeated recessions. Whether these sharp ups and downs could have been prevented under a fiat money standard cannot be known.

The Gold Exchange Standard: 1925–1931

The gold standard broke down during World War I and was briefly reinstated from 1925 to 1931 as the Gold Exchange Standard. Under this standard, the United States and England could hold only gold reserves, but other nations could hold both gold and dollars or pounds as reserves. In 1931, England departed from gold in the face of massive gold and capital flows, owing to an unrealistic exchange rate, and the Gold Exchange Standard was finished.

Following the devaluation of sterling, 25 other nations devalued their currencies to maintain trade competitiveness. These *beggar-thy-neighbor devaluations*, in which nations cheapened their currencies in order to increase their exports at others' expense and reduce imports, led to a trade war. Many economists and policymakers believed that the protectionist exchange rate and trade policy fueled the global depression. In order to avoid such destructive economic policies in the future, the Allied nations agreed to a new postwar monetary system at a conference held in Bretton Woods, New Hampshire, in 1944. The conference also created two new institutions—the International Monetary Fund (IMF) and the International Bank for Reconstruction and Development (World Bank)—to implement the new system.

The Bretton Woods System: 1946–1971

Under the *Bretton Woods Agreement*, implemented in 1946, each government pledged to maintain a fixed, or pegged, exchange rate for its currency vis-à-vis the dollar or gold. Since one ounce of gold was set equal to $35, fixing a currency's gold price was equivalent to setting its exchange rate relative to the dollar. For

The Bretton Woods system returned the world to a gold standard.

example, the Deutsche mark was set equal to 1/140 of an ounce of gold, meaning it was worth $0.25 ($35/140). The exchange rate was allowed to fluctuate only within 1% of its stated par value (usually less in practice).

The fixed exchange rates were maintained by official intervention in the foreign exchange markets. The intervention took the form of purchases and sales of dollars by foreign central banks against their own currencies whenever the supply and demand conditions in the market caused rates to deviate from the agreed-upon par values. The IMF stood ready to provide the necessary foreign exchange to member nations defending their currencies against pressure resulting from temporary factors. Any dollars acquired by the monetary authorities in the process of such intervention could then be exchanged for gold at the U.S. Treasury, at a fixed price of $35 per ounce.

These technical aspects of the system had important practical implications for all trading nations participating in it. In principle, the stability of exchange rates removed a great deal of uncertainty from international trade and investment transactions, thus promoting their growth for the benefit of all the participants. Also, the functioning of the system imposed a degree of discipline on the participating nations' economic policies.

Periodic foreign exchange crises arose when governments failed to make necessary adjustments to their economic policies.

For example, a country that followed policies leading to a higher rate of inflation than that experienced by its trading partners would experience a balance-of-payments deficit as its goods became more expensive, reducing its exports and increasing its imports. The necessary consequences of the deficit would be an increase in the supply of the deficit country's currency on the foreign exchange markets. The excess supply would depress the exchange value of that country's currency, forcing its authorities to intervene. The country would be obligated to "buy" with its reserves the excess supply of its own currency, effectively reducing the domestic money supply. Moreover, as the country's reserves were gradually depleted through intervention, the authorities would be forced, sooner or later, to change economic policies in order to eliminate the source of the reserve-draining deficit. The reduction in the money supply and the adoption of restrictive policies would reduce the country's inflation, thus bringing it in line with the rest of the world.

Changes in these fixed rates were permitted only in the case of fundamental disequilibrium. In over 25 years of operation, however, fundamental disequilibrium was never adequately defined. This ambiguity proved useful to governments because they perceived large political costs to any exchange rate changes. Most governments were also unwilling to coordinate their monetary policies, even though this coordination was necessary to maintain existing currency values.

The reluctance of governments to adjust currency values or to make the necessary economic adjustments to ratify the current values of their currencies led to periodic foreign exchange crises. Dramatic battles between the central banks and the foreign exchange markets ensued. Those battles were invariably won by the markets. However, because devaluation or revaluation was used only as a last resort, exchange rate changes were infrequent and large.

In fact, Bretton Woods was a fixed exchange rate system in name only. Of 21 major industrial countries, only the United States and Japan had no change in par value during the period 1946–1971. Of the 21 countries, 12 devalued their curren-cies more than 30% against the dollar, 4 had revaluations, and 4 were floating their currencies by mid-1971 when the system collapsed.

The maintenance of price stability under the Bretton Woods system was largely the responsibility of the United States. As long as the system remained intact, all currencies were subject to the same rate of inflation as the U.S. dollar. If the United States kept the price of gold at $35 an ounce, it would stabilize prices around the world.

Unfortunately, the Federal Reserve did not arrange monetary policy to keep gold at $35. The U.S. government avoided this discipline by using every means of keeping gold at $35 except the one that counted—restricting the issuance of dollars. The United States issued nonmarketable Treasury bonds as a substitute for redemption of foreign gold holdings; prohibited U.S. citizens from holding gold abroad as well as at home; abolished the gold cover for U.S. dollars; elimi-nated private redemption of gold; restricted capital outflows by MNCs; and pressured other governments not to convert dollars for gold. The deathblow for the system came on August 15, 1971, when President Nixon, convinced that the "run" on the dollar was reaching alarming proportions, abruptly ordered U.S. authorities to terminate convertibility even for central banks. At the same time, he devalued the dollar to deal with America's emerging trade deficit.

The fixed exchange rate system collapsed along with the dissolution of the gold standard. There are two related reasons for the collapse of the Bretton Woods system. First, inflation reared its ugly head in the United States. In the mid-1960s, the Johnson administration financed the escalating war in Vietnam and its equally expensive Great Society programs by, in effect, printing money instead of raising taxes. As a result, it was difficult for the United States to maintain the price of gold at $35 an ounce without resorting to the various dilatory tactics referred to above.

> The Bretton Woods system broke down because the United States issued too many dollars.

Second, the fixed exchange rate system collapsed because some countries—primarily West Germany, Japan, and Switzerland—refused to accept the inflation that a fixed exchange rate with the dollar would have imposed on them. Thus, the dollar depreciated sharply relative to the currencies of these three countries.

The Post–Bretton Woods System: 1971 to the Present

In December 1971, under the *Smithsonian Agreement*, the dollar was devalued to 1/38 of an ounce of gold, and other currencies were revalued by agreed-on amounts vis-à-vis the dollar. After months of such last-ditch efforts to set new fixed rates, the world officially turned to floating exchange rates in 1973.

OPEC and the Oil Crisis of 1973–1974. October 1973 marked the beginning of successful efforts by OPEC to raise the price of oil. By 1974, oil prices had quadrupled. Nations responded in various ways to the vast shift of resources to the oil-exporting countries. Some nations, such as the United States, tried to offset the effect of higher energy bills by boosting spending, pursuing expansionary monetary policies, and controlling the price of oil. The result was high inflation, economic dislocation, and a misallocation of resources, without bringing about the real economic growth that was desired. Other nations, such as Japan, allowed the price of oil to rise to its market level and followed more prudent monetary policies.

The first group of nations experienced balance-of-payments deficits (because their governments kept intervening in the foreign exchange market to maintain overvalued currencies); the second group of nations, along with the OPEC nations, wound up with balance-of-payments surpluses. These surpluses were recycled to debtor nations, setting the stage for the international debt crisis of the 1980s.

U.S. Dollar Crisis of 1977–1978.   During 1977–1978, the value of the dollar plummeted, and U.S. balance-of-payments difficulties were exacerbated as the Carter administration pursued an expansionary monetary policy that was significantly out of line with other strong currencies. A run on the dollar was provoked, in part, by Treasury Secretary Michael Blumenthal's 1977 announcement that the dollar was overvalued. The turnaround in the dollar's fortunes can be dated to October 6, 1979, when the Fed announced a major change in its conduct of monetary policy. From here on, in order to curb inflation and inflationary expectations, it would focus its efforts on stabilizing the money supply, even if that meant more volatile interest rates. Prior to this date, the Fed had attempted to stabilize interest rates, indirectly causing the money supply to be highly variable.

> The dollar's ups and downs during the past 15 years can be traced largely to changes in U.S. economic policy.

The Rising Dollar: 1980–1983.   This shift had its desired effect on both the inflation rate and the value of the U.S. dollar. During President Reagan's first term in office (1981–1984), inflation plummeted and the dollar rebounded extraordinarily. This rebound has been attributed to vigorous economic expansion in the United States and to high real interest rates (due largely to strong economic growth) that combined to attract capital from around the world.

The Sinking Dollar: 1985–1987.   The dollar peaked in March 1985 and then began a long downhill slide. The slide is largely attributable to changes in government policy and relative national economic performances. Most important was the slowdown in U.S. economic growth relative to growth in the rest of the world. However, this factor was compounded by the effects of foreign exchange market intervention and confusing signals concerning U.S. monetary and fiscal policies.

By September 1985, the dollar had fallen about 15% from its March high. But this decline was considered inadequate to dent the growing U.S. trade deficit. In late September of 1985, the Group of Five, or *G-5 nations* (the United States, France, Japan, Great Britain and West Germany), met at the Plaza Hotel in New York City at the initiative of U.S. Treasury Secretary James Baker . His purpose was to defuse mounting protectionist pressures associated with the U.S. trade deficit. The outcome was the *Plaza Agreement*, a coordinated program designed to force down the dollar against other major currencies and thereby improve American competitiveness.

The policy to bring down the value of the dollar worked too well. The dollar slid so fast during 1986 that the central banks of Japan, Germany, and Britain reversed their policies and began buying dollars to stem the dollar's decline. Believing that the dollar had declined enough, and in fact showed signs of "overshooting" its equilibrium level, the United States, Japan, West Germany, France, Britain, Canada and Italy—also known as the Group of Seven or *G-7 nations*—met again in February 1987 and agreed to an ambitious plan to slow the dollar's fall. The *Louvre Accord*, named for the Paris landmark where it was negotiated, called for the G-7 nations to support the falling dollar by pegging exchange rates within a narrow, undisclosed range, while they also moved to bring their economic policies into line.

The United States promised to cut its bulging budget deficit; the Germans and Japanese agreed to stimulate their economies to offset slowing growth in the United States. However, as always, it proved much easier to talk about coordinating policy than to change it. The United States failed to cut its deficit. At the same time, inflation-sensitive governments in Bonn and Tokyo resisted U.S. pressure for major tax cuts, increases in money growth rates, or spending increases to stimulate their economies. They chose instead to limit their actions to token measures. The hoped-for economic cooperation faded, and the dollar continued to fall (see Exhibit 3.7).

International policy co-ordination has proven easier in theory than in practice.

The failure of the Louvre Accord provides further proof that currency manipulation is fruitless in a world of sovereign states. Intervening in currency markets—even strong statements of an intention to intervene—can have a pow-

Exhibit 3.7 Effects of Government Actions and Statements on the Value of 1987 Dollar

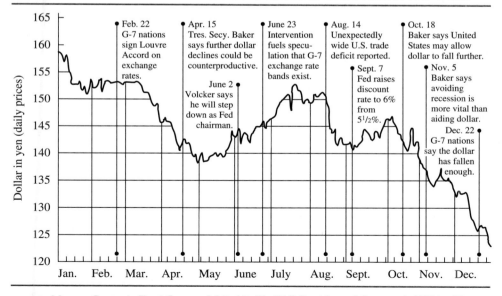

Only changes in basic economic policies can have long-term effects on a currency's value.

erful effect on exchange rates for a while. The dollar, for instance, dropped 5% the day after the Plaza Agreement was announced. But intervention has a lasting effect only if it is accompanied by equally lasting changes in monetary and fiscal policies. Short-term intervention is costly and merely delays the inevitable triumph of the market's judgment.

Recent History: 1988–1993.   Beginning in early 1988, the U.S. dollar rallied somewhat and then maintained its strength against most currencies through 1989. It fell sharply again in 1990 but then stayed basically flat in 1991 and 1992, while posting sharp intra-year swings. Its future course is unpredictable given the absence of an anchor for its value.

ILLUSTRATION: Iraq Invades Kuwait

Following the Iraqi invasion of Kuwait in August 1990, investors initially sought refuge in the dollar and it surged in value. Then they had second thoughts, switched out of dollars, and the dollar slumped. The reversal reflected investor nervousness about the possibility that the United States would repeat its past mistakes. In particular, the reaction of many Americans to the rise in the price of oil following the invasion evoked memories of the 1970s. Large oil companies—attacked unmercifully by politicians and the media throughout the 1970s—were once again in the spotlight, accused of profiteering on the Persian Gulf crisis and threatened with new price controls. At the same time, U.S. Treasury policymakers began pushing again for a falling dollar to improve American trade competitiveness. In other words, the dollar's fall reflected lack of confidence in the ability of the U.S. political system to deal with economic crises and its willingness to protect the integrity of the dollar. The subsequent war in the Persian Gulf and its successful conclusion, brought a reminder of American strength and renewed prospects for the U.S. economy—and a stronger dollar. The dollar's strength was reinforced by doubts about how well German economic integration was working.

Assessment of the Floating-Rate System

At the time floating rates were adopted in 1973, proponents said that the new system would reduce economic volatility and facilitate free trade. In particular, floating exchange rates would offset international differences in inflation rates so that trade, wages, employment, and output would not have to adjust. High-inflation countries would see their currencies depreciate, allowing their firms to stay competitive without having to cut wages or employment. At the same time, currency appreciation would not place firms in low-inflation countries at a competitive disadvantage. Real exchange rates would stabilize, even if permitted to float in principle, since the underlying conditions affecting trade and the relative productivity of capital would change only gradually. And if countries would coordinate their monetary policies to achieve a convergence of inflation rates, then nominal exchange rates would also stabilize.

The experience to date, however, is disappointing. The dollar's ups and downs have had little to do with actual inflation, and a lot to do with expectations of future government policies and economic conditions. Put another way, real exchange rate volatility has increased, not decreased, since floating began. Partly, this instability reflects nonmonetary (or real) shocks to the world economy, such as changing oil prices and shifting competitiveness among countries, but these real shocks were not obviously greater during the 1980s than they were in earlier periods. Instead, uncertainty over future government policies has increased.

Given this evidence, a number of economists and others have called for a return to fixed exchange rates. To the extent that fixed exchange rates more tightly constrain the types of monetary and other policies governments can pursue, this should make expectations less volatile and, hence, reduce fluctuations in the real exchange rate.

Although history offers no convincing model for a system that will lead to long-term exchange rate stability, it does point to two basic requirements. First, the system must be credible. If the market expects an exchange rate to be changed, the battle to keep it fixed is already lost. Second, the system must have price stability built into its very core. Without price stability the system will not be credible. Recall that under a fixed-rate system, each member must accept the group's inflation rate as its own. Only a zero rate of inflation will be mutually acceptable. If the inflation rate is much above zero, prudent governments will defect from the system.

Even with tightly coordinated monetary policies, freely floating exchange rates would still exhibit some volatility because of real economic shocks. But this volatility is not necessarily a bad thing since it could make adjustment to these shocks easier. For example, it has been argued that flexible exchange rates permitted the United States to cope with the buildup in defense spending in the early 1980s and the later slowdown in defense spending. When the United States increased defense spending, this expanded aggregate demand and shifted output toward defense. The stronger dollar attracted imports, which helped satisfy the civilian demand. As the United States cut back on defense spending, the weakening dollar helped boost U.S. exports, making up for some of the decline in defense. To the extent this argument is correct, the dollar's movements helped buffer the effects of defense spending shifts on American living standards.

As uncertainty over future government policies has increased, so has exchange rate volatility.

3.3 THE EUROPEAN MONETARY SYSTEM

A review of the *European Monetary System* provides valuable insights into the operation of a target-zone system and illustrates the problems that such mechanisms are likely to encounter. Perhaps the most important lesson that the EMS illustrates is that the exchange rate stability afforded by any target-zone arrangement requires a coordination of economic policy objectives and practices. Nations should achieve convergence of those economic variables that directly affect exchange rates—variables such as fiscal deficits, monetary growth rates, and real economic growth differentials.

Although the system helped keep its member currencies in a remarkably narrow zone of stability between 1987 and 1992, it has had a history of ups and downs. In its early years, the exchange-rate mechanism offered little anti-inflationary discipline, with Italy and France undergoing regular devaluations to offset higher inflation than in West Germany. By January 1987, the values of the EMS currencies had been realigned 12 times despite heavy central bank intervention. Relative to their positions in March 1979, the Deutsche mark and the Dutch guilder soared, while the French franc and the Italian lira nose-dived. For example, between 1979 and 1988, the franc devalued relative to the DM by over 50%.

EMS member states have allowed political priorities to dominate exchange rate considerations.

The reason for the past failure of the European Monetary System to provide the currency stability it promised is straightforward: Germany's economic policymakers, responding to an electorate hypersensitive to inflation, have put a premium on price stability; in contrast, the French have generally pursued a more expansive monetary policy in response to high domestic unemployment. Moreover, neither country has been willing to permit exchange rate considerations to override political priorities.

Consider, for example, the situation in early 1983. Both Germany and France were facing a general election in early March, and each government was reluctant to undertake economic measures that could adversely affect the outcome. The German government was reluctant to revalue the Deutsche mark for fear that a change would reduce the country's ability to export and, thus, increase domestic unemployment. In France, the Socialist government of Francois Mitterrand was reluctant to devalue the franc for fear that such a step (the third since it took office in May 1981) would deal a blow to the national "prestige" and would amount to an admission of failure of its domestic economic policies. Consequently, even though the pressures in the foreign exchange markets mounted, each government stood by its increasingly misaligned currency exchange rates.

The politically motivated intransigence proved costly to the French treasury. In early March, while the political debates raged on, the exchange markets were turned into "sure bet" gambling casinos. The French government is reported to have spent over $5 billion in two weeks to defend its overvalued currency, mostly to the benefit of the speculators. Finally, by mid-March and with the elections behind them, the two governments turned their attention to the exchange rates. The outcome was a 2.5% devaluation of the French franc and a 3.5% revaluation of the Deutsche mark.

The experience of the EMS also demonstrates once again that foreign exchange market intervention not supported by a change in a nation's monetary policy has only a limited influence on exchange rates. The heavy intervention preceding the January 12, 1987, EMS realignment was generally not accompanied by changes in national monetary policies. Germany, in particular, made only small adjustments to monetary policy in response to the exchange rate pressures. Consequently, the intervention failed to contain speculation, and a realignment became unavoidable.

Exhibit 3.8 United States and German Monetary Policies in Conflict

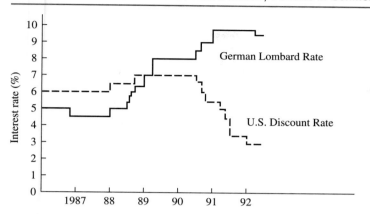

(a) Gap in Key Interest Rates Created by U.S. Federal Reserve and German Bundesbank Led to Turmoil in the Foreign Exchange Market

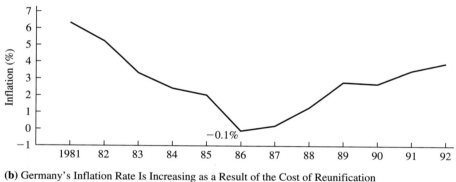

(b) Germany's Inflation Rate Is Increasing as a Result of the Cost of Reunification

SOURCE: Based on data from the Bundesbank and U.S. Federal Reserve, November 1992.

The Currency Crisis of September 1992

The same attempt to maintain increasingly misaligned exchange rates in the EMS occurred again in 1992. And once again, the system broke down, in September 1992. The catalyst for the September currency crisis was the decision by the Bundesbank to tighten monetary policy and force up German interest rates (see Exhibit 3.8) to battle inflationary pressures associated with the spiraling costs of bailing out the former East Germany. During this same period, the Federal Reserve had been cutting rates to revive the U.S. economy. This divergence in monetary policies caused the Deutsche mark to rise and the dollar to plunge. That, in turn, put the weaker currencies in the ERM under pressure. To defend their currency parities with the DM, the other member countries had to match the high interest rates in Germany (see Exhibit 3.9). The deflationary effects of high interest rates were accompanied by a prolonged economic slump

The currency crisis of September 1992 stemmed from misaligned exchange rates.

Exhibit 3.9 Defending the ERM Requires High Interest Rates in Europe

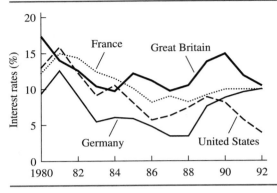

SOURCE: Data from OECD and Federal Reserve, September 30, 1992.

and high unemployment in Britain, France, Italy, Spain, and most other EMS members.

As the costs of maintaining exchange rate stability rose, the markets began betting that some countries with weaker economies would devalue their currencies or withdraw them from the ERM altogether rather than maintain painfully high interest rates at a time of rising unemployment. In effect, the markets were predicting that countries like Britain, Italy, and Spain would be more concerned about economic growth whereas the Bundesbank would continue to wage a relentless battle against its ancient enemy—inflation. Although the Bundesbank lowered the Lombard rate (the rate charged for supplemental bank borrowing) by 25 basis points to reduce currency speculation, the markets viewed the German move as "too little, too late" and renewed their attack.

The threat of a currency realignment forced European governments to raise their interest rates.

The mere possibility of a currency realignment meant that nations had to raise their interest rates dramatically to halt speculative attacks on their currencies: 15% in Britain and Italy, 13.75% in Spain, 13% in France, and an extraordinary 500% in Sweden. They also intervened aggressively in the foreign exchange markets. British, French, Italian, Spanish, and Swedish central banks together spent the equivalent of roughly $100 billion trying to prop up their currencies, with the Bank of England reported to have spent $15 billion–$20 billion in just one day to support the pound. The Bundesbank spent another $50 billion in DM to support the ERM. But all to no avail.

Ironically, the Bundesbank found itself a victim of its own anti-inflation strategy. Its interventions to maintain the ERM caused its money supply to bulge (just propping up the lira forced it to create more marks in one week than it would normally pump out in a year). Obviously, the Bundesbank could not continue with this level of intervention without endangering its monetary policy and its cherished German price stability.

On September 14, the central banks capitulated, but not before losing an estimated $4 billion to $6 billion in their mostly futile attempt to maintain the

ERM. For example, the Bank of England borrowed DM 33 billion from the Bundesbank when a pound was worth DM 2.78. It had to repay this money at the less favorable rate. At a rate of DM 2.50:£1, a devaluation of 10%, the extra cost would be £1.3 billion (33 billion/2.50 – 33 billion/2.78). As noted earlier, despite these costly efforts, Britain and Italy were forced to drop out of the ERM and Spain, Portugal, and Ireland devalued their currencies within the ERM. In addition, Sweden, Norway, and Finland were forced to abandon their currencies' unofficial links to the ERM.

With hindsight, Europe's economy—and the ERM itself—would look much healthier had there been a big revaluation of the DM against all other member currencies in the early days of German reunification. A stronger Deutsche mark would have dampened inflationary pressures in Germany and so allowed the Bundesbank to cut interest rates sooner. This is what the Bundesbank wanted, but the other members refused. In effect, the central banks brought September's debacle upon themselves because the exchange rates they were defending may have made political sense for the European leaders committed to the European Community but no longer made any economic sense.

The bottom line is that the maintenance of target zones narrow enough to eliminate the uncertainty associated with exchange rate volatility requires a close degree of macroeconomic coordination. Ironically, if nations maintain a mutually consistent and stable set of monetary, fiscal, and trade policies, a system of rigid target zones becomes unnecessary. Coordination and cooperation by themselves could maintain exchange rate stability. The principal argument, therefore, for a target-zone arrangement is that it could provide the mechanism to induce such coordination and cooperation.

Maintenance of a fixed-rate system or target-zone arrangement requires close coordination of macro-economic policies.

Unfortunately, the experience to date is mixed. Bretton Woods, for example, broke down when politics overrode economics; instead of changing policies to stay with the system, the major countries of the world simply dropped the system. Similarly, the Louvre Accord has produced more bickering than cooperation.

On the other hand, despite its recent problems, the EMS did achieve some significant success. By improving monetary policy coordination among its member states, the EMS has succeeded in narrowing inflation differentials in Europe. In 1980 the gap between the highest inflation rate (Italy's 21.2%) and the lowest (West Germany's 3.5%) was 16 percentage points. By 1990 the gap had narrowed to less than four percentage points. The narrowing of inflation rates, in turn, reduced exchange rate volatility until 1992. Indeed, from January 1987 to September 1992 currencies remained fixed. Moreover, the importance of Germany to the European economy and the Bundesbank's unwillingness to compromise its monetary policy mean that—the recent turmoil notwithstanding—other members of the EMS have been forced to adjust their monetary policies to more closely mimic Germany's low-inflation policy. As a result, inflation rates have tended to converge toward Germany's lower rate. For example, in 1990 the Netherlands, France, Belgium, Denmark, and Ireland all had inflation rates within one percentage point of Germany's (see Exhibit 3.10). In effect, the EMS has moved to a Deutsche-mark standard. Conversely, the gap between British and German infla-

Exhibit 3.10 The European Monetary System Forces Convergence Toward Germany's Inflation Rate

tion widened over time. In recognition of the benefits to be derived from a strong and stable monetary system, Prime Minister Thatcher finally relented on "monetary sovereignty" in late 1990 and entered Britain in the EMS (only to pull out two years later).

The EMS could not escape from market forces.

However, the EMS was based on Germany continuing to deliver low inflation rates and low interest rates. As long as Germany lived up to its end of the bargain, the benefits to other EMS members of following the Bundesbank's policies would exceed the costs. But once the German government broke that compact, by running huge and inflationary deficits, the costs to most members of following a Bundesbank monetary policy designed to counter the effects of the government's fiscal policies exceeded the benefits. Put another way, the existing exchange rates became unrealistic given what would have been required of the various members to maintain those exchange rates. In the end, there was no real escape from market forces.

Monetary Union

Even as it becomes less likely, many politicians and commentators point to the recent turmoil in the EMS as increasing the need for the European Community to move towards *monetary union*. Under this scenario, formalized in the *Maastricht Treaty*, the EC nations would establish a single central bank with the sole power to issue a single European currency by 1999. In order to join this monetary union, European nations would have to meet tough standards on inflation, currency stability, and deficit spending.

Business would clearly benefit from monetary union through lower cross-border currency conversion costs. For example, Philips, the giant Dutch electronics company, estimates that a single European currency would save it $300 million a year in currency transaction costs. Overall, the EC Commission estimates that businesses in Europe spend $13 billion a year converting money from one EC currency to another. Ordinary citizens also bear some substantial currency conversion costs. A tourist who left Paris with 1,000 francs and visited the other 11 EC countries, each exchanging her money for the local currency but not spending any of it, would find herself with less than 500 francs when she returned to Paris.

Adopting a common currency would also eliminate the risk of currency fluctuations. This would encourage the flow of trade and investments among member countries and more efficient allocation of resources within the region as a whole. Moreover, monetary union—such as exists among the 50 states of the United States, where the exchange rate between states is immutably set at 1—would provide the ultimate in coordination of monetary policy. Inflation rates under monetary union would converge, but not in the same way as in the current system. The common inflation rate would be decided by the monetary policy of the European central bank. It would tend to reflect the average preferences of the people running the bank, rather than giving automatic weight to the most anti-inflationary nation as in the current system. Thus, in order for the *European Monetary Union* (EMU) to be an improvement over the current state of affairs, the new European central bank must be as averse to inflation as is the central bank Europe in effect already has—the Bundesbank.

To ensure the EMU's inflation-fighting success, the new central bankers would have to be granted independence along with a statutory duty to devote monetary policy to keeping the price level stable. One way to protect the central bank's independence is to appoint the governing body, as in the United States and Germany, on long-term contracts that cut across national electoral cycles. Only then would a European central bank be able to do what William McChesney Martin, a former Fed chairman, said a sound central bank must always do: "take away the punch-bowl just when the party gets going."

Monetary union would reduce currency conversion costs and the risk of currency fluctuations.

ILLUSTRATION: German Monetary Union

As a first step toward economic reunification, East and West Germany formed a monetary union. On July 2, 1990, the East German mark or Ostmark was replaced by the Deutsche mark as the single German currency. It was agreed that East Germans would trade their Ostmarks to the West German Bundesbank for Deutsche marks at an exchange rate fixed in advance. In addition, the East German central bank had to cede its power to issue currency or create bank balances; otherwise, the Bundesbank would lose control over the money supply. At the same time, restrictions on movements of capital across the border were eliminated, making it possible for East Germans to hold bank accounts in West Germany and for West Germans to invest freely in East Germany. All transactions would be denominated in DM.

Most economists believed that a key to smooth transition toward German monetary union—and ultimately economic integration—was to get the exchange rate between Deutsche marks and Ostmarks right. Valuing the DM too high would destroy the worth of East German savings. But overvaluing the Ostmark would keep East German wages and goods from being competitive. Businesses in East Germany would suffer, leading to a further exodus of workers to West Germany.

Most economists felt that the best approach would be to err on the side of undervaluation, making industry in eastern Germany more competitive and attracting investors from western Germany and other countries. In the event, Chancellor Helmut Kohl decided on political grounds to convert East German savings, debts, wages, and prices from Ostmarks into DM at vastly overvalued rates ranging between one and two Ostmarks to one Deutsche mark. The resulting expansion in the DM money supply helped contribute to the inflationary pressures facing Germany. As we have already seen, the Bundesbank responded to unification-induced inflation by raising real interest rates, leading to the breakdown of the EMS.

Central banks profit from money creation.

Another important issue in forming a monetary union is who gets the benefits of *seigniorage*—the profit to the central bank from money creation. In other words, who gets to spend the proceeds from printing money? In the United States, the answer is the federal government. In the case of Europe, however, this issue has not been resolved yet.

3.4. SUMMARY AND CONCLUSIONS

This chapter studied the process of exchange rate determination under four different market mechanisms—free float, managed float, target-zone system, and fixed-rate system—as well as the current hybrid system. In the latter three systems, governments intervene in the currency markets in various ways to affect the exchange rate.

Regardless of the form of intervention, however, fixed rates do not remain fixed for long. Neither do floating rates. The basic reason that exchange rates don't stay fixed for long in either a fixed- or floating-rate system is that governments subordinate exchange rate considerations to domestic political considerations.

We saw that the gold standard is a specific type of fixed exchange rate system, one that required participating countries to maintain the value of their currencies in terms of gold. Calls for a new gold standard remind us of the fundamental lack of trust in fiat money due to the historical unwillingness of the monetary authorities to desist from tampering with the money supply.

Finally, we conclude that intervention to maintain a disequilibrium rate is generally ineffective or injurious when pursued over lengthy periods of time. Seldom have policymakers been able to outsmart for any extended period the collective judgment of buyers and sellers. The current volatile market environment, a consequence of unstable U.S. and world financial conditions, cannot be arbitrarily directed by government officials for long.

Examining U.S. experience since the abandonment of fixed rates, we find that free-market forces did correctly reflect economic realities thereafter. The dollar's value dropped sharply between 1973 and 1980 when the United States experienced high inflation and weakened economic conditions. Beginning in 1981, the dollar's value rose when American policies dramatically changed under the leadership of the Federal Reserve and a new president, but fell when foreign economies strengthened relative to the U.S. economy. Nonetheless, the resulting shifts in U.S. cost competitiveness have led many to question the current international monetary system.

The principal alternative to the current system of floating currencies with its economic volatility is a fixed exchange rate system. History offers no entirely convincing model for how such a system should be constructed, but it does point to two requirements. To succeed in reducing economic volatility, a system of fixed exchange rates must be credible, and it must have price stability built into its very fabric. Otherwise, the market's expectations of exchange rate changes combined with an unsatisfactory rate of inflation will lead to periodic battles among central banks and between central banks and the financial markets. The recent experiences of the European Monetary System point to the costs associated with the maintenance of exchange rates at unrealistic levels. These experiences also point out that, in the end, there is no real escape from market forces.

A final lesson learned is that one must be realistic in what one can expect from a currency system. In particular, no currency system can achieve what many politicians seem to expect of it—a way to keep all the benefits of economic policy for their own nation while passing along the costs to foreigners (who don't vote) or to future generations (who don't vote yet).

QUESTIONS

1. Have exchange rate movements under the current system of managed floating been excessive? Explain.

2. Why has speculation failed to smooth exchange rate movements?

3. Is a floating-rate system more inflationary than a fixed-rate system? Explain.

4. Find a recent example of a nation's foreign exchange market intervention and note what the government's justification was. Does this justification make economic sense?

5. Gold has been called "the ultimate burglar alarm." Explain what this expression means.

6. Since 1979, the price of gold has fallen by over 60%. What could explain such a steep price decline? Consider the roles of inflation and new financial instruments such as swaps and options that can provide lower-cost inflation hedges.

7. Comment on the following statement: "A system of floating exchange rate fails when governments ignore the verdict of the exchange markets on their policies and resort to direct controls over trade and capital flows."

8. Suppose nations attempt to pursue independent monetary and fiscal policies. How will exchange rates behave?

9. Will coordination of economic policies make exchange rates more or less stable? Explain.

10. The experiences of fixed exchange rate systems and target-zone arrangements have not been entirely satisfactory.

   a. What lessons can economists draw from the breakdown of the Bretton Woods system?

   b. What lessons can economists draw from the exchange rate experiences of the European Monetary System?

11. Despite official parity between the Deutsche mark and the Ostmark, the black market rate in early 1990 was about ten Ostmarks for one Deutsche mark. What problems might setting the exchange rate at one Ostmark for each DM create for Germany?

12. Historically, Spain has had high inflation and has seen its peseta continuously depreciate. In 1989, though, Spain joined the EMS and pegged the peseta to the DM. According to a Spanish banker, EMS membership means that "the government has less capability to manage the currency but, on the other hand, the people are more trusting of the currency for that reason."

   a. What underlies the peseta's historical weakness?

   b. Comment on the banker's statement.

   c. What are the likely consequences of EMS membership on the Spanish public's willingness to save and invest?

13. When Britain announced its entry into the exchange-rate mechanism of the EMS on October 5, 1990, the price of British gilts (long-term government bonds) soared and sterling rose in value.

   a. What might account for these price jumps?

   b. Sterling entered the ERM at a central rate against the DM of DM 2.95, and it is allowed to move within a band of plus and minus 6% of this rate. What are sterling's upper and lower rates against the DM?

14. In discussing European Monetary Union, a recent government report stressed a need to make the central bank accountable to the "democratic process." What are the likely consequences for price stability and exchange rate stability in the EMS if the "Eurofed" becomes accountable to the "democratic process?"

15. Comment on the following headline in *The Wall Street Journal* (January 11, 1993): "Germany's Rate Cut Takes Pressure Off French Franc, and the Rest of the EMS."

PROBLEMS

1. The central rates within the ERM for the French franc and DM are FF 6.90403:ECU 1 and DM 2.05853:ECU 1, respectively.

   a. What is the cross-exchange rate between the franc and the mark?

   b. Given a 2.25% margin on either side of the central rate, what are the upper and lower intervention limits for France and Germany?

2. On Friday, September 13, 1992, the lira was worth DM 0.0013065. Over the weekend, the lira devalued against the DM to DM 0.0012613.

   a. By how much has the lira devalued against the DM?

   b. By how much has the DM appreciated against the lira?

   c. Suppose Italy borrowed DM 4 billion, which it sold to prop up the lira. What were the Bank of Italy's lira losses on this currency intervention?

   d. Suppose Germany spent DM 24 billion in an attempt to defend the lira. What were the Bundesbank's DM losses on this currency intervention?

   3. Panama adopted the U.S. dollar as its official paper money in 1904. There is currently about $400 million to $500 million in U.S. dollars circulating in Panama. If interest rates on U.S. Treasury securities are 7%, what is the value of the seigniorage that Panama is forgoing by using the U.S. dollar instead of its own-issue money?

BIBLIOGRAPHY

Bordo, Michael David. "The Classical Gold Standard: Some Lessons for Today." *Federal Reserve Bank of St. Louis Review*, May 1981, pp. 2–17.

Coombs, Charles A. *The Arena of International Finance*. New York: John Wiley & Sons, 1976.

Friedman, Milton, and Robert V. Roosa. "Free Versus Fixed Exchange Rates: A Debate." *Journal of Portfolio Management*, Spring 1977, pp. 68–73.

4 The Balance of Payments and International Economic Linkages

I had a trade deficit in 1986 because I took a vacation in France. I didn't worry about it; I enjoyed it.

> Herbert Stein
> Chairman of the Council
> of Economic Advisors under
> Presidents Nixon and Ford

We have almost a crisis in trade and this is the year Congress will try to turn it around with trade legislation.

> Lloyd Bentsen
> U.S. Senator from Texas (1987)

Despite all the cries for protectionism to cure the trade deficit, protectionism will not lower the trade deficit.

> Phil Gramm
> U.S. Senator from Texas (1986)

CHAPTER LEARNING OBJECTIVES

- To distinguish between the current account, capital account, and official reserves account and describe the links among these accounts
- To calculate a nation's balance-of-payments accounts from data on its international transactions
- To identify the links between domestic economic behavior and the international flows of goods and capital and describe how these links are reflected in the various balance-of-payments accounts
- To describe the causes and likely consequences of the current U.S. trade deficit
- To list the proposed solutions to the U.S. trade deficit and analyze their likely economic consequences

A key theme of this book is that companies today operate within a global marketplace, and they can ignore this fact only at their peril. In line with this theme, the purpose of this chapter is to present the financial and real linkages between the domestic and world economies and examine how these linkages affect business viability. The chapter identifies the basic forces underlying the flows of goods, services, and capital between countries and relates these flows to key political, economic, and cultural factors.

Politicians and the business press realize the importance of these trade and capital flows. They pay attention to the balance of payments, on which these flows are recorded, and to the massive and continuing U.S. trade deficits. As we will see in Chapter 5, government foreign exchange policies are often geared toward dealing with balance-of-payments problems. But as the three quotes above indicate, many people disagree on the nature of the trade deficit problem and its solution. In the process of studying the balance of payments, this chapter will sort out some of these issues.

4.1 BALANCE-OF-PAYMENTS CATEGORIES

The *balance of payments* is an accounting statement that summarizes all the economic transactions between residents of the home country and residents of all other countries. Balance-of-payments statistics are published quarterly in the United States by the Commerce Department and include such transactions as trade in goods and services, transfer payments, loans, and short- and long-term investments. The statistics are followed closely by bankers and business people, economists, and foreign exchange traders; the publication affects the value of the home currency if these figures are more, or less, favorable than anticipated.

The balance of payments summarizes a nation's international economic transactions.

— Currency inflows are recorded as *credits,* and outflows are recorded as *debits.* Credits show up with a plus sign, and debits have a minus sign. There are three major balance-of-payments categories:
— *Current account,* which records flows of goods, services, and transfers
— *Capital account,* which shows public and private investment and lending activities
— *Official reserves account,* which measures changes in holdings of gold and foreign currencies—*reserve assets*—by official monetary institutions

Exports of goods and services are credits; imports of goods and services are debits. Interest and dividends are treated as services because they represent payment for the use of capital. Capital inflows appear as credits since the nation is selling (exporting) to foreigners valuable assets—buildings, land, stock, bonds, and other financial claims—and receiving cash in return. Capital outflows show up as debits because they represent purchases (imports) of valuable foreign assets. The increase in a nation's official reserves also shows up as a debit item because the purchase of gold and other reserve assets is equivalent to importing these assets.

Balance-of-payments accounting is based on double-entry bookkeeping.

The balance-of-payments statement is based on double-entry bookkeeping; every economic transaction recorded as a credit brings about an equal and offsetting debit entry, and vice versa. For example, if a foreigner sells a painting to a U.S. resident, a debit is recorded to indicate an increase in purchases made by the United States (the painting); a credit is recorded to reflect an increase in liabilities to the foreigner (payment for the painting).

Because double-entry bookkeeping ensures that debits equal credits, the sum of all transactions is zero. That is, the sum of the balance on the current account, capital account, and official reserves account must equal zero.

These features of balance-of-payments accounting are illustrated in Exhibit 4.1, which shows the U.S. balance of payments for 1992, and in Exhibit 4.2, which gives examples of entries in the U.S. balance-of-payments accounts.

Exhibit 4.1   The U.S. Balance of Payments for 1992 (U.S. $ Billions)

Credits		Debits	
a: Exports of civilian goods	$439.3	b: Imports of civilian goods	$535.5
c: Military sales abroad	10.9	d: Military purchases abroad	13.4
	Trade balance	$= a + c - (b + d)$	
		$=$ Deficit of 98.7	
e: Exports of services (investment income and fees earned, foreign tourism in United States, etc.)	276.8	f: Imports of services (investment income paid out, U.S. tourism abroad, etc.)	209.1
		g: Net unilateral transfers (gifts)	31.4
	Current-account balance	$= a + c + e - (b + d + f + g)$	
		$=$ Deficit of 62.4	
h: Foreign private investment in United States	80.1	i: U.S. private investment overseas	47.8
j: Foreign official lending in United States	40.3	k: U.S. government lending overseas	1.0
	Capital-account balance	$= h + j - (i + k)$	
		$=$ Surplus of 71.6	
		l: Net increase in U.S. official reserves	3.9
	Official reserves balance	$=$ Deficit of 3.9	
m: Statistical discrepancy	13.1		

SOURCE: Data from *Survey of Current Business*, U.S. Department of Commerce, March 1993.

Exhibit 4.2   Examples of Entries in the U.S. Balance-of-Payments Accounts

Credits	*Debits*
Current Account	
a: Sales of wheat to Great Britain; sales of computers to Germany	*b:* Purchases of oil from Saudi Arabia; purchases of Japanese automobiles
c: Sales of Phantom jets to Canada	*d:* Payments to Korean workers at U.S. bases in South Korea
e: Interest earnings on loans to Argentina; profits on U.S.-owned auto plants abroad; licensing fees earned by Lotus 1-2-3; spending by Japanese tourists at Disneyland	*f:* Profits on sales by Nestle's U.S. affiliate; hotel bills of U.S. tourists in Paris
	g: Remittances by Mexican-Americans to relatives in Mexico; Social Security payments to Americans living in Italy; economic aid to Pakistan
Capital Account	
h: Purchases by the Japanese of U.S. real estate; increases in Arab bank deposits in New York banks; purchases by the French of IBM stock; investment in plant expansion in Ohio by Honda	*i:* New investment in a German chemical plant by Du Pont; increases in U.S. bank loans to Mexico; deposits in Swiss banks by Americans; purchases of Japanese stocks and bonds by Americans
j: Purchases of U.S. Treasury bonds by Bank of Japan; increases in holdings of New York bank deposits by Saudi Arabian government	*k:* Deposits of funds by the U.S. Treasury in British banks; purchases of Swiss-franc bonds by the Federal Reserve
Official Reserve Account	
	l: Purchases of gold by the U.S. Treasury; increases in holdings of Japanese yen by the Federal Reserve

Current Account

The balance on current account reflects the net flow of goods, services, and unilateral transfers (gifts). It includes exports and imports of merchandise (trade balance), military transactions, and service transactions (invisibles). The service account includes investment income (interest and dividends), tourism, financial charges (banking and insurance), and transportation expenses (shipping and air travel). *Unilateral transfers* include pensions, remittances, and other transfers for which no specific services are rendered. In 1992, for example, the U.S. balance of trade registered a deficit of $98.7 billion, while the overall current-account deficit was $62.4 billion, a difference of $36.3 billion.

The current-account balance reflects the net flow of goods, services, and gifts.

The U.S. current-account deficit at $62.4 billion in 1992 is the world's largest, but as a percent of GNP the deficit has fallen to 0.9% in 1992—one fourth its peak in 1987. Eleven industrial countries—including Germany—had larger deficits than the United States as a percent of GNP in 1992.

Capital Account

The capital account shows public and private lending and investment activities.

Capital-account transactions affect a nation's wealth and net creditor position. These transactions are classified as either portfolio, direct, or short-term investments. *Portfolio investments* are purchases of financial assets with a maturity greater than one year, while *short-term investments* involve securities with a maturity of less than one year. *Direct investments* are those where management control is exerted. Government borrowing and lending is included in the balance on capital account. As shown in Exhibit 4.1, the U.S. balance on capital account in 1992 was a surplus of $71.6 billion.

Official Reserves Account

The change in official reserves measures a nation's surplus or deficit on its current- and capital-account transactions by netting reserve liabilities from reserve assets. For example, a surplus will lead to an increase in official holdings of foreign currencies and/or gold; a deficit will normally cause a reduction in these assets. However, U.S. balance-of-payments deficits have not been matched exactly by net changes in reserve assets because foreigners have been willing to hold many billions of dollars (over $100 billion it is estimated) for liquidity and other purposes. Instead of being converted into foreign currencies, many dollars have been placed on deposit in the Eurodollar market. For most countries, though, balance-of-payments deficits and reserve declines are closely correlated. A drop in reserves will occur, for instance, when a nation sells gold to acquire foreign currencies that it can then use to meet a deficit in its balance of payments.

Balance-of-Payments Measures

There are a number of balance-of-payments definitions available. The *basic balance* focuses on transactions that are considered to be fundamental to the economic health of a currency. Thus, it includes the balance on current account and long-term capital, but it excludes such ephemeral items as short-term capital flows—mainly bank deposits—that are heavily influenced by temporary factors—short-run monetary policy, changes in interest differentials, and anticipations of currency fluctuations.

The *net liquidity balance* measures the change in private domestic borrowing or lending that is required to keep payments in balance without adjusting official reserves. Nonliquid, private, short-term capital flows and errors and omissions are included in the balance, while liquid assets and liabilities are excluded.

The *official reserve transactions balance* measures the adjustment required in official reserves to achieve balance-of-payments equilibrium. The assumption here is that official transactions are different from private transactions.

Each of these measures has shortcomings, primarily because of the increasing complexity of international financial transactions. For example, changes in the official reserve balance may now reflect investment flows as well as central bank intervention. Similarly, critics of the basic balance argue that the distinction between short- and long-term capital flows has become blurred. Direct investment is still determined by longer-term factors, but investment in stocks and bonds can be just as speculative as bank deposits and sold just as quickly. The astute international financial manager, therefore, must analyze the payments figures rather than rely on a single summarizing number.

The Missing Numbers

In going over the numbers in Exhibit 4.1, you will note an item referred to as *statistical discrepancy*. This number reflects errors and omissions in collecting data on international transactions. In 1992, that item was $13.1 on the plus side. (A plus figure reflects a mysterious inflow of funds; a minus amount reflects an outflow.) The statistical discrepancy in 1990 was even higher, a huge $66.8 billion.

This discrepancy coincided with such worrisome foreign events as the Iraqi invasion of Kuwait, the turmoil in Iran, the unrest in Central and Latin America, and the upheaval in the Soviet Union. Many experts believe that the statistical discrepancy is primarily the result of foreigners surreptitiously moving money into what they deem to be a safe political haven—the United States.

4.2 THE INTERNATIONAL FLOW OF GOODS, SERVICES, AND CAPITAL

This section provides an analytical framework that links the international flows of goods and capital to domestic economic behavior. The framework consists of a set of basic *macroeconomic accounting identities* that link domestic spending and production to savings, consumption, and investment behavior, and thence to the capital-account and current-account balances. By manipulating these equations, we will identify the nature of the links between the U.S. and world economies and assess the effects on the domestic economy of international economic policies, and vice versa. As we shall see in the next section, ignoring these links leads to political solutions to international economic problems—such as the trade deficit—that create greater problems. At the same time, authors of domestic policy changes are often unaware of the effect these changes can have on the country's international economic affairs.

Basic macroeconomic accounting identities link domestic spending and production to the current-account and capital-account balances.

Domestic Savings and Investment and the Capital Account

The national income and product accounts provide an accounting framework for recording our national product and showing how its components are affected by international transactions. This framework begins with the observation that *national income,* which is the same as *national product,* is either spent on consumption or saved:

$$\text{National product} = \text{Consumption} + \text{Savings} \qquad (4.1)$$

Similarly, *national expenditure,* the total amount that the nation spends on goods and services, can be divided into spending on consumption and spending on domestic real investment. *Real investment* refers to plant and equipment, R&D, and other expenditures designed to increase the nation's productive capacity. This equation provides the second national accounting identity:

$$\text{National spending} = \text{Consumption} + \text{Investment} \quad (4.2)$$

Subtracting Equation 4.2 from Equation 4.1 yields a new identity:

$$\text{National income} - \text{National spending} = \text{Savings} - \text{Investment} \quad (4.3)$$

A nation whose income exceeds its spending will have a domestic savings surplus that must be invested abroad.

This identity says if a nation's income exceeds its spending, then savings will exceed domestic investment, yielding surplus capital. The surplus capital must be invested overseas (if it were invested domestically there wouldn't be a capital surplus). In other words, savings equals domestic investment plus net foreign investment. Net foreign investment equals the nation's net public and private capital outflows plus the increase in official reserves. The net private and public capital outflows equal the capital-account deficit if the outflow is positive (a capital-account surplus if negative), while the net increase in official reserves equals the balance on official reserves account. In a freely floating exchange rate system—that is, no government intervention and no official reserve transactions—excess savings will equal the capital-account deficit. Alternatively, a national savings deficit will equal the capital-account surplus (net borrowing from abroad); this borrowing finances the excess of national spending over national income.

A nation that produces more (less) than it spends will have a net capital outflow (inflow).

Here is the bottom line: A nation that produces more than it spends will save more than it invests domestically and will have a net capital outflow. This capital outflow will appear as some combination of a capital-account deficit and an increase in official reserves. Conversely, a nation that spends more than it produces will invest domestically more than it saves and have a net capital inflow. This capital inflow will appear as some combination of a capital-account surplus and a reduction in official reserves.

The Link Between the Current and Capital Accounts

Beginning again with national product, we can subtract from it spending on domestic goods and services. The remaining goods and services must equal exports. Similarly, if we subtract spending on domestic goods and services from total expenditures, the remaining spending must be on imports. Combining these two identities leads to another national income identity:

$$\text{National income} - \text{National spending} = \text{Exports} - \text{Imports} \quad (4.4)$$

Equation 4.4 says that a current-account surplus arises when national output exceeds domestic expenditures; similarly, a current-account deficit is due to domestic expenditures exceeding domestic output. Exhibit 4.3 illustrates this latter point for the United States. Moreover, when Equation 4.4 is combined with Equation 4.3, we have a new identity:

Exhibit 4.3 Trade Balance Falls as Spending Rises Relative to GNP

NOTE: Total spending is "Gross Domestic Purchases"; trade balance is "Net Exports of Goods and Services."

SOURCE: Data from "National Income and Product Accounts Tables," *Survey of Current Business,* U.S. Department of Commerce, various issues.

$$\text{Savings} - \text{Investment} = \text{Exports} - \text{Imports} \qquad (4.5)$$

According to Equation 4.5, if a nation's savings exceed its investment, then that nation will run a current-account surplus. This equation explains the Japanese current-account surplus: The Japanese have an extremely high savings rate, both in absolute terms and relative to their investment rate. Conversely, a nation, such as the United States, that saves less than it invests must run a current-account deficit. Noting that savings minus investment equals net foreign investment, we have the following identity:

> The current-account balance must equal the net capital outflow.

$$\text{Net foreign investment} = \text{Exports} - \text{Imports} \qquad (4.6)$$

Equation 4.6 says that the balance on the current account must equal the net capital outflow; that is, any foreign exchange earned by selling abroad must either be spent on imports or exchanged for claims against foreigners. The net amount of these IOUs equals the nation's capital outflow. If the current account is in surplus, then the country must be a net exporter of capital; a current-account deficit indicates that the nation is a net capital importer. This equation explains why Japan, with its large current-account surpluses, is a major capital exporter, while the United States, with its large current-account deficits, is a major capital importer. Bearing in mind that trade is goods plus services, to say that the United States has a *trade deficit* with Japan is simply to say that the United States is buying more goods and services from Japan than Japan is buying from the United States, and that Japan is investing more in the United States than the United States is investing in Japan. Between the United States and Japan, any deficit in the current account is exactly equal to the surplus in the capital account. Otherwise, there would be an imbalance in the foreign exchange market, and the exchange rate would change.

> Japan is using its large current-account surplus to invest in the United States.

Another interpretation of Equation 4.6 is that the excess of goods and services bought over goods and services produced domestically must be acquired through foreign trade and must be financed by an equal amount of borrowing from abroad (the capital-account surplus and/or official reserves deficit). Thus, in a freely floating exchange rate system, the current-account balance and the capital-account balance must exactly offset each other. With government intervention in the foreign exchange market, the sum of the current-account balance plus the capital-account balance plus the balance on official reserves account must be zero. These relations are shown in Exhibit 4.4.

To improve the current-account balance, domestic savings must be increased relative to domestic investment.

These identities are useful because they allow us to assess the efficacy of proposed "solutions" for improving the current-account balance. It is clear that a nation cannot reduce its current-account deficit nor increase its current-account surplus unless it meets two conditions: (1) Raise national product relative to national spending, and (2) increase savings relative to domestic investment. A proposal to improve the current-account balance by reducing imports (say, via higher tariffs) that doesn't affect national output/spending and national savings/investment leaves the trade deficit the same; and the proposal cannot achieve its objective without violating fundamental accounting identities.

These accounting identities also suggest that a current-account surplus is not necessarily a sign of economic vigor nor is a current-account deficit necessarily a sign of weakness. Indeed, economically healthy nations that provide good investment opportunities tend to run trade deficits (since this is the only way to run a capital-account surplus). The United States ran trade deficits from early Colonial

Exhibit 4.4 Linking National Economic Activity with Balance-of-Payments Accounts: Basic Identities

---

Our national product (Y) − Our total spending (E)
minus Our spending for consumption   minus Our spending for consumption

---

=   Our national savings (S) − Our investment in new real assets (I_d)
= Net foreign investment, or the net increase in claims on foreigners and official reserve assets, e.g., gold (I_f)

Our national product (Y) − Our total spending (E)
minus Our spending on our own goods   minus Our spending on our own
     and services   goods and services

=   Our exports of goods and services (X) − Our imports of goods and services (M)
= Balance on current account
= −(Balance on capital and official reserves accounts)

$$Y - E = S - I_d = X - M = I_f$$

Conclusions: A nation that produces more than it spends will save more than it invests, export more than it imports, and wind up with a capital outflow. A nation that spends more than it produces will invest more than it saves, import more than it exports, and wind up with a capital inflow.

times to just prior to World War I, as Europeans sent investment money and goods to develop the continent. During these 300 years as a debtor nation—a net importer of capital—the United States progressed from the status of a minor colony to the world's strongest power. Conversely, it ran surpluses while the infamous Smoot-Hawley tariff helped sink the world into depression. Similarly, during the 1980s Latin America ran current-account surpluses because its dismal economic prospects made it unable to attract foreign capital. As Latin America's prospects improved in the early 1990s, money flowed in and it began running capital-account surpluses again—matched by offsetting current-account deficits.

Government Budget Deficits and Current-Account Deficits

Up to now, government spending and taxation have been included in aggregate domestic spending and income figures. By differentiating between the government and private sectors, we can see the effect of a government deficit on the current-account deficit.

National spending can be divided into household spending plus private investment plus government spending. Household spending, in turn, equals national income less the sum of private savings and taxes. Combining these terms yields the following identity:

$$\begin{aligned} \text{National spending} &= \text{Household spending} + \text{Private investment} + \text{Government spending} \\ &= \text{National income} - \text{Private savings} - \text{Taxes} + \text{Private investment} + \text{Government spending} \end{aligned} \tag{4.7}$$

Rearranging Equation 4.7 yields a new expression for excess spending:

$$\text{National spending} - \text{National income} = \text{Private investment} - \text{Private savings} + \text{Government budget deficit} \tag{4.8}$$

where the *government budget deficit* equals government spending minus taxes. Equation 4.8 says that excess national spending is composed of two parts: the excess of private domestic investment over private savings and the total government (federal, state, and local) deficit. Since national spending minus national product equals the net capital inflow, Equation 4.8 also says that the nation's excess spending equals its net borrowing from abroad.

A government budget deficit will worsen a nation's current-account deficit.

Rearranging and combining Equations 4.4 and 4.8 provides a new accounting identity:

$$\text{Current account balance} = \text{Savings surplus} - \text{Government budget deficit} \tag{4.9}$$

Equation 4.9 reveals that a nation's current-account balance is identically equal to its private savings-investment balance less the government budget deficit. According to this expression, a nation running a current-account deficit is not saving enough to finance its private investment and government budget deficit.

Conversely, a nation running a current-account surplus is saving more than is needed to finance its private investment and government deficit.

In 1986, for example, private savings in the United States totaled $681 billion; private investment equaled $686 billion; and the government budget deficit amounted to $143 billion. Excess domestic spending thus equaled $148 billion, and the United States experienced a $143 billion current-account deficit. The $5 billion discrepancy reflects errors and omissions in the measurements of international transactions plus other small adjustments.

Exhibit 4.5 presents similar data for the United States between 1980 and 1992, along with the averages for the period 1973 to 1979. To facilitate comparisons over time, the data are expressed as percentages of gross national product (GNP). The table shows that the increase in the U.S. current-account deficit during the 1980s was associated with an increase in the total government budget deficit and with a narrowing in private savings relative to private investment. As savings relative to investment rose beginning in 1989, the current account deficit narrowed, even as the government deficit continued to grow. The growth in the total government

The U.S. current-account deficit during the 1980s was closely related to the federal deficit.

Exhibit 4.5 U.S. National Income Accounts and the Current-Account Deficit, 1973–1992 (%GNP)

Year	Gross Private Savings	Gross Private Investment	Savings Less Investment	Total Government Deficit	Current-Account Balance*
1973–79 (average)	18.0	16.8	1.2	−0.9	0.1
1980	17.5	16.0	1.5	−1.3	0.5
1981	18.0	16.9	2.9	−1.0	0.3
1982	18.3	14.7	3.6	−3.6	0.0
1983	17.4	14.7	2.7	−3.8	−1.0
1984	17.9	17.6	0.3	−2.7	−2.4
1985	17.2	16.5	0.7	−3.4	−2.9
1986	16.2	16.3	−0.1	−3.4	−3.4
1987	14.7	15.7	−0.8	−2.3	−3.5
1988	15.1	15.4	−0.3	−2.0	−2.5
1989	15.0	14.8	0.2	−1.7	−1.9
1990	15.4	14.4	1.0	−2.5	−1.6
1991	15.8	12.7	3.1	−3.4	−0.1
1992**	16.4	12.9	3.5	−4.8	−0.9

*The sum of the savings-investment balance and the government budget deficit should equal the current-account balance. Any discrepancy between these figures is due to rounding or minor data adjustments.

**Preliminary data.

SOURCE: *Economic Report of the President*, (Washington, D.C.: U.S. Government Printing Office, January 1993, Tables B–20, B–26, and B-100.

budget deficit reflects the huge federal budget deficit, since state and local governments typically run surpluses. In general, a current-account deficit represents a decision to consume, both publicly and privately, and to invest more than the nation currently is producing.

The purpose of Exhibit 4.5 is not to specify a channel of causation, but simply to show a tautological relationship among private savings, private investment, the government budget deficit, and the current-account balance. Nevertheless, the important implication is that steps taken to correct the current-account deficit can only be effective if they also change private savings, private investment, and/or the government deficit. Policies or events that fail to affect both sides of the relationship shown in Equation 4.9 will not alter the current-account deficit.

4.3 COPING WITH THE CURRENT-ACCOUNT DEFICIT

Conventional wisdom suggests some oft-repeated solutions to a current-account deficit. The principal suggestions are currency devaluation and protectionism. Yet, there are important, though subtle, reasons why neither is likely to work.

Currency Depreciation

An overvalued currency acts as a tax on exports and a subsidy to imports, reducing the former and increasing the latter. The result, as we saw in Chapter 2, is that a nation maintaining an overvalued currency will run a trade deficit. Permitting the currency to return to its equilibrium level will help reduce the trade deficit.

Many academics, politicians, and business people also believe that devaluation can reduce a trade deficit in a floating-rate system. Key to the effectiveness of devaluation is sluggish adjustment of nominal prices, which translates changes in nominal exchange rates into changes in real (inflation-adjusted) exchange rates. This view of exchange rate changes implies a systematic relation between the exchange rate and the current-account balance. For example, it implies that the current U.S. trade deficit will be reduced eventually by a fall in the value of the dollar.

One proposed solution to the U.S. current-account deficit is to devalue the dollar and make U.S. goods more competitive.

By contrast, we saw in Chapter 2 that all exchange rates do is to equate currency supplies and demands; they do not determine the distribution of these currency flows between trade flows (the current-account balance) and capital flows (the capital-account balance). This view of exchange rates predicts that there is no simple relation between the exchange rate and the current-account balance. Trade deficits do not "cause" currency depreciation, nor does currency depreciation by itself help reduce a trade deficit: That is, both exchange rate changes and trade balances are determined by more fundamental economic factors.

These diametrically opposed theories can be evaluated by studying evidence on trade deficits and exchange rate changes. A good place to start is with recent U.S. experience.

From 1976 to 1980, the value of the dollar declined as the current-account deficit for the United States first worsened and then improved; but from 1980 to 1985, the dollar strengthened even as the current account steadily deteriorated. Many analysts attributed the rise in the U.S. trade deficit in the early 1980s to the sharp rise in the value of the U.S. dollar over that period. As the dollar rose in value against the currencies of America's trading partners, it took fewer dollars to buy a given amount of foreign goods and more foreign currencies to buy a fixed amount of U.S. goods. Responding to these price changes, Americans bought more foreign goods; and foreign consumers reduced their purchases of U.S.-made goods. U.S. imports increased and exports declined.

Historical experience indicates that currency devaluation will not cure a trade deficit.

After reaching its peak in early March 1985, the value of the dollar began to decline. This decline was actively encouraged by the United States and by several foreign governments in hope of reducing the U.S. trade deficit. Conventional wisdom suggested that the very same basic economic forces affecting the trade account during the dollar's run-up would now be working in the opposite direction, reducing the U.S. trade deficit. As Exhibit 4.6 documents, however, the theory didn't work. The U.S. trade deficit kept rising, reaching new record levels month after month. By 1987, it had risen to $150 billion and remained at that level in 1988. What went wrong?

J-Curve Theory. One explanation is based on the J-curve theory, illustrated in Exhibit 4.7. The letter J describes a curve that, viewed from left to right, goes down sharply for a short time, flattens out, then rises steeply for an extended period. That's how J-curve proponents have been expecting the U.S. trade deficit to behave. According to the *J-curve theory,* a country's trade deficit worsens just after its currency depreciates because price effects will dominate the effect on volume of imports in the short run: That is, the higher cost of imports will more

Exhibit 4.6   The Dollar and the Deficit

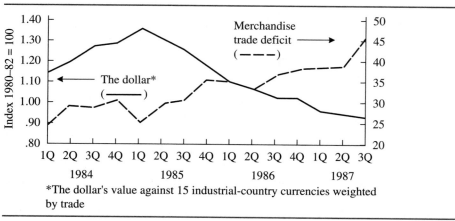

*The dollar's value against 15 industrial-country currencies weighted by trade

SOURCE: Data from *World Financial Markets,* Morgan Guaranty Trust Company; and *Survey of Current Business,* U.S. Department of Commerce.

Exhibit 4.7 The Theoretical J-Curve

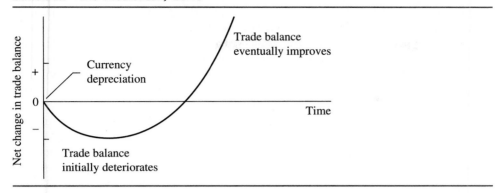

than offset the reduced volume of imports. Thus, the J-curve says that a decline in the value of the dollar should be followed by a temporary worsening in the trade deficit before its longer term improvement.

J-curve theory predicts that currency devaluation will initially worsen and then improve a nation's trade deficit.

The initial worsening of the trade deficit occurred as predicted in 1985 but it wasn't until over four years later, in 1989, that the trade deficit started coming down. Moreover, what little improvement occurred in 1989 may owe more to the jump in Social Security taxes, which reduced the federal budget deficit, than to depreciation of the dollar. In other words, the upturn of the J-curve has proved elusive.

U.S. Deficits and the Demand for U.S. Assets. Another possible reason for the failure of dollar devaluation to cure the persistent U.S. trade deficit is that the earlier analysis mixed up cause and effect. The argument that the strong dollar was the main culprit of the massive U.S. trade deficit rested on the obvious fact that the dollar's high price made it cheaper to import than to export. But that was not the complete picture. The dollar's price was not a cause nor even a symptom of the problem. It is axiomatic that price is a reflection of a fundamental value in the market. To argue that the high dollar hurt the U.S. economy does not explain how or why the price got there.

Instead of one causing the other, the strong dollar and the trade deficit may both have resulted from foreign demand for U.S. assets.

Here is a plausible explanation. For a variety of reasons, including an increasingly attractive investment climate in the United States and added political and economic turmoil elsewhere in the world, foreign investors in the early 1980s wanted to expand their holdings of U.S. assets. They bid up the value of the dollar to a level at which Americans were willing to exchange their assets for foreign goods and services. The result was a capital-account surplus balanced by a current-account deficit. In effect, the capital-account surplus drove the current-account deficit. The net result was excess American spending financed by borrowing from abroad.

Adding fuel to the current-account deficit, particularly after 1982, was the growth of the federal government's budget deficit. The U.S. budget deficit could only be funded in one of three ways: restricting investment, increasing savings, or

The price of the dollar determines the terms on which the rest of the world is willing to finance the U.S. budget deficit.

exporting debt. The United States rejected the first alternative, was unable to accomplish the second, and thus relied heavily on the third. Accordingly, the trade deficit was the equilibrating factor that enabled the United States to satisfy its extra large debt appetite. The price of the dollar determined the terms on which the rest of the world was willing to finance that deficit. When foreigners wanted to hold U.S. assets, the terms were quite attractive (they were willing to pay a high price for dollars); when foreigners no longer found U.S. assets so desirable, the financing terms became more onerous (they reduced the price they were willing to pay for dollars). However, since private savings were insufficient to finance private investment plus the government deficit, the U.S. current-account deficit persisted even as the lower dollar led Americans to consume fewer foreign goods and services. How could this be? It occurred because devaluation without a change in savings and spending behavior meant that the lower volume of imports cost more dollars: That is, Americans were buying less abroad, but paying more.

In general, unless the drop in imports exceeds the devaluation-induced increase in import prices, the total import bill in dollars will actually increase. For example, if a foreign currency appreciation of 20% causes an increase of 15% in the dollar price of imports, the volume of imports must drop by at least 15% for the dollar amount of imports to drop. At the same time, the dollar volume of exports should rise following dollar depreciation. The net effect of devaluation on the current account, therefore, depends on the price elasticities of export and import demand.

Unless the federal budget deficit shrinks, the current-account deficit will disappear only if the U.S. private savings rate rises significantly or the rate of investment falls. Hence, currency devaluation will work only if some mechanism is in place that leads to a rise in private savings, a cut in private investment, or a reduction in the government budget deficit. Otherwise, any rise in exports is offset by the adverse effects of higher-priced imports.

Although a policy of forcing down the dollar may not improve the current account balance, it does have two clear-cut effects. It makes Americans poorer, since it takes a greater volume of domestic output to acquire a unit of imports. Dollar depreciation also reduces the incentives U.S. industry has to improve international competitiveness by cutting costs and increasing productivity.

Protectionism

Another response to a current-account deficit is *protectionism*—that is, the imposition of tariffs, quotas, or other forms of restraint against foreign imports. A *tariff* is essentially a tax that is imposed on a foreign product sold in a country. Its purpose is to increase the price of the product, thereby discouraging purchase of that product and encouraging the purchase of a substitute, domestically produced product. A *quota* specifies the quantity of particular products that can be imported to a country, typically an amount that is considerably less than the amount currently being imported. By restricting the supply relative to the demand, the quota causes the price of foreign products to rise. In both cases, the results are ultimately a rise in the price of products consumers buy, an erosion of purchasing power, and a collective decline in the standard of living.

These results present a powerful argument against selective trade restrictions as a means of correcting a nation's trade imbalance. An even more powerful argument is that such restrictions don't work. Either other imports rise or exports fall. This conclusion follows from the basic national income accounting identity: Savings – Investment = Exports – Imports. Unless saving or investment behavior changes, this identity says that a $1 reduction in imports will lead to a $1 decrease in exports.

The mechanism that brings about this result depends upon the basic market forces that shape the supply and demand for currencies in the foreign exchange market. For example, when the U.S. government imposes restrictions on steel imports, the reduction in purchases of foreign steel effectively reduces the U.S. demand for foreign exchange. Fewer dollars tendered for foreign exchange means a higher value for the dollar. The higher-valued dollar raises the price of U.S. goods sold overseas and causes proportionately lower sales of U.S. exports. A higher-valued dollar also lowers the cost in the United States of foreign goods, thereby encouraging the purchase of those imported goods on which there is no tariff. Thus, any reduction in imports from tariffs or quotas will be offset by the reduction in exports and increase in other imports.

Restrictions on importing steel will also raise the price of steel, reducing the competitiveness of U.S. users of steel, such as automakers and capital goods manufacturers. Their ability to compete will be constrained both at home and abroad. Ironically, it is the most efficient and most internationally competitive producers—those who are exporting or are able to compete against imports—who are being punished, while the inefficient producers are being sheltered.

Protectionism is likely to reduce both imports and exports by the same amount, leaving the trade deficit unchanged.

Ending Foreign Ownership of Domestic Assets

One approach that would eliminate a current-account deficit is to forbid foreigners from owning domestic assets. If foreigners cannot hold claims on the nation, they will export an amount equal in value to what they are willing to import, ending net capital inflows. The microeconomic adjustment mechanism that will balance imports and exports under this policy is as follows.

The cessation of foreign capital inflows, by reducing the available supply of capital, will raise real domestic interest rates. Higher interest rates will stimulate more savings because the opportunity cost of consumption rises with the real interest rate; higher rates will cause domestic investment to fall because fewer projects will have positive net present values. The outcome will be a balance between savings/investment and elimination of excess domestic spending that caused the current-account deficit in the first place. Although such an approach would work, most observers would consider the resulting slower economic growth too high a price to pay to eliminate a current-account deficit.

Ending foreign ownership of domestic assets would eliminate a trade deficit but slow economic growth.

Although many observers are troubled by the role of foreign investors in U.S. financial markets, as long as Americans continue to spend more than they produce, there will be a continuing need for foreign capital. This foreign capital is helping to improve America's industrial base, while at the same time providing capital gains to those Americans who are selling their assets to foreigners. Foreign investors often introduce improved management, better production, or new technology that increases the quality and variety of goods available to U.S. consumers, who benefit from lower prices as well. Investment—even foreign investment—makes labor more productive. And higher labor productivity leads to higher wages—whether the factory's owners live across town or across the Pacific. Restrictions on foreign investment may also provoke reciprocal restrictions by foreign governments.

Boosting the Savings Rate

One way to reduce the trade deficit is to boost the national savings rate.

As we have seen, a low savings rate tends to lead to a current-account deficit. Thus, another way to reduce the current-account deficit would be to stimulate savings behavior. Yet, the data indicate that the rate of U.S. private savings has declined over time. In particular, personal savings, which averaged about 8% of disposable income in the 1970s, slid to 4.3% in 1987 and stayed below 5% through 1992. Future U.S. wealth will be impaired if the low U.S. personal savings rate persists.

One possible explanation for the decline in personal savings is that Social Security benefits expanded greatly during the 1970s. By attenuating the link between savings behavior and retirement income, Social Security may have reduced the incentive for Americans to save for retirement. By contrast, Japan—which has only a rudimentary social security system and no welfare to speak of—has an extraordinarily high personal savings rate. Presumably, the inability of the Japanese to throw themselves on the mercy of the state has affected their willingness to save for a rainy day.

Similarly, changes in tax regulations and tax rates may greatly affect savings and investment behavior and, therefore, the nation's trade and capital flows. Thus, purely domestic policies may have dramatic—and unanticipated—consequences for a nation's international economic transactions. The lesson is clear: In an integrated world economy, everything connects to everything else; politicians can't tinker with one parameter without affecting the entire system.

Current-Account Deficits and Unemployment

One rationale for attempting to eliminate a current-account deficit is that such a deficit leads to unemployment. Underlying this rationale is the notion that imported goods and services are substituting for domestic goods and services and costing domestic jobs. It is argued that reducing imports would raise domestic production and employment. However, the view that reducing a current-account deficit promotes jobs is based on single-entry bookkeeping.

If a country buys fewer foreign goods and services, it will demand less foreign exchange. As discussed above, this result will raise the value of the domestic currency, thereby reducing exports and encouraging the purchase of other imports. Jobs are saved in some industries, but other jobs are lost by the decline in exports and rise in other imports. According to this line of reasoning, the net impact of a trade deficit or surplus on jobs should be nil.

Judging by the claims of some politicians, however, it would appear that the economic performance of the United States has been dismal because of its huge current-account deficits. But if the alternative story is correct—that a current-account deficit reflects excess spending and has little to do with the health of an economy—then there should be no necessary relation between economic performance and the current-account balance.

The appropriate way to settle this dispute is to examine the evidence. Here are some facts:

1. Although its current-account deficit nearly quadrupled between 1982 and 1987, the United States created over 13 million new jobs during this period, more than Europe and Japan combined in the past decade.
2. Between 1983 and 1987, U.S. unemployment declined by 28%; the unemployment rate in Japan rose by 17%; and the unemployment rate in the Common Market countries rose by more than 20%.
3. Between 1982 and 1986 as the trade deficit increased, the United States gained 406,000 jobs in manufacturing.
4. Not only did the number of jobs in manufacturing increase in the United States, but real wages in manufacturing, which declined by 7% from 1977 to 1981 (when the United States was generally running a current-account surplus), increased by 6% from 1982 to 1986.

The large U.S. trade deficit during the 1980s does not appear to have harmed U.S. economic performance.

In short, from 1982 to 1986, the trade deficit soared, but the United States created jobs 3 times as fast as Japan and 20 times as fast as West Germany. Also, in the same time period, America's GNP grew 43% faster than that of Japan or West Germany, even though both nations had huge trade surpluses with the United States.

In general, no systematic relationship between net exports and economic growth should be expected. Exhibit 4.8 shows the annual growth rate of U.S. real GNP from 1970 to 1986, together with the real value of the current account. Strong

Exhibit 4.8 No Systematic Relationship Between Current Account and Economic Growth

SOURCE: Carl Walsh, "The Trade Balance and the Economic Outlook," *Weekly Letter,* March 6, 1987. Federal Reserve Bank of San Francisco.

Trade deficits, by them-
selves, are neither
good nor bad.

output growth has been associated with both an improving current account, as in 1978, and a worsening current account, as in 1984. The evidence shows that current-account surpluses—in and of themselves—are neither good nor bad. They are not correlated with growth, decline, competitiveness, or weakness. What matters is why they occur.

ILLUSTRATION: Germany's Current Account Surplus Turns Into a Deficit

The process of international payments equilibrium and its tie to both macroeconomic factors and exchange rates is shown in the case of Germany. With its mature industrial economy and aging population, western Germany has long run a current-account surplus. Modernization of the eastern German economy changed that. To finance reunification, Germany had to shift from being a large capital exporter to being a capital importer. This it did, as shown in Exhibit 4.9. For example, Germany's current account moved from a surplus of DM 70 billion (about 3% of GDP) in 1990 to a deficit of DM 30 billion (about 1.5% of GDP) in 1991. Such a drastic change could be brought about in one of two ways.

One possibility would have been to reduce domestic demand in Germany by private and government consumption or investment. However, cuts in capital spending would be unwise since they would mean less productive capacity in the future. Private consumption would have to be curbed through tax increases, which—even if temporary—would be unpopular, to say the least. Cutting non-

Exhibit 4.9 Reunification Turns Germany's Current-Account Surplus into a Deficit That Exceeds the U.S. Deficit (% of GDP)

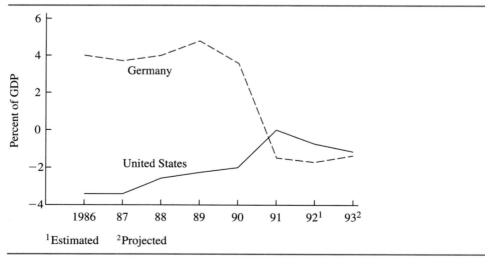

¹Estimated   ²Projected

SOURCE: Adapted from *The Economist*, January 30, 1993, p. 59. © 1993 The Economist Newspaper Group, Inc. Used with permission.

unification-related government expenditures would have been politically difficult as well, given the strong constituencies behind that spending.

The other alternative was to reduce demand for German exports and, at the
same time, rely to a greater extent on imports to meet domestic demand. This
path—which Germany chose—required its goods to become relatively more expensive to its trading partners (mostly fellow members of the EMS), and foreign
goods relatively less expensive to Germans. This shift in relative prices could be
accomplished through some combination of higher inflation in Germany, appreciation of the DM, depreciation of foreign currencies relative to the DM, or
deflation in fellow EMS members.

As we saw in Chapter 3, Germany was unwilling to accept inflation and the
ERM prevented exchange rate changes. That left only deflation in other EMS
countries—until it too proved unacceptable and the system broke down in September 1992.

The Bottom Line on Current-Account Deficits and Surpluses

To summarize the previous discussion of current-account deficits and surpluses,
consider the following stylized facts. Suppose that the United States is a country
whose citizens, for one reason or another, have a low propensity to save. And
suppose also that for a variety of reasons, the United States is an attractive place
to invest. Finally, suppose that in the rest of the world, people have high propensities to save, but their opportunities for investment are less attractive. In these
circumstances, there will be a flow of capital from the rest of the world and a
corresponding net inflow of goods and services to the United States. The United
States would have a current-account deficit.

Trade flows tend to adjust to national preferences for con-sumption, savings, and investment.

In the above situation, the current-account deficit would not be viewed as a
problem. Rather, it would be viewed as an efficient adaptation to different savings
propensities and investment opportunities in the United States and the rest of the
world. From this perspective, a current-account deficit becomes a solution, not a
problem.

The real problem, if there is one, is either too much consumption and thus too
little savings or too much investment. Regardless of what one's opinions are, the
situation confronting the United States and the rest of the world is an expression
of national preferences, to which trade flows have adjusted in a timely manner.
An economist has no further wisdom to shed on this matter.

What are the long-term consequences for the United States or for any other
nation that runs a current-account deficit? Here, an economist can speak with
some authority. If the current-account deficit and resulting capital-account surplus finances productive domestic investment, then the nation is better off; the
returns from these added investments will service the foreign debts with income
left over to increase living standards. Conversely, a capital-account surplus that
finances consumption will increase the nation's well-being today at the expense
of its future well-being. That trade-off, however, has little to do with the balance
of payments per se.

4.4 SUMMARY AND CONCLUSIONS

The balance of payments is an accounting statement of the international transactions of one nation over a specific period. The statement shows the sum of economic transactions of individuals, businesses, and government agencies located in one nation with those located in the rest of the world during the period. Thus, the U.S. balance of payments for a given year is an accounting of all transactions between U.S. residents and residents of all other countries during that year.

The statement is based on double-entry bookkeeping; every economic transaction recorded as a credit brings about an equal and offsetting debit entry, and vice versa. A debit entry shows a purchase of foreign goods, services, or assets, or a decline in liabilities to foreigners. A credit entry shows a sale of domestic goods, services, or assets, or an increase in liabilities to foreigners. For example, if a foreign company sells a car to a U.S. resident, a debit is recorded to indicate an increase in purchases made by the United States (the car); a credit is recorded to reflect an increase in liabilities to the foreigner (payment for the car).

The balance of payments is often divided into several different components. Each shows a particular kind of transaction, such as merchandise exports or foreign purchases of U.S. government securities. Transactions that represent purchases and sales of goods and services in the current period are called the current account; those that represent capital transactions are called the capital account. Changes in official reserves appear on the official reserves account.

Because double-entry bookkeeping ensures that debits equal credits, the sum of all transactions is zero. In the absence of official reserve transactions, a capital-account surplus must offset the current-account deficit; and a capital-account deficit must offset a current-account surplus.

The United States is presently running a large current-account deficit. Much public discussion about why the United States imports more than it exports has focused on claims of unfair trading practices or the high value of the dollar (the latter claim seems less realistic today). However, economic theory indicates that the total size of the current-account deficit is a macroeconomic phenomenon; there is a basic accounting identity that a nation's current-account deficit reflects excess domestic spending. Equivalently, a current-account deficit equals the excess of domestic investment over domestic savings. Explicitly taking government into account yields a new relation: The domestic spending balance equals the private savings-investment balance minus the government budget deficit. Since private savings and investment are approximately in balance for the United States, the trade deficit can be traced to the federal budget deficit.

Failure to consider the elementary economic accounting identities can mislead policymakers into relying on dollar depreciation, trade restrictions, or trade subsidies in order to reduce U.S. trade deficits without doing anything about excess domestic spending. To reduce the current-account deficit, domestic savings must rise; private investment must decline; or the government deficit must be reduced. Absent any of these changes, the current-account deficit will not diminish, regardless of the trade barriers imposed or the amount of dollar depreciation.

QUESTIONS

1. In a freely floating exchange rate system, if the current account is running a deficit, what are the consequences for the nation's balance on capital account and its overall balance of payments?

2. As the inflation-adjusted value of the U.S. dollar rises, what is likely to happen to the U.S. balance on current account?

3. Currently, social security is minimal in Japan. Suppose Japan institutes a comprehensive social security system. How is this policy switch likely to affect Japan's trade surplus?

4. Suppose Lufthansa buys $400 million worth of Boeing jets in 1994 and is financed by the U.S. Eximbank with a five-year loan that has no principal or interest payments due until 1995. What is the net impact of this sale on the U.S. current account, capital account, and overall balance of payments for 1994?

5. How does a trade deficit affect the current-account balance?

6. On which balance-of-payments account does tourism show up?

7. Suppose the United States expropriates all foreign holdings of American assets. What will happen to the U.S. current-account deficit? What will likely happen to U.S. savings and investment? Why?

8. What happens to Mexico's ability to repay its foreign loans if the United States restricts imports of Mexican agricultural produce?

9. In order for Brazil to service its foreign debts without borrowing more money, what must be true of its trade balance?

10. Suppose the United States imposes import restrictions on Japanese steel. What is likely to happen to the U.S. current-account deficit? What else is likely to happen?

11. Suppose that Brazil starts welcoming foreign investment with open arms. How is this likely to affect the value of the cruzeiro? The Brazilian current-account balance?

12. In 1990, Germany's current-account surplus was over $50 billion. However, it is estimated that the process of reunification will require that Germany invest several hundred billion dollars in its eastern states over the coming decade.

    a. What implications does this huge investment have for Germany's current-account balance in the future? Explain.

    b. How should the Deutsche mark's value change to facilitate the necessary shift in Germany's economy?

13. Suppose that the trade imbalances of the 1980s largely disappear during the 1990s. What is likely to happen to the huge global capital flows of the 1980s? What is the link between the trade imbalances and the global movement of capital?

14. In 1990, Japan's Ministry of International Trade and Investment (MITI) proposed that firms be given a tax credit equal to 5% of the value of its increased imports. The purpose of this tax subsidy is to encourage Japanese imports of foreign products and thereby reduce Japan's persistent trade surplus. At the same time, the Japanese government announced that it will reduce its budget deficit during the coming year.

a. What are the likely consequences of the tax subsidy plan on Japan's trade balance, the value of the yen, and the competitiveness of Japanese firms?

b. What are the likely consequences of a lower Japanese budget deficit on Japan's trade balance?

15. During 1992, Japan entered a recession. However, at the same time, its current-account surplus hit a record. Is there a contradiction between Japan's large trade surplus and a weak national economy? Explain.

16. What will strong economic growth do for the U.S. balance on current account? How about a U.S. recession?

PROBLEMS

1. The following transactions (expressed in U.S. $ billions) take place during a year. Calculate the U.S. merchandise-trade, current-account, capital-account, and official reserves balances.

a. The United States exports $300 of goods and receives payment in the form of foreign demand deposits abroad.

b. The United States imports $225 of goods and pays for them by drawing down its foreign demand deposits.

c. The United States pays $15 to foreigners in dividends drawn on U.S. demand deposits here.

d. American tourists spend $30 overseas using traveler's checks drawn on U.S. banks here.

e. Americans buy foreign stocks with $60, using foreign demand deposits held abroad.

f. The U.S. government sells $45 in gold for foreign demand deposits abroad. g.In a currency support operation, the U.S. government uses its foreign demand deposits to purchase $8 from private foreigners in the United States.

2. Ruritania is calculating its balance of payments for the year. As usual, its data are perfectly accurate. All of the transactions for the year are listed below (in Rur$ millions). Fill in the correct number for each balance-of-payments account a through j.

a. Ruritania received weapons worth $200 from the United States under its military aid program; no payment is necessary.

b. A Ruritanian firm exported $400 of cloth and received an IOU from the foreign importer.

c. A Ruritanian resident paid $10 in interest on a loan from a foreigner; the check was drawn on a domestic Ruritanian bank.

d. Foreign tourists visited Ruritania and spent $100 in traveler's checks drawn on foreign banks.

e. The Ruritanian central bank sold $60 in gold to a foreign government and received U.S. Treasury bills in return.

f. A foreign central bank deposited $120 in a private domestic Ruritanian bank and paid with a check drawn on a private bank in the United States.

1. Exports
    a. goods
    b. services
    Imports
    c. goods
    d. services
    e. unilateral transfers
2. Ruritanian assets abroad
    f. privately owned
    g. officially owned
3. Foreign assets in Ruritania
    h. privately owned
    i. officially owned
    j. current account

3.* Select a country and undertake an analysis of that country's balance of payments for 8 to 12 years, subject to availability of data. The analysis must include examinations (presentation of statistical data with discussion) of the trade balance, current-account balance, capital-account balance, basic balance, and overall balance. Your report should also address the following issues:

   a. What accounts for swings in these various balances over time?

   b. What is the relationship between shifts in the current-account balance and changes in savings and investment? How do government budget deficits and surpluses relate to the savings-investment and current-account balances?

*Project suggested by Donald T. Buck.

5 The Foreign Exchange Market

The Spaniards coming into the West Indies, had many commodities of the country which they needed, brought unto them by the inhabitants, to who when they offered them money, goodly pieces of gold coin, the Indians, taking the money, would put it into their mouths, and spit it out to the Spaniards again, signifying that they could not eat it, or make use of it, and therefore would not part with their commodities for money, unless they had such other commodities as would serve their use.

Edward Leigh (1671)

CHAPTER LEARNING OBJECTIVES

- To describe the organization of the foreign exchange market and distinguish between the spot and forward markets
- To distinguish between different methods of foreign exchange quotation and convert from one method of quotation to another
- To read and explain foreign-currency quotations as they appear in *The Wall Street Journal*
- To identify profitable currency arbitrage opportunities and calculate the profits associated with these arbitrage opportunities
- To describe the mechanics of spot currency transactions
- To explain how forward contracts can be used to reduce currency risk
- To list the major users of forward contracts and describe their motives
- To calculate forward premiums and discounts

The volume of international transactions has grown enormously since the end of World War II. U.S. exports of goods and services now total almost 13% of gross national product, or about $760 billion annually. For both Canada and Great Britain, this figure exceeds 25%. Imports are about the same size. Similarly, annual capital flows involving hundreds of billions of dollars occur between the United States and other nations. International trade and investment of this magnitude would not be possible without the ability to buy and sell foreign currencies. Currencies must be bought and sold because the U.S. dollar is not the acceptable means of payment in most other countries. Investors, tourists, exporters, and importers must exchange dollars for foreign currencies, and vice versa.

The trading of currencies takes place in foreign exchange markets whose primary function is to facilitate international trade and investment. Knowledge of the operation and mechanics of these markets, therefore, is important for any fundamental understanding of international financial management. The purpose of this chapter is to provide this information. It discusses the organization of the most important foreign exchange market—the interbank market—including the spot market, the market in which currencies are traded for immediate delivery, and the forward market, in which currencies are traded for future delivery. Chapter 6 examines the currency futures and options markets.

5.1 ORGANIZATION OF THE FOREIGN EXCHANGE MARKET

If there were a single international currency, there would be no need for a foreign exchange market. As it is, in any international transaction, at least one party is dealing in a foreign currency. The purpose of the *foreign exchange market* is to permit transfers of purchasing power denominated in one currency to another— that is, to trade one currency for another currency. For example, a Japanese exporter sells automobiles to a U.S. dealer for dollars, and a U.S. manufacturer sells machine tools to a Japanese company for yen. Ultimately, however, the U.S. company will likely be interested in receiving dollars, whereas the Japanese exporter will want yen. Similarly, an American investor in Swiss-franc-denominated bonds must convert dollars into francs, and Swiss purchasers of U.S. Treasury bills require dollars to complete these transactions. Because it would be inconvenient, to say the least, for individual buyers and sellers of foreign exchange to seek out one another, a foreign exchange market has developed to act as an intermediary.

The foreign exchange market permits people to exchange purchasing power denominated in different currencies.

Most currency transactions are channeled through the worldwide *interbank market,* the wholesale market in which major banks trade with one another. This market is normally referred to as *the* foreign exchange market. In the *spot market,* currencies are traded for immediate delivery, which is actually within two business days after the transaction has been concluded. In the *forward market,* contracts are made to buy or sell currencies for future delivery.

Major banks trade with one another in the interbank market.

The foreign exchange market is not a physical place; rather, it is an electronically linked network of banks, foreign exchange brokers, and dealers whose function is to bring together buyers and sellers of foreign exchange. It is not confined to any one country but is dispersed throughout the leading financial centers of the world: London, New York City, Paris, Zurich, Amsterdam, Tokyo, Toronto, Milan, Frankfurt, and other cities.

Trading is generally done by telephone or telex machine. Foreign exchange traders in each bank usually operate out of a separate foreign exchange trading room. Each trader has several telephones and is surrounded by terminals displaying up-to-the-minute information. It is a hectic existence, and many traders burn out by age 35. Most transactions are based on oral communications; written confirmation occurs later. Hence, an informal code of moral conduct has evolved over time in which the foreign exchange dealers' word is their bond.

The Participants

Major foreign ex-
change market partici-
pants include large
commercial banks,
MNCs, and central
banks.

The major participants in the foreign exchange market are the large commercial banks; foreign exchange brokers in the interbank market; commercial customers, primarily multinational corporations; and central banks, which intervene in the market from time to time to smooth exchange rate fluctuations or to maintain target exchange rates. Central bank intervention involving buying or selling in the market is often indistinguishable from the foreign exchange dealings of commercial banks or of other private participants.

Only the head offices or regional offices of the major commercial banks are actually marketmakers—that is, actively deal in foreign exchange for their own accounts. These banks stand ready to buy or sell any of the major currencies on a more or less continuous basis. A large fraction of the interbank transactions in the United States is conducted through *foreign exchange brokers,* specialists in matching net supplier and demander banks. These brokers, of whom there are about a half dozen at present (located in New York City), receive a small commission on all trades. Some brokers tend to specialize in certain currencies, but they all handle major currencies such as the pound sterling, Canadian dollar, Deutsche mark, and Swiss franc.

Commercial and central bank customers buy and sell foreign exchange through their banks. However, most small banks and local offices of major banks do not deal directly in the interbank market. Rather, they typically will have a credit line with a large bank or with their home office. Thus, transactions with local banks will involve an extra step. The customer deals with a local bank that in turn deals with its head office or a major bank. The various linkages between banks and their customers are depicted in Exhibit 5.1. Note that the diagram includes linkages with currency futures and options markets, which we will examine in the next chapter.

Electronic Trading. In April 1992, Reuters, the news company that supplies the foreign exchange market with the screen quotations used in telephone trading, introduced a new service, Dealing 2000–2. This service adds automatic execution to the package, so creating a genuine screen-based market. Other quote vendors, like Telerate and Quotron are building their own automatic systems. These systems offer automated matching. Traders can enter buy and sell orders directly into their terminals on an anonymous basis and these prices will be visible to all market participants. Another trader, anywhere in the world, can execute a trade by simply hitting two buttons.

The introduction of automated trading should reduce the cost of trading, partly by eliminating foreign exchange brokers. The new systems will replicate the order-matching and the anonymity that brokers offer, and they will do it more cheaply. At the same time, automated systems threaten the oligopoly of informa-

Exhibit 5.1 Structure of Foreign Exchange Markets

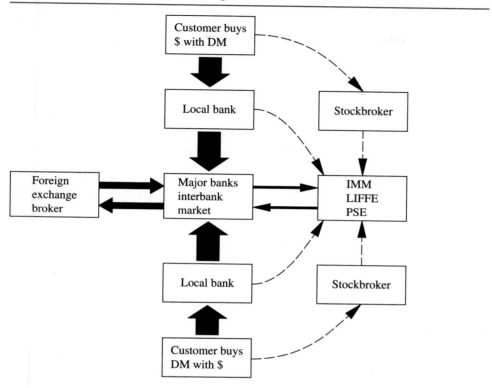

NOTE: The International Money Market (IMM) Chicago trades foreign exchange futures and DM futures options. The London International Financial Futures Exchange (LIFFE) trades foreign exchange futures. The Philadelphia Stock Exchange (PSE) trades foreign currency options.

SOURCE: *Review,* Federal Reserve Bank of St. Louis, March 1984, p. 9.

tion that has underpinned the profits of those who now do most foreign exchange business. These new systems will gather information on the prices and quantities of currencies as they are actually traded. They could make possible a foreign exchange ticker tape like the stock market tickers that reveal details of share trades, disseminating information that until now the traders have profitably kept to themselves.

Automated trading threatens the information oligopoly held by currency traders today.

Size

The foreign exchange market is by far the largest financial market in the world. A recent estimate placed the average foreign exchange trading volume in 1992 at over $1 trillion daily, or $250 trillion a year.[1] This figure compares with an average

[1]This estimate appeared in *The Economist,* September 26, 1992, p. 94.

The foreign exchange market is the largest financial market in the world.

daily trading volume of about $7 billion on the New York Stock Exchange. Indeed, the New York Stock Exchange's biggest day, Black Monday (October 19, 1987), was only $21 billion, or 4% of the daily foreign exchange volume. As another benchmark, the U.S. gross national product was approximately $6 trillion in 1992.

According to recent data from the world's central banks, London is the world's largest currency trading market, and increasing its lead, with daily turnover in 1992 estimated at $303 billion.[2] New York is second, at about $192 billion, followed by Tokyo, at $128 billion. The U.S. share has remained fairly stable in recent years. Exhibit 5.2 shows that the world foreign exchange market has grown by over 50% in volume between 1989 and 1992, and by over 200% since 1986, far outpacing the growth of international trade and the world's output of goods and services. This explosive growth has been attributed to the growing integration of the world's economies and financial markets, as well as a growing desire on the part of companies and financial institutions to more actively manage their currency risk exposure.

Exhibit 5.2 Average Daily Foreign Exchange Trading

SOURCE: Bank of England and U.S. Federal Reserve.

[2]The results of this survey were reported in *The Economist*, December 12, 1992, p. 116.

Among smaller foreign exchange markets, the central banks reported average daily volume in Singapore at $75 billion, Zurich at $71 billion, Hong Kong at $64 billion, Frankfurt at $57 billion, and Paris at $35 billion. Forward trading now accounts for 47% of total trading in London. The share of spot trading has fallen from 73% in 1986 to 50% in 1992 (options and futures account for the remaining 3% of foreign exchange trading). In 1989 sterling-dollar trades were the most common, but they have been overtaken by dollar-DM trading, which now accounts for 23% of turnover.

5.2 THE SPOT MARKET

This section examines the spot market in foreign exchange. It covers spot quotations, transaction costs, and the mechanics of spot trading.

Spot Quotations

Almost all major newspapers print a daily list of exchange rates. For major currencies, up to four different *foreign exchange quotes* (prices) are displayed. One is the *spot price*. The others might include the 30-day, 90-day, and 180-day *forward prices*. These quotes are for trades among dealers in the interbank market. When interbank trades involve dollars (about 60% of such trades do), these rates will be expressed in either *American terms* (numbers of U.S. dollars per unit of foreign currency) or *European terms* (number of foreign-currency units per U.S. dollar). In *The Wall Street Journal,* quotes in both American and European terms are listed side by side (see Exhibit 5.3.) For example, on April 29, 1993, the American quote for the Swiss franc was SFr 1 = $0.7018, and the European quote was $1 = SFr 1.4250. Nowadays, in trades involving dollars, all except U.K. and Irish exchange rates are expressed in European terms.

> Most banks quote all currencies against the U.S. dollar when trading among themselves.

In their dealings with nonbank customers, banks in most countries use a system of *direct quotation*. A direct exchange rate quote gives the home currency price of a certain quantity of the foreign currency quoted (usually 100 units, but only one unit in the case of the U.S. dollar or the pound sterling). For example, the price of foreign currency is expressed in French francs (FF) in France and in Deutsche marks (DM) in Germany. Thus, in France, the Deutsche mark might be quoted at FF 4 while, in Germany, the franc would be quoted at DM 0.25.

> The financial press contains daily spot and forward quotations for most major currencies.

There are exceptions to this rule, though. Banks in Great Britain quote the value of the pound sterling (£) in terms of the foreign currency—for example, £1 = $1.4420. This method of *indirect quotation* is also used in the United States for domestic purposes and for the Canadian dollar. In their foreign exchange activities abroad, however, U.S. banks adhere to the European method of direct quotation.

Banks do not normally charge a commission on their currency transactions, but profit from the spread between the buying and selling rates. Quotes are always given in pairs because a dealer usually does not know whether a prospective customer is in the market to buy or to sell a foreign currency. The first rate is the buy, or bid, price; the second is the sell, or ask, or offer, rate. Suppose the

Exhibit 5.3 Foreign Exchange Rate Quotations

EXCHANGE RATES

Thursday, April 29, 1993

The New York foreign exchange selling rates below apply to trading among banks in amounts of $1 million and more, as quoted at 3 p.m. Eastern time by Bankers Trust Co., Telerate and other sources. Retail transactions provide fewer units of foreign currency per dollar.

Country	U.S. $ equiv. Thurs.	U.S. $ equiv. Wed.	Currency per U.S. $ Thurs.	Currency per U.S. $ Wed.
Argentina (Peso)	1.01	1.01	.99	.99
Australia (Dollar)	.7110	.7136	1.4065	1.4013
Austria (Schilling)	.09005	.08993	11.10	11.12
Bahrain (Dinar)	2.6522	2.6522	.3771	.3771
Belgium (Franc)	.03080	.03076	32.47	32.51
Brazil (Cruzeiro)	.0000328	.0000332	30506.03	30104.07
Britain (Pound)	1.5743	1.5735	.6352	.6355
30-Day Forward	1.5703	1.5700	.6368	.6369
90-Day Forward	1.5626	1.5623	.6400	.6401
180-Day Forward	1.5519	1.5518	.6444	.6444
Canada (Dollar)	.7855	.7866	1.2731	1.2713
30-Day Forward	.7843	.7854	1.2750	1.2733
90-Day Forward	.7816	.7822	1.2794	1.2785
180-Day Forward	.7768	.7774	1.2873	1.2864
Czech. Rep. (Koruna)				
Commercial rate	.0358680	.0361011	27.8800	27.7000
Chile (Peso)	.002556	.002557	391.23	391.07
China (Renminbi)	.174856	.174856	5.7190	5.7190
Colombia (Peso)	.001518	.001518	658.75	658.75
Denmark (Krone)	.1646	.1644	6.0741	6.0841
Ecuador (Sucre)				
Floating rate	.000556	.000556	1800.02	1800.02
Finland (Markka)	.18432	.18481	5.4253	5.4108
France (Franc)	.18788	.18753	5.3225	5.3325
30-Day Forward	.18705	.18677	5.3462	5.3541
90-Day Forward	.18561	.18528	5.3875	5.3971
180-Day Forward	.18369	.18333	5.4440	5.4545
Germany (Mark)	.6335	.6327	1.5785	1.5805
30-Day Forward	.6284	.6304	1.5914	1.5864
90-Day Forward	.6263	.6256	1.5967	1.5985
180-Day Forward	.6205	.6199	1.6115	1.6131
Greece (Drachma)	.004663	.004657	214.45	214.75
Hong Kong (Dollar)	.12937	.12941	7.7295	7.7275
Hungary (Forint)	.0116496	.0117082	85.8400	85.4100
India (Rupee)	.03214	.03214	31.11	31.11
Indonesia (Rupiah)	.0004836	.0004836	2068.04	2068.04
Ireland (Punt)	1.5432	1.5432	.6480	.6480
Israel (Shekel)	.3727	.3755	2.6834	2.6633
Italy (Lira)	.0006761	.0006825	1479.07	1465.14
Japan (Yen)	.009003	.008909	111.07	112.25
30-Day Forward	.009003	.008908	111.08	112.26
90-Day Forward	.009003	.008908	111.08	112.26
180-Day Forward	.009004	.008909	111.06	112.24
Jordan (Dinar)	1.4984	1.4984	.6674	.6674
Kuwait (Dinar)	3.3322	3.3322	.3001	.3001
Lebanon (Pound)	.000574	.000574	1742.00	1742.00
Malaysia (Ringgit)	.3891	.3890	2.5700	2.5705
Malta (Lira)	2.7586	2.7586	.3625	.3625
Mexico (Peso)				
Floating rate	.3231540	.3231540	3.0945	3.0945
Netherland (Guilder) ...	.5639	.5631	1.7734	1.7758
New Zealand (Dollar) .	.5430	.5436	1.8416	1.8396
Norway (Krone)	.1498	.1498	6.6734	6.6773
Pakistan (Rupee)	.0376	.0376	26.57	26.57
Peru (New Sol)	.5287	.5370	1.89	1.86
Philippines (Peso)	.03883	.03883	25.75	25.75
Poland (Zloty)	.00006333	.00006328	15791.00	15803.01
Portugal (Escudo)	.006833	.006831	146.36	146.39
Saudi Arabia (Riyal) ..	.26702	.26702	3.7450	3.7450
Singapore (Dollar)	.6194	.6182	1.6145	1.6175
Slovak Rep. (Koruna) .	.0358680	.0361011	27.8800	27.7000
South Africa (Rand)				
Commercial rate	.3171	.3170	3.1538	3.1545
Financial rate	.2188	.2155	4.5700	4.6400
South Korea (Won)	.0012564	.0012569	795.90	795.60
Spain (Peseta)	.008653	.008647	115.56	115.65
Sweden (Krona)	.1373	.1384	7.2848	7.2268
Switzerland (Franc) ...	.7018	.6998	1.4250	1.4290
30-Day Forward	.7004	.6986	1.4277	1.4315
90-Day Forward	.6982	.6963	1.4323	1.4362
180-Day Forward	.6959	.6942	1.4369	1.4405
Taiwan (Dollar)	.039063	.039002	25.60	25.64
Thailand (Baht)	.03976	.03976	25.15	25.15
Turkey (Lira)	.0001045	.0001043	9570.00	9592.00
United Arab (Dirham) .	.2723	.2723	3.6725	3.6725
Uruguay (New Peso)				
Financial	z.265957	z.257201	z3.76	z3.89
Venezuela (Bolivar)				
Floating rate	.01181	.01183	84.66	84.56
SDR	1.42019	1.41686	.70413	.70579
ECU	1.23830	1.23730	....	....

Special Drawing Rights (SDR) are based on exchange rates for the U.S., German, British, French and Japanese currencies. Source: International Monetary Fund.

European Currency Unit (ECU) is based on a basket of community currencies.

z-Reflects change in currency earlier this year.

SOURCE: *The Wall Street Journal*, April 30, 1993, p. C13. Reprinted with permission of *The Wall Street Journal*, © Dow Jones & Company, Inc. 1993. All rights reserved worldwide.

> Currency quotations are given in pairs, the first being the bid or buy rate and the second being the ask or sell rate.

pound sterling is quoted at $1.4419–36. This quote means that banks are willing to buy pounds at $1.4419 and sell them at $1.4436. In practice, dealers do not quote the full rate to each other; instead, they quote only the last two digits of the decimal. Thus, sterling would be quoted at 19-36 in the above example. Any dealer who isn't sufficiently up-to-date to know the preceding numbers will not remain in business for long.

Transaction Costs. The *bid-ask spread*—that is, the spread between bid and ask rates for a currency—is based on the breadth and depth of the market for that currency as well as on the currency's volatility. This spread is usually stated as a percentage cost of transacting in the foreign exchange market, which is computed as follows:

$$\text{Percent spread} = \frac{\text{Ask price} - \text{Bid price}}{\text{Ask price}} \times 100$$

For example, with pound sterling quoted at \$1.4419–36, the percentage spread equals 0.12%:

$$\text{Percent spread} = \frac{1.4436 - 1.4419}{1.4436} = 0.12\%$$

For widely traded currencies, such as the pound, DM, and yen, the spread might be on the order of 0.1–0.5%.[3] Less heavily traded currencies have higher spreads. These spreads have widened appreciably for most currencies since the general switch to floating rates in early 1973.

The bid-ask spread is narrower for widely traded currencies and for less volatile currencies.

The quotes found in the financial press are not those that individuals or firms would get at a local bank. Unless otherwise specified, these quotes are for transactions in the interbank market exceeding \$1 million. (The standard transaction amount in the interbank market is now \$3 million.) But competition ensures that individual customers receive rates that reflect, even if they do not necessarily equal, interbank quotations. For example, a trader may believe that he or she can trade a little more favorably than the market rates indicate—that is, buy from a customer at a slightly lower rate or sell at a somewhat higher rate than the market rate. Thus, if the current spot rate for the Swiss franc is \$0.6967–72, the bank may quote a customer a rate of \$0.6964–75. On the other hand, a bank that is temporarily short in a currency may be willing to pay a slightly more favorable rate; or if the bank has overbought, it may be willing to sell at a lower rate.

For these reasons, many corporations will shop around at several banks for quotes before committing themselves to a transaction. On large transactions customers also may get a rate break inasmuch as it ordinarily does not take much more effort to process a large order than a small order.

The market for traveler's checks and smaller currency exchanges, such as might be made by a traveler going abroad, is quite separate from the interbank market. The spread on these smaller exchanges is much wider than that in the interbank market, reflecting the higher average costs banks incur on such transactions. As a result, individuals and firms involved in smaller retail transactions generally pay a higher price when buying and receive a lower price when selling foreign exchange than those quoted in newspapers.

Cross Rates. Because most currencies are quoted against the dollar, it may be necessary to work out the *cross rates* for currencies other than the dollar. For example, if the Deutsche mark is selling for \$0.60 and the buying rate for the French franc is \$0.15, then the DM/FF cross rate is DM 1 = FF 4. A somewhat more complicated cross-rate calculation would be the following. Suppose that we have the following European quotes for the Japanese yen and the South Korean won:

Japanese yen	¥135.62/U.S.\$1
South Korean won	W763.89/U.S.\$1

[3]See, for example, Jacob A. Frenkel and Richard M. Levich, "Transaction Costs and Interest Arbitrage: Tranquil versus Turbulent Periods," *Journal of Political Economy*, November–December 1977, pp. 1209–1228.

In this case, the cross rate of yen per won can be calculated as follows:

$$\frac{\text{Japanese yen/U.S. dollar}}{\text{Korean won/U.S. dollar}} = \frac{\yen135.62/\text{U.S. \$1}}{\text{W}763.89/\text{U.S. \$1}} = \yen0.17754/\text{W1}$$

Exhibit 5.4 contains cross rates for major currencies on April 29, 1993.

ILLUSTRATION: Calculating the Direct Quote for the Pound in Frankfurt

Suppose that sterling is quoted at $1.4419–36, while the Deutsche mark is quoted at $0.6250–67. What is the direct quote for the pound in Frankfurt?

Solution. The bid rate for the pound in Frankfurt can be found by realizing that selling pounds for DM is equivalent to combining two transactions: (1) selling pounds for dollars at the rate of $1.4419 and (2) converting those dollars into DM 1.4419/0.6267 = DM 2.3008 per pound at the ask rate of $0.6267. Similarly, the DM cost of buying one pound (the ask rate) can be found by first buying $1.4436 (the ask rate for £1) with DM and then using those dollars to buy one pound. Because buying dollars for DM is equivalent to selling DM for dollars (at the bid rate of $0.6250), it will take DM 1.4436/0.6250 = DM 2.3098 to acquire the $1.7036 necessary to buy one pound. Thus, the direct quotes for the pound in Frankfurt are DM 2.3008–3098.

A growing percentage of foreign exchange trades don't involve the dollar.

Currency Arbitrage. Until recently, the pervasive practice among bank dealers was to quote all currencies against the U.S. dollar when trading among themselves. Now, however, about 40% of all currency trades don't involve the dollar, and that percentage is growing.[4] For example, Swiss banks may quote the Deut-

Exhibit 5.4 Key Currency Cross Rates

Key Currency Cross Rates Late New York Trading Apr. 29, 1993

	Dollar	Pound	SFranc	Guilder	Yen	Lira	D-Mark	FFranc	CdnDlr
Canada	1.2718	1.9999	.89155	.71699	.01146	.00086	.80545	.23899	....
France	5.3215	8.368	3.7305	3.0001	.04794	.00359	3.3702	....	4.1842
Germany	1.5790	2.4830	1.1069	.89018	.01423	.00107	....	.29672	1.2415
Italy	1482.5	2331.2	1039.26	835.78	13.356	....	938.89	278.59	1165.7
Japan	111.00	174.55	77.813	62.578	....	.07487	70.298	20.859	87.28
Netherlands	1.7738	2.7893	1.2435	....	.01598	.00120	1.1234	.33333	1.3947
Switzerland	1.4265	2.2432	....	.80421	.01285	.00096	.90342	.26806	1.1216
U.K.	.63593	....	.44580	.35851	.00573	.00043	.40274	.11950	.50002
U.S.	....	1.5725	.70102	.56376	.00901	.00067	.63331	.18792	.78629

Source: Telerate

[4]This estimate appeared in *The Wall Street Journal*, March 1, 1991, p. C1.

sche mark against the Swiss franc, and German banks may quote pounds sterling in terms of Deutsche marks. Exchange traders are continually alert to the possibility of taking advantage, through *currency arbitrage transactions,* of exchange rate inconsistencies in different money centers. These transactions involve buying a currency in one market and selling it in another. Such activities tend to keep exchange rates uniform in the various markets.

Traders take advantages of differences in exchange rate quotations among markets through currency arbitrage.

For example, suppose that the pound sterling is bid at $1.9809 in New York, and the Deutsche mark at $0.6251 in Frankfurt. At the same time, London banks are offering pounds sterling at DM 3.1650. An astute trader would sell dollars for Deutsche marks in Frankfurt, use the Deutsche marks to acquire pounds sterling in London, and sell the pounds in New York.

Specifically, if the trader begins in New York with $1 million, the trader could acquire DM 1,599,744.04 for $1,000,000 in Frankfurt, sell these Deutsche marks for £505,448.35 in London, and resell the pounds in New York for $1,001,242.64. Thus, a few minutes' work would yield a profit of $1,242.64. In effect, the trader would, by arbitraging through the DM, be able to acquire sterling at $1.9784 in London ($0.6251 × 3.1650) and sell it at $1.9809 in New York. This sequence of transactions, known as *triangular currency arbitrage,* is depicted in Exhibit 5.5.

In the preceding example, the arbitrage transactions would tend to cause the Deutsche mark to appreciate vis-à-vis the dollar in Frankfurt and to depreciate against the pound sterling in London; at the same time, sterling would tend to fall

Exhibit 5.5 Triangular Currency Arbitrage

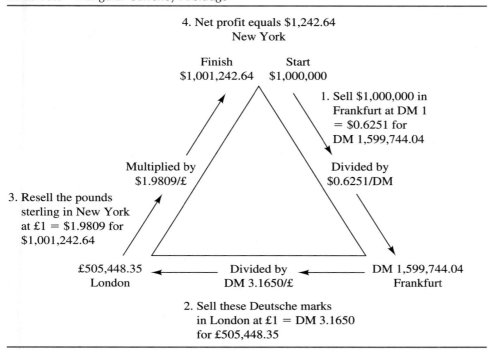

4. Net profit equals $1,242.64
New York

Finish   Start
$1,001,242.64 $1,000,000

1. Sell $1,000,000 in Frankfurt at DM 1 = $0.6251 for DM 1,599,744.04

Multiplied by $1.9809/£

Divided by $0.6251/DM

3. Resell the pounds sterling in New York at £1 = $1.9809 for $1,001,242.64

£505,448.35 ← Divided by ← DM 1,599,744.04
London   DM 3.1650/£   Frankfurt

2. Sell these Deutsche marks in London at £1 = DM 3.1650 for £505,448.35

Ready access to information has reduced opportunities for profitable currency arbitrage.

in New York. Opportunities for such profitable currency arbitrage have been greatly reduced in recent years, given the extensive network of people—aided by high-speed, computerized information systems—who are continually collecting, comparing, and acting on currency quotes in all financial markets. The practice of quoting rates against the dollar makes currency arbitrage even simpler. The result of this activity is that rates for a specific currency tend to be the same everywhere, with only minimal deviations due to transaction costs.

ILLUSTRATION: Calculating the Direct Quote for the Deutsche Mark in New York

If the direct quote for the dollar is DM 2.5 in Frankfurt, and transaction costs are 0.4%, what are the minimum and maximum possible direct quotes for the DM in New York?

Solution. An arbitrageur who converted $1 into DM in Frankfurt would receive DM 2.5×0.996, after paying transaction costs of 0.4%. Converting these DM into dollars in New York at a direct quote of e, the arbitrageur would keep $2.5 \times 0.996 \times e \times 0.996$. Because in equilibrium this quantity must be less than or equal to $1 (otherwise there would be a money machine), $e < 1/[2.5(0.996)^2] = \$0.4032$. Alternatively, if the arbitrageur converted $1 into DM in New York at a rate of e, took those DM to Frankfurt, and exchanged them for dollars, the arbitrageur would wind up—after paying transaction costs in both New York and Frankfurt—with $(1/e) \times 0.996 \times (1/2.5) \times 0.996$. Because this quantity must be less than or equal to $1, the result is $(0.996)^2 \times (1/2.5e) < 1$ or $e > \$0.3968$. Combining these two inequalities yields $\$0.3968 < e < \$0.4032$.

Settlement Date. The *value date* for spot transactions, the date on which the monies must be paid to the parties involved, is set as the second working day after the date on which the transaction is concluded. Thus, a spot deal entered into on Thursday in Paris will not be settled until the following Monday (French banks are closed on Saturdays and Sundays). It is possible, although unusual, to get one-day or even same-day value, but the rates will be adjusted to reflect interest differentials on the currencies involved.

Bankers acting as marketmakers, by taking positions in foreign currencies, expose themselves to exchange risk.

Exchange Risk. Bankers also act as marketmakers, as well as agents, by taking positions in foreign currencies, thereby exposing themselves to *exchange risk*. The immediate adjustment of quotes as traders receive and interpret new political and economic information is the source of both exchange losses and gains by banks active in the foreign exchange market. For instance, suppose that a trader quotes a rate of £1:$1.3012 for £500,000, and it is accepted. The bank will receive $650,600 in return for the £500,000. If the bank doesn't have an offsetting transaction, it may decide within a few minutes to cover its exposed position in the interbank market. If during this brief delay, news of a lower-than-expected British trade deficit reaches the market, the trader may be unable to purchase pounds at a rate lower than $1.3101. Since it will cost the bank $655,050 to acquire £500,000 at this new rate, the result is a $4,450 ($655,050 – $650,600) exchange loss on a relatively small transaction within just a few minutes. Equally possible, of course, is a gain if the dollar strengthens against the pound.

Clearly, as a trader becomes more and more uncertain about the rate at which she can offset a given currency contract with other dealers or customers, she will demand a greater profit to bear this added risk. This expectation translates into a wider bid-ask spread. For example, during a period of volatility in the exchange rate between the French franc and U.S. dollar, a trader will probably quote a customer a bid for francs that is distinctly lower than the last observed bid in the interbank market; the trader will attempt to reduce the risk of buying francs at a price higher than that at which she can eventually resell them. Similarly, the trader may quote an ask price for francs that is above the current ask price.

The Mechanics of Spot Transactions

The simplest way to explain the process of actually settling transactions in the spot market is to work through an example. Suppose a U.S. importer requires FF 1 million to pay his French supplier. After receiving and accepting a verbal quote from the trader of a U.S. bank, the importer will be asked to specify two accounts: (1) the account in a U.S. bank that he wants debited for the equivalent dollar amount at the agreed exchange rate and (2) the French supplier's account that is to be credited by FF 1 million.

Upon completion of the verbal agreement, the trader will forward a dealing slip containing the relevant information to the settlement section of her bank. That same day, a *contract note*—that includes the amount of the foreign currency, the dollar equivalent at the agreed rate, and confirmation of the payment instructions—will be sent to the importer. The settlement section will then cable the bank's correspondent (or branch) in Paris, requesting transfer of FF 1 million from its *nostro account*—that is, working balances maintained with the correspondent to facilitate delivery and receipt of currencies—to the account specified by the importer. On the value date, the U.S. bank will debit the importer's account, and the exporter will have his account credited by the French correspondent.

At the time of the initial agreement, the trader provides a clerk with the pertinent details of the transaction. The clerk, in turn, constantly updates a *position sheet* that shows the bank's position by currency (as well as by maturities of forward contracts). A number of the major international banks have fully computerized this process to ensure accurate and instantaneous information on individual transactions and on the bank's cumulative currency exposure at any time. The head trader will monitor this information for evidence of possible fraud or excessive exposure in a given currency.

Because spot transactions are normally settled two working days later, a bank is never certain until one or two days after the deal is concluded whether the payment due the bank has actually been made. To keep this credit risk in bounds,

Foreign exchange transactions are based on verbal agreements, later supplemented by a contract note.

most banks will transact large amounts only with prime names (other banks or corporate customers).

5.3 THE FORWARD MARKET

Forward exchange operations carry the same credit risk as spot transactions, but for longer periods of time; however, there are significant exchange risks involved.

A *forward contract* between a bank and a customer (which could be another bank) calls for delivery, at a fixed future date, of a specified amount of one currency against dollar payment; the exchange rate is fixed at the time the contract is entered into. Although the Deutsche mark is the most widely traded currency at present, active forward markets exist for the pound sterling, the Canadian dollar, the Japanese yen, and the major Continental currencies—particularly the Swiss franc, French franc, Belgian franc, Italian lira, and Dutch guilder. In general, forward markets for the currencies of less-developed countries (LDCs) are either limited or nonexistent.

> Companies can reduce their exchange risk by using forward contracts to lock in the exchange rate on future currency transactions.

In a typical forward transaction, for example, a U.S. company buys textiles from England with payment of £1 million due in 90 days. The importer, thus, is *short* pounds—that is, it owes pounds for future delivery. Suppose the present price of the pound is $1.71. Over the next 90 days, however, the pound might rise against the dollar, raising the dollar cost of the textiles. The importer can guard against this exchange risk by immediately negotiating a 90-day forward contract with a bank at a price of, say, £1 = $1.72. According to the forward contract, in 90 days the bank will give the importer £1 million (which it will use to pay for its textile order), and the importer will give the bank $1.72 million, which is the dollar equivalent of £1 million at the forward rate of $1.72.

In technical terms, the importer is offsetting a short position in pounds by going *long* in the forward market—that is, by buying pounds for future delivery. Exhibit 5.6 plots the importer's dollar cost of the textile shipment with and without the use of a forward contract. It also shows the gain or loss on the forward contract as a function of the contracted forward price and the spot price of the pound when the contract matures.

The gains and losses from long and short forward positions are related to the difference between the contracted forward price and the spot price of the underlying currency at the time the contract matures. In the case of the textile order, the importer is committed to buy pounds at $1.72 apiece. If the spot rate in 90 days is less than $1.72, the importer will suffer an implicit loss on the forward contract because it is buying pounds for more than its prevailing value. But if the spot rate in 90 days exceeds $1.72, the importer will enjoy an implicit profit because the contract obliges the bank to sell the pounds at a price less than its current value.

Three points are worth noting. First, the gain or loss on the forward contract is unrelated to the current spot rate of $1.71. Second, the forward contract gain or loss exactly offsets the change in the dollar cost of the textile order that is associated with movements in the pound's value. For example, if the spot price of the

Exhibit 5.6 Hedging a Future Payment with a Forward Contract

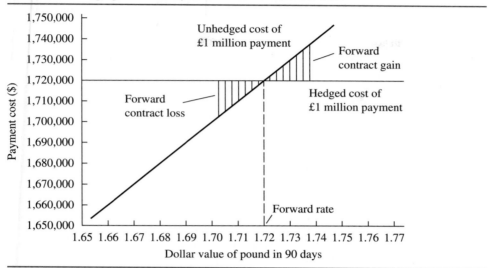

pound in 90 days is $1.75, the importer's cost of delivery is $1.75 million. However, the forward contract has a gain of $30,000, or 1,000,000 × (1.75 − 1.72). The net cost of the textile order when covering with a forward contract is $1.72 million, no matter what happens to the spot exchange rate in 90 days. (Chapter 9 elaborates on the use of forward contracts to manage exchange risk.) Third, the forward contract is not an option contract. Both parties must perform the agreed-upon behavior, unlike the situation with an option where the buyer can choose whether to exercise the contract or allow it to expire. The bank must deliver the pounds, and the importer must buy them at the prearranged price. Options are discussed in Chapter 6.

Forward Market Participants

The major participants in the forward market can be categorized as arbitrageurs, traders, hedgers, and speculators.

Arbitrageurs seek to earn risk-free profits by taking advantage of differences in interest rates among countries. They use forward contracts to eliminate the exchange risk involved in transferring their funds from one nation to another.

Traders use forward contracts to eliminate or cover the risk of loss on export or import orders that are denominated in foreign currencies. More generally, a forward-covering transaction relates to a specific payment or receipt expected at a specified point in time.

Hedgers, mostly multinational firms, engage in forward contracts to protect the home currency value of various foreign-currency-denominated assets and liabilities on their balance sheets that are not to be realized over the life of the contracts.

Major users of forward contracts include arbitragers, traders, hedgers, and speculators.

Arbitrageurs, traders, and hedgers seek to reduce (or eliminate, if possible) their exchange risks by "locking in" the exchange rate on future trade or financial operations.

In contrast to these three types of forward market participants, *speculators* actively expose themselves to currency risk by buying or selling currencies forward in order to profit from exchange rate fluctuations. Their degree of participation does not depend on their business transactions in other currencies; instead, it is based on prevailing forward rates and their expectations for spot exchange rates in the future.

Forward Quotations

Forward rates can be expressed in two ways. Commercial customers are usually quoted the actual price, otherwise known as the *outright rate*. In the interbank market, however, dealers quote the forward rate only as a discount from, or a premium on, the spot rate. This forward differential is known as the *swap rate*. A foreign currency is at a *forward discount* if the forward rate expressed in dollars is below the spot rate, whereas a *forward premium* exists if the forward rate is above the spot rate. As we shall see in Chapter 7, the forward premium or discount is closely related to the difference in interest rates on the two currencies.

A foreign currency is at a forward discount (premium) if the forward rate expressed in dollars is below (above) the spot rate.

According to Exhibit 5.3, spot Japanese yen on April 29, 1993, sold at $0.009003 while 180-day forward yen were priced at $0.009004. Based on these rates, the swap rate for the 180-day forward yen was quoted as a 1-point premium (0.009004 − 0.009003), where a point or "pip" refers to the last digit quoted. Similarly, because the 180-day British pound was quoted at $1.5519 while the spot pound was $1.5743, the 180-day forward British pound sold at a 224-point discount. Alternatively, the discount or premium may be expressed as an annualized percentage deviation from the spot rate using the following formula:

$$\frac{\text{Foreign premium}}{\text{or discount}} = \frac{\text{Forward rate} - \text{Spot rate}}{\text{Spot rate}} \times \frac{12}{\substack{\text{Forward contract} \\ \text{length in months}}}$$

Thus, on April 29, 1993, the six-month forward Japanese yen was selling at a 0.02% annualized premium:

$$\frac{\text{Forward premium}}{\text{annualized}} = \frac{0.009004 - 0.009003}{0.009003} \times \frac{12}{6} = 0.005$$

The six-month British pound was selling at a 2.85% annualized discount:

$$\frac{\text{Forward discount}}{\text{annualized}} = \frac{1.5519 - 1.5743}{1.5743} \times \frac{12}{6} = -0.0285$$

A swap rate can be converted into an outright rate by adding the premium (in points) to, or subtracting the discount (in points) from, the spot rate. Although the swap rates do not carry plus or minus signs, you can determine whether the forward rate is at a discount or premium using the following rule: When the forward bid in points is smaller than the offer rate in points, the forward rate is at a premium and the points should be added to the spot price to compute the outright quote. Conversely, if the bid in points exceeds the offer in points, the forward rate is at a discount and the points must be subtracted from the spot price to get the outright quotes.[5]

Suppose, for example, that the following quotes are received for spot, one-month, three-month, and six-month Swiss francs (SFr) and pounds sterling:

£:$2.0015–30   19–17   26–22   42–35
SFr:$0.6963–68   4–6   9–14   25–38

The outright rates are

Maturity	£			SFr		
	Bid	Ask	Spread (%)	Bid	Ask	Spread (%)
Spot	$2.0015	$2.0030	0.075	$0.6963	$0.6969	0.086
One-month	1.9996	2.0013	0.085	0.6967	0.6974	0.100
Three-month	1.9989	2.0008	0.095	0.6972	0.6982	0.143
Six-month	1.9973	1.9995	0.110	0.6988	0.7006	0.257

Thus, the Swiss franc is selling at a premium against the dollar and the pound is selling at a discount. Note the slightly wider percentage spread between outright bid and offer on the Swiss franc compared with the spread on the pound. This difference is due to the broader market in pounds. Note too the widening of spreads over time for both currencies. This widening is caused by the greater uncertainty surrounding future exchange rates.

Exchange Risk. Spreads in the forward market are a function of both the breadth of the market (volume of transactions) in a given currency and the risks associated with forward contracts. The risks, in turn, are based on the variability of future spot rates. Even if the spot market is stable, there is no guarantee that future rates will remain invariant. This uncertainty will be reflected in the forward market. Furthermore, because beliefs about distant exchange rates are typically less secure than those about nearer-term rates, uncertainty will increase with lengthening maturities of forward contracts. Dealers will quote wider spreads on longer-term forward contracts to compensate themselves for the risk of being unable to profitably reverse their positions. Moreover, the greater unpredictability of future spot rates may reduce the number of market participants. This increased thinness will further widen the bid-ask spread because it magnifies the dealer's risk in taking even a temporary position in the forward market.

The bid-ask spread on forward contracts rises with currency volatility and contract maturity.

Cross Rates. Forward cross rates are figured in much the same way as spot cross-rates. For instance, suppose a customer wants to sell one-month forward lire (Lit) against Dutch guilder (Dfl) delivery. The market rates (expressed in European terms of foreign currency units per dollar) are

[5]This rule is based on two factors: (1) The buying rate, be it for spot or forward delivery, is always less than the selling price, and (2) the forward bid-ask spread always exceeds the spot bid-ask spread.

Lit:$ spot	1,890.00–1,892.00
One-month forward	1,894.25–1,897.50
Dfl:$ spot	3.4582–3.4600
One-month forward	3.4530–3.4553

Based on these rates, the forward cross rate for selling lire against guilders is found as follows: Forward lire are sold for dollars—that is, dollars are bought at the lira forward selling price of Lit 1,897.50 = $1—and are simultaneously sold for one-month forward guilders at a rate of Dfl 3.4530. Thus, Lit 1,897.50 = Dfl 3.4530 or the forward selling price for lire against guilders is Lit 1,897.50/3.4530 = Lit 549.52. Similarly, the forward buying rate for lire against guilders is Lit 1,894.25/3.4553 = Lit 548.22. The spot selling rate is Lit 1,892.0/3.4582 = Lit 547.11. Hence, the forward discount on selling lire against Dfl delivery equals (549.52 − 547.11)/547.11 = 0.0044 or 5.29% per annum (0.0044 × 12 = 0.0529).

Forward Contract Maturities

Forward contracts going out past one year are available for widely traded currencies.

Forward contracts are normally available for one-month, two-month, three-month, six-month, or 12-month delivery. Banks will also tailor forward contracts for odd maturities (e.g., 77 days) to meet their customers' needs. Longer-term forward contracts can usually be arranged for widely traded currencies, such as the pound sterling, Deutsche mark, or Japanese yen; however, the bid-ask spread tends to widen for longer maturities. As with spot rates, these spreads have widened for almost all currencies since the early 1970s, probably because of the greater turbulence in foreign exchange markets. For widely traded currencies, the three-month bid-ask spread can vary from 0.1% to 1%.

5.4 SUMMARY AND CONCLUSIONS

In this chapter, we saw that the primary function of the foreign exchange market is to transfer purchasing power denominated in one currency to another, and thereby facilitate international trade and investment. The foreign exchange market consists of two tiers: the interbank market, in which major banks trade with each other, and the retail market, in which banks deal with their commercial customers.

In the spot market, currencies are traded for settlement within two business days after the transaction has been concluded. In the forward market, contracts are made to buy or sell currencies for future delivery. Spot and forward quotations are given in either American terms—the dollar price of a foreign currency—or in European terms—the foreign-currency price of a dollar. Quotations can also be expressed on a direct basis—the home-currency price of another currency—or an indirect basis—the foreign-currency price of the home currency.

The major participants in the forward market were categorized as arbitrageurs, traders, hedgers, and speculators. Forward rates can be stated on an outright basis, or as a discount from, or a premium on, the spot rate. This forward differential is known as the swap rate. Because all currencies are quoted against the dollar, the exchange rate between two nondollar currencies—known as a cross rate—must be calculated on the basis of their direct quotes against the dollar.

QUESTIONS

1. Answer the following questions based on data in Exhibit 5.3.
   a. How many Swiss francs can you get for one dollar?
   b. How many dollars can you get for one Swiss franc?
   c. What is the three-month forward rate for the Swiss franc?
   d. Is the Swiss franc selling at a forward premium or discount?
   e. What is the 90-day forward discount or premium on the Swiss franc?

2. What risks confront dealers in the foreign exchange market? How can they cope with those risks?

3. Suppose a currency increases in volatility. What is likely to happen to its bid-ask spread? Why?

4. Who are the principal users of the forward market? What are their motives?

5. How does a company pay for the foreign exchange services of a commercial bank?

6. The spot rate on the Deutsche mark is $0.63, and the 180-day forward rate is $0.64. What are possible reasons for the difference between the two rates?

PROBLEMS

1. The $:DM exchange rate is DM 1 = $0.35, and the DM:FF exchange rate is FF 1 = DM 0.31. What is the FF:$ exchange rate?

2. Suppose the direct quote for sterling in New York is 1.1110–5. What is the direct quote for dollars in London?

3. Suppose the spot quote on the Deutsche mark is $0.3302–10, and the spot quote on the French franc is $0.1180–90.
   a. What is the direct spot quote for the franc in Frankfurt?
   b. Compute the percentage bid-ask spreads on the DM and franc.

4. The spot and 90-day forward rates for the pound are $1.1376 and $1.1350, respectively. What is the forward premium or discount on the pound?

5. Suppose you observe the following direct spot quotations in New York and Toronto, respectively: 0.8000–50 and 1.2500–60. What are the arbitrage profits per $1 million?

6. Suppose the DM is quoted at 0.2074–80 in London, and the pound sterling is quoted at 4.7010–32 in Frankfurt.
   a. Is there a profitable arbitrage situation? Describe it.
   b. Compute the percentage bid-ask spreads on the pound and DM.

7. Assuming no transaction costs, suppose £1 = $2.4110 in New York, $1 = FF 3.997 in Paris, and FF 1 = £0.1088 in London. How could you profit from these rates?

8. Using the data in Exhibit 5.3, calculate the 30-day, 90-day, and 180-day forward discounts for the British pound.

9. An investor wishes to buy French francs spot (at $0.1080) and sell French francs forward for 180 days (at $0.1086).

    a. What is the swap rate on French francs?

    b. What is the premium on 180-day French francs?

10. Assume the pound sterling is worth FF 9.80 in Paris and SFr 5.40 in Zurich.

    a. Show how British arbitrageurs can make profits given that the Swiss franc is worth two French francs. What would be the profit per pound transacted?

    b. What would be the eventual outcome on exchange rates in Paris and Zurich given these arbitrage activities?

    c. Rework part a, assuming that transaction costs amount to 0.6% of the amount transacted. What would be the profit per pound transacted?

    d. Suppose the Swiss franc is quoted at FF 2 in Zurich. Given a transaction cost of 0.6% of the amount transacted, what are the minimum/maximum French franc prices for the Swiss franc that you would expect to see quoted in Paris?

11. Examine the following currency cross rates. The quotes are expressed as units of the currency represented in the left-hand column per unit of currency shown in the top row. Consider the dollar rates to be the quotes off which the cross rates are set.

	DM	FF	£	¥	U.S.$
DM	—	0.29570–76	2.4256–67	0.01276–78	1.5780–86
FF	3.3818–25	—	8.2031–41	0.04315–19	5.3021–33
£	0.41227–35	0.12381–90	—	0.00526–29	0.6502–10
¥	78.381–496	23.178–251	190.121–390	—	123.569–707

    a. Do any triangular arbitrage opportunities exist among these currencies? Assume that any deviations from the theoretical cross rates of 5 points or less are due to transaction costs.

    b. How much profit could be made from a $5 million transaction associated with each arbitrage opportunity?

BIBLIOGRAPHY

Chrystal, K. Alec. "A Guide to Foreign Exchange Markets." *Federal Reserve Bank of St. Louis Review,* March 1984, pp. 5–18.

Kubarych, Roger M. *Foreign Exchange Markets in the United States.* New York: Federal Reserve Bank of New York, 1983.

Currency Futures and Options Markets

6

I dipt into the future far as human eye could see, Saw the vision of the world and all the wonder that would be.

Tennyson

CHAPTER LEARNING OBJECTIVES

- To explain what currency futures, options, and futures options contracts are and to describe the organization of the markets in which these contracts are traded
- To distinguish between currency forward and futures contracts
- To distinguish between currency futures and options contracts
- To describe the advantages and disadvantages of futures contracts relative to forward contracts
- To explain how currency futures and options contracts can be used to manage currency risk
- To identify the basic factors that determine the value of a currency option
- To read and interpret the prices of currency futures, options, and futures options contracts as they appear in *The Wall Street Journal*

Foreign currency futures and options contracts are a new breed of financial instrument. This chapter describes the nature of these contracts and shows how they can be used to manage foreign exchange risk or take speculative positions on currency movements. It also shows how to read the prices of these contracts as they appear in the financial press.

6.1 FUTURES CONTRACTS

Currency futures contracts are patterned after grain and commodity futures contracts.

In 1972, the *Chicago Mercantile Exchange* opened its *International Monetary Market* (IMM) division. The IMM provides an outlet for currency speculators and for those looking to reduce their currency risks. Trade takes place in *currency futures,* which are contracts for specific quantities of given currencies; the exchange rate is fixed at the time the contract is entered into, and the delivery date is set by the board of directors of the IMM. These contracts, which represented the first step in the development of financial futures, are patterned after those for grain and commodity futures contracts, which have been traded on Chicago's exchanges for over 100 years.

Currency futures contracts are currently available for the British pound, Canadian dollar, Deutsche mark, Swiss franc, Japanese yen, and Australian dollar. The IMM is continually experimenting with new contracts. Those that meet the minimum volume requirements are added and those that don't are dropped. For example, the IMM recently added a DM/¥ cross-rate contract, while dropping contracts in the Dutch guilder, French franc, Mexican peso, and European Currency Unit. Private individuals are encouraged, rather than discouraged, to participate in the market. Contract sizes are standardized according to amount of foreign currency—for example, £62,500, C$100,000, SFr 125,000. Exhibit 6.1 shows

Exhibit 6.1 Contract Specifications for Foreign Currency Futures

	Australian Dollar	British Pound	Canadian Dollar	Deutsche Mark	Japanese Yen	Swiss Franc
Contract Size	A$100,000	£62,500	C$100,000	DM 125,000	¥12,500,000	SFr 125,000
Symbol	AD	BP	CD	DM	JY	SF
Margin Requirements*						
Initial	$1,215	$4,050	$1,080	$2,700	$1,890	$4,050
Maintenance	900	3,000	800	2,000	1,400	3,000
Mimimum Price Change	0.0001 (1 pt.)	0.0002 (2 pts.)	0.0001 (1 pt.)	0.0001 (1 pt.)	0.000001 (1 pt.)	0.0001 (1 pt.)
Value of 1 Point	$10.00	$6.25	$10.00	$12.50	$12.50	$12.50
Months Traded	January, March, April, June, July, September, October, December and spot month					
Regular Trading hours	7:20 A.M.–2:00 P.M. (Central time)					
Last Day of Trading	Second business day before Third Wednesday of the delivery month					

*Margin requirements are subject to change. These margins are as of December 8, 1992

SOURCE: *Minimum Performance Bond Requirements and Contract Specifications,* Chicago Mercantile Exchange, December 8, 1992.

contract specifications. Leverage is high; margin requirements average less than 4% of the value of the futures contract. The leverage assures that investors' fortunes will be decided by tiny swings in exchange rates.

The contract specifications in Exhibit 6.1 show the margin requirements. The *initial margin* shows how much money must be in the account balance when the contract is entered into. This amount is $2,000 in the case of the pound. A *margin call* is issued if—because of losses on the futures contract—the balance in the account falls below the *maintenance margin,* which is $1,500 for the pound. At that time, enough new money must be added to the account balance to bring it up to the maintenance margin. For example, if you start with an initial balance of $2,000 in your account on a pound futures contract and your contract loses, say, $700 in value, you must add $200 ($2,000 – $700 + $200 = $1,500).

Instead of using the bid-ask spreads found in the interbank market, traders charge commissions. Though commissions will vary, a *round trip*—that is, one buy and one sell—costs as little as $15. This cost works out to less than 0.05% of the value of a sterling contract. The low cost, along with the high degree of leverage, has provided a major inducement for speculators to participate in the market. Other market participants include importers and exporters, companies with foreign-currency assets and liabilities, and bankers.

Traders charge commissions on futures contracts rather than using the bid-ask spreads found in the forward market.

Although volume in the futures market is still small compared to the forward market, Exhibit 6.2 shows that it grew rapidly until 1992. The IMM can be viewed as an expanding part of a growing foreign exchange market. As we will see shortly, the different segments of this market are linked by arbitrage.

A notable feature of the IMM and other futures markets is that deals are struck by brokers face to face on a trading floor, rather than over the telephone. There are a number of other, more important distinctions between the futures and forward markets.

Forward Contract Versus Futures Contract

One way to understand futures contracts is to compare them to forward contracts. *Futures contracts* are standardized contracts that trade on organized futures markets. Because contract sizes and maturities are standardized, all participants in the market are familiar with the types of contracts available, and trading is facilitated. Forward contracts, on the other hand, are private deals between two individuals who can sign any type of contract they agree on. For example, two individuals may sign a forward contract for DM 70,000 in 20 months to be paid in Belgian francs. However, IMM contracts trade only in round lots of DM 125,000 priced in U.S. dollars and with a limited range of maturities available. With only a few standardized contracts traded, the trading volume in available contracts is higher, leading to superior liquidity, smaller price fluctuations, and lower transaction costs in the futures market.

Futures contracts are standardized contracts traded on an organized exchange, whereas forward contracts are nonstandardized private deals.

The organization of futures trading with a clearing house reduces the default risks of trading. The exchange members, in effect, guarantee both sides of a contract. In contrast, a forward contract is a private deal between two par-

Exhibit 6.2 IMM Currency Futures Trading Volume, 1975–1993

*January–March 1993 annualized

SOURCE: Chicago Mercantile Exchange.

ties and is subject to the risk that either side may default on the terms of the agreement.

Futures contracts are marked to market, meaning that contract profits and losses are paid over each day at the end of trading.

Profits and losses of futures contracts are paid over every day at the end of trading, a practice called *marking to market.* This daily-settlement feature can best be illustrated with an example. On Tuesday morning, an investor takes a long position in a Swiss-franc futures contract that matures on Thursday afternoon. The agreed-upon price is $0.75 for SFr 125,000. To begin, the investor must put $1,700 into her initial margin account. At the close of trading on Tuesday, the futures price has risen to $0.755. Due to daily settlement, three things occur. First, the investor receives her cash profit of $625 (125,000 × 0.005). Second, the existing futures contract with a price of $0.75 is canceled. Third, the investor receives a new futures contract with the prevailing price of $0.755. Thus, the value of the futures contracts is set to zero at the end of each trading day.

At Wednesday close, the price has declined to $0.752. The investor must pay the $375 loss (125,000 × 0.003) to the other side of the contract and trade in her old contract for a new one with a price of $0.752. At Thursday close, the price drops to $0.74, and the contract matures. The investor pays her $1,500 loss to the other side and takes delivery of the Swiss francs, paying the prevailing price of $0.74. Exhibit 6.3 details the daily settlement process.

Exhibit 6.3 An Example of Daily Settlement with a Futures Contract

Time	Action	Cash Flow
Tuesday morning	Investor buys SFr futures contract that matures in two days. Price is $0.75.	None
Tuesday close	Futures price rises to $0.755. Position is marked to market.	Investor receives 125,000 × (0.755 − 0.75) = $625.
Wednesday close	Futures price drops to $0.752. Position is marked to market.	Investor pays 125,000 × (0.755 − 0.752) = $375.
Thursday close	Futures price drops to $0.74. (1) Contract is marked to market. (2) Investor takes delivery of SFr 125,000.	(1) Investor pays 125,000 × (0.752 − 0.74) = $1,500. (2) Investor pays 125,000 × 0.74 = $92,500.

Daily settlement reduces the default risk of futures contracts relative to forward contracts. Every day, futures investors must pay over any losses or receive any gains from the day's price movements. These gains or losses are generally added to or subtracted from the investor's margin account. An insolvent investor with an unprofitable position would be forced into default after only one day's trading, rather than being allowed to build up huge losses that lead to one large default at the time the contract matures (as could occur with a forward contract). For example, if the investor decided to keep her contract in force, rather than closing it out on Wednesday, she would have had a margin call for $850 ($1,700 + $625 − $375 − $1,500 + $850 = $1,300) in order to meet her $1,300 maintenance margin.

Daily settlement reduces default risk.

Futures contracts also can be closed out easily with an *offsetting trade.* For example, if a company's long position in DM futures has proved to be profitable, it need not literally take delivery of the DM at the time the contract matures. Rather, the company can sell futures contracts on a like amount of DM just prior to the maturity of the long position. The two positions cancel on the books of the futures exchange and the company receives its profit in cash. These and other differences between forward and futures contracts are summarized in Exhibit 6.4.

Advantages and Disadvantages of Futures Contracts. The smaller size of a futures contract and the freedom to liquidate the contract at any time before its maturity in a well-organized futures market differentiate the futures contract from the forward contract. These features of the futures contract attract many users. On the other hand, the limited number of currencies traded, the limited delivery dates, and the rigid contractual amounts of currencies to be delivered are disadvantages of the futures contract to many commercial users. Only by chance will contracts

Futures contracts are useful for speculators and for customers with a stable and continuous stream of foreign currency payments or receipts.

Exhibit 6.4 Basic Differences Between Forward and Futures Contracts

1. *Trading:*
   Forward contracts are traded by telephone or telex.
   Futures contracts are traded in a competitive arena.
2. *Regulation:*
   The forward market is self-regulating.
   The IMM is regulated by the Commodity Futures Trading Commission.
3. *Frequency of Delivery:*
   More than 90% of all forward contracts are settled by actual delivery.
   By contrast, less than 1% of the IMM futures contracts are settled by delivery.
4. *Size of Contract:*
   Forward contracts are individually tailored and tend to be much larger than the standardized contracts on the futures market.
   Futures contracts are standardized in terms of currency amount.
5. *Delivery date:*
   Banks offer forward contracts for delivery on any date.
   IMM futures contracts are available for delivery on only a few specified dates a year.
6. *Settlement:*
   Forward contract settlement occurs on the date agreed upon between the bank and its customer.
   Futures contract settlements are made daily via the Exchange's Clearing House; gains on position values may be withdrawn and losses are collected daily. This practice is known as marking to market.
7. *Quotes:*
   Forward prices generally are quoted in European terms (units of local currency per U.S. dollar).
   Futures contracts are quoted in American terms (dollars per one foreign-currency unit).
8. *Transaction Costs:*
   Costs of forward contracts based on bid-ask spread.
   Futures contracts entail brokerage fees for buy and sell orders.
9. *Margins:*
   Margins are not required in the forward market.
   Margins are required of all participants in the futures market.
10. *Credit Risk:*
    The credit risk is borne by each party to a forward contract. Credit limits must therefore be set for each customer.
    The Exchange's Clearing House becomes the opposite side to each futures contract, thereby reducing credit risk substantially.

---

conform exactly to corporate requirements. The contracts are of value mainly to those commercial customers who have a fairly stable and continuous stream of payments or receipts in the traded foreign currencies.

Arbitrage Between the Futures and Forward Markets. Arbitrageurs play an important role on the IMM. They translate IMM futures rates into interbank forward rates and, by realizing profit opportunities, keep IMM futures rates in line with bank forward rates.

ILLUSTRATION: Forward-Futures Arbitrage

Suppose that the interbank forward bid for June 18 on pounds sterling is $1.2927 at the same time that the price of IMM sterling futures for delivery on June 18 is $1.2915. How could the dealer use arbitrage to profit from this situation?

Solution. The dealer would simultaneously buy the June sterling futures contract for $80,718.75 (62,500 × $1.2915) and sell an equivalent amount of sterling forward, worth $80,793.75 (62,500 × $1.2927), for June delivery. Upon settlement, the dealer would earn a profit of $75. Alternatively, if the markets come back together before June 18, the dealer could unwind his position (by simultaneously buying £62,500 forward and selling a futures contract, both for delivery on June 18) and earn the same $75 profit. Although the amount of profit on this transaction is tiny, it becomes $7,500 if 100 futures contracts are traded.

Such arbitrage transactions will bid up the futures price and bid down the forward price until approximate equality is restored. The word approximate is used because there is a difference between the two contracts. Unlike the forward contract, where gains or losses are not realized until maturity, marking to market means that day-to-day futures contract gains (or losses) will have to be invested (or borrowed) at uncertain future interest rates. However, a study of actual rates for the British pound, Canadian dollar, Deutsche mark, Swiss franc, and Japanese yen found that forward and futures prices do not differ significantly from each other.[1]

6.2 CURRENCY OPTIONS

Whatever advantages the forward or the futures contract might hold for their purchaser, they have a common disadvantage: While they protect the holder against the risk of adverse movements in exchange rates, they eliminate the possibility of gaining a windfall profit from favorable movements. This was apparently one of the considerations that led some commercial banks to offer *currency options* to their customers. Exchange-traded currency options were first offered in 1983 by the *Philadelphia Stock Exchange* (PHLX). Currency options are now one of the fastest growing segments of the global foreign exchange market, now accounting for as much as 7% of daily trading volume.

> Currency options give holders the right, but not the obligation, to sell (put) or buy (call) the contracted currency at a set price and expiration date.

In principle, an *option* is a financial instrument that gives the holder the right—but not the obligation—to sell (put) or buy (call) another financial instrument at a set price and expiration date. The seller of the put option or call option must fulfill the contract if the buyer so desires it. Because the option not to buy or

---

[1]Bradford Cornell and Marc Reinganum, "Forward and Futures Prices: Evidence from the Foreign Exchange Markets," *Journal of Finance,* December 1981, pp. 1035–1045.

sell has value, the buyer must pay the seller of the option some premium for this privilege. As applied to foreign currencies, *call options* give the customer the right to purchase, and *put options* give the right to sell, the contracted currencies at the *expiration date*. An *American option* can be exercised at any time up to the expiration date; a *European option* can only be exercised at maturity.

An option that would be profitable to exercise at the current exchange rate is said to be *in-the-money*. Conversely, an *out-of-the-money* option is one that would not be profitable to exercise at the current exchange rate. The price at which the option is exercised is called the *exercise price* or *strike price*. An option whose exercise price is the same as the spot exchange rate is termed *at-the-money*.

Using Currency Options

An out-of-the-money option is worthless on its expiration date.

To see how currency options might be used, consider a U.S. importer that has a DM 62,500 payment to make to a German exporter in 60 days. The importer could purchase a European call option to have the Deutsche marks delivered to it at a specified exchange rate (the strike price) on the due date. Suppose the option premium is $0.02 per DM, and the exercise price is $0.64. The importer has paid $1,250 for a DM 64 call option, which gives it the right to buy DM 62,500 at a price of $0.64 per mark at the end of 60 days. If at the time the importer's payment falls due, the value of the Deutsche mark has risen to, say, $0.70, the option would be in-the-money. In this case, the importer exercises its call option, and purchases Deutsche marks for $0.64. The importer would earn a profit of $3,750 (62,500 × 0.06), which would more than cover the $1,250 cost of the option. If the rate has declined below the contracted rate to, say, $0.60, the DM 64 option would be out-of-the-money. Consequently, the importer would let the option expire and purchase the Deutsche marks in the spot market. Despite losing the $1,250 option premium, the importer would still be $1,250 better off than if it had locked in a rate of $0.64 with a forward or futures contract.

Exhibit 6.5 illustrates the importer's gains or losses on the call option. At a spot rate on expiration of $0.64 or lower, the option will not be exercised, resulting in a loss of the $1,250 option premium. Between $0.64 and $0.66, the option will be exercised, but the gain is insufficient to cover the premium. The *break-even price*—where the gain on the option just equals the option premium—is $0.66. Above $0.66 per DM, the option is sufficiently deep in-the-money to cover the option premium and yield a—potentially unlimited—net profit. Since this is a zero-sum game, the profit from selling a call is the mirror image of the profit from buying the call.

In contrast, a put option at the same terms (exercise price of $0.64 and put premium of $0.02 per DM) would be in-the-money at a spot price of $0.60 and out-of-the-money at $0.70. Exhibit 6.6 illustrates the profits available on this DM put option. If the spot price falls to, say, $0.58, the holder of a put option will deliver DM 62,500 worth $36,250 (0.58 × 62,500) and receive $40,000 (0.64 × 62,500). The option holder's profit, net of the $1,250 option premium, is $2,500. As the spot price falls further, the value of the put option rises. At the extreme, if the spot rate falls to 0, the buyer's profit on the contract will reach $38,750 (0.64 ×

Exhibit 6.5 Profit from Buying a Call Option for Various Spot Prices at Expiration

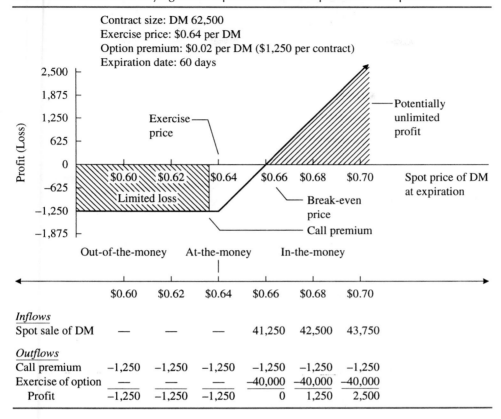

Contract size: DM 62,500
Exercise price: $0.64 per DM
Option premium: $0.02 per DM ($1,250 per contract)
Expiration date: 60 days

	$0.60	$0.62	$0.64	$0.66	$0.68	$0.70
Inflows						
Spot sale of DM	—	—	—	41,250	42,500	43,750
Outflows						
Call premium	−1,250	−1,250	−1,250	−1,250	−1,250	−1,250
Exercise of option	—	—	—	−40,000	−40,000	−40,000
Profit	−1,250	−1,250	−1,250	0	1,250	2,500

62,500 − 1,250). Below a spot rate of $0.62, the gain on the put option will more than cover the $1,250 option premium. Between $0.62—the break-even price for the put option—and $0.64, the holder would exercise the option, but the gain will be less than the option premium. At spot prices above $0.64, the holder would not exercise the option and so would lose the $1,250 premium. Both the put and the call options will be at-the-money if the spot rate in 60 days is $0.64, and the call or put option buyer will lose the $1,250 option premium.

An in-the-money option will show a loss if the gain is less than the option premium.

ILLUSTRATION: *Speculating With a Japanese Yen Call Option*

In March, a speculator who is gambling that the yen will appreciate against the dollar pays $680 to buy a yen June 81 call option. This option gives the speculator the right to buy yen in June at an exchange rate of ¥1 = $0.0081 (the 81 in the contract description is expressed in hundredths of a cent). By the expiration date in June, the yen spot price has risen to $0.0083. Since the call option is in-the-

Exhibit 6.6 Profit from Buying a Put Option for Various Spot Prices at Expiration

Contract size: DM 62,500
Exercise price: $0.64 per DM
Option premium: $0.02 per DM ($1,250 per contract)
Expiration date: 60 days

	$0.58	$0.60	$0.62	$0.64	$0.66	$0.68
Inflows						
Exercise of option	40,000	40,000	40,000	—	—	—
Outflows						
Put premium	−1,250	−1,250	−1,250	−1,250	−1,250	−1,250
Spot purchase of DM	−36,250	−37,500	−38,750	—	—	—
Profit	2,500	1,250	0	−1,250	−1,250	−1,250

money by .02 cents, the investor will realize a gain of $625 ($.0002 × 6,250,000)) on the option contract. This amount, less the $680 paid for the option, produces a loss on the contract of $55.

Currency options can be used to hedge contingent foreign currency cash flows.

Typical users of currency options might be financial firms holding large investments overseas where sizable unrealized gains had occurred because of exchange rate changes and where these gains were thought likely to be partially or fully reversed. Limited use of currency options has also been made by firms that have a foreign currency inflow or outflow that is possibly forthcoming, but not definitely. In such cases, where future foreign-currency cash flows are contingent on an event such as acceptance of a bid, long call or put positions can be safer hedges than either futures or forwards.

For example, assume that a U.S. investor makes a firm bid in pounds sterling to buy a piece of real estate in London. If the firm wishes to hedge the dollar cost of the bid, it could buy pounds forward so that if the pound sterling appreciates, the gain on the forward contract would offset the increased dollar cost of the prospective investment. But, if the bid is eventually rejected, and if the pound has fallen in the interim, losses from the forward position would have no offset. If no forward cover is taken and the pound appreciates, the real estate will cost more than expected.

Currency call options can provide a better hedge in such a case. Purchased-pound call options would provide protection against a rising pound; and yet, if the bid were rejected and the pound had fallen, the uncovered hedge loss would be limited to the premium paid for the calls. Note that a U.S. company in the opposite position, such as one bidding on a British project, whose receipt of future pound cash inflows is contingent on acceptance of its bid, would use a long pound put position to provide the safest hedge.

Currency options can also be used by pure speculators, those without an underlying foreign-currency transaction to protect against. The presence of speculators in the options markets adds to the breadth and depth of these markets, thereby making them more liquid and lowering transactions costs and risk.

Currency options can also be used by speculators.

Option Pricing and Valuation

From a theoretical standpoint, the value of an option is comprised of two components: intrinsic value and time value. The *intrinsic value* of the option is the amount by which the option is in-the-money, or $S - E$, where S is the current spot price and E the exercise price. In other words, the intrinsic value equals the immediate exercise value of the option. Thus, the further into the money an option is, the more valuable it is. An out-of-the-money option has no intrinsic value. For example, the intrinsic value of a call option on Swiss francs with an exercise price of $0.74 and a spot rate of $0.77 would be $0.03 per franc. The intrinsic value of the option for spot rates less than the exercise price is zero. Any excess of the option value over its intrinsic value is called the *time value* of the contract. An option will generally sell for at least its intrinsic value. The more out-of-the-money an option is, the lower the option price. These features are shown in Exhibit 6.7.

Options have both intrinsic value and time value.

During the time remaining before an option expires, the exchange rate can move so as to make exercising the option profitable or more profitable. That is, an out-of-the-money option can move into the money, or one already in-the-money can become more so. The chance that an option will become profitable or more profitable is always greater than zero. Consequently, the time value of an option is always positive for an out-of-the-money option and is usually positive for an in-the-money option. Moreover, the more time that remains until an option expires, the higher the time value tends to be. For example, an option with six months remaining until expiration will tend to have a higher price than an option with the same strike price but with only three months until expiration. As the option approaches its maturity, the time value declines to zero.

The value of an American option always exceeds its intrinsic value because the time value is always positive up to the expiration date. For example, if $S > E$,

Exhibit 6.7 The Value of a Call Option Prior to Maturity

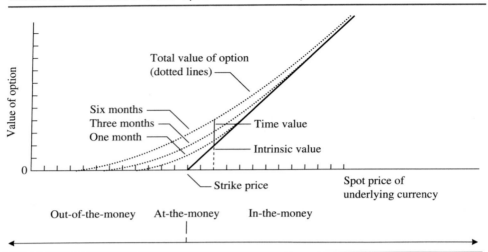

then $C(E) > S - E$, where $C(E)$ is the dollar price of an American call option on one unit of foreign currency. However, the case is more ambiguous for European options because increasing the time to maturity may not increase its value, given that it can only be exercised on the maturity date.[2] That is, a European currency option may be in-the-money before expiration, yet it may be out-of-the-money by the maturity date.

The value of a currency option rises with both contract maturity and increases in exchange rate volatility.

Before expiration, an out-of-the-money option has only time value, but an in-the-money option has both time value and intrinsic value. At expiration, an option can have only intrinsic value. The time value of a currency option reflects the probability that its intrinsic value will increase before expiration; this probability depends, among other things, on the volatility of the exchange rate. An increase in currency volatility increases the chance of an extremely high or low exchange rate at the time the option expires. The chance of a very high exchange rate benefits the call owner. The chance of a very low exchange rate, however, is irrelevant; the option will be worthless for any exchange rate less than the striking price, whether the exchange rate is "low" or "very low." Inasmuch as the effect of increased volatility is beneficial, the value of the call option is higher. Put options similarly benefit from increased volatility in the exchange rate.

Another aspect of time value involves interest rates. In general, options have a present intrinsic value, determined by the exercise price and price of the underlying asset. Since the option is a claim on a specified amount of an asset over a period of time into the future, that claim must have a return in line with market

[2]For a technical discussion of foreign currency option pricing, see Mark B. Garman and Steven W. Kohlhagen, "Foreign Currency Option Values," *Journal of International Money and Finance*, December 1983, pp. 231–238.

interest rates on comparable instruments. Therefore, a rise in the interest rate will cause call values to rise and put values to fall.

Pricing foreign-currency options is more complex because it requires consideration of both domestic and foreign interest rates. A foreign currency is normally at a forward premium or discount vis-à-vis the domestic currency. As we will see in Chapter 7, this premium or discount is determined by relative interest rates. Consequently, for foreign-currency options, call values rise and put values fall when the domestic interest rate increases or the foreign interest rate decreases.

The price of a currency option is affected by both domestic and foreign interest rates.

The flip side of a more valuable put or call option is a higher option premium. Hence, options become more expensive when exchange rate volatility rises. Similarly, when the domestic-foreign interest differential increases, call options become more expensive and put options less expensive.

Using Forward or Futures Contracts Versus Options Contracts

Suppose that on July 1, an American company makes a sale for which it will receive DM 125,000 on September 1. The firm will want to convert those DM into dollars, so it is exposed to the risk that the mark will fall below its current spot rate of $0.6922 in the meantime. The firm can protect itself against a declining Deutsche mark by selling its expected DM receipts forward (using a futures contract) or by buying a DM put option.

Exhibit 6.8 shows possible results for each choice, using options with strike prices just above and just below the spot exchange of July 1 ($0.68 and $0.70). The example assumes a DM decline to $0.6542 and the consequent price adjustments of associated futures and options contracts. The put quotes are the option premiums per DM. Thus, the dollar premium associated with a particular quote equals the quote multiplied by the number of DM covered by the put options. For example, the quote of $0.0059 for a September put option with a strike price of 68 (in cents) represents a premium for covering the exporter's DM 125,000 transaction equal to $0.0059 × 125,000 = $737.50.

In the above example, a decision to remain unhedged would yield a loss of 125,000 × (0.6922 − 0.6542) or $4750. The outcomes of the various hedge possibilities are shown in Exhibit 6.9.

Exhibit 6.8 Declining Exchange Rate Scenario

	July 1	*September 1*
Spot	$0.6922	$0.6542
September futures	0.6956	0.6558
September 68 put	0.0059	0.0250
September 70 put	0.0144	0.0447

Exhibit 6.9 Hedging Alternatives: Offsetting a $4,750 Loss Due to a Declining DM

Result of Selling Futures
  (0.6956 − 0.6558) × 125,000 = $4,975 profit

Results of Buying Put Options
  68 put: (0.0250 − 0.0059) × 125,000 = $2,387.50 profit
  70 put: (0.0447 − 0.0144) × 125,000 = $3,787.50 profit

Futures or forward contracts are better suited than options to hedge known future foreign currency cash flows.

Exhibit 6.9 demonstrates the following differences between the futures and options hedging strategies:

1. The futures hedge offers the closest offset to the loss due to the decline of the Deutsche mark.
2. The purchase of the in-the-money put option (the 70 strike price) offers greater protection (but at a higher premium) than the out-of-the-money put (the 68 strike price).

Note that the September futures price is unequal to the spot rate on September 1 because settlement is not until later in the month. As the DM declines in value, the company would suffer a larger loss on its DM receivables, to be offset by a further increase in the value of the put and futures contracts.

While the company wants to protect against the possibility of a DM depreciation, what would happen if the DM appreciates? To answer this question—so as to fully assess the options and futures hedge strategies—assume the hypothetical conditions in Exhibit 6.10.

In this scenario, the rise in the DM would increase the value of the unhedged position by 125,000 × (0.7338 − 0.6922), or $5200. This gain would be offset by losses on the futures or options contracts, as shown in Exhibit 6.11.

We can see that the futures hedge again provides the closest offset. However, because these hedges generate losses, the company would be better served under this scenario by the smallest offset. With rapidly rising exchange rates, the company would benefit most from hedging with a long put position as opposed to a futures contract; conversely, with rapidly falling exchange rates, the company would benefit most from hedging with a futures contract.

Exhibit 6.10 Rising Exchange Rate Scenario

	July 1	September 1
Spot	$0.6922	$0.7338
September futures	0.6956	0.7374
September 68 put	0.0059	0.0001
September 70 put	0.0144	0.0001

Exhibit 6.11   Hedging Alternatives: Offsetting a $5,200 Gain Due to a Rising DM

Result of Selling Futures
  $(0.7374 - 0.6956) \times 125{,}000 = \$5{,}225$ loss

Results of Buying Put Options
  68 put: $(0.0059 - 0.0001) \times 125{,}000 = \$725$ loss
  70 put: $(0.0144 - 0.0001) \times 125{,}000 = \$1{,}787.50$ loss

Market Structure

Options are purchased and traded either on an organized exchange (such as the PHLX) or in the *over-the-counter* (OTC) *market. Exchange-traded options* or *listed options* are standardized contracts with predetermined exercise prices, standard maturities (one, three, six, nine, and 12 months), and fixed maturities (March, June, September, and December). Options on the PHLX are available in the ECU and seven currencies—Deutsche mark, pound sterling, French franc, Swiss franc, Japanese yen, Canadian dollar, and Australian dollar—and are traded in standard contracts half the size of the IMM futures contracts (some of which no longer exist). Cross-rate options are also available for the DM/¥, £/DM, and £/¥. By taking the U.S. dollar out of the equation, cross-rate options allow one to hedge directly the currency risk that arises when dealing with non-dollar currencies. Contract specifications are shown in Exhibit 6.12. The PHLX trades both American-style and European-style currency options. It also trades month-end options, which insure the availability of a short-term (at most, a two- or sometimes three-week) currency option at all times, and long-term options, which extend the available expiration months on PHLX dollar-based and cross-rate contracts—providing for 18-, 24-, 30-, and 36-month European-style options.

> Currency options are traded both on organized exchanges and in the over-the-counter markets.

Other organized options exchanges are located in Amsterdam (European Options Exchange), Chicago (Chicago Mercantile Exchange), and Montreal (Montreal Stock Exchange).

Trading volume in exchange-traded currency options has grown dramatically since their introduction in 1983, with more than 10 million contracts representing approximately $500 billion in underlying value traded in 1990. Exhibit 6.13 shows the growth in contract volume on the PHLX since 1983.

OTC options are contracts whose specifications are generally negotiated as to the amount, exercise price and rights, underlying instrument, and expiration. *OTC currency options* are traded by commercial and investment banks in virtually all financial centers. OTC activity is concentrated in London and New York and it centers on the major currencies, most often involving U.S. dollars against pounds sterling, Deutsche marks, Swiss francs, Japanese yen, and Canadian dollars. Branches of foreign banks in the major financial centers are generally willing to write options against the currency of their home country. For example, Australian banks in London write options on the Australian dollar. OTC options are generally traded in round lots, commonly $5–10 million in New York and $2–3

Exhibit 6.12 Philadelphia Stock Exchange Currency Options Specifications

	Australian Dollar	British Pound	Canadian Dollar	Deutsche Mark	European Currency Unit	Swiss Franc	French Franc	Japanese Yen
Symbol								
American style	XAD	XBP	XCD	XDM	ECU	XSF	XFF	XJY
European style	CAD	CBP	CCD	CDM	n.a.	CSF	CFF	CJY
Contract size	A$50,000	£31,250	C$50,000	DM 62,500	ECU 62,500	SFr 62,500	FF 250,000	¥6,250,000
Exercise Price Intervals	1¢	2.5¢	0.5¢	1¢*	2¢	1¢*	0.25¢	0.01¢*
Premium Quotations	Cents per unit	Cents per unit	Cents per unit	Cents per unit	Cents per unit	Cents per unit	Tenths of a cent per unit	Hundredths of a cent per unit
Minimum Price Change	$0.(00)01	$0.(00)01	$0.(00)01	$0.(00)01	$0.(00)01	$0.(00)01	$0.(000)02	$0.(0000)01
Minimum Contract Price Change	$5.00	$3.125	$5.00	$6.25	$6.25	$6.25	$5.00	$6.25

Expiration Months & Cycle _____ March, June, September, and December + 2 near-term months _____

Exercise Notice _____ No automatic exercise of in-the-money options _____

Expiration Date _____ Friday before third Wednesday of the month _____

Expiration Settlement Date _____ Third Wednesday of expiring month _____

Daily Price Limits _____ None _____

Issuer & Guarantor _____ Options Clearing Corporation (OCC) _____

Margin for Uncovered Writer Option premium plus 4% of the underlying contract value less _____ out-of-the-money amount, if any, to a minimum of the option premium plus 3/4% of the underlying contract value. Contract value equal spots price times unit of currency per contract.

Position & Exercise Limits _____ 100,000 contracts _____

Trading Hours ____ EST 6:00 P.M.–10:00 P.M./ 11:30 P.M.–2:30 P.M.—EDT 7:00 P.M.–11:00 P.M. /12:30 A.M.–2:30 P.M.** ____

*Half-point strike prices for DM (0.5¢), SFr (0.5¢), and ¥ (0.005¢) in the two near-term months only.

**The trading week commences on Sunday evening and ends on Friday afternoon.

SOURCE: Philadelphia Stock Exchange, 1992.

million in London. The average maturity of OTC options ranges from two to six months, and very few options are written for more than one year. American options are most common, but European options are popular in Switzerland and Germany because of familiarity.

The OTC options market
consists of a retail
market and a whole-
sale market.

The OTC options market consists of two sectors: (1) a *retail market* composed of nonbank customers who purchase from banks what amounts to customized insurance against adverse exchange rate movements and (2) a *wholesale market*

Exhibit 6.13 PHLX Currency Options Trading Volume, 1983–1992

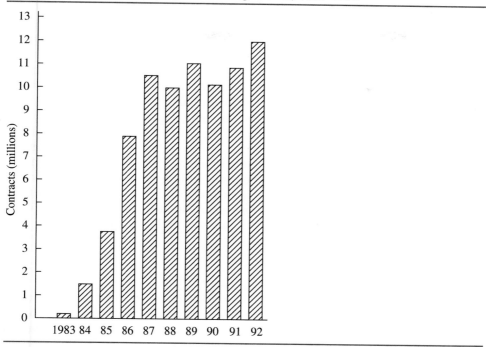

SOURCE: Philadelphia Stock Exchange, 1992.

among commercial banks, investment banks, and specialized trading firms; this market may include interbank OTC trading or trading on the organized exchanges. The interbank market in currency options is analogous to the interbank markets in spot and forward exchange. Banks use the wholesale market to hedge or "reinsure" the risks undertaken in trading with customers and to take speculative positions in options.

Most retail customers for OTC options are either corporations active in international trade or financial institutions with multicurrency asset portfolios. These customers could purchase foreign exchange puts or calls on organized exchanges, but they generally turn to the banks for options in order to find precisely the terms that match their needs. Contracts are generally tailored with regard to amount, strike price, expiration date, and currency.

OTC currency options predate exchange-traded options by many years, but trading in OTC options grew rapidly at the same time that PHLX trading began. For example, OTC trading volume in foreign currency options was estimated at $10 billion daily in 1988, double the volume in 1986.[3] The acceleration in the growth of options trading in both markets appears to spring from the desire by

[3]These estimates appear in *The Economist,* May 28, 1988, p. 82.

companies to manage foreign-currency risks more effectively and, in particular, from an increased willingness to pay a fee in order to transfer such risks to another party. Most commentators suggest that corporate demand has increased because the greater volatility of exchange rates has increasingly exposed firms to risks from developments that are difficult to predict and beyond their control.

The growth of listed options, especially for "wholesale" purposes, is apparently putting pressure on the OTC markets for greater standardization in interbank trading. In some instances, OTC foreign currency options are traded for expiration on the third Wednesday of March, June, September, and December, to coincide with expiration dates on the U.S. exchanges.

The buyer of an option can lose only the premium, whereas the seller's potential loss is unlimited.

Although the buyer of an option can lose only the premium paid for the option, the seller's risk of loss is potentially unlimited. Because of this asymmetry between income and risk, few customers are willing to write options. For this reason, the market structure is distinctly asymmetrical when compared with the ordinary market for spot and forward foreign exchange—where there is a balance between customers purchasing or selling currency and where the interbank market likewise has a reasonable balance.

Futures Options

In January 1984, the IMM introduced a market in options on Deutsche-mark futures contracts. Since then the *futures option* market has grown to include options on futures in British pounds, Japanese yen, Swiss francs, and Canadian dollars as well. Trading involves purchases and sales of puts and calls on a contract calling for delivery of a standard IMM futures contract in the currency rather than the currency itself. When exercised, the holder receives a short or long position in the currency futures contract that expires one week after the expiration of the option contract. Once the option contract is exercised and the futures contract delivered, the holder may sell the contract on the IMM at a price that provides the holder with exactly the same profit as the holder would have realized with a straight currency option. The introduction of the futures option has been hailed by many observers as an important step toward providing traders and investors with a greater variety of instruments to reduce the risks associated with international business and investment.

6.3 READING CURRENCY FUTURES AND OPTIONS PRICES

Futures and options prices appear daily in the financial press and are straightforward to read.

Futures and exchange-listed options prices appear daily in the financial press. Exhibit 6.14 shows prices for April 29, 1993, as displayed in *The Wall Street Journal* on the following day. Futures prices on the IMM are listed for six currencies, with one to four contracts quoted for each currency: June and September 1993 for all but the Australian dollar, and December 1993 and March 1994 for some currencies. Included are the opening and last settlement (settle) prices, the change from the previous trading day, the range for the day, and the number of contracts outstanding (open interest). For example, the June Deutsche mark futures con-

Exhibit 6.14 Foreign Currency Futures and Options Quotations

FUTURES

JAPAN YEN (CME) – 12.5 million yen; $ per yen (.00)

	Open	High	Low	Settle	Change	Lifetime High	Lifetime Low	Open Interest
June	.8935	.9022	.8918	.9003	+ .0086	.9155	.7745	71,298
Sept	.8946	.9020	.8929	.9002	+ .0085	.9160	.7945	4,140
Dec	.8990	.9016	.8990	.9006	+ .0084	.9150	.7970	728

Est vol 25,653; vol Wed 27,239; open int 76,172, −844.

DEUTSCHEMARK (CME) – 125,000 marks; $ per mark

	Open	High	Low	Settle	Change	Lifetime High	Lifetime Low	Open Interest
June	.6297	.6334	.6273	.6298	+ .0008	.6920	.5883	120,863
Sept	.6238	.6268	.6212	.6234	+ .0007	.6720	.5860	7,379
Dec	.6200	.6200	.6180	.6186	+ .0007	.6650	.5830	351

Est vol 49,751; vol Wed 46,926; open int 128,604, −6.

CANADIAN DOLLAR (CME) – 100,000 dlrs.; $ per Can $

	Open	High	Low	Settle	Change	Lifetime High	Lifetime Low	Open Interest
June	.7850	.7861	.7830	.7835	− .0007	.8360	.7532	26,583
Sept	.7802	.7815	.7789	.7787	− .0007	.8335	.7515	1,789
Dec	.7760	.7760	.7734	.7734	− .0007	.8310	.7470	982
Mr94	.7705	.7705	.7700	.7683	− .0007	.7860	.7550	805
June	.7640	.7640	.7638	.7638	− .0001	.7805	.7515	179

Est vol 3,715; vol Wed 9,092; open int 30,388, +1,455.

BRITISH POUND (CME) – 62,500 pds.; $ per pound

	Open	High	Low	Settle	Change	Lifetime High	Lifetime Low	Open Interest
June	1.5680	1.5750	1.5618	1.5682	− .0008	1.9100	1.4020	43,750
Sept	1.5600	1.5640	1.5520	1.5572	− .0012	1.5800	1.3980	1,723

Est vol 13,375; vol Wed 9,834; open int 45,569, +259.

SWISS FRANC (CME) – 125,000 francs; $ per franc

	Open	High	Low	Settle	Change	Lifetime High	Lifetime Low	Open Interest
June	.6987	.7032	.6960	.7000	+ .0016	.8070	.6405	46,707
Sept	.7000	.7005	.6940	.6973	+ .0013	.7100	.6380	3,168
Dec	.6965	.6990	.6930	.6957	+ .0011	.7010	.6400	235

Est vol 24,275; vol 21,476; open int 50,132, +2,259.

AUSTRALIAN DOLLAR (CME) – 100,000 dlrs.; $ per A.$

	Open	High	Low	Settle	Change	Lifetime High	Lifetime Low	Open Interest
June	.7125	.7145	.7075	.7092	− .0036	.7242	.6590	3,368

Est vol 562; vol Wed 527; open int 3,394, −51.

U.S. DOLLAR INDEX (FINEX) – 1,000 times USDX

	Open	High	Low	Settle	Change	Lifetime High	Lifetime Low	Open Interest
June	89.92	90.15	89.45	89.77	− .14	97.20	82.55	6,462
Sept	90.92	91.22	90.75	90.87	− .15	97.10	90.75	1,232

Est vol 1,800; vol Wed 1,279; open int 7,701, −36.
The index: High 89.53; Low 88.90; Close 89.25 −.06

(a)

FUTURES OPTIONS

JAPANESE YEN (CME)
12,500,000 yen; cents per 100 yen

Strike Price	Calls – Settle May	Calls – Settle Jun	Calls – Settle Jly	Puts – Settle May	Puts – Settle Jun	Puts – Settle Jly
8900	1.29	1.84	....	0.26	0.81	1.22
8950	0.95	1.55	....	0.42	1.02	....
9000	0.68	1.29	1.71	0.65	1.26	1.69
9050	0.46	1.07	1.49	0.93	1.54	....
9100	0.32	0.88	1.29	1.29	1.85	2.26
9150	0.22	0.72	1.11	1.69	2.18	....

Est. vol. 8,714;
Wed vol. 8,526 calls; 4,693 puts
Op. Int. Wed 39,883 calls; 39,937 puts

DEUTSCHEMARK (CME)
125,000 marks; cents per mark

Strike Price	Calls – Settle May	Calls – Settle Jun	Calls – Settle Jly	Puts – Settle May	Puts – Settle Jun	Puts – Settle Jly
6200	1.14	1.57	1.58	0.16	0.59	1.24
6250	0.79	1.26	1.32	0.31	0.78	1.48
6300	0.49	0.99	1.10	0.51	1.01	1.75
6350	0.29	0.77	0.91	0.81	1.29	....
6400	0.16	0.59	0.74	1.18	1.60	2.38
6450	0.08	0.45	0.60	....	....	....

Est. vol. 18,442;
Wed vol. 4,585 calls; 8,914 puts
Op. Int. Wed 177,363 calls; 135,204 puts

CANADIAN DOLLAR (CME)
100,000 Can.$, cents per Can.$

Strike Price	Calls – Settle May	Calls – Settle Jun	Calls – Settle Jly	Puts – Settle May	Puts – Settle Jun	Puts – Settle Jly
7750	....	1.19	....	0.10	0.34	....
7800	....	0.86	....	0.22	0.51	....
7850	0.27	0.60	....	0.42	0.75	....
7900	0.12	0.40	....	0.77	1.05	....
7950	0.05	0.25	....	1.20	1.40	....
8000	0.02	0.15	....	1.67	1.79	....

Est. vol. 541;
Wed vol. 264 calls; 648 puts
Op. Int. Wed 3,877 calls; 4,983 puts

BRITISH POUND (CME)
62,500 pounds; cents per pound

Strike Price	Calls – Settle May	Calls – Settle Jun	Calls – Settle Jly	Puts – Settle May	Puts – Settle Jun	Puts – Settle Jly
1525	4.52	5.40	5.58	0.20	1.10	2.38
1550	2.44	3.74	4.16	0.62	1.92	3.44
1575	1.04	2.40	2.98	1.72	3.08	4.74
1600	0.36	1.48	2.08	3.54	4.64	....
1625	0.14	0.86	1.40	....	6.52	....
1650	0.08	0.50	0.92	....	8.64	....

Est. vol. 1,257;
Wed vol. 563 calls; 311 puts
Op. int. Wed 15,481 calls; 11,589 puts

SWISS FRANC (CME)
125,000 francs; cents per franc

Strike Price	Calls – Settle May	Calls – Settle Jun	Calls – Settle Jly	Puts – Settle May	Puts – Settle Jun	Puts – Settle Jly
6905	1.23	1.78	2.10	0.23	0.78	....
6950	0.88	1.48	1.83	0.38	0.98	....
7000	0.59	1.22	1.60	0.59	1.22	....
7050	0.38	0.99	....	0.88	....	....
7100	0.24	0.79	1.17	1.24	1.79	....
7150	0.14	0.63	....	....	....	....

Est. vol. 1,278;
Wed vol. 894 calls; 1,147 puts
Op. Int. We 12,433 calls; 17,827 puts

(b)

OPTIONS
PHILADELPHIA EXCHANGE

	Calls Vol.	Calls Last	Puts Vol.	Puts Last
Canadian Dollar				**78.57**
50,000 Canadian Dollars EOM-cents per unit.				
78½ Apr	...	...	200	0.09
80 Apr	...	...	50	1.42
50,000 Canadian Dollars-cents per unit.				
77½ Sep	...	...	10	1.02
78 Jun	...	...	5	0.65
79 Sep	...	...	5	1.84
79½ Jun	...	...	2	1.39
80 Sep	1	0.54	...	...
ECU				**123.94**
62,500 European Currency Units EOM-cents per unit.				
120 Jun	...	...	4	1.26
122 Apr	6	2.01	...	...
124 Jun	4	2.06	...	...
62,500 European Currency Units-cents per unit.				
122 May	...	...	4	0.72
French Franc				**188.19**
250,000 French Francs EOM-10ths of a unit per unit.				
18¼ May	...	...	10	0.86
250,000 French Francs-10ths of a cent per unit.				
18 Sep	...	...	66	3.66
250,000 French Francs-European Style.				
18 Jun	7556	7.32	...	...
GMark-JYen				**70.34**
62,500 GMark-JYen cross EOM.				
70½ Apr	...	...	10	0.22
62,500 German Mark-Japanese Yen cross.				
73 Jun	160	0.41	...	...
German Mark				**63.43**
62,500 German Marks EOM-cents per unit.				
61½ Apr	...	...	1175	0.02
62 Apr	...	...	1100	0.05
62½ Apr	...	...	826	0.05
63 Apr	266	0.43	235	0.10
63½ Apr	805	0.19	...	...
64 Apr	490	0.07	...	...
62,500 German Marks-European Style.				
59 Jun	...	...	60	0.10
61 Sep	...	...	2600	1.25
62½ Jun	...	...	5	0.44
62½ Jun	...	...	50	0.82
63½ May	...	...	20	0.80
64 Jun	50	0.71	...	...
65 Sep	...	...	900	3.44
65½ May	25	0.07	...	...
66 May	25	0.06	...	...
62,500 German Marks-cents per unit.				
56 Jun	32	7.38	...	...
59 Sep	...	...	4	0.73
60 Jun	5	3.13	152	0.22
60 Sep	...	...	1	0.93
60½ May	...	...	1	0.12
61½ May	...	...	2	0.11
61½ Jun	2	2.00	131	0.42
62 May	2	1.30	100	0.23
62 Jun	6	1.80	654	0.75
62 Sep	...	...	9	1.78
62½ Jun	...	...	31	0.96
63 May	100	0.82	...	...
63 Jun	...	...	20	1.02
63 Sep	2	1.67	6	2.34
63½ May	436	0.56	410	0.70
63½ Jun	414	0.98	...	...
64 May	3856	0.28	...	...
64 Jun	47	0.67	...	...
Japanese Yen				**90.19**
6,250,000 Japanese Yen EOM-100ths of a cent per unit.				
87 May	...	...	40	0.28
88 Apr	...	...	120	0.07
89 Apr	...	...	379	0.19
89 May	...	...	50	0.87
90 Apr	145	0.35	...	...
91 Apr	110	0.09	...	...
93 Jun	400	0.44	...	...
6,250,000 Japanese Yen EOM.				
88½ Apr	...	...	165	0.05
89½ Apr	50	0.42	30	0.33
90½ Apr	245	0.17	...	...
91½ Apr	105	0.10	...	...

(c)

SOURCE: *The Wall Street Journal,* April 30, 1993, p. C13. Excerpted with permission of *The Wall Street Journal,* © Dow Jones & Company, Inc. 1993. All rights reserved worldwide.

tract opened at $0.6297 per DM and closed at $0.6298 per DM. Futures prices are shown in Exhibit 6.14a.

The Chicago Mercantile Exchange trades options on currency futures contracts.

Exhibit 6.14b shows the Chicago Mercantile Exchange (IMM) options on this same futures contract. To interpret the numbers in this column, consider the call options. These are rights to buy the June DM futures contract at specified prices—the strike prices. For example, the call option with a strike price of 62 means that you can purchase an option to buy a June DM futures contract, up to the June settlement date, for $0.6200 per mark. This option will cost $0.0180 per Deutsche mark, or $2,250, plus brokerage commission for a DM 125,000 contract. The price is high because the option is in-the-money. In contrast, the June futures option with a strike price of 64, which is well out-of-the-money, costs only $0.0071 per mark, or $887.50 for one contract. These option prices indicate that the market expects the dollar price of the Deutsche mark to exceed $0.6200 but not to rise much above $0.6400 by June.

A futures call option allows you to buy the relevant futures contract, which is settled at maturity. On the other hand, the Philadelphia call options contract is an option to buy foreign exchange spot, which is settled when the call option is exercised; the buyer receives foreign currency immediately.

Price quotes usually reflect this difference. For example, PHLX call options for the June DM (shown in Exhibit 6.14c), with strike price $0.6400 are $0.0059 per mark (versus $0.0071 for the June futures call option), or $368.75, plus brokerage fees for one contract of DM 62,500. Brokerage fees here would be about the same as on the IMM: about $16 per transaction round trip, per contract.

Exhibit 6.15 summarizes how to read price quotations for futures and options on futures using a DM illustration.

6.4 SUMMARY AND CONCLUSIONS

In this chapter, we have examined the currency futures and options markets and looked at some of the institutional characteristics and mechanics of these markets. We saw that currency futures and options offer alternative hedging (and speculative) mechanisms for companies and individuals. Like forward contracts, futures contracts must be settled at maturity. By contrast, currency options give the owner the right but not the obligation to buy (call option) or sell (put option) the contracted currency. An American option can be exercised at any time up to the expiration date; a European option can only be exercised at maturity.

Futures contracts are standardized contracts that trade on organized exchanges. Forward contracts, on the other hand, are custom-tailored contracts, typically entered into between a bank and its customers. Options contracts are sold on both organized exchanges and in the over-the-counter market. Like forward contracts, OTC options are contracts whose specifications are generally negotiated as to the terms and conditions between a bank and its customers.

Exhibit 6.15 How to Read Futures and Futures Options Quotations

Futures

Prices represent the open, high, low, and settlement (or closing) price for the previous day.

One day's change in the settlement price

The extreme prices recorded for the contract over its trading life

GERMAN MARK (IMM)—125,000 marks; $ per mark

The number of contracts still in effect at the end of the previous day's trading session. Each unit represents a buyer *and* a seller who still have a contract position.

	Open	High	Low	Settle	Chg	Lifetime high	Low	Open interest
Mar.	.5415	.5452	.5401	.5436	−.0011	.5520	.4370	56,576
June	.5435	.5472	.5422	.5459	−.0011	.5538	.4850	1,839
Sept.	.5460	.5494	.5460	.5483	−.0010	.5525	.4868	270

Est. vol. 26,426; vol. Thur. 35,278; open int. 58,706, — 1,399.

Contract delivery months that are currently traded

Number of trades transacted in the previous two trading sessions

The total of the right column, and the change from the prior trading day

Options on Futures

Closing prices for call options*

Closing prices for put options*

GERMAN MARK (CME)—125,000 marks; cents per mark

Most active strike prices

Expiration month

Strike price	Calls–Settle			Puts–Settle		
	Feb-C	Mar-C	Apr-C	Feb-P	Mar-P	Apr-P
52	2.46	2.63	....	0.11	0.29	....
53	1.63	1.87	2.21	0.28	0.52	0.65
54	0.96	1.27	1.60	0.60	0.91	....
55	0.50	0.80	....	1.14	1.44	....
56	0.25	0.50	....	....	2.13	....
57	....	0.30	....	....	....	....

Est. vol. 8,145, Thur. vol. 9,077 calls, 9,024 puts
Open interest Thur.; 47,855 calls, 46,767 puts

Volume of options transacted in the previous two trading sessions. Each unit represents both the buyer *and* the seller.

The number of options that were still open positions at the end of the previous day's trading session.

* The dollar price represented by a premium quotation equals the quote multiplied by the number of currency units covered in the underlying futures. For example, a quote of 0.50¢ for a 55 call represents a dollar premium of 0.50¢ × DM 125,000 = $625.

SOURCE: *Opportunities in Currency Trading,* Chicago Mercantile Exchange, 1986, p. 25.

QUESTIONS

1.   On April 1, the spot price of the British pound was $1.86 and the price of the June futures contract was $1.85. During April the pound appreciated, so that by May 1 it was selling for $1.91. What do you think happened to the price of the June pound futures contract during April? Explain.

2.   Suppose that Texas Instruments must pay a French supplier FF 10 million in 90 days.
     a. Explain how TI can use currency futures to hedge its exchange risk. How many futures contracts will TI need to fully protect itself?
     b. Explain how TI can use currency options to hedge its exchange risk. How many options contracts will TI need to fully protect itself?
     c. Discuss the advantages and disadvantages of using currency futures versus currency options to hedge TI's exchange risk.

3.   Since a forward market already existed, why was it necessary to establish currency futures and currency options contracts?

4.   What are the basic differences between forward and futures contracts? Between futures and options contracts?

5.   What is the last day of trading and the settlement day for the IMM Australian dollar futures for September of the current year?

6.   Which contract is likely to be more valuable, an American or a European call option? Explain.

7.   In Exhibit 6.7, the value of the call option is shown as approaching its intrinsic value as the option goes deeper and deeper in-the-money or further and further out-of-the-money. Explain why this is so.

8.   Suppose that Bechtel Group wants to hedge a bid on a Japanese construction project. But since the yen exposure is contingent on acceptance of its bid, Bechtel decides to buy a put option for the ¥15 billion bid amount rather than sell it forward. In order to reduce its hedging cost, however, Bechtel simultaneously sells a call option for ¥15 billion with the same strike price. Bechtel reasons that it wants to protect its downside risk on the contract and is willing to sacrifice the upside potential in order to collect the call premium. Comment on Bechtel's hedging strategy.

PROBLEMS

1.   On Monday morning, an investor takes a long position in a pound futures contract that matures on Wednesday afternoon. The agreed-upon price is $1.78 for £62,500. At the close of trading on Monday, the futures price has risen to $1.79. At Tuesday close, the price rises further to $1.80. At Wednesday close, the price falls to $1.785, and the contract matures. The investor takes delivery of the pounds at the prevailing price of $1.785. Detail the daily settlement process (see Exhibit 6.3). What will be the investor's profit (loss)?

2.   On Monday morning, an investor takes a short position in a DM futures contract that matures on Wednesday afternoon. The agreed-upon price is $0.6370 for DM 125,000. At the close of trading on Monday, the futures price has fallen to $0.6315. At Tuesday close, the

price falls further to $0.6291. At Wednesday close, the price rises to $0.6420, and the contract matures. The investor delivers the Deutsche marks at the prevailing price of $0.6420. Detail the daily settlement process (see Exhibit 6.3). What will be the investor's profit (loss)?

3. Suppose that the forward ask price for March 20 on DM is $0.7127 at the same time that the price of IMM mark futures for delivery on March 20 is $0.7145. How could an arbitrageur profit from this situation? What will be the arbitrageur's profit per futures contract (contract size is DM 125,000)?

4. On August 6, you go long one IMM yen futures contract at an opening price of $0.00812. The settlement prices for August 6, 7, and 8 are $0.00791, $0.00845, and $0.00894, respectively. On August 9, you close out the contract at a price of $0.00857. Your round-trip commission is $31.48.

    a. Calculate the daily cash flows on your account. Be sure to take into account your required margin and any margin calls.

    b. What is your cash balance with your broker on the morning of August 10?

5. Suppose that DEC buys a Swiss franc futures contract (contract size is SFr 125,000) at a price of $0.83. If the spot rate for the Swiss franc at the date of settlement is SFr 1 = $0.8250, what is DEC's gain or loss on this contract?

6. On January 10, Volkswagen agrees to import auto parts worth $7 million from the United States. The parts will be delivered on March 4 and are payable immediately in dollars. VW decides to hedge its dollar position by entering into IMM futures contracts. The spot rate is DM 1.8347/$1 and the March futures price is DM 1.8002.

    a. Calculate the number of futures contracts that VW must buy to offset its dollar exchange risk on the parts contract.

    b. On March 4, the spot rate turns out to be DM 1.7952, while the March futures price is DM 1.7968. Calculate VW's net DM gain or loss on its futures position. Compare this figure with VW's gain or loss on its unhedged position.

7. Citicorp sells a call option on Deutsche marks (contract size is DM 500,000) at a premium of $0.04 per DM. If the exercise price is $0.71 and the spot price of the mark at date of expiration is $0.73, what is Citicorp's profit (loss) on the call option?

8. Ford buys a French franc put option (contract size is FF 250,000) at a premium of $0.01 per franc. If the exercise price is $0.21 and the spot price of the franc at date of expiration is $0.216, what is Ford's profit (loss) on the put option?

9. Apex Corporation must pay its Japanese supplier ¥125 million in three months. It is thinking of buying 20 yen call options (contract size is ¥6.25 million) at a strike price of $0.00800 in order to protect against the risk of a rising yen. The premium is 0.015 cents per yen. Alternatively, Apex could buy 10 three-month yen futures contracts (contract size is ¥12.5 million) at a price of $0.007940/¥. The current spot rate is ¥1 = $0.007823. Apex's treasurer believes that the most likely value for the yen in 90 days is $0.007900, but the yen could go as high as $0.008400 or as low as $0.007500.

    a. Diagram Apex's gains and losses on the call option position and the futures position within its range of expected prices (see Exhibit 6.5). Ignore transaction costs and margins.

    b. Calculate what Apex would gain or lose on the option and futures positions if the yen settled at its most likely value.

    c. What is Apex's break-even future spot price on the option contract? On the futures contract?

d. Calculate and diagram the corresponding profit and loss and break-even positions on the futures and options contracts for the sellers of these contracts.

10. Biogen expects to receive royalty payments totaling £1.25 million next month. It is interested in protecting these receipts against a drop in the value of the pound. It can sell 30-day pound futures at a price of \$1.6513/£ or it can buy pound put options with a strike price of \$1.6612 at a premium of 2.0 cents per pound. The spot price of the pound is currently \$1.6560, and the pound is expected to trade in the range of \$1.6250 to \$1.70100. Biogen's treasurer believes that the most likely price of the pound in 30 days will be \$1.6400.

    a. How many futures contracts will Biogen need to protect its receipts? How many options contracts?

    b. Diagram Biogen's profit and loss on the put option position and the futures position within its range of expected exchange rates (see Exhibit 6.6). Ignore transaction costs and margins.

    c. Calculate what Biogen would gain or lose on the option and futures positions within the range of expected future exchange rates and if the pound settled at its most likely value.

    d. What is Biogen's break-even future spot price on the option contract? On the futures contract?

    e. Calculate and diagram the corresponding profit and loss and break-even positions on the futures and options contracts for those who took the other side of these contracts.

BIBLIOGRAPHY

Using Currency Futures and Options. Chicago: Chicago Mercantile Exchange, 1987.

Garman, Mark B., and Steven W. Kohlhagen. "Foreign Currency Option Values." *Journal of International Money and Finance,* December 1983, pp. 231–238.

Parity Conditions in International Finance and Currency Forecasting

7

It is not for its own sake that men desire money, but for the sake of what they can purchase with it.

Adam Smith (1776)

CHAPTER LEARNING OBJECTIVES

- To describe the meaning of "the law of one price" and its importance to the study of international finance
- To explain how arbitrage links goods prices and asset returns internationally
- To list and describe the five key theoretical relationships among spot exchange rates, forward exchange rates, inflation rates, and interest rates that result from international arbitrage activities
- To differentiate between the real and nominal exchange rate and the real and nominal interest rate
- To list and describe the four requirements for successful currency forecasting
- To identify a five-stage procedure for forecasting exchange rates in a fixed-rate system
- To describe how to forecast exchange rates in a floating-rate system using the predictions already embodied in interest and forward rates
- To describe the meaning and likelihood of forecasting success in both fixed-rate and floating-rate systems

On the basis of the flows of goods and capital discussed in Chapter 4, this chapter presents a simple, yet elegant, set of equilibrium relationships that should apply to product prices, interest rates, and spot and forward exchange rates if markets are not impeded. These relationships, or *parity conditions,* provide the foundation for much of the remainder of this text; they should be clearly understood before you proceed further. The final section of this chapter examines the usefulness of a number of

KEY TERMS

black-market exchange rate
charting
controlled exchange rate
covered interest arbitrage
covered interest differential
currency forecasting
Fisher effect (FE)
fundamental analysis
inflation differential
interest parity
interest rate differential
interest rate parity (IRP)
international Fisher effect (IFE)
law of one price
market-based forecasts
model-based forecasts
nominal exchange rate
nominal interest rate
parity conditions
purchasing power parity (PPP)
real exchange rate
real interest rate
technical analysis
trend analysis
unbiased forward rate (UFR)
unbiased predictor

models and methodologies in profitably forecasting currency changes under both fixed-rate and floating-rate systems.

7.1 ARBITRAGE AND THE LAW OF ONE PRICE

The law of one price says that exchange-adjusted prices of identical tradeable goods and assets must be within transactions costs of equality worldwide.

In competitive markets, characterized by numerous buyers and sellers having low-cost access to information, exchange-adjusted prices of identical tradable goods and financial assets must be within transaction costs of equality worldwide. This idea, referred to as the *law of one price,* is enforced by international arbitrageurs who follow the profit-guaranteeing dictum of "buy low, sell high" and prevent all but trivial deviations from equality. Similarly, in the absence of market imperfections, risk-adjusted expected returns on financial assets in different markets should be equal.

Five key theoretical economic relationships, which are depicted in Exhibit 7.1, result from these arbitrage activities.

— Purchasing power parity (PPP)
— Fisher effect (FE)
— International Fisher effect (IFE)
— Interest rate parity (IRP)
— Forward rates as unbiased predictors of future spot rates (UFR)

The framework of Exhibit 7.1 emphasizes the links among prices, spot exchange rates, interest rates, and forward exchange rates. According to the diagram, if

Exhibit 7.1 Five Key Theoretical Relationships Among Spot Rates, Forward Rates, Inflation Rates, and Interest Rates

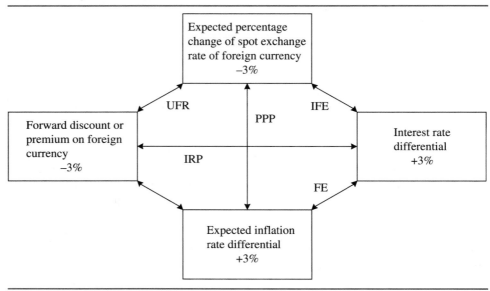

inflation in, say, France is expected to exceed inflation in the United States by 3% for the coming year, then the French franc should decline in value by about 3% relative to the dollar. By the same token, the one-year forward French franc should sell at a 3% discount relative to the U.S. dollar. Similarly, one-year interest rates in France should be about 3% higher than one-year interest rates on securities of comparable risk in the United States.

The common denominator of these parity conditions is the adjustment of the various rates and prices to inflation. According to modern monetary theory, inflation is the logical outcome of an expansion of the money supply in excess of real output growth. Although this view of the origin of inflation is not universally subscribed to, it has a solid microeconomic foundation. In particular, it is a basic precept of price theory that as the supply of one commodity increases relative to supplies of all other commodities, the price of the first commodity must decline relative to the prices of other commodities. Thus, for example, a bumper crop of corn should cause corn's value in exchange—its exchange rate—to decline. Similarly, as the supply of money increases relative to the supply of goods and services, the purchasing power of money—the exchange rate between money and goods—must decline.

Money supply growth, inflation, interest rates, and exchange rates are linked to each other through arbitrage.

The mechanism that brings this adjustment about is simple and direct. Suppose, for example, that the supply of U.S. dollars exceeds the amount that individuals desire to hold. In order to reduce their excess holdings of money, individuals increase their spending on goods, services, and securities, causing U.S. prices to rise.

ILLUSTRATION: *Bolivia Ends Its Hyperinflation*

In the Spring of 1985, Bolivia's inflation rate was running at 25,000% a year, one of the highest rates in history. At the time, Bolivian government revenues covered less than 15% of its spending, with most of the rest being paid for by printing new pesos. Inflation threatened the very fabric of society. Prices changed by the minute, and people literally carried money around in suitcases. Currency, which was printed abroad, was the third-largest import in 1984. The two-inch stack of money needed to buy a chocolate bar far outweighed the candy. The government eventually solved the stacks-of-money problem by issuing 1-million-, 2-million-, and 10-million-peso notes. But its failure to solve the inflation problem led to its replacement by a new government that announced an anti-inflation program on August 29. The program had two basic thrusts: Cut spending and shut down the printing presses. To cut spending, the new government adopted the simple rule that it would not spend more than it received. Each day the finance minister signed checks only up to the value of the revenues the treasury had received that day. By October, the monthly inflation rate had fallen to zero, from more than 60% in August. Economists consider this performance to be an extraordinary verification of basic monetary theory.

Inflation and currency
depreciation are jointly
determined by domes-
tic money supply
growth relative to
money demand growth.

A further link in the chain relating money supply growth, inflation, interest rates, and exchange rates is the notion that money is neutral. That is, money should have no impact on real variables. Thus, for example, a 10% increase in the supply of money relative to the demand for money should cause prices to rise by 10%. This view has important implications for international finance. Specifically, although a change in the quantity of money will affect prices and exchange rates, this change should not affect the rate at which domestic goods are exchanged for foreign goods or the rate at which goods today are exchanged for goods in the future. These ideas are formalized as purchasing power parity and the Fisher effect, respectively. We will examine them here briefly and then in greater detail in Sections 7.2 and 7.3, respectively.

The international analogue to inflation is home-currency depreciation relative to foreign currencies. The analogy derives from the observation that inflation involves a change in the exchange rate between the home currency and domestic goods, whereas home-currency depreciation—a decline in the foreign currency value of the home currency—results in a change in the exchange rate between the home currency and foreign goods.

That inflation and currency depreciation are related is no accident. Excess money-supply growth, through its impact on the rate of aggregate spending, affects the demand for goods produced abroad as well as goods produced domestically. In turn, the domestic demand for foreign currencies changes and, consequently, the foreign exchange value of the domestic currency changes. Thus, the rate of domestic inflation and changes in the exchange rate are jointly determined by the rate of domestic money growth relative to the growth of the amount that people—domestic and foreign—want to hold.

International arbitrage
enforces the law of
one price.

If international arbitrage enforces the law of one price, then the exchange rate between the home currency and domestic goods must equal the exchange rate between the home currency and foreign goods. In other words, a unit of home currency (HC) should have the same purchasing power worldwide. Thus, if a dollar buys a pound of bread in the United States, it should also buy a pound of bread in Great Britain. For this to happen, the foreign exchange rate must change by (approximately) the difference between the domestic and foreign rates of inflation. This relationship is called *purchasing power parity* (PPP).

Similarly, the *nominal interest rate,* the price quoted on lending and borrowing transactions, determines the exchange rate between current and future dollars (or any other currency). For example, an interest rate of 10% on a one-year loan means that one dollar today is being exchanged for 1.1 dollars a year from now. But what really matters according to the *Fisher effect* is the exchange rate between current and future purchasing power, as measured by the real interest rate. Simply put, the lender is concerned with how many more goods can be obtained in the future by forgoing consumption today, while the borrower wants to know how much future consumption must be sacrificed to obtain more goods today. This condition is the case regardless of whether the borrower and lender are located in the same or different countries. As a result, if the exchange rate between current and future goods—the *real interest rate*—varies from one country to the next, arbitrage between domestic and foreign capital markets, in the form of international capital flows, should occur. These flows will tend to equalize real interest rates across countries. By looking more closely at these and related parity conditions, we can see how they can be formalized and used for management purposes.

7.2 PURCHASING POWER PARITY (PPP)

Purchasing power parity (PPP) was first stated in a rigorous manner by the Swedish economist Gustav Cassel in 1918; he used it as the basis for recommending a new set of official exchange rates at the end of World War I that would allow for the resumption of normal trade relations.[1] Since then, PPP has been widely used by central banks as a guide to establishing new par values for their currencies when the old ones were clearly in disequilibrium. From a management standpoint, purchasing power parity is often used to forecast future exchange rates, for purposes ranging from deciding on the currency denomination of long-term debt issues to determining in which countries to build plants.

> Purchasing power parity says that currencies with high rates of inflation should depreciate relative to currencies with lower rates of inflation.

In its *absolute* version, purchasing power parity states that exchange-adjusted price levels should be identical worldwide. In other words, a unit of home currency (HC) should have the same purchasing power around the world. This theory is just an application of the law of one price to national price levels rather than to individual prices. (That is, it rests on the assumption that free trade will equalize the price of any good in all countries; otherwise, arbitrage opportunities would exist.) However, absolute PPP ignores the effects on free trade of transportation costs, tariffs, quotas and other restrictions, and product differentiation.

The *relative* version of purchasing power parity, which is used more commonly now, states that the exchange rate between the home currency and any foreign currency will adjust to reflect changes in the prices levels of the two countries. For example, if inflation is 5% in the United States and 1% in Japan, then in order to equalize the dollar price of goods in the two countries, the dollar value of the Japanese yen must rise by about 4%.

Formally, if i_h and i_f are the periodic price level increases (rates of inflation) for the home country and the foreign country, respectively; e_0 is the dollar (HC) value of one unit of foreign currency at the beginning of the period; and e_t is the spot exchange rate in period t, then

$$\frac{e_t}{e_0} = \frac{(1 + i_h)^t}{(1 + i_f)^t} \tag{7.1}$$

For example, if the United States and Germany are running annual inflation rates of 5% and 3%, respectively, and the spot rate is DM 1 = $0.75, then according to Equation 7.1 the value of the DM in three years should be

$$e_3 = 0.75 \left(\frac{1.05}{1.03} \right)^3 = \$0.7945$$

[1]Gustav Cassel, "Abnormal Deviations in International Exchanges," *Economic Journal*, December 1981, pp. 413–415.

The one-period version of Equation 7.1 is commonly used. It is

$$\frac{e_1}{e_0} = \frac{1 + i_h}{1 + i_f} \tag{7.2}$$

ILLUSTRATION: Calculating the PPP Rate for the DM

Suppose the current U.S. price level is at 112 while the German price level is at 107, relative to base price levels of 100. If the initial value of the Deutsche mark was $0.48, then according to PPP, the dollar value of the DM should have risen to approximately $0.5024 (0.48 × 112/107), an appreciation of 4.67%. On the other hand, if the German price level now equals 119, then the Deutsche mark should have depreciated by about 5.88%, to $0.4518 (0.48 × 112/119).

Purchasing power parity is often represented by the following approximation of Equation 7.2:[2]

$$\frac{e_1 - e_0}{e_0} = i_h - i_f \tag{7.3}$$

That is, the exchange rate change during a period should equal the *inflation differential* for that same time period. In effect, PPP says that *currencies with high rates of inflation should devalue relative to currencies with lower rates of inflation.*

Equation 7.3 is illustrated in Exhibit 7.2. The vertical axis measures the percentage currency change, and the horizontal axis shows the inflation differential. Equilibrium is reached on the parity line, which contains all those points at which these two differentials are equal. At point A, for example, the 3% inflation differential is just offset by the 3% appreciation of the foreign currency relative to the home currency. Point B, on the other hand, depicts a situation of disequilibrium, where the inflation differential of 3% is greater than the appreciation of 1% in the HC value of the foreign currency.

The Lesson of Purchasing Power Parity

Only changes in the real exchange rate will affect the relative competitive positions of domestic firms and their foreign competitors.

Purchasing power parity bears an important message: Just as the price of goods in one year cannot be meaningfully compared to the price of goods in another year without adjusting for interim inflation, so exchange rate changes may indicate nothing more than the reality that countries have different inflation rates. In fact, according to PPP, exchange rate movements should just cancel out changes in the foreign price level relative to the domestic price level. These offsetting movements should have no effects on the relative competitive positions of do-

---

[2]Subtracting 1 from both sides of Equation 7.2 yields

$$\frac{e_1 - e_0}{e_0} = \frac{i_h - i_f}{1 + i_f}$$

Equation 7.3 follows if i_f is relatively small.

Exhibit 7.2 Purchasing Power Parity

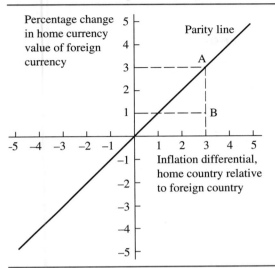

mestic firms and their foreign competitors. Thus, changes in the *nominal exchange rate*—that is, the actual exchange rate—may be of little significance in determining the true effects of currency changes on a firm and a nation. In terms of currency changes affecting relative competitiveness, therefore, the focus must be not on nominal exchange rate changes but instead on changes in the real purchasing power of one currency relative to another. Here we consider the concept of the real exchange rate.

As defined in Chapter 4, the *real exchange rate* is the nominal exchange rate adjusted for changes in the relative purchasing power of each currency since some base period.[3] If changes in the nominal exchange rate are fully offset by changes in the relative price levels between the two countries, then the real exchange rate remains unchanged. Alternatively, a change in the real exchange rate is equivalent to a deviation from PPP.

The distinction between the nominal exchange rate and the real exchange rate has important implications for foreign exchange risk measurement and management. As we will see in Chapter 10, if the real exchange rate remains constant (i.e., if purchasing power parity holds), currency gains or losses from nominal exchange rate changes will generally be offset over time by the effects of differences in relative rates of inflation, thereby reducing the net impact of nominal devaluations and revaluations. Deviations from purchasing power parity, however, will lead to real exchange gains and losses.

> Deviations from purchasing power parity cause real exchange rate changes.

[3]In technical terms, the real exchange rate at time t, e_t', is designated as

$$e_t' = e_0 \frac{(1 + i_h)^t}{(1 + i_f)^t}$$

where the various parameters are the same as those defined previously.

Expected Inflation and Exchange Rate Changes

Changes in expected, as well as actual, inflation will cause exchange rate changes. An increase in a currency's expected rate of inflation, all other things being equal, makes that currency more expensive to hold over time (because its value is being eroded at a faster rate) and less in demand at the same price. Consequently, the value of higher-inflation currencies will tend to be depressed relative to the value of lower-inflation currencies, other things being equal.

Empirical Evidence

PPP holds up well in the long run, but not so well over shorter time periods.

The strictest version of purchasing power parity—that all goods and financial assets obey the law of one price—is demonstrably false. The risks and costs of shipping goods internationally, as well as government-erected barriers to trade and capital flows, are at times high enough to cause exchange-adjusted prices to systematically differ between countries. On the other hand, there is clearly a relationship between relative inflation rates and changes in exchange rates. This relationship is shown in Exhibit 7.3, which compares the relative change in the purchasing power of 22 currencies (as measured by their relative inflation rates) with the relative change in the exchange rates for those currencies for the period 1982 through 1988. As expected, those currencies with the largest relative decline (gain) in purchasing power saw the sharpest erosion (appreciation) in their foreign exchange values.

Exhibit 7.3 Purchasing Power Parity: Empirical Data, 1982–1988

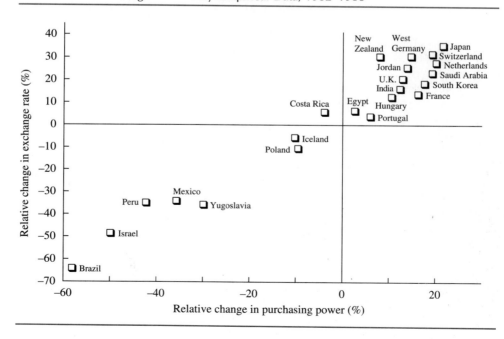

The general conclusion from empirical studies of PPP is that the theory holds up well in the long run, but not as well over shorter time periods.[4] A common explanation for the failure of PPP to hold is that goods prices are sticky, leading to short-term violations of the law of one price. Adjustment to PPP eventually occurs, but it does so with a lag. An alternative explanation for the failure of most tests to support PPP in the short run is that these tests ignore the problems caused by the combination of differently constructed price indices, relative price changes, and nontraded goods and services.

One problem arises because the price indices used to measure inflation vary substantially between countries as to the goods and services included in the "market basket" and the weighting formula used. Thus, changes in the relative prices of various goods and services will cause differently constructed indices to deviate from each other, falsely signaling deviations from PPP. Measured deviations from PPP tend to be far smaller when using the same weights than when using different weights in calculating the U.S. and foreign price indices.

In addition, relative price changes could lead to changes in the equilibrium exchange rate, even in the absence of changes in the general level of prices. For example, an increase in the relative price of oil will lead to an increase in the exchange rates of oil-exporting countries, even if other prices adjust so as to keep all price levels constant. In general, a relative price change that increases a nation's wealth will also increase the value of its currency. Similarly, an increase in the real interest rate in one nation relative to real interest rates elsewhere will induce flows of foreign capital to the first nation. The result will be an increase in the real value of that nation's currency.

Finally, price indices heavily weighted with nontraded goods and services will provide misleading information about a nation's international competitiveness. Over the longer term, increases in the price of medical care or the cost of education will affect the cost of producing traded goods. But, in the short run, such price changes will have little effect on the exchange rate.

PPP measures are distorted by nontraded goods and relative price changes.

Exhibit 7.4 shows the often substantial gaps that can arise between nontraded goods and services between countries. You can't easily substitute a Hong Kong Big Mac costing $0.98 for a Paris Big Mac at $2.97. Similarly, if you're in Tokyo and you don't like the $316 price of a room at the Hotel Okura, you can't easily substitute a $124 room at the Alameda Plaza hotel in Kansas City. Because PPP is driven by arbitrage, including such prices in estimating PPP will not help to determine whether exchange rates are in equilibrium.

Despite the problems caused by relative price changes, most tests of relative PPP as a long-term theory of exchange rate determination seem to support its validity. The reason is that over long periods of time with a moderate inflation differential, the general trend in the price level ratio will tend to dominate the effects of relative price changes. This factor also explains why standard tests of PPP support it even in the short run during periods of hyperinflation: With high

---

[4]See for example Henry J. Galliot, "Purchasing Power Parity as an Explanation of Long-Term Changes in Exchange Rates," *Journal of Money, Credit, and Banking*, August 1971, pp. 348–357.

process of arbitrage would continue, in the absence of government intervention, until expected real returns were equalized.

In equilibrium, then, with no government interference, it should follow that the nominal interest rate differential will approximately equal the anticipated inflation rate differential, or

$$\frac{1 + r_h}{1 + r_f} = \frac{1 + i_h}{1 + i_f} \qquad\qquad (7.5)$$

where r_h and r_f are the nominal home- and foreign-currency interest rates, respectively.

Currencies with higher rates of inflation should have higher interest rates than currencies with lower inflation rates.

If r_f and i_f are relatively small, then this exact relationship can be approximated by Equation 7.6:[5]

$$r_h - r_f = i_h - i_f \qquad\qquad (7.6)$$

In effect, the generalized version of the Fisher effect says that *currencies with high rates of inflation should bear higher interest rates than currencies with lower rates of inflation.*

For example, if inflation rates in the United States and the United Kingdom are 4% and 7%, respectively, the Fisher effect says that nominal interest rates should be about 3% higher in the United Kingdom than in the United States. A graph of Equation 7.6 is shown in Exhibit 7.5. The horizontal axis shows the expected difference in inflation rates between the home country and the foreign

Exhibit 7.5 The Fisher Effect

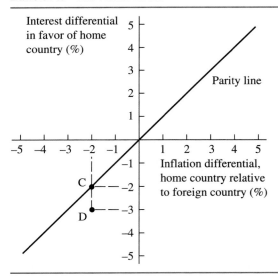

[5]Equation 7.5 can be converted into Equation 7.6 by subtracting 1 from both sides and assuming that r_f and i_f are relatively small.

country, and the vertical axis shows the interest differential between the two countries for the same time period. The parity line shows all points for which $r_h - r_f = i_h - i_f$.

Point C, for example, is a position of equilibrium since the 2% higher rate of inflation in the foreign country ($i_h - i_f = -2\%$) is just offset by the 2% lower HC interest rate ($r_h - r_f = -2\%$). At point D, however, where the real rate of return in the home country is 1% higher than in the foreign country (an inflation differential of 3% versus an interest differential of only 2%), funds should flow from the foreign country to the home country to take advantage of the real differential. This flow will continue until expected real returns are again equal.

Empirical Evidence

Exhibit 7.6 illustrates the relationship between interest rates and subsequent inflation rates for 20 countries during the period 1982 through 1988. It is evident from the graph that nations with higher inflation rates generally have higher interest rates. Thus, the empirical evidence is consistent with the hypothesis that most of the variation in nominal interest rates across countries can be attributed to differences in inflationary expectations.

Real interest rates tend to be equalized across countries.

The proposition that expected real returns are equal between countries cannot be tested directly. However, many observers believe it unlikely that significant real interest differentials could long survive in the increasingly internationalized capital markets. Most market participants agree that arbitrage, via the huge pool

Exhibit 7.6 Fisher Effect: Empirical Data, 1982–1988

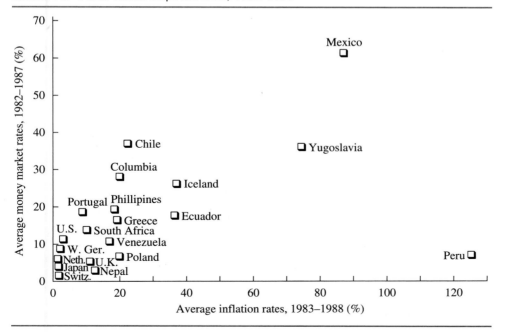

of liquid capital that operates in international markets these days, is forcing pre-tax real interest rates to converge across all the major nations.

The result has been to homogenize markets around the world, eroding much—although not all—of the real interest rate differentials between comparable domestic and offshore securities, and strengthening the link between assets that are denominated in different currencies but carry similar credit risks.[6] To the extent that real interest differentials do exist, they must be due to either currency risk or some form of political risk.

A real interest rate differential could exist without being arbitraged away if investors strongly prefer to hold domestic assets in order to avoid currency risk, even if the expected real return on foreign assets was higher. Despite this theoretical possibility, the data indicate a convergence in real interest rates internationally, even if they don't appear to be equal.[7]

Absent currency risk, the only way to reintroduce real interest rate differentials in this closely integrated world economy is for countries to pursue sharply differing tax policies, impose regulatory barriers to the free flow of capital, or consciously present varying risks for would-be investors. None of these options is attractive to policymakers of the major industrial countries.

Political risk can cause real interest rates to differ across countries.

In many developing countries, however, currency controls and other government policies impose political risk on foreign investors. In effect, political risk can drive a wedge between the returns available to domestic investors and those available to foreign investors. For example, if political risk in Brazil causes foreign investors to demand a 7% higher interest rate than they demand elsewhere, then foreign investors would consider a 10% expected real return in Brazil to be equivalent to a 3% expected real return in the United States. Hence, real interest rates in developing countries can exceed those in developed countries without presenting attractive arbitrage opportunities to foreign investors. The combination of a relative shortage of capital and high political risk in most developing countries is likely to cause real interest rates in these countries to exceed real interest rates in the developed countries.

7.4 THE INTERNATIONAL FISHER EFFECT (IFE)

The key to understanding the impact of relative changes in nominal interest rates among countries on the foreign exchange value of a nation's currency is to recall the implications of PPP and the generalized Fisher effect. PPP implies that exchange rates will move to offset changes in inflation rate differentials. Thus, a rise in the U.S. inflation rate relative to those of other countries will be associated with

---

[6]An offshore security is one denominated in the home currency but issued abroad. They are generally referred to as Eurosecurities.

[7]See, for example, Frederick S. Mishkin, "Are Real Interest Rates Equal Across Countries? An International Investigation of Parity Conditions," *Journal of Finance*, December 1984, pp. 1345–1357. He finds that although capital markets may be integrated, real interest rates appear to differ across countries because of currency risk.

a fall in the dollar's value. It will also be associated with a rise in the U.S. interest rate relative to foreign interest rates. Combine these two conditions and the result is the *international Fisher effect*:

$$\frac{(1+r_h)^t}{(1+r_f)^t} = \frac{\overline{e}_t}{e_0} \tag{7.7}$$

where $\overline{e}_t$ is the expected exchange rate in period t. The single period analogue to Equation 7.7 is

$$\frac{1+r_h}{1+r_f} = \frac{\overline{e}_1}{e_0} \tag{7.8}$$

According to Equation 7.8, the expected return from investing at home, $1 + r_h$, should equal the expected HC return from investing abroad, $(1 + r_f)\overline{e}_1/e_0$. As discussed in the previous section, however, despite the intuitive appeal of equal expected returns, domestic and foreign expected returns might not equilibrate if the element of currency risk restrained the process of international arbitrage.

> The expected HC returns from investing at home and abroad should be equal.

ILLUSTRATION: Using the IFE to Forecast U.S.$ and SFr Rates

In July, the one-year interest rate is 4% on Swiss francs and 13% on U.S. dollars.
a. If the current exchange rate is SFr 1 = $0.63, what is the expected future exchange rate in one year?

Solution. According to the international Fisher effect, the spot exchange rate expected in one year equals $0.63 \times 1.13/1.04 = \$0.6845$.

b. If a change in expectations regarding future U.S. inflation causes the expected future spot rate to rise to $0.70, what should happen to the U.S. interest rate?

Solution. If r_{us} is the unknown U.S. interest rate, and the Swiss interest rate stayed at 4% (because there has been no change in expectations of Swiss inflation), then according to the international Fisher effect, $0.70/0.63 = (1 + r_{us})/1.04$, or $r_{us} = 15.56\%$.

If r_f is relatively small, Equation 7.9 provides a reasonable approximation to the international Fisher effect (IFE):[8]

$$r_h - r_f = \frac{\overline{e}_1 - e_0}{e_0} \tag{7.9}$$

---

[8]Subtracting 1 from both sides of Equation 7.8 yields

$$\frac{\overline{e}_1 - e_0}{e_0} = \frac{r_h - r_f}{1 + r_f}$$

Equation 7.9 follows if r_f is relatively small.

The international Fisher effect says that currencies with low interest rates are expected to appreciate relative to currencies with high interest rates.

In effect, the IFE says that *currencies with low interest rates are expected to appreciate relative to currencies with high interest rates.*

A graph of Equation 7.9 is shown in Exhibit 7.7. The vertical axis shows the expected change in the home-currency value of the foreign currency, and the horizontal axis shows the interest differential between the two countries for the same time period. The parity line shows all points for which $r_h - r_f = (e_1 - e_0)/e_0$.

Point E is a position of equilibrium because it lies on the parity line, with the 4% interest differential in favor of the home country just offset by the anticipated 4% appreciation in the HC value of the foreign currency. Point F, however, illustrates a situation of disequilibrium. If the foreign currency is expected to appreciate by 3% in terms of the HC, but the interest differential in favor of the home country is only 2%, then funds would flow from the home to the foreign country to take advantage of the higher exchange-adjusted returns there. This capital flow will continue until exchange-adjusted returns are equal in both nations.

Essentially what the IFE says is that arbitrage between financial markets—in the form of international capital flows—should ensure that the interest differential between any two countries is an *unbiased predictor* of the future change in the spot rate of exchange. This condition does not mean, however, that the interest differential is an especially accurate predictor; it just means that prediction errors tend to cancel out over time. Moreover, an implicit assumption that underlies IFE is that investors view foreign and domestic assets as perfect substitutes. To the extent that this condition is violated (see the discussion on the Fisher effect) and investors require a risk premium (in the form of a higher expected real return) to hold foreign assets, IFE will not hold exactly.

Exhibit 7.7 International Fisher Effect

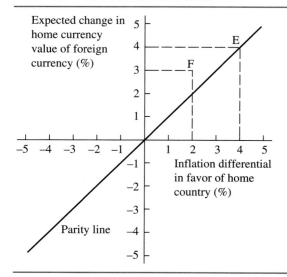

Empirical Evidence

As predicted, there is a clear tendency for currencies with high interest rates (for example, Mexico and Brazil) to depreciate and those with low interest rates (for example, Japan and Switzerland) to appreciate. This is shown in Exhibit 7.8, which graphs the nominal interest differential (relative to the U.S. interest rate) against exchange rate changes (relative to the U.S. dollar) for 22 currencies over the period 1982 to 1988. The ability of interest differentials to anticipate currency changes is also supported by several empirical studies that indicate the long-run tendency for these differentials to offset exchange rate changes.[9] Thus, at any given time, currencies bearing higher nominal interest rates can reasonably be expected to depreciate relative to currencies bearing lower interest rates.

> Empirical evidence indicates that currencies with high (low) interest rates tend to depreciate (appreciate).

However, the effect on exchange rates of a change in the nominal interest differential is not so easily determined. According to the Fisher effect, changes in the nominal interest differential can be due to changes in either the real interest differential or relative inflationary expectations. These two possibilities have op-

Exhibit 7.8 International Fisher Effect: Empirical Data, 1982–1988

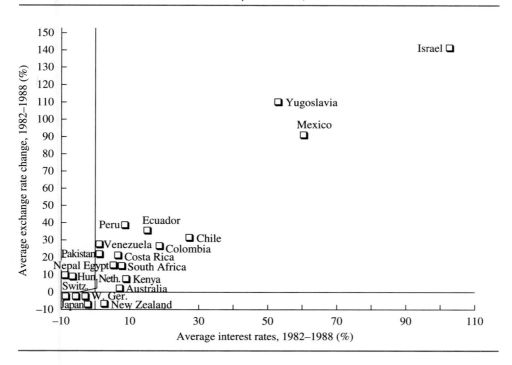

[9]See, for example, Ian H. Giddy and Gunter Dufey, "The Random Behavior of Flexible Exchange Rates," *Journal of International Business Studies*, Spring 1975, pp. 1–32; and Robert A. Aliber and Clyde P. Stickney, "Accounting Measures of Foreign Exchange Exposure: The Long and Short of It," *The Accounting Review*, January 1975, pp. 44–57.

The effect on exchange rates of a change in interest rates depends on whether that change is real or is due to a change in expected inflation.

posite effects on currency values. For example, suppose that the nominal interest differential widens in favor of the United States. If this spread is due to a rise in the real interest rate in the United States relative to that of other countries, the value of the dollar will rise. Alternatively, if the change in the nominal interest differential is caused by an increase in inflationary expectations for the United States, the dollar's value will drop.

The key to understanding short-run changes in the value of the dollar or other currency, then, is to distinguish changes in nominal interest rate differentials that are caused by changes in real interest rate differentials from those caused by changes in relative inflation expectations. Historically, changes in the nominal interest differential have been dominated, at times, by changes in the real interest differential; at other times, they have been dominated by changes in relative inflation expectations. Consequently, there is no stable, predictable relationship between changes in the nominal interest differential and exchange rate changes.

7.5 INTEREST RATE PARITY THEORY (IRP)

The movement of funds between two currencies to take advantage of *interest rate differentials* is also a major determinant of the spread between forward and spot rates. In fact, the forward discount or premium is closely related to the interest differential between the two currencies.

According to interest rate parity theory, the currency of the country with a lower interest rate should be at a forward premium in terms of the currency of the country with the higher rate. More specifically, in an efficient market with no transaction costs, the interest differential should be (approximately) equal to the forward differential. When this condition is met, the forward rate is said to be at *interest parity*, and equilibrium prevails in the money markets.

Interest parity ensures that the return on a hedged (or "covered") foreign investment will just equal the domestic interest rate on investments of identical risk, thereby eliminating the possibility of having a money machine. When this condition holds, the *covered interest differential*—the difference between the domestic interest rate and the hedged foreign rate—is zero. If the covered interest differential between two money markets is nonzero, there is an arbitrage incentive to move money from one market to the other.

Covered interest arbitrage forces interest rates on different currencies to be at parity with each other.

For example, suppose the interest rate on pounds sterling is 12% in London, and the interest rate on a comparable dollar investment in New York is 7%. The pound spot rate is $1.75 and the one-year forward rate is $1.68. These rates imply a forward discount on sterling of 4% [(1.68 − 1.75)/1.75] and a covered yield on sterling approximately equal to 8% (12% − 4%). Since there is a covered interest differential in favor of London, funds will flow from New York to London. This movement of money to take advantage of a covered interest differential is known as *covered interest arbitrage*.

To illustrate the profits associated with covered interest arbitrage, we will assume that the borrowing and lending rates are identical and the bid-ask spread in the spot and forward markets is zero. Here are the steps the arbitrageur can take to profit from the discrepancy in rates based on a $1 million transaction. Specifically, the arbitrageur will

1. Borrow $1,000,000 in New York at an interest rate of 7%. This means that at the end of one year, the arbitrageur must repay principal plus interest of $1,070,000.
2. Immediately convert the $1,000,000 to pounds at the spot rate of £1 = $1.75. This yields £571,428.57 available for investment.
3. Invest the principal of £571,428.57 in London at 12% for one year. At the end of the year, the arbitrageur will have £640,000.
4. Simultaneously with the other transactions, sell the £640,000 in principal plus interest forward at a rate of £1 = $1.68 for delivery in one year. This transaction will yield $1,075,200 next year.
5. At the end of the year, collect the £640,000, deliver it to the bank's foreign exchange department in return for $1,075,200, and use $1,070,000 to repay the loan. The arbitrageur will earn $5,200 on this set of transactions.

The transactions associated with covered interest arbitrage will affect prices in both the money and foreign exchange markets. As pounds are bought spot and sold forward, boosting the spot rate and lowering the forward rate, the forward discount will tend to widen. Simultaneously, as money flows from New York, interest rates there will tend to increase; at the same time, the inflow of funds to London will depress interest rates there. The process of covered interest arbitrage will continue until interest parity is achieved, unless there is government interference.

If this process is interfered with, covered interest differentials between national money markets will not be arbitraged away. Interference often occurs since many governments regulate and restrict flows of capital across their borders. Moreover, just the risk of controls will be sufficient to yield prolonged deviations from interest rate parity.

Government intervention can cause persistent covered interest differentials.

The relationship between the spot and forward rates and interest rates in a free market can be shown graphically, as in Exhibit 7.9. Plotted on the vertical axis is the interest differential in favor of the home country. The horizontal axis plots the percentage forward discount (negative) or premium (positive) on the foreign currency relative to the home currency. The interest parity line joins those points for which the forward exchange rate is in equilibrium with the interest differential. For example, if the interest differential in favor of the foreign country is 2%, then the currency of that country must be selling at a 2% forward discount for equilibrium to exist.

Point G indicates a situation of disequilibrium. Here, the interest differential is 2%, whereas the forward premium on the foreign currency is 3%. The transfer of funds abroad with exchange risks covered will yield an additional 1% annually. At point H, the forward premium remains at 3%, but the interest differential increases to 4%. Now it becomes profitable to reverse the flow of funds. The 4% higher interest rate more than makes up for the 3% loss on the forward exchange transaction, leading to a 1% increase in the interest yield.

In reality, the interest parity line is a band because transaction costs, arising from the spread on spot and forward contracts and brokerage fees on security

Exhibit 7.9 Interest Rate Parity Theory

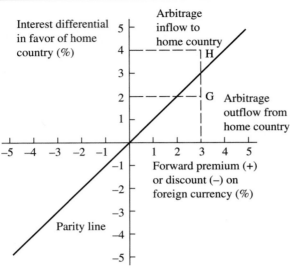

purchases and sales, cause effective yields to be lower than nominal yields. For example, if transaction costs are 0.75%, then a covered yield of only 0.5% will not be sufficient to induce a flow of funds. That is, for interest arbitrage to occur, the covered yield must be at least equal to the transaction costs involved.

Interest rate parity holds when the interest differential is approximately equal to the forward differential.

The covered interest arbitrage relationship can be stated formally. Let e_0 be the current spot rate (dollar value of one unit of foreign currency), and f_1 the end-of-period forward rate. If r_h and r_f are the prevailing interest rates in New York and, say, London, respectively, then one dollar invested in New York will yield $1 + r_h$ at the end of the period; the same dollar invested in London will be worth $(1 + r_f)f_1/e_0$ dollars at maturity. This latter result can be seen as follows: One dollar will convert into $1/e_0$ pounds that, when invested at r_f, will yield $(1 + r_f)/e_0$ pounds at the end of the period. By selling the proceeds forward today, this amount will be worth $(1 + r_f)f_1/e_0$ dollars when the investment matures.

Therefore, it can be seen that funds will flow from New York to London if and only if

$$1 + r_h < \frac{(1 + r_f)f_1}{e_0}$$

Conversely, funds will flow from London to New York if and only if

$$1 + r_h > \frac{(1 + r_f)f_1}{e_0}$$

Interest rate parity holds when there are no covered interest arbitrage opportunities. Based on the previous discussion, this no-arbitrage condition can be stated as follows:

$$\frac{1+r_h}{1+r_f} = \frac{f_1}{e_0} \tag{7.10}$$

ILLUSTRATION: *Using IRP to Calculate the $/¥ Forward Rate*

The interest rate in the United States is 10%; in Japan, the comparable rate is 7%. The spot rate for the yen is $0.003800. If interest rate parity holds, what is the 90-day forward rate?

Solution. According to interest rate parity, the 90-day forward differential on the yen f_{90} should be

$$f_{90} = \$0.003800\left[\left(1+\frac{0.10}{4}\right)\left(1+\frac{0.07}{4}\right)\right]$$

In other words, the 90-day forward Japanese yen should be selling at an annualized premium of about 2.95% ($4 \times 0.000028/0.0038$).

Interest rate parity is often approximated by Equation 7.11:[10]

$$r_h - r_f = \frac{f_1 - e_0}{e_0} \tag{7.11}$$

In effect, interest rate parity says that *high interest rates on a currency are offset by forward discounts and that low interest rates are offset by forward premiums.*

High (low) interest rates on a currency are offset by forward discounts (premiums).

Empirical Evidence

Interest rate parity is one of the best-documented relationships in international finance. In fact, in the Eurocurrency markets, the forward rate is calculated from the interest differential between the two currencies using the no-arbitrage condition. Deviations from interest parity do occur between national capital markets, however, owing to capital controls (or the threat of them), the imposition of taxes on interest payments to foreigners, and transaction costs. However, as we can see in Exhibit 7.10, these deviations tend to be small and short-lived.

7.6 THE RELATIONSHIP BETWEEN THE FORWARD RATE AND THE FUTURE SPOT RATE

Our current understanding of the workings of the foreign exchange market suggests that, in the absence of government intervention in the market, both the spot rate and the forward rate are influenced heavily by current expectations of future

---

[10]Subtracting 1 from both sides of Equation 7.10 yields $(f_1 - e_0)/e_0 = (r_h - r_f)/(1 + r_f)$. Equation 7.11 follows if r_f is relatively small.

Exhibit 7.10 Uncovered and Covered Interest Rate Differentials (U.S. $ Versus Other Currencies)

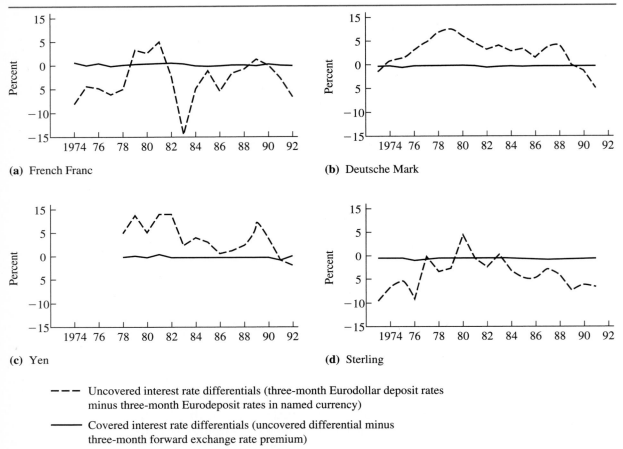

(a) French Franc

(b) Deutsche Mark

(c) Yen

(d) Sterling

– – – Uncovered interest rate differentials (three-month Eurodollar deposit rates minus three-month Eurodeposit rates in named currency)

——— Covered interest rate differentials (uncovered differential minus three-month forward exchange rate premium)

SOURCE: Data from DRI, IMF, and Datastream International reported in "A Survey of the World Economy," *The Economist*, September 19, 1992, p. 23. © 1993 The Economist Newspaper Group, Inc. Reprinted with permission.

events; and both rates move in tandem, with the link between them based on interest differentials. New information, such as a change in interest rate differentials, is reflected almost immediately in both spot and forward rates.

Suppose a depreciation of pounds sterling is anticipated. Recipients of sterling will begin selling sterling forward, while sterling-area dollar earners will slow their sales of dollars in the forward market. These actions will tend to depress the price of forward sterling. At the same time, banks will probably try to even out their long (net purchaser) positions in forward sterling by selling sterling spot. In addition, sterling-area recipients of dollars will tend to delay converting dollars into sterling, and earners of sterling will speed up their collection and conversion of sterling. In this way, pressure from the forward market is transmitted to the spot market, and vice versa.

Equilibrium is achieved only when the forward differential equals the expected change in the exchange rate. At this point, there is no longer any incentive to buy or sell the currency forward. This condition is illustrated in Exhibit 7.11. The vertical axis measures the expected change in the home currency (HC) value of the foreign currency, and the horizontal axis shows the forward discount or premium on the foreign currency. Parity prevails at point I, for example, where the expected foreign currency depreciation of 2% is just matched by the 2% forward discount on the foreign currency. Point J, however, is a position of disequilibrium because the expected 4% depreciation of the foreign currency exceeds the 3% forward discount on the foreign currency. We would, therefore, expect to see speculators selling the foreign currency forward for home currency, taking a 3% discount in the expectation of covering their commitment with 4% fewer units of HC.

A formal statement of the *unbiased nature of the forward rate* (UFR) is that the forward rate should reflect the expected future spot rate on the date of settlement of the forward contract:

> The forward rate should reflect the expected future spot rate on the date of settlement.

$$f_1 = \overline{e_1} \qquad\qquad (7.12)$$

where e_1 is the expected future exchange rate at time 1 (units of home currency per unit of foreign currency) and f_1 is the forward rate for settlement at time 1.

Exhibit 7.11 Relationship Between the Forward Rate and the Future Spot Rate

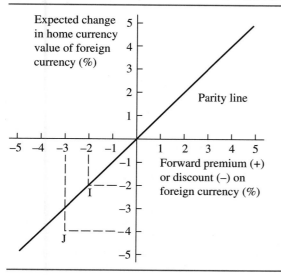

ILLUSTRATION: *Using UFR to Forecast the Future $/DM Spot Rate*

If the 90-day forward rate is DM 1 = $0.5987, what is the expected value of the DM in 90 days?

Solution. Arbitrage should ensure that the market expects the spot value of the DM in 90 days to be about $0.5987.

Equation 7.12 can be transformed into the one reflected in the parity line appearing in Exhibit 7.13, which is that the forward differential equals the expected change in the exchange rate, by subtracting 1 (e_0/e_0), from both sides, where e_0 is the current spot rate (HC per unit of foreign currency):

$$\frac{f_1 - e_0}{e_0} = \frac{\overline{e_1} - e_0}{e_0} \tag{7.13}$$

It should be noted that market efficiency requires that people process information and form reasonable expectations; it does require that $f_1 = e_1$. Market efficiency allows for the possibility that risk-averse investors will demand a risk premium on forward contracts, much the same as they demand compensation for bearing the risk of investing in stocks. In this case, the forward rate will not reflect exclusively the expectation of the future spot rate.

The principal argument against the existence of a risk premium is that currency risk is largely diversifiable. If foreign exchange risk can be diversified away, no risk premium need be paid for holding a forward contract; the forward rate and expected future spot rate will be approximately equal. Ultimately, therefore, the unbiased nature of forward rates is an empirical, and not a theoretical, issue.

Empirical Evidence

Forward rates tend to be unbiased, though inaccurate, predictors of future spot rates.

A number of studies have examined the relation between forward rates and future spot rates.[11] Of course, it would be unrealistic to expect a perfect correlation between forward and future spot rates since the future spot rate will be influenced by events, such as an oil crisis, that can be forecast only imperfectly, if at all.

Nonetheless, the general conclusion from early studies was that forward rates are unbiased predictors of future spot rates. But more recent studies, using more powerful econometric techniques, argue that the forward rate is a biased predictor, probably because of a risk premium.[12] However, the premium appears to change signs—being positive at some times and negative at other times—and

[11]See, for example, Ian Giddy and Gunter Dufey, "The Random Behavior of Flexible Exchange Rates," *Journal of International Business Studies*, Spring 1975, pp. 1–32; and Bradford Cornell, "Spot Rates, Forward Rates, and Market Efficiency," *Journal of Financial Economics*, January 1977, pp. 55–65.

[12]See, for example, L. P. Hansen and R. J. Hodrick, "Forward Rates as Optimal Predictions of Future Spot Rates," *Journal of Political Economy*, October 1980, pp. 829–853.

averages near zero. In the absence of a detailed econometric model, therefore, it would not be stretching things to treat the forward rate as an unbiased forecast of the future spot rate.

7.7 CURRENCY FORECASTING

Forecasting exchange rates has become an occupational hazard for financial executives of multinational corporations. The potential for periodic—and unpredictable—government intervention makes currency forecasting all the more difficult. But this has not dampened the enthusiasm for currency forecasts, nor the willingness of economists and others to supply them. Unfortunately, though, enthusiasm and willingness are not sufficient conditions for success.

Requirements for Successful Currency Forecasting

Currency forecasting can lead to consistent profits only if the forecaster meets at least one of the following four criteria.[13] He or she

— Has exclusive use of a superior forecasting model
— Has consistent access to information before other investors
— Exploits small, temporary deviations from equilibrium
— Can predict the nature of government intervention in the foreign exchange market

The first two conditions are self-correcting. Successful forecasting breeds imitators, while the second situation is unlikely to last long in the highly informed world of international finance. The third situation describes how foreign exchange traders actually earn their living and also why deviations from equilibrium are not likely to last long. The fourth situation is the one worth searching out. Countries that insist on managing their exchange rates, and are willing to take losses to achieve their target rates, present speculators with potentially profitable opportunities. Simply put, consistently profitable predictions are possible in the long run only if it is not necessary to outguess the market to win.

As a general rule, when forecasting in a fixed-rate system, the focus must be on the governmental decision-making structure because the decision to devalue or revalue at a given time is clearly political. During the Bretton Woods system, for example, many speculators did quite well by "stepping into the shoes of the key decision makers" to forecast their likely behavior. The basic forecasting methodology in a fixed-rate system, therefore, involves first ascertaining the pressure on a currency to devalue or revalue and then determining how long the nation's political leaders can, and will, persist with this particular level of disequilibrium. Exhibit 7.12 depicts a five-step procedure for performing this analysis. In the case of a floating-rate system, where government intervention is sporadic or nonex-

Successful currency forecasting is most likely when governments are willing to spend money to achieve noneconomic objectives.

[13]These criteria were suggested by Giddy and Dufey, "Random Behavior of Flexible Exchange Rates."

Exhibit 7.12 Forecasting in a Fixed-Rate System

istent, currency prognosticators have the choice of using either market- or model-based forecasts, neither of which guarantees success.

Market-Based Forecasts

So far, we have identified several equilibrium relationships that should exist between exchange rates and interest rates. The empirical evidence on these relationships implies that, in general, the financial markets of developed countries efficiently incorporate expected currency changes in the cost of money and forward exchange. This means that currency forecasts can be obtained by extracting the predictions already embodied in interest and forward rates.

Interest rates and forward rates contain implicit currency forecasts.

Forward Rates. *Market-based forecasts* of exchange rate changes can be derived most simply from current forward rates. Specifically, f_1—the forward rate for one period from now—will usually suffice for an unbiased estimate of the spot rate as of that date. In other words, f_1 should equal e_1, where e_1 is the expected future spot rate.

Interest Rates. Although forward rates provide simple and easy to use currency forecasts, their forecasting horizon is limited to about one year because of the general absence of longer-term forward contracts. Interest rate differentials can be used to supply exchange rate predictions beyond one year. For example, suppose five-year interest rates on dollars and Deutsche marks are 12% and 8%, respectively. If the current spot rate for the DM is $0.40 and the (unknown) value of the DM in five years is e_5, then $1.00 invested today in Deutsche marks will be worth $(1.08)^5 e_5 / 0.4$ dollars at the end of five years; if invested in the dollar security, it will be worth $(1.12)^5$ in five years. The market's forecast of e_5 can be found by assuming that investors demand equal returns on dollar and DM securities, or

$$\frac{(1.08)^5 e_5}{0.4} = (1.12)^5$$

Thus, the five-year DM spot rate implied by the relative interest rates is $e_5 = \$0.4798$ ($0.40 \times 1.12^5 / 1.08^5$).

Model-Based Forecasts

The two principal model-based approaches to currency prediction are known as fundamental analysis and technical analysis. Each approach has its advocates and detractors.

Currency forecasting models rely on either fundamental analysis or technical analysis.

Fundamental Analysis. *Fundamental analysis* is the most common approach to forecasting future exchange rates. It relies on painstaking examination of the macroeconomic variables and policies that are likely to influence a currency's prospects. The variables examined include relative inflation and interest rates, national income growth, and changes in money supplies. The interpretation of these variables and their implications for future exchange rates depend on the analyst's model of exchange rate determination.

The simplest form of fundamental analysis involves the use of PPP. We have previously seen the value of PPP in explaining exchange rate changes. Its application in currency forecasting is straightforward.

ILLUSTRATION: Using PPP to Forecast the Peseta's Future Spot Rate

The U.S. inflation rate is expected to average about 4% annually, while the Spanish rate of inflation is expected to average about 9% annually. If the current spot rate for the peseta is $0.008, what is the expected spot rate in two years?

Solution. According to PPP (Equation 7.1), the expected spot rate for the peseta in two years is $0.008 \times (1.04/1.09)^2 = \$0.00728$.

Most analysts use more complicated forecasting models whose analysis usually centers on how the different macroeconomic variables are likely to affect the demand and supply for a given foreign currency. The currency's future value is then determined by estimating the exchange rate at which supply just equals demand—when any current-account imbalance is just matched by a net capital flow.

Technical Analysis. *Technical analysis* is the antithesis of fundamental analysis in that it focuses exclusively on past price and volume movements—while totally ignoring economic and political factors—to forecast currency winners and losers. Success depends on whether technical analysts can discover price patterns that repeat themselves and are, therefore, useful for forecasting.

There are two primary methods of technical analysis: *charting* and *trend analysis*. Chartists examine bar charts or use more sophisticated computer-based extrapolation techniques to find recurring price patterns. They then issue buy or sell recommendations if prices diverge from their past pattern. Trend-following systems seek to identify price trends via various mathematical computations.

Model Evaluation

Currency forecasting is unlikely to be consistently profitable in an efficient market.

The possibility that either fundamental or technical analysis can be used to profitably forecast exchange rates is inconsistent with the efficient market hypothesis, which says that current exchange rates reflect all publicly available information. Because markets are forward looking, exchange rates will fluctuate randomly as market participants assess and then react to new information, much as security and commodity prices in other asset markets respond to news. Thus, exchange rate movements are unpredictable; otherwise, it would be possible to earn arbitrage profits. Such profits could not persist in a market—like the foreign exchange market—that is characterized by free entry and exit and an almost unlimited amount of money, time, and energy that participants are willing to commit in pursuit of profit opportunities.

Despite the theoretical skepticism over successful currency forecasting, a study of 14 forecast advisory services by Richard Levich indicates that the profits associated with using several of these forecasts seem too good to be explained by chance.[14] Of course, if the forward rate contains a risk premium, these returns would have to be adjusted for the risks borne by speculators. It is also questionable whether currency forecasters would continue selling their information rather than acting on it themselves if they truly believed it could yield excess risk-adjusted returns.

Forecasting Controlled Exchange Rates

A major problem in currency forecasting is that the widespread existence of exchange controls, as well as restrictions on imports and capital flows, often masks the true pressures on a currency to devalue. In such situations, forward markets and capital markets are invariably nonexistent or subject to such stringent controls that interest and forward differentials are of little practical use in providing market-based forecasts of exchange rate changes. An alternative forecasting approach in such a controlled environment is to use *black-market exchange rates* as useful indicators of devaluation pressure on the nation's currency.

Black-market exchange rates for a number of countries are regularly reported in *Pick's Currency Yearbook and Reports*. These black markets for foreign exchange are likely to appear whenever exchange controls cause a divergence between the equilibrium exchange rate and the official, or *controlled, exchange rate*. Those potential buyers of foreign exchange without access to the central banks will have an incentive to find another market in which to buy foreign currency. Similarly, sellers of foreign exchange will prefer to sell their holdings at the higher black-market rate.

The black-market rate depends on the difference between the official and equilibrium exchange rates, as well as on the expected penalties for illegal transactions. The existence of these penalties and the fact that some transactions do go through at the official rate mean that the black-market rate is not influenced by exactly the same set of supply-and-demand forces that influences the free-market rate. Therefore, the black-market rate in itself cannot be regarded as indicative of the true equilibrium rate that would prevail in the absence of controls. Economists normally assume that for an overvalued currency, the hypothetical equilibrium rate lies somewhere between the official rate and the black-market rate.

The usefulness of the black-market rate is that it is a good indicator of where the official rate is likely to go if the monetary authorities give in to market pressure. However, although the official rate can be expected to move toward the black-market rate, we should not expect to see it coincide with that rate due to the bias induced by government sanctions. The black-market rate seems to be most

Black-market exchange rates are a useful indicator of future changes in controlled currencies.

---

[14]Richard M. Levich, "The Use and Analysis of Foreign Exchange Forecasts: Current Issues and Evidence," paper presented at the Euromoney Treasury Consultancy Program, New York, September 4–5, 1980.

accurate in forecasting the official rate one month ahead and is progressively less accurate as a forecaster of the future official rate for longer time periods.[15]

Exhibit 7.13(a) graphs monthly movements in the official and black-market rates for the Brazilian cruzeiro from December 1968 to March 1977. Exhibit 7.13(b) graphs monthly movements in the two rates from 1981 to 1983. The data clearly show that the black-market cruzeiro rate is invariably above the official rate and is a useful indicator of future devaluations.

Exhibit 7.13 Black Market Versus Official Exchange Rates: Brazillian Cruzeiro

(a) 1968–1977

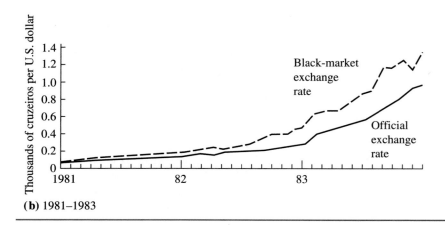

(b) 1981–1983

[15]See, for example, Ian H. Giddy, "Black Market Exchange Rates as a Forecasting Tool," working paper, Columbia University, May 1978.

7.8 SUMMARY AND CONCLUSIONS

We have examined five relationships, or parity conditions, that should apply to spot rates, inflation rates, and interest rates in different currencies: purchasing power parity, the Fisher effect, the international Fisher effect, interest rate parity, and the forward rate as an unbiased forecast of the future spot rate. These parity conditions follow from the law of one price, the notion that in the absence of market imperfections, arbitrage ensures that exchange-adjusted prices of identical traded goods and financial assets are within transaction costs worldwide.

The technical description of these five equilibrium relationships is summarized as follows:

— Purchasing power parity

$$\frac{e_t}{e_0} = \frac{(1 + i_h)^t}{(1 + i_f)^t}$$

where e_t = the home currency value of the foreign currency at time t
e_0 = the home currency value of the foreign currency at time 0
i_h = the periodic domestic inflation rate
i_f = the periodic foreign inflation rate

— Fisher effect

$$1 + r = (1 + a)(1 + i)$$

where r = the nominal rate of interest
a = the real rate of interest
i = the rate of expected inflation

Generalized version of Fisher effect

$$\frac{(1 + r_h)^t}{(1 + r_f)^t} = \frac{(1 + i_h)^t}{(1 + i_f)^t}$$

where r_h = the periodic home currency interest rate
r_f = the periodic foreign currency interest rate

— International Fisher effect

$$\frac{(1 + r_h)^t}{(1 + r_f)^t} = \frac{\overline{e_t}}{e_0}$$

where $\overline{e_t}$ = the expected home currency value of the foreign currency at time t

— The forward rate as an unbiased predictor of the future spot rate

$$f_1 = \overline{e_1}$$

where $\overline{e_1}$ = the expected home currency value of the foreign currency at time 1
f_1 = the forward rate for delivery of the foreign currency at time 1

— Interest rate parity

$$\frac{1+r_h}{1+r_f} = \frac{f_1}{e_0}$$

Despite the mathematical precision with which these parity conditions are expressed, they are only approximations to reality. A variety of factors can lead to significant and prolonged deviations from parity. For example, both currency risk and inflation risk may cause real interest rates to differ across countries.

The chapter also defined the real exchange rate as the nominal, or actual, exchange rate adjusted for changes in the relative purchasing power of each currency since some base period.

Finally, we analyzed a series of forecasting models that purport to outperform the market's own forecasts of future exchange rates as embodied in interest and forward differentials. We concluded that the foreign exchange market is no different from any other financial market in its susceptibility to profitable predictions.

Those who have inside information about events that will affect the value of a currency or a security should benefit handsomely. Those who do not have this access will have to trust either to luck or to the existence of a market imperfection, such as government intervention, to assure themselves of above average, risk-adjusted profits. In fact, given the widespread availability of information and the many knowledgeable participants in the foreign exchange market, only the latter situation—government manipulation of exchange rates—holds the promise of superior returns from currency forecasting. When governments spend money to control exchange rates, this money flows into the hands of private participants who bet against the government. The trick is to predict government actions.

QUESTIONS

1. What are some reasons for deviations from purchasing power parity?

2. Under what circumstances can purchasing power parity be applied?

3. One proposal to stabilize the international monetary system involves setting exchange rates at their purchasing power parity rates. Once exchange rates are correctly aligned (according to PPP), each nation would adjust its monetary policy so as to maintain them. What problems might arise from using the PPP rate as a guide to the equilibrium exchange rate?

4. If the average rate of inflation in the world rises from 5% to 7%, what will be the effect on the U.S. dollar's forward premium or discount relative to foreign currencies?

5. Comment on the following statement. "It makes sense to borrow during times of high inflation because you can repay the loan in cheaper dollars."

6. Which is likely to be higher, a 150% cruzeiro return in Brazil or a 15% dollar return in the United States?

7. The interest rate in England is 12%, while in Switzerland it is 5%. What are possible reasons for this interest rate differential? What is the most likely reason?

8. In Exhibit 7.6, Peru and Chile stand out as countries whose interest rates are not consistent with their inflation experience.

    a. How would you characterize the real interest rates of Peru and Chile (e.g., close to zero, highly positive, highly negative)?

    b. What might account for Peru's low interest rate relative to its high inflation rate? What are the likely consequences of this low interest rate?

    c. What might account for Chile's high interest rate relative to its inflation rate? What are the likely consequences of this high interest rate?

    d. In Exhibit 7.10, Peru is shown as having a small interest differential and yet a large average exchange rate change. How would you reconcile this experience with the international Fisher effect and with your answer to part b?

  9. A number of countries (e.g., Pakistan, Hungary, Venezuela) are shown in Exhibit 7.10 as having a small or negative interest rate differential and a large average annual depreciation against the dollar. How would you explain these data? Can you reconcile these data with the international Fisher effect?

10. The empirical evidence shows that there is no consistent relationship between the spot exchange rate and the nominal interest rate differential. Why might this be?

11. During 1988, the U.S. prime rate—the rate of interest banks charge on loans to their best customers—stood at 9.5%. Japan's prime rate, meanwhile, was about 3.5%. Pointing to that discrepancy, a number of commentators argued that the cost of capital must come down for U.S. business to remain competitive with Japanese companies. What additional information would you need to properly assess this claim? Why might interest rates be lower in Japan than in the United States?

12. In the late 1960s, Firestone Tire decided that Swiss francs at 2% were cheaper than U.S. dollars at 8% and borrowed about SFr 500 million. Comment on this choice.

13. Comment on the following quote from a story in *The Wall Street Journal* (August 27, 1984, p. 6) that discusses the improving outlook for Britain's economy: "Recovery here will probably last longer than in the U.S. because there isn't a huge budget deficit to pressure interest rates higher."

14. In early 1989, Japanese interest rates were about 4 percentage points below U.S. rates. The wide difference between Japanese and U.S. interest rates prompted some U.S. real estate developers to borrow in yen to finance their projects. Comment on this strategy.

15. In early 1990, Japanese and German interest rates rose while U.S. rates fell. At the same time, the yen and DM fell against the U.S. dollar. What might explain the divergent trends in interest rates?

16. In late December 1990, one-year German Treasury bills yielded 9.1%, whereas one-year U.S. Treasury bills yielded 6.9%. At the same time, the inflation rate during 1990 was 6.3% in the United States, double the German rate of 3.1%.

    a. Are these inflation and interest rates consistent with the Fisher effect?

    b. What might explain this difference in interest rates between the United States and Germany?

17. The spot rate on the Deutsche mark is $0.63, and the 180-day forward rate is $0.64. What are possible reasons for the difference between the two rates?

18. What factors might lead to persistent covered interest arbitrage opportunities among countries?

19. Comment on the following headline that appeared in *The Wall Street Journal* (December 19, 1990, p. C10): "Dollar Falls Across the Board as Fed Cuts Discount Rate to 6.5% From 7%." The discount rate is the interest rate the Fed charges member banks for loans.

20. In late 1990, the U.S. government announced that it might try to reduce the budget deficit by imposing a 0.5% transfer tax on all sales and purchases of securities in the United States, with the exception of Treasury securities. It projected the tax would raise $10 billion in federal revenues—an amount arrived at by multiplying 0.5% by the value of the $2 trillion trading on the New York Stock Exchange each year.

   a. What are the likely consequences of this tax? Consider its effects on trading volume in the United States and stock and bond prices.

   b. Why does the U.S. government plan to exclude its securities from this tax?

   c. Critically assess the government's estimates of the revenue it will raise from this tax.

21. "The U.S. government's economic policies, particularly as they affect the U.S. budget deficit, are severely constrained by the world's financial markets." Discuss.

22. "High real interest rates can be a cause for celebration, not alarm." Discuss.

23. In an integrated world capital market, will higher interest rates in, say Japan, mean higher interest rates in, say, the United States?

PROBLEMS

1. From base price levels of 100 in 1987, West German and U.S. price levels in 1988 stood at 102 and 106, respectively. If the 1987 $:DM exchange rate was $0.54, what should the exchange rate be in 1988? In fact, the exchange rate in 1988 was DM 1 = $0.56. What might account for the discrepancy? (Price levels were measured using the consumer price index.)

2. Two countries, the United States and England, produce only one good, wheat. Suppose the price of wheat in the United States is $3.25 and in England it is £1.35.

   a. According to the law of one price, what should the $:£ spot exchange rate be?

   b. Suppose the price of wheat over the next year is expected to rise to $3.50 in the United States and to £1.60 in England. What should the one-year $:£ forward rate be?

   c. If the U.S. government imposes a tariff of $0.50 per bushel on wheat imported from England, what is the maximum possible change in the spot exchange rate that could occur?

3. In July, the one-year interest rate is 12% on British pounds and 9% on U.S. dollars.

   a. If the current exchange rate is $1.63:£1, what is the expected future exchange rate in one year?

   b. Suppose a change in expectations regarding future U.S. inflation causes the expected future spot rate to decline to $1.52:£1. What should happen to the U.S. interest rate?

4. If expected inflation is 100% and the real required return is 5%, what will the nominal interest rate be according to the Fisher effect?

5. Suppose that in Japan the interest rate is 8% and inflation is expected to be 3%. Meanwhile, the expected inflation rate in France is 12%, and the English interest rate is 14%. To the nearest whole number, what is the best estimate of the one-year forward exchange premium (discount) at which the pound will be selling relative to the French franc?

6. Chase Econometrics has just published projected inflation rates for the United States and Germany for the next five years. U.S. inflation is expected to be 10% per year, while German inflation is expected to be 4% per year. If the current exchange rate is DM 1 = $0.50, forecast the exchange rates for the next five years.

7. The inflation rate in Great Britain is expected to be 4% per year, and the inflation rate in France is expected to be 6% per year. If the current spot rate is £1 = FF 12.50, what is the expected spot rate in two years?

8. If the $:¥ spot rate is $1 = ¥218 and interest rates in Tokyo and New York are 6% and 12%, respectively, what is the expected $:¥ exchange rate one year hence?

9. Suppose three-year deposit rates on Eurodollars and Eurofrancs (Swiss) are 12% and 7%, respectively. If the current spot rate for the Swiss franc is $0.3985, what is the spot rate implied by these interest rates for the franc three years from now?

10. Assume the interest rate is 11% on pounds sterling and 8% on Deutsche marks. If the Deutsche mark is selling at a one-year forward premium of 4% against the pound, is there an arbitrage opportunity? Explain.

11. Suppose that on January 1, the cost of borrowing French francs for the year is 18%. During the year, U.S. inflation is 5%, and French inflation is 9%. At the same time, the exchange rate changes from FF 1 = $0.15 on January 1 to FF 1 = $0.10 on December 31. What was the real U.S. dollar cost of borrowing francs for the year?

12. In late 1990, following Britain's entry into the exchange-rate mechanism of the European Monetary System, 10-year British Treasury bonds yielded 11.5%, whereas the German equivalent offered a yield of just 9%. Under terms of its entry, Britain established a central rate against the DM of DM 2.95 and pledged to maintain this rate within a band of plus and minus 6%.

   a. By how much would sterling have to fall against the DM over a 10-year period for the German bond to offer a higher overall return than the British one? Assume the Treasuries are zero-coupon bonds with no interest paid until maturity.

   b. How does the exchange rate established in part a compare to the lower limit that the British government is pledged to maintain for sterling against the DM?

   c. What accounts for the difference between the two rates? Does this difference violate the international Fisher effect?

13. Suppose the Eurosterling rate is 15%, and the Eurodollar rate is 11.5%. What is the forward premium on the dollar? Explain.

14. If the Swiss franc is $0.68 on the spot market and the 180-day forward rate is $0.70, what is the annualized interest rate in the United States over the next six months? The annualized interest rate in Switzerland is 2%.

15. The interest rate in the United States is 8%; in Japan the comparable rate is 2%. The spot rate for the yen is $0.007692. If interest rate parity holds, what is the 90-day forward rate on the Japanese yen?

16. Suppose today's spot exchange rate is $0.51:DM 1. The six-month interest rates on dollars and DM are 13% and 6%, respectively. The six-month forward rate is $0.5170:DM 1. A foreign exchange advisory service has predicted that the DM will appreciate to $0.54:DM 1 within six months.

   a. How would you use forward contracts to profit in the above situation?

   b. How would you use borrowing and lending transactions to profit?

17. Suppose the spot rates for the Deutsche mark, pound sterling, and Swiss franc are $0.32, $1.13, and $0.38, respectively. The associated 90-day interest rates (annualized) are 8%, 16%, and 4%; the U.S. 90-day rate (annualized) is 12%. What is the 90-day forward rate on an ACU (ACU 1 = DM 1 + £1 + SFr 1) if interest parity holds?

18. Suppose that three-month interest rates (annualized) in Japan and the United States are 7% and 9%, respectively. If the spot rate is ¥142:$1 and the 90-day forward rate is ¥139:$1:

    a. Where would you invest?

    b. Where would you borrow?

    c. What arbitrage opportunity do these figures present?

    d. Assuming no transaction costs, what would be your arbitrage profit per dollar or dollar-equivalent borrowed?

BIBLIOGRAPHY

Dufey, Gunter, and Ian H. Giddy. *The International Money Market.* Englewood Cliffs, N.J.: Prentice-Hall, 1978.

————. "Forecasting Exchange Rates in a Floating World." *Euromoney,* November 1975, pp. 28–35.

Gailliot, Henry J. "Purchasing Power Parity as an Explanation of Long-Term Changes in Exchange Rates." *Journal of Money, Credit, and Banking,* August 1970, pp. 348–357.

Giddy, Ian H. "An Integrated Theory of Exchange Rate Equilibrium." *Journal of Financial and Quantitative Analysis,* December 1976, pp. 883–892.

————, and Gunter Dufey. "The Random Behavior of Flexible Exchange Rates," *Journal of International Business Studies,* Spring 1975, pp. 1–32.

Levich, Richard M. "Analyzing the Accuracy of Foreign Exchange Advisory Services: Theory and Evidence." In *Exchange Risk and Exposure.* Richard Levich and Clas Wihlborg, eds. Lexington, Mass: D.C. Heath, 1980.

Officer, Lawrence H. "The Purchasing-Power-Parity Theory of Exchange Rates: A Review Article." *IMF Staff Papers,* March 1976, pp. 1–60.

Case I.1 OIL LEVIES: THE ECONOMIC IMPLICATIONS

BACKGROUND

The combination of weakening oil prices and the failure of Congress to deal with the budget deficit by cutting spending has led some to see the possibility of achieving two objectives at once: (1) protecting U.S. oil producers from "cheap" foreign competition and (2) reducing the budget deficit. The solution is an oil-import fee or tariff. A tax on imported crude and refined products that matches a world oil-price decline, for example, would leave oil and refined-product prices in the United States unchanged. Thus, it is argued, such a tax will have little effect on U.S. economic activity. It merely represents a transfer of funds from foreign oil producers to the U.S. Treasury. Moreover, it would provide some price relief to struggling U.S. refineries and encourage the production of U.S. oil. Finally, at the current level of imports, a $5/barrel tariff on foreign crude oil and a separate tariff of $10/barrel-equivalent on refined products would raise more than $11.5 billion a year.

QUESTIONS

1. Suppose the tariff were levied solely on imported crude. In an integrated world economy, who will bear the burden of the import tariff? Who will benefit? Why? What will be the longer-term consequences?

2. If a $10/barrel tariff were levied on imported refined products (but no tariff were levied on crude oil), who would bear the burden of such a tariff? Who would benefit? Why? What will be the longer-term consequences?

3. What would be the economic consequences of the combined $5/barrel tariff on imported crude and a $10/barrel tariff on refined oil products? How would these tariffs affect domestic consumers, oil producers, refiners, companies competing against imports, and exporters?

4. How would these proposed import levies affect foreign suppliers to the United States of crude oil and refined products?

5. During the 1970s, price controls on crude oil—but not on refined products—were in effect in the United States. Based on your previous analysis, what differences would you expect to see between heating oil and gasoline prices in New York and in Rotterdam (the major refining center in northwestern Europe)?

Case I.2 PRESIDENT CARTER LECTURES THE FOREIGN EXCHANGE MARKETS

At a press conference in March 1978, President Jimmy Carter—responding to a falling dollar—lectured the international financial markets as follows:

> I've spent a lot of time studying about the American dollar, its value in international monetary markets, the causes of its recent deterioration as it relates to other major currencies. I can say with complete assurance that the basic principles of monetary values are not being adequately addressed on the current international monetary market.*

President Carter then offered three reasons why the dollar should improve: (1) the "rapidly increasing" attractiveness of investment in the U.S. economy due to high nominal interest rates, (2) an end to growth in oil imports, and (3) a decline in the real growth of the U.S. economy relative to the rest of the world's economic growth.

QUESTIONS

1. How were financial markets likely to respond to President Carter's lecture? Explain.

2. At the time President Carter made his remarks, the inflation rate was running at about 10% annually and accelerating as the Federal Reserve continued to pump up the money supply to finance the growing government budget deficit. Meanwhile, the interest rate on long-term Treasury bonds had risen to about 8.5%. Was President Carter correct in his assessment of the positive effects on the dollar of the higher interest rates? Explain. Note that during 1977, the movement of private capital had switched to an outflow of $6.6 billion in the second half of the year, from an inflow of $2.9 billion in the first half.

3. Comment on the consequences of a reduction in U.S. oil imports for the value of the U.S. dollar. Next, consider that President Carter's energy policy involved heavily taxing U.S. oil production, imposing price controls on domestically produced crude oil and gasoline, and providing rebates to users of heating oil. How was this energy policy likely to affect the value of the dollar? Explain.

4. What were the likely consequences of the slowdown in U.S. economic growth for the value of the U.S. dollar? For the U.S. trade balance?

5. If President Carter had listened to the financial markets instead of trying to lecture them, what might he have heard? That is, what were the markets trying to tell him about his policies?

*Adapted from "President Canute," *The Wall Street Journal*, March 8, 1978, p. 16. Used with permission.

Foreign Exchange
Risk Management

Measuring Accounting Exposure $\boldsymbol{8}$

The stream of time sweeps away errors, and leaves the truth for the inheritance of humanity.

Georg Brandes

CHAPTER LEARNING OBJECTIVES

- To define translation and transaction exposure and distinguish between the two
- To describe the four principal currency translation methods available and to calculate translation exposure using these different methods
- To describe and apply the past (FASB-8) and present (FASB-52) currency translation methods prescribed by the Financial Accounting Standards Board
- To distinguish between accounting measures of exposure and the economic effects of currency changes on the value of a firm
- To assess the relevance for chief financial officers of accounting measures of exposure as opposed to economic measures of exposure

KEY TERMS

accounting exposure
balance-sheet exposure
current exchange rate
current/noncurrent method
current rate method
economic exposure
Financial Accounting
    Standards Board
foreign exchange risk
functional currency
historical exchange rate
hyperinflationary country
monetary/nonmonetary
    method
reporting currency
Statement of Financial
    Accounting Standards
    No. 8
Statement of Financial
    Accounting Standards
    No. 52
temporal method
transaction exposure
translation exposure

The general concept of *exposure* refers to the degree to which a company is affected by exchange rate changes. *Accounting exposure* arises from the need, for purposes of reporting and consolidation, to convert the financial statements of foreign operations from the local currencies (LC) involved to the home currency (HC). If exchange rates have changed since the previous reporting period, this *translation*, or restatement, of those assets, liabilities, revenues, expenses, gains, and losses that are denominated in foreign currencies will result in foreign exchange gains or losses. The possible extent of these gains or losses is measured by the translation exposure figures. The rules that govern translation are devised by an accounting association such as the *Financial Accounting Standards Board* in the United States, the parent firm's government, or the firm itself.

This chapter presents alternative accounting methods for determining translation exposure, focusing on *Statements of Financial Accounting Standards No. 8* and *No. 52*—the past (No. 8) and present (No. 52) currency translation methods prescribed by the Financial Accounting Standards Board (FASB). The chapter also discusses the differences between accounting requirements and economic reality, making recommendations to accountants and financial executives on how to adjust reporting standards in order to reconcile those differences. The next chapter discusses how companies can manage their accounting exposure.

8.1 ALTERNATIVE CURRENCY TRANSLATION METHODS

Companies with international operations will have foreign-currency-denominated assets and liabilities, revenues, and expenses. However, because home-country investors and the entire financial community are interested in home-currency values, the foreign currency balance-sheet accounts and income statement must be assigned HC values. In particular, the financial statements of an MNC's overseas subsidiaries must be translated from local currency to home currency prior to consolidation with the parent's financial statements.

Translation exposure arises from the need to convert foreign currency accounts, revenues, and expenses into the home currency.

If currency values change, foreign exchange translation gains or losses may result. Assets and liabilities that are translated at the current (postchange) exchange rate are considered to be exposed; those translated at a historical (prechange) exchange rate will maintain their historic HC values and, hence, are regarded as not exposed. *Translation exposure* is simply the difference between exposed assets and exposed liabilities. The controversies among accountants center on which assets and liabilities are exposed and on when accounting-derived foreign exchange gains and losses should be recognized (reported on the income statement). A crucial point to realize in putting these controversies in perspective is that such gains or losses are of an accounting nature—that is, no cash flows are necessarily involved.

Four principal translation methods are available: the current/noncurrent method, the monetary/nonmonetary method, the temporal method, and the current rate method. In practice, there are also variations of each method.

Current/Noncurrent Method

At one time, the *current/noncurrent method*, whose underlying theoretical basis is maturity, was used by almost all U.S. multinationals. With this method, all the foreign subsidiary's current assets and liabilities are translated into home currency at the *current exchange rate*. Each noncurrent asset or liability is translated at its *historical exchange rate*; that is, at the rate in effect at the time the asset was acquired or the liability incurred. Hence, a foreign subsidiary with positive local-currency working capital will give rise to a translation loss (gain) from a devaluation (revaluation) with the current/noncurrent method, and vice versa if working capital is negative.

The income statement is translated at the average exchange rate of the period, except for those revenues and expense items associated with noncurrent assets or liabilities. The latter items, such as depreciation expense, are translated at the same rates as the corresponding balance-sheet items. Thus, it is possible to see different revenue and expense items with similar maturities being translated at different rates.

Monetary/Nonmonetary Method

The *monetary/nonmonetary method* differentiates between *monetary* assets and liabilities—that is, those items that represent a claim to receive, or an obligation to pay, a fixed amount of foreign currency units—and *nonmonetary*, or physical, assets and liabilities. Monetary items (for example, cash, accounts payable and receivable, and long-term debt) are translated at the current rate; nonmonetary items (for example, inventory, fixed assets, and long-term investments) are translated at historical rates.

Income statement items are translated at the average exchange rate during the period, except for revenue and expense items related to nonmonetary assets and liabilities. The latter items, primarily depreciation expense and cost of goods sold, are translated at the same rate as the corresponding balance-sheet items. As a result, the cost of goods sold may be translated at a rate different from that used to translate sales.

Temporal Method

This method appears to be a modified version of the monetary/nonmonetary method. The only difference is that under the monetary/nonmonetary method, inventory is always translated at the historical rate. Under the *temporal method*, inventory is normally translated at the historical rate, but it can be translated at the current rate if the inventory is shown on the balance sheet at market values. Despite the similarities, however, the theoretical basis of each method is different. The choice of exchange rate for translation is based on the type of asset or liability in the monetary/nonmonetary method; in the temporal method, it is based on the underlying approach to evaluating cost (historical versus market). Under a historical cost accounting system, as the United States now has, most accounting theoreticians would probably argue that the temporal method is the appropriate method for translation.

The four principal translation methods are the current/noncurrent, monetary/nonmonetary, temporal, and current rate methods.

Income statement items are normally translated at an average rate for the reporting period. However, cost of goods sold and depreciation and amortization charges related to balance-sheet items carried at past prices are translated at historical rates.

Current Rate Method

The *current rate method* is the simplest; all balance-sheet and income items are translated at the current rate. As the method recommended by the Institute of Chartered Accountants of England and Wales and the Institute of Chartered Accountants of Scotland, it is widely employed by British companies. Under this method, if a firm's foreign-currency-denominated assets exceed its foreign-currency-denominated liabilities, a devaluation must result in a loss and a revaluation, in a gain. One variation is to translate all assets and liabilities except net fixed assets at the current rate.

Exhibit 8.1 applies the four different methods to a hypothetical balance sheet that is affected by both a 25% devaluation and a revaluation of 37.5%. Depending on the method chosen, the translation results for the devaluation can range from

Exhibit 8.1 Financial Statement Impact of Translation Alternatives (U.S. $ Thousands)

	Local Currency	U.S. Dollars Prior to Exchange Rate Change (LC 4 = $1)	After Devaluation of Local Currency (LC 5 = $1) Monetary/Non-monetary	Temporal	Current/Non-current	Current Rates for All Assets and Liabilities	After Recaluation of Local Currency (LC 2.5 = $1) Monetary/Non-Monetary	Temporal	Current/Non-current	Current Rates for All Assets and Liabilities
Assets										
Current assets										
Cash, marketable securities, and receivables	2,600	$ 650	$ 520	$ 520	$ 520	$ 520	$1,040	$1,040	$1,040	$1,040
Inventory (at cost)	3,600	900	900	720	720	720	900	1,440	1,440	1,440
Prepaid expenses	200	50	50	50	40	40	50	50	80	80
Total current assets	6,400	1,600	1,470	1,290	1,280	1,280	1,990	2,530	2,560	2,560
Fixed assets less accumulated depreciation	3,600	900	900	900	900	720	900	900	900	1,440
Goodwill	1,000	250	250	250	250	200	250	250	250	400
Total assets	LC 11,000	$2,750	$2,620	$2,440	$2,430	$2,200	$3,140	$3,680	$3,710	$4,400
Liabilities										
Current liabilities	3,400	850	680	680	680	680	1,360	1,360	1,360	1,360
Long-term debt	3,000	750	600	600	750	600	1,200	1,200	750	1,200
Deferred income taxes	500	125	100	100	125	100	200	200	125	200
Total liabilities	6,900	1,725	1,380	1,380	1,555	1,380	2,760	2,760	2,235	2,760
Capital stock	1,500	375	375	375	375	375	375	375	375	375
Retained earnings	2,600	650	865	685	500	445	5	545	1,100	1,265
Total equity	4,100	1,025	1,240	1,060	875	820	380	920	1,475	1,640
Total liabilities plus equity	LC 11,000	$2,750	$2,620	$2,440	$2,430	$2,200	$3,140	$3,680	$3,710	$4,400
Translation Gain (Loss)	—	—	$ 215	$ 35	$ (150)	$ (205)	$ (645)	$ (105)	$ 450	$ 615

a loss of $205,000 to a gain of $215,000; revaluation results can vary from a gain of $615,000 to a loss of $645,000.

8.2 STATEMENT OF FINANCIAL ACCOUNTING STANDARDS NO. 8

Such a wide variation in results as those of Exhibit 8.1 led the Financial Accounting Standards Board to issue a new ruling: *Statement of Financial Accounting Standards No. 8* (FASB-8). FASB-8 established uniform standards for the translation into dollars of foreign-currency-denominated financial statements and transactions of U.S.-based multinational companies.

FASB-8, which was based on the temporal method, became effective on January 1, 1976. Its principal virtue was its consistency with generally accepted accounting practice that requires balance-sheet items to be valued (translated) according to their underlying measurement basis (that is, current or historical).

Almost immediately upon its adoption, controversy ensued over FASB-8. A major source of corporate dissatisfaction with FASB-8 was the ruling that all reserves for currency losses be disallowed. Before FASB-8, many companies established a reserve and were able to defer unrealized translation gains and losses by adding them to, or charging them against, the reserve. In that way corporations generally were able to cushion the impact of sharp changes in currency values on reported earnings. With FASB-8, however, fluctuating values of pesos, pounds, marks, Canadian dollars, Australian dollars, and other foreign currencies often had far more impact on profit-and-loss statements than did the sales and profit margins of multinational manufacturers' product lines.

The experience of Sony, the Japanese electronics producer, which follows U.S. accounting rules because its shares are traded on the New York Stock Exchange, illustrates the impact of FASB-8. In 1979, Sony's consolidated second-quarter earnings were reduced by a foreign exchange loss of $49.3 million, whereas in 1978, the second-quarter net was restated to include a $19.3 million gain on currency conversion—a $68.6 million swing in pre-tax net income that might never be realized. The result was a 49% slump in Sony's second-quarter consolidated earnings, despite a near tripling in operating earnings from a year earlier. For the first half of 1979, Sony reported that net earnings had declined by 36% from the year before, despite a 98% increase in operating earnings. Sony's plight was caused almost entirely by an $84.8 million earnings movement resulting from a 1979 first-half foreign exchange loss of $59.4 million, compared to a gain of $26.4 million a year earlier.

FASB-8 was an attempt to establish a uniform translation standard, to end the wide variation in results that previously existed.

8.3 STATEMENT OF FINANCIAL ACCOUNTING STANDARDS NO. 52

In 1981, widespread dissatisfaction by corporate executives over FASB-8 led to a new translation standard: *Statement of Financial Accounting Standards No. 52*

Widespread dissatisfaction with FASB-8 led to the adoption of FASB-52, which mandated use of the current rate method.

(FASB-52). According to FASB-52, firms must use the current rate method to translate foreign-currency-denominated assets and liabilities into dollars. All foreign currency revenue and expense items on the income statement must be translated at either the exchange rate in effect on the date these items are recognized or at an appropriately weighted average exchange rate for the period. The most important aspect of the new standard is that unlike the case with FASB-8, most FASB-52 translation gains and losses bypass the income statement and are accumulated in a separate equity account on the parent's balance sheet. This account is usually called something like "cumulative translation adjustment."

FASB-52 differentiates for the first time between the functional currency and the reporting currency. An affiliate's *functional currency* is the currency of the primary economic environment in which the affiliate generates and expends cash. If the enterprise's operations are relatively self-contained and integrated within a particular country, the functional currency would generally be the currency of that country. An example of this case would be an English affiliate that both manufactures and sells most of its output in England. Alternatively, if the foreign affiliate's operations are a direct and integral component or extension of the parent company's operations, the functional currency would be the U.S. dollar. An example would be a Hong Kong assembly plant for radios that sources the components in the United States and sells the assembled radios in the United States. It is also possible that the functional currency is neither the local currency nor the dollar but, rather, is a third currency. However, in the remainder of this chapter, we will assume that if the functional currency is not the local currency, then it is the U.S. dollar.

FASB-52 distinguishes between the functional currency and the reporting currency.

Guidelines for selecting the appropriate functional currency are presented in Exhibit 8.2. There is sufficient ambiguity, however, to give companies some leeway in selecting the functional currency. However, in the case of a *hyperinflationary country*—defined as one that has cumulative inflation of approximately 100% or more over a three-year period—the functional currency must be the dollar.

Companies will usually explain in the notes to their annual report how they accounted for foreign currency translation. A typical statement is that found in Dow Chemical's 1989 Annual Report:

> The U.S. dollar has been used as the functional currency throughout the world except for operations in Germany and Japan, for which local currencies have been used. Effective December 31, 1988, the functional currency of the subsidiary companies in six European countries was changed to the local currency. These countries are Belgium, France, Italy, the Netherlands, Spain, and U.K. The impact on the balance sheet is noted in the Consolidated Statement of Stockholders' Equity. This change did not impact income in 1988.
>
> Where the U.S. dollar is used as the functional currency, foreign currency gains and losses are reflected in income currently. Translation gains and losses of those operations that use local currencies as the functional currency, and the effects of exchange rate changes on transactions designated as hedges of net foreign investments are included as a separate component of stockholders' equity.

The *reporting currency* is the currency in which the parent firm prepares its own financial statements; that is, U.S. dollars for a U.S. firm. FASB-52 requires that

Exhibit 8.2 Factors Indicating the Appropriate Functional Currency

Foreign Unit's	*Local Currency Indicators*	*Dollar Indicators*
Cash flows	Primarily in the local currency; do not directly affect parent company cash flows	Direct impact on parent company; cash flow available for remittance
Sales prices	Not responsive to exchange rate changes in the short run; determined more by local conditions	Determined more by world-wide competition; affected in the short run by exchange rate changes
Sales market	Active local market for entity's products	Products sold primarily in the United States; sales contracts denominated in dollars
Expenses	Labor, materials, and other costs denominated primarily in local currency	Inputs primarily from sources in the United States or otherwise denominated in dollars
Financing	Primarily in local currency; operations generate sufficient funds to service these debts	Primarily from the parent company or otherwise denominated in dollars; operations don't generate sufficient dollars to service its dollar debts
Intercompany transactions	Few intracorporate transactions; little connection between local and parent operations	High volume of intracorporate transactions; extensive interrelationship between local and parent operations

the financial statements of a foreign unit first be stated in the functional currency, using generally accepted accounting principles of the United States. At each balance-sheet date, any assets and liabilities denominated in a currency other than the functional currency of the recording entity must be adjusted to reflect the current exchange rate on that date. Transaction gains and losses that result from adjusting assets and liabilities denominated in a currency other than the functional currency, or from settling such items, generally must appear on the foreign unit's income statement. The only exceptions to the general requirement to include transaction gains and losses in income as they arise are listed as follows:

1. Gains and losses attributable to a foreign-currency transaction that is designated as an economic hedge of a net investment in a foreign entity must be included in the separate component of shareholders' equity in which adjustments arising from translating foreign-currency financial statements are accumulated. An example of such a transaction would be a Deutsche mark borrowing by a U.S. parent. The transaction would be designated as a hedge of the parent's net investment in its German subsidiary. See, for example, the statement in Dow's 1989 Annual Report.

Under FASB-52, transaction gains or losses are generally included in the income statement, whereas translation gains or losses are not.

2. Gains and losses attributable to intercompany foreign-currency transactions that are of a long-term investment nature must be included in the separate component of shareholders' equity. The parties to the transaction in this case are accounted for by the equity method in the reporting entity's financial statements.

3. Gains and losses attributable to foreign-currency transactions that hedge identifiable foreign-currency commitments are to be deferred and included in the measurement on the basis of the related foreign transactions.

The requirements regarding translation of transactions apply both to transactions entered into by a U.S. company and denominated in a currency other than the U.S. dollar and to transactions entered into by a foreign affiliate of a U.S. company and denominated in a currency other than its functional currency. Thus, for example, if a German subsidiary of a U.S. company owed $180,000 and the DM declined from $0.60 to $0.50, the Deutsche mark amount of the liability would increase from DM 300,000 (180,000/0.60) to DM 360,000 (180,000/0.50), for a loss of DM 60,000. If the subsidiary's functional currency is the Deutsche mark, the DM 60,000 loss must be translated into dollars at the average exchange rate for the period (say $0.55), and the resulting amount ($33,000) must be included as a transaction loss in the U.S. company's consolidated statement of income. This loss results even though the liability is denominated in the parent company's reporting currency because the subsidiary's functional currency is the Deutsche mark, and its financial statements must be measured in terms of that currency. Under FASB-8, there was no gain or loss included in consolidated net income on debt denominated in the parent company's reporting currency. Similarly, under FASB-52, if the subsidiary's functional currency is the U.S. dollar, no gain or loss would arise on the $180,000 liability.

After all financial statements have been converted into the functional currency, the functional currency statements are then translated into dollars, with translation gains and losses flowing directly into the parent's foreign exchange equity account.

If the functional currency is the dollar, the unit's local currency financial statements must be remeasured in dollars. The objective of the remeasurement process is to produce the same results that would have been reported if the accounting records had been kept in dollars rather than the local currency. Translation of the local currency accounts into dollars takes place according to the temporal method previously required by FASB-8; thus, the resulting translation gains and losses *must* be included in the income statement.

Most firms select the local currency as the functional currency.

A large majority of firms have opted for the local currency as the functional currency for most of their subsidiaries. The major exceptions are those subsidiaries operating in Latin American and other highly inflationary countries that must use the dollar as their functional currency.

Application of FASB No. 52

Sterling Ltd.—the British subsidiary of a U.S. company—started business and acquired fixed assets at the beginning of a year when the exchange rate for the pound sterling was £1 = $1.50. The average exchange rate for the period was $1.40, the rate at the end of the period was $1.30, and the historical rate for inventory was $1.45. Refer to Exhibits 8.3 and 8.4 for the discussion that follows.

During the year, Sterling Ltd. has income after tax of £20 million, which goes into retained earnings—that is, no dividends are paid. Thus, retained earnings rise from £0 to £20 million. Exhibit 8.3 shows how the income statement would be translated into dollars under two alternatives: (1) The functional currency is the pound sterling, and (2) the functional currency is the U.S. dollar. The second alternative yields results similar to those under FASB-8.

If the functional currency is the pound sterling, Sterling Ltd. will have a translation loss of $22 million, which bypasses the income statement (because the functional currency is identical to the local currency) and appears on the balance sheet as a separate item called *cumulative translation adjustment* under the share-holder's equity account. The translation loss is calculated as the number that reconciles the equity account with the remaining translated accounts to balance assets with liabilities and equity. Exhibit 8.4 shows the balance-sheet translations for Sterling Ltd. under the two alternative functional currencies.

Similarly, if the dollar is the functional currency, the foreign exchange translation gain of $108 million, which appears on Sterling Ltd.'s income statement (because the functional currency differs from the local currency), is calculated as the difference between translated income before currency gains ($23 million) and the retained earnings figure ($131 million). This amount just balances Sterling Ltd.'s books.

Exhibit 8.3 Translation of Sterling Ltd.'s Income Statement Under FASB–52 (Millions)

| | Pounds Sterling | Functional Currency | | | |
| | | Pound Sterling | | U.S. Dollar | |
	Pounds Sterling	Rates Used	U.S. Dollars	Rates Used	U.S. Dollars
Revenue	£120	1.40	$168	1.40	$168
Cost of goods sold	(50)	1.40	(70)	1.45	(73)
Depreciation	(20)	1.40	(28)	1.50	(30)
Other expenses, net	(10)	1.40	(14)	1.40	(14)
Foreign exchange gain					108
Income before taxes	40		56		159
Income taxes	(20)	1.40	(28)		(28)
Net income	£ 20		$ 28		$131
Ratios					
Net income to revenue	0.17		0.17		0.78
Gross profit to revenue	0.58		0.58		0.57
Debt to equity	7.33		7.33		4.07

Exhibit 8.4 Translation of Sterling Ltd.'s Balance Sheet Under FASB–52 (Millions)

| | | Functional Currency | | | |
| | | Pound Sterling | | U.S. Dollar | |
	Pounds Sterling	*Rates Used*	*U.S. Dollars*	*Rates Used*	*U.S. Dollars*
Assets					
Cash	£ 120	1.30	$ 130	1.30	$ 130
Receivables	200	1.30	260	1.30	260
Inventory	300	1.30	390	1.45	435
Fixed assets, net	400	1.30	520	1.50	600
Total assets	£1,000		$1,300		$1,425
Liabilities					
Current liabilities	180	1.30	234	1.30	234
Long-term debt	700	1.30	910	1.30	910
Stockholders' equity					
Common stock	100	1.50	150	1.50	150
Retained earnings	20		28		131
Cumulative translation adjustment			(22)		
Total liabilities plus equity	£1,000		$1,300		$1,425

Two comments are appropriate here.

1. Fluctuations in reported earnings in the example above are reduced significantly under FASB-52 when the local currency is the functional currency, as compared to the case when the U.S. dollar is the functional currency. Using the U.S. dollar as the functional currency is similar to the situation that prevailed when FASB-8 was in effect.

2. Key financial ratios and relationships—such as net income-to-revenue, gross profit, and debt-to-equity—are the same when translated into dollars under FASB-52, using the local currency as the functional currency, as they are in the local-currency financial statements. These ratios and relationships were significantly different under FASB-8, represented here by using the dollar as the functional currency. The ratios appear at the bottom of Exhibit 8.3.

8.4 TRANSACTION EXPOSURE

Companies often include transaction exposure as part of their accounting exposure. *Transaction exposure* stems from the possibility of incurring future exchange gains or losses on transactions already entered into and denominated in a foreign currency. For example, when IBM sells a mainframe computer to Royal Dutch

Shell in England, it typically will not be paid until a later date. If that sale is priced in pounds, IBM has a pound transaction exposure.

A company's transaction exposure is measured currency by currency and equals the difference between contractually fixed future cash inflows and outflows in each currency. Some of these unsettled transactions, including foreign-currency-denominated debt and accounts receivable, are already listed on the firm's balance sheet. But other obligations, such as contracts for future sales or purchases, are not.

8.5 ACCOUNTING PRACTICE AND ECONOMIC REALITY

Many multinationals have responded to increased currency volatility by devoting more resources to the management of *foreign exchange risk*. In order to develop an effective strategy for managing currency risk, management must first determine what is at risk. This determination requires an appropriate definition of foreign exchange risk. However, there is a major discrepancy between accounting practice and economic reality in terms of measuring exposure.

Accounting measures of exposure focus on the effect of currency changes on previous decisions of the firm, as reflected in the book values of assets acquired and liabilities incurred in the past. However, book values—which represent historical cost—and market values—which reflect future cash flows—of assets and liabilities typically differ. Therefore, *retrospective* accounting techniques, no matter how refined, cannot truly account for the economic (that is, cash flow) effects of a devaluation or revaluation on the value of a firm because these effects are primarily *prospective* in nature.

Since the change in accounting net worth produced by a movement in exchange rates often bears little relationship to the change in the market value of the firm, information derived from a historical-cost accounting system can provide a misleading picture of a firm's true economic exposure. Here, *economic exposure* is defined as the extent to which the value of the firm—as measured by the present value of its expected cash flows—will change when exchange rates change. Although all items on a firm's balance sheet represent future cash flows, not all future flows appear there. Moreover, these items are not adjusted to reflect the distorting effects of inflation and relative price changes on their associated future cash flows.

The definition of exposure based on market value assumes that management's goal is to maximize the value of the firm. Whether management actually behaves in this fashion has been vigorously debated. Some managers will undoubtedly prefer to pursue other objectives. Nevertheless, the assumption that management seeks to maximize (risk-adjusted) cash flow remains standard in much of the finance literature. Moreover, the principle of maximizing stockholder wealth provides a rational guide to financial decision making.

Our evolving understanding of what exchange risk is, however, is often at odds with current management practice. Many top managers seem to be preoccupied with potential accounting-based currency gains or losses; perhaps these man-

> There is a major discrepancy between accounting practice and economic reality in terms of measuring exposure to exchange rate changes.

agers believe that the stock market evaluates a firm on the basis of its reported earnings or changes in accounting net worth, regardless of the underlying cash flows. Or perhaps their compensation is tied to earnings instead of market value. For whatever reason, failure to distinguish between the accounting description of foreign exchange risk and the business reality of the effects of currency movements can cause corporate executives to make serious errors of judgment.

Recommendations for International Financial Executives

Companies should focus on the economic effects of currency changes rather than the accounting effects.

Most chief executives want to generate the smooth pattern of year-to-year earnings gains so cherished by security analysts. That is probably why empirical research by academicians, as well as statements by practitioners, show such a strong relationship between accounting translation methods and corporate financial policies that are designed to manage currency risk. But since the real effect of currency changes is on a firm's future cash flows, it is obvious that information based on retrospective accounting techniques may bear no relationship to a firm's actual operating results. Furthermore, basing management decisions on these flawed accounting data can lead to financial policies that will adversely affect the real economic growth of foreign operations.

The myopia of acting on the basis of *balance-sheet exposure* rather than economic impact has been scathingly portrayed by Gunter Dufey.[1] In Dufey's example, the French subsidiary of an American multinational corporation was instructed to reduce its working-capital balances in light of a forecasted French-franc devaluation. To do so would have forced it to curtail its operations; however, the French subsidiary was selling all of its output to other subsidiaries located in Germany and Belgium. Because the dollar value of its output would remain constant while franc costs expressed in dollars would decline, a 10% franc devaluation was expected to increase the French subsidiary's dollar profitability by over 25%. The French manager, therefore, argued (correctly) that the plant should begin expanding its operations, rather than contracting them, to take advantage of the anticipated devaluation.

To be sure, the distortions associated with accounting measures of exposure do not mean that accounting statements are irrelevant; clearly the statements serve a useful purpose and are necessary for consolidating the results of a worldwide network of operating units. The danger is that the results will be misinterpreted—not by financial executives, but by stockholders, bankers, security analysts, and the board of directors. In fact, financial managers generally are aware of the misleading nature of many of these results. Despite that knowledge, however, most financial executives undertake cosmetic exchange risk management actions because they worry that others will not understand the real, as opposed to the accounting, effects of currency changes. Clearly, if the capital markets did not rationally price corporate securities, managers would be hard pressed to design a foreign exchange strategy that could be expected to maximize the firm's value.

---

[1]Gunter Dufey, "Corporate Finance and Exchange Rate Variations," *Financial Management*, Summer 1978, pp. 51–57.

Is there a solution to this dichotomy between accounting and economic reality? Fortunately, the problem may be more apparent than real. A large body of research on financial markets suggests that investors are relatively sophisticated in responding to publicly available information; they appear able to understand detailed financial statements and properly interpret various accounting conventions behind corporate balance sheets and income statements.

Although the view of efficient capital markets in which stock prices correctly reflect all available information is not universally held, there is a good deal of empirical evidence that investors can effectively discriminate between accounting gimmickry and economic reality. In particular, when accounting numbers diverge significantly from cash flows, changes in security prices generally reflect changes in cash flows rather than reported earnings. Consider, as an example, changes in accounting practices for reporting (but not tax) purposes, such as switching depreciation and/or inventory valuation methods, that affect reported earnings but not cash flows. The changes do not appear to have any discernible, statistically significant effect on security prices.[2]

> Empirical evidence indicates that investors can distinguish between accounting gimmickry and economic reality.

The implication of these results for multinational firms is that as long as there is complete disclosure, it probably doesn't matter which translation method is used. In an efficient market, translation gains or losses will be placed in a proper perspective by investors and, therefore, should not affect an MNC's stock price. To help the market correctly interpret the translation outcomes, though, companies should clearly and openly disclose which translation methods they use. Furthermore, nothing prevents management from including a note in the financial statement explaining its view of the economic consequences of exchange rate changes.

Despite its inconclusive nature, the debate over the adoption by the Financial Accounting Standards Board of new currency translation methods has helped increase Wall Street's insight into the effects of currency changes on foreign operations. The debate has focused attention on the all-important distinction between the accounting and the cash-flow approaches to measuring exposure.

Against that background, a number of multinational firms are now taking a longer-term look at their degree of exchange risk. This look involves an examination of the risk due to the potential impact of uncertain exchange rate changes on future cash flows. Chapter 10 looks more closely at what constitutes this real exposure.

8.6 SUMMARY AND CONCLUSIONS

In this chapter, we have examined the concept of exposure to exchange rate changes from the perspective of the accountant. The accountant's concern is the

---

[2]See, for example, Robert S. Kaplan and Richard Roll, "Investory Evaluation of Accounting Information: Some Empirical Evidence," *Journal of Business*, April 1972, pp. 225–257.

appropriate way to translate foreign-currency-denominated items on financial statements to their home-currency values. If currency values change, translation gains or losses may result. We have surveyed the four principal translation methods available: the current/noncurrent method, the monetary/nonmonetary method, the temporal method, and the current rate method. In addition, we analyzed the past and present translation methods mandated by the Financial Accounting Standards Board, FASB-8 and FASB-52, respectively.

Regardless of the translation method selected, measuring accounting exposure is conceptually the same. It involves determining which foreign-currency-denominated assets and liabilities will be translated at the current (postchange) exchange rate and which will be translated at the historical (prechange) exchange rate. The former items are considered to be exposed, while the latter items are regarded as not exposed. Translation exposure is simply the difference between exposed assets and exposed liabilities.

By far the most important feature of the accounting definition of exposure is the exclusive focus on the balance-sheet effects of currency changes. We saw that this focus is misplaced since it has led the accounting profession to ignore the more important effect that these changes may have on future cash flows.

QUESTIONS

1. What is translation exposure? Transaction exposure?
2. What are the basic translation methods? How do they differ?
3. Why was FASB-8 so widely criticized? How did the Financial Accounting Standards Board respond to this criticism?

PROBLEMS

1. Suppose that on January 1, American Golf's French subsidiary, Golf du France, had a balance sheet that showed current assets of FF 1 million; current liabilities of FF 300,000; total assets of FF 2.5 million; and total liabilities of FF 900,000. On December 31, Golf du France's balance sheet in francs was unchanged from the figures given above, but the franc had declined in value from $0.1270 at the start of the year to $0.1180 at the end of the year. Under FASB-52, what is the translation amount to be shown on American Golf's equity account for the year if the franc is the functional currency? How would your answer change if the dollar were the functional currency?

2. Suppose that at the start and at the end of the year, Bell U.K. had current assets of £1 million, fixed assets of £2 million, and current liabilities of £1 million. Bell has no long-term liabilities. If the pound depreciated during that year from $1.50 to $1.30, what is the FASB-52 translation gain (loss) to be included in the equity account of Bell's U.S. parent?

3. Zapata Auto Parts, the Mexican affiliate of American Diversified, Inc., had the following balance sheet on January 1, 1992:

Assets (Ps Millions)			Liabilities (Ps Millions)		
Cash, marketable securities	Ps	1,000	Current liabilities	Ps	47,000
Accounts receivable		50,000	Long-term debt		12,000
Inventory		32,000	Equity		135,000
Net fixed assets		111,000		Ps	194,000
	Ps	194,000			

The exchange rate on January 1, 1992 was Ps 8,000 = $1.

a. What is Zapata's FASB-52 peso translation exposure on January 1, 1992?

b. Suppose the exchange rate on December 31, 1992 is Ps 12,000. What will be Zapata's translation loss for the year?

c. Zapata can borrow an additional Ps 15,000. What will this do to its translation exposure if it uses the funds to pay a dividend to its parent? If it uses the funds to increase its cash position?

BIBLIOGRAPHY

Accounting for the Translation of Foreign Currency Transactions and Foreign Currency Financial Statements, Statement of Financial Accounting Standards No. 8. Stamford, Conn.: Financial Accounting Standards Board, October 1975.

Dukes, Roland. *An Empirical Investigation of the Effects of Statement of Financial Accounting Standards No. 8 on Security Return Behavior.* Stamford, Conn.: Financial Accounting Standards Board, 1978.

Evans, Thomas G., William R. Folks, Jr., and Michael Jilling. *The Impact of Statement of Financial Accounting Standards No. 8 on the Foreign Exchange Risk Management Practices of American Multinationals.* Stamford, Conn.: Financial Accounting Standards Board, November 1978.

Statement of Financial Accounting Standards No. 52. Stamford, Conn.: Financial Accounting Standards Board, December 1981.

Giddy, Ian H. "What Is FAS No. 8's Effect on the Market's Valuation of Corporate Stock Prices?" *Business International Money Report*, May 26, 1978, p. 165.

9 Managing Accounting Exposure

KEY TERMS

currency risk sharing
exposure netting
forward market hedge
funds adjustment
hard currency
hedging
money market hedge
neutral zone
opportunity cost
price adjustment clauses
risk shifting
soft currency

Unfortunately the values of today's currencies oscillate wildly—to the despair of international companies that want to plan ahead.

The Economist, May 28, 1988, p. 81

CHAPTER LEARNING OBJECTIVES

- To identify the basic hedging strategy and techniques used by firms to manage their currency transaction and translation risks
- To explain how a forward market hedge works.
- To explain how a money market hedge works
- To describe how foreign currency contract prices should be set to factor in exchange rate change expectations
- To describe how currency risk sharing arrangements work
- To explain when foreign currency options are the preferred hedging technique
- To describe the costs associated with using the different hedging techniques
- To describe and assess the economic soundness of the various corporate hedging objectives
- To explain the advantages and disadvantages of centralizing foreign exchange risk management

The pressure to monitor and manage foreign currency risks has led many companies to develop sophisticated computer-based systems to keep track of their foreign exchange exposure and aid in managing that exposure. This chapter deals with the management of accounting exposure, including both translation and transaction exposure. Management of accounting exposure centers around the concept of hedging. *Hedging* a particular currency exposure means establishing an offsetting currency position such that whatever is lost or gained on the original currency exposure is exactly offset by a corresponding foreign exchange gain or loss on the currency hedge. Regardless of what happens to the future exchange rate, therefore, hedging locks in a dollar (home currency) value for the currency exposure. In this way, hedging can protect a firm from unforeseen currency movements.

A variety of hedging techniques are available, but before a firm uses them it must decide on which exposures to manage. Once the firm has determined the exposure position it intends to manage, how should it manage that position? How much of that position should it hedge, and which exposure-reducing technique(s) should it employ? In addition, how should exchange rate considerations be incorporated into operating decisions that will affect the firm's exchange risk posture? This chapter deals with these and other issues.

9.1 MANAGING TRANSACTION EXPOSURE

A transaction exposure arises whenever a company is committed to a foreign currency-denominated transaction. Since the transaction will result in a future foreign currency cash inflow or outflow, any change in the exchange rate between the time the transaction is entered into and the time it is settled in cash will lead to a change in the dollar (HC) amount of the cash inflow or outflow. Protective measures to guard against transaction exposure involve entering into foreign currency transactions whose cash flows exactly offset the cash flows of the transaction exposure.

These protective measures include using forward contracts, price adjustment clauses, currency options, and borrowing or lending in the foreign currency. Alternatively, the company could try to invoice all transactions in dollars and to avoid transaction exposure entirely. However, eliminating transaction exposure doesn't eliminate all foreign exchange risk. The firm is still subject to exchange risk on its future revenues and costs—its operating cash flows.

We will now look at the various techniques for managing transaction exposure by examining the case of General Electric's Deutsche mark exposure. Suppose that on January 1, GE is awarded a contract to supply turbine blades to Lufthansa, the German airline. On December 31, GE will receive payment of DM 25 million for these blades. The most direct way for GE to hedge this receivable is to sell a DM 25 million forward contract for delivery in one year. Alternatively, it can use a money market hedge, which would involve borrowing DM 25 million for one year, converting it into dollars, and investing the proceeds in a security that matures on December 31. As we will see, if interest rate parity holds, both methods will yield the same results. GE can also manage its transaction exposure through risk shifting, risk sharing, exposure netting, and currency options.

Transaction exposure can be managed by entering into offsetting foreign currency transactions.

Forward Market Hedge

In a *forward market hedge,* a company that is long a foreign currency will sell the foreign currency forward, whereas a company that is short a foreign currency will buy the currency forward. In this way, the company can fix the dollar value of future foreign currency cash flow. For example, by selling forward the proceeds from its sale of turbine blades, GE can effectively transform the currency denomination of its DM 25 million receivable from Deutsche marks to dollars, thereby eliminating all currency risk on the sale. For example, suppose the current spot price for the Deutsche mark is DM 1 = $0.40, and the one-year forward rate is DM

1 = \$0.3828. Then, a forward sale of DM 25 million for delivery in one year will yield GE \$9.57 million on December 31. Exhibit 9.1 shows the cash-flow consequences of combining the forward sale with the Deutsche mark receivable, given three possible exchange rate scenarios.

Regardless of what happens to the future spot rate, Exhibit 9.1 demonstrates that GE still gets to collect \$9.57 million on its turbine sale. Any exchange gain or loss on the forward contract will be offset by a corresponding exchange loss or gain on the receivable. The effects of this transaction can also be seen with the following simple T-account describing GE's position as of December 31:

In a forward market hedge, any exchange gain or loss on the forward contract will be offset by a corresponding exchange loss or gain on the underlying transaction.

December 31: GE T-Account (Millions)

Account receivable	DM 25	Forward contract payment	DM 25
Forward contract receipt	\$9.57		

Without hedging, GE will have a DM 25 million asset whose value will fluctuate with the exchange rate. The forward contract creates an equal DM liability, offset by an asset worth \$9.57 million dollars. The DM asset and liability cancel each other out, and GE is left with a \$9.57 million asset.

The True Cost of Hedging. Exhibit 9.1 also shows that the true cost of hedging can't be calculated in advance because it depends on the future spot rate, which is unknown at the time the forward contract is entered into. In the example above, the actual cost of hedging can vary from +\$430,000 to –\$570,000; a plus (+) represents a cost, and a minus (–) represents a negative cost or a gain. In percentage terms, the cost varies from –5.7% to +4.3%.

This example points out the distinction between the traditional method of calculating the cost of a forward contract and the correct method, which measures its opportunity cost. Specifically, the cost of a forward contract is usually measured as its forward discount or premium:

$$\frac{f_1 - e_0}{e_0}$$

where e_0 is the current spot rate (dollar price) of the foreign currency and f_1 is the forward rate. In GE's case, this cost would equal 4.3%.

Exhibit 9.1   Possible Outcomes of Forward Market Hedge as of December 31

Spot Exchange Rate	Value of Original Receivable (1)	+	Gain (Loss) on Forward Contract (2)	=	Total Cash Flow (3)
DM 1 = \$0.40	\$10,000,000		(\$430,000)		\$9,570,000
DM 1 = \$0.3828	9,570,000		0		9,570,000
DM 1 = \$0.36	9,000,000		570,000		9,570,000

However, this approach is wrong because the relevant comparison must be between the dollars per unit of foreign currency received with hedging, f_1, and the dollars received in the absence of hedging, e_1, where e_1 is the future (unknown) spot rate on the date of settlement. That is, the real cost of hedging is an *opportunity cost*. In particular, if the forward contract had not been entered into, the future value of each unit of foreign currency would have been e_1 dollars. Thus, the true dollar cost of the forward contract per dollar's worth of foreign currency sold forward equals

$$\frac{f_1 - e_1}{e_0}$$

In fact, in an efficient market, the expected cost (value) of a forward contract must be zero. Otherwise, there would be an arbitrage opportunity. Suppose, for example, that management at General Electric believes that despite a one-year forward rate of $0.3828, the Deutsche mark will actually be worth about $0.3910 on December 31. Then GE could profit by buying (rather than selling) Deutsche marks forward for one year at $0.3828 and, on December 31, completing the contract by selling Deutsche marks in the spot market at $0.3910. If GE is correct, it will earn $0.0082 (0.3910 − 0.3828) per Deutsche mark sold forward. On a DM 25 million forward contract, this would amount to $205,000—a substantial reward for a few minutes of work.

As we saw in Chapter 7, the prospect of such rewards would not go unrecognized for long, which is why the forward rate is likely to be an unbiased estimate of the future spot rate. Therefore, unless GE or any other company has some special information about the future spot rate that it has good reason to believe is not adequately reflected in the forward rate, it should accept the forward rate's predictive validity as a working hypothesis and avoid speculative activities. After the fact, of course, the actual cost of a forward contract will turn out to be positive or negative (unless the future spot rate equals the forward rate), but the sign can't be predicted in advance.

The true cost of hedging is an opportunity cost that depends on the future spot rate on the date of settlement.

In an efficient market, the expected cost of a forward contract is zero.

Money Market Hedge

An alternative to a forward market hedge is to use a money market hedge. A *money market hedge* involves simultaneous borrowing and lending activities in two different currencies to lock in the dollar value of a future foreign currency cash flow. For example, suppose Deutsche mark and U.S. dollar interest rates are 15% and 10%, respectively. Using a money market hedge, General Electric will borrow DM 25/1.15 million = DM 21.74 million for one year, convert it into $8.7 million in the spot market, and invest the $8.7 million for one year. On December 31, GE will receive 1.10 × $8.7 million = $9.57 million from its dollar investment. GE will use these dollars to pay back the 1.15 × DM 21.74 million = DM 25 million it owes in principal and interest. As Exhibit 9.2 shows, the exchange gain or loss on the borrowing and lending transactions exactly offsets the dollar loss or gain on GE's DM receivable.

Exhibit 9.2 Possible Outcomes of Money Market Hedge on December 31

Spot Exchange Rate	Value of Original Receivable (1)	+	Gain (Loss) on Money Market Hedge (2)	=	Total Cash Flow (3)
DM 1 = $0.40	$10,000,000		($430,000)		$9,570,000
DM 1 = $0.3828	9,570,000		0		9,570,000
DM 1 = $0.36	9,000,000		570,000		9,570,000

A money market hedge uses simultaneous borrowing and lending activities in two different currencies to eliminate a transaction exposure.

The gain or loss on the money market hedge can be calculated simply by subtracting the cost of repaying the DM debt from the dollar value of the investment. For example, in the case of an end-of-year spot rate of $0.40, the DM 25 million in principal and interest will cost $10 million to repay. The return on the dollar investment is only $9.57 million, leaving a loss of $430,000.

We can also view the effects of this transaction with the simple T-account used earlier:

December 31: GE T-Account (Millions)

Account receivable	DM 25	Loan repayment	DM 25
Investment return (including interest)	$9.57	(including intreest)	

As before, the DM asset and liability (the loan repayment) cancel each other out, and GE is left with a $9.57 million asset (its investment).

The equality of the net cash flows from the forward market and money market hedges is not coincidental. The interest rates and forward and spot rates were selected so that interest rate parity holds. In effect, the simultaneous borrowing and lending transactions associated with a money market hedge enable GE to create a "homemade" forward contract. The effective rate on this forward contract will equal the actual forward rate if interest rate parity holds. Otherwise, a covered interest arbitrage opportunity would exist.

Risk Shifting

MNCs can eliminate transaction risk by pricing all contracts in the home currency.

General Electric could have avoided its transaction exposure altogether if Lufthansa had allowed it to price the sale of turbine blades in dollars. Dollar invoicing, however, does not eliminate currency risk; it simply shifts that risk from GE to Lufthansa (which now has dollar exposure). Lufthansa may or may not be better able, or more willing, to bear it. Despite the fact that this form of *risk shifting* is a zero-sum game, it is common in international business. Firms typically attempt to invoice exports in strong currencies and imports in weak currencies.

Is it possible to gain from risk shifting? Not if one is dealing with informed customers or suppliers. To see why, consider the GE-Lufthansa deal. If Lufthansa is willing to be invoiced in dollars for the turbine blades, that must be because

Lufthansa calculates that its Deutsche mark equivalent cost will be no higher than the DM 25 million price it was originally prepared to pay. Since Lufthansa does not have to pay for the turbine blades until December 31, its cost will be based on the spot price of the dollars as of that date. By buying dollars forward at the one-year forward rate of DM 1 = $0.3828, Lufthansa can convert a dollar price of P into a DM cost of $P/0.3828$. Thus, the maximum dollar price P_M that Lufthansa should be willing to pay for the turbine blades is the solution to

$$\frac{P_M}{0.3828} = \text{DM 25 million}$$

or

$$P_M = \$9.57 \text{ million}$$

Considering that GE can guarantee itself $9.57 million by pricing in Deutsche marks and selling the resulting DM 25 million forward, it will certainly not accept a lower dollar price. The bottom line is that both Lufthansa and General Electric will be indifferent between a U.S. dollar price and a Deutsche mark price only if the two prices are equal at the forward exchange rate. Therefore, because the Deutsche mark price arrived at through arm's-length negotiations is DM 25 million, the dollar price that is equally acceptable to Lufthansa and GE can only be $9.57 million. Otherwise, one or both of the parties involved in the negotiations has ignored the possibility of currency changes. Such naiveté is unlikely to exist for long in the highly competitive world of international business.

Pricing Decisions

Notwithstanding the view expressed above, top management has sometimes failed to take anticipated exchange rate changes into account when making operating decisions, leaving financial management with the essentially impossible task, through purely financial operations, of recovering a loss already incurred at the time of the initial transaction. To illustrate this type of error, suppose that GE has priced Lufthansa's order of turbine blades at $10 million and then, because Lufthansa demands to be quoted a price in Deutsche marks, converts the dollar price to a Deutsche mark quote of DM 25 million, using the spot rate of DM 1 = $0.40.

Foreign currency contract prices should factor in possible exchange rate changes.

In reality, the quote is worth only $9.57 million—even though it is booked at $10 million—because that is the risk-free price that GE can guarantee for itself by using the forward market. If GE management wanted to sell the blades for $10 million, it should have set a Deutsche mark price equal to DM 10,000,000/0.3828 = DM 26.12 million. Thus, GE lost $430,000 the moment it signed the contract (assuming that Lufthansa would have agreed to the higher price rather than turn to another supplier). This loss is not an exchange loss; it is a loss due to management inattentiveness.

The general rule on credit sales overseas is to convert between the foreign currency price and the dollar price by using the forward rate, not the spot rate. If the dollar price is high enough, the exporter should follow through with the sale.

The dollar price on foreign sales should be converted into a foreign currency price based on the forward rate, not the spot rate.

Similarly, if the dollar price on a foreign-currency-denominated import is low enough, the importer should follow through on the purchase. All this rule does is to recognize that a Deutsche mark (or any other foreign currency) tomorrow is not the same as a Deutsche mark today. This rule is the international analogue to the insight that a dollar tomorrow is not the same as a dollar today.

In the case of a sequence of payments to be received at several points in time, the foreign currency price should be a weighted average of the forward rates for delivery on those dates.

ILLUSTRATION: Weyerhaeuser Quotes a French Franc Price for Its Lumber

Weyerhaeuser is asked to quote a price in French francs for lumber sales to a French company. The lumber will be shipped and paid for in four equal, quarterly installments. Weyerhaeuser requires a minimum price of $1 million to accept this contract. If P_F is the French franc price contracted for, then Weyerhaeuser will receive $0.25 P_F$ every three months, beginning 90 days from now. Suppose the spot and forward rates for the French franc are as follows:

Spot	90-Day	180-Day	270-Day	360-Day
$0.1772	$0.1767	$0.1761	$0.1758	$0.1751

Based on these forward rates, the certainty-equivalent dollar value of this franc revenue is $0.25P_F(0.1767 + 0.1761 + 0.1758 + 0.1751)$ or $0.25P_F(0.7037) = \$0.1759P_F$. In order for Weyerhaeuser to realize $1 million from this sale, the minimum French franc price must be the solution to

$$\$0.1759P_F = \$1,000,000$$

or

$$P_F = FF5,685,048$$

At any lower franc price, Weyerhaeuser cannot be assured of receiving the $1 million it demands for this sale. Note that the spot rate did not enter into any of these calculations.

Exposure Netting

Exposure netting involves offsetting exposures in one currency with exposures in the same or another currency, where exchange rates are expected to move in such a way that losses (gains) on the first exposed position should be offset by gains (losses) on the second currency exposure. This portfolio approach to hedging recognizes that the total variability or risk of a currency exposure portfolio should be less than the sum of the individual variabilities of each currency exposure considered in isolation. The assumption underlying exposure netting is that the net gain or loss on the entire currency exposure portfolio is what matters, rather than the gain or loss on any individual monetary unit.

It is easy to see, for example, that a DM 1 million receivable and DM 1 million payable cancel each other out, with no net (before-tax) exposure. It may be less obvious that such exposure netting can also be accomplished by using positions in different currencies. But companies practice multicurrency exposure netting all the time. According to Frederick Dietz of B.F. Goodrich, the U.S.-based tire manufacturer: "We might be willing to tolerate a short position in Swiss francs if we had a long position in Deutsche marks. They're fellow travelers. We look at our exposures as a portfolio."[1]

In practice, exposure netting involves one of three possibilities:

1. A firm can offset a long position in a currency with a short position in that same currency.
2. If the exchange rate movements of two currencies are positively correlated (for example, the Swiss franc and Deutsche mark), then the firm can offset a long position in one currency with a short position in the other.
3. If the currency movements are negatively correlated, then short (or long) positions can be used to offset each other.

Exposure netting involves offsetting exposure in one currency with exposure in the same or another currency.

Currency Risk Sharing

In addition to, or instead of, a traditional hedge, General Electric and Lufthansa can agree to share the currency risks associated with their turbine blade contract. *Currency risk sharing* can be implemented by developing a customized hedge contract imbedded in the underlying trade transaction. This hedge contract typically takes the form of a *price adjustment clause*, whereby a base price is adjusted to reflect certain exchange rate changes. For example, the base price could be set at DM 25 million, but the parties would share the currency risk beyond a neutral zone. The *neutral zone* represents the currency range in which risk is not shared.

Companies can agree to share the exchange risk on their contracts.

Suppose the neutral zone is specified as a band of exchange rates: $0.39–0.41:DM 1, with a base rate of DM 1 = $0.40. This means that the exchange rate can fall as far as $0.39:DM 1 or rise as high as $0.41:DM 1 without reopening the contract. Within the neutral zone, Lufthansa must pay GE the dollar equivalent of DM 25 million at the base rate of $0.40, or $10 million. Thus, Lufthansa's cost can vary from DM 24.39 million to DM 25.64 million (10,000,000/0.41 to 10,000,000/0.39). But if the DM depreciates from $0.40 to, say, $0.35, the actual rate will have moved $0.04 beyond the lower boundary of the neutral zone ($0.39:DM 1). This amount is shared equally. Thus, the exchange rate actually used in settling the transaction is $0.38:DM 1 ($0.40 − .04/2). The new price of the turbine blades becomes DM 25,000,000 × 0.38 or $9.5 million. Lufthansa's cost rises to DM 27.14 million (9,500,000/0.35). In the absence of a risk-sharing agreement, the contract value to GE would have been $8.75 million. Of course, if the Deutsche mark appreciates beyond the upper bound to, say, $0.45, GE does not get the full benefit of the DM's rise in value. Instead, the new contract exchange rate becomes $0.42

[1]"How Corporations Are Playing the Currency Game," *Institutional Investor,* May 1976, p. 31.

(0.40 + 0.04/2). GE collects DM 25,000,000 × 0.42, or $10.5 million; and Lufthansa pays a price of DM 23.33 million (10,500,000/0.45).

Exhibit 9.3 compares the currency risk protection features of the currency risk-sharing arrangement with that of a traditional forward contract (at a forward rate of $0.3828) and a no-hedge alternative. Within the neutral zone, the dollar value of GE's contract under the risk-sharing agreement stays at $10 million. This situation is equivalent to Lufthansa selling GE a forward contract at the current spot rate of $0.40. Beyond the neutral zone, the contract's dollar value rises or falls only half as much under the risk-sharing agreement as under the no-hedge alternative. The value of the hedged contract remains the same, regardless of the exchange rate.

Foreign Currency Options

Companies often have contingent foreign currency cash flows that can't be hedged with forward contracts.

Thus far, we have examined how firms can hedge known foreign currency transaction exposures. Yet, in many circumstances, the firm is uncertain whether the hedged foreign currency cash inflow or outflow will materialize. For example, the previous assumption was that GE learned on January 1 that it had won a contract to supply turbine blades to Lufthansa. But suppose that although GE's bid on the contract was submitted on January 1, the announcement of the winning bid would not be until April 1. During the three-month period from January 1 to April 1, GE does not know whether it will receive a payment of DM 25 million on December 31 or not. This uncertainty has important consequences for the appropriate hedging strategy.

Exhibit 9.3 Currency Risk Sharing: GE and Lufthansa

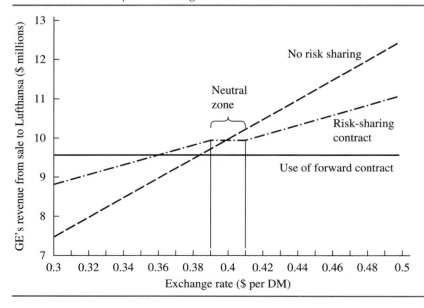

GE would like to guarantee that the exchange rate doesn't move against it between the time it bids and the time it gets paid, should it win the contract. The danger of not hedging is that its bid will be selected and the Deutsche mark will decline in value, possibly wiping out GE's anticipated profit margin. For example, if the forward rate on April 1 for delivery December 31 falls to DM 1 = $0.36, the value of the contract will drop from $9.57 million to $9 million, for a loss in value of $570,000.

The apparent solution is for GE to sell the anticipated DM 25 million receivable forward on January 1. However, if GE does that and loses the bid on the contract, it still has to sell the currency—which it will have to get by buying on the open market, perhaps at a big loss. For example, suppose the forward rate on April 1 for December 31 delivery has risen to $0.4008. To eliminate all currency risk on its original forward contract, GE would have to buy DM 25 million forward at a price of $0.4008. The result would be a loss of $450,000 [(0.3828 − 0.4008) × 25,000,000] on the forward contract entered into on January 1 at a rate of $0.3828.

Until recently, GE or any company that bid on a contract denominated in a foreign currency and was not assured of success would be unable to resolve its foreign exchange risk dilemma. The advent of *currency options* has changed all that. Specifically, the solution to managing its currency risk in this case is for GE, at the time of its bid, to purchase an option to sell DM 25 million on December 31. For example, suppose that on January 1, GE can buy for $100,000 the right to sell Citibank DM 25 million on December 31 at a price of $0.3828 per Deutsche mark. If it enters into this option contract with Citibank, GE will guarantee itself a minimum price ($9.57 million) should its bid be selected, while simultaneously ensuring that if it lost the bid, its loss would be limited to the price paid for the option contract (the premium of $100,000). Should the spot price of the Deutsche mark on December 31 exceed $0.3828, GE would let its option contract expire unexercised and convert the DM 25 million at the prevailing spot rate.

> Currency options can be used to hedge contingent foreign currency cash flows.

As we saw in Chapter 3, two types of options are available to manage exchange risk. A *put option*, such as the one appropriate to GE's situation, gives the buyer the right, but not the obligation, to sell a specified number of foreign currency units to the option seller at a fixed dollar price, up to the option's expiration date. Alternatively, a *call option* is the right, but not the obligation, to buy the foreign currency at a specified dollar price, up to the expiration date.

A call option is valuable, for example, when a firm has offered to buy a foreign asset, such as another firm, at a fixed foreign currency price, but is uncertain whether its bid will be accepted. By buying a call option on the foreign currency, the firm can lock in a maximum dollar price for its tender offer, while limiting its downside risk to the call premium in the event its bid is rejected.

Currency options are a valuable risk-management tool in other situations as well. Conventional transaction exposure management says you wait until your sales are booked or your orders placed before hedging them. But if a company does that, it faces potential losses from exchange rate movements because the foreign currency price doesn't necessarily adjust right away to changes in the value of the dollar. As a matter of policy, to avoid confusing customers and salespeople, most companies don't change their price list every time the exchange rate changes. Unless and until the foreign currency price changes, the unhedged company may suffer a decrease in its profit margin. Because of the uncertainty of anticipated sales or purchases, however, forward contracts are an imperfect tool to hedge the exposure.

For example, a company that commits to a foreign currency price list for, say, three months has a foreign currency exposure that depends on the unknown volume of sales at those prices during this period. Thus, the company does not know what volume of forward contracts to enter into to protect its profit margin on these sales. For the price of the premium, currency put options allow the company to insure its profit margin against adverse movements in the foreign currency while guaranteeing fixed prices to foreign customers. Without options, the firm might be forced to raise its foreign currency prices sooner than the competitive situation warranted.

ILLUSTRATION: Hewlett-Packard Uses Currency Options to Protect Its Profit Margins

Hewlett-Packard, the California-based computer firm, uses currency options to protect its dollar profit margins on products built in the United States but sold in Europe. The firm needs to be able to lower local currency (LC) prices if the dollar weakens and hold LC prices steady for about three months (the price adjustment period) if the dollar strengthens.

Suppose H-P sells anticipated DM sales forward at DM 2.5:$1 to lock in a dollar value for those sales. If one month later the dollar weakens to DM 2:$1, H-P faces tremendous competitive pressure to lower its Deutsche mark prices. H-P would now be locked into a loss on the forward contracts that would not be offset by a gain on its sales (because it had to cut DM prices). With DM put options, H-P would just let them expire, and it would lose only the put premium. Conversely, options help H-P delay LC price increases when the dollar strengthens until it can raise them without suffering a competitive disadvantage. The reduced profit margin on local sales is offset by the gain on the put option.

Currency options can be used to hedge exposure to shifts in a competitor's currency.

Currency options can also be used to hedge exposure to shifts in a competitor's currency. Companies competing with firms from other nations may find their products at a price disadvantage if a major competitor's currency weakens, allowing the competitor to reduce its prices. Thus, the company will be exposed to fluctuations in the competitor's currency even if it has no sales in that currency. For example, a Swiss engine manufacturer selling in Germany will be placed at a competitive disadvantage if dollar depreciation allows its principal competitor, located in the United States, to sell at a lower price in Germany. Purchasing out-of-the-money put options on the dollar and selling them for a profit if they move into the money (which will happen if the dollar depreciates enough) will allow the Swiss firm to partly compensate for its lost competitiveness. Since the exposure is not contractually set, forward contracts are again not as useful as options in this situation.

The ideal use of forward contracts is when the exposure has a straight risk-reward profile: Forward contract gains or losses are exactly offset by losses or gains on the underlying transaction. But if the transaction exposure is uncertain, because the volume and/or the foreign currency prices of the items being bought or sold are unknown, a forward contract won't match it. By contrast, currency options are a good hedging tool in situations in which the quantity of foreign exchange to be received or paid out is uncertain.

ILLUSTRATION: How Cadbury Schweppes Uses Currency Options

Cadbury Schweppes, the British candy manufacturer, uses currency options to hedge uncertain payables. The price of its key product input, cocoa, is quoted in sterling but is really a dollar-based product. That is, as the value of the dollar changes, the sterling price of cocoa changes as well. The objective of the company's foreign exchange strategy is to eliminate the currency element in the decision to purchase the commodity, thus leaving the company's buyers able to concentrate on fundamentals. However, this task is complicated by the fact that the company's projections of its future purchases is highly uncertain.

As a result, Cadbury Schweppes has turned to currency options. After netting its total exposure, the company covers with forward contracts a base number of exposed, known payables. It covers the remaining—uncertain—portion with options. The options act as an insurance policy.

The general rules to follow when choosing between currency options and forward contracts for hedging purposes are summarized as follows:

1. When the quantity of a foreign currency cash outflow is known, buy the currency forward; when the quantity is unknown, buy a call option on the currency.
2. When the quantity of a foreign currency cash inflow is known, sell the currency forward; when the quantity is unknown, buy a put option on the currency.
3. When the quantity of a foreign currency cash flow is partially known and partially uncertain, use a forward contract to hedge the known portion and an option to hedge the maximum value of the uncertain remainder.[2]

Forward contracts can be used to hedge the known portion of foreign currency cash flows, and options for the uncertain remainder.

These rules presume that the financial manager's objective is to reduce risk and not to speculate on the direction or volatility of future currency movements. They also presume that both forward and options contracts are fairly priced. In an efficient market, the expected value or cost of either of these contracts should

---

[2]For elaboration, see Ian H. Giddy, "The Foreign Exchange Options as a Hedging Tool," *Midland Corporate Finance Journal,* Fall 1983, pp. 32–42.

be zero. Any other result would introduce the possibility of arbitrage profits. The presence of such profits would attract arbitrageurs as surely as bees are attracted to honey. Their subsequent attempts to profit from inappropriate prices will return these prices to their equilibrium values.

9.2 MANAGING TRANSLATION EXPOSURE

To hedge translation exposure, decrease soft currency assets (hard currency liabilities) and increase soft currency liabilities (hard currency assets).

Firms have three available methods for managing their translation exposure: (1) adjusting fund flows, (2) entering into forward contracts, and (3) exposure netting. The basic hedging strategy for reducing translation exposure shown in Exhibit 9.4 uses these methods. Essentially, the strategy involves increasing *hard-currency* (likely to appreciate) assets and decreasing *soft-currency* (likely to depreciate) assets, while simultaneously decreasing hard-currency liabilities and increasing soft-currency liabilities. For example, if a devaluation appears likely, the basic hedging strategy would be executed as follows: Reduce the level of cash, tighten credit terms to decrease accounts receivable, increase LC borrowing, delay accounts payable, and sell the weak currency forward.

Despite their prevalence among firms, however, these hedging activities are not automatically valuable. If the market already recognizes the likelihood of currency appreciation or depreciation, this recognition will be reflected in the costs of the various hedging techniques. Only if the firm's anticipations differ from the market's and are also superior to the market's can hedging lead to reduced costs. Otherwise, the principal value of hedging would be to protect a firm from unforeseen currency fluctuations.

Funds Adjustment

Most techniques for hedging an impending local currency (LC) devaluation reduce LC assets or increase LC liabilities, thereby generating LC cash. If accounting exposure is to be reduced, these funds must be converted into hard-currency assets. For example, a company will reduce its translation loss if, before an LC devaluation, it converts some of its LC cash holdings to the home currency. This conversion can be accomplished, either directly or indirectly, by means of various funds adjustment techniques.

Funds adjustment involves altering either the amounts or the currencies (or both) of the planned cash flows of the parent and/or its subsidiaries to reduce the

Exhibit 9.4 Basic Strategy for Hedging Translation Exposure

	Assets	Liabilities
Hard currencies (Likely to appreciate)	Increase	Decrease
Soft currencies (Likely to depreciate)	Decrease	Increase

firm's local currency accounting exposure. If an LC devaluation is anticipated, direct funds-adjustment methods include pricing exports in hard currencies and imports in the local currency, investing in hard-currency securities, and replacing hard-currency borrowings with local currency loans. The indirect methods, which will be elaborated on in Chapter 15, include adjusting transfer prices on the sale of goods between affiliates; speeding up the payment of dividends, fees, and royalties; and adjusting the leads and lags of intersubsidiary accounts. The latter method, which is the one most frequently used by multinationals, involves speeding up the payment of intersubsidiary accounts payable and delaying the collection of intersubsidiary accounts receivable. These hedging procedures for devaluations would be reversed for revaluations (see Exhibit 9.5).

Some of these techniques or tools may require considerable lead time and—as is the case with a transfer price—once they are introduced, they cannot be easily changed. In addition, techniques such as transfer price, fee and royalty, and dividend flow adjustments fall into the realm of corporate policy and are not usually under the treasurer's control (although this situation may be changing). It is, therefore, incumbent on the treasurer to educate other decisionmakers about the impact of these tools on the costs and management of corporate exposure.

Although entering forward contracts is the most popular coverage technique, leading and lagging of payables and receivables is almost as important. For those countries in which a formal market in LC forward contracts doesn't exist, leading

Forward contracts are the most popular hedging tool.

Exhibit 9.5 Basic Hedging Techniques

Depreciation	Appreciation
— Sell local currency forward	— Buy local currency forward
— Reduce levels of local-currency cash and marketable securities	— Increase levels of local-currency cash and marketable securities
— Tighten credit (reduce local-currency receivables)	— Relax local-currency credit terms
— Delay collection of hard-currency receivables	— Speed up collection of soft-currency receivables
— Increase imports of hard-currency goods	— Reduce imports of soft-currency goods
— Borrow locally	— Reduce local borrowing
— Delay payment of accounts payable	— Speed up payment of accounts payable
— Speed up dividend and fee remittances to parent and other subsidiaries	— Delay dividend and fee remittances to parent and other subsidiaries
— Speed up payment of intersubsidiary accounts payable	— Delay payment of intersubsidiary accounts payable
— Delay collection of intersubsidiary accounts receivable	— Speed up collection of intersubsidiary accounts receivable
— Invoice exports in foreign currency and imports in local currency	— Invoice exports in local currency and imports in foreign currency

and lagging and LC borrowing are the most important techniques. The bulk of international business, however, is conducted in those few currencies for which forward markets do exist.

Forward contracts can reduce a firm's translation exposure by creating an offsetting asset or liability in the foreign currency. For example, suppose that IBM U.K. has translation exposure of £40 million (that is, sterling assets exceed sterling liabilities by that amount). IBM U.K. can eliminate its entire translation exposure by selling £40 million forward. Any loss (gain) on its translation exposure will then be offset by a corresponding gain (loss) on its forward contract. Note, however, that the gain (or loss) on the forward contract is of a cash-flow nature and is netted against an unrealized translation loss (or gain).

Selecting convenient (less-risky) currencies for invoicing exports and imports and adjusting transfer prices are two techniques that are less frequently used, perhaps because of constraints on the use of those techniques. It is often difficult, for instance, to make a customer or supplier accept billing in a particular currency.

Exposure netting is an additional exchange management technique that is available to multinational firms with positions in more than one foreign currency or with offsetting positions in the same currency. As defined earlier, this technique involves offsetting exposures in one currency with exposures in the same or another currency such that gains and losses on the two currency positions will offset each other.

Evaluating Alternative Hedging Mechanisms

Firms should adjust fund flows whenever it is profitable to do so on a covered basis, regardless of the impact on accounting exposure.

Ordinarily, the selection of a funds-adjustment strategy cannot proceed by evaluating each possible technique separately without risking suboptimization; for example, whether or not a firm chooses to borrow locally is not independent of its decision to use or not use those funds to import additional hard-currency inventory. However, where the level of forward contracts that the financial manager can enter into is unrestricted, the following two-stage methodology allows the optimal level of forward transactions to be determined apart from the selection of what funds-adjustment techniques to use.[3] Moreover, this methodology is valid regardless of the manager's (or firm's) attitude toward risk.

Stage 1: Compute the profit associated with each funds-adjustment technique on a covered after-tax basis. Transactions that are profitable on a covered basis ought to be undertaken regardless of whether they increase or decrease the firm's accounting exposure. However, such activities should not be termed *hedging;* rather, they involve the use of *arbitrage* to exploit market distortions.

Stage 2: Any unwanted exposure resulting from the first stage can be corrected in the forward market. Stage two is the selection of an optimal level of forward transactions based on the firm's initial exposure, adjusted for the impact on exposure of decisions made in Stage 1. Where the forward market is nonexistent, or where access to it is limited, the firm must determine both what techniques to use and what their appropriate levels are. In the latter case, a

[3]This methodology is presented in William R. Folks, Jr., "Decision Analysis for Exchange Risk Management," *Financial Management,* Winter 1972, pp. 101–112.

comparison of the net cost of a funds-adjustment technique with the anticipated currency depreciation will indicate whether or not the hedging transaction is profitable on an expected-value basis.

9.3 DESIGNING A HEDGING STRATEGY

Management's objectives will largely determine its decision about the specific hedging tactics and strategy to pursue. These objectives, in turn, should reflect management's view of the world, particularly its beliefs about how markets work. The quality, or value to the shareholders, of a particular hedging strategy is, therefore, related to the congruence between those perceptions and the realities of the business environment.

The view taken here is that the basic purpose of hedging is to reduce exchange risk, where exchange risk is defined as that element of cash-flow variability that is due to currency fluctuations. Underlying the selection of a definition of exchange risk based on market value is the assumption that management's primary objective is to maximize the value of the firm. Hence, the focus is on the cash-flow effects of currency changes.

In operational terms, hedging to reduce the variance of cash flows translates into the following exposure management goal: to arrange a firm's financial affairs in such a way that however the exchange rate may move in the future, the effects on dollar returns are minimized. This objective is not universally subscribed to, however. Instead, many firms follow a selective hedging policy designed to protect against anticipated currency movements. But, if financial markets are efficient, firms cannot hedge against *expected* exchange rate changes. Interest rates, forward rates, and sales-contract prices should already reflect currency changes that are anticipated, thereby offsetting the loss-reducing benefits of hedging with higher costs. In the case of Mexico, for instance, the one-year forward discount in the futures market was close to 100% just before the peso was floated in 1982. The unavoidable conclusion is that a firm can protect itself only against *unexpected* currency changes.

Other standard techniques for responding to anticipated currency changes were summarized in Exhibit 9.5. Such techniques, however, are vastly overrated. If a devaluation is unlikely, they are costly and inefficient ways of doing business. If a devaluation is expected, the cost of using the techniques (like the cost of local borrowing) rises to reflect the anticipated devaluation. Just prior to the August 1982 peso devaluation, for example, every company in Mexico was trying to delay peso payments. Of course, this technique cannot produce a net gain because one company's payable is another company's receivable. As another example, if one company wants peso trade credit, another must offer it. Assuming that both the borrower and the lender are rational, a deal will not be struck until the interest cost rises to reflect the expected decline in the peso.

Even shifting funds from one country to another is not a costless means of hedging. The net effect of speeding up remittances while delaying receipt of intercompany receivables is to force a subsidiary in a devaluation-prone country

Corporate hedging objectives should reflect management's beliefs about how financial markets work.

to increase its local currency borrowings to finance the additional working capital requirements. The net cost of shifting funds, therefore, is the cost of the LC loan minus the profit generated from the use of the funds—for example, prepaying a hard-currency loan—with both adjusted for expected exchange rate changes. As mentioned previously, loans in local currencies subject to devaluation fears carry higher interest rates that are likely to offset any gains from LC devaluation.

Reducing the level of cash holdings to lower exposure can adversely affect a subsidiary's operations, while selling LC-denominated marketable securities can entail an opportunity cost (the lower interest rate on hard-currency securities). A firm with excess cash or marketable securities should reduce its holdings regardless of whether a devaluation is anticipated. Once cash balances are at the minimum level, however, any further reductions will involve real costs that must be weighed against the expected benefits.

Risk shifting by invoicing exports in the foreign currency and imports in the local currency may cause the loss of valuable sales or may reduce a firm's ability to extract concessions on import prices. Similarly, tightening credit may reduce profits more than costs.

Hedging exchange risk costs money and should be evaluated like any other purchase of insurance.

To summarize, hedging exchange risk costs money and should be scrutinized like any other purchase of insurance. The costs of these hedging techniques are summarized in Exhibit 9.6.

A company can benefit from the preceding techniques only to the extent that it can estimate the probability and timing of a devaluation more accurately than the general market can. Attempting to profit from foreign exchange forecasting, however, is speculating rather than hedging. The hedger is well advised to assume that the market knows as much as he or she does. Those who feel that they have superior information may choose to speculate, but this activity should not be confused with hedging.

Under some circumstances, it is possible for a company to benefit at the expense of the local government without speculating. Such a circumstance would involve the judicious use of market imperfections and/or existing tax asymmetries. In the case of an overvalued currency, such as the Mexican peso in 1982, if exchange controls are not imposed to prevent capital outflows and if hard currency can be acquired at the official exchange rate, then money can be moved out of the country via intercompany payments. For instance, a subsidiary can speed payments of intercompany accounts payable, make immediate purchases from other subsidiaries, or speed remittances to the parent. Unfortunately, governments are not unaware of these tactics. During a currency crisis, when hard currency is scarce, the local government can be expected to block such transfers or at least make them more expensive.

Another often-cited reason for market imperfection is that individual investors may not have equal access to capital markets. For example, since forward exchange markets exist only for the major currencies, hedging often requires local borrowing in heavily regulated capital markets. As a legal citizen of many nations, the MNC normally has greater access to these markets.

Similarly, if forward contract losses are treated as a cost of doing business, whereas gains are taxed at a lower capital gains rate, the firm can engage in tax

Exhibit 9.6 Cost of the Basic Hedging Techniques

Depreciation	Costs
— Sell local currency forward	— Transaction costs; difference between forward and future spot rates
— Reduce levels of local-currency cash and marketable securities	— Operational problems; opportunity cost (loss of higher interest rates on LC securities)
— Tighten credit (reduce local receivables)	— Lost sales and profits
— Delay collection of hard-currency receivables	— Cost of financing additional receivables
— Increase imports of hard-currency goods	— Financing and holding costs
— Borrow locally	— Higher interest rates
— Delay payment of accounts payable	— Harm to credit reputation
— Speed up dividend and fee remittances to parent and other subsidiaries	— Borrowing cost if funds not available or loss of higher interest rates if LC securities must be sold
— Speed up payment of intersubsidiary accounts payable	— Opportunity cost of money
— Delay collection of intersubsidiary accounts receivable	— Opportunity cost of money
— Invoice exports in foreign currency and imports in local currency	— Lost export sales or lower price; premium price for imports

arbitrage. In the absence of financial market imperfections or tax asymmetries, however, the net expected value of hedging over time should be zero. But, despite the questionable value to shareholders of hedging balance-sheet exposure or even transaction exposure, managers often try to reduce these exposures because they are evaluated, at least in part, on translation or transaction gains or losses.

Companies can take advantage of tax asymmetries and market imperfections to lower their cost of hedging.

Centralization Versus Decentralization

In the area of foreign exchange risk management, there are good arguments both for and against centralization. Favoring centralization is the reasonable assumption that local treasurers want to optimize their own financial and exposure positions, regardless of the overall corporate situation. An example is a multibillion-dollar U.S. consumer goods firm that gives its affiliates a free hand in deciding on their hedging policies. The firm's local treasurers ignored the possibilities available to the corporation to trade off positive and negative currency exposure positions by consolidating exposure worldwide. If subsidiary A sells to subsidiary B in sterling, then from the corporate perspective, these sterling exposures net out on a consolidated translation basis (but only before tax). If A and/or B hedge their sterling positions, however, unnecessary hedging takes place or a zero sterling exposure turns into a positive or negative position. Furthermore, in their dealings

Centralization of exchange risk management reduces the amount of hedging needed to achieve a given level of safety.

with external customers, some affiliates may wind up with a positive exposure and others with a negative exposure in the same currency. Through lack of knowledge or incentive, individual subsidiaries may undertake hedging actions that increase rather than decrease overall corporate exposure in a given currency.

A further benefit of centralized exposure management is the ability to take advantage, through exposure netting, of the portfolio effect discussed previously. Thus, centralization of exchange risk management should reduce the amount of hedging required to achieve a given level of safety.

Once the company has decided on the maximum currency exposure it is willing to tolerate, it can then select the cheapest option(s) worldwide to hedge its remaining exposure. Tax effects can be crucial at this stage, both in computing the amounts to hedge and the costs involved, but only headquarters will have the required global perspective. Centralized management is also needed to take advantage of the before-tax hedging cost variations that are likely to exist among subsidiaries because of market imperfections.

All these arguments for centralization of currency risk management are powerful. Against the benefits must be weighed the loss of local knowledge and the lack of incentive for local managers to take advantage of particular situations that only they may be familiar with. Companies that decentralize the hedging decision may allow local units to manage their own exposures by engaging in forward contracts with a central unit at negotiated rates. The central unit, in turn, may or may not lay off these contracts in the marketplace.

9.4 ILLUSTRATION: MANAGING TRANSACTION EXPOSURE FOR THE TORONTO BLUE JAYS

During the first half of the 1985 baseball season, the Toronto Blue Jays, an American League expansion team, had the best won-lost record in the major leagues. Yet their profits at the gate did not match their performance at the plate. Attendance was up, and so were ticket prices, but the Blue Jays budgeted for a loss of more than C$2 million in 1985. The reason: The Blue Jays get most of their revenue in the form of Canadian dollars (C$) but pay most of their bills in U.S. dollars.

Projected 1985 expenses included about $19 million in U.S. dollars and the equivalent of only about $4.5 million in Canadian currency. Projected revenues of roughly $21 million were almost all in Canadian dollars except for income from a U.S. television package and 20% of gate receipts from the Jays' games in U.S. ballparks. As a result of this imbalance of currency inflows and outflows, it was estimated that each $0.01 drop of the Canadian dollar against its U.S. counterpart cost the Jays about C$135,000 in 1985.

Although major-league teams usually lose money, it was believed that the Jays' ecstatic fans would have made the team profitable in 1985 if it weren't for the currency problem. The magnitude of this problem is indicated by the changed fortune of the Canadian dollar. When the Toronto franchise was created in 1976, the Canadian currency was worth $1.04; at midseason 1985, it was trading at about $0.73.

The biggest expense in 1985 was U.S. $10 million for players' salaries. (All major-league ballplayers are paid in U.S. dollars; none of the Jays' players are Canadians anyway.) By 1989, that figure had reached about U.S. $18 million. At an exchange rate of $0.80, a 1 cent drop in the Canadian dollar added C$285,000 to annual salary costs.

Like other businesses with foreign exchange problems, the Blue Jays and their fellow sufferers, the Montreal Expos, make forward purchases of U.S. dollars to protect against swings in exchange rates. Late in 1984, for example, the Jays contracted to buy about 60% of the team's projected 1985 U.S. currency needs at about 75 cents per Canadian dollar. The profit on this position enabled the team to offset most of the losses on its U.S. dollar outflows.

9.5 SUMMARY AND CONCLUSIONS

Firms normally cope with anticipated currency changes by engaging in forward contracts, borrowing locally, and adjusting their pricing and credit policies. However, there is reason to question the value of much of this activity. In fact, we have seen that, in normal circumstances, hedging cannot provide protection against expected exchange rate changes.

A number of empirical studies indicate that forward rates provide an unbiased estimate of future spot rates. Furthermore, according to the international Fisher effect, in the absence of government controls, interest rate differentials among countries should equal anticipated currency devaluations or revaluations. Empirical research substantiates that over time, gains or losses on debt in hard currencies tend to be offset by low interest rates; in soft currencies, they will be offset by higher interest rates unless, of course, there are various barriers that preclude equalization of real interest rates.

In fact, no other results would be consistent with the existence of a well-informed market with numerous participants—as is represented by the international financial community. Persistent differences between forward and future spot rates, for instance, would provide profitable opportunities for speculators. However, the very act of buying or selling forward to take advantage of these differences would tend to bring about equality between hedging costs and expected currency changes.

The other hedging methods, which involve factoring anticipated exchange rate changes into pricing and credit decisions, can be profitable only at the expense of others. Thus, to consistently gain by these trade-term adjustments, it is necessary to deal continuously with less-knowledgeable people. Certainly, though, a policy predicated on the continued existence of naive firms is unlikely to be viable for very long in the highly competitive and well-informed world of international business. The real value to a firm of factoring currency change expectations into its pricing and credit decisions is to prevent others from profiting at its expense.

The basic value of hedging, therefore, is to protect a company against unexpected exchange rate changes; however, by definition, these changes are unpredictable and, consequently, impossible to profit from. Of course, to the extent that a government does not permit interest and/or forward rates to fully adjust to market expectations, a firm with access to these financial instruments can expect, on average, to gain from currency changes. Nevertheless, the very nature of these imperfections severely restricts a company's ability to engage in such profitable financial operations.

QUESTIONS

1. A U.S. firm has fully hedged its sterling receivables and has bought credit insurance to cover the risk of default. Has this firm eliminated all risk on these receivables? Explain.

2. What is the basic translation hedging strategy? How does it work?

3. What alternative hedging transactions are available to a company seeking to hedge the translation exposure of its German subsidiary?

4. Referring to Question 3, how would the appropriate hedge change if the German affiliate's functional currency is the U.S. dollar?

5. Multinational firms can always reduce the foreign exchange risk faced by their foreign affiliates by borrowing in the local currency. True or false? Why?

6. Can hedging provide protection against expected exchange rate changes? Explain.

7. What is the domestic counterpart to exchange risk? Explain.

8. If a currency that a company is long in threatens to weaken, many companies will sell that currency forward. Comment on this policy.

9. Instead of its previous policy of always hedging its foreign currency receivables, Sun Microsystems has decided to hedge only when it believes the dollar will strengthen. Otherwise, it will go uncovered. Comment on this new policy.

10. Studies have shown that in trade dealings between nations that have high and volatile inflation rates, most export prices are quoted in dollars. What might account for this finding?

PROBLEMS

1. In March, Multinational Industries, Inc., assessed the September spot rate for sterling at the following rates:

$1.30/£ with probability 0.15
$1.35/£ with probability 0.20
$1.40/£ with probability 0.25
$1.45/£ with probability 0.20
$1.50/£ with probability 0.20

a. What is the expected spot rate for September?
b. If the six-month forward rate is $1.40, should the firm sell forward its pound receivables due in September?
c. What factors are likely to affect the firm's hedging decision?

2. An importer has a payment of £8 million due in 90 days.

a. If the 90-day pound forward rate is $1.4201, what is the hedged cost of making that payment?

b. If the spot rate expected in 90 days is $1.4050, what is the expected cost of payment?

c. What factors will influence the hedging decision?

3. A foreign exchange trader assesses the French franc exchange rate three months hence as follows:

$0.11 with probability 0.25
$0.13 with probability 0.50
$0.15 with probability 0.25

The 90-day forward rate is $0.12.

a. Will the trader buy or sell French francs forward against the dollar if she is concerned solely with expected values? In what volume?

b. In reality, what is likely to limit the trader's speculative activities?

c. Suppose the trader revises her probability assessment as follows:

$0.09 with probability 0.33
$0.13 with probability 0.33
$0.17 with probability 0.33

Assuming the forward rate remains at $0.12, do you think this new assessment will affect the trader's decision?

4. International Worldwide would like to execute a money market hedge to cover a ¥250,000,000 shipment from Japan of sound systems it will receive in six months. The current exchange rate for yen is ¥124 = $1.

a. How would International structure the hedge? What would it do to hedge the Japanese yen it must pay in six months? The annual yen interest rate is 4%.

b. The yen may rise to as much as ¥140 = $1 or fall to ¥115 = $1. What will the total dollar cash flow be in six months in either case?

5. An investment manager hedges a portfolio of Bunds (German government bonds) with a 6-month forward contract. The current spot rate is DM1.64:$1 and the 180-day forward rate is DM 1.61:$1. At the end of the 6-month period, the Bunds have risen in value by 3.75% (in DM terms), while the spot rate is now DM 1.46:$1.

a. If the Bunds earn interest at the annual rate of 5%, paid semi-annually, what is the investment manager's total dollar return on the hedged Bunds?

b. What would the return on the Bunds have been without hedging?

c. What was the true cost of the forward contract?

6. A French corporate treasurer expects to receive a DM 11 million payment in 90 days from a German customer. The current spot rate is DM 0.29870:FF 1 and the 90-day forward rate is DM 0.29631:FF 1. In addition, the annualized three-month EuroDM and Eurofranc (French) rates are 9.8% and 12.3%, respectively.

a. What is the hedged value of the DM receivable using the forward contract?

b. Describe how the French treasurer could use a money market hedge to lock in the franc value of the DM receivable. What is the hedged value of the DM receivable? What is the effective forward rate that the treasurer can obtain using this money market hedge?

c. Given your answers in parts a and b, is there an arbitrage opportunity? How could the treasurer take advantage of it?

7. Magnetronics, Inc., a U.S. company, owes its Taiwanese supplier NT$205 million in three months. The company wishes to hedge its NT$ payable. The current spot rate is NT$1 = U.S.$0.03987, while the three-month forward rate is NT$1 = U.S.$0.04051. Magnetronics can also borrow/lend U.S. dollars at an annualized interest rate of 12% and Taiwanese dollars at an annualized interest rate of 8%.

a. What is the U.S. dollar accounting entry for this payable?

b. What is the minimum U.S. dollar cost that Magnetronics can lock in for this payable? Describe the procedure it would use to get this price.

8.* Metalgesselschaft, a leading German metal processor, has scheduled a supply of 20,000 metric tons of copper for October 1. On April 1, copper is quoted on the London Metals Exchange at £562 per metric ton for immediate delivery and £605 per metric ton for delivery on October 1. Monthly storage costs are £10 for a metric ton in London and DM 30 in Hamburg, payable on the first day of storage. Exchange rate quotations are as follows: The pound is worth DM 3.61 on April 1 and is selling at a 6.3% annual discount. The opportunity cost of capital for Metalgesselschaft is estimated at 8% annually, and the pound sterling is expected to depreciate at a yearly rate of 6.3% throughout the next 12 months.

Compute the Deutsche mark cost for Metalgesselschaft on April 1 of the following options:

a. Buy 20,000 metric tons of copper on April 1 and store it in London until October 1.

b. Buy a forward contract of 20,000 metric tons on April 1, for delivery in six months. Cover sterling debt by purchasing forward pounds sterling on April 1.

c. Buy 20,000 metric tons of copper on October 1. Can you identify other options available to Metalgesselschaft? Which one would you recommend?

9. In January 1988, Arco bought a 24.3% stake in the British oil firm Britoil PLC. It intended to buy a further $1 billion worth of Britoil stock if Britoil was agreeable. However, Arco was uncertain whether Britoil, which had expressed a strong desire to remain independent, would accept its bid. To guard against the possibility of a pound appreciation in the interim, Arco decided to convert $1 billion into pounds and place them on deposit in London, pending the outcome of its discussions with Britoil's management. What exchange risk does Arco face and has it chosen the best way to protect itself from that risk?

10. Sumitomo Chemical of Japan has one week in which to negotiate a contract to supply products to a U.S. company at a dollar price that will remain fixed for one year. What advice would you give Sumitomo?

11. Kemp & Beatley, Inc., is a New York importer of table linens and accessories. It hedges all its import orders using forward contracts. Does Kemp & Beatley face any exchange risk? Explain.

12. U.S. Farm-Raised Fish Trading Co., a catfish concern in Jackson, Mississippi, tells its Japanese customers that it wants to be paid in dollars. According to its director of export marketing, this simple strategy eliminates all its currency risk. Is he right? Why?

13. The Montreal Expos are a major-league baseball team located in Montreal, Canada. What currency risk is faced by the Expos, and how can this exchange risk be managed?

14. Westinghouse recently had to put together a $50 million bid, denominated in Swiss francs, to upgrade a Swiss power plant. If it won, Westinghouse expected to pay subcontractors and suppliers in five currencies. The payment schedule for the contract stretched over a five-year period.

a. How should Westinghouse establish the Swiss franc price of its $50 million bid?

b. What exposure does Westinghouse face on this bid? How can it hedge that exposure?

*Problem contributed by Laurent Jacque.

15. Liz Claiborne contracts out much of its production to foreign manufacturers. As such, the company faces currency risk.
   a. What currency risk does Liz Claiborne face?
   b. How might Liz Claiborne go about hedging its currency risk?
   c. What danger does it face from locking in currency rates today?

BIBLIOGRAPHY

Cornell, Bradford, and Alan C. Shapiro. "Managing Foreign Exchange Risks." *Midland Corporate Finance Journal*, Fall 1983, pp. 16–31.

Dufey, Gunter, and S.L. Srinivasulu. "The Case for Corporate Management of Foreign Exchange Risk." *Financial Management*, Summer 1984, pp. 54–62.

Giddy, Ian H. "The Foreign Exchange Option as a Hedging Tool." *Midland Corporate Finance Journal*, Fall 1983, pp. 32–42.

Goeltz, Richard K. "Managing Liquid Funds on an International Scope," unpublished paper. New York: Joseph E. Seagram and Sons, 1971.

Shapiro, Alan C., and David P. Rutenberg. "Managing Exchange Risks in a Floating World." *Financial Management*, Summer 1976, pp. 48–58.

Srinivasulu, Sam, and Edward Massura. "Sharing Currency Risks in Long-Term Contracts." *Business International Money Reports*, February 23, 1987, pp. 57–59.

10 Measuring Economic Exposure

Let's face it. If you've got 75% of your assets in the U.S. and 50% of your sales outside it, and the dollar's strong, you've got problems.

> Donald V. Fites
> President
> Caterpillar Inc.

CHAPTER LEARNING OBJECTIVES

- To define economic exposure and exchange risk and distinguish between the two
- To define operating exposure and distinguish between it and transaction exposure
- To describe the economic consequences of exchange rate changes
- To identify the basic factors that determine the foreign exchange risk faced by a particular company or project
- To calculate the real exchange rate and describe the consequences of real exchange rate changes
- To calculate economic exposure given a particular exchange rate change and specific cost and revenue scenarios
- To determine a firm's true economic exposure and susceptibility to exchange risk using regression analysis

Chapter 8 focused on the accounting effects of currency changes. As we saw in that chapter, the adoption of FASB-52 has helped to moderate the wild swings in the translated earnings of overseas subsidiaries. Nevertheless, the problem of coping with volatile currencies remains essentially unchanged. Fluctuations in exchange rates will continue to have "real" effects on the cash profitability of foreign subsidiaries—complicating overseas selling, pricing, buying, and plant-location decisions.

This chapter develops an appropriate definition of foreign exchange risk. It discusses the nature and origins of exchange risk and presents a theory of the *economic*, as distinguished from the accounting, consequences of currency changes on a firm's value. The chapter also illustrates how economic exposure can be measured and provides an operational measure of exchange risk.

10.1 FOREIGN EXCHANGE RISK AND ECONOMIC EXPOSURE

The most important aspect of foreign exchange risk management is to incorporate currency change expectations into *all* basic corporate decisions. In performing this task, the firm must know what is at risk. However, there is a major discrepancy between accounting practice and economic reality in terms of measuring *exposure*, which is the degree to which a company is affected by exchange rate changes.

As we saw in Chapter 8, those who use an accounting definition of exposure—whether FASB-8, FASB-52, or some other method—divide the balance sheet's assets and liabilities into those accounts that will be affected by exchange rate changes and those that will not. In contrast, economic theory focuses on the impact of an exchange rate change on future cash flows; that is, *economic exposure* is based on the extent to which the value of the firm—as measured by the present value of its expected future cash flows—will change when exchange rates change.

> Economic exposure focuses on the cash flow effects of exchange rate changes.

Specifically, if PV is the present value of a firm, then that firm is exposed to currency risk if $\Delta PV / \Delta e$ is not equal to zero, where ΔPV is the change in the firm's present value associated with an exchange rate change, Δe. *Exchange risk*, in turn, is defined as the variability in the firm's value that is caused by uncertain exchange rate changes. Thus, exchange risk is viewed as the possibility that currency fluctuations can alter the expected amounts or variability of the firm's future cash flows.

Economic exposure can be separated into two components: transaction exposure and operating exposure. We saw that *transaction exposure* stems from exchange gains or losses on foreign-currency-denominated contractual obligations. Although transaction exposure is often included under accounting exposure, as it was in Chapter 8, it is more properly a cash-flow exposure and, hence, part of economic exposure. However, even if the company prices all contracts in dollars or otherwise hedges its transaction exposure, the residual exposure—longer-term operating exposure—still remains.

Operating exposure arises because currency fluctuations can alter a company's future revenues and costs—that is, its operating cash flows. Consequently, measuring a firm's operating exposure requires a longer-term perspective, viewing the firm as an ongoing concern with operations whose cost and price competitiveness could be affected by exchange rate changes.

Thus, the firm faces operating exposure the moment it invests in servicing a market subject to foreign competition or in sourcing goods or inputs abroad. This investment includes new-product development, a distribution network, foreign supply contracts, or production facilities. Transaction exposure arises later on, and only if the company's commitments lead it to engage in foreign-currency-denominated sales or purchases. Exhibit 10.1 shows the time pattern of economic exposure.

The measurement of economic exposure is made especially difficult because it is impossible to assess the effects of an exchange rate change without simultaneously considering the impact on cash flows of the underlying relative rates of

Exhibit 10.1 The Time Pattern of Economic Exposure

Noncontractual	Quasi-contractual	Contractual	
Investment in new product development, distribution facilities, brand name, marketing, foreign production capacity, foreign supplier relationships	Quote foreign currency price, receive a foreign currency price quote	Ship product/bill customers in foreign currency, receive bill for supplies in foreign currency	Collect foreign currency receivables, pay foreign currency liabilities

A company's operating exposure, also termed competitive exposure, is only affected by changes in the real exchange rate.

inflation associated with each currency. Reconsidering the concept of the real exchange rate will help clarify the discussion of exposure. As presented in Chapter 7, the *real exchange rate* is defined as the nominal exchange rate (for example, the number of dollars per franc) adjusted for changes in the relative purchasing power of each currency since some base period. Specifically,

$$e_t' = e_t \times \frac{(1 + i_{f,t})}{(1 + i_{h,t})}$$

where e_t' = the real exchange rate (home currency per one unit of foreign currency) at time t

e_t = the nominal exchange rate (home currency per one unit of foreign currency) at time t

$i_{f,t}$ = the amount of foreign inflation between times 0 and t

$i_{h,t}$ = the amount of domestic inflation between times 0 and t

Importance of the Real Exchange Rate

The distinction between the nominal exchange rate and the real exchange rate is important because of their vastly different implications for exchange risk. A dramatic change in the nominal exchange rate accompanied by an equal change in the price level should have no effects on the relative competitive positions of domestic firms and their foreign competitors and, therefore, will not alter real cash flows. Alternatively, if the real exchange rate changes, it will cause relative price changes—changes in the ratio of domestic goods' prices to prices of foreign goods. In terms of currency changes affecting relative competitiveness, therefore, the focus must be not on nominal exchange rate changes, but instead on changes in the purchasing power of one currency relative to another.

Inflation and Exchange Risk

Let us begin by holding relative prices constant and looking only at the effects of general inflation. This condition means that if the inflation rate is 10%, the price of every good in the economy rises by 10%. In addition, we will initially assume that all goods are traded in a competitive world market without transaction costs, tariffs, or taxes of any kind. Given these conditions, economic theory tells us that the law of one price must prevail. That is, the price of any good, measured in a common currency, must be equal in all countries.

If the law of one price holds and if there is no variation in the relative prices of goods or services, then the rate of change in the exchange rate must equal the difference between the inflation rates in the two countries. The implications of a constant real exchange rate—that is, PPP holds—are worth exploring further. To begin, purchasing power parity does not imply that exchange rate changes will necessarily be small or easy to forecast. If a country has high and unpredictable inflation (for example, Argentina), then the country's exchange rate will also fluctuate randomly.

> If PPP holds, then nominal exchange rate changes will not affect an MNC's competitive position.

Nonetheless, without relative price changes, a multinational company faces no real operating exchange risk. As long as the firm avoids contracts fixed in foreign-currency terms, its foreign cash flows will vary with the foreign rate of inflation. Because the exchange rate also depends on the difference between the foreign and the domestic rates of inflation, the movement of the exchange rate exactly cancels the change in the foreign price level, leaving real dollar cash flows unaffected.

ILLUSTRATION: Calculating the Effect of Exchange Rate Changes and Inflation on Apex Spain

Apex Spain, the Spanish subsidiary of Apex Company, produces and sells medical imaging devices in Spain. At the current peseta exchange rate of Ptas. 1 = $0.01, the devices cost Ptas. 40,000 ($400) to produce and sell for Ptas. 100,000 ($1000). The profit margin of Ptas. 60,000 provides a dollar margin of $600. Suppose that Spanish inflation during the year is 20%, while the U.S. inflation rate is zero. All prices and costs are assumed to move in line with inflation. Assuming that purchasing power parity holds, the peseta will devalue to $0.0083 (0.01 × 1/1.2). Since the real value of the peseta stays at $0.01 (0.0083 × 1.2/1.0), Apex Spain's dollar profit margin will remain at $600. These effects are shown in Exhibit 10.2.

Of course, the above conclusion does not hold if the firm enters into contracts fixed in terms of the foreign currency. Examples of such contracts are debt with fixed interest rates, long-term leases, labor contracts, and rent. However, if the real exchange rate remains constant, the risk introduced by entering into fixed contracts is not exchange risk; it is inflation risk. For instance, a Mexican firm with fixed-rate debt in pesos faces the same risk as the subsidiary of an American firm with peso debt. If the rate of inflation declines, the real interest cost of the debt rises, and the real cash flow of both companies falls. The solution to the problem of inflation risk is to avoid writing contracts fixed in nominal terms in countries with unpredictable inflation. If the contracts are indexed and if the real exchange rate remains constant, exchange risk is eliminated.

> Transaction exposure can be eliminated by avoiding contracts fixed in foreign currency terms.

Exhibit 10.2 The Effects of Nominal Exchange Rate Changes and Inflation on Apex Spain

Price Level	Spain	United States
Beginning of year	100	100
End of year	120	100

Exchange Rate	Beginning of Year	End of Year
Nominal Rate	Ptas. 1 = $0.01	Ptas. 1 = $0.0083
Real Rate	Ptas. 1 = $0.01	Ptas. 1 = $0.0083 × 1.2/1 = $0.01

	Beginning of Year		End of Year	
Profit Impact	Pesetas	U.S. Dollars	Pesetas	U.S. Dollars
Price*	Ptas. 100,000	$1,000	Ptas. 120,000	$1,000
Cost of production*	40,000	400	48,000	400
Profit margin	Ptas. 60,000	$ 600	Ptas. 72,000	$ 600

*Peseta prices and costs are assumed to increase at the 20% rate of Spanish inflation.

Real Exchange Rate Changes and Exchange Risk

In general, a decline in the real value of a nation's currency makes its exports and import-competing goods more competitive. Conversely, an appreciating currency hurts the nation's exporters and those producers competing with imports.

During the late 1970s, for example, worldwide demand for Swiss franc-denominated assets caused the Swiss franc to appreciate in real terms. As a result, Swiss watchmakers were squeezed. Because of competition from Japanese companies, Swiss firms could not significantly raise the dollar price of watches sold in the United States. Yet, at the same time, the *dollar* cost of Swiss labor was rising because the franc was appreciating against the dollar.

An increase (decrease) in the real value of the dollar hurts (helps) U.S. companies facing foreign competition both at home and abroad.

American companies faced similar problems when the real value of the dollar began rising against other currencies during the early 1980s. U.S. exporters found themselves with the Hobson's choice of either keeping dollar prices constant and losing sales volume (because foreign currency prices rose in line with the appreciating dollar) or setting prices in the foreign currency to maintain market share, with a corresponding erosion in dollar revenues and profit margins. At the same time, the dollar cost of American labor remained the same or rose in line with U.S. inflation. The combination of lower dollar revenues and unchanged or higher dollar costs resulted in severe hardship for those U.S. companies selling abroad. Similarly, U.S. manufacturers competing domestically with imports whose dollar prices were declining saw both their profit margins and sales volumes reduced. But now the shoe is on the other foot, as Japanese firms attempt to cope with a yen that appreciated by more than 100% in real terms between 1985 and 1989.

ILLUSTRATION: *Yen Appreciation Harms Japanese TV Producers*

For most of 1985, the yen traded at about ¥240 = $1. By 1988, the yen's value had risen to about ¥130 = $1, without a commensurate increase in U.S. inflation. This rise had a highly negative impact on Japanese TV manufacturers. If it cost, say, ¥100,000 to build a color TV in Japan, ship it to the United States, and earn a normal profit, that TV could be sold in 1985 for about $417 (100,000/240). However, in 1988, the price would have had to be about $769 (100,000/130) for Japanese firms to break even. Because other U.S. prices haven't risen, as the Japanese firms raise their dollar price to compensate for yen appreciation, Americans buy fewer Japanese color TVs, and yen revenues fall. If the Japanese TV producers decide to keep their price constant at $417 to preserve market share in the United States, they will have to cut their yen price to about ¥54,210 (417 × 130). Whether they hold the line on yen prices or cut them, real yen appreciation is bad news for Japanese TV manufacturers.

Alternatively, Industrias Penoles, the Mexican firm that is the world's largest refiner of newly mined silver, increased its dollar profits by over 200% following the real devaluation of the Mexican peso relative to the dollar in 1982. The reason for the firm's success is that its costs, which are in pesos, declined in dollar terms, while the dollar value of its revenues, which are derived from exports, held steady.

To summarize, the economic impact of a currency change on a firm depends on whether the exchange rate change is fully offset by the difference in inflation rates or whether (because of price controls, a shift in monetary policy, or some other reason) the real exchange rate and, hence, relative prices change. It is these relative price changes that ultimately determine a firm's long-run exposure.

A less obvious point is that a firm may face more exchange risk if nominal exchange rates do *not* change. Consider, for example, a Brazilian shoe manufacturer producing for export to the United States and Europe. If the Brazilian cruzeiro's exchange rate remains fixed in the face of Brazil's typically high rate of inflation, then both the cruzeiro's real exchange rate and the manufacturer's dollar costs of production will rise. Therefore, unless the cruzeiro devalues, the Brazilian exporter will be placed at a competitive disadvantage vis-à-vis producers located in countries with less rapidly rising costs, such as Taiwan and South Korea.

A fixed exchange rate may lead to more, not less, exchange risk.

ILLUSTRATION: *Chile Mismanages Its Exchange Rate*

A particularly dramatic illustration of the unfortunate effects of a fixed nominal exchange rate combined with high domestic inflation is provided by Chile. As part of its plan to bring down the rate of Chilean inflation, the government fixed the exchange rate in the middle of 1979 at 39 pesos to the U.S. dollar. Over the next two and one-half years, the Chilean price level rose 60%, while U.S. prices rose by only about 30%. Thus, by early 1982, the Chilean peso had appreciated in real terms by approximately 23% (1.6/1.3 – 1) against the U.S. dollar. These data are summarized in Exhibit 10.3.

An 18% "corrective" devaluation was enacted in June 1982. But the artificially high peso had already done its double damage to the Chilean economy: It made Chile's manufactured products more expensive abroad, pricing many of them out of international trade; and it made imports cheaper, undercutting Chilean domestic industries. The effects of the overvalued peso were devastating. Banks became insolvent, factories and copper smelters were thrown into bankruptcy, copper mines were closed, construction projects were shut down, and farms were put on the auction block. Unemployment approached 25%, and some areas of Chile resembled industrial graveyards.

An increase in the real value of a currency acts as a tax on exports and a subsidy on imports.

The Chilean example illustrates a critical point: *An increase in the real value of a currency acts as a tax on exports and a subsidy on imports.* Hence, firms that export or that compete with imports are hurt by an appreciating home currency. Conversely, such firms benefit from home-currency depreciation. These general principles identify a company's economic exposure.

Exhibit 10.3   Nominal and Real Exchange Rates for Chile, 1979–1982

Price Level	Chile	United States		
1979	100	100		
1982	160	130		
Nominal Exchange Rate	1979	Ps. 1 = $0.02564		
	1982	Ps. 1 = $0.02564		
Real Exchange Rate	1979	Ps. 1 = $0.02564		
	1982	Ps. 1 = $0.02564 $\times \dfrac{1.60}{1.30}$		
		= $0.03156		

Increase in Real Value of the Chilean Peso $\dfrac{0.03156 - 0.02564}{0.02564}$ = 23.1%

Result: Economic Devastation

—Loss of export markets
—Loss of domestic markets to imports
—Massive unemployment
—Numerous bankruptcies
—Numerous bank failures

10.2 THE ECONOMIC CONSEQUENCES OF EXCHANGE RATE CHANGES

We now examine more closely the specifics of a firm's economic exposure. Solely for the purpose of exposition, the discussion of exposure is divided into its component parts: transaction exposure and real operating exposure.

Transaction Exposure

Transaction exposure arises out of the various types of transactions that require settlement in a foreign currency. Examples are cross-border trade, borrowing and lending in foreign currencies, and the local purchasing and sales activities of foreign subsidiaries. Strictly speaking, of course, the items already on a firm's balance sheet, such as loans and receivables, capture some of these transactions. However, a detailed transaction exposure report must also contain a number of off-balance-sheet items as well, including future sales and purchases, lease payments, forward contracts, loan repayments, and other contractual or anticipated foreign-currency receipts and disbursements.

> Transaction exposure includes both on- and off-balance-sheet items.

In terms of measuring economic exposure, though, a transaction exposure report, no matter how detailed, has a fundamental flaw: the assumption that local-currency cost and revenue streams remain constant following an exchange rate change.

That assumption does not permit an evaluation of the typical adjustments that consumers and firms can be expected to undertake under conditions of currency change. Hence, attempting to measure the likely exchange gain or loss by simply multiplying the projected predevaluation (prerevaluation) local-currency cash flows by the forecast devaluation (revaluation) percentage will lead to misleading results. Given the close relationship between nominal exchange rate changes and inflation as expressed in purchasing power parity, measuring exposure to a currency change without reference to the accompanying inflation is also a misguided task.

We will now examine more closely the typical demand and cost effects that result from a real exchange rate change and how these effects combine to determine a firm's true operating exposure. In general, an appreciating real exchange rate can be expected to have the opposite effects. The dollar is assumed to be the home currency.

Operating Exposure

A real exchange rate change affects a number of aspects of the firm's operations. With respect to dollar (HC) appreciation, the key issue for a domestic firm is its degree of *pricing flexibility*—that is, can the firm maintain its dollar margins both at home and abroad? Can the company maintain its dollar price on domestic sales in the face of lower-priced foreign imports? In the case of foreign sales, can the firm raise its foreign currency selling price sufficiently to preserve its dollar profit margin?

The answers to these questions depend largely on the *price elasticity of demand*. The less price elastic the demand, the more price flexibility a company will have to respond to exchange rate changes. Price elasticity, in turn, depends on the degree of competition and the location of key competitors. The more *differentiated* (distinct) a company's products are, the less competition it will face and the greater its ability will be to maintain its domestic currency prices both at home and abroad. Examples here are IBM and Daimler-Benz (producer of Mercedes Benz cars). Similarly, if most competitors are based in the home country, then all will face the same change in their cost structure from home currency appreciation, and all can raise their foreign currency prices without putting any of them at a competitive disadvantage relative to their domestic competitors. Examples of this situation are in the precision instrumentation and high-end telecommunications industries, in which virtually all the important players are U.S.-based companies.

Conversely, the less differentiated a company's products are and the more internationally diversified its competitors (for example, the low-priced end of the auto industry) are, the greater the price elasticity of demand for its products will be and the less pricing flexibility it will have. These companies face the greatest amount of exchange risk.

The greater pricing flexibility held by companies with differentiated products reduces their exchange risk.

ILLUSTRATION: Product Differentiation and Susceptibility to Exchange Risk of the U.S. Apparel and Textile Industries

The U.S. textile and apparel industries are highly competitive, with each composed of many small manufacturers. In addition, nearly every country has a textile industry, and apparel industries are also common to most countries.

Despite these similarities, the textile industry exists in a more-competitive environment than the apparel industry because textile products are more standardized than apparel products. Buyers of textiles can easily switch from a firm that sells a standard good at a higher price to one that sells virtually the same good at a lower price. Because they are more differentiated, the products of competing apparel firms are viewed as more distinct and are less sensitive than textile goods to changes in prices. Thus, even though both textile and apparel firms operate in highly competitive industries, apparel firms—with their greater degree of pricing flexibility—are less subject to exchange risk than textile firms.

Another important determinant of a company's susceptibility to exchange risk is its ability to shift production and the sourcing of inputs among countries. The greater a company's flexibility to substitute between home-country and foreign-country inputs or production, the less exchange risk the company will face. Other things being equal, firms with worldwide production systems can cope with currency changes by increasing production in a nation whose currency has undergone a real devaluation and decreasing production in a nation whose currency has revalued in real terms.

With respect to a multinational corporation's foreign operations, the determinants of its economic exposure will be similar to those just mentioned. A foreign subsidiary selling goods or services in its local market will generally be unable to raise its local-currency selling price to the full extent of an LC devaluation, causing it to register a decline in its postdevaluation dollar revenues. However, because an LC devaluation will also reduce import competition, the more import competition the subsidiary was facing prior to the devaluation, the smaller its dollar revenue decline will be.

The harmful effects of LC devaluation will be mitigated somewhat since the devaluation should lower the subsidiary's dollar production costs, particularly those attributable to local inputs. However, the higher the import content of local inputs, the less dollar production costs will decline. Inputs used in the export or import-competing sectors will decline less in dollar price than other domestic inputs.

An MNC using its foreign subsidiary as an export platform will be benefited by an LC devaluation since its export revenues should stay about the same, whereas its dollar costs will decline. The net result will be a jump in dollar profits for the exporter.

Local-currency movements can also affect the dollar value of the depreciation tax shield. The cash flow associated with the tax write-off of depreciable assets can have a substantial present value, particularly for a capital-intensive corporation. Unless indexation of fixed assets is permitted (as in Argentina, Brazil, and Israel), the dollar value of the local-currency-denominated tax shield will unambiguously decline by the percentage of nominal devaluation.

The major conclusion is that the sector of the economy in which a firm operates (export, import-competing, or purely domestic), the sources of the firm's inputs (imports, domestic traded or nontraded goods), and fluctuations in the real exchange rate are far more important in delineating the firm's true economic exposure than is any accounting definition. The economic effects are summarized in Exhibit 10.4.

A surprising implication of this analysis is that domestic facilities that supply foreign markets normally entail much greater exchange risk than do foreign facilities supplying local markets. The explanation is that material and labor used in a domestic plant are paid for in the home currency while the products are sold in a foreign currency. For example, take a Japanese company such as Nissan Motors that builds a plant to produce cars for export, primarily to the United States. The company will incur an exchange risk from the point at which it invests in facilities to supply a foreign market (the United States) because its yen expenses will be matched with dollar revenues rather than yen revenues. The point seems obvious; however, all too frequently, firms neglect those effects when analyzing a proposed foreign investment.

Similarly, a firm (or its affiliate) producing solely for the domestic market and using only domestic sources of inputs can be strongly affected by currency changes, even though its accounting exposure is zero. Consider, for example,

Domestic facilities that supply foreign markets normally entail more exchange risk than do foreign facilities supplying local markets.

Exhibit 10.4 Characteristic Economic Effects of Exchange Rate Changes on MNCs

Cash-Flow Categories	Relevant Economic Factors	Devaluation Impact	Revaluation Impact
Revenue		Parent-Currency Revenue Impact	Parent-Currency Revenue Impact
Export sales	Price-sensitive demand	Increase (+ +)	Decrease (– –)
	Price-insensitive demand	Slight increase (+)	Slight decrease (–)
Local sales	Weak prior import competition	Sharp decline (– –)	Increase (+ +)
	Strong prior import competition	Decrease (–) (less than devaluation %)	Slight increase (+)
Costs		Parent-Currency Cost Impact	Parent-Currency Cost Impact
Domestic inputs	Low import content	Decrease (– –)	Increase (+ +)
	High import content/inputs used in export or import-competing sectors	Slight decrease (–)	Slight increase (+)
Imported inputs	Small local market	Remain the same (0)	Remain the same (0)
	Large local market	Slight decrease (–)	Slight increase (+)
Depreciation		Cash-Flow Impact	Cash-Flow Impact
Fixed assets	No asset valuation adjustment	Decrease by devaluation % (– –)	Increase by revaluation % (+ +)
	Asset valuation adjustment	Decrease (–)	Increase (+)

NOTE: To interpret the above chart, and taking the impact of a devaluation on local demand as an example, it is assumed that if import competition is weak, local prices will climb slightly, if at all; in such a case, there would be a sharp contraction in parent-company revenue. If imports generate strong competition, local-currency prices are expected to increase, although not to the full extent of the devaluation; in this instance, only a moderate decline in parent-company revenue would be registered.

SOURCE: Alan C. Shapiro, "Developing a Profitable Exposure Management System." Reprinted from p. 188 of the June 17, 1977, issue of *Business International Money Report*, with the permission of Business International Corporation (New York).

American Motors (now a Chrysler subsidiary), which produces and sells cars only in the United States and uses only U.S. labor and materials. Because it buys and sells only in dollars, by U.S. accounting standards it has no balance-sheet exposure. However, its principal emphasis has been on the compact, economy-minded end of the auto market—the segment most subject to competition from less-expensive Korean, Japanese, Italian, and German imports. Dollar devaluations have certainly enhanced American Motors' competitive position or, at least, have slowed down its erosion, enabling the company to enjoy higher dollar profits than it would have in the absence of these currency changes. Appreciation of the dollar has had opposite effects.

10.3 IDENTIFYING ECONOMIC EXPOSURE

At this point it makes sense to illustrate some of the concepts just discussed by examining several firms to see in what ways they may be susceptible to exchange risk. The companies are Aspen Skiing Company, Petróleos Mexicanos, and Toyota Motor Company.

Aspen Skiing Company

Aspen owns and operates ski resorts in the Colorado Rockies, catering primarily to Americans. It buys all its supplies in dollars and uses only American labor and materials. All guests pay in dollars. Because it buys and sells only in dollars, by U.S. standards it has no accounting exposure. Yet, Aspen Skiing Company does face economic exposure because changes in the value of the dollar affect its competitive position. For example, the strong dollar in the early 1980s adversely affected the company because it led to bargains abroad that offered stiff competition for domestic resorts, including the Rocky Mountain ski areas.

> Aspen Skiing Company faces exchange risk because changes in the value of the dollar affect its competitive position.

Despite record snowfalls in the Rockies during the early 1980s, many Americans decided to ski in the European Alps instead. Although air fare to the Alps cost much more than a flight to Colorado, the difference between expenses on the ground made a European ski holiday less expensive. For example, in January 1984, American Express offered a basic one-week ski package in Aspen for $439 per person, including double-occupancy lodging, lift ticket and free rental car or bus transfer from Denver.[1] Throw in round-trip air fare between New York and Denver of $300 and the trip's cost totaled $739.

At the same time, skiers could spend a week in Chamonix in the French Alps for $234, including lodging, lift ticket, breakfast and a bus transfer from Geneva, Switzerland. Adding in round-trip air fare from New York of $579 brought the trip's cost to $813. The Alpine vacation became less expensive than the one in the Rockies when the cost of meals was included: an estimated $50 a day in Aspen versus $30 a day in Chamonix.

In effect, Aspen Skiing Company is operating in a global market for skiing or, more broadly, vacation services. As the dollar appreciates in real terms, both foreigners and Americans find less-expensive skiing and vacation alternatives outside the United States. In addition, even if California and other West Coast skiers find that high transportation costs continue to make it more expensive to ski in Europe than in the Rockies, they are not restricted to the American Rockies. They have the choice of skiing in the Canadian Rockies, where the skiing is fine and their dollars go further.

Conversely, a depreciating dollar makes Aspen Skiing Company more competitive and should increase its revenues and profits. In either event, the use of American products and labor means that its costs will not be significantly affected by exchange rate fluctuations.

[1]Report in *The Wall Street Journal,* January 17, 1984, p. 1

Petróleos Mexicanos

Petróleos Mexicanos, or Pemex, is the Mexican national oil company. It is the largest company in Mexico and ranked number 40 in the 1992 *Fortune Directory* of the biggest non-U.S. industrial companies. Most of its sales are overseas. Suppose Pemex borrows U.S. dollars. If the peso devalues, is Pemex a better or worse credit risk?

Petróleos Mexicanos is helped by a peso devaluation because its revenues are in dollars and costs are in pesos.

The instinctive response of most people is that peso devaluation makes Pemex a poorer credit risk. This response is wrong. Consider Pemex's revenues. Assume that it exports all its oil. Because oil is priced in dollars, Pemex's dollar revenues will remain the same following peso devaluation. Its dollar costs, however, will change. Most of its operating costs are denominated in pesos. These costs include labor, local supplies, services, and materials. Although the peso amount of these costs may go up somewhat, they will not rise to the extent of the devaluation of the peso. Hence, the dollar amount of peso costs will decline. Pemex also uses a variety of sophisticated equipment and services to aid in oil exploration, drilling, and production. Because these inputs are generally from foreign sources, their dollar costs are likely to be unaffected by peso devaluation. Inasmuch as some costs will fall in dollar terms and other costs will stay the same, the overall effect of peso devaluation is a decline in Pemex's dollar costs.

Since its dollar revenue will stay the same while the dollar amount of its costs will fall, the net effect on Pemex of a peso devaluation is to increase its dollar cash flow. Hence, it becomes a better credit risk in terms of its ability to service dollar debt.

Might this conclusion be reversed if it turns out that Pemex sells much of its oil domestically? Surprisingly, the answer is no if we add the further condition that the Mexican government doesn't impose oil price controls. Suppose the price of oil is $20 a barrel. If the initial peso exchange rate is Ps 1 = $0.04, that means that the price of oil in Mexico must be Ps 500 a barrel. Otherwise, there would be an arbitrage opportunity because oil transportation costs are a small fraction of the price of oil. If the peso now devalues to $0.02, the price of oil must rise to Ps 1,000. Consider what would happen if the price stayed at Ps 500. The dollar equivalent price would now be $10. But why would Pemex sell oil in Mexico for $10 a barrel when it could sell the same oil outside Mexico for $20 a barrel? It wouldn't do so unless there were price controls in Mexico and the government allocated a certain amount of oil to the Mexican market at this price. Hence, in the absence of government intervention, the peso price of oil must rise to Ps 1,000 and Pemex's dollars profits will rise whether it exports all or part of its oil.

This situation points out the important distinction between the currency of denomination and the currency of determination. The *currency of denomination* is the currency in which contracts are stated. For example, oil prices in Mexico are stated in pesos. However, although the currency of denomination for oil sales in Mexico is the peso, the peso price itself is determined by the dollar price of oil; that is, as the peso:dollar exchange rate changes, the peso price of oil changes to equate the dollar-equivalent price of oil in Mexico with the dollar price of oil in the world market. Thus, the *currency of determination* for Pemex's domestic oil sales is the U.S. dollar.

Toyota Motor Company

Toyota is the largest Japanese auto company and the fourth largest non-U.S. industrial firm in the world. Over half of its sales are overseas, primarily in the United States. If the yen appreciates, Toyota has the choice of keeping its yen price constant or its dollar price constant. If Toyota holds its yen price constant, the dollar price of its auto exports will rise and sales volume will decline. On the other hand, if Toyota decides to maintain its U.S. market share, it must hold its dollar price constant. In either case, its yen revenues will fall.

Even if Toyota decides to focus on the Japanese market, it will face the *flow-back effect*, as previously exported products flow back into the home market. Flow-back occurs because other Japanese firms find that a high yen makes it difficult to export their cars and so they emphasize Japanese sales as well. The result is increased domestic competition and lower profit margins on domestic sales.

Toyota's yen production costs will also be affected by yen appreciation. Steel, copper, aluminum, oil (from which plastics are made), and other materials that go into making a car are all imported. As the yen appreciates, the yen cost of these imported materials will decline. Yen costs of labor and domestic services, products, and equipment will likely stay the same. The net effect of lower yen costs for some inputs and constant yen costs for other inputs is a reduction in overall yen costs of production.

The net effect on profits of lower yen revenues and lower yen costs is an empirical question. This question can be answered by examining the profit consequences of yen appreciation. Here, the answer is unambiguous: Yen appreciation hurts Toyota; the reduction in its revenues more than offsets the reduction in its costs.

These three examples illustrate a progression of ideas. Aspen Skiing Company's revenues were affected by exchange rate changes, but its costs were largely unaffected. By contrast, Pemex's costs were affected by exchange rate changes, but not its revenues. Toyota had both its costs and its revenues affected by exchange rate changes. The process of examining these companies includes a systematic approach to identifying a company's exposure to exchange risk. Exhibit 10.5 summarizes this approach by presenting a series of questions that underlie the analysis of economic exposure.

Toyota Motors' yen revenues and yen costs will fall with yen appreciation.

10.4 CALCULATING ECONOMIC EXPOSURE

We will now work through a hypothetical, though comprehensive, example illustrating all the various aspects of exposure that have been discussed so far. This example emphasizes the quantitative, rather than qualitative, determination of economic exposure. It shows how critical the underlying assumptions are.

Exhibit 10.5 Key Questions to Ask That Help to Identify Exchange Risk

1. Where is the company selling?
   Domestic versus foreign sales breakdown
2. Who are the company's key competitors?
   Domestic versus foreign companies
3. How sensitive is demand to price?
   Price-sensitive demand versus price-insensitive demand
4. Where is the company producing?
   Domestic production versus foreign production
5. Where are the company's inputs coming from?
   Domestic inputs versus foreign inputs
6. How are the company's inputs or outputs priced?
   Priced in a world market or in a domestic market; the currency of determination as opposed to the currency of denomination

---

Calculating economic exposure depends critically on the assumptions as to the amounts and exchange rate sensitivities of future cash flows.

Spectrum Manufacturing AB is the wholly owned Swedish affiliate of a U.S. multinational industrial plastics firm. It manufactures patented sheet plastic in Sweden, with 60% of its output currently being sold in Sweden and the remaining 40% exported to other European countries. Spectrum uses only Swedish labor in its manufacturing process, but it use both local and foreign sources of raw material. The effective Swedish tax rate on corporate profits is 40%, and the annual depreciation charge on plant and equipment, in Swedish kronor (SKr), is SKr 900,000. In addition, Spectrum AB has outstanding SKr 3 million in debt, with interest payable at 10% annually.

Exhibit 10.6 presents Spectrum's projected sales, costs, after-tax income, and cash flow for the coming year, based on the current exchange rate of SKr 4 = $1. All sales are invoiced in kronor (singular, krona).

Spectrum's Accounting Exposure

Exhibit 10.7 shows Spectrum's balance sheet before and after an exchange rate change. To contrast the economic and accounting approaches to measuring exposure, the Swedish krona is assumed to devalue by 20%, from SKr 4 = $1 to SKr 5 = $1. The third column of Exhibit 10.7 shows that under the current rate method mandated by FASB-52, Spectrum will have a translation loss of $685,000. Use of the monetary/nonmonetary method leads to a much smaller reported loss of $50,000.

Spectrum's Economic Exposure

On the basis of current information, it is impossible to determine just what the economic impact of the krona devaluation will be. Therefore, three different scenarios have been constructed, with varying degrees of plausibility, and Spectrum's economic exposure has been calculated under each scenario. The three scenarios are

Exhibit 10.6 Summary of Projected Operations for Spectrum Manufacturing AB: Base Case

	Units (Hundred Thousands)	Unit Price (SKr)	Total
Domestic sales	6	20	SKr 12,000,000
Export sales	4	20	8,000,000
Total revenue			20,000,000
Total operating expeditures			10,800,000
Overhead expenses			3,500,000
Interest on krona debt @ 10%			300,000
Depreciation			900,000
Net profit before tax			SKr 4,500,000
Income tax @ 40%			1,800,000
Profit after tax			SKr 2,700,000
Add back depreciation			900,000
Net cash flow in kronor			SKr 3,600,000
Net cash flow in dollars (SKr 4 = $1)			$900,000

1. All variables remain the same.
2. Krona sales prices and all costs rise; volume remains the same.
3. There are partial increases in prices, costs, and volume.

Scenario 1: All variables remain the same. If all prices remain the same (in kronor) and sales volume doesn't change, then Spectrum's krona cash flow will stay at SKr 3,600,000. At the new exchange rate, this amount will equal $720,000 (3,600,000/5). Then the net loss in dollar operating cash flow in year one can be calculated as follows:

First-year cash flow (SKr 4 = $1)	$900,000
First-year cash flow (SKr 5 = $1)	720,000
Net loss from devaluation	$180,000

Moreover, this loss will continue until relative prices adjust. Part of this loss, however, will be offset by the $150,000 gain that will be realized when the SKr 3 million loan is repaid (3 million × 0.05).[2] If a three-year adjustment process is assumed and the krona loan will be repaid at the end of year three, then the present value of the economic loss from operations associated with the krona devaluation, using a 15% discount rate, equals $312,420:

---

[2]No Swedish taxes will be owed on this gain because SKr 3 million were borrowed and SKr 3 million were repaid. These tax effects are elaborated on in Chapters 13 and 19.

Exhibit 10.7 Impact of Krona Devaluation on Spectrum AB's Financial Statement Under FASB–52

	Kronor	U.S. Dollars Before Krona Devaluation (SKr 4 = $1)	U.S. Dollars After Krona Devaluation (SKr 5 = $1) Current Rate	Monetary/ Nonmonetary
Assets				
Cash	SKr 1,000,000	$ 250,000	$ 200,000	$ 200,000
Accounts receivable	5,000,000	1,250,000	1,000,000	1,000,000
Inventory	2,700,000	675,000	540,000	675,000
Net fixed assets	10,000,000	2,500,000	2,000,000	2,500,000
Total assets	SKr 18,700,000	$4,675,000	$3,740,000	$4,375,000
Liabilities				
Accounts payable	2,000,000	500,000	400,000	400,000
Long-term debt	3,000,000	750,000	600,000	600,000
Equity	13,700,000	3,425,000	2,740,000	3,375,000
Total liabilities plus equity	SKr 18,700,000	$4,675,000	$3,740,000	$4,375,000
Translation Gain (Loss)			$ (685,000)	$ (50,000)

Year	Postdevaluation Cash Flow (1)	–	Predevaluation Cash Flow (2)	=	Change in Cash Flow (3)	×	15% Present Value Factor (4)	=	Present Value (5)
1	$720,000		$900,000		–$180,000		0.870		–$156.600
2	720,000		900,000		– 180,000		0.756		– 136,080
3	870,000*		900,000		– 30,000		0.658		– 19,740
							Net loss		–$312,420

*Includes a gain of $150,000 on loan repayment.

This loss is primarily due to the inability to raise the sales price. The resulting constant krona profit margin translates into a 20% reduction in dollar profits. The economic loss of $312,420 contrasts with the accounting recognition of a $685,000 foreign exchange loss. In reality, of course, the prices, costs, volume, and input mix are unlikely to remain fixed. The discussion will now focus on the economic effects of some of these potential adjustments.

Scenario 2: Krona sales price and all costs rise; volume remains the same. It is assumed here that all costs and prices increase in proportion to the krona devaluation, but unit volume remains the same. However, the operating cash flow in kronor does not rise to the same extent because depreciation, which is based on historical cost, remains at SKr 900,000. As a potential offset, interest payments also hold steady at SKr 300,000. Working through the numbers in Exhibit 10.8 gives us an operating cash flow of $891,000.

Exhibit 10.8 Summary of Projected Operations for Spectrum Manufacturing AB: Scenario 2

	Units (Hundred Thousands)	Unit Price (SKr)	Total	
Domestic sales	6	25	SKr 15,000,000	
Export sales	4	25	10,000,000	
Total revenue				25,000,000
Total operating expeditures				13,500,000
Overhead expenses				4,375,000
Interest on krona debt @ 10%				300,000
Depreciation				T 900,000
Net profit before tax				SKr 5,925,000
Income tax @ 40%				2,370,000
Profit after tax				SKr 3,555,000
Add back depreciation				900,000
Net cash flow in kronor				SKr 4,455,000
Net cash flow in dollars (SKr 5 = $1)				$891,000

The $9,000 reduction in cash flow equals the decreased dollar value of the SKr 900,000 depreciation tax shield less the decreased dollar cost of paying the SKr 300,000 in interest. Before devaluation, the tax shield was worth $(900,000 \times 0.4)/4$ dollars, or $90,000. After devaluation, the dollar value of the tax shield declines to $(900,000 \times 0.4)/5$ dollars = $72,000, or a loss of $18,000 in cash flow. Similarly, the dollar cost of paying SKr 300,000 in interest declines by $15,000 to $60,000 (from $75,000). After tax, this decrease in interest expense equals $9,000. Adding the two figures (–$18,000 + $9,000) yields a net loss of $9,000 annually in operating cash flow.

The net economic gain over the coming three years, relative to predevaluation expectations, is $78,220.

Year	Postdevaluation Cash Flow (1)	–	Predevaluation Cash Flow (2)	=	Change in Cash Flow (3)	×	15% Present Value Factor (4)	=	Present Value (5)
1	$ 891,000		$900,000		–$9,000		0.870		–$7.830
2	891,000		900,000		– 9,000		0.756		– 6,800
3	1,041,000*		900,000		–141,000		0.658		92,780
							Net gain		$78,220

*Includes a gain of $150,000 on loan repayment.

Most of this gain in economic value comes from the gain on repayment of the krona loan.

Scenario 3: Partial increases in prices, costs, and volumes. In the most realistic situation, all variables will adjust somewhat. It is assumed here that the sales price at home rises by 10% to SKr 22, and the export price is raised to SKr 24—still providing a competitive advantage in dollar terms over foreign products. The result is a 20% increase in domestic sales and a 15% increase in export sales.

Local input prices are assumed to go up, but the dollar price of imported material stays at its predevaluation level. As a result of the change in relative cost, some substitutions are made between domestic and imported goods. The result is an increase in SKr unit cost of approximately 17%. Overhead expenses rise by only 10% because some components of this account, such as rent and local taxes, are fixed in value.

The net result of all these adjustments is an operating cash flow of $1,010,800, which is a gain of $110,800 over the predevaluation level of $900,000. This scenario is shown in Exhibit 10.9.

Over the next three years, cash flows and the firm's economic value will change as follows:

Exhibit 10.9 Summary of Projected Operations for Spectrum Manufacturing AB: Scenario 3

	Units (Hundred Thousands)	Unit Price (SKr)	Total
Domestic sales	7.2	22	SKr 15,840,000
Export sales	4.6	24	11,040,000
Total revenue			26,880,000
Total operating expeditures			14,906,000
Overhead expenses			3,850,000
Interest on krona debt @ 10%			300,000
Depreciation			900,000
Net profit before tax			SKr 6,924,000
Income tax @ 40%			2,769,000
Profit after tax			SKr 4,154,000
Add back depreciation			900,000
Net cash flow in kronor			SKr 5,054,000
Net cash flow in dollars (SKr 5 = $1)			$1,010,800

Year	Postdevaluation Cash Flow (1)	–	Predevaluation Cash Flow (2)	=	Change in Cash Flow (3)	×	15% Present Value Factor (4)	=	Present Value (5)
1	$1,010,800		$900,000		$110,800		0.870		$ 96.396
2	1,010,800		900,000		110,800		0.756		83,765
3	1,160,800*		900,000		260,800		0.658		171,606
							Net gain		$351,767

*Includes a gain of $150,000 on loan repayment.

Thus, under this scenario, the economic value of the firm will increase by $351,767. This gain reflects the increase in operating cash flow combined with the gain on loan repayment.

Case Analysis. The three preceding scenarios demonstrate the sensitivity of a firm's economic exposure to assumptions concerning its price elasticity of demand; its ability to adjust its mix of inputs as relative costs change; its pricing flexibility; subsequent local inflation; and its use of local-currency financing. Perhaps most important of all, this example makes clear the lack of any necessary relationship between accounting-derived measures of exchange gains or losses and the true impact of currency changes on a firm's economic value. The economic effects of this devaluation under the three alternative scenarios are summarized in Exhibit 10.10.

10.5 AN OPERATIONAL MEASURE OF EXCHANGE RISK

The preceding example demonstrates that determining a firm's true economic exposure is a daunting task, requiring a singular ability to forecast the amounts and exchange rate sensitivities of future cash flows. Most firms that follow the

Exhibit 10.10 Summary of Economic Exposure Impact of Krona Devaluation on Spectrum Manufacturing AB

Year	Forecast Change in Cash Flows		
	Scenario 1	Scenario 2	Scenario 3
1	–$180,000	–$ 9,000	$110,800
2	– 180,000	– 9,000	110,800
3	– 30,000*	141,000*	260,800*
Change in present value (15% discount factor)	–$312,420	$ 78,220	$351,767

*Includes a gain of $150,000 on loan repayment

economic approach to managing exposure, therefore, must settle for a measure of their economic exposure and the resulting exchange risk that is often supported by nothing more substantial than intuition.

This section presents a workable approach to determine a firm's true economic exposure and susceptibility to exchange risk. The approach avoids the problem of using seat-of-the-pants estimates in performing the necessary calculations.[3] The technique is straightforward to apply; and it requires only historical data from the firm's actual operations or, in the case of a *de novo* venture, data from a comparable business.

Regression analysis can help determine a company's economic exposure.

This approach is based on the following operational definition of the exchange risk faced by a parent or one of its foreign affiliates: *A company faces exchange risk to the extent that variations in the dollar value of the unit's cash flows are correlated with variations in the nominal exchange rate.* This correlation is precisely what a *regression analysis* seeks to establish. A simple and straightforward way to implement this definition, therefore, is to regress actual cash flows from past periods, converted into their dollar values, on the average exchange rate during the corresponding period. Specifically, this approach involves running the following regression:[4]

$$CF_t = a + \beta EXCH_t + u_t \tag{10.1}$$

where CF_t = the dollar value of total affiliate (parent) cash flows in period t
   $EXCH_t$ = the average nominal exchange rate (dollar value of one unit of the foreign currency) during period t
   u = a random error term with mean 0

The output from such a regression includes three key parameters: (1) the foreign exchange beta (β) coefficient, which measures the sensitivity of dollar cash flows to exchange rate changes; (2) the t-statistic, which measures the statistical significance of the beta coefficient; and (3) the R^2, which measures the fraction of cash flow variability explained by variation in the exchange rate. The higher the beta coefficient, the greater the impact of a given exchange rate change on the dollar value of cash flows. Conversely, the lower the beta coefficient, the less exposed the firm is to exchange rate changes. A larger t-statistic means a higher level of confidence in the value of the beta coefficient.

However, even if a firm has a large and statistically significant beta coefficient and thus faces real exchange risk, this situation does not necessarily mean that currency fluctuations are an important determinant of overall firm risk. What really matters is the percentage of total corporate cash-flow variability that is due to these currency fluctuations. Thus, the most important parameter, in terms of its impact on the firm's exposure management policy, is the regression's R^2. For

[3]This section is based on C. Kent Garner and Alan C. Shapiro, "A Practical Method of Assessing Foreign Exchange Risk," *Midland Corporate Finance Journal*, Fall 1984, pp. 6–17.

[4]The application of the regression approach to measuring exposure to currency risk is illustrated in Garner and Shapiro, "A Practical method of Assessing Foreign Exchange Risk;" and in Michael Adler and Bernard Dumas, "Exposure to Currency Risk: Definition and Measurement," *Financial Management*, Summer 1984, pp. 41–50.

example, if exchange rate changes explain only 1% of total cash-flow variability, the firm should not devote much in the way of resources to foreign exchange risk management, even if the beta coefficient is large and statistically significant.

The higher the percentage of cash-flow variability explained by exchange rate changes, the more exchange risk the company has.

Limitations

The validity of this method is clearly dependent on the sensitivity of future cash flows to exchange rate changes being similar to their historical sensitivity. In the absence of additional information, this assumption seems to be reasonable. But the firm may have reason to modify the implementation of this method. For example, the nominal foreign-currency tax shield provided by a foreign affiliate's depreciation is fully exposed to the effects of currency fluctuations. If the amount of depreciation in the future is expected to differ significantly from its historical values, then the depreciation tax shield should be removed from the cash flows used in the regression analysis and treated separately. Similarly, if the firm has recently entered into a large purchase or sales contract fixed in terms of the foreign currency, it might decide to consider the resulting transaction exposure apart from its operating exposure.

10.6 ILLUSTRATION: LAKER AIRWAYS

The crash of Sir Freddie Laker's Skytrain had little to do with the failure of its navigational equipment or its landing gear; indeed, it can be largely attributed to misguided management decisions. Laker's management erred in selecting the financing mode for the acquisition of the aircraft fleet that would accommodate the booming transatlantic business spearheaded by Sir Freddie's sound concept of a "no-frill, low-fare, stand-by" air travel package.

In 1981, Laker was a highly leveraged firm with a debt of more than $400 million. The debt resulted from the mortgage financing provided by the U.S. Eximbank and the U.S. aircraft manufacturer McDonnell Douglas. As most major airlines do, Laker Airways incurred three major categories of cost: (1) fuel, typically paid for in U.S. dollars (even though the United Kingdom is more than self-sufficient in oil); (2) operating costs incurred in sterling (administrative expenses and salaries), but with a nonnegligible dollar cost component (advertising and booking in the United States); and (3) financing costs from the purchase of U.S.-made aircraft, denominated in dollars. Revenues accruing from the sale of transatlantic airfare were about evenly divided between sterling and dollars. The dollar fares, however, were based on the assumption of a rate of $2.25 to the pound. The imbalance in the currency denomination of cash flows (dollar-denominated cash outflows far exceeding dollar-denominated cash inflows) left Laker vulnerable to a sterling depreciation below the budgeted exchange rate of £1 = $2.25. Indeed, the dramatic plunge of the exchange rate to £1 = $1.60 over the 1981–1982 period brought Laker Airways to default.

Could Laker have hedged its "natural" dollar liability exposure? The first option of indexing the sale of sterling airfare to the day-to-day exchange rate was not a viable alternative. Advertisements, based on a set sterling fare, would have had to be revised almost daily and would have discouraged the "price-elastic, budget-conscious" clientele of the company. Another possibility would have been for Laker to direct more of its marketing efforts toward American travelers, thereby giving it a more diversified demand structure. When the pound devalued against the dollar, fewer British tourists would vacation in the United States, but more Americans would travel to Britain. Laker could also have financed the acquisition of DC 10 aircraft in sterling rather than in dollars, thereby more closely matching its pound outflows with its pound inflows. This example points out that the currency denomination of debt financing can ill afford to be determined apart from the currency risk faced by the firm's total business portfolio.

10.7 SUMMARY AND CONCLUSIONS

In this chapter, we have examined the concept of exposure to exchange rate changes from the perspective of the economist. We have seen that the focus of the accounting profession on the balance-sheet impact of currency changes has led accountants to ignore the more important effect that these changes may have on future cash flows. Moreover, it is now apparent that currency risk and inflation risk are intertwined—that through the theory of purchasing power parity, these risks are, to a large extent, offsetting. Hence, for firms incurring costs and selling products in foreign countries, the net effect of currency appreciations and depreciations may be less important in the long run.

One implication of this close association between inflation and currency fluctuations is that to measure exposure properly, we must focus on inflation-adjusted, or real, exchange rates instead of on nominal, or actual, exchange rates. Therefore, economic exposure has been defined as the extent to which the value of a firm is affected by currency fluctuations, inclusive of price level changes. Thus, any accounting measure that focuses on the firm's past activities and decisions, as reflected in its current balance-sheet accounts, is likely to be misleading.

Although exchange risk is conceptually easy to identify, it is difficult in practice to determine what the actual economic impact of a currency change will be. For a given firm, this impact depends on a great number of variables including the location of its major markets and competitors, supply and demand elasticities, substitutability of inputs, and offsetting inflation. We did see a technique, however, that avoids many of these problems by using regression analysis to determine an operation's exposure to exchange risk. However, its applicability is limited by the assumption that the past is representative of the future.

QUESTIONS

1.   Please answer the following questions.
    a. Define exposure, differentiating between accounting and economic exposure. What role does inflation play?

b. Describe at least three circumstances under which economic exposure is likely to exist.

c. Of what relevance are the international Fisher effect and purchasing power parity to your answers to parts a and b?

d. What is exchange risk, as distinct from exposure?

2. Under what circumstances might multinational firms be less subject to exchange risk than purely domestic firms in the same industry?

3. Should Laker have financed its purchase of DC 10 aircraft by borrowing sterling from a British bank rather than using the dollar-denominated financing supplied by McDonnell Douglas and the Eximbank? Explain.

4. Many business people and the business press are convinced that the devalued dollar offers a significant advantage to foreign bidders for American companies and real estate. Comment on this position.

5. The sharp decline of the U.S. dollar since 1985 has significantly improved the profitability of U.S. firms both at home and abroad.

a. In what sense is this profit improvement false prosperity?

b. How would you incorporate the decline in the dollar in evaluating management performance? In making investment decisions?

6. E & J Gallo is the largest vintner in the United States. It gets its grapes in California (some of which it grows itself) and sells its wines throughout the United States. Does Gallo face currency risk? Why and how?

7. Chrysler Motors exports vans to Europe in competition with the Japanese. Similarly, Digital Equipment exports computers to Europe. However, its biggest competitors are all American companies—IBM, Hewlett-Packard, and Tandem. Assuming all else is equal, which of these companies—Chrysler or Digital—is likely to benefit more from a weak dollar? Explain.

8. Saint-Gobain, a French firm, and Pilkington PLC, a British firm, are arch rivals in the European flat-glass business. Following Britain's exit from the ERM in September 1992, the pound fell by 15% against the franc.

a. What was the likely impact on Saint-Gobain's profitability of the pound devaluation?

b. What was the likely impact on Pilkington's profitability of the pound devaluation?

PROBLEMS

Problems 1 and 2 are based on the Spectrum Manufacturing AB case (scenarios 1, 2, and 3) presented in Section 10.4. Calculate Spectrum's economic exposure under the following new scenarios:

1. *Scenario 4: Sales and import prices rise; domestic materials substituted for imported materials; other variables remain the same.*

a. Spectrum is able to raise the krona price of its sheet plastic to SKr 25 to exactly offset the effect of the devaluation.

b. Because of domestic materials substitutions, krona operating expenditures rise by only 4% relative to the base case.

c. Physical sales volume stays at its predevaluation level.

2. *Scenario 5: Volume and import prices rise; other variables remain the same.*

   a. The krona sales price is held constant at SKr 20.

   b. Unit sales volume rises by 50%, both domestically and abroad, owing to the lower dollar price.

   c. Because krona costs of local labor and materials stay the same, krona unit operating expenditures rise by only 5.6%.

   d. The firm's various overhead expenses do not change.

3. Hilton International is considering investing in a new Swiss hotel. The required initial investment is $1.5 million (or SFr 2.38 million at the current exchange rate of $0.63 = SFr 1). Profits for the first 10 years will be reinvested, at which time Hilton will sell out to its partner. Based on projected earnings, Hilton's share of this hotel will be worth SFr 3.88 million in 10 years.

   a. What factors are relevant in evaluating this investment?

   b. How will fluctuations in the value of the Swiss franc affect this investment?

   c. How would you forecast the $:SFr exchange rate 10 years ahead?

4. A proposed foreign investment involves a plant whose entire output of 1 million units per annum is to be exported. With a selling price of $10 per unit, the yearly revenue from this investment equals $10 million. At the present rate of exchange, dollar costs of local production equal $6 per unit. A 10% devaluation is expected to lower unit costs by $0.30, while a 15% devaluation will reduce these costs by an additional $0.15. Suppose a devaluation of either 10% or 15% is likely, with respective probabilities of 0.4 and 0.2 (the probability of no currency change is 0.4). Depreciation at the current exchange rate equals $1 million annually, while the local tax rate is 40%.

   a. What will annual dollar cash flows be if no devaluation occurs?

   b. Given the currency scenario described above, what is the expected value of annual after-tax dollar cash flows assuming no repatriation of profits to the United States?

5. On January 1, the U.S. dollar:Japanese yen exchange rate is $1 = ¥250. During the year, U.S. inflation is 4% and Japanese inflation is 2%. On December 31, the exchange rate is $1 = ¥235. What are the likely competitive effects of this exchange rate change on Caterpillar Inc., the American earth-moving equipment manufacturer, whose toughest competitor is Japan's Komatsu?

6. Mucho Macho is the leading beer in Patagonia, with a 65% share of the market. Because of trade barriers, it faces essentially no import competition. Exports account for less than 2% of sales. Although some of its raw material is bought overseas, the large majority of the value added is provided by locally supplied goods and services. Over the past five years, Patagonian prices have risen by 300%, while U.S. prices have risen by about 10%. During this time period, the value of the Patagonian peso has dropped from P 1 = $1.00 to P 1 = $0.50.

   a. What has happened to the real value of the peso over the past five years? Has it gone up or down? A little or a lot?

   b. What has the high inflation over the past five years likely done to Mucho Macho's peso profits? Has it moved profits up or down? A lot or a little? Explain.

   c. Based on your answer to part a, what has been the likely effect of the change in the peso's real value on Mucho Macho's peso profits converted into dollars? Have dollar-equivalent profits gone up or down? A lot or a little? Explain.

   d. Mucho Macho has applied for a dollar loan to finance its expansion. Were you to look solely at its past financial statements in judging its creditworthiness, what would be your likely response to Mucho Macho's dollar loan request?

e. What foreign exchange risk would such a dollar loan face? Explain.

7. In 1990, General Electric acquired Tungsram Ltd., a Hungarian light bulb manufacturer. Hungary's inflation rate was 28% in 1990 and 35% in 1991, while the forint (Hungary's currency) was devalued 5% and 15%, respectively, during those years. Corresponding inflation for the U.S. was 6.1% in 1990 and 3.1% in 1991.

a. What has happened to the competitiveness of GE's Hungarian operations during 1990 and 1991? Explain.

b. In early 1992, GE announced that it would cut back its capital investment in Tungsram. What might have been the purpose of GE's publicly announced cutback?

8. You are asked to lend money for a major commercial real estate development in the town of Calexico, which is on the California side of the Mexican border. There is some talk about a further devaluation of the Mexican peso. What information do you need to assess the creditworthiness of this project?

9. About two-thirds of all California almonds are exported. The ups and downs of the U.S. dollar, therefore, cause headaches for almond growers. To avoid these problems, a grower decides to concentrate on domestic sales. Does that grower bear exchange risk? Why and how?

10. Aldridge Washmon Co. is one of the largest distributors of heavy farming equipment in Brownsville, Texas, located on the border with Mexico. The time is late 1981. Sales have increased dramatically over the past two years, and Aldridge is requesting an expansion of its credit line. What information would you as a banker need before you accede to its request?

11. Assess the likely consequences of a declining dollar on Fluor Corporation, the international construction-engineering contractor based in Irvine, California. Most of Fluor's value-added involves project design and management, while most of its costs are for U.S. labor in design, engineering, and construction-management services.

12. The European chemical industry pays for an estimated 79% of its oil-based feedstock in dollars. Thus, its costs are declining sharply because of the drop in the price of oil combined with the sharp decline in the value of the dollar. What is the likely impact of the dollar's decline on the European chemical industry's profits? Will it now be more competitive relative to the American chemical industry?

13. Cooper Industries is a maker of compressors, pneumatic tools, and electrical equipment. It doesn't face much foreign competition in the United States, and exports account for only 7% of its sales. Does it face exchange risk?

14. The Edmonton Oilers (Canada) of the National Hockey League are two-time defending Stanley Cup champions. (The Stanley Cup playoff is hockey's equivalent of football's Super Bowl or baseball's World Series.) As is true of all NHL teams, most of the Oilers' players are Canadian. How are the Oilers affected by changes in the Canadian-dollar/U.S.-dollar exchange rate?

15. South Korean companies such as Goldstar, Samsung, and Daewoo have captured more than 10% of the U.S. color TV market with their small, low-priced TV sets. They are also becoming more significant exporters of videocassette recorders and small microwave ovens. What currency risk do these firms face?

16. Thomasville Plastics Corp. has contracted to buy $1.1 million worth of Japanese plastic-injection molding machines. The contract price is set in dollars. Does Thomasville bear any currency risk associated with this purchase? Explain.

BIBLIOGRAPHY

Adler, Michael, and Bernard Dumas. "Exposure to Currency Risk: Definition and Measurement." *Financial Management*, Summer 1984, pp. 41–50.

Cornell, Bradford, and Alan C. Shapiro. "Managing Foreign Exchange Risks." *Midland Corporate Finance Journal*, Fall 1983, pp. 16–31.

Eaker, Mark R. "The Numeraire Problem and Foreign Exchange Risk." *Journal of Finance*, May 1981, pp. 419–426.

Garner, C. Kent, and Alan C. Shapiro. "A Practical Method of Assessing Foreign Exchange Risk." *Midland Corporate Finance Journal*, Fall 1984, pp. 6–17.

Giddy, Ian H. "Exchange Risk: Whose View?" *Financial Management*, Summer 1977, pp. 23–33.

Lessard, Donald R., and John B. Lightstone. "Volatile Exchange Rates Can Put Operations at Risk." *Harvard Business Review*, July-August 1986, pp. 107–114.

Shapiro, Alan C. "Exchange Rate Changes, Inflation, and the Value of the Multinational Corporation." *Journal of Finance*, May 1975, pp. 485–502.

Managing Economic Exposure

11

We concluded there's enough risk in the car business without trying to get rich in foreign exchange; so our policy is essentially defensive.

Executive at Ford Motor Co.

CHAPTER LEARNING OBJECTIVES

- To identify the basic considerations that enter into the design of a strategy for managing operating exposure
- To describe the marketing, production, and financial strategies that are appropriate for coping with the economic consequences of exchange rate changes
- To explain how companies can develop contingency plans to cope with exchange risk and the consequences of their ability to rapidly respond to currency changes
- To describe an approach that companies can use to integrate currency considerations into the general management process
- To identify the role of the financial executive in facilitating the operation of an integrated exchange risk management program

The explosive rise of the dollar's value that began in 1981 cut deeply into the ability of American manufacturers to export their products, even as it gave a welcome boost to the U.S. sales of foreign companies. While still paying attention to the short-term balance sheet effects of the strong dollar, most firms responded to its economic consequences by making the longer-term operating adjustments described in the headline above. These firms are now well positioned to take advantage of the stunning reversal of the dollar's fortunes that began in 1985.

Based on these and similar experiences, this chapter discusses the basic considerations that go into the design of a strategy for managing foreign exchange risk, along with the marketing, production, and financial management strategies that are appropriate for coping with the economic consequences of exchange rate changes. Its basic message is straightforward: Since currency risk affects all facets of a company's operations, it should not be the concern of financial managers alone. Operating managers, in particular, should develop marketing and production initiatives that help to ensure profitability over the long run. They should also

253

devise anticipatory or proactive, rather than reactive, strategic alternatives in order to gain competitive leverage internationally.

The focus on the real (economic) effects of currency changes and how to cope with the associated risks suggests that a sensible strategy for exchange risk management is one that is designed to protect the dollar (HC) earning power of the company as a whole. But whereas firms can easily hedge exposures based on projected foreign currency cash flows, *competitive exposures*—those arising from competition with firms based in other currencies—are longer-term, harder to quantify, and cannot be dealt with solely through financial hedging techniques. Rather, they require making the longer-term operating adjustments that are described in this chapter.

11.1 AN OVERVIEW OF OPERATING EXPOSURE MANAGEMENT

In order for a currency depreciation or appreciation to significantly affect a firm's value, it must lead to changes in the relative prices either of the firm's inputs or of the products bought or sold in various countries. The impact of these currency-induced relative price changes on corporate revenues and costs depends on the extent of the firm's commitment to international business, its competitive environment, and its degree of operational flexibility.

Companies can manage their operating exposure by altering their marketing and production policies.

To the extent that exchange rate changes do bring about relative price changes, the firm's competitive situation will be altered. As a result, management may wish to adjust its production process or its marketing mix to accommodate the new set of relative prices.

By making the necessary marketing and production revisions, companies can either counteract the harmful effects of, or capitalize on the opportunities presented by, a currency appreciation or depreciation. We turn again here to the concept of the real exchange rate (discussed in Chapter 7 and elaborated on in Chapter 10). The distinction between the nominal and the real exchange rates has important implications for those marketing and production decisions that bear on exchange risk. As we saw in Chapter 10, nominal currency changes that are fully offset by differential inflation do not entail a material degree of real exchange risk for a firm unless that firm has major contractual agreements in the foreign currency. A real exchange rate change, however, can strongly affect the competitive positions of local firms and their foreign competitors.

The following are some of the proactive marketing and production strategies that a firm can pursue in response to anticipated or actual real exchange rate changes.

Marketing Initiatives	*Production Initiatives*
Market selection	Product sourcing
Product strategy	Input mix
Pricing strategy	Plant location
Promotional strategy	Raising productivity

The appropriate response to an anticipated or actual real exchange rate change depends crucially on the length of time that real change is expected to persist. For example, following a real home currency appreciation, the exporter has to decide whether, and how much, to raise its foreign currency prices. If the change were expected to be temporary and if regaining market share would be expensive, the exporter would probably prefer to maintain its foreign currency prices at existing levels. Although this response would mean a temporary reduction in unit profitability, the alternative—raising prices now and reducing them later when the real exchange rate declined—could be even more costly. A longer-lasting change in the real exchange rate, however, would probably lead the firm to raise its foreign currency prices, at the expense of losing some export sales. Assuming a still more permanent shift, management might choose to build production facilities overseas. Alternatively, if the cost of regaining market share is sufficiently great, the firm can hold foreign currency prices constant and count on shifting production overseas to preserve its longer-term profitability.

> The appropriate marketing and production responses to a currency change depend on how long that change is expected to persist.

These considerations are illustrated by the experience of Millipore Corp., a Bedford, Massachusetts, maker of industrial equipment for domestic and foreign companies. Confronted by the strong dollar, Millipore decided to cut prices in dollar terms on some products and hold back increases on others to maintain its market share against foreign competition. Although earnings were damaged in the short run, Millipore's management decided that it would be more expensive in the long run to regain market share. To cope with the pressure on its profit margins, Millipore opened a plant in Japan and expanded another one in France.

In general, real exchange rate movements that narrow the gap between the current rate and the equilibrium rate are likely to be longer lasting than are those that widen the gap. Neither, however, will be permanent. Rather, in a world without an anchor for currency values, there will be a sequence of equilibrium rates, each of which has its own implications for marketing and production strategies.

11.2 MARKETING MANAGEMENT OF EXCHANGE RISK

The design of a firm's marketing strategy under conditions of home currency (HC) fluctuation presents considerable opportunity for gaining competitive leverage.[1] Thus one of the international marketing manager's tasks should be to identify the likely effects of a currency change and then act on them by adjusting pricing and product policies.

Market Selection

Major strategic considerations for an exporter are the markets in which to sell—that is, *market selection*—and the relative marketing support to devote to each market. As a result of the strong dollar, for example, some discouraged U.S. firms

[1]This section is based on Alan C. Shapiro and Thomas S. Robertson, "Managing Foreign Exchange Risks: The Role of Market Strategy," working paper, The Wharton School, University of Pennsylvania, 1976.

The international marketing manager should identify the likely effects of a currency change and then adjust pricing and product policies accordingly.

pulled out of markets that foreign competition made unprofitable. From the perspective of foreign companies, however, the strong U.S. dollar was a golden opportunity to gain market share at the expense of their U.S. rivals. Japanese and European companies also used their dollar cost advantage to carve out market share against American competitors in third markets. The subsequent drop in the dollar helped U.S. firms turn the tables on their foreign competitors, both at home and abroad.

It is also necessary to consider the issue of *market segmentation* within individual countries. A firm that sells differentiated products to more affluent customers may not be harmed as much by a foreign currency devaluation as will a mass marketer. On the other hand, following a depreciation of the home currency, a firm that sells primarily to upper-income groups may find it is now able to penetrate mass markets abroad.

ILLUSTRATION: U.S. Textile Mills Cope with Currency Risk

Thanks to mammoth modernization efforts, the productivity of U.S. textile mills is now the highest in the world. Nevertheless, although American textile manufacturers are currently on an equal footing with those of Italy and Japan, their costs are 30% to 40% higher for products like lightweight shirting than costs in the Latin American and East Asian newly industrialized countries. Thus, the industry is concentrating on sophisticated materials like industrial fabrics and on goods such as sheets and towels that require little direct labor.

American producers are also competing by developing a service edge in the domestic market. For example, the industry developed a computerized inventory management and ordering program, called Quick Response, that provides close coordination between textile mills, apparel manufacturers, and retailers. The system cuts in half the time between a fabric order and delivery of the garment to a retailer and gives all the parties better information for planning, thereby placing foreign manufacturers at a competitive disadvantage. In response, Japanese companies—and even some Korean ones—are looking to set up U.S. factories.

Market selection and market segmentation provide the basic parameters within which a company may adjust its marketing mix over time. In the short term, however, neither of these two basic strategic choices can be altered in reaction to actual or anticipated currency changes. Instead, the firm must select certain tactical responses such as adjustments of pricing, promotional, and credit policies. In the long run, if the real exchange rate change persists, the firm will have to revise its marketing strategy.

Pricing Strategy

Two key issues that must be addressed when developing a *pricing strategy* in the face of currency volatility are whether to emphasize market share or profit margin and how frequently to adjust prices.

Market Share Versus Profit Margin. In the wake of a rising dollar, a U.S. firm selling overseas or competing at home against foreign imports faces a Hobson's choice: Does it keep its dollar price constant to preserve its profit margin and, thereby, lose sales volume, or does it cut its dollar price to maintain market share and, thereby, suffer a reduced profit margin? Conversely, does the firm use a weaker dollar to regain ground lost to foreign competitors, or does it use the weak dollar to raise prices and recoup losses incurred from the strong dollar?

To begin the analysis, a firm selling overseas should follow the standard economic proposition of setting the price that maximizes dollar profits (by equating marginal revenues and marginal costs). In making this determination, however, profits should be translated using the forward exchange rate that reflects the true expected dollar value of the receipts upon collection.

Following appreciation of the dollar, which is equivalent to a foreign currency (FC) depreciation, a firm selling overseas should consider opportunities to increase the FC prices of its products. The problem, of course, is that local producers now will have a competitive cost advantage, limiting an exporter's ability to recoup dollar profits by raising FC selling prices.

At best, therefore, an exporter will be able to raise its product prices by the extent of the FC devaluation. For example, suppose Avon is selling cosmetics in England priced at £2.00 when the exchange rate is £1 = $1.80. This gives Avon revenue of $3.60 per unit. If the pound devalues to £1 = $1.50, Avon's revenue will fall to $3.00, unless it can raise its selling price to £2.40 (2.40 × 1.5 = 3.60). At worst, in an extremely competitive situation, the exporter will be forced to absorb a reduction in home currency revenues equal to the percentage decline in the value of the local currency. For example, if Avon can't raise its pound price, its new dollar price of $3.00 represents a 16.7% decline in revenue, the same percentage decline as the drop in the value of the pound [(1.80 − 1.50)/1.80].

In the most likely case, foreign currency prices can be raised somewhat, and the exporter will make up the difference through a lower profit margin on its foreign sales.

Under conditions of dollar depreciation, it follows that U.S. exports will gain a competitive price advantage on the world market. An exporter now has the option of increasing unit profitability—that is, *price skimming*—or expanding its market share—*penetration pricing*. The decision is influenced by such factors as whether this change is likely to persist, economies of scale, the cost structure of expanding output, consumer price sensitivity, and the likelihood of attracting competition if high unit profitability is obvious.

The greater the *price elasticity of demand*—the change in demand for a given change in price—the greater the incentive to hold down price and thereby expand sales and revenues. Similarly, if significant *economies of scale* exist, it will generally be worthwhile to hold down price, expand demand, and thereby lower unit production costs. The reverse is true if economies of scale are nonexistent or if price elasticity is low.

Historically, many of the exports of U.S. multinationals appear to have fit the latter category (low price elasticity of demand) because they were technologically innovative or differentiated, often without close substitutes. Thus, there was a

An MNC must decide whether to go for market share or profit margin when coping with currency movements.

The higher the price elasticity of demand for its products, the more currency risk an MNC faces.

pronounced tendency for U.S. firms not to decrease prices after the real dollar devaluations of the 1970s.

Similarly, following dollar appreciation in the early 1980s, European and Japanese automakers were able to keep the dollar prices up on their car exports to the United States. European cars figure largely in the luxury car market, which is fairly insensitive to price swings. Import quotas enabled the Japanese car companies to avoid the price cutting they find necessary in their highly competitive home market. This factor, combined with the strong dollar, resulted in the major Japanese automakers earning about 80% of their 1984 worldwide profits in the United States.

By the late 1980s, however, the United States was no longer the across-the-board leader in the development and application of new technology to manufactured goods. As the U.S. technological edge has eroded, more American companies have faced competition from companies in other industrial nations. Absent other strategies to reduce costs or the price sensitivity of demand, these American firms have become more subject to exchange risk.

In general, firms dealing in commodities, such as table wines, face more exchange risk than those selling differentiated products, such as Mercedes Benzes. For example, when French winemakers refused to cut their franc prices as the dollar declined, French table wine exports to the United States dropped about 27% in 1987.

In deciding whether to raise prices following a foreign currency devaluation, companies must consider not just sales that will be lost today, but also the likelihood of losing future sales as well. The reason is that once they build market share, foreign firms are unlikely to pull back. For example, foreign capital goods manufacturers used the period when they had a price advantage to build strong U.S. distribution and service networks. U.S. firms that hadn't previously bought foreign-made equipment became loyal customers. When the dollar fell, foreign firms opened U.S. plants to supply their distribution systems and hold onto their customers.

The same is true in many other markets as well: *A customer who is lost may be lost forever.* Americans who discover California wines may not switch back to French wines even after a franc devaluation. Similarly, in the auto business, a customer who is satisfied with a foreign model may stick with that brand for a long time.

Frequency of Price Adjustments. Firms in international competition differ in their ability and willingness to adjust prices in response to exchange rate changes. Some firms constantly adjust their prices for exchange rate changes. However, other companies feel that stable prices are a key ingredient in maintaining their customer base. For example, customers who have invested in machinery or other assets that operate best with supplies from the selling firm may value a contract that is fixed in both price and quantity. Similarly, the company may try to shield risk-averse customers by offering them prices fixed in their local currency for a certain period of time.

As the U.S. technological lead has eroded, American companies have become more subject to exchange risk.

MNCs often shield customers from exchange rate changes by offering them prices fixed in their local currency for a certain period of time.

It is important also not to neglect the effect of frequent price changes on the exporter's distributors, who must constantly adjust their margins to conform to the prices they pay. A number of firms now have different list prices for domestic and foreign customers in order to shield their foreign customers—especially those who sell through catalogues—from continual revisions of overseas prices.

Turning now to domestic pricing after devaluation, a domestic firm facing strong import competition may have much greater latitude in pricing. It then has the choice of potentially raising prices consistent with import price increases or of holding prices constant in order to improve market share. Again, the strategy depends on such variables as economies of scale and *consumer price sensitivity*.

In early 1978, for instance, General Motors and Ford took advantage of price increases on competitive foreign autos to raise prices on their Chevette and Pinto models. The prices of those small cars had previously been held down, and even reduced, in an attempt to combat the growing market share of West German and Japanese imports. However, the declining value of the U.S. dollar relative to the Deutsche mark and yen led the West German and Japanese automakers to raise their dollar prices. The price increases by the U.S. manufacturers, which were less than the sharp rise in import prices, improved profit margins and kept U.S. cars competitive with their foreign rivals.

Promotional Strategy

Promotional strategy should similarly take into account anticipated exchange rate changes. A key issue in any marketing program is the size of the promotional budget for advertising, personal selling, and merchandising. Promotional decisions should explicitly build in exchange rates, especially in allocating budgets among countries. The appreciation of the U.S. dollar in the early 1980s illustrates these promotional considerations. European countries wooed U.S. skiers from the Rocky Mountains with campaigns capitalizing on their lower costs and comparable Alpine skiing.

A firm exporting its products after a domestic devaluation may well find that the return per dollar expenditure on advertising or selling is increased because of the product's improved price positioning. A foreign currency devaluation, on the other hand, is likely to reduce the return on marketing expenditures and may require a more fundamental shift in the firm's product policy.

Product Strategy

Companies often respond to exchange risk by altering their *product strategy*, which deals with such areas as new-product introduction, product line decisions, and product innovation. One way to cope with exchange rate fluctuations is to change the timing of the introduction of new products. For example, because of the competitive price advantage, the period after a home currency depreciation may be the ideal time to develop a brand franchise. Societe Claude Havrey, a French maker of women's clothes, began its U.S. sales push in 1984, after a significant strengthening of the dollar against the French franc. According to the export sales manager, "If the dollar were weak, we might have waited a while

Currency movements may affect the timing of new product introductions.

before starting. You have to choose the right time to start—the hard part is implanting yourself in the foreign market."[2] The strong dollar enabled the firm to price its clothes competitively in the United States.

Exchange rate fluctuations also affect product line decisions. Following home currency devaluation, a firm will potentially be able to expand its product line and cover a wider spectrum of consumers both at home and abroad. Conversely, following appreciation of the home currency, a firm may have to reorient its product line and target it to a higher-income, more quality conscious, less price sensitive constituency. Volkswagen, for example, achieved its export prominence on the basis of low-priced, stripped-down, low-maintenance cars. The appreciation of the Deutsche mark in the early 1970s, however, effectively ended VW's ability to compete primarily on the basis of price. The company lost over $310 million in 1974 alone attempting to maintain its market share by lowering DM prices. To compete in the long run, Volkswagen was forced to revise its product line and sell relatively high priced cars to middle-income consumers, from an extended product line, on the basis of quality and styling rather than cost.

The equivalent strategy for firms selling to the industrial, rather than consumer, market and confronting a strong home currency is *product innovation*, financed by an expanded research-and-development (R&D) budget. Kollmorgen Corp., a Connecticut-based electronic components company, responded to the strong dollar in part by increasing its R&D budget by 40%. According to Kollmorgen's chairman, Robert Swiggett, "We're not counting on being able to increase foreign sales very substantially unless we can keep introducing new product lines. That Bunsen burner is burning an awful lot brighter these days."[3]

11.3 PRODUCTION MANAGEMENT OF EXCHANGE RISK

MNCs can cope with operating exposure through global sourcing and shifting production locations.

The adjustments discussed so far involve attempts to alter the dollar value of foreign currency revenues. But sometimes exchange rates move so much that pricing or other marketing strategies can't save the product. This was the case for U.S. firms in the early 1980s and for Japanese firms in the late 1980s. Firms facing this situation must either drop uncompetitive products or cut their costs.

Product sourcing and *plant location* are the principal variables that companies manipulate to manage competitive risks that can't be dealt with through marketing changes alone. Consider, for example, the possible responses of U.S. firms to a strong dollar. The basic strategy would involve shifting the firm's manufacturing base overseas, but this can be accomplished in more than one way.

Input Mix

Outright additions to facilities overseas naturally accomplish a manufacturing shift. A more flexible solution is to change the *input mix* by purchasing more

[2]*The Wall Street Journal,* January 18, 1984, p. 16.
[3]*The Wall Street Journal,* August 1, 1984, p. 16.

components overseas. Following the rise of the dollar in the early 1980s, most U.S. companies increased their global sourcing. For example, Caterpillar responded to the soaring U.S. dollar and a tenacious competitor, Japan's Komatsu, by "shopping the world" for components. More than 50% of the pistons that the company uses in the United States now come from abroad, mainly from a Brazilian company. Some work previously done by Caterpillar's Milwaukee plant was moved in 1984 to a subsidiary in Mexico. Caterpillar also stopped most U.S. production of lift trucks and began importing a new line—complete with Cat's yellow paint and logo—from South Korea's Daewoo.

Foreign sourcing and outsourcing allow companies to take advantage of currency changes.

ILLUSTRATION: *Japanese Automakers Outsource to Cope with a Rising Yen*

Japanese automakers have protected themselves against the rising yen by purchasing a significant percentage of intermediate components from independent suppliers. This practice, called *outsourcing*, gives them the flexibility to shift purchases of intermediate inputs toward suppliers with costs least affected by exchange rate changes. Some of these inputs come from South Korea and Taiwan, nations whose currencies have been closely linked to the U.S. dollar. Thus, even if such intermediate goods were not priced in dollars, their yen-equivalent prices tend to decline with the dollar and, thereby, lessen the impact of a falling dollar on the cost of Japanese cars sold in the United States.

Outsourcing in countries whose currencies are linked to the currency of the export market also creates competitive pressures on domestic suppliers of the same intermediate goods. To cope in such an environment, domestic suppliers must themselves have flexible arrangements with their own input suppliers. In many cases, these smaller firms can survive because they have greater ability to recontract their costs than do the larger firms specializing in assembly and distribution. When the suppliers are faced with the reality of an exchange rate change that reduces the competitive price of their outputs, they are able to recontract with their own inputs (typically by lowering wages) to reduce costs sufficiently to remain economically viable.

For a firm already manufacturing overseas, the cost savings associated with using a higher proportion of domestically produced goods and services, following local currency depreciation, will depend on subsequent domestic price behavior. Goods and services used in international trade, or with a high import content, will exhibit greater dollar (HC) price increases than those with a low import content or with little involvement in international trade.

For the longer term, when increasing production capacity, the firm should consider the option of designing new facilities that provide added flexibility in making substitutions among various sources of goods. Maxwell House, for instance, can blend the same coffee whether using coffee beans from Brazil, the Ivory Coast, or other producers. The advantages of being able to respond to relative price differences among domestic and imported inputs must be weighed, of course, against the extra design and construction costs.

Shifting Production Among Plants

MNCs can reduce their exchange risk by allocating production among their several plants in line with changing costs.

Multinational firms with worldwide production systems can allocate production among their several plants in line with the changing dollar costs of production, increasing production in a nation whose currency has devalued, and decreasing production in a country where there has been a revaluation. Contrary to conventional wisdom, therefore, multinational firms may well be subject to less exchange risk than an exporter, given the MNC's greater ability to adjust its production (and marketing) operations on a global basis, in line with changing relative production costs.

A good example of this flexibility is provided by Westinghouse Electric Corp. of Pittsburgh, Pennsylvania. Westinghouse can quote its customers prices from numerous foreign affiliates: gas turbines from Canada, generators from Spain, circuit breakers and robotics from Britain, and electrical equipment from Brazil. Its sourcing decisions take into account both the effect of currency values and subsidized export financing available from foreign governments.

Of course, the theoretical ability to shift production is more limited in reality. The limitations depend on many factors, not the least of which is the power of the local labor unions involved. However, the innovative nature of the typical MNC means a continued generation of new products. The sourcing of those new products among the firm's various plants can certainly be done with an eye to the costs involved.

A strategy of *production shifting* presupposes that the MNC has already created a portfolio of plants worldwide. For example, as part of its global sourcing strategy, Caterpillar now has dual sources, domestic and foreign, for some products. These sources allow Caterpillar to "load" the plant that offers the best economies of production, given exchange rates at any moment. But multiple plants also create manufacturing redundancies and impede cost cutting.

The benefits of a global portfolio of plants must be traded off against the potential loss of economies of scale.

The cost of multiple sourcing is especially great where there are economies of scale that would ordinarily dictate the establishment of only one or two plants to service the global market. But most firms have found that in a world of uncertainty, significant benefits may be derived from production diversification. Hence, despite the higher unit costs associated with smaller plants, currency risk may provide one more reason for the use of multiple production facilities.

The case of the auto industry illustrates the potential value of maintaining a globally balanced distribution of production facilities in the face of fluctuating exchange rates. For auto manufacturers in Japan and Sweden, among other countries, with all their production facilities located domestically, it has been feast or famine. When the home currency appreciates, as in the 1970s, the firms' exports suffer from a lack of cost competitiveness. On the other hand, a real depreciation of the home currency, as in the early 1980s, is a time of high profits.

By contrast, Ford and General Motors, with their worldwide manufacturing facilities, have substantial leeway in reallocating various stages of production among their several plants in line with relative production and transportation costs. For example, Ford can shift production among the United States, Spain, Germany, Great Britain, Brazil, and Mexico.

Plant Location

A firm without foreign facilities that is exporting to a competitive market whose currency has devalued may find that sourcing components abroad is insufficient to maintain unit profitability. Despite its previous hesitancy, the firm may have to locate new plants abroad. For example, the economic response by the Japanese to the strong yen is well under way. Many Japanese companies have found that building new plants in the United States is equally profitable to expanding plants in Japan.

Third-country plant locations are also a viable alternative in many cases, depending especially on the labor intensity of production or the projections for further monetary realignments. Many Japanese firms, for example, have shifted production offshore—to Taiwan, South Korea, Singapore, and other developing nations, as well to as the United States—in order to cope with the high yen.

Before making such a major commitment of its resources, management should attempt to assess the length of time a particular country will retain its cost advantage. If the devaluation was due to inflationary conditions that are expected to persist, a country's apparent cost advantage may soon reverse itself. In Mexico, for example, the wholesale price index rose 18% relative to U.S. prices between January 1969 and May 1976. This rise led to a 20% peso devaluation in September 1976. Within one month, though, the Mexican government allowed organized labor to raise its wages by 35%–40%. As a result, the devaluation's effectiveness was nullified, and the government was forced to devalue the peso again in less than two months. Once again, however, the Mexican government fixed the nominal value of the peso while inflation persisted at a high level.

Yet, shifting production abroad when the home currency rises is not always the best approach. Toyota Motors, for example, decided it was cheaper to produce parts in high volume in efficient Japanese factories that are close to domestic suppliers and to assembly plants. Producing at home also improves coordination between design and manufacturing and avoids problems of quality control. For firms that rely heavily on such coordination and closeness to suppliers, raising domestic productivity is preferable to producing abroad.

As an alternative to shifting production abroad, companies with a strong home currency can try to improve their productivity at home.

Raising Productivity

Many U.S. companies assaulted by foreign competition made prodigious efforts to improve their productivity—closing inefficient plants, automating heavily, and negotiating wage and benefit cutbacks and work-rule concessions with unions. Many also began programs to heighten productivity and improve product quality through employee motivation. These cost cuts now stand U.S. firms in good stead as the firms attempt to use the weaker dollar to gain back market share lost to foreign competitors.

ILLUSTRATION: The American Paper and Pulp Industry Restructures

The restructuring of the American paper and pulp industry is a classic case. It enjoys comparative advantages galore. With a $110 billion domestic market, the industry can achieve tremendous economies of scale. Then there are the fast-sprouting Southern pines, which mature in half the time it takes northern types.

But plenty of other countries were giving the United States a hard time even before the dollar rose. The Finns have offset their high costs by pioneering new technologies. The Brazilians, with abundant and cheap power supplies, are the low-cost pulp producers.

The phenomenal restructuring wave that swept America, swallowing giants like Crown Zellerbach, St. Regis, and Diamond International, has rationalized product lines, held down compensation, and retired old machinery. Today the industry boasts some of the most modern facilities, probably the highest productivity, and quite possibly the fiercest cost-cutting management in the world. These strengths, and the dollar's fall, helped manufacturers regain overseas markets.

Others, most notably the steel and auto industries, have successfully sought government import restrictions. But import quotas illustrate a dilemma facing U.S. industry. Bicycle manufacturers, for example, sought government restrictions on imports of finished bicycles; at the same time, they tried to save money by importing more parts and materials from foreign suppliers.

Planning for Exchange Rate Changes

The marketing and production strategies advocated thus far assume knowledge of exchange rate changes. Even if currency changes are unpredictable, however, contingency plans can be made. This planning involves developing several plausible currency scenarios (see Chapter 10), analyzing the effects of each scenario on the firm's competitive position, and deciding on strategies to deal with these possibilities.

Companies can use scenario analysis to plan for unpredictable currency movements.

When a currency change actually occurs, the firm is able to quickly adjust its marketing and production strategies in line with the plan. Given the substantial costs of gathering and processing information, a firm should focus on scenarios that have a high probability of occurrence and that would also strongly impact it.

ILLUSTRATION: Kodak Plans for Currency Changes

Historically, Eastman Kodak focused its exchange risk management efforts on hedging near-term transactions. It now looks at exchange-rate movements from a strategic perspective. Kodak's moment of truth came in the early 1980s when the strong dollar enabled overseas rivals such as Fuji Photo Film of Japan to cut prices and make significant inroads into its market share. This episode convinced Kodak that it had been defining its currency risk too narrowly. It appointed a new foreign-exchange planning director, David Fiedler, at the end of 1985. According to Mr. Fiedler, "We were finding a lot of things that didn't fit our definition [of exposure] very well, and yet would have a real economic impact on the corpora-tion."[4] To make sure such risks no longer go unrecognized, Mr. Fiedler now spends about 25% of his time briefing Kodak's operating managers on foreign exchange planning. Kodak's new approach figured in a 1988 decision against putting in a factory in Mexico. Kodak decided to locate the plant elsewhere because of its assessment of the peso's relative strength. In the past, currency risk would have been ignored in such project assessments. According to Kodak's chief financial officer, before their reassessment of the company's foreign exchange risk management policy, its financial officers "would do essentially nothing to assess the possible exchange impact until it got to the point of signing contracts for equipment."[5]

The ability to plan for volatile exchange rates has fundamental implications for exchange risk management because there is no longer such a thing as the "natural" or "equilibrium" rate. Rather, there is a sequence of equilibrium rates, each of which has its own implications for corporate strategy. Success in such an environ-ment—where change is the only constant—depends on a company's ability to react to change within a shorter time horizon than ever before. To cope, companies must develop competitive options—such as outsourcing, flexible manufacturing sys-tems, a global network of production facilities, and shorter product cycles.

In a volatile world, these investments in flexibility are likely to yield high returns. For example, flexible manufacturing systems permit faster production response times to shifting market demand. Similarly, foreign facilities, even if they are uneconomical at the moment, can pay off by enabling companies to shift production in response to changing exchange rates or other relative cost shocks.

The greatest boost to competitiveness comes from compressing the time it takes to bring new and improved products to market. The edge a company gets from shorter *product cycles* is dramatic: Not only can it charge a premium price for its exclusive products, but it can also incorporate more up-to-date technology in its goods and respond faster to emerging market niches and changes in taste. Often held up as the ideal is the speedy way that retailers such as The Limited operate (see Chapter 1, Exhibit 1.2): If they see an item catching on with the public, they can have it manufactured in quantity and on their shelves within perhaps three weeks.

Shortening the product cycle can greatly reduce a company's operating exposure.

This speedy delivery is harder for a company that produces, say, automobiles or heavy machinery. Apparently, however, radical improvements in new-product delivery time are within reach even in these industries. In response to *endaka*—the soaring yen—which made their old products less competitive, Japanese automak-ers are making a frantic effort to reduce—from four years to less than two years—the time between the initial design and the actual production of a new car. With better planning and more competitive options, corporations can now change their strategies substantially before the impact of any currency change can make itself felt.

[4]Quoted in Christopher J. Chipello, "The Market Watcher," *The Wall Street Journal,* September 23, 1988, p. 14.
[5]Quoted in Chipello, "The Market Watcher."

As a result, the adjustment period following a large exchange rate change has been compressed dramatically. The 100% appreciation of the Japanese yen against the dollar from 1985 to 1988, for example, sparked some changes in Japanese corporate strategy that are likely to be long-lasting: increased production in the United States and East Asia to cope with the high yen and to protect their foreign markets from any trade backlash; purchasing more parts overseas to take advantage of lower costs; upscaling to reduce the price sensitivity of their products and broaden their markets; massive cost-reduction programs in their Japanese plants, with a long-term impact on production technology; and an increase in joint ventures between competitors.

ILLUSTRATION: *Toshiba Copes with a Rising Yen by Cutting Costs*

By 1988, Toshiba's cost cutting reduced its cost-to-sales ratio to where it was before the yen began rising. The company shifted production of low-tech products to developing nations and moved domestic production to high-value-added products. At a VCR plant outside of Tokyo, it halved the number of assembly-line workers by minimizing inventories and simplifying operations. Other cost-reducing international activities included production of color picture tubes with Westinghouse in the United States, photocopier production in a joint venture with Rhone-Poulenc in France, assembly of video cassette recorders in Tennessee, production of similar VCRs in West Germany, and establishment of a new plant in California for assembling and testing telephones and medical electronics equipment. Overall, Toshiba is estimated to have saved ¥115 billion—¥53 billion by redesigning products, ¥47 billion in parts cutbacks and lower raw material costs, and ¥15 billion in greater operating efficiency. Similarly, by 1989, with the dollar around ¥125, Fujitsu Fanuc, a robot maker had streamlined itself so thoroughly and differentiated its products so effectively that it estimated it could break even with only a fifth of its plant in use and a dollar down to ¥70.

11.4 FINANCIAL MANAGEMENT OF EXCHANGE RISK

MNCs should structure their financing to give themselves breathing room while they undertake the necessary strategic marketing and production adjustments.

The one attribute that all the strategic marketing and production adjustments have in common is that they take time to accomplish in a cost-effective manner. The role of financial management in this process is to structure the firm's liabilities in such a way that during the time the strategic operational adjustments are underway, the reduction in asset earnings is matched by a corresponding decrease in the cost of servicing these liabilities.

One possibility is to finance the portion of a firm's assets used to create export profits so that any shortfall in operating cash flows due to an exchange rate change is offset by a reduction in debt servicing expenses. For example, a firm that has developed a sizable export market should hold a portion of its liabilities in that country's currency. The portion to be held in the foreign currency depends on the size of the loss in profitability associated with a given currency change. No more definite recommendations are possible because the currency effects will vary from one company to another.

Volkswagen is a case in point. To hedge its operating exposure, VW should have used dollar financing in proportion to its net dollar cash flow from U.S. sales. This strategy would have cushioned the impact of the DM revaluation that almost brought VW to its knees. For the longer term, though, VW could only manage its competitive exposure by developing new products with lower price elasticities of demand and by establishing production facilities in lower-cost nations.

A company exporting to a foreign country should be partially financed in the currency of that country.

The implementation of a hedging policy is likely to be quite difficult in practice, if only because the specific cash-flow effects of a given currency change are hard to predict. Trained personnel are required to implement and monitor an active hedging program. Consequently, hedging should be undertaken only when the effects of anticipated exchange rate changes are expected to be significant.

A highly simplified example can illustrate the application of the financing rule developed previously; namely, that the liability structure of the combined MNC—parent and subsidiaries—should be set up in such a way that any change in the inflow on assets due to a currency change should be matched by a corresponding change in the outflow on the liabilities used to fund those assets. Consider the effect of a local currency change on the subsidiary depicted in Exhibit 11.1. In the absence of any exchange rate changes, the subsidiary is

Exhibit 11.1 Statement of Projected Cash Flow

	Units (hundred thousands)	Unit Price (LC)	Total	
LC 1 = $0.25				
Domestic sales	4	20	8,000,000	
Export sales	4	20	8,000,000	
Total revenue				16,000,000
Local labor (hours)	8	10	8,000,000	
Local material	8	3	2,400,000	
Imported material	6	4	2,400,000	
Total expeditures				12,800,000
Net Cash Flow from Operations				LC 3,200,000
Net Cash Flow from Operations				$800,000
LC 1 = $0.20				
Domestic sales	3	24	7,200,000	
Export sales	5	24	12,000,000	
Total revenue				19,200,000
Local labor (hours)	8	12	9,600,000	
Local material	10	3.5	3,500,000	
Imported material	4.5	5	2,250,000	
Total expeditures				15,350,000
Net Cash Flow from Operations				LC 3,850,000
Net Cash Flow from Operations				$770,000

forecast to have an operating profit of $800,000. If a predicted 20% devaluation of the local currency from LC 1 = $0.25 to LC 1 = $0.20 occurs, the subsidiary's LC profitability is expected to rise to LC 3.85 million from LC 3.2 million because of price increases. However, that LC profit rise still entails a loss of $30,000, despite a reduction in the dollar cost of production.

Suppose the subsidiary requires assets equaling LC 20 million, or $5 million at the current exchange rate. It can finance these assets by borrowing dollars at 8% and converting them into their local currency equivalent, or it can use LC funds at 10%. How can the parent structure its subsidiary's financing in such a way that a 20% devaluation will reduce the cost of servicing the subsidiary's liabilities by $30,000 and thus balance operating losses with a decrease in cash outflows?

Actually, a simple procedure is readily available. If S is the dollar outflow on local debt service, then it is necessary that $0.2S$, the dollar gain on devaluation, equal $30,000, the operating loss on devaluation. Hence, $S = \$150,000$, or LC 600,000 at the current exchange rate. At a local currency interest rate of 10%, that debt service amount corresponds to local currency debt of LC 6 million. The remaining LC 14 million can be provided by borrowing $3.5 million. Exhibit 11.2 illustrates the offsetting cash effects associated with such a financial structure.

> The impact on debt servicing charges should offset the impact on operating cash flows.

This example would certainly become more complex if the effects of taxes, depreciation, and working capital were included. Although the execution becomes more difficult, a rough equivalence between operating losses (gains) and debt service gains (losses) can still be achieved as long as all cash flows are accounted for. The inclusion of other foreign operations just requires the aggregation of the cash-flow effects over all affiliates because the corporation's total exchange risk is based on the sum of the changes of the profit contributions of each individual subsidiary.

As mentioned earlier, this approach concentrates exclusively on risk reduction rather than on cost reduction. Where financial market imperfections are

Exhibit 11.2 Effect of Financial Structure on Net Cash Flow

	LC 1 = $0.25		LC 1 = $0.20	
	Local Currency	Dollars	Local Currency	Dollars
Operating cash flows	LC 3,200,000	$800,000	LC 3,850,000	$770,000
Debt service requirements:				
Local currency debt	600,000	150,000	600,000	120,000
Dollar debt	1,120,000	280,000	1,400,000	280,000
Total debt service outflow	1,720,000	430,000	2,000,000	400,000
Net cash flow	LC 1,480,000	$370,000	LC 1,850,000	$370,000

significant, a firm might consider exposing itself to more exchange risk in order to lower its expected financing costs.

11.5 SUMMARY AND CONCLUSIONS

We have seen in this chapter that currency risk affects all facets of a company's operations; therefore, it should not be the concern of financial managers alone. Operating managers, in particular, should develop marketing and production initiatives that help to ensure profitability over the long run. They should also devise anticipatory or proactive, rather than reactive, strategic alternatives in order to gain competitive leverage internationally.

The key to effective exposure management is to integrate currency considerations into the general management process. One approach used by a number of MNCs to develop the necessary coordination among executives responsible for different aspects of exchange risk management is to establish a committee for managing foreign currency exposure. Besides financial executives, such committees should—and often do—include the senior officers of the company such as the vice president-international, top marketing and production executives, the director of corporate planning, and the chief executive officer. This arrangement is desirable because top executives are exposed to the problems of exchange risk management, so they can incorporate currency expectations into their own decisions.

In this kind of integrated exchange risk program, the role of the financial executive is fourfold: (1) to provide local operating management with forecasts of inflation and exchange rates, (2) to identify and highlight the risks of competitive exposure, (3) to structure evaluation criteria such that operating managers are not rewarded or penalized for the effects of unanticipated currency changes, and (4) to estimate and hedge whatever operating exposure remains after the appropriate marketing and production strategies have been put in place.

QUESTIONS

1. Why should managers focus on marketing and production strategies to cope with foreign exchange risk?

2. What marketing and production techniques can firms initiate to cope with exchange risk?

3. What is the role of finance in protecting against exchange risk?

4. Comment on the following statement: "The sharp appreciation of the U.S. dollar during the early 1980s might have been the best thing that ever happened to American industry."

5. In what sense is the boost in profits of American companies due to a falling dollar artificial?

6. How does a shorter product-cycle time help companies reduce the exchange risk they face?

7. Why do exchange rate changes bring feast or famine for Volvo, but neither feast nor famine for Ford? Consider the distribution and concentration of their production facilities worldwide.

8. In order to cut costs when the dollar was at its peak, Caterpillar shifted production of small construction equipment overseas. By contrast, Caterpillar's main competitors in that area, Deere & Co. and J.I. Case, make most of their small construction equipment in the United States. What are the most likely competitive consequences of this restructuring?

PROBLEMS

1.* Nissan produces a car that sells in Japan for ¥1.8 million. On September 1, the beginning of the model year, the exchange rate is ¥150:$1. Consequently, Nissan sets the U.S. sticker price at $12,000. By October 1, the exchange rate has dropped to ¥125:$1. Nissan is upset because it now receives only $12,000 × 125 = ¥1.5 million per sale.
  a. What scenarios are consistent with the U.S. dollar's depreciation?
  b. What alternatives are open to Nissan to improve its situation?
  c. How should Nissan respond in this situation?
  d. Suppose that on November 1, the U.S. Federal Reserve intervenes to rescue the dollar, and the exchange rate adjusts to ¥220:$1 by the following July. What problems and/or opportunities does this situation present for Nissan and for General Motors?

2.* Middle American Corporation (MAC) produces a line of corn silk cosmetics. All of the inputs are purchased domestically and processed at the factory in Des Moines, Iowa. Sales are only in the United States, primarily west of the Mississippi.
  a. Is there any sense in which MAC is exposed to the risk of foreign exchange rate changes that effect large multinational firms? If yes, how could MAC protect itself from these risks?
  b. If MAC opens a sales office in Paris, will this move increase its exposure to exchange rate risks? Explain.

3.* Gizmo, U.S.A. is investigating medium-term financing of $10 million in order to build an addition to its factory in Toledo, Ohio. Gizmo's bank has suggested the following alternatives:

Type of Loan	Rate (%)
Three-year U.S. dollar loan	14
Three-year Deutsche mark loan	8
Three-year Swiss franc loan	4

  a. What information does Gizmo require to decide among the three alternatives?
  b. Suppose the factory will be built in Geneva, Switzerland, rather than Toledo. How does this affect your answer in part a?

*Problems 1–3 contributed by Richard M. Levich.

4. Chemex, a U.S. maker of specialty chemicals, exports 40% of its $600 million in annual sales: 5% goes to Canada and 7% each to Japan, Britain, Germany, France, and Italy. It incurs all its costs in U.S. dollars, while most of its export sales are priced in the local currency.
  a. How is Chemex affected by exchange rate changes?
  b. Distinguish between Chemex's transaction exposure and its operating exposure.
  c. How can Chemex protect itself against transaction exposure?
  d. What financial, marketing, and production techniques can Chemex use to protect itself against operating exposure?
  e. Can Chemex eliminate its operating exposure by hedging its position every time it makes a foreign sale or by pricing all foreign sales in dollars? Why or why not?

5. In September 1992, Dow Chemical reacted to the currency chaos in Europe by switching to DM pricing for all its products in Europe. The purpose, said a Dow executive, was to shift currency risk from Dow to its European customers. Moreover, said the Dow executive, the policy was fairer: By setting the same DM price throughout Europe, Dow's new policy would nullify any advantage that a Dow customer in one company might have over competitors in another country based on currency swings.
  a. What is Dow really trying to accomplish with its new pricing policy?
  b. What is the likelihood that this new policy will reduce Dow's currency risk?
  c. How are Dow's customers likely to respond to this new policy?

6. Boeing Commercial Airplane Co. manufactures all its planes in the United States and prices them in dollars, even the 50% of its sales destined for overseas markets. Assess Boeing's currency risk. How can it cope with this risk?

7. Matsushita exports about half of its TV set production to the United States under its Panasonic, Quasar, and Technics brand names. It prices its products in yen. Suppose the yen moves from ¥130 = $1 to ¥110 = $1. What currency risk is Matsushita facing? How can it cope with this currency risk?

8. Lyle Shipping, a British company, has chartered out ships at fixed-U.S.-dollar freight rates. How can Lyle use financing to hedge against its exposure? How will your recommendation affect Lyle's translation exposure? Lyle uses the current rate method to translate foreign currency assets and liabilities. However, the charters are off-balance-sheet items.

9. When the dollar was strong, and it could no longer earn a reasonable profit margin on European sales, Osmose International gave up its government permits to sell its chemical wood preservatives in much of Europe. "Why pay for a permit when you can't sell anything there anyway?" explained its president.
  a. What response do you have for the president of Osmose?
  b. How might you go about assessing the trade-offs involved for Osmose?

10. Texas Instruments (TI) manufactures integrated circuits and memory chips that it sells around the world. It has major markets in Europe. TI's primary competitors are Japanese companies.
  a. What factors will influence TI's exposure to movements in the dollar value of European currencies?
  b. Does TI's European business have yen exposure? Explain.
  c. How can TI use financing to reduce its yen exposure, to the extent this exposure exists?

BIBLIOGRAPHY

Dufey, Gunter. "Corporate Financial Policies and Floating Exchange Rates." Address presented at the meeting of the International Fiscal Association in Rome, October 14, 1974.

Lessard, Donald R., and John B. Lightstone. "Volatile Exchange Rates Can Put Operations at Risk." *Harvard Business Review*, July–August 1986, pp. 107–114.

Shapiro, Alan C., and Thomas S. Robertson. "Managing Foreign Exchange Risks: The Role of Marketing Strategy." Working paper, The Wharton School, University of Pennsylvania, 1976.

Case II.1 ROLLS-ROYCE LIMITED

Rolls-Royce Limited, the British aeroengine manufacturer, suffered a loss of £58 million in 1979 on worldwide sales of £848 million. The company's annual report for 1979 (page 4) blamed the loss on the dramatic revaluation of the pound sterling against the dollar, from £1 = $1.71 in early 1977 to £1 = $2.12 by the end of 1979:

The most important was the effect of the continued weakness of the U.S. dollar against sterling. The large civil engines which Rolls Royce produces are supplied to American air frames. Because of U.S. dominance in civil aviation, both as producer and customer, these engines are usually priced in U.S. dollars and escalated according to U.S. indices. . . .

A closer look at Rolls-Royce competitive position in the global market for jet engines reveals the sources of its dollar exposure. For the previous several years, Rolls-Royce export sales had accounted for a stable 40% of total sales and had beend irected at the U.S. market. This market is dominated by two U.S. competitors, Pratt and Whitney Aircraft Group (United Technologies) and General Electric's aerospace division. As the clients of its mainstay engine, the RB 211, were U.S. aircraft manufacturers (Boeing's 747SP and 747,200 and Lockheed's L1011), Rolls-Royce had little choice in the currency denomination of its export sales but to use the dollar.

Indeed, Rolls-Royce won some huge engine contracts in 1978 and 1979 that were fixed in dollar terms. Rolls-Royce operating costs, ont he other hand, were almost exclusively incurred in sterling (wages, components, and debt servicing). These contracts were mostly pegged to an exchange rate of about $1.80 for the pound, and Rolls-Royce officials, in fact, expected the pound to fall further to $1.65. Hence, they didn't cover their dollar exposures. If the officials were correct, and the dollar strengthened, Rolls-Royce would enjoy windfall profits. When the dollar weakened instead, the combined effect of fixed dollar revenues and sterling costs resulted in foreign exchange losses in 1979 on its U.S. engine contracts that were estimated by *The Wall Street Journal* (March 11, 1980, p. 6) to be equivalent to as much as $200 mikllion.

QUESTIONS

1. Describe the factors you would need to know to assess the economic impact on Rolls-Royce of the change in the dollar:sterling exchange rate. Does inflation affect Rolls-Royce's exposure?

2. Given these factors, how would you calculate Rolls-Royce's economic exposure?

3. Suppose Rolls-Royce had hedged its dollar contracts. Would it now be facing any economic exposure? How about inflation risk?

4. What alternative financing management strategies might Rolls-Royce have followed that would hvae reduced or eliminated its economic exposure on the U.S. engine contracts?

5. What nonfinancial tactics might Rolls-Royce now initiate to reduce its exposure on the remaining engines to be supplied under the contracts? On future business (e.g., diversification of export sales)?

6. What additional information would you require to ascertain the validity of the statement that "the more engines produced and sold under the previously negotiated contracts, the greater Rolls-Royce's losses will be?

Case II.2 THE MEXICAN PESO

The basic purpose of this case is to have you conduct an in-depth analysis of government macroeconomic policies on firms and banks doing business with that country. The vehicle being used is the Mexican peso. See Exhibit II 2.1 for statistics related to exchange rates and price indexes in the United States and Mexico for the period 1975–1992. Using these data, please address the following questions.

1. What are the causes of the continuing devaluation of the peso since August 1976? Analyze both the immediate causes (e.g., balance-of-payments deficits) and longer-term, more fundamental causes (e.g., inflation, the political and economic environment). Concentrate especially on the 1982 and subsequent devaluations of the peso.

2. What role did oil price changes play in Mexico's difficulties?

3. What indicators of peso devaluation prior to 1982 were there?

4. What were the likely effects of the peso devaluation between 1976 and January 1982 on
   a. Mexican companies?
   b. Foreign firms operating in Mexico?
   c. U.S. companies in border towns catering to Mexicans?

5. Redo question 4, focusing on the effects of peso devaluation subsequent to February 1982.

6. In August 1982, the Mexican government devaluated the peso, froze all dollar accounts in Mexican banks, and imposed currency controls. What were the government's objectives? How did these actions affect the black market value of the peso? Why?

7. How did the Mexican government's expropriation of Mexico City real estate, following the September 1985 earthquake, affect the value of the peso and why?

8. Consider the trust factor with respect to Mexican policies. What have been the probable effects of trust or its lack on investment in Mexico, Mexican citizens' investment choices, and the peso's value?

9. Are dollar loans to the Mexican government and Mexican companies exposed to exchange risk? Explain.

10. How did Mexico's economic policies contribute to its debt crisis? How have subsequent government policies affected Mexico's financial health?

11. What has happened to the competitiveness of Mexican industry subsequent to 1985?

Exhibit II.2.1 Exchange Rates

Year:Quarter	Nominal Exchange Rates (Period Average)		CPI Mexico	CPI United States
	Peso/Dollar	Dollar/Peso		
75:1	12.5	0.08000	100.0	100.0
75:2	12.5	0.08000	103.2	101.9
75:3	12.5	0.08000	107.0	104.1
75:4	12.5	0.08000	110.4	105.8
76:1	12.5	0.08000	115.2	106.8
76:2	12.5	0.08000	118.2	108.2
76:3	19.9	0.05038	122.0	109.8
76:4	20.0	0.05013	137.3	111.0
77:1	22.7	0.04407	149.1	113.0
77:2	23.0	0.04348	155.7	115.5
77:3	22.7	0.04407	162.4	117.1
77:4	22.7	0.04399	168.6	118.5
78:1	22.7	0.04398	177.7	120.4
78:2	22.8	0.04384	183.9	123.6
78:3	22.7	0.04399	191.4	126.5
78:4	22.7	0.04401	197.6	129.0
79:1	22.8	0.04380	209.5	132.3
79:2	22.8	0.04378	217.0	136.8
79:3	22.8	0.04390	225.2	141.3
79:4	22.8	0.04386	235.6	145.4
80:1	22.9	0.04376	256.8	151.1
80:2	22.9	0.04361	271.5	156.6
80:3	23.1	0.04337	289.3	159.4
80:4	23.3	0.04301	303.9	163.7
81:1	23.8	0.04209	328.5	168.0
81:2	24.4	0.04103	348.4	171.9
81:3	25.2	0.03968	365.9	176.9
81:4	26.3	0.03804	389.4	179.3
82:1	45.5	0.02198	435.0	180.9
82:2	48.0	0.02082	501.5	183.5
82:3	50.0	0.02000	606.1	187.0
82:4	96.5	0.01036	730.8	187.5
83:1	102.0	0.00980	926.2	187.3
83:2	120.0	0.00833	1076.9	189.7
83:3	132.0	0.00758	1217.2	191.9
83:4	143.9	0.00695	1369.6	193.6
84:1	155.8	0.00642	1601.9	195.7
84:2	167.6	0.00597	1807.3	197.9
84:3	179.6	0.00557	1987.7	200.1
84:4	192.6	0.00519	2196.5	201.5
85:1	208.9	0.00479	2552.7	202.8

(continues)

Exhibit II.2.1 Continued

Year:Quarter	Nominal Exchange Rates (Period Average)		CPI Mexico	CPI United States
	Peso/Dollar	Dollar/Peso		
85:2	228.0	0.00439	2800.9	205.3
85:3	305.1	0.00328	3097.0	206.7
85:4	371.7	0.00269	3527.5	212.6
86:1	473.6	0.00211	4254.7	213.1
86:2	575.4	0.00174	4957.8	212.6
86:3	752.0	0.00133	5930.4	214.3
86:4	923.5	0.00108	7164.7	215.4
87:1	1126.0	0.00089	8909.4	217.8
87:2	1353.7	0.00074	11120.8	220.7
87:3	1570.8	0.00064	13889.6	223.1
87:4	2209.7	0.00045	15228.2	225.0
88:1	2281.0	0.00044	29116.0	229.4
88:2	2281.0	0.00044	32453.0	232.2
88:3	2281.0	0.00044	33924.0	235.3
88:4	2281.0	0.00044	34968.1	237.7
89:1	2369.0	0.00042	36943.5	240.5
89:2	2460.0	0.00041	38435.6	244.3
89:3	2551.0	0.00039	39687.9	246.4
89:4	2641.0	0.00038	41501.0	248.7
90:1	2733.0	0.00037	45621.2	253.0
90:2	2817.0	0.00035	48104.5	255.5
90:3	2890.6	0.00034	50789.0	260.0
90:4	2945.4	0.00034	53783.8	264.3
91:1	2981.0	0.00033	57724.0	266.4
91:2	3018.2	0.00033	59812.3	267.9
91:3	3055.8	0.00033	61442.0	270.0
91:4	3071.0	0.00033	64257.0	272.1
92:1	3083.5	0.00032	67738.6	274.0
92:2	3122.3	0.00032		276.2

Multinational Working Capital Management

Short-Term Financing 12

Money is a wonderful thing, but it is possible to pay too high a price for it.

Anonymous

CHAPTER LEARNING OBJECTIVES

- To identify the key factors associated with developing a short-term overseas financing strategy
- To describe and evaluate the objectives that a firm might use to arrive at its borrowing strategy, including deciding where and in which currencies to borrow
- To describe the available short-term borrowing options
- To calculate and compare the effective after-tax dollar costs of alternative borrowing options

KEY TERMS

banker's acceptance
break-even analysis
cleanup clause
commercial paper (CP)
compensating balance
  requirements
discounting
effective interest rate
Euro-commercial paper
  (Euro-CP)
Euronotes
intercompany loan
line of credit
overdraft
political risk
revolving credit agreement
systematic risk
term loan
total risk

Financing the working capital requirements of a multinational corporation's foreign affiliates poses a complex decision problem. This complexity stems from the large number of financing options available to the subsidiary of an MNC. Subsidiaries have access to funds from sister affiliates and the parent, as well as from external sources. This chapter focuses on developing policies for borrowing from either within or without the corporation when the risk of exchange rate changes is present and different tax rates and regulations are in effect.

This chapter is concerned with the following five aspects of developing a short-term overseas financing strategy: (1) identifying the key factors, (2) formulating and evaluating objectives, (3) describing available short-term borrowing options, (4) developing a methodology for calculating and comparing the effective after-tax dollar costs of these alternatives, and (5) integrating the borrowing strategy with exposure management considerations.

12.1   KEY FACTORS IN SHORT-TERM FINANCING STRATEGY

Expected costs and risk, the basic determinants of any funding strategy, are strongly influenced in an international context by six key factors.

Six key factors influence the expected cost and risk of a short-term financing strategy.

1. If forward contracts are unavailable, the crucial issue is whether differences in nominal interest rates among currencies are matched by anticipated exchange rate changes. For example, is the difference between an 8% dollar interest rate and a 3% Swiss franc interest rate due solely to expectations that the dollar will devalue by 5% relative to the franc? The key issue here, in other words, is whether there are deviations from the international Fisher effect. If deviations do exist, then expected dollar borrowing costs will vary by currency, leading to a decision problem. Trade-offs must then be made between the expected borrowing costs and the exchange risks associated with each financing option.

2. The element of exchange risk is the second key factor. Many firms borrow locally to provide an offsetting liability for their exposed local currency assets. On the other hand, borrowing a foreign currency in which the firm has no exposure will increase its exchange risk. What matters is the covariance between the operating and financing cash flows. That is, the risks associated with borrowing in a specific currency are related to the firm's degree of exposure in that currency.

3. The third essential element is the firm's degree of risk aversion. The more risk averse the firm (or its management) is, the higher the price it should be willing to pay to reduce its currency exposure. Risk aversion affects the company's risk-cost trade-off and consequently, in the absence of forward contracts, influences the selection of currencies it will use to finance its foreign operations.

4. If forward contracts are available, however, currency risk should not be a factor in the firm's borrowing strategy. Instead, relative borrowing costs, calculated on a covered basis, become the sole determinant of which currencies to borrow in. The key issue here is whether the nominal interest differential equals the forward differential—that is, whether interest rate parity holds. If it does hold, then in the absence of tax considerations, the currency denomination of the firm's debt is irrelevant. Covered after-tax costs can differ among currencies because of government capital controls or the threat of such controls. Due to this added element of risk, the annualized forward discount or premium may not offset the difference between the interest rate on the LC loan versus the dollar loan—that is, interest rate parity will not hold.

5. Even if interest rate parity does hold before tax, the currency denomination of corporate borrowings does matter where tax asymmetries are present. These tax asymmetries are based on the differential treatment of foreign exchange gains and losses on either forward contracts or loan repayments. For example, English firms or affiliates have a disincentive to borrow in strong currencies because Inland Revenue, the British tax agency, taxes exchange gains on foreign currency borrowings, but disallows the deductibility of exchange losses on the same loans. An opposite incentive (to borrow in stronger currencies) is created in countries such as Australia that may permit exchange gains on forward contracts to be taxed at a lower rate than the rate at which forward contract losses are deductible. In such a case, even if interest parity holds before tax, after-tax forward contract gains may be greater than after-tax interest costs. Such tax asymmetries lead to possibilities of borrowing arbitrage, even if interest rate parity holds before tax. The essential point is that, in comparing relative borrowing costs, these costs must be computed on an after-tax covered basis.

6. A final factor that may enter into the borrowing decision is *political risk*. Even if local financing is not the minimum cost option, multinationals will often still try to maximize their local borrowings if they believe that expropriation or exchange controls are serious possibilities. If either event occurs, an MNC has fewer assets at risk if it has used local, rather than external, financing.

12.2 SHORT-TERM FINANCING OBJECTIVES

This section considers four possible objectives that can guide a firm in deciding where and in which currencies to borrow.

1. *Minimize expected cost.* By ignoring risk, this objective reduces information requirements, allows borrowing options to be evaluated on an individual basis without considering the correlation between loan cash flows and operating cash flows, and lends itself readily to break-even analysis (see Section 12.4). One problem with this approach is that if risk affects the company's operating cash flows (see Chapter 1, Section 1.3), the validity of using expected cost alone is questionable. If forward contracts are available, however, there is a theoretically justifiable reason for ignoring risk; namely, loan costs should be evaluated on a covered (riskless) basis. In that case, minimizing expected cost is the same as minimizing actual cost.

Short-term financing objectives tend to trade off expected cost and risk.

2. *Minimize risk without regard to cost.* A firm that followed this advice to its logical conclusion would dispose of all its assets and invest the proceeds in government securities. In other words, this objective is impractical and contrary to shareholder interests.

3. *Trade off expected cost and systematic risk.* The advantage of this objective is that, like the first objective, it allows a company to evaluate different loans without considering the relationship between loan cash flows and operating cash flows from operations. Moreover, it is consistent with shareholder preferences as described by the capital asset pricing model. In practical terms, however, there is probably little difference between expected borrowing costs adjusted for *systematic risk* and expected borrowing costs without that adjustment. This lack of difference is because the correlation between currency fluctuations and a well-diversified portfolio of risky assets is likely to be quite small.

4. *Trade off expected cost and total risk.* The theoretical rationale for this approach was described in Chapter 1. Basically, it relies on the existence of potentially substantial costs of financial distress. On a more practical level,

management generally prefers greater stability of cash flows (regardless of investor preferences). Management will typically self-insure against most losses, but might decide to use the financial markets to hedge against the risk of large losses. To implement this approach, it is necessary to take into account the covariances between operating and financing cash flows. This approach (trading off expected cost and total risk) is valid only where forward contracts are unavailable. Otherwise, selecting the lowest-cost borrowing option, calculated on a covered after-tax basis, is the only justifiable objective.[1]

12.3 SHORT-TERM FINANCING OPTIONS

Firms typically prefer to finance the temporary component of current assets with short-term funds. This section briefly describes three short-term financing options that may be available to an MNC: (1) the intercompany loan, (2) the local currency loan, and (3) Euronotes and Euro-commercial paper.

Intercompany Financing

The parent or a sister affiliate may provide short-term financing in the form of an intercompany loan.

A frequent means of affiliate financing is to have either the parent company or sister affiliate provide an *intercompany loan*. At times, however, these loans may be limited in amount or duration by official exchange controls, such as the restrictions between 1968 and 1974 imposed by the U.S. government's Office of Foreign Direct Investment. In addition, interest rates on intercompany loans are frequently required to fall within set limits. Normally, the lender's government will want the interest rate on an intercompany loan to be set as high as possible for both tax and balance-of-payments purposes, while the borrower's government will demand a low interest rate for similar reasons. The relevant parameters in establishing the cost of such a loan include the lender's opportunity cost of funds, the interest rate set, tax rates and regulations, the currency of denomination of the loan, and expected exchange rate movements over the term of the loan.

Local Currency Financing

Like most domestic firms, affiliates of multinational corporations generally attempt to finance their working capital requirements locally, for both convenience and exposure management purposes. Since all industrial nations and most LDCs have well-developed commercial banking systems, firms desiring local financing generally turn there first. The major forms of bank financing include overdrafts, discounting, and term loans. Nonbank sources of funds include commercial paper and factoring (see Chapter 13, Section 13.3).

Bank Loans. Loans from commercial banks are the dominant form of short-term interest-bearing financing used around the world. These loans are described as *self-liquidating* because they are usually used to finance temporary increases in

---

[1]These possible objectives are suggested by Donald R. Lessard, "Currency and Tax Considerations in International Financing," Teaching Note No. 3, Massachusetts Institute of Technology, Spring 1979.

accounts receivable and inventory. These increases in working capital are soon converted into cash, which is used to repay the loan.

Bank loans are the dominant form of short-term financing used around the world.

Short-term bank credits are typically unsecured. The borrower signs a note evidencing its obligation to repay the loan when it is due, along with accrued interest. Most notes are payable in 90 days; the loans must, therefore, be repaid or renewed every 90 days. The need to periodically roll over bank loans gives a bank substantial control over the use of its funds, reducing the need to impose severe restrictions on the firm. To further ensure that short-term credits are not being used for permanent financing, a bank will usually insert a *cleanup clause* requiring the company to be completely out of debt to the bank for a period of at least 30 days during the year.

Forms of Bank Credit. Bank credit provides a highly flexible form of financing because it is readily expandable and, therefore, serves as a financial reserve. Whenever the firm needs extra short-term funds that can't be met by trade credit, it is likely to turn first to bank credit. Unsecured bank loans may be extended under a line of credit, under a revolving-credit arrangement, or on a transaction basis. Bank loans can be originated either in the domestic or Eurodollar market.

1. *Term loans.* Term loans are straight loans, often unsecured, that are made for a fixed period of time, usually 90 days. They are attractive because they give corporate treasurers complete control over the timing of repayments. A term loan is typically made for a specific purpose with specific conditions and is repaid in a single lump sum. The loan provisions are contained in the promissory note that is signed by the customer. This type of loan is used most often by borrowers who have an infrequent need for bank credit.

2. *Line of credit.* Arranging separate loans for frequent borrowers is a relatively expensive means of doing business. One way to reduce these transaction costs is to use a line of credit. This informal agreement permits the company to borrow up to a stated maximum amount from the bank. The firm can draw down its line of credit when it requires funds and pay back the loan balance when it has excess cash. Although the bank is not legally obligated to honor the line-of-credit agreement, it almost always does unless it or the firm encounters financial difficulties. A line of credit is usually good for one year, with renewals renegotiated every year.

3. *Overdrafts.* In countries other than the United States, banks tend to lend through overdrafts. An overdraft is simply a line of credit against which drafts (checks) can be drawn (written) up to a specified maximum amount. These overdraft lines are often extended and expanded year after year, thus providing, in effect, a form of medium-term financing. The borrower pays interest on the debit balance only.

4. *Revolving credit agreement.* A revolving credit agreement is similar to a line of credit except that now the bank (or syndicate of banks) is *legally committed* to extend credit up to the stated maximum. The firm pays interest on its outstanding borrowings plus a commitment fee, ranging between 0.125% and 0.5% per annum, on the *unused* portion of the credit line. Revolving credit agreements are usually renegotiated every two or three years.

The danger that short-term credits are being used to fund long-term requirements is particularly acute with a revolving credit line that is continuously renewed. Inserting an out-of-debt period under a cleanup clause validates the temporary need for funds.

Discounting is the pre-
ferred short-term
financing technique in
many European coun-
tries.

5. *Discounting.* The discounting of trade bills is the preferred short-term financing technique in many European countries—especially in France, Italy, Belgium, and, to a lesser extent, Germany. It is also widespread in Latin America, particularly in Argentina, Brazil, and Mexico. These bills often can be rediscounted with the central bank.

Discounting usually results from the following set of transactions. A manufacturer selling goods to a retailer on credit draws a bill on the buyer, payable in, say, 30 days. The buyer endorses (accepts) the bill or gets his or her bank to accept it, at which point it becomes a *banker's acceptance*. The manufacturer then takes the bill to his or her bank, and the bank accepts it for a fee if the buyer's bank has not already accepted it. The bill is then sold at a discount to the manufacturer's bank or to a money market dealer. The rate of interest varies with the term of the bill and the general level of local money market interest rates.

The popularity of discounting in European countries stems from the fact that according to European commercial law, which is based on the Code Napoleon, the claim of the bill holder is independent of the claim represented by the underlying transaction. (For example, the bill holder must be paid even if the buyer objects to the quality of the merchandise.) This right makes the bill easily negotiable and enhances its liquidity (or tradability), thereby lowering the cost of discounting relative to other forms of credit.

Interest Rates on Bank Loans. The interest rate on bank loans is based on personal negotiation between the banker and the borrower. The loan rate charged to a specific customer reflects that customer's creditworthiness, previous relationship with the bank, the maturity of the loan, and other factors. Ultimately, of course, bank interest rates are based on the same factors as the interest rates on the financial securities issued by a borrower: the risk-free return, which reflects the time value of money, plus a risk premium based on the borrower's credit risk. However, there are certain bank loan pricing conventions that you should be familiar with.

Interest on a loan can be paid at maturity or in advance. Each payment method gives a different effective interest rate, even if the quoted rate is the same. The *effective interest rate* is defined as follows:

$$\text{Effective interest rate} = \frac{\text{Annual interest paid}}{\text{Funds received}}$$

Suppose you borrow $10,000 for one year at 11% interest. If the interest is paid at maturity, you owe the lender $11,100 at the end of the year. This payment method yields an effective interest rate of 11%, the same as the stated interest rate:

$$\text{Effective interest rate when} \atop \text{interest is paid at maturity} = \frac{\$1,100}{\$10,000} = 11\%$$

If the loan is quoted on a *discount basis*, the bank deducts the interest in advance. On the $10,000 loan, you will receive only $8,900 and must repay $10,000 in one year. The effective rate of interest exceeds 11% because you are paying interest on $10,000, but only have the use of $8,900:

The effective interest rate on a bank loan typically exceeds the stated interest rate.

$$\text{Effective interest rate} \atop \text{on discounted loan} = \frac{\$1,100}{\$8,900} = 12.4\%$$

An extreme illustration of the difference in the effective interest rate between paying interest at maturity and paying interest in advance is provided by the Mexican banking system. In 1985, the nominal interest rate on a peso bank loan was 70%, about 15 percentage points higher than the inflation rate. But high as it was, the nominal figure didn't tell the whole story. By collecting interest in advance, Mexican banks boosted the effective rate dramatically. Consider, for example, the cost of a Ps 10,000 loan. By collecting interest of 70%, or Ps 7,000, in advance, the bank actually loaned out only Ps 3,000 and received Ps 10,000 at maturity. The effective interest rate on the loan is 233%:

$$\text{Effective interest rate} \atop \text{on Mexican loan} = \frac{\text{Ps } 7,000}{\text{Ps } 3,000} = 233\%$$

Compensating Balances. Many banks require borrowers to hold from 10% to 20% of their outstanding loan balance on deposit in a noninterest-bearing account. These *compensating balance requirements* raise the effective cost of a bank credit since not all of the loan is available to the firm:

$$\text{Effective interest} \atop \text{rate with compensating} \atop \text{balance requirements} = \frac{\text{Annual interest paid}}{\text{Usable funds}}$$

Usable funds equal the net amount of the loan less the compensating balance requirement.

Returning to the previous example, suppose you borrow $10,000 at 11% interest paid at maturity, and the compensating balance requirement is 15%, or $1,500. Thus, the $10,000 loan provides only $8,500 in usable funds for an effective interest rate of 12.9%:

$$\text{Effective interest rate when} \atop \text{interest is paid at maturity} = \frac{\$1,100}{\$8,500} = 12.9\%$$

If the interest is prepaid, the amount of usable funds declines by a further $1,100—that is, to $7,400—and the effective interest rate rises to 14.9%:

$$\text{Effective interest rate} \atop \text{on discounted loan} = \frac{\$1,100}{\$7,400} = 14.9\%$$

In both instances, the compensating balance requirement raises the effective interest rate above the stated interest rate. This higher rate is the case even if the bank pays interest on the compensating balance deposit because the loan rate invariably exceeds the deposit rate.

Commercial paper is a favorite short-term non-bank financing method for MNCs.

Commercial Paper.   One alternative to borrowing short term from a bank is to issue commercial paper. *Commercial paper* (CP) is a short-term unsecured promissory note that is generally sold by large corporations on a discount basis to institutional investors and to other corporations. Because commercial paper is unsecured and bears only the name of the issuer, the market has generally been dominated by the largest, most creditworthy companies.

Commercial paper is one of the most-favored short-term nonbank financing methods for MNCs. But CP markets are not all alike. Perhaps the most telling difference is the depth and popularity of CP markets, as best measured by the amount outstanding. The United States dwarfs all other national markets. In September 1987, U.S. commercial paper outstanding was $350 billion. By contrast, CP outstanding in the Netherlands was only about $300 million.

Available maturities are fairly standard across the spectrum, but average maturities—reflecting the terms companies actually use—vary from 20–25 days in the United States to over three months in the Netherlands. The minimum denomination of paper also varies widely: In Australia, Canada, Sweden, and the United States, firms can issue CP in much smaller amounts than in other markets. In most countries, the instrument is issued at a discount, with the full face value of the note redeemed upon maturity. In other markets, however, interest-bearing instruments are also offered.

MNCs are substituting commercial paper for bank loans because of the interest savings.

By going directly to the market rather than relying on a financial intermediary such as a bank, large, well-known corporations can save substantial interest costs, often on the order of 1% or more. In addition, because commercial paper is sold directly to large institutions, U.S. CP is exempt from SEC registration requirements. This exemption reduces the time and expense of readying an issue of commercial paper for sale.

There are three major noninterest costs associated with using commercial paper as a source of short-term funds: (1) back-up lines of credit, (2) fees to commercial banks, and (3) rating service fees. In most cases, issuers back their paper 100% with lines of credit from commercial banks. Because its average maturity is very short, commercial paper poses the risk that an issuer might not be able to pay off or roll over maturing paper. Consequently, issuers use back-up lines as insurance against periods of financial stress or tight money, when lenders ration money directly rather than raise interest rates. For example, the market for Texaco paper, which provided the bulk of its short-term financing, disappeared following the $11.1 billion judgment against it. Texaco replaced these funds by drawing on its bank lines of credit.

Back-up lines are usually paid for through compensating balances, typically about 10% of the unused portion of the credit line plus 20% of the amount of credit actually used. As an alternative to compensating balances, issuers sometimes pay straight fees ranging from 0.375% to 0.75% of the line of credit; this explicit pricing procedure has been used increasingly in recent years.

Another cost associated with issuing commercial paper is fees paid to the large commercial banks that act as issuing and paying agents for the paper issuers and handle all the associated paper work. Finally, rating services charge fees ranging from $5,000 to $25,000 per year for ratings, depending on the rating service. Credit ratings are not legally required by any nation, but they are often essential for placing paper.

Euronotes and Euro-Commercial Paper

A recent innovation in nonbank short-term credits that bears a strong resemblance to commercial paper is the so-called Euronote. *Euronotes* are short-term notes usually denominated in dollars and issued by corporations and governments. The prefix "Euro" indicates that the notes are issued outside the country in whose currency they are denominated. The interest rates are adjusted each time the notes are rolled over. Euronotes are often called *Euro-commercial paper* (Euro-CP, for short). Typically, though, the name Euro-CP is reserved for those Euronotes that are not underwritten.

There are some differences between the U.S. commercial paper and the Euro-CP markets. For one thing, the average maturity of Euro-CP is about twice as long as the average maturity of U.S. CP. Also, Euro-CP is actively traded in a secondary market, but most U.S. CP is held to maturity by the original investors. Central banks, commercial banks, and corporations are important parts of the investor base for particular segments of the Euro-CP market; the most important holders of U.S. CP are money market funds, which are not very important in the Euro-CP market. In addition, the distribution of U.S. issuers in the Euro-CP market is of significantly lower quality than the distribution of U.S. issuers in the U.S.-CP market. An explanation of this finding may lie in the importance of banks as buyers of less-than-prime paper in the Euro-CP market.

Although similar, the U.S. CP and the Euro-CP markets differ in some important respects.

Another important difference in practice between the two markets is in the area of ratings. Only about 45% of active Euro-CP issuers at year-end 1986 were rated. Credit ratings in the United States, on the other hand, are ubiquitous. This difference may prove transitory, however, as investors become accustomed to the concept and the rating agencies facilitate the use of their services. For example, Standard and Poor's Corporation charges an entity with a U.S. rating only $5,000 on top of the $25,000 annual U.S. fee for a Euro-CP rating. Moody's has gone a step further by making its CP ratings global paper ratings that are applicable in any market or currency.

12.4 CALCULATING THE DOLLAR COSTS OF ALTERNATIVE FINANCING OPTIONS

This section presents explicit formulas to compute the effective dollar costs of a local currency loan and a dollar loan for both the no-tax and tax cases.[2] These cost

[2]This section draws on material on Alan C. Shapiro, "Evaluating Financing Costs for Multinational Subsidiaries," *Journal of International Business Studies*, Fall 1975, pp. 25–32.

formulas can be used to calculate the least expensive financing source for each future exchange rate. A computer can easily perform this analysis—called *break-even analysis*—and determine the range of future exchange rates within which each particular financing option is cheapest.

With this break-even analysis, the treasurer can readily see the amount of currency appreciation or depreciation necessary to make one type of borrowing less expensive than another. The treasurer will then compare the firm's actual forecast of currency change, determined objectively or subjectively, with this benchmark.

The logic of this break-even analysis can be extended to financing alternatives other than the two that are presented in this section. In all situations, the cost of each source of funds must be calculated in terms of the relevant parameters (for example, nominal interest rate, tax rate, and future exchange rate) and the expense compared with that of all other possibilities. These calculations and comparisons will differ little from those that are performed here.

Suppose that Du Pont's Brazilian affiliate requires funds to finance its working capital needs for one year. It can borrow cruzeiros at 45% or dollars at 11%. To determine an appropriate borrowing strategy, this section will first develop explicit cost expressions for each of these loans using the numbers given above. These expressions will then be generalized to obtain analytical cost formulas that are usable under a variety of circumstances.

Case 1: No Taxes

In the absence of taxes and forward contracts, costing these loans is relatively straightforward.

1. *Local currency loan.* Suppose the current exchange rate e_0 ($\$e_0 =$ Cr\$1) is Cr\$1 = \$0.0025 = 1/400, or Cr\$400 = \$1. Then, the cruzeiro cost of repaying the principal plus interest (45%) at the end of one year on one dollar's worth of cruzeiros is $400(1.45) =$ Cr\$580. The dollar cost is $400(1.45)e_1$, where e_1 is the (unknown) ending exchange rate. Subtracting the dollar principal yields an effective dollar cost of $400(1.45)e_1 - 1$. For example, if the ending exchange rate is \$0.002 (or Cr\$500 = \$1), then the cost per dollar borrowed equals

$$(400)(1.45)(0.002) - 1 = 0.16 \; or \; 16\%$$

The cost of a local currency loan equals the interest expense less the exchange gain (loss) on loan repayment.

A simpler expression for the borrowing cost can be found by substituting $1/e_0$ for 400, yielding $1.45(e_1/e_0) - 1$. This expression equals $0.45(1 - d) - d$, where d is the (unknown) cruzeiro devaluation and is defined as $d = (e_0 - e_1)/e_0$. Thus, the effective dollar interest rate on borrowed cruzeiros equals $0.45(1 - d) - d$. In general, the dollar (HC) cost of borrowing local currency at an interest rate of r_L and a currency change of d is the sum of the dollar interest cost less the exchange gain (loss) on repaying the principal:

$$\frac{\text{Dollar cost}}{\text{of LC loan}} = \text{Interest} - \text{Exchange gain (loss)}$$

(12.1)

$$= r_L(1 - d) - d$$

The first term in Equation 12.1 is the dollar interest cost (paid at year end after an LC devaluation of d); the second term is the exchange gain or loss involved in repaying an LC loan valued at $1 at the beginning of the year with local currency worth $(1 - d)$ dollars at year end. As before, $d = (e_0 - e_1)/e_0$, where e_0 and e_1 are the beginning and ending exchange rates (LC 1 = $\$e$).

2. *Dollar loan.* The Brazilian affiliate can borrow dollars at 11%. In general, the cost of a dollar (HC) loan to the affiliate is the interest rate on the dollar (HC) loan r_H.

Analysis.   The cruzeiro loan costs $0.45(1 - d) - d$, and the dollar loan costs 11%. To find the break-even rate of currency depreciation at which the dollar cost of cruzeiro borrowing is just equal to the cost of dollar financing, equate the two costs and solve for d:

$$0.45(1 - d) - d = 0.11$$

or

$$d = \frac{(0.45 - 0.11)}{1.45} = 0.234$$

In other words, the Brazilian cruzeiro must devalue by 23.4%, to Cr$522 = $1, before it is less expensive to borrow cruzeiros at 45% than dollars at 11%. Ignoring the factor of exchange risk, the borrowing decision rule is as follows:

Break-even analysis can establish the amount of currency change that equates the costs of local currency and dollar financing.

If $d < 23.4\%$, borrow dollars

If $d > 23.4\%$, borrow cruzeiros

Each of these cost formulas can be represented as a straight line with a positive intercept (equal to the effective interest rate when $d = 0$) and a negative (or zero) slope equal to the coefficient of the d term. The points at which these lines intersect (unless they are parallel) provide the break-even values of d. These straight-line equations are plotted in Exhibit 12.1. A cruzeiro devaluation of 31% will yield an effective interest rate of zero on the cruzeiro loan.

In the general case, the break-even rate of currency change is found by equating the dollar costs of dollar and local currency financing:

$$r_H = r_L(1 - d) - d \tag{12.2}$$

The solution to Equation 12.2 is

$$d^* = \frac{r_L - r_H}{1 + r_L} \tag{12.3}$$

If the international Fisher effect holds, then we saw in Chapter 7 (Equation 7.8) that d^*, the breakeven amount of currency change, also equals the expected LC devaluation (revaluation); that is, the expected cruzeiro devaluation should equal 23.4% unless there is reason to believe that some form of market imperfection is not permitting interest rates to adjust to reflect anticipated currency changes.

Exhibit 12.1   Loan Cost Comparisons: No Taxes

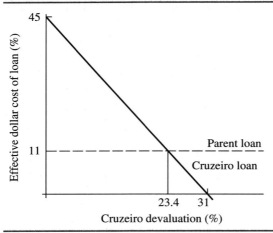

Case 2: Taxes

Taxes complicate the calculation of effective interest rates on local currency and dollar financing.

Taxes complicate the calculating of various loan costs. Suppose the effective tax rate on the earnings of Du Pont's Brazilian affiliate is 40%.

1. *Local currency loan.* The interest expense on one dollar's worth of cruzeiros is $0.45 \times 400 = Cr\$180$. After Brazilian tax, this cost is $180 \times (1 - 0.40) = Cr\$108$. The total after-tax cruzeiro cost of repaying the loan plus interest equals Cr$508 (the principal amount of Cr$400 plus the after-tax interest expense of Cr$108). The dollar cost equals $508e_1$. Subtracting the dollar principal produces the after-tax dollar cost of $508e_1 - 1$. This cost can be separated into two terms:

$$0.45 \times \frac{e_1}{e_0} \times 0.6 + \frac{e_1}{e_0} - 1$$

Substituting d for $(e_0 - e_1)/e_0$ yields

$$0.45(1 - d)0.6 - d = 0.27(1 - d) - d$$

The first term is the after-tax dollar interest cost of the cruzeiro interest expense, and the second term is the gain from the reduced dollar cost of repaying the cruzeiro principal.

In general, the after-tax dollar cost of borrowing in the local currency for a foreign affiliate equals the after-tax interest expense less the exchange gain (loss) on principal repayment, or

$$\begin{matrix} \text{After-tax dollar} \\ \text{cost of LC loan} \end{matrix} = \text{Interest cost} - \text{Exchange gain (loss)} \qquad \textbf{(12.4)}$$

$$= r_L(1 - d)(1 - t_a) - d$$

where t_a is the affiliate's marginal tax rate. The first term in Equation 12.4 is the after-tax dollar interest cost paid at year end after an LC devaluation (revaluation) of d; the second is the exchange gain or loss in dollars of repaying a local currency loan valued at one dollar with local currency worth $(1 - d)$ dollars at the end of the year. The gain or loss has no tax effect for the affiliate because the same amount of local currency was borrowed and repaid.

2. *Dollar loan.* The after-tax cost of a dollar loan equals the Brazilian affiliate's after-tax interest expense, $0.11(1 - 0.4)$, minus the dollar value to the Brazilian affiliate of the tax write-off on the increased number of cruzeiros necessary to repay the dollar principal following a cruzeiro devaluation, $0.4d$. This latter term is calculated in the following way: The dollar loan is converted to $1/e_0$ cruzeiros, or Cr\$400. The number of cruzeiros needed to repay this principal equals $1/e_1$ or an increase of

$$\frac{1}{e_1} - 400 = \frac{1}{e_1} - \frac{1}{e_0}$$

This extra expense is tax-deductible. The cruzeiro value of this tax deduction is $0.40(1/e_1 - 1/e_0)$, with a dollar value equal to $0.4(1/e_1 - 1/e_0)e_1$, or $0.4d$. Adding these two components yields a cost of dollar financing equal to

The added expense of repaying a foreign currency loan following LC devaluation is ordinarily tax deductible.

$$0.11(1 - 0.4) - 0.4d = 0.066 - 0.4d$$

We can generalize this analysis as follows: The total cost of the dollar loan is the after-tax interest expense less the tax write-off associated with the dollar principal repayment, or

$$\frac{\text{After-tax cost}}{\text{of dollar loan}} = \frac{\text{Interest cost}}{\text{to subsidiary}} - \text{Tax gain (loss)} \tag{12.5}$$

$$= r_H(1 - t_a) - dt_a$$

The only change from the no-tax case, other than using after-tax instead of before-tax interest rates, is the addition of the second term, dt_a. This term equals the dollar value of the tax write-off (cost) associated with the increased (decreased) amount of local currency required to repay the dollar principal following an LC depreciation (appreciation).

Similarly, an LC revaluation will lead to a foreign exchange gain that is taxable, resulting in an increase in taxes equaling dt_a dollars. Hence, due to the tax effects, an LC devaluation will decrease the total cost of the dollar (HC) loan, and an LC revaluation will increase it.

Analysis. As in case 1, we will set the cost of dollar financing, $0.066 - 0.4d$, equal to the cost of local currency financing, $0.27(1 - d) - d$, in order to find the break-even rate of cruzeiro depreciation necessary to leave the firm indifferent between borrowing in dollars or cruzeiros.

The break-even value of d occurs when

$$0.066 - 0.4d = 0.27(1 - d) - d$$

or

$$d = 0.234$$

Thus, the cruzeiro must devalue by 23.4% to Cr$522 = $1 before it is cheaper to borrow cruzeiros at 45% than dollars at 11%. This is the same break-even exchange rate as in the before-tax case. Although taxes affect the after-tax costs of the dollar and LC loans, they don't affect the relative desirability of the two loans. That is, if one loan has a lower cost before tax, it will also be less costly on an after-tax basis.

As in the no-tax case, effective dollar interest rates can be graphically illustrated as a function of alternative rates of cruzeiro devaluation. The intersection of the lines in Exhibit 12.2 provides the break-even values of cruzeiro devaluation—that is, the devaluation percentages at which the firm would just be indifferent between one form of financing and another. Surprisingly, perhaps the most visible effect of taxes is the negative after-tax costs of the two loans at the break-even rate of currency depreciation.[3] In contrast, the interest rate of 11% at the break-even level of cruzeiro depreciation in the no-tax case is highly positive.

In general, the break-even rate of currency appreciation or depreciation can be found by equating the dollar costs of local currency and dollar financing and solving for d:

$$r_H(1 - t_a) - dt_a = r_L(1 - d)(1 - t_a) - d$$

or

$$d^* = \frac{r_L(1 - t_a) - r_H(1 - t_a)}{1 + r_L)(1 - t_a)} = \frac{r_L - r_H}{1 + r_L} \qquad (12.6)$$

The tax rates cancel out and we are left with the same break-even value for d as in the before-tax case (see Equation 12.3). This result is the same as in the case of Du Pont's Brazilian affiliate and demonstrates that the earlier result was not a fluke.

Exhibit 12.2 Loan Cost Comparisons: Taxes

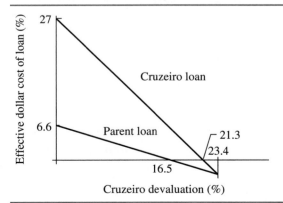

[3]The negative after-tax loan costs here are analogous to the negative real after-tax interest expenses often encountered during periods of high inflation.

12.5 SUMMARY AND CONCLUSIONS

This chapter has examined the various short-term financing alternatives available to a firm, focusing on parent company loans, local currency bank loans, and commercial paper. We saw how factors such as relative interest rates, anticipated currency changes, tax rates, the existence of forward contracts, and economic exposure combine to affect a firm's short-term borrowing choices. Various objectives that a firm might use to arrive at its borrowing strategy were evaluated. It was concluded that if forward contracts exist, the only valid objective is to minimize covered after-tax interest costs. In the absence of forward contracts, firms can either attempt to minimize expected costs or establish some trade-off between reducing expected costs and reducing the degree of cash-flow exposure. The latter goal involves offsetting operating cash inflows in a currency with financing cash outflows in that same currency.

This chapter also developed formulas to compute effective dollar costs of loans denominated in dollars (home currency) or local currency in the presence and absence of taxes. These formulas were then used to calculate the break-even rates of currency appreciation or depreciation that would equalize the costs of borrowing in the local currency or in the home currency.

QUESTIONS

1. Comment on the following statement: "One should borrow in those currencies expected to depreciate and invest in those expected to appreciate."

2. How can taxes affect the choice of currency denomination for loans?

3. How can the choice of currency denomination of loans enable a firm to reduce its exchange risk?

4. What are the three basic types of bank loans? Describe their differences.

5. How does each of the following affect the relationship of stated and effective interest rates?

   a. The lending bank requires the borrower to repay principal and interest at the end of the borrowing period only.

   b. The lending bank requires the borrower to maintain a compensating balance.

   c. Interest is deducted from the amount borrowed before the borrower receives the proceeds.

   d. What is the likely ranking of the above from least to most expensive?

6. Explain the characteristics of commercial paper that tend to limit its use to financially sound firms.

PROBLEMS

1. Apex Supplies borrows FF 1 million at 12%, payable in one year. If Apex is required to maintain a compensating balance of 20%, what is the effective percentage cost of its loan (in FF)?

2. The Olivera Corp., a manufacturer of olive oil products, needs to acquire Lit 100 million in funds today to expand a pimento-stuffing facility. Banca di Roma has offered them a choice of an 11% loan payable at maturity or a 10% loan on a discount basis. Which loan should Olivera choose?

3. To finance production of its new F-16 bubble gum, Hong Kong-based Top Gum Co. has been offered a one-year loan of HK$1.25 million at 9% payable at maturity with a 10% compensating balance.
  a. What is the effective interest rate on this loan (in HK$)?
  b. If the compensating balance requirement is 20%, what will be the effective interest rate?
  c. If the compensating balance is 10%, but the loan is on a discount basis, what will be the effective interest rate?
  d. If the company requires HK$1.25 million, how much must it borrow in part c to receive this amount?

4. If Consolidated Corp. issues a Eurobond denominated in yen, the 7% interest rate on the $1-million, one-year borrowing will be 2% less than rates in the United States. However, ConCorp would have to pay back the principal and interest in Japanese yen. Currently, the exchange rate is ¥183 = $1. By how much could the yen rise against the dollar before the Euroyen bond would lose its advantage to ConCorp?

5. Although the one-year interest rate is 10% in the United States, one-year, yen-denominated corporate bonds in Japan yield only 5%.
  a. Does this present a riskless opportunity to raise capital at low yen interest rates?
  b. Suppose the current exchange rate is ¥140 = $1. What is the lowest future exchange rate at which borrowing yen would be no more expensive than borrowing U.S. dollars?

6. Ford can borrow dollars at 12% or pesos at 80% for one year. The peso:dollar exchange rate is expected to move from $1 = Ps 3300 currently to $1 = Ps 4500 by year's end.
  a. What is the expected after-tax dollar cost of borrowing dollars for one year if the Mexican corporate tax rate is 53%?
  b. What is Ford's expected after-tax dollar cost of borrowing pesos for one year?
  c. At what end-of-year exchange rate will the after-tax peso cost of borrowing dollars equal the after-tax peso cost of borrowing pesos?

7. The manager of an English subsidiary of a U.S. firm is trying to decide whether to borrow, for one year, dollars at 7.8% or pounds sterling at 12%. If the current value of the pound is $1.70, at what end-of-year exchange rate would the firm be indifferent now between borrowing dollars and pounds?

8. Suppose that a firm located in Belgium can borrow dollars at 8% or Belgian francs at 14%.
  a. If the Belgian franc is expected to depreciate from BF 58 = $1 at the beginning of the year to BF 61 = $1 at the end of the year, what is the expected before-tax dollar cost of the Belgian franc loan?
  b. If the Belgian corporate tax rate is 42%, what is the expected after-tax dollar cost of borrowing dollars, assuming the same currency change scenario?
  c. Given the expected exchange rate change, which currency yields the lower expected after-tax dollar cost?

BIBLIOGRAPHY

Financing Foreign Operations. New York: Business International Corporation, various issues.

Lessard, Donald R. "Currency and Tax Considerations in International Financing." Teaching Note No. 3, Massachusetts Institute of Technology, Spring 1979.

Shapiro, Alan C. "Evaluating Financing Costs for Multinational Subsidiaries." *Journal of International Business Studies*, Fall 1975, pp. 25–32.

————. Chapter 29 in *Modern Corporate Finance*. New York: Macmillan, 1990.

13 Financing Foreign Trade

The development of a new product is a three-step process: first, a U.S. firm announces an invention; second, the Russians claim they made the same discovery 20 years ago; third, the Japanese start exporting it.

Anonymous

KEY TERMS

banker's acceptance
Bankers' Association for
  Foreign Trade
bill of exchange
bill of lading (B/L)
buyback
buyer credits
cash in advance
clean B/L
clean draft
clean L/C
commercial invoice
confirmed L/C
consignment
consular invoice
countertrade
discounting
documentary draft
documentary L/C
draft
export-credit insurance
Export-Import Bank
  (Eximbank)
factoring
Foreign Credit Insurance
  Association (FCIA)
forfaiting
foul B/L
irrevocable L/C
letter of credit (L/C)
open account selling
order B/L
Private Export Funding
  Corporation (PEFCO)
received-for-shipment B/L
recourse
revocable L/C
sight draft
straight B/L
supplier credits
time draft
trade acceptance
transferable L/C
unconfirmed L/C

CHAPTER LEARNING OBJECTIVES

- To describe the five principal means of payment in international trade
- To explain from the standpoint of an exporter the advantages and disadvantages associated with each means of arranging payment
- To identify the necessary documentation associated with each payment procedure
- To describe the primary functions associated with the use of the basic trade-financing instruments and documents
- To describe the different methods of private sector export financing
- To explain the benefits and costs of factoring
- To identify the different government-sponsored export-financing and credit insurance programs
- To describe the trends and consequences of public sector export financing
- To define countertrade and describe the specific forms it takes
- To explain the costs and benefits to both parties of countertrade transactions

Most multinational corporations are heavily involved in foreign trade in addition to their other international activities. The financing of trade-related working capital requires large amounts of money, as well as financial services such as letters of credit and acceptances. It is vital, therefore, that the multinational financial executive have knowledge of the institutions and documentary procedures that have evolved over the centuries to facilitate the international movement of goods. Much of the material in this chapter is descriptive in nature, but interspersed throughout will be discussions of the role of these special financial techniques and their associated advantages and disadvantages.

The main purpose of this chapter is to describe and analyze the various payment terms possible in international trade, along with the necessary documentation associated with each procedure. It also examines the different methods and sources of export financing and credit insurance that are available from the public sector. The final section discusses the rise of countertrade, a sophisticated word for barter.

13.1 PAYMENT TERMS IN INTERNATIONAL TRADE

Every shipment abroad requires some kind of financing while in transit. The exporter also needs financing to buy or manufacture its goods. Similarly, the importer has to carry these goods in inventory until the goods are sold. Then, it must finance its customers' receivables.

A financially strong exporter can finance the entire trade cycle out of its own funds by extending credit until the importer has converted these goods into cash. Alternatively, the importer can finance the entire cycle by paying cash in advance. Usually, however, some in-between approach is chosen, involving a combination of financing by the exporter, the importer, and one or more financial intermediaries.

The various means of payment in international trade impose different risks on the exporter.

The five principal means of payment in international trade, ranked in terms of increasing risk to the exporter, are

— Cash in advance
— Letter of credit
— Draft
— Consignment
— Open account

As a general rule, the greater the protection afforded the exporter, the less convenient are the payment terms for the buyer (importer). Some of these methods, however, are designed to protect both parties against commercial and/or political risks. It is up to the exporter when choosing among these payment methods to weigh the benefits in risk reduction against the cost of lost sales.

The five basic means of payment are discussed in the following paragraphs.

Cash in Advance

Cash in advance affords the exporter the greatest protection because payment is received either before shipment or upon arrival of the goods. This method also allows the exporter to avoid tying up its own funds. Although less common than in the past, cash payment upon presentation of documents is still widespread.

Cash in advance minimizes payment risk, but importers will often balk at this payment method.

Cash terms are used where there is political instability in the importing country or where the buyer's credit is doubtful. Political crises or exchange controls in the purchaser's country may cause payment delays or even prevent fund transfers, leading to a demand for cash in advance. In addition, where goods are made to order, prepayment is usually demanded, both to finance production and to reduce marketing risks.

Letter of Credit

Importers will often balk at paying cash in advance, however, and will demand credit terms instead. When credit is extended, the *letter of credit* (L/C) offers the exporter the greatest degree of safety.

If the importer is not well known to the exporter or if exchange restrictions exist or are possible in the importer's country, the exporter selling on credit may wish to have the importer's promise of payment backed by a foreign or domestic bank. On the other hand, the importer may not wish to pay the exporter until it is reasonably certain that the merchandise has been shipped in good condition. A letter of credit satisfies both of these conditions.

The letter of credit (L/C) is a bank guarantee of payment provided that certain stipulated conditions are met.

In essence, the letter of credit is a letter addressed to the seller, written and signed by a bank acting on behalf of the buyer. In the letter, the bank promises it will honor drafts drawn on itself if the seller conforms to the specific conditions set forth in the L/C. (The draft, which is a written order to pay, is discussed in the next part of this section.) Through an L/C, the bank substitutes its own commitment to pay for that of its customer (the importer). The letter of credit, therefore, becomes a financial contract between the issuing bank and a designated beneficiary that is separate from the commercial transaction.

The advantages to the exporter are as follows:

1. Most important, an L/C eliminates credit risk if the bank that opens it is of undoubted standing. Therefore, the firm need check only on the credit reputation of the issuing bank.
2. An L/C also reduces the danger that payment will be delayed or withheld due to exchange controls or other political acts. Countries generally permit local banks to honor their letters of credit. Failure to honor them could severely damage the country's credit standing and credibility.
3. An L/C reduces uncertainty. The exporter knows all the requirements for payment because they are clearly stipulated on the L/C.
4. The L/C can also guard against preshipment risks. The exporter who manufactures under contract a specialized piece of equipment runs the risk of contract cancellation before shipment. Opening a letter of credit will provide protection during the manufacturing phase.
5. Last, and certainly not least, the L/C facilitates financing because it ensures the exporter a ready buyer for its product. It also becomes especially easy to create a banker's acceptance—a draft accepted by a bank.

The L/C contains advantages for both the importer and the exporter.

Most advantages of an L/C are realized by the seller; nevertheless, there are some advantages to the buyer as well.

1. Because payment is only in compliance with the L/C's stipulated conditions, the importer is able to ascertain that the merchandise is actually shipped on, or before, a certain date by requiring an on-board bill of lading. The importer can also require an inspection certificate.
2. Any documents required are carefully inspected by clerks with years of experience. Moreover, the bank bears responsibility for any oversight.

3. Because an L/C is about as good as cash in advance, the importer can usually command better credit terms and/or prices.
4. Some exporters will sell only on a letter of credit. Willingness to provide one expands a firm's sources of supply.
5. L/C financing may be cheaper than the alternatives. There is no tie-up of cash if the L/C substitutes for cash in advance.
6. If prepayment is required, the importer is better off depositing its money with a bank than with the seller because it is then easier to recover the deposit if the seller is unable or unwilling to make a proper shipment.

The mechanics of letter-of-credit financing are quite simple. To illustrate its application, consider the case of U.S.A. Importers, Inc., of Los Angeles. The company is buying spare auto parts worth $38,000 from Japan Exporters, Inc., of Tokyo, Japan. U.S.A. Importers applies for, and receives, a letter of credit for $38,000 from its bank, Wells Fargo. The actual L/C is shown in Exhibit 13.1. Exhibit 13.2, in turn, shows the relationships between the three parties to the letter of credit.

After Japan Exporters has shipped the goods, it draws a draft against the issuing bank (Wells Fargo) and presents it, along with the required documents, to its own bank, the Bank of Tokyo. The Bank of Tokyo, in turn, forwards the bank draft and attached documents to Wells Fargo; Wells Fargo pays the draft upon receiving evidence that all conditions set forth in the L/C have been met. Exhibit 13.3 details the sequence of steps in the L/C transaction.

Most L/Cs issued in connection with commercial transactions are *documentary*—that is, the seller must submit, together with the draft, any necessary invoices and the like. The documents required from Japan Exporters are listed on the face of the letter of credit in Exhibit 13.1 following the words "accompanied by the following documents." A *nondocumentary*, or *clean*, L/C is normally used in other than commercial transactions.

The letter of credit can be revocable or irrevocable. A *revocable L/C* is a means of arranging payment, but it does not carry a guarantee. It can be revoked, without notice, at any time up to the time a draft is presented to the issuing bank. An *irrevocable L/C*, on the other hand, cannot be revoked without the specific permission of all parties concerned, including the exporter. Most credits between unrelated parties are irrevocable; otherwise, the advantage of commitment to pay is lost. In the case of Japan Exporters, the L/C is irrevocable.

The essential feature of the irrevocable L/C is that it substitutes the bank's name for the importer's.

Although the essential character of a letter of credit—the substitution of the bank's name for the merchant's—is absent with a revocable credit, this type of L/C is useful in some respects. Just the fact that a bank is willing to open a letter of credit for the importer gives an indication of the customer's creditworthiness. Thus, it is safer than sending goods on a collection basis, where payment is made by a draft only after the goods have been shipped. Of equal, if not greater, importance is the probability that imports covered by letters of credit will be given priority in the allocation of foreign exchange should currency controls be imposed.

A letter of credit can also be confirmed or unconfirmed. A *confirmed L/C* is an L/C issued by one bank and confirmed by another, obligating both banks to

Exhibit 13.1 Letter of Credit

SOURCE: Used with permission of Wells Fargo Bank.

Exhibit 13.2 Relationships Between the Three Parties to a Letter of Credit

Wells Fargo Bank
(issuing bank)

The relationship between the issuing bank (Wells Fargo) and the beneficiary (Japan Exporters) is governed by the terms of the credit as issued by that bank.

The relationship between the importer (U.S.A. Importers) and the issuing bank (Wells Fargo) is governed by the terms of the application and agreement for the letter of credit.

The relationship between Japan Exporters and U.S.A. Importers is governed by the sales contract.

Japan Exporters
(exporter)

U.S.A. Importers
(importer)

SOURCE: Adapted from *Export and Import Financing Procedures*. First National Bank of Chicago, p. 22.

honor any drafts drawn in compliance. An *unconfirmed L/C* is the obligation of only the issuing bank.

An exporter will prefer an irrevocable letter of credit by the importer's bank with confirmation by a domestic bank. In this way, the exporter need look no further than a bank in its own country for compliance with terms of the letter of credit. For example, if the Bank of Tokyo had confirmed the letter of credit issued by Wells Fargo and Wells Fargo, for whatever reason, fails to honor its irrevocable L/C, Japan Exporters can collect $38,000 from the Bank of Tokyo, assuming that Japan Exporters has met all the necessary conditions. This arrangement serves two purposes. Most exporters are not in a position to evaluate or deal with a foreign bank directly should difficulties arise. Domestic confirmation avoids this problem. In addition, should the foreign bank be unable to fulfill its commitment to pay, whether because of foreign exchange controls or political directives, that is of no concern to the exporter. The domestic confirming bank must still honor all drafts in full.

The confirmed L/C protects the exporter against problems with the bank that issued the L/C.

Thus, the three main types of L/C, in order of safety for the exporter, are (1) the irrevocable, confirmed L/C; (2) the irrevocable, unconfirmed L/C; and (3) the revocable L/C. Selecting the type of L/C to use depends on an evaluation of the risks associated with the transaction and the relative costs involved. One of the costs is the possibility of lost sales if the importer can get better credit terms elsewhere.

An exporter who acts as an intermediary may have to provide some assurance to its supplier that the supplier will be paid. It can provide this assurance by transferring or assigning the proceeds of the letter of credit opened in its name to the manufacturer.

A *transferable L/C* is one under which the beneficiary has the right to instruct the paying bank to make the credit available to one or more secondary beneficiaries. No L/C is transferable unless specifically authorized in the credit; more-

Exhibit 13.3　Example of Letter of Credit Financing of U.S. Imports

————— Process preceding creation of L/C
————— Process after creation of L/C

over, it can be transferred only once. The stipulated documents are transferred along with the L/C.

An *assignment*, in contrast to a transfer, assigns part or all of the proceeds to another party, but does not transfer to the party the required documents. This provision is not as safe to the assignee as a transfer because the assignee does not have control of the required merchandise and documentation.

The Draft

The draft is an unconditional written order to pay commonly used in international trade.

Commonly used in international trade, a *draft* is an unconditional order in writing—usually signed by the exporter (seller) and addressed to the importer (buyer) or the importer's agent—ordering the importer to pay on demand, or at a fixed or determinable future date, the amount specified on its face. Such an instrument, also known as a *bill of exchange*, serves three important functions:

— To provide written evidence, in clear and simple terms, of a financial obligation
— To enable both parties to potentially reduce their costs of financing
— To provide a negotiable and unconditional instrument (That is, payment must be made to any holder in due course despite any disputes over the underlying commercial transaction.)

Using a draft also enables an exporter to employ its bank as a collection agent. The bank forwards the draft or bill of exchange to the foreign buyer (either directly or through a branch or correspondent bank), collects on the draft, and then remits the proceeds to the exporter. The bank has all the necessary documents for control of the merchandise and turns them over to the importer only when the draft has been paid or accepted in accordance with the exporter's instructions.

The conditions for a draft to be negotiable under the U.S. Uniform Commercial Code are that it must be

— In writing
— Signed by the issuer (drawer)
— An unconditional order to pay
— A certain sum of money
— Payable on demand or at a definite future time
— Payable to order of bearer

There are usually three parties to a draft. The party who signs and sends the draft to the second party is called the *drawer*; payment is made to the third party, the *payee*. Normally, the drawer and payee are the same person. The party to whom the draft is addressed is the *drawee*, who may be either the buyer or if a letter of credit was used, the buyer's bank. In the case of a confirmed L/C, the drawee would be the confirming bank.

The three parties to a draft are the drawer, the payee, and the drawee.

In the previous example, Japan Exporters is the drawer and the Bank of Tokyo is the payee. The drawee is Wells Fargo under the terms of the L/C. This information is included in the draft shown in Exhibit 13.4.

Drafts may be either sight or time drafts. *Sight drafts* must be paid on presentation or else dishonored. *Time drafts* are payable at some specified future date and as such become a useful financing device. The maturity of a time draft is known as its *usance* or *tenor*. As mentioned earlier, to qualify as a negotiable instrument, the date of payment must be determinable. For example, a time draft payable "upon delivery of goods" is not specific enough, given the vagaries of ocean freight, and, hence, will likely nullify its negotiability. As shown in Exhibit 13.4, the draft drawn under the letter of credit by Japan Exporters is a time draft with a tenor of 90 days, indicated by the words "at ninety days sight." Thus, the draft will mature on August 24, 90 days after it was drawn (May 26).

A time draft becomes an *acceptance* after being accepted by the drawee. Accepting a draft means writing *accepted* across its face, followed by an authorized person's signature and the date. The party accepting a draft incurs the obligation to pay it at maturity. A draft accepted by a bank becomes a *banker's acceptance*; one drawn on and accepted by a commercial enterprise is termed a *trade acceptance*. Exhibit 13.5 is the time draft in Exhibit 13.4 after being accepted by Wells Fargo.

The exporter can hold the acceptance or sell it at a discount from face value to its bank, to some other bank, or to an acceptance dealer. The discount normally is less than the prevailing prime rate for bank loans. These acceptances enjoy a wide market and are an important tool in the financing of international trade.

Exhibt 13.4 Time Draft

TOKYO, JAPAN	MAY 26	, 19 XX No. 712

AT NINETY DAYS _____ SIGHT OF THIS **ORIGINAL** OF EXCHANGE (DUPLICATE UNPAID)

PAY TO THE ORDER OF ___ BANK OF TOKYO _____ U.S. $ 38,000.00

THE SUM OF ___ THIRTY EIGHT THOUSAND AND NO/100 * U.S. Dollars

DRAWN UNDER LETTER OF CREDIT NO.	DATED	ISSUED BY
X Y Z 9000	MAY 6, 19XX	WELLS FARGO BANK

To WELLS FARGO BANK   *SPECIMEN*

770 WILSHIRE BLVD.

LOS ANGELES, CALIFORNIA   JAPAN EXPORTERS INC.

SOURCE: Used by permission of Wells Fargo Bank.

They are discussed in more detail in the next section. An acceptance can be transferred from one holder to another simply by endorsement.

Drafts can be clean or documentary. A *clean draft*, one unaccompanied by any other papers, is normally used only for nontrade remittances. Its primary purpose is to put pressure on a recalcitrant debtor that must pay or accept the draft or else face damage to its credit reputation.

Most drafts used in international trade are accompanied by documents to be delivered to the drawee on payment or acceptance of the draft.

Most drafts used in international trade are documentary. A *documentary draft*, which can be either sight or time, is accompanied by documents that are to be delivered to the drawee on payment or acceptance of the draft. Typically, these documents include the bill of lading in negotiable form, the commercial invoice, the consular invoice where required, and an insurance certificate. The bill of lading in negotiable form is the most important document because it gives its holder the right to control the goods covered. A documentary sight draft is also known as a D/P (documents against payment) draft; if documents are delivered on acceptance, it is a D/A draft.

There are two significant aspects to shipping goods under documentary time drafts for acceptance. First, the exporter is extending credit to the importer for the usance of the draft. Second, the exporter is relinquishing control of the goods in return for a signature on the acceptance to assure it of payment.

It is important to bear in mind that sight drafts are not always paid at presentation, nor are time drafts always paid at maturity. Firms can get bank statistics on the promptness of sight and time draft payments, by country, from bank publications such as Chase Manhattan's *Collection Experience* bulletin.

Unless a bank has accepted a draft, the exporter must ultimately look to the importer for payment. Thus, use of a sight or accepted time draft is warranted only when the exporter has faith in the importer's financial strength and integrity.

Exhibit 13.5 Banker's Acceptance

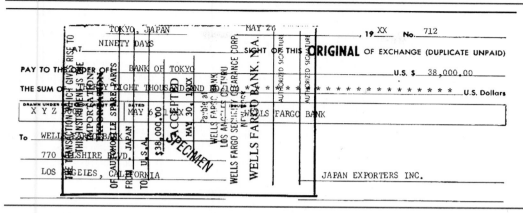

SOURCE: Used by permission of Wells Fargo Bank.

Consignment

Goods sent on *consignment* are only shipped to the importer, but they are not sold. The exporter (consignor) retains title to the goods until the importer (consignee) has sold them to a third party. This arrangement is normally made only with a related company because of the large risks involved. There is little evidence of the buyer's obligation to pay, and should the buyer default, it will prove difficult to collect.

The seller must carefully consider the credit risks involved and also the availability of foreign exchange in the importer's country. Imports covered by documentary drafts receive priority over imports shipped on consignment.

Open Account

Open account selling is shipping goods first and billing the importer later. The credit terms are arranged between the buyer and the seller, but the seller has little evidence of the importer's obligation to pay a certain amount at a certain date. Sales on open account, therefore, are made only to a foreign affiliate or to a customer with which the exporter has a long history of favorable business dealings. However, open account sales have greatly expanded due to the major increase in international trade, the improvement in credit information about importers, and the greater familiarity with exporting in general. The benefits include greater flexibility (no specific payment dates are set) and involve lower costs, including fewer bank charges than with other methods of payment. As with shipping on consignment, the possibility of currency controls is an important factor because of the low priority in allocating foreign exchange normally accorded this type of transaction.

Exhibit 13.6 summarizes some of the advantages and disadvantages associated with the various means of arranging payment in international trade.

Goods that are shipped to the importer with payment to be made later are subject to the risk of currency controls.

Exhibit 13.6 International Methods of Payment: Advantages and Disadvantages (Ranked by Risk)

Method	Risk*	Chief Advantage	Chief Disadvantage
Cash in advance	L	No credit extension required	Can limit sales potential, disturb some potential customers
Sight draft	M/L	Retains control and title; ensures payment before goods are delivered	If customer does not or cannot accept goods, goods remain at port of entry and no payment is due.
Letters of credit Irrevocable Revocable	 M M/H	Banks accept responsibility to pay; payment upon presentation of papers; costs go to buyer	If revocable, terms can change during contract work.
Time draft	M/H	Lowers customer resistance by allowing extended payment after receipt of goods	Same as sight draft, plus goods are delivered before payment is due or received
Consignment sales	M/H	Facilitates delivery; lowers customer resistance	Capital tied up until sales; must establish distributor's creditworthiness; need political risk insurance in some countries; increased risk from currency controls
Open account	H	Simplified procedure; no customer resistance	High risk; seller must finance production; increased risk from currency controls

*L: low risk; M: medium risk; H: high risk

Collecting Overdue Accounts

Typically, 1%–3% of a company's export sales go uncollected. Small businesses, however, take more risks than do large ones, often selling on terms other than a confirmed letter of credit. One reason is that they are eager to develop a new market opportunity; another reason is that they aren't as well versed in the mechanics of foreign sales. Thus, their percentage of uncollected export sales may be higher than is that of large companies.

Once an account becomes delinquent, sellers have three options: (1) They can try to collect the account themselves; (2) they can hire an attorney who is experienced in international law; or (3) they can engage the services of a collection agency.

The first step is for sellers to attempt to recover the money themselves. Turning the bill over to a collection agency or a lawyer too quickly will hurt the customer relationship. However, after several telephone calls, telexes, and/or personal visits, the firm must decide whether to write the account off or pursue it further.

The cost of hiring a high-priced U.S. lawyer, who then contacts an expensive foreign lawyer, is a deterrent to following the second option for receivables of less than $100,000. With such a relatively small amount, a collection agency would usually be more appropriate. Unlike lawyers, who charge by the hour for their services, regardless of the amount recovered, collection agencies work on a percentage basis. A typical fee is 20%–25% of the amount collected, but if the claim is over $25,000 or so, the agency will often negotiate a more favorable rate.

Collecting overdue accounts in a foreign country is a frustrating and expensive process.

Even with professional help, there are no guarantees of collecting on foreign receivables. This reality puts a premium on checking a customer's credit prior to filling an order. However, getting credit information on specific foreign firms is often difficult.

One good source of credit information is the U.S. Department of Commerce's International Trade Administration (ITA). Its *World Data Trade Reports* covers nearly 200,000 foreign establishments and can be obtained from district offices of ITA for $75. Other places to check on the creditworthiness of foreign companies and governments are export management companies and the international departments of commercial banks. Also, Dun & Bradstreet International publishes *Principal International Businesses*, a book with information on about 50,000 foreign enterprises in 133 countries.

The National Association of Credit Management collects data on how much time it takes to collect on the average bill from importers in various foreign countries. Exhibit 13.7, which contains these data for the second quarter of 1992, shows the wide variation in collection times by country.

Exhibit 13.7 Your Check Is Not in the Mail Yet: Length of Time Required for U.S. Companies to Collect on the Average Bill from Concerns in Selected Foreign Countries in the Second Quarter of 1992

Country	Number of Days
Iran	337
Kenya	129
Argentina	123
Brazil	119
Italy	90
India	80
Mexico	74
Taiwan	73
United Kingdom	70
Japan	58
Germany	54

SOURCE: Michael Selz, "Small Firms Hit Foreign Obstacles in Billing Overseas," *The Wall Street Journal*, December 18, 1992, p. B2. Reprinted by permission of *The Wall Street Journal*, © Dow Jones & Company, Inc. 1992. All rights reserved worldwide.

Banks and Trade Financing

Historically, banks have been involved in only a single step in international trade transactions such as providing a loan or a letter of credit. But as financing has become an integral part of many trade transactions, U.S. banks—especially major money center banks—have evolved as well. They have gone from financing individual trade deals to providing comprehensive solutions to trade needs. This includes combining bank lending with subsidized funds from government export agencies, international leasing, and other nonbank financing sources, along with political and economic risk insurance.

13.2 DOCUMENTS IN INTERNATIONAL TRADE

The most important supporting document required in commercial bank financing of exports is the bill of lading. Of secondary importance are the commercial invoice, consular invoice, and insurance certificate.

Bill of Lading

The bill of lading is the document covering actual shipment of the merchandise by a common carrier and title.

Of the shipping documents, the *bill of lading* (B/L) is the most important. It serves three main and separate functions:

1. It is a contract between the carrier and shipper (exporter) in which the former agrees to carry the goods from port of shipment to port of destination.
2. It is the shipper's receipt for the goods.
3. The negotiable B/L, its most common form, is a document that establishes control over the goods.

A bill of lading can be either a straight or order B/L. A *straight B/L* consigns the goods to a specific party, normally the importer, and is not negotiable. Because title cannot be transferred to a third party merely by endorsement and delivery, a straight B/L is not good collateral and, therefore, is used only when no financing is involved.

Most trade transactions do involve financing, which requires transfer of title, so the vast majority of bills of lading are order B/Ls. Under an *order B/L*, the goods are consigned to the order of a named party, usually the exporter. In this way, the exporter retains title to the merchandise until it endorses the B/L on the reverse side. The exporter's representative may endorse to a specific party or endorse it in blank by simply signing his or her name. The shipper delivers the cargo in the port of destination to the bearer of the endorsed order B/L, who must surrender it.

Because an order B/L represents goods in transit that are probably readily marketable and fully insured, this document is generally considered to be good collateral by banks. It is required under L/C financing and for discounting of drafts.

Bills of lading can also be classified in several other ways. An *on-board* B/L certifies that the goods have actually been placed on board the vessel. By contrast, a *received-for-shipment* B/L merely acknowledges that the carrier has received the goods for shipment. It does not state that the ship is in port or that space is available. The cargo can, therefore, sit on the dock for weeks, or even months, before it is shipped. When goods are seasonal or perishable, therefore, the received-for-shipment B/L is never satisfactory to either the shipper or the importer. A received-for-shipment B/L can easily be converted into an on-board B/L by stamping it "on-board" and supplying the name of the vessel, the date, and the signature of the captain or the captain's representative.

A *clean B/L* indicates that the goods were received in apparently good condition. However, the carrier is not obligated to check beyond the external visual appearance of the boxes. If boxes are damaged or in poor condition, this observation is noted on the B/L, which then becomes a *foul B/L*. It is important that the exporter get a clean B/L—that is, one with no such notation—because foul B/Ls are generally not acceptable under a letter of credit.

Commercial Invoice

A *commercial invoice* contains an authoritative description of the merchandise shipped, including full details on quality, grades, price per unit, and total value. It also contains the names and addresses of the exporter and importer, the number of packages, any distinguishing external marks, the payment terms, other expenses such as transportation and insurance charges, any fees collectible from the importer, the name of the vessel, the ports of departure and destination, and any required export or import permit numbers.

Trade documents that are necessary but of lesser importance include commercial and consular invoices and the insurance receipts.

Insurance

All cargoes going abroad are insured. Most of the insurance contracts used today are under an *open*, or *floating*, policy. This policy automatically covers all shipments made by the exporter, thereby eliminating the necessity of arranging individual insurance for each shipment. To evidence insurance for a shipment under an open policy, the exporter makes out an *insurance certificate* on forms supplied by the insurance company. This certificate contains information on the goods shipped. All entries must conform exactly with the information on the B/L, on the commercial invoice and, where required, on the consular invoice.

Consular Invoice

Exports to many countries require a special *consular invoice*. This invoice, which varies in its details and information requirements from nation to nation, is presented to the local consul in exchange for a visa. The form must be filled out very carefully, for even trivial inaccuracies can lead to substantial fines and delays in customs clearance. The consular invoice does not convey any title to the goods being shipped and is not negotiable.

13.3 FINANCING TECHNIQUES IN INTERNATIONAL TRADE

In addition to straight bank financing, there are several other techniques available for trade financing: bankers' acceptances, discounting, factoring, and forfaiting.

Bankers' Acceptances

The banker's acceptance is a time draft drawn on a bank that the bank agrees to pay on maturity.

Bankers' acceptances have played an important role in financing international trade for many centuries. As we saw in the previous section, a banker's acceptance is a time draft drawn on a bank. By "accepting" the draft, the bank makes an unconditional promise to pay the holder of the draft a stated amount on a specified day. Thus, the bank effectively substitutes its own credit for that of a borrower, and in the process, it creates a negotiable instrument that may be freely traded.

An importer of goods can use a banker's acceptance to finance its purchase until the goods can be resold.

Creating an Acceptance. A typical acceptance transaction is shown in Exhibit 13.7. An importer of goods seeks credit to finance its purchase until the goods can be resold. The importer requests its bank to issue a letter of credit on its behalf, authorizing the foreign exporter to draw a time draft on the bank in payment for the goods. Based on this authorization, the exporter ships the goods on an order B/L made out to itself and presents a time draft and the endorsed shipping documents to its bank. The foreign bank then forwards the draft and the appropriate shipping documents to the importer's bank; the importer's bank accepts the draft and, thus, creates a banker's acceptance. The exporter discounts the draft with the accepting bank and receives payment for the shipment. The shipping documents are delivered to the importer, and the importer may now claim the shipment. The accepting bank may either buy (discount) the B/A and hold it in its own portfolio or sell (rediscount) the B/A in the money market; in Exhibit 13.8, the bank sells the acceptance in the money market.

Terms of Acceptance Financing. Typical maturities on bankers' acceptances are 30 days, 90 days, and 180 days, with the average being 90 days. Maturities can be tailored, though, to cover the entire period needed to ship and dispose of the goods financed.

For an investor, a banker's acceptance is a close substitute for other bank liabilities, such as certificates of deposit (CDs). Consequently, bankers' acceptances trade at rates very close to those on CDs. Market yields, however, do not give a complete picture of the costs of acceptance financing to the borrower because the accepting bank levies a fee, or commission, for accepting the draft. The fee varies depending on the maturity of the draft as well as the creditworthiness of the borrower, but it averages less than 1% per annum. The bank also receives a fee if a letter of credit is involved. In addition, the bank may hope to realize a profit on the difference between the price at which it purchases and the price at which it resells the acceptance.

On the maturity date of the acceptance, the accepting bank is required to pay the current holder the amount stated on the draft. The holder of a bank acceptance

Exhibit 13.8 Example of Banker's Acceptance Financing of U.S. Imports: Created, Discounted, Sold, and Paid at Maturity

— — — —   Process preceding creation of B/A
——————   Process after creation of B/A

SOURCE: "Bankers' Acceptances," Jeremy G. Duffield and Bruce J. Summers, in *Instruments of the Money Market,* Timothy Q. Cook and Bruce J. Summers, eds. Federal Reserve Bank of Richmond, 1981, p. 116. Used with permission.

has recourse for the full amount of the draft from the last endorser in the event of the importer's unwillingness or inability to pay at maturity. The authenticity of an accepted draft is separated from the underlying commercial transaction and may not be dishonored for reason of a dispute between the exporter and importer. This factor, of course, significantly enhances its marketability and reduces its riskiness.

In recent years, the demand for acceptance financing has fallen off. One factor has been the increased availability of funding from nonbank investors in the U.S. commercial paper market. Prime commercial paper generally trades at rates near those on acceptance liabilities of prime banks; for firms with access to this market, the overall cost—including placement fees charged by dealers and fees for back-up line of credit—is usually below the all-in cost of acceptance financing.

Evaluating the Cost of Acceptance Financing. Suppose that the discount rate on a $1 million acceptance for 90 days is 9.8% per annum and the acceptance fee is 1% per annum. If the exporter chooses to hold the acceptance, then in 90 days it will receive the face amount less the acceptance fee:

Face amount of acceptance	$1,000,000
Less: 1% per annum commission for 90 days	−5,000
Amount received by exporter in 90 days	$995,000

Alternatively, the exporter can sell the acceptance at a 2.45% discount (9.8%/4) and receive $970,500 immediately:

Face amount of acceptance	$1,000,000
Less: 1% per annum commission for 90 days	−5,000
Less: 9.8% per annum discount for 90 days	−24,500
Amount received by exporter immediately	$970,500

Whether the exporter should discount the acceptance or wait depends on the opportunity cost of money. Suppose that the exporter's opportunity cost of money is 10.2%. Then the present value of holding onto the acceptance is $995,000/(1 + (.102/4)), or $970,258. In this case, the exporter would come out ahead by selling the acceptance.

Discounting

A trade draft can be converted into cash my means of discounting.

Even if a trade draft is not accepted by a bank, the exporter can still convert the trade draft into cash by means of *discounting*. The exporter places the draft with a bank or other financial institution and, in turn, receives the face value of the draft less interest and commissions. By insuring the draft against both commercial and political risks, the exporter will often pay a lower interest rate. If losses covered by the insurer do occur, the insuring agency will reimburse the exporter or any institution to which the exporter transfers the draft.

The discount rate for trade paper is often lower than interest rates on overdrafts, bank loans, and other forms of local funding. This lower rate is usually a result of export promotion policies that lead to direct or indirect subsidies of rates on export paper. Discounting may be done with or without *recourse*. With recourse, the bank can collect from the exporter if the importer fails to pay the bill when due. The bank bears the collection risk if the draft is sold without recourse.

Factoring

Firms with a substantial export business and companies too small to afford a foreign credit and collections department can turn to a *factor*. Factors buy a company's receivables at a discount, thereby accelerating their conversion into cash. Most factoring is done on a *nonrecourse* basis, which means that the factor assumes all the credit and political risks except for those involving disputes between the transacting parties. The exporter assumes these risks in factoring *with recourse*.

Firms with a substantial export business can sell their receivables to a factor for cash.

Factoring is becoming increasingly popular as a trade financing vehicle. The value of world exports financed through factoring now exceeds $10 billion. By using a factor, a firm can ensure that its terms are in accord with local practice and are competitive. For instance, customers can be offered payment on open account rather than being asked for a letter of credit or stiffer credit requirements. If the margin on its factored sales is not sufficiently profitable, then the firm can bear the credit risks itself or forgo that business. Even if an exporter chooses not to discount its foreign receivables with a factor, it can still use the factor's extensive credit information files to ascertain the creditworthiness of prospective customers.

An exporter that has established an ongoing relationship with a factor will submit new orders directly to the factor. After evaluating the creditworthiness of the new claim, the factor will make a recourse/nonrecourse decision within two days to two weeks, depending on the availability of information.

Although the factors may consider their fees to be nominal considering the services provided, they are not cheap. Export factoring fees are determined on an individual company basis and are related to the annual turnover (usually a minimum of $500,000 to $1 million is necessary), the average invoice size (smaller invoices are more expensive because of the fixed information-gathering costs), the creditability of the claims, and the terms of sale. In general, these fees run from 1.75% to 2% of sales.

Factoring is expensive but may be of great value to the occasional exporter.

Evaluating the Cost of Factoring. Suppose that a factor will buy an exporter's receivables at a 2.5% per *month* discount. In addition, the factor will charge an extra 1.75% fee for nonrecourse financing. If the exporter decides to factor $1 million in 90-day receivables without nonrecourse, then it will receive $907,500 today:

Face amount of receivable	$1,000,000
Less: 1.75% nonrecourse fee	−17,500
Less: 3% monthly factoring fee	−75,000
Amount received by exporter	$907,500

On an annualized basis, factoring is costing this company 4 × (7.5% + 1.75%), or 37%. Despite these high costs, factoring can be quite worthwhile to many firms for one principal reason: The cost of bearing the credit risk associated with a given receivable can be substantially lower to a factor than to the selling firm. First, the factor's greater credit information makes it more knowledgeable of the actual, as opposed to the perceived, risks involved and, thereby, reduces its required risk premium. Second, by holding a well-diversified portfolio of receivables, the factor can eliminate some of the risks associated with individual receivables.

Factors are often better able to asses and bear credit risk.

In general, factoring is most useful for (1) the occasional exporter and (2) the exporter having a geographically diverse portfolio of accounts receivable. In both cases, it would be organizationally difficult and expensive to internalize the accounts receivable collection process. Such companies would generally be small or else be involved on a limited scale in foreign markets.

Forfaiting

The specialized factoring technique known as forfaiting is sometimes used in the case of extreme credit risk. *Forfaiting* is the discounting—at a fixed rate without recourse—of medium-term export receivables denominated in fully convertible currencies (U.S. dollar, Swiss franc, Deutsche mark). This technique is usually used in the case of capital-goods exports with a five-year maturity and repayment in semiannual installments. The discount is set at a fixed rate: about 1.25% above the local cost of funds.

Forfaiting is especially popular in Western Europe (primarily in Switzerland and Austria), and many forfaiting houses are subsidiaries of major international banks, such as Credit Suisse. These houses also provide help with administrative and collection problems.

13.4 GOVERNMENT SOURCES OF EXPORT FINANCING AND CREDIT INSURANCE

Governments often provide subsidized export credits to boost exports.

In the race for export orders, particularly for capital equipment and other "big-ticket" items requiring long repayment arrangements, most governments of developed countries have attempted to provide their domestic exporters with a competitive edge in the form of low-cost export financing and concessionary rates on political and economic risk insurance. Nearly every developed nation has its own export-import agency for development and trade financing.

Export Financing

Procedures for extending credit vary greatly among agencies. Many agencies offer funds in advance of the actual export contract, whereas private sources extend financing only after the sale has been made. Some programs extend credit only to the supplier—called *supplier credits*—to pass on to the importer; others grant credit directly to the buyer—called *buyer credits*—who then pays the supplier. The difference is that in the first arrangement, the supplier bears the credit risk, whereas in the latter case, the government is the risk bearer. Of course, the government often provides credit insurance in conjunction with supplier credits.

Export-Import Bank. The *Export-Import Bank* (*Eximbank*) is the only U.S. government agency dedicated solely to financing and facilitating U.S. exports. Eximbank loans provide competitive, fixed-rate financing for U.S. export sales facing foreign competition backed with subsidized official financing. Evidence of foreign competition is not required for exports produced by small businesses where the loan amount is $2.5 million or less. Eximbank also provides guarantees of loans made by others. The loan and guarantee programs cover up to 85% of the U.S. export value and have repayment terms of one year or more.

Eximbank operations generally conform to five basic principles:

1. Loans are made for the specific purpose of financing U.S. exports of goods and services. If a U.S. export item contains foreign-made components, Eximbank will cover up to 100% of the U.S. content of exports provided that the total amount financed or guaranteed does not exceed 85% of the total contract price of the item and that the total U.S. content accounts for at least half of the contract price.

2. Eximbank will not provide financing unless private capital is unavailable in the amounts required. It supplements, rather than competes with private capital.

3. Loans must have reasonable assurance of repayment and must be for projects that have a favorable impact on the country's economic and social well-being. The host government must be aware of, and not object to, the project.

4. Fees and premiums charged for guarantees and insurance are based on the risks covered.

5. In authorizing loans and other financial assistance, Eximbank is obliged to take into account any adverse effects on the U.S. economy or balance of payments that might occur.

The Export-Import Bank (Eximbank) is a U.S. government agency dedicated to financing and facilitating U.S. exports.

The interest rates on Eximbank's loans are based on an international arrangement among the 22 members of the Organization for Economic Cooperation and Development (OECD). The purpose of the arrangement, which sets minimum rates that an official export finance agency must charge on export credits, is to limit the interest subsidies used by many industrial countries to gain competitive advantage vis-à-vis other nations. The OECD minimum rates are based on the weighted average interest rate on government bond issues denominated in the U.S. dollar, German mark, British pound, French franc, and Japanese yen. In this way, rates on export credits are brought closer to market interest rates.

Eximbank extends direct loans to foreign buyers of U.S. exports and intermediary loans to financial institutions that extend loans to the foreign buyers. Both direct and intermediary loans are provided when U.S. exporters face officially subsidized foreign competition.

Eximbank's medium-term loans to intermediaries (where the loan amount is $10 million or less and the term is seven years or less) are structured as "standby" loan commitments. The intermediary may request disbursement by Eximbank at any time during the term of the underlying debt obligation.

Eximbank guarantees provide repayment protection for private sector loans to creditworthy buyers of exported U.S. goods and services. The guarantees are available alone or may be combined with an intermediary loan. Most guarantees provide comprehensive coverage of both political and commercial risks. Eximbank will also guarantee payments on cross-border or international leases.

Exporters may also have access to an Eximbank program that guarantees export-related working-capital loans to creditworthy small and medium-sized businesses. Since all Eximbank guarantees carry the full faith and credit of the U.S. government, loans provided under these guarantee programs are made at close to the risk-free interest rate. In effect, low-cost guarantees are another form of government-subsidized export financing.

Repayment terms vary with the project and type of equipment purchased. For capital goods, long-term credits are normally provided for a period of five years to ten years. Loans for projects and large product acquisitions are eligible for longer terms, while lower-unit-value items receive shorter terms. Loan amortization is made in semiannual installments, beginning six months after delivery of the exported equipment. Another program run by Eximbank provides a *preliminary commitment* that outlines the amount, terms, and conditions of financing it will extend to importers of U.S. goods and services. This commitment gives U.S. firms a competitive advantage in bidding on foreign projects because it enables the firms to offer financing along with their equipment proposals. Preliminary commitments are issued without cost (there is a $100 processing fee) or obligation to applicants.

Eximbank terms depend on the risk of the transaction and the degree of competition from foreign export financing agencies.

Eximbank charges a front-end *exposure fee*, assessed on each disbursement of a loan by Eximbank or the guaranteed or intermediary lender. Exposure fees, which are adjusted periodically, vary according to the term of the loan, the classification of the borrower or guarantor, and the borrower's country. For exposure-fee purposes, Eximbank classifies countries in five country categories according to risk. Under each country category, there are three borrower/guarantor classifications:

— Class I: Sovereign borrowers or guarantors, or for political-risks-only cover
— Class II: Creditworthy nonsovereign public institutions or banks, or highly creditworthy private buyers
— Class III: Other creditworthy private buyers

In recent years, Eximbank has become more aggressive in fighting perceived abuses by foreign export-credit agencies. One area that Eximbank has targeted is foreign *mixed-credit financing*—the practice of tying grants and low-interest loans to the acceptance of specific commercial contracts. For years, U.S. capital-equipment exporters, engineering firms, and high-tech producers have lost overseas bids to foreign firms backed by government mixed credits. Eximbank now offers its own mixed credits. It will even offer mixed-credit deals before the fact. Any deal that has a chance of attracting a foreign mixed-credit bid is considered. However, an Eximbank spokesperson noted, "This is not an export promotion. We are not out there to match every mixed credit. We're out to end mixed credits, and will only offer one if it helps us to make a specific negotiating point."[1]

Private Export Funding Corporation. The *Private Export Funding Corporation* (PEFCO) was created in 1970 by the *Bankers' Association for Foreign Trade* to mobilize private capital for financing the export of big-ticket items by U.S. firms. It purchases the medium- to long-term debt obligations of importers of U.S. products

---

[1]"How U.S. Firms Benefit from Eximbank's War on Foreign Mixed Credits," *Business International Money Report,* February 10, 1986, p. 41.

at fixed interest rates. PEFCO finances its portfolio of foreign importer loans through the sale of its own securities. Eximbank fully guarantees repayment of all PEFCO foreign obligations.

PEFCO normally extends its credits jointly with one or more commercial banks and Eximbank. The maturity of the importers' notes purchased by PEFCO varies from 2.5 years to 12 years; the banks take the short-term maturity and Eximbank, the long-term portion of a PEFCO loan. Much of this money goes to finance purchases of U.S.-manufactured jet aircraft and related equipment such as jet engines.

Trends. There are several trends in public-source export financing. These trends include

1. *A shift from supplier to buyer credits*: Many capital goods exports that cannot be financed under the traditional medium-term supplier credits become feasible under buyer credits, where the payment period can be stretched up to 20 years.
2. *A growing emphasis on acting as catalysts to attract private capital*: This action includes participating with private sources, either as a member of a financial consortium or as a partner with an individual private investor, in supplying export credits.
3. *Public agencies as a source of refinancing*: Public agencies are becoming an important source for refinancing loans made by bankers and private financiers. Refinancing enables a private creditor to discount its export loans with the government.
4. *Attempts to limit competition among agencies*: The virtual export-credit war among governments has led to several attempts to agree upon and coordinate financing terms. These attempts, however, have been honored more in the breach than in the observance.

> Government export financing agencies are shifting to buyer credits and are acting as catalysts to attract private capital.

The Effect of Export-Credit Subsidies

The benefits of the Eximbank do not come free of charge. Through much of the 1980s, the Eximbank has absorbed losses of more than $250 million a year. In fiscal 1987, it posted a record loss of $387 million. The bank borrows through the U.S. Treasury, which means that the credit terms it receives are first rate. However, lending below the market to help U.S. companies export ensures a persistent deficit. The obligation that American taxpayers take on to support this activity translates into a credit break for foreign firms that buy U.S. airplanes and the like.

Although the Eximbank claims that cut-rate loans are necessary to allow U.S. firms to compete with foreign exporters, the truth is that the Eximbank loans subsidize less than 3% of American merchandise exports. Another argument used by Eximbank officials is that their activities are justified because foreign governments subsidize exports. But a nation that subsidizes exports simply gives away part of its wealth. Moreover, there is reason to question whether export subsidies really improve the balance of trade. Any increase in exports achieved by a subsidy would necessarily increase the demand for dollars by foreign purchasers of U.S.

goods. The increase in demand would boost the dollar's value. Dollar appreciation would, of course, encourage further imports and discourage unsubsidized exports. Since savings and investment are unaffected by these subsidies, the trade deficit is unlikely to respond to export subsidies.

Export-Credit Insurance

Export financing covered by government credit insurance, also known as *export-credit insurance*, provides protection against losses from political and/or commercial risks. It serves as collateral for the credit and is often indispensable in making the sale. The insurance does not usually provide an ironclad guarantee against all risks, however. Having this insurance results in lowering the cost of borrowing from private institutions because the government agency is bearing those risks set forth in the insurance policy. The financing is nonrecourse to the extent that risks and losses are covered. Often, however, the insurer requires additional security in the form of a guarantee by a foreign local bank or a certificate from the foreign central bank that foreign exchange is available for repayment of the interest and principal.

The purpose of export-credit insurance is to encourage a nation's export sales by protecting domestic exporters against nonpayment by importers. The existence of medium- and long-term credit insurance policies makes banks more willing to provide nonrecourse financing of big-ticket items that require lengthy repayment maturities, provided the goods in question have been delivered and accepted.

Foreign Credit Insurance Association. In the United States, the export-credit insurance program is administered by the *Foreign Credit Insurance Association* (FCIA). The FCIA is a cooperative effort of Eximbank and a group of approximately 50 of the leading marine, casualty, and property insurance companies. FCIA insurance offers protection from political and commercial risks to U.S. exporters: The private insurers cover commercial risks, and the Eximbank covers political risks. The exporter (or the financial institution providing the loan) must self-insure that portion not covered by the FCIA.

Short-term insurance is available for export credits up to 180 days (360 days for bulk agricultural commodities and consumer durables) from the date of shipment. Coverage is of two types: comprehensive (90%–100% of political and 90%–95% of commercial risks) and political only (90%–100% coverage). Coinsurance is required presumably because of the element of moral hazard: the possibility that exporters might take unreasonable risks knowing that they would still be paid in full.

Rather than sell insurance on a case-by-case basis, the FCIA approves discretionary limits within which each exporter can approve its own credits. Insurance rates are based on the terms of sale, type of buyer, and the country of destination. The FCIA also offers preshipment insurance up to 180 days from the time of sale.

Medium-term insurance, guaranteed by Eximbank and covering big-ticket items sold on credit usually from 181 days to 5 years, is available on a case-by-case basis. As with short-term coverage, the exporter must reside in, and ship from, the United States. However, the FCIA will provide medium-term coverage for that portion only of the value-added that originated in the United States. As before, the rates depend on the terms of sale and the destination.

Under the FCIA lease insurance program, lessors of U.S. equipment and related services can cover both the stream of lease payments and the fair market value of products leased outside the United States. The FCIA charges a risk-based premium that is determined by country, lease term, and the type of lease.

13.5 COUNTERTRADE

In recent years, more and more multinationals have had to resort to *countertrade* to sell overseas: purchasing local products to offset the exports of their own products to that market. Countertrade transactions can often be complex and cumbersome. They may involve two-way or three-way transactions, especially where a company is forced to accept unrelated goods for resale by outsiders.

If swapping goods for goods sounds less efficient than using cash or credit, that's because it is less efficient; but it is preferable to having no sales in a given market. More firms are finding it increasingly difficult to conduct business without being prepared to countertrade. Although precise numbers are impossible to come by, this transaction is growing in importance. One recent estimate places countertrade volume at from 20% to 30% of all international trade.[2]

When a company exports to a nation requiring countertrade, it must take back goods that the country can't (or won't try to) sell in international markets. To unload these goods, the company usually has to cut the prices at which the goods are nominally valued in the barter arrangement. Recognizing this necessity, the firm will typically pad the price of the goods it sells to its countertrade customer. When a German machine-tool maker sells to Rumania, for instance, it might raise prices by 20%. Then, when it unloads the blouses it gets in return, the premium covers the reduction in price.

Usually, an exporting company wants to avoid the trouble of marketing those blouses, so it hands over the 10% premium to a countertrade specialist. This middleman splits the premium with a blouse buyer, keeping perhaps 2% and passing the remaining 8% along in price cuts. The result: Rumania pays above the market for imports, making international trade less attractive than it should be, and dumps its own goods through backdoor price shaving. In the long run, however, the practice is self-defeating. Having failed to set up continuing relationships with customers, Rumania never learns what the market really wants— what style blouses, for instance—or how it might improve its competitiveness.

Countertrade takes several specific forms.

1. *Barter*: a direct exchange of goods between two parties without the use of money. For example, Iran might swap oil for guns.

More and more MNCs have resorted to countertrade in recent years to sell overseas.

[2]Thomas R. Hofstedt, "An Overview of Countertrade," July 29, 1987, unpublished.

2. *Counterpurchase*: also known as parallel barter, the sale and purchase of goods that are unrelated to each other. For example, Pepsico sold soft drinks to the former Soviet Union for vodka.
3. *Buyback*: repayment of the original purchase price through the sale of a related product. For example, Western European countries delivered various pipeline materials to the Soviet Union for construction of a gas pipeline from Siberian gas fields and in return will purchase 28 billion cubic meters of gas per year.

Countertrade is viewed as a necessary evil by the firms involved.

The unanswered question in countertrade is, Why go through such a convoluted sales process? Why not sell the goods directly at their market price (which is what ultimately happens anyway) using experts to handle the marketing? One argument is that countertrade enables members of cartels such as OPEC to undercut an agreed-upon price without formally doing so. Another argument is that countertrade keeps bureaucrats busy in centrally planned economies. Countertrade may also reduce the risk faced by a country that contracts for a new manufacturing facility. If the contractor's payment is received in the form of goods supplied by the facility, the contractor has an added incentive to do quality work and to ensure that the plant's technology is suitable for the skill levels of the available workers.

Regardless of its reason for being, countertrading is replete with problems for the firms involved. First, the goods that can be taken in countertrade are usually undesirable. Those that could be readily converted into cash have already been converted. So, although a firm shipping computers to Brazil might prefer to take coffee beans in return, the only goods available might be Brazilian shoes. Second, the trading details are difficult to work out (how many tons of naphtha is a pile of shoddy Eastern European goods worth?). The inevitable result is a very high ratio of talk to action, with only a small percentage of deals that are talked about getting done. And lost deals cost money.

Until recently, most countertrade centered on the governmental foreign trade organizations (FTOs) of Eastern European countries. In order to sell a machine or an entire plant to an FTO, a Western firm might be required to take at least some of its pay in goods (for example, tomatoes, linen, and machine parts). Sometimes these deals will stretch over a period of several years. Centered in Vienna, the countertrade experts in this business use their contacts with Eastern European officials and their knowledge of available products to earn their keep. However, the restructuring currently taking place in Eastern Europe has already reduced the scale and profitability of their business.

The loss of Eastern European business, however, has been more than offset by the explosive growth in countertrade with Third World countries. The basis for the new wave of countertrade is the cutting off of bank credit to developing nations. Third World countertrade involves more commodities and fewer hard-to-sell manufactured goods. A typical deal, arranged by Sears World Trade, involved bartering U.S. breeding swine for Dominican sugar. Another countertrader swapped BMWs for Ecuadoran tuna fish.

In an effort to make it easier for Third World countries to buy their products, big manufacturers—including General Motors, General Electric, and Caterpillar—

have set up countertrading subsidiaries. Having sold auto and truck parts to Mexico, for example, GM's countertrade subsidiary, Motors Trading Corp., arranged tour groups to the country and imported Mexican slippers and gloves. Similarly, arms manufacturers selling to developing countries are often forced to accept local products in return—for example, Iraqi oil for French Exocet missiles or Peruvian anchovies for Spanish Piranha patrol boats.

Authorities in countertrading countries are concerned that goods taken in countertrade will cannibalize their existing cash markets. Proving that countertrade goods go to new markets is difficult enough in the area of manufactured goods; it's impossible for commodities, whose ultimate use cannot be identified with its source. For example, some Indonesian rubber taken in countertrade will invariably displace rubber that Indonesia sells for cash.

Interest in countertrade and its variations appears to be growing, even among developed countries, despite the obvious difficulties it presents to the firms and countries involved. For example, in order for McDonnell Douglas to sell F-15s to the Japanese air force, it had to offset the cost to Japan in currency and jobs by agreeing to teach Japanese manufacturers to make military aircraft.

The growth in countertrade is reflected in the scramble for experienced specialists. It has been said that a good countertrader combines the avarice and opportunism of a commodities trader, the inventiveness and political sensitivity of a crooked bureaucrat, and the technical knowledge of a machine-tool salesperson.

Countertrading countries try to ensure that goods taken in countertrade will not cannibalize their existing cash exports.

13.6 SUMMARY AND CONCLUSIONS

In this chapter, we have examined a number of different financing arrangements and documents involved in international trade. The most important documents encountered in bank-related financing are the draft, which is a written order to pay; the letter of credit, which is a bank guarantee of payment provided that certain stipulated conditions are met; and the bill of lading, the document covering actual shipment of the merchandise by a common carrier and title. Documents of lesser importance include commercial and consular invoices and the insurance certificate.

— These instruments serve four primary functions:
— To reduce both buyer and seller risk
— To pinpoint who bears those risks that remain
— To facilitate the transfer of risk to a third party
— To facilitate financing

Each instrument evolved over time as a rational response to the additional risks in international trade posed by greater distances, the lack of familiarity between exporters and importers, the possibility of government imposition of exchange controls, and the greater costs involved in bringing suit against a party domiciled in another nation. Were it not for the latter two factors and publicly financed export promotion programs, we might expect that, with the passage of time, the financial arrangements in international trade would differ little from those encountered in purely domestic commercial transactions.

We also examined some of the government-sponsored export financing programs and credit insurance programs. The number of these institutions and their operating scope have grown steadily, in line with national export drives. From the standpoint of international financial managers, the most significant difference between public and private sources of financing is that public lending agencies offer their funds and credit insurance at less than normal commercial rates. The multinational firm can take advantage of these subsidized rates by structuring its marketing and production programs in accord with the different national financial programs.

QUESTIONS

1. The principal problem in analyzing different forms of export financing is the distribution of risks between the exporter and the importer. Analyze the following export financing instruments in this respect.
    a. Confirmed, revocable letter of credit
    b. Confirmed, irrevocable letter of credit
    c. Open account credit
    d. Time draft, D/A
    e. Cash with order
    f. Cash in advance
    g. Consignment
    h. Sight draft

2. In order to "meet the competition" from its counterparts overseas, Eximbank will mechanically match the terms of a loan provided by a rival export-financing agency—including the interest rate—when it finances U.S. exports.
    a. What problems might arise from this rule of matching nominal interest rates?
    b. As of January 15, 1988, the minimum interest rate on government-supplied export credits to rich countries was set at a flat rate of 10.4% for all nations providing such credits. What problems might arise with this rule? Comment on which governments would push for such a rule. Which would be against it?
    c. How should minimum interest rates on export credits be set so as to ensure comparability across countries?
    d. Suppose that instead of subsidizing interest rates, governments turn to export insurance subsidies. Is this move an improvement vis-à-vis export-credit subsidies? Explain.
    e. Why has the U.S. government fought against export-credit subsidies?

3. One of the purposes of Eximbank is to absorb credit risks on export sales that the private sector will not accept. Comment on this purpose.

4. Comment on the following statement: "Eximbank does not compete with private financial institutions. It offers assistance only in cases in which the export-credit transaction would not take place without its help. Eximbank does not offer direct-loan assistance to foreign buyers when private institutions will provide comparable financing on reasonable terms."

5. What is countertrade? Why is it termed a sophisticated form of barter?

6. What are some benefits and costs of countertrade for the parties involved?

PROBLEMS

1. L.A. Cellular has received an order for phone switches from Singapore. The switches will be exported under the terms of a letter of credit issued by Sumitomo Bank on behalf of Singapore Telecommunications. Under the terms of the L/C, the face value of the export order, $12 million, will be paid six months after Sumitomo accepts a draft drawn by L.A. Cellular. The current discount rate on 6-month acceptances is 8.5% per annum and the acceptance fee is 1.25% per annum. In addition, there is a flat commission, equal to 0.5% of the face amount of the accepted draft, that must be paid if it is sold.

    a. How much cash will L.A. Cellular receive if it holds the acceptance until maturity?

    b. How much cash will it receive if it sells the acceptance at once?

    c. Suppose L.A. Cellular's opportunity cost of funds is 8.75% per annum. If it wishes to maximize the present value of its acceptance, should it discount the acceptance?

2. Suppose Minnesota Machines (MM) is trying to price an export order from Russia. Payment is due nine months after shipping. Given the risks involved, MM would like to factor its receivable without recourse. The factor will charge a monthly discount of 2% plus a fee equal to 1.5% of the face value of the receivable for the nonrecourse financing.

    a. If Minnesota Machines desires revenue of $2.5 million from the sale, after paying all factoring charges, what is the minimum acceptable price it should charge?

    b. Alternatively, CountyBank has offered to discount the receivable, but with recourse, at an annual rate of 14% plus a 1% fee. What price will net MM the $2.5 million it desires to clear from the sale?

    c. Based on your answers to parts a and b, should Minnesota Machines discount or factor its Russian receivables? MM is competing against Nippon Machines for the order, so the higher MM's price, the lower the probability that its bid will be accepted. What other considerations should influence MM's decision?

    d. What other alternatives might be available to MM to finance its sale to Russia?

BIBLIOGRAPHY

Financing Foreign Operations. New York: Business International Corporation, various issues.

Methods of Export Financing, 2nd ed. New York: Chase World Information Corporation, 1976.

Schneider, Gerhard W. *Export-Import Financing*. New York: The Ronald Press, 1974.

14 Current Asset Management

A penny saved is a penny earned.
    Benjamin Franklin

CHAPTER LEARNING OBJECTIVES

- To describe the basic objectives of international cash management
- To identify the advantages of a centralized international cash management program
- To describe the techniques that MNCs can use to expedite the collection of funds both within a foreign country and across borders, and to more effectively manage their disbursements
- To define payments netting and explain its benefits
- To identify the basic techniques and guidelines for globally managing a marketable securities portfolio
- To describe the techniques available to an MNC with operating subsidiaries in many countries to economize on cash and marketable securities
- To describe the techniques companies can use for international cash planning and budgeting
- To identify the basic problems MNCs have in managing their bank relations and describe how MNCs can cope with these problems
- To describe the circumstances under which an MNC may benefit by easing its credit terms on foreign sales
- To describe a five-step approach that firms can use to compare the expected benefits and costs associated with extending credit internationally
- To identify the inventory management problems faced by MNCs and the techniques that they can use to deal with these problems

The management of *working capital* in the multinational corporation is similar to its domestic counterpart. Both are concerned with selecting that combination of *current assets*—cash, marketable securities, accounts receivable, and inventory—that will maximize the value of the firm. The essential differences between domestic and international working-capital management include the impact of currency fluctuations, potential exchange controls, and multiple tax jurisdictions on these decisions, in addition to the wider range of short-term financing and investment options available.

Chapter 15 discusses the mechanisms by which the multinational firm can shift liquid assets among its various affiliates; it also examines the tax and other consequences of these maneuvers. This chapter deals with the management of working-capital items available to each affiliate. The focus includes discussions of international cash, accounts receivable, and inventory management.

14.1 INTERNATIONAL CASH MANAGEMENT

International money managers attempt to attain on a worldwide basis the traditional domestic objectives of cash management: (1) bringing the company's cash resources within control as quickly and efficiently as possible and (2) achieving the optimum conservation and utilization of these funds. Accomplishing the first goal requires establishing accurate, timely forecasting and reporting systems, improving cash collections and disbursements, and decreasing the cost of moving funds among affiliates. The second objective is achieved by minimizing the required level of cash balances, making money available when and where it is needed, and increasing the risk-adjusted return on those funds that can be invested.

The principles of domestic and international cash management are identical. The latter is a more complicated exercise, however, and not only because of its wider scope and the need to recognize the customs and practices of other countries. When considering the movement of funds across national borders, a number of external factors inhibit adjustment and constrain the money manager. The most obvious is a set of restrictions that impedes the free flow of money into or out of a country. Numerous examples exist: the former U.S. Office of Foreign Direct Investment (OFDI) restrictions, Germany's Bardepot, and the requirements of many countries that their exporters repatriate the proceeds of foreign sales within a specific period. These regulations impede the free flow of capital and, thereby, hinder an international cash management program.

The principals of domestic and international cash management are the same, but the latter is a more complicated exercise.

There is really only one generalization that can be made about this type of regulation: Controls become more stringent during periods of crisis, precisely when financial managers want to act. Thus, a large premium is placed on foresight, planning, and anticipation. Government restrictions must be scrutinized on a country-by-country basis to determine realistic options and limits of action.

Other complicating factors in international money management include multiple tax jurisdictions and currencies and the relative absence of internationally integrated interchange facilities—such as are available domestically in the United States and in other Western nations—for moving cash swiftly from one location to another. Despite these difficulties, however, MNCs may have significant opportunities for improving their global cash management. For example, multinationals can often achieve higher returns overseas on short-term investments that are denied to purely domestic corporations, and the MNCs can frequently keep a higher proportion of these returns after tax by taking advantage of various tax laws and treaties. In addition, by considering all corporate funds as belonging to a central reservoir or "pool" and managing it as such (where permitted by the exchange control authorities), overall returns can be increased while simultaneously reducing the required level of cash and marketable securities worldwide.

This section is divided into seven key areas of *international cash management*: (1) organization, (2) collection and disbursement of funds, (3) netting of interaffiliate payments, (4) investment of excess funds, (5) establishment of an optimal level of worldwide corporate cash balances, (6) cash planning and budgeting, and (7) bank relations.

Organization

When compared to a system of autonomous operating units, a fully centralized international cash management program offers a number of advantages:

There is a growing tendency by MNCs to centralize their international cash management.

1. The corporation is able to operate with a smaller amount of cash; pools of excess liquidity are absorbed and eliminated; each operation will maintain transactions balances only and not hold speculative or precautionary ones.
2. By reducing total assets, profitability is enhanced and financing costs are reduced.
3. The headquarters staff, with its purview of all corporate activity, can recognize problems and opportunities that an individual unit might not perceive.
4. All decisions can be made using the overall corporate benefit as the criterion.
5. By increasing the volume of foreign exchange and other transactions done through headquarters, banks provide better foreign exchange quotes and better service.
6. Greater expertise in cash and portfolio management exists if one group is responsible for these activities.
7. Less will be lost in the event of an expropriation or currency controls restricting the transfer of funds because the corporation's total assets at risk in a foreign country can be reduced.

The forgoing benefits have long been understood by many experienced multinational firms. Today the combination of volatile currency and interest rate fluctuations, questions of capital availability, increasingly complex organizations and operating arrangements, and a growing emphasis on profitability virtually mandates a highly centralized international cash management system. There is also a trend to place much greater responsibility in corporate headquarters.

Centralization does not necessarily imply control by corporate headquarters of all facets of cash management. Instead, a concentration of decision making at a sufficiently high level within the corporation is required so that all pertinent information is readily available and can be used to optimize the firm's position.

Collection and Disbursement of Funds

Accelerating *collections* both within a foreign country and across borders is a key element of international cash management. Material potential benefits exist because long delays are often encountered in collecting receivables, particularly on export sales, and in transferring funds among affiliates and corporate headquarters. Allowing for mail time and bank processing, delays of eight to ten business days are common from the moment an importer pays an invoice to the time when the exporter is credited with *good funds*—that is, when the funds are available for use. Given high interest rates, wide fluctuations in the foreign exchange markets, and the periodic imposition of credit restrictions that have characterized financial markets in recent years, cash in transit has become more expensive and more exposed to risk.

With increasing frequency, corporate management is participating in the establishment of an affiliate's credit policy and the monitoring of collection performance. The principal goals of this intervention are to minimize *float*—that is, the transit time of payments—to reduce the investment in accounts receivable, and to lower banking fees and other transaction costs. By converting receivables into cash as rapidly as possible, a company can increase its portfolio or reduce its borrowing and, thus, earn a higher investment return or save interest expense.

Considering either national or international collections, accelerating the receipt of funds usually involves the following: (1) defining and analyzing the different available payment channels, (2) selecting the most efficient method (which can vary by country and by customer), and (3) giving specific instructions regarding procedures to the firm's customers and banks.

In addressing the first two points, the full costs of using the various methods must be determined, and the inherent delay of each must be calculated. There are two main sources of delay in the collections process: the time between the dates of payment and of receipt and the time for the payment to clear through the banking system. Inasmuch as banks will be as "inefficient" as possible to increase their float, understanding the subtleties of domestic and international money transfers is requisite if a firm is to reduce the time that funds are held and extract the maximum value from its banking relationships. Exhibit 14.1 lists the different methods multinationals use to expedite their collection of receivables.

With respect to payment instructions to customers and banks, the use of *cable remittances* is a crucial means for companies to minimize delays in receipt of payments and in conversion of payments into cash, especially in Europe because European banks tend to defer the value of good funds when the payment is made by check or draft.

Turning to international cash movements, having all affiliates transfer funds by telex enables the corporation to better plan because the vagaries of mail time

> Accelerating collections to reduce float is a key element of international cash management.

Exhibit 14.1 How Multinationals Expedite Their Collection of Receivables

Procedures for Expediting Receipt of Payments	Procedures for Expediting Conversion of Payments into Cash
Cable remittances	Cable remittances
Mobilization centers	Establishing accounts in customers' banks
Lock boxes	Negotiations with banks on value-dating
Electronic fund transfers	

are eliminated. Third parties, too, will be asked to use wire transfers. For most amounts, the fees required for telex are less than the savings generated by putting the money to use more quickly.

One of the cash manager's biggest problems is that bank-to-bank wire transfers do not always operate with great efficiency or reliability. Delays, crediting the wrong account, availability of funds, and many other operational problems are common. One solution to these problems is to be found in the *SWIFT* network (Society for Worldwide Interbank Financial Telecommunications). SWIFT has standardized international message formats and employs a dedicated computer network to support funds transfer messages.

The SWIFT network improves the efficiency and reliability of international fund transfers among member banks.

The SWIFT network connects over 900 banks in North America, Western Europe, and the Far East. Its mission is to quickly transmit standard forms to allow its member banks to automatically process data by computer. All types of customer and bank transfers are transmitted as well as foreign exchange deals, bank account statements, and administrative messages. To use SWIFT the corporate client must deal with domestic banks that are subscribers and with foreign banks that are highly automated.

To cope with some of the transmittal delays associated with checks or drafts, customers are instructed to remit to "mobilization" points that are centrally located in regions with large sales volumes. These funds are managed centrally or are transmitted to the selling subsidiary. For example, European customers may be told to make all payments to Switzerland, where the corporation maintains a staff specializing in cash and portfolio management and collections.

Sometimes customers are asked to pay directly into a designated account at a branch of the bank that is mobilizing the MNC's funds internationally. This method is particularly useful when banks have large branch networks. Another technique used is to have customers remit funds to a designated *lock box*, which is a postal box in the company's name. One or more times daily, a local bank opens the mail received at the lock box and deposits any checks immediately.

Multinational banks now provide firms with rapid transfers of their funds among branches in different countries, generally giving their customers *same-day value*—that is, funds are credited that same day. Rapid transfers can also be accomplished through a bank's correspondent network, although it becomes somewhat more difficult to arrange same-day value for funds.

MNCs today insist that their banks have leading-edge electronic banking systems.

Chief financial officers are increasingly relying on computers and worldwide telecommunications networks to help manage the company cash portfolio. Many multinational firms will not deal with a bank that doesn't have a leading-edge electronic banking system.

At the heart of today's high-tech corporate treasuries are the *treasury workstation* software packages that many big banks sell as supplements to their cash management systems. Linking the company with its bank and branch offices, the workstations let treasury personnel compute a company's worldwide cash position on a "real-time" basis, meaning that the second a transaction is made in, say, Rio de Janeiro, it is electronically recorded in Tokyo as well. This simultaneous record keeping lets companies keep their funds active at all times. Treasury personnel can use their workstations to initiate fund transfers from units with surplus cash to those units that require funds, thereby reducing the level of bank borrowings.

ILLUSTRATION: *International Cash Management at National Semiconductor*

After computerizing its cash management system, National Semiconductor was able to save significant interest expenses by quickly transferring money from locations with surplus cash to those needing money. In a typical transaction, the company shifted a surplus $500,000 from its Japanese account to its Philippine operations—avoiding the need to borrow the half million dollars and saving several thousand dollars in interest expense. Before computerization, it would have taken five or six days to discover the surplus.

Management of *disbursements* is a delicate balancing act: holding onto funds versus staying on good terms with suppliers. It requires a detailed knowledge of individual country and supplier nuances, as well as the myriad of payment instruments and banking services available around the world. Exhibit 14.2 presents some questions that corporate treasurers should address in reviewing their disbursement policies.

Payments Netting in International Cash Management

Many multinational corporations are now in the process of rationalizing their production on a global basis. This process involves a highly coordinated international interchange of materials, parts, subassemblies, and finished products among the various units of the MNC, with many affiliates both buying from, and selling to, each other.

The high volume of interaffiliate trade leads to substantial interaffiliate fund flows.

The importance of these physical flows to the international financial executive is that they are accompanied by a heavy volume of *interaffiliate fund flows*. Of

---

Exhibit 14.2 Reviewing Disbursements: Auditing Payment Instruments

1. What payment instruments are you using to pay suppliers, employees, and government entities (e.g., checks, drafts, wire transfers, direct deposits)?
2. What are the total disbursements made through each of these instruments annually?
3. What is the mail and clearing float for these instruments in each country?
4. What techniques, such as remote disbursement, are being used to prolong the payment cycle?
5. How long does it take suppliers to process the various instruments and present them for payment?
6. What are the bank charges and internal processing costs for each instrument?
7. Are banking services such as controlled disbursement and zero-balance accounts used where available?

Payments netting reduces the volume and cost of intercompany fund flows.

particular importance is the fact that there is a measurable cost associated with these cross-border fund transfers, including the cost of purchasing foreign exchange (the foreign exchange spread), the opportunity cost of float (time in transit), and other transaction costs, such as cable charges. These transaction costs are estimated to vary from 0.25% to 1.5% of the volume transferred. Thus, there is a clear incentive to minimize the total volume of intercompany fund flows. This can be achieved by payments netting.

Bilateral and Multilateral Netting. The idea behind a *payments netting* system is very simple: Payments among affiliates go back and forth, whereas only a netted amount need be transferred. Suppose, for example, the German subsidiary of an MNC sells goods worth $1 million to its Italian affiliate that in turn sells goods worth $2 million to the German unit. The combined flows total $3 million. On a net basis, however, the German unit need remit only $1 million to the Italian unit. This type of *bilateral netting* is valuable, though, only if subsidiaries sell back and forth to each other.

Bilateral netting would be of little use where there is a more complex structure of internal sales, such as in the situation depicted in Exhibit 14.3 where no company both buys from, and sells to, any one affiliate. Note, however, that each affiliate's inflows equal its outflows. On a multilateral basis, therefore, total transfers would net out to zero.

Since a large percentage of multinational transactions are internal—leading to a relatively large volume of interaffiliate payments—the payoff from *multilateral netting* can be large, relative to the costs of such a system. Many companies find they can eliminate 50% or more their intercompany transactions through multilateral netting, with annual savings in foreign exchange transactions costs and bank transfer charges that average about 1.5% per dollar netted. For example, SmithKline Beckman estimates that it saves $300,000 annually in foreign exchange transactions costs and bank transfer charges by using a multilateral netting system.[1]

Exhibit 14.3 Multilateral Netting

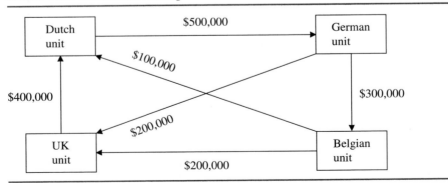

---

[1]"How Centralized Systems Benefit Managerial Control: SmithKline Beckman," *Business International Money Report*, June 23, 1986, p. 198.

Similarly, Baxter International estimates it saves $200,000 per year by eliminating approximately 60% of its intercompany transactions through netting.[2]

Information Requirements. Essential to any netting scheme is a centralized control point that can collect and record detailed information on the intracorporate accounts of each participating affiliate at specified time intervals. The control point, called a *netting center*, is a subsidiary company set up in a location with minimal exchange controls for trade transactions.

The netting center will use a matrix of payables and receivables to determine the net payer or creditor position of each affiliate at the date of clearing. An example of such a matrix is provided in Exhibit 14.4. It is assumed that there is a U.S. parent corporation with subsidiaries in France, Belgium, and Sweden. Each of the amounts due to and from the affiliated companies is converted into a common currency (the U.S. dollar in this example) and entered onto the matrix. Note that in an intercompany system, the payables will always equal the receivables on both a gross basis and a net basis. Typically, to minimize the impact of currency changes on the amounts scheduled for transfer, the exchange rate at which these transactions occur is fixed during the week that netting takes place.

The netting center coordinates payment flows among the MNC's various units.

Without netting, the total payments in the system would equal $44 million. Multilateral netting will pare these transfers to $12 million, a net reduction of 73%. If all payments and disbursements are made through a central pool, the payers in the system—Sweden and Belgium in this example—will remit the local currency equivalent of their net obligations to the pool, where those currencies

Exhibit 14.4 Intercompany Payments Matrix (U.S. $ Millions)

	Paying Affiliates				
Receiving Affiliates	United States	France	Sweden	Belgium	Total
United States	—	8	7	4	19
France	6	—	4	2	12
Sweden	2	0	—	3	5
Belgium	1	2	5	—	8
Total	9	10	16	9	44

	Receipt	Payment	Net Receipt	Net Payment
United States	19	9	10	—
France	12	10	2	—
Sweden	5	16	—	11
Belgium	8	9	—	1

[2]*Solving International Financial and Currency Problems* (New York: Business International Corporation, 1976), p. 29.

are sold in exchange for the receiving units' currencies. Alternatively, the payers can be asked to remit funds directly to specified recipients.

The choice of which affiliate(s) each payer pays depends on the relative costs of transferring funds between each pair of affiliates. The per unit costs of sending funds between two affiliates can vary significantly from month to month because one subsidiary may receive payment from a third party in a currency that is needed by the other subsidiary. By using this currency for payment, one or more foreign exchange conversions can be eliminated. This conclusion implies that the cost of sending funds from Germany to France, for example, can differ greatly from the cost of moving money from France to Germany.

For example, Volvo has a policy of transferring a currency, without conversion, to a unit needing that currency to pay a creditor.[3] To see how this policy works, suppose that Volvo Sweden buys automotive components from a German manufacturer and Volvo Belgium purchases automotive kits from Volvo Sweden. At the same time, a German dealer buys automobiles from Volvo Belgium and pays in Deutsche marks. Volvo Belgium will then use these DM to pay Volvo Sweden, which in turn will use them to pay its German creditor.

Foreign Exchange Controls. Before implementing a payments netting system, a company needs to know whether any restrictions on netting exist. Firms may sometimes be barred from netting or be required to obtain permission from the local monetary authorities.

The value of netting rises with the volume of intercompany transactions.

Analysis. The higher the volume of intercompany transactions and the more back-and-forth selling that takes place, the more worthwhile netting is likely to be. A useful approach to evaluating a netting system would be to establish the direct cost savings of the netting system and then use this figure as a benchmark against which to measure the costs of implementation and operation. These set-up costs have been estimated at less than $20,000.[4]

An additional benefit from running a netting system is the tighter control that management can exert over corporate fund flows. The same information required to operate a netting system will also enable an MNC to shift funds in response to expectations of currency movements, changing interest differentials, and tax differentials.

ILLUSTRATION: *Cost/Benefit Analysis of an International Cash Management System*

Although company A already operates a multilateral netting system, it commissioned a study to show where additional improvements in cash management

---

[3]Op cit, p. 32.

[4]"The State of the Art," *New Techniques in International Exposure and Cash Management*, vol. 1 (New York: Business International Corporation, 1977), p. 244.

could be made.[5] The firm proposed to establish a finance company (FINCO) in Europe. FINCO'S primary function would be to act as a collecting and paying agent for divisions of company A that export to third parties. All receivables would be gathered into the international branch network of bank X. Each branch would handle receivables denominated in the currency of its country of domicile. These branch accounts would be monitored by both FINCO and the exporting unit via the bank's electronic reporting facility.

Intercompany payments and third-party collection payments from FINCO to each exporter would be included in the existing multilateral netting system, which would be administered by FINCO. Payments for imports from third-party suppliers would also be included. Finally, the netting system would be expanded to include intercompany payments from operations in the United States, Canada, and one additional European country.

The feasibility study examined six basic savings components and two cost components. The realizable, annualized savings are summarized below:

Savings Component	Cost Savings
1. Optimized multilateral netting	$ 29,000
2. Reduced remittance-processing time by customer and remitting bank	26,000
3. Reduction in cross-border transfer float by collecting currencies in their home country	46,000
4. Reduction in cross-border transfer commissions and charges by collecting currencies in their home country	41,000
5. Use of incoming foreign currencies to source outgoing foreign payments in the same currencies	16,000
6. Use of interest-bearing accounts	8,000
Total Estimated Annual Savings	$166,000

Cost Component	Cost
1. Computer time-sharing charges for accessing Bank X's system	$ 17,000
2. Communications charges for additional cross-border funds transfers	13,000
Total Estimated Annual Costs	$ 30,000
Total Net Savings	$136,000

Management of the Short-Term Investment Portfolio

A major task of international cash management is to determine the levels and currency denominations of the multinational group's investment in cash balances and money market instruments. Firms with seasonal or cyclical cash flows have special problems, such as spacing investment maturities to coincide with pro-jected needs. To manage this investment properly requires (1) a forecast of future cash needs based on the company's current budget and past experience and (2) an

---

[5]This illustration appears in "Cost/Benefit Analysis of One Company's Cash Management System," *Business International Money Report*, April 14, 1986, pp. 119–120.

estimate of a minimum cash position for the coming period. These projections should take into account the effects of inflation and anticipated currency changes on future cash flows.

Successful management of an MNC's required cash balances and of any excess funds generated by the firm and its affiliates depends largely on the astute selection of appropriate short-term money market instruments. Rewarding opportunities exist in many countries, but the choice of an investment medium depends on government regulations, the structure of the market, and the tax laws, all of which vary widely. Available money instruments differ among the major markets, and at times, foreign firms are denied access to existing investment opportunities. Only a few markets, such as the broad and diversified U.S. market and the Eurocurrency markets, are truly free and international. Capsule summaries of key money market instruments are provided in Exhibit 14.5.

> The value of taking advantage of higher investment returns overseas must be traded off against the transaction costs involved.

Once corporate headquarters has fully identified the present and future needs of its affiliates, it must then decide on a policy for managing its liquid assets worldwide. This policy must recognize that the value of shifting funds across national borders to earn the highest possible risk-adjusted return depends not only on the risk-adjusted yield differential, but also on the transaction costs involved. In fact, the basic reason for holding cash in several currencies simultaneously is the existence of currency conversion costs. If these costs are zero and government regulations permit, all cash balances should be held in the currency having the highest effective risk-adjusted return net of withdrawal costs.

Given that transaction costs do exist, the appropriate currency denomination mix of an MNC's investment in money and near-money assets is probably more a function of the currencies in which it has actual and projected inflows and outflows than of effective yield differentials or government regulations. The reason why is simple: Despite government controls, it would be highly unusual to see an annualized risk-adjusted interest differential of even 2%. Although seemingly large, a 2% annual differential yields only an additional 0.167% for a 30-day investment or 0.5% extra for a 90-day investment. Such small differentials can easily be offset by foreign exchange transaction costs. Thus, even large annualized risk-adjusted interest spreads may not justify shifting funds for short-term placements.

Portfolio Guidelines. Common-sense guidelines for globally managing the marketable securities portfolio are as follows:

1. Diversify the instruments in the portfolio to maximize the yield for a given level of risk. Don't invest only in government securities. Eurodollar and other instruments may be nearly as safe.
2. Review the portfolio daily to decide which securities should be liquidated and what new investments should be made.
3. In revising the portfolio, make sure that the incremental interest earned more than compensates for such added costs as clerical work, the income lost between investments, fixed charges such as the foreign exchange spread, and commissions on the sale and purchase of securities.
4. If rapid conversion to cash is an important consideration, then carefully evaluate the security's marketability (liquidity). Ready markets exist for some securities, but not for others.

Exhibit 14.5 Key Money Market Instruments

Instrument	Borrower	Maturities	Comments
Treasury bills (T-bills)	Central governments of many countries	Up to 1 year	Safest and most-liquid short-term investment
Federal funds (U.S.)	U.S. commercial banks temporarily short of legal reserve requirements	Overnight to 3 days	Suitable for very short-term investment of large amounts ($1 million or more)
Government agency notes (U.S.)	Issued by U.S. government agencies such as Federal National Mortgage Association	30 days to 270 days	Similar to local authority notes in the United Kingdom. Both offer slightly higher yields than T-bills.
Demand deposits	Commercial banks	On demand	Governments sometimes impose restrictions on interest rates banks can offer (as in the U.S.).
Time deposits	Commercial banks	Negotiable but advance notice usually required	Governments sometimes regulate interest rates and/or maturities.
Deposits with nonbank financial institutions	Nonbank financial institutions	Negotiable	Usually offer higher yields than banks do
Certificates of deposit (CDs)	Commercial banks	Negotiable but normally 30, 60, or 90 days	Negotiable papers representing a term bank deposit; more liquid than straight deposits since they can be sold
Bankers' acceptances	Bills of exchange guaranteed by a commercial bank	Up to 180 days	Highest-quality investment next to T-bills
Commercial paper (also known as trade paper or, in the United Kingdom, fine trade bills)	Large corporations with high credit ratings	30 days to 270 days	Negotiable, unsecured promissory notes; available in all major money markets
Temporary corporate loans	Corporations	Negotiable	Usually offer higher returns than those available from financial institutions but are not liquid since they must be held to maturity

5. Tailor the maturity of the investment to the firm's projected cash needs, or be sure a secondary market for the investment with high liquidity exists.
6. Carefully consider opportunities for covered or uncovered interest arbitrage.

Optimal Worldwide Cash Levels

Centralized cash management typically involves the transfer of an affiliate's cash in excess of minimal operating requirements into a centrally managed account, or *cash pool.* Some firms have established a special corporate entity that collects and disburses funds through a single bank account.

With cash pooling, each affiliate need hold locally only the minimum cash balance required for transactions purposes. All precautionary balances are held by the parent or in the pool. As long as the demands for cash by the various units are reasonably independent of each other, centralized cash management can provide an equivalent degree of protection with a lower level of cash reserves.

Another benefit from pooling is that either less borrowing need be done or more excess funds are available for investment where returns will be maximized. Consequently, interest expenses are reduced or investment income is increased. In addition, the larger the pool of funds, the more worthwhile it becomes for a firm to invest in cash management expertise. Furthermore, pooling permits exposure arising from holding foreign currency cash balances to be centrally managed.

Evaluation and Control. Taking over control of an affiliate's cash reserves can create motivational problems for local managers unless some adjustments are made to the way in which these managers are evaluated. One possible approach is to relieve local managers of profit responsibility for their excess funds. The problem with this solution is that it provides no incentive for local managers to take advantage of specific opportunities that only they may be aware of.

An alternative approach is to present local managers with interest rates for borrowing or lending funds to the pool that reflect the opportunity cost of money to the parent corporation. In setting these *internal interest rates* (IIRs), the corporate treasurer, in effect, is acting as a bank, offering to borrow or lend currencies at given rates. By examining these IIRs, local treasurers will have a greater awareness of the opportunity cost of their idle cash balances, as well as an added incentive to act on this information. In many instances, they will prefer to transfer at least part of their cash balances (where permitted) to a central pool in order to earn a greater return. To make pooling work, managers must have access to the central pool whenever they require money.

ILLUSTRATION: An Italian Cash Management System

An Italian firm has created a centralized cash management system for its 140 operating units within Italy. At the center is a holding company that manages banking relations, borrowings, and investments. In the words of the firm's treasurer, "We put ourselves in front of the companies as a real bank and say, 'If you have a surplus to place, I will pay you the best rates.' If the company finds something better than that, they are free to place the funds outside the group. But this doesn't happen very often."[6] In this way, the company avoids being overdrawn with one bank while investing with another.

---

[6]"Central Cash Management Step by Step: The European Approach," *Business International Money Report*, October 19, 1984, p. 331.

Cash pooling enables the MNC to minimize its level of cash reserves to achieve a given financial safety level.

Cash Planning and Budgeting

The key to the successful global coordination of a firm's cash and marketable securities is a good reporting system. Cash receipts must be reported and forecast in a comprehensive, accurate, and timely manner. If the headquarters staff is to fully and economically use the company's worldwide cash resources, they must know the financial positions of affiliates, the forecast cash needs or surpluses, the anticipated cash inflows and outflows, local and international money market conditions, and likely currency movements.

As a result of rapid and pronounced changes in the international monetary arena, the need for more frequent reports has become acute. Firms that had been content to receive information quarterly now require monthly, weekly, or even daily data. Key figures are often transmitted by telex or fax machine instead of by mail.

Multinational Cash Mobilization. A *multinational cash mobilization* system is designed to optimize the use of funds by tracking current and near-term cash positions. The information gathered can be used to aid a multilateral netting system, to increase the operational efficiency of a centralized cash pool, and to determine more effective short-term borrowing and investment policies.

The operation of a multinational cash mobilization system is illustrated here with a simple example centered around a firm's four European affiliates. Assume the European headquarters maintains a regional cash pool in London for its operating units located in England, France, Germany, and Italy. Each day, at the close of banking hours, every affiliate reports to London its current cash balances in *cleared funds*—that is, its cash accounts net of all receipts and disbursements that have cleared during the day. All balances are reported in a common currency, which is assumed here to be the U.S. dollar, with local currencies translated at rates designated by the manager of the central pool.

One report format is presented in Exhibit 14.6. It contains the end-of-day balance as well as a revised five-day forecast. According to the report for July 12, the Italian affiliate has a cash balance of $400,000. This balance means the affiliate could have disbursed an additional $400,000 that day without creating a cash deficit or having to use its overdraft facilities. The French affiliate, on the other hand, has a negative cash balance of $150,000, which it is presumably covering with an overdraft. Alternatively, it might have borrowed funds from the pool to cover this deficit. The British and German subsidiaries report cash surpluses of $100,000 and $350,000, respectively.

The manager of the central pool can then assemble these individual reports into a more usable form, such as that depicted in Exhibit 14.7. This report shows the cash balance for each affiliate, its required minimum operating cash balance, and the resultant cash surplus or deficit for each affiliate individually and for the region as a whole. According to the report, both the German and Italian affiliates ended the day with funds in excess of their operating needs, while the English unit wound up with $25,000 less than it normally requires in operating funds (even though it had $100,000 in cash). The French affiliate was short $250,000,

A good reporting system is the key to successful global coordination of a firm's cash and marketable securities.

Cash reporting should be done in cleared funds, which is money that is available for immediate use.

Exhibit 14.6 Daily Cash Reports of European Central Cash Pool (U.S. $ Thousands)

Date: *July 12, 199X*
Affiliate: *France*
Cash Position: *–150*
Five-Day Forecast:

Day	Deposit	Disburse	Net
1	400	200	+200
2	125	225	–100
3	300	700	–400
4	275	275	0
5	250	100	+150
		Net for period	–150

Date: *July 12, 199X*
Affiliate: *Germany*
Cash Position: *+350*
Five-Day Forecast:

Day	Deposit	Disburse	Net
1	430	50	+380
2	360	760	–400
3	500	370	+130
4	750	230	+520
5	450	120	+330
		Net for period	+960

Date: *July 12, 199X*
Affiliate: *Italy*
Cash Position: *+400*
Five-Day Forecast:

Day	Deposit	Disburse	Net
1	240	340	–100
2	400	275	+125
3	480	205	+275
4	90	240	–150
5	300	245	+ 55
		Net for period	+205

Date: *July 12, 199X*
Affiliate: *England*
Cash Position: *+100*
Five-Day Forecast:

Day	Deposit	Disburse	Net
1	100	50	+ 50
2	260	110	+150
3	150	350	–200
4	300	50	+250
5	200	300	–100
		Net for period	+150

The data from affiliate cash reports can be used to decide how to cover any deficits and where to invest surplus funds.

including its operating deficit and minimum required balances. For the European region as a whole, however, there was excess cash of $75,000.

The information contained in these reports can be used to decide how to cover any deficits and where to invest temporary surplus funds. Netting can also

Exhibit 14.7 Aggregate Cash Position of European Central Cash Pool (U.S. $ Thousands)

Affiliate	Daily Cash Position, July 12, 199X		
	Closing Balance	Minimum Required	Cash Balance Surplus (Deficit)
France	–150	100	–250
Germany	+350	250	100
Italy	+400	150	250
England	+100	125	– 25
Regional surplus (deficit)			+ 75

be facilitated by breaking down each affiliate's aggregate inflows and outflows into their individual currency components. This breakdown will aid in deciding what netting operations to perform and in which currencies.

The cash forecasts contained in the daily reports can aid in determining when to transfer funds to or from the central pool and the maturities of any borrowings or investments. For example, although the Italian subsidiary currently has $250,000 in excess funds, it projects a deficit tomorrow of $100,000. One possible strategy is to have the Italian unit remit $250,000 to the pool today and, in turn, have the pool return $100,000 tomorrow to cover the projected deficit. However, unless interest differentials are large and/or transaction costs are minimal, it may be preferable to instruct the Italian unit to remit only $150,000 to the pool and invest the remaining $100,000 overnight in Italy.

Similarly, the five-day forecast shown in Exhibit 14.8, based on the data provided in Exhibit 14.7, indicates that the $75,000 European regional surplus generated today can be invested for at least two days before it is required (because of the cash deficit forecasted two days from today).

The cash mobilization system illustrated here has been greatly simplified in order to bring out some key details. In reality, such a system should include longer-term forecasts of cash flows broken down by currency, forecasts of inter-company transactions (for netting purposes), and interest rates paid by the pool (for decentralized decision making).

Bank Relations

Good bank relations are central to a company's international cash management effort. Although some companies may be quite pleased with their banks' services, others may not even realize that they are being poorly served by their banks. Poor cash management services mean lost interest revenues, overpriced services, and inappropriate or redundant services. Many firms that have conducted a bank relations audit find that they are dealing with too many banks. Here are some considerations involved in auditing the company's banks.

Good bank relations are important to international cash management, but many firms mismanage their bank relations.

Exhibit 14.8 Five-Day Cash Forecast of European Central Cash Pool (U.S. $ Thousands)

Affiliate	+1	+2	+3	+4	+5	Five-Day Total
France	+200	−100	−400	0	+150	−150
Germany	+380	−400	+130	+520	+330	+960
Italy	−100	+125	+275	−150	+ 55	+205
England	+ 50	+150	−200	+250	−100	+150
Forecast regional surplus (deficit) by day	+530	−225	−195	+620	+435	+1165

Days from July 12, 199X

Some common problems in bank relations are

1. *Too many relations*: Using too many banks can be expensive. It also invariably generates idle balances, higher compensating balances, more check-clearing float, suboptimal rates on foreign exchange and loans, a heavier administrative workload, and diminished control over every aspect of banking relations.

2. *High banking costs*: To keep a lid on bank expenses, treasury management must carefully track not only the direct costs of banking services—including rates, spreads, and commissions—but also the indirect costs rising from check float, *value-dating*—that is, when value is given for funds—and compensating balances. This monitoring is especially important in developing countries of Latin America and Asia; in these countries, compensating balance requirements may range as high as 30%–35%, and check-clearing times may drag on for days or even weeks. It also pays off in such European countries as Italy, where banks enjoy value-dating periods of as long as 20–25 days.

3. *Inadequate reporting*: Banks often don't provide immediate information on collections and account balances. This delay can cause excessive amounts of idle cash and prolonged float. To avoid such problems, firms should instruct their banks to provide daily balance information and to clearly distinguish between *ledger* and *collected balances*—that is, posted totals versus immediately available funds.

4. *Excessive clearing delays*: In many countries, bank float can rob firms of funds availability. In such nations as Mexico, Spain, Italy, and Indonesia, checks drawn on banks located in remote areas can take weeks to clear to headquarters accounts in the capital city. Fortunately, firms that negotiate for better float times often meet with success. Whatever method is used to reduce clearing time, it is crucial that companies constantly check up on their banks to ensure that funds are credited to accounts as expected.

MNCs should determine the value of the bank services they receive and the value of the business they generate for each bank they deal with.

Negotiating better service is easier if the company is a valued customer. Demonstrating that it is a valuable customer requires the firm to have ongoing discussions with its bankers to determine the precise value of each type of banking activity and the value of the business it generates for each bank. Armed with this information, the firm should make up a monthly report that details the value of its banking business. By compiling this report, the company knows precisely how much business it is giving to each bank it uses. With such information in hand, the firm can negotiate better terms and better service from its banks.

14.2 ACCOUNTS RECEIVABLE MANAGEMENT

Firms grant trade credit to customers, both domestically and internationally, because they expect the investment in receivables to be profitable, either by expanding sales volume or by retaining sales that otherwise would be lost to competitors. Some companies also earn a profit on the financing charges they levy on credit sales.

The need to scrutinize *credit terms* is particularly important in countries experiencing rapid rates of inflation. The incentive for customers to defer payment, liquidating their debts with less valuable money in the future, is great. Furthermore, credit standards abroad are often more relaxed than in the home market, especially in countries lacking alternative sources of credit for small customers. To remain competitive, MNCs may feel compelled to loosen their own credit standards. Finally, the compensation system in many companies tends to reward higher sales more than it penalizes an increased investment in accounts receivable. Local managers frequently have an incentive to expand sales even if the MNC overall does not benefit.

The effort to better manage receivables overseas will not get far if finance and marketing don't coordinate their efforts. In many companies, finance and marketing work at cross purposes. Marketing thinks about selling, and finance thinks about speeding up cash flows. One way to ease the tensions between finance and marketing is to educate the sales force on how credit and collection affect company profits. Another way is to tie bonuses for salespeople to *collected* sales or to adjust sales bonuses for the interest cost of credit sales. Forcing managers to bear the opportunity cost of working capital ensures that their credit, inventory, and other working-capital decisions will be more economical.

> To better manage receivables overseas, salespeople must understand how credit and collection affect company profits.

ILLUSTRATION: Nestle Charges for Working Capital

Nestle charges local subsidiary managers for the interest expense of net working capital using an internally devised standard rate. The inclusion of this finance charge encourages country managers to keep a tight rein on accounts receivable and inventory because the lower the net working capital, the lower the theoretical interest charge, and the higher their profits.

Credit Extension

Two key credit decisions to be made by an firm selling abroad are the amount of credit to extend and the currency in which credit sales are to be billed. Nothing need be added here to Chapter 10's discussion (see Section 9.1) of the latter decision except to note that competitors will often resolve the currency-of-denomination issue.

> Companies selling abroad must decide in which currencies to extend credit.

The easier the credit terms are, the more sales are likely to be made. Generosity is not always the best policy. Balanced against higher revenues must be the risk of default, increased interest expense on the larger investment in receivables, and the deterioration (through currency devaluation) of the dollar value of accounts receivable denominated in the buyer's currency. These additional costs may be partly offset if liberalized credit terms enhance a firm's ability to raise its prices.

The bias of most personnel evaluation systems is in favor of higher revenues, but another factor often tends to increase accounts receivable in foreign countries. An uneconomic expansion of local sales may occur if managers are credited with

One way to better manage receivables overseas is to adjust sales bonuses for the interest and currency costs of credit sales.

dollar sales when accounts receivable are denominated in the local currency. Sales managers should be charged for the expected depreciation in the value of local currency accounts receivable. For instance, if the current exchange rate is LC 1 = $0.10, but the expected exchange rate 90 days hence (or the three-month forward rate) is $0.09, managers providing three-month credit terms should be credited with only $0.90 for each dollar in sales booked at the current spot rate.

Whether judging the implications of inflation, devaluation, or both, it must be remembered that when a unit of inventory is sold on credit, a real asset has been transformed into a monetary asset. The opportunity to raise the local currency selling price of the item to maintain its dollar value is lost. This point is obvious, but is frequently disregarded.

Assuming that both buyer and seller have access to credit at the same cost and reflect in their decisions anticipated currency changes and inflation, it should normally make no difference to a potential customer whether it receives additional credit or an equivalent cash discount. However, the MNC may benefit by revising its credit terms in three circumstances:

An MNC may benefit by revising its credit terms to foreign customers under three circumstances.

1. The buyer and seller hold different opinions concerning the future course of inflation or currency changes, leading one of the two to prefer term/price discount trade-offs (that is, a lower price if paid within a specified period).
2. The MNC has a lower risk-adjusted cost of credit than does its customer because of market imperfections. In other words, the buyer's higher financing cost must not be a result of its greater riskiness.
3. During periods of credit restraint in a country, the affiliate of an MNC may have access to funds (because of its parent) that local companies do not have and may thereby gain a marketing advantage over its competitors. Absolute availability of money, rather than its cost, may be critical.

The following five-step approach enables a firm to compare the expected benefits and costs associated with extending credit internationally:

Firms should compare the expected costs and benefits of extending credit internationally.

1. Calculate the current cost of extending credit.
2. Calculate the cost of extending credit under the revised credit policy.
3. Using the information from steps 1 and 2, calculate incremental credit costs under the revised credit policy.
4. Ignoring credit costs, calculate incremental profits under the revised credit policy.
5. If, and only if, incremental profits exceed incremental credit costs, select the new credit policy.

ILLUSTRATION: Evaluating Credit Extension Overseas

Suppose a subsidiary in France currently has annual sales of $1 million with 90-day credit terms. It is believed that sales will increase by 6%, or $60,000, if terms are extended to 120 days. Of these additional sales, the cost of goods sold is $35,000. Monthly credit expenses are 1% in financing charges. In addition, the French franc is expected to depreciate an average of 0.5% every 30 days.

Ignoring currency changes for the moment, but considering financing costs, the value today of one dollar of receivables to be collected at the end of 90 days is approximately $0.97. Taking into account the 1.5% ($3 \times 0.5\%$) expected French franc depreciation over the 90-day period, this value declines to $0.97(1 - 0.015)$, or 0.955, implying a 4.5% cost of carrying French franc receivables for three months. Similarly, one dollar of receivables collected 120 days from now is worth $(1 - 4 \times 0.01)(1 - 0.02)$ today, or 0.941. Then the incremental cost of carrying French franc receivables for the fourth month equals $0.955 - 0.941$ dollars, or 1.4%.

Applying the five-step evaluation approach and using the information generated above, 90-day credit costs are currently $\$1,000,000 \times 0.045 = \$45,000$. Lengthening terms to 120 days will raise this cost to $\$1,000,000 \times 0.059 = \$59,000$. The cost of carrying for 120 days the incremental sales of $\$60,000$ is $\$60,000 \times 0.059 = \$3,540$. Thus, incremental credit costs under the new policy equal $\$59,000 + \$3,540 - \$45,000 = \$17,540$. Since this amount is less than the incremental profit of $\$25,000$ ($60,000 - 35,000$), it is worthwhile providing a fourth month of credit.

In the general case, let ΔS and ΔC be the incremental sales and costs associated with an easing of credit terms. If the expected credit cost per unit of sales revenues, R, is expected to increase to $R + \Delta R$ because of a more lenient credit policy, then terms should be eased if, and only if, incremental profits are greater than incremental credit costs, or

$$\Delta S - \Delta C \geq S\Delta R + \Delta S(R + \Delta R)$$

It should be noted that R reflects forecasted changes in currency values as well as the cost of funds over the longer collection period. This analysis can also be used to ascertain whether it would be worthwhile to tighten credit, accepting lower sales but reducing credit costs at the same time.

This same methodology of comparing incremental benefits and costs can be used to solve some of the important problems firms face in trying to manage inventory abroad.

14.3 INVENTORY MANAGEMENT

Inventory in the form of raw materials, work in process, or finished goods is held (1) to facilitate the production process by both ensuring that supplies are at hand when needed and allowing a more even rate of production and (2) to make certain that goods are available for delivery at the time of sale.

Although, conceptually, the inventory management problems faced by multinational firms are not unique, they may be exaggerated in the case of foreign operations. For instance, MNCs typically find it more difficult to control their overseas inventory and realize inventory turnover objectives. There are a variety of reasons: long and variable transit times if ocean transportation is used, lengthy customs proceedings, dock strikes, import controls, higher duties, supply disruption, and anticipated changes in currency values.

MNCs typically find it more difficult to control their overseas inventory and to realize inventory turnover objectives.

Production Location and Inventory Control

Overseas production locations often led to higher inventories.

Many U.S. companies have eschewed domestic manufacturing for offshore production to take advantage of both low-wage labor and a grab bag of tax holidays, low-interest loans, and other government largess. But a number of firms have found that low manufacturing cost isn't everything. Aside from the strategic advantages associated with U.S. production, such as maintaining close contact with domestic customers, onshore manufacturing allows for a more efficient use of capital. In particular, because of the delays in international shipment of goods and potential supply disruptions, firms producing abroad typically hold larger work-in-process and finished goods inventories. The result is higher inventory-carrying costs.

ILLUSTRATION: Cypress Semiconductor Decides to Stay Onshore

The added inventory expenses that foreign manufacture would entail is an important reason that Cypress Semiconductor decided to manufacture integrated circuits in San Jose, California, instead of going abroad. Because Cypress makes relatively expensive circuits (they average around $8 apiece), time-consuming international shipments would have tied up the company's capital in a very expensive way. Even though offshore production would save about $0.032 per chip in labor costs, the company estimated that the labor saving would be more than offset by combined shipping and customs duties of $0.025, and an additional $0.16 in the capital cost of holding inventory.

According to Cypress chairman L.J. Sevin, "Some people just look at the labor rates, but it's inventory cost that matters. It's simply cheaper to sell a part in one week than in five or six. You have to figure out what you could have done with the inventory or the money you could have made simply by pulling the interest on the dollars you have tied up in the part."[7]

The estimate of 16 cents in carrying cost can be backed out as follows: As the preceding quotation indicates, parts manufactured abroad were expected to spend an extra five weeks or so in transit. This means that parts manufactured abroad would spend five more weeks in work-in-process inventory than would parts manufactured domestically. Assuming an opportunity cost of 20% (not an unreasonable number considering the volatility of the semiconductor market) and an average cost per chip of $8, the added inventory-related interest expense associated with overseas production equals:

$$\frac{\text{Added interest}}{\text{expense}} = \frac{\text{Opportunity cost}}{\text{of funds}} \times \frac{\text{Added time}}{\text{in transit}} \times \frac{\text{Cost per}}{\text{part}}$$

$$= 0.20 \times 5/52 \times \$8 = \$0.154$$

---

[7]Joel Kotkin, "The Case for Manufacturing in America," *Inc.*, March 1985, p. 54.

Advance Inventory Purchases

In many developing countries, forward contracts for foreign currency are limited in availability or nonexistent. In addition, restrictions often preclude free remittances, making it difficult, if not impossible, to convert excess funds into hard currency. One means of hedging is to engage in anticipatory purchases of goods, especially imported items. The trade-off is owning goods for which local currency prices may increase, thereby maintaining the dollar value of the asset even if devaluation occurs, versus forgoing the return on local money market investments.

> Companies can partially hedge their currency risk, albeit at a cost, by buying imported goods in advance.

For example, suppose that Volkswagen do Brasil is trying to decide how many months' worth of components to carry in inventory. The present price of a component is DM 100, and this price is rising at the rate of 0.5% monthly. The Deutsche mark holding cost is estimated at 1% monthly, including insurance, warehousing, and spoilage, but excluding the opportunity cost of funds. Under these circumstances, where holding costs exceed anticipated cost increases by 0.5% monthly, Volkswagen should maintain the minimum parts inventory necessary to achieve its targeted output in Brazil.

Assume now that Volkswagen has excess cruzeiro balances in Brazil on which it is earning a nominal monthly rate of 2%. However, under Brazil's system of minidevaluation, the cruzeiro is expected to devalue against the Deutsche mark by 3% in each of the next three months, 2% in the fourth month, and 1% thereafter. Since other investment opportunities are limited or nonexistent because of currency and financial market controls, VW's opportunity cost of funds in Deutsche marks (the 2% nominal rate it earns on cruzeiros less the expected devaluation) for the next six months, month by month, equals

Month	Opportunity Cost of Funds (%)
1	−1
2	−1
3	−1
4	0
5	1
6	1

Adding this opportunity cost of funds to the previously given monthly holding costs of 1% yields the total monthly individual and cumulative DM costs of carrying inventory for the next six months:

Beginning Month	Total Monthly Carrying Cost (%)	Cumulative Carrying Cost (5 months)	Cumulative Price Increase (%)
1	0	0	0.0
2	0	0	0.5
3	0	0	1.0

(continues)

Beginning Month	Total Monthly Carrying Cost (%)	Cumulative Carrying Cost (5 months)	Cumulative Price Increase (%)
4	1	1	1.5
5	2	3	2.0
6	2	5	2.5

Based on the cumulative carrying costs and price increases, it is now apparent that the existence of anticipated cruzeiro devaluations, unmatched by correspondingly higher nominal interest rates—that is, the international Fisher effect is not expected to hold—should lead Volkswagen do Brasil to hedge a portion of its cash balances by purchasing four months' worth of inventory at today's prices (and at today's DM:cruzeiro exchange rate). In other words, it will pay Volkswagen to purchase this amount of inventory in advance in order to minimize losses in the real value of its cruzeiro cash balances. This conclusion is illustrated in Exhibit 14.9.

Inventory Stockpiling

MNCs can protect against supply disruptions by advance purchases of imported goods, but stockpiling inventory is very expensive.

Because of long delivery lead times, the often limited availability of transport for economically sized shipments, and currency restrictions, the problem of supply failure is of particular importance for any firm that is dependent on foreign sources. These conditions may make the knowledge and execution of an optimal stocking policy, under a threat of a disruption to supply, more critical in the MNC than in the firm that purchases domestically.

The traditional response to such risks has been advance purchases. Holding large amounts of inventory can be quite expensive, though. In fact, the high cost of *inventory stockpiling*—including financing, insurance, storage, and obsoles-

Exhibit 14.9 The Value of Advance Purchases of Inventory

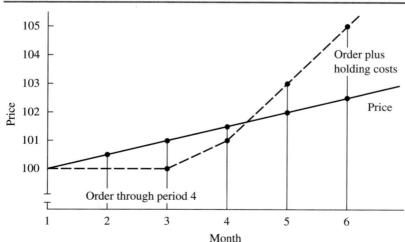

cence—has led many companies to identify low inventories with effective management. In contrast, production and sales managers typically desire a relatively large inventory, particularly when a cutoff in supply is anticipated.

Some firms do not charge their managers interest on the money tied up in inventory. A danger is that managers in these companies may take advantage of this situation by stockpiling sufficient quantities of material or goods before a potential cutoff in order to have close to a zero stock-out probability. Such a policy, established without regard to the trade-offs involved, can be very costly. For example, "In Singapore possible curtailment in shipments of air conditioners led to such heavy advance ordering that for the next two years the market was completely saturated because the warehouses were full of air conditioners."[8] Such an asymmetrical reward structure will distort the trade-offs involved. The profit performances of those managers who are receiving the benefits of additional inventory on hand should be adjusted to reflect the added costs of stockpiling.

> Charging managers for the cost of stockpiling inventory will make them more sensitive to the tradeoffs involved.

It is obvious that as the probability of disruption increases or as holding costs go down, more inventory should be ordered. Similarly, if the cost of a stock-out rises or if future supplies are expected to be more expensive, it will pay to stockpile additional inventory. Conversely, if these parameters move in the opposite direction, less inventory should be stockpiled.

14.4 ILLUSTRATION: AMERICAN EXPRESS

In early 1980, American Express (Amex) completed an eight-month study of the cash cycles of its travel, credit card, and traveler's check businesses operating in seven European countries.[9] On the basis of that project, Amex developed an international cash management system that was expected to yield cash gains—increased investments or reduced borrowing—of about $35 million in Europe alone. About half of these savings were projected to come from accelerated receipts and better control of disbursements. The other half of projected gains represented improved bank-balance control, reduced bank charges, improved value-dating, and better control of foreign exchange.

The components of the system are collection and disbursement methods, bank-account architecture, balance targeting, and foreign exchange management. The worldwide system is controlled on a regional basis, with some direction from the corporate treasurer's office in New York. A regional treasurer's office in Brighton, England, controls cash, financing, and foreign exchange transactions for Europe, the Middle East, and Africa.

The most advantageous collection and disbursement method for every operating division in each country was found by analyzing the timing of mail and clearing floats. This analysis involved

[8]Sidney Robbins and Robert B. Stobaugh, *Money in the Multinational Enterprise* (New York: Basic Books, 1973), p. 113.

[9]This section is adapted from Lars H. Thunell, "The American Express Formula," *Euromoney*, March 1980, pp. 121–127.

— Establishing what payment methods were used by customers in each country because checks are not necessarily the primary method of payment in Europe
— Measuring the mail time between certain sending and receiving points
— Identifying clearing systems and practices, which vary considerably among countries
— Analyzing for each method of payment the value-dating practice, the times for processing check deposits, and the bank charges per item

Using these data, Amex changed some of its collection and disbursement methods. For example, it installed interception points in Europe to minimize the collection float.

Next, Amex centralized the management of all its bank accounts in Europe on a regional basis. Allowing each subsidiary to set up its own independent bank account has the merit of simplicity, but it leads to a costly proliferation of different pools of funds. Amex restructured its bank accounts, eliminating some and ensuring that funds could move freely among the remaining accounts. By pooling its surplus funds, Amex can invest them for longer periods and also cut down on the chance that one subsidiary will be borrowing funds while another has surplus funds. Conversely, by combining the borrowing needs of various operations, Amex can use term financing and dispense with more expensive overdrafts. Reducing the number of accounts made cash management less complicated and also reduced banking charges.

The particular form of bank-account architecture used by Amex is a modular account structure that links separate accounts in each country with a master account. Management, on a daily basis, has only to focus on the one account through which all the country accounts have access to borrowing and investment facilities.

Balance targeting is used to control bank-account balances. The target is an average balance set for each account that reflects compensating balances, goodwill funds kept to foster the banking relationship, and the accuracy of cash forecasting. Aside from the target balance, the minimum information needed each morning to manage an account by balance targeting is the available opening balance and expected debits and credits.

Foreign exchange management in Amex's international cash management system focuses on its transaction exposure. This exposure, which is due to the multicurrency denomination of traveler's checks and credit card charges, fluctuates on a daily basis.

Procedures to control these exposures and to coordinate foreign exchange transactions center on how Amex finances its working capital from country to country, as well as the manner in which interaffiliate debts are settled. For example, if increased spending by cardholders creates the need for more working capital, Amex must decide whether to raise funds in local currency or in dollars. As a general rule, day-to-day cash is obtained at the local level through overdrafts or overnight funds.

To settle indebtedness among divisions, Amex uses interaffiliate settlements. For example, if a French cardholder uses her card in Germany, the French credit card office pays the German office, which in turn pays the German restaurant or hotel in Deutsche marks. Amex uses netting, coordinated by the regional treasurer's office in Brighton, to reduce settlement charges. For example, suppose that a German cardholder used his card in France at the same time the French cardholder charged with her card in Germany. Instead of two transactions, one foreign exchange transaction settles the differences between the two offices.

14.5 SUMMARY AND CONCLUSIONS

This chapter has examined the diverse elements involved in international cash, accounts receivable, and inventory management. We saw that although the objectives of cash management are the same for the MNC as for the domestic firm—to accelerate the collection of funds and optimize their use—the key ingredients to successful management differ. The wider investment options available to the multinational firm were discussed, as were the concepts of multilateral netting, cash pooling, and multinational cash mobilization. As multinational firms develop more efficient and comprehensive information-gathering systems, the international cash management options available to them will increase. Accompanying these options will be even more sophisticated management techniques than currently exist.

Similarly, we saw that inventory and receivable management in the MNC involve the familiar cost-minimizing strategy of investing in these assets up to the point at which the marginal cost of extending another dollar of credit or purchasing one more unit of inventory is just equal to the additional expected benefits to be derived. These benefits accrue in the form of maintaining or increasing the value of other current assets—such as cash and marketable securities—increasing sales revenue, or reducing inventory stock-out costs.

We have also seen that most of the inventory and receivables management problems that arise internationally have close parallels in the purely domestic firm. Currency changes have effects that are similar to those of inflation, and supply disruptions are not unique to international business. The differences that do exist are more in degree than in kind.

The major reason why inflation, currency changes, and supply disruptions generally cause more concern in the multinational rather than the domestic firm is that multinationals are often restricted in their ability to deal with these problems because of financial market constraints or import controls. Where financial markets are free to reflect anticipated economic events, there is no need to hedge against the loss of purchasing power by inventorying physical assets; financial securities or forward contracts are cheaper and more- effective hedging media. Similarly, there is less likelihood of government policies disrupting the flow of supplies among regions within a country than among countries.

QUESTIONS

1. Today's high interest rates put a premium on careful management of cash and marketable securities.

    a. What techniques are available to an MNC with operating subsidiaries in many countries to economize on these short-term assets?

    b. What are the advantages and disadvantages of centralizing the cash management function?

    c. What can the firm do to enhance the advantages and reduce the disadvantages described in part b?

2. Standard advice given to firms exporting to soft currency countries is to invoice in their own currency. Critically analyze this recommendation and suggest a framework that will help a financial manager to decide whether or not to stipulate hard-currency invoicing in export contracts.

    a. Under what circumstances does this advice make sense?

    b. Are these circumstances consistent with market efficiency?

    c. Are there any circumstances under which importer and exporter will mutually agree on an invoicing currency?

3. Suppose a subsidiary is all-equity financed and, hence, has no interest expenses. Does it still make sense to charge local managers for the working capital tied up in their operations? Explain.

PROBLEMS

1. A $1.5 billion Italian multinational manufacturing company has a total of $600 million in intercompany trade flows and settles accounts in 13 currencies. It also has about $400 million in third-party trade flows. Intercompany settlements are all made manually, there are no predefined remittance channels for either intercompany or third-party payments, and the methods and currencies of payment are determined by each unit independently of the other units. Payment terms for both intercompany and third-party accounts are identical. What techniques might help this company better manage its affairs?

2. A major U.S. conglomerate operates eight large, independent subsidiaries in France that regularly trade with each other on an arm's length basis. Some of the units are relatively mature and are net generators of cash; others are growing rapidly and need cash. In addition, these units trade with a number of other units located in other countries. They all have dealings with third parties in other countries as well. A recent audit revealed that these units maintained eight separate accounts at the same bank. What potential areas of improvement are there in this company's cash management?

3. SmithKline Beckman, the health-care products multinational, has 105 affiliates worldwide. There is a great deal of intercompany sales, dividend flows, and fee and royalty payments. Each unit makes its intercompany credit, payments, and hedging decisions independently. What advantages might SKB realize from centralizing international cash management and foreign exchange management?

4. Pfizer, the pharmaceutical company, generates approximately 52% of its sales overseas. A consulting study of treasury management revealed that the international division had its own treasury group that reported to the president of the international division. Both the domestic and the international treasury groups managed sizable cash portfolios. Moreover, Pfizer Inc. was significantly increasing its issues of U.S. commercial paper, and Pfizer International had cash surpluses. Intercompany sales were made on an arm's length basis, with no coordination of payments or credit terms. Each foreign unit would report monthly on what its bank balances were. All banking relations were managed locally. What profitable opportunities has Pfizer overlooked?

5. A major food and beverage manufacturer with three major divisions, 150 countries of operation, and international revenues accounting for 15% of total revenues of $6 billion conducted a treasury audit. It gathered data in the following areas: (a) local reports put out by the subsidiaries; (b) cross-border reports prepared by regional headquarters; (c) the system's organization; (d) transmission of data between subsidiaries, regional headquarters, and parent headquarters; (e) possible computerization of local reporting systems; (f) local-bank-balance reports; and (g) the accuracy of cash forecasts. What information should the company be looking for in each of these areas and why?

6. Twenty different divisions of Union Carbide sell to thousands of customers in more than 50 countries throughout the world. The proceeds are received in the form of drafts, checks, and letters of credit. Controlling the flow of funds from each transaction is an extremely complex task. Union Carbide wants to reduce the collection float to improve its cash flow. What are some techniques that might help to achieve this objective?

7. RJR Nabisco, the tobacco and consumer products company, sells in more than 160 countries around the world. RJR collects, disburses, or invests more than $50 million each day in up to 80 different currencies. Much of the fund flows involve interaffiliate flows. In the mid-1980s, RJR's Corporate Treasury group discovered that combined borrowing of all RJR units totaled approximately $120 million to $130 million on a daily basis. Simultaneously, short-term investments entered into by RJR units ranged from $90 million to $100 million daily. Moreover, there was no central management of the fund flows. What are your recommendations to improve RJR's international cash management? Where and how might savings be achieved?

8. Newport Circuits is trying to decide whether to shift production overseas of its relatively expensive integrated circuits (they average around $11 each). Offshore assembly would save about 11.1 cents per chip in labor costs. But by producing offshore, it would take about five weeks to get the parts to customers, in contrast to one week with domestic manufacturing. Thus, offshore production would force Newport to carry another four weeks of inventory. In addition, offshore production would entail combined shipping and customs duty costs of 3.2 cents. Suppose Newport's cost of funds is 15%. Will it save money by shifting production offshore?

9. Tiger Car Corp., a leading Japanese automaker, is considering a proposal to locate a factory abroad in Tennessee. Although labor costs would rise by ¥33,000 per car, the time in transit for the cars (to be sold in the United States) would be reduced by 65 days. Tigers sell for ¥825,000, and TCC's cost of funds is 12.5%. Should TCC locate the plant in Tennessee?

BIBLIOGRAPHY

Goeltz, Richard K. "Managing Liquid Funds Internationally." *Columbia Journal of World Business*, July–August 1972, pp. 59–65.

Prindl, Andreas R. "International Money Management II: Systems and Techniques." *Euromoney*, October 1971.

Robbins, Sidney, and Robert B. Stobaugh. *Money in the Multinational Enterprise*. New York: Basic Books, 1973.

Shapiro, Alan C. "International Cash Management: The Determination of Multicurrency Cash Balances." *Journal of Financial and Quantitative Analysis*, December 1976, pp. 893–900.

———. "Payments Netting in International Cash Management." *Journal of International Business Studies*, Fall 1978, pp. 51–58.

Managing the Multinational Financial System

15

An injudicious tax offers a great temptation to smuggling. But the penalties of smuggling must rise in proportion to the temptation. The law, contrary to all the ordinary principles of justice, first creates the temptation, and then punishes those who yield to it.

Adam Smith (1776)

CHAPTER LEARNING OBJECTIVES

- To identify the principal transfer mechanisms that MNCs can use to move money and profits among their various affiliates and to describe their tax, currency control, and cash management implications
- To identify the three principal arbitrage opportunities available to MNCs that stems from their ability to shift profits and funds internally
- To describe the costs and benefits associated with each transfer mechanism, as well as the constraints on their use
- To identify the factors that affect a multinational firm's ability to benefit from its internal financial transfer system
- To describe the information an MNC needs to take full advantage of its internal financial system

The multinational corporation possesses a unique characteristic: the ability to shift funds and accounting profits among its various units through internal financial transfer mechanisms. Collectively, these mechanisms make up the *multinational financial system*. As we saw in Chapter 1, *internal financial transactions* are inherent in the MNC's global approach to international operations, specifically the highly coordinated international interchange of goods (material, parts, subassemblies, and finished products), services (technology, management skills, trademarks, and patents), and capital (equity and debt) that is the hallmark of the modern multinational firm. Indeed, almost 40% of U.S. imports and exports are transactions between U.S. firms and their foreign affiliates or parents.

The purpose of this chapter is to analyze the benefits, costs, and constraints associated with the multinational financial system. This analysis includes (1) identifying the conditions under which use of this system will increase the value of the firm relative to what it would be if all financial transactions were made at arm's length through external financial channels, (2) describing and evaluating the various channels for moving money and profits internationally, and (3) specifying the design principles for a global approach to managing international fund transfers. We will examine the objectives of such an approach and the various behavioral, informational, legal, and economic factors that help determine its degree of success.

15.1 THE VALUE OF THE MULTINATIONAL FINANCIAL SYSTEM

The value of the MNC's network of financial linkages stems from the wide variations in national tax systems and significant costs and barriers associated with international financial transfers. Exhibit 15.1 summarizes the various factors that enhance the value of internal, relative to external, financial transactions. These restrictions are usually imposed to allow nations to maintain artificial values (usually inflated) for their currencies. In addition, capital controls are necessary when governments set the cost of local funds at a lower-than-market rate when currency risks are accounted for—that is, when government regulations do not allow the international Fisher effect or interest rate parity to hold.

Consequently, the ability to transfer funds and to reallocate profits internally presents multinationals with three different types of arbitrage opportunities.

The multinational financial system enables MNCs to arbitrage tax systems, financial markets, and regulatory systems.

1. *Tax arbitrage*: MNCs can reduce their tax burden by shifting profits from units located in high-tax nations to those in lower-tax nations. Or, they may shift profits from units in a taxpaying position to those with tax losses.
2. *Financial market arbitrage*: By transferring funds among units, MNCs may be able to circumvent exchange controls, earn higher risk-adjusted yields on excess funds, reduce their risk-adjusted cost of borrowed funds, and tap previously unavailable capital sources.
3. *Regulatory system arbitrage*: When subsidiary profits are a function of government regulations (for example, when a government agency sets allowable prices on the firm's goods) or union pressure, rather than the marketplace, the ability to disguise true profitability by reallocating profits among units may give the multinational firm a negotiating advantage.[1]

---

[1]See Donald R. Lessard, in "Transfer Prices, Taxes, and Financial Markets: Implications of Internal Financial Transfers Within the Multinational Firm," in *The Economic Effects of Multinational Corporations*, Robert G. Hawkins, ed. (Greenwich, Conn.: JAI Press, 1979); and David R. Rutenberg, "Maneuvering Liquid Assets in a Multinational Company," *Management Science*, June 1970, pp. B–671–684.

Exhibit 15.1 Market Imperfections That Enchance the Value of Internal Financial Transactions

Formal Barriers to International Transactions
— Quantitative restrictions (exchange controls) and direct taxes on international movements of funds
— Differential taxation of income streams according to nationality and global tax situation of the owners
— Restrictions by nationality of investor and/or investment on access to domestic capital markets

Informal Barriers to International Transactions
— Costs of obtaining information
— Difficulty of enforcing contracts across national boundaries
— Transaction costs
— Traditional investment patterns

Imperfections in Domestic Capital Markets
— Ceilings on interest rates
— Mandatory credit allocations
— Limited legal and institutional protection for minority shareholders
— Limited liquidity due to thinness of markets
— High transaction costs due to small market size and/or monopolistic practices of key financial institutions
— Difficulty of obtaining information needed to evaluate securities

SOURCE: Donald R. Lessard, "Transfer Prices, Taxes, and Financial Markets: Implications of Internal Financial Transfers Within the Multinational Firm," in Robert G. Hawkins, ed., *The Economic Effects of Multinational Corporations* (Greenwich, Conn.: JAI Press, 1979). Reprinted by permission of the publisher.

A fourth possible arbitrage opportunity is the ability to permit an affiliate to negate the effect of credit restraint or controls in its country of operation. If a government limits access to additional borrowing locally, then the firm able to draw on external sources of funds not only can achieve greater short-term profits but also may be able to attain a more powerful market position over the long term.

15.2 INTERCOMPANY FUND-FLOW MECHANISMS: COSTS AND BENEFITS

The MNC can be visualized as *unbundling* the total flow of funds between each pair of affiliates into separate components that are associated with resources transferred in the form of products, capital, services, and technology. For example, dividends, interest, and loan repayments can be matched against capital invested as equity or debt; fees, royalties, or corporate overhead can be charged for various corporate services, trademarks, or licenses.

The different channels available to the multinational enterprise for moving money and profits internationally include transfer pricing, fee and royalty adjustments, leading and lagging, intercompany loans, dividend adjustments, and investing in the form of debt versus equity. This section examines the costs, benefits, and constraints associated with each of these methods of effecting *intercompany fund flows*: It begins by sketching out some of the tax consequences for U.S.-based MNCs of interaffiliate financial transfers.

Tax Factors

Total tax payments on intercompany fund transfers depend on the tax regulations of both the host and recipient nations.

Total tax payments on intercompany fund transfers are dependent on the tax regulations of both the host and the recipient nations. The host country ordinarily has two types of taxes that directly affect tax costs: corporate income taxes and withholding taxes on dividend, interest, and fee remittances. In addition, several countries, such as Germany and Japan, tax retained earnings at a different (usually higher) rate than earnings paid out as dividends.

Many recipient nations, including the United States, tax income remitted from abroad at the regular corporate tax rate. Where this rate is higher than the foreign tax rate, dividend and other payments will normally entail an incremental tax cost. There are a number of countries, however—such as Canada, the Netherlands, and France—that do not impose any additional taxes on foreign-source income.

As an offset to these additional taxes, most countries, including the United States, provide tax credits for affiliate taxes already paid on the same income. For example, if a subsidiary located overseas has $100 in pre-tax income, pays $30 in local tax, and then remits the remaining $70 to its U.S. parent in the form of a dividend, the U.S. Internal Revenue Service (IRS) will impose a $34 tax (0.34 × $100), but will then provide a dollar-for-dollar *foreign tax credit* (FTC) for the $30 already paid in foreign taxes, leaving the parent with a bill for the remaining $4. Foreign tax credits from other remittances can be used to offset these additional taxes. For example, if a foreign subsidiary earns $100 before tax, pays $45 in local tax, and then remits the remaining $55 in the form of a dividend, the parent will wind up with an FTC of $11, the difference between the $34 U.S. tax owed and the $45 foreign tax paid.

Transfer Pricing

The pricing of goods and services traded internally is one of the most sensitive of all management subjects, and executives are typically reluctant to discuss it. Each government normally presumes that multinationals use *transfer pricing* to its country's detriment. For this reason, a number of home and host governments have set up policing mechanisms to review the transfer pricing policies of MNCs.

The most important uses of transfer pricing include (1) reducing taxes, (2) reducing tariffs, and (3) avoiding exchange controls. Transfer prices may also be used to increase the MNC's share of profits from a joint venture and to disguise an affiliate's true profitability.

Tax Effects. To illustrate the tax effects associated with a change in transfer price, suppose that affiliate A produces 100,000 circuit boards for $10 apiece and sells them to affiliate B. Affiliate B, in turn, sells these boards for $22 apiece to an unrelated customer. As shown in Exhibit 15.2, pre-tax profit for the consolidated company is $1 million regardless of the price at which the goods are transferred from affiliate A to affiliate B.

Nevertheless, because affiliate A's tax rate is 30% while affiliate B's tax rate is 50%, consolidated after-tax income will differ depending on the transfer price used. Under the low-markup policy, in which affiliate A sets a unit transfer price of $15, affiliate A pays taxes of $120,000 and affiliate B pays $300,000, for a total tax bill of $420,000 and a consolidated net income of $580,000. Switching to a high-markup policy (a transfer price of $18), affiliate A's taxes rise to $210,000 while affiliate B's decline to $150,000, for combined tax payments of $360,000 and consolidated net income of $640,000. The result of this transfer price increase is to lower total taxes paid by $60,000 and raise consolidated income by the same amount.

In effect, profits are being shifted from a higher to a lower tax jurisdiction. In the extreme case, an affiliate may be in a loss position because of high start-up costs, heavy depreciation charges, or substantial investments that are expensed. Consequently, it has a zero effective tax rate, and profits channeled to that unit can be received tax free. The basic rule of thumb to follow if the objective is to minimize taxes is as follows: If affiliate A is selling goods to affiliate B, and t_A and t_B are the marginal tax rates of affiliate A and affiliate B, respectively, then

If $t_A > t_B$, set the transfer price as low as possible

If $t_A < t_B$, set the transfer price as high as possible

MNCs can reduce taxes by using transfer prices to shift profits from the high-tax to the low-tax nation.

Exhibit 15.2 Tax Effect of High Versus Low Transfer Price ($ Thousands)

	Affiliate A	Affiliate B	Affiliates A + B
Low-Markup Policy			
Revenue	1,500	2,200	2,200
Cost of goods solds	1,000	1,500	1,000
Gross profit	500	700	1,200
Other expenses	100	100	200
Income before taxes	400	600	1,000
Taxes (30%/50%)	120	300	420
Net income	280	300	580
High-Markup Policy			
Revenue	1,800	2,200	2,200
Cost of goods sold	1,000	1,800	1,000
Gross profit	800	400	1,200
Other expenses	100	100	200
Income before taxes	700	300	1,000
Taxes (30%/50%)	210	150	360
Net income	490	150	640

Tariffs. The introduction of tariffs complicates this decision rule. Suppose that affiliate B must pay *ad valorem* import duties—tariffs that are set as a percentage of the value of the imported goods—at the rate of 10%. Then, raising the transfer price will increase the duties that affiliate B must pay, assuming that the tariff is levied on the invoice (transfer) price. The combined tax-plus-tariff effects of the transfer price change are shown in Exhibit 15.3.

Tariff considerations complicate the optimal transfer price decision.

Under the low-markup policy, import tariffs of $150,000 are paid. Affiliate B's taxes will decline by $75,000 because tariffs are tax-deductible. Total taxes plus tariffs paid are $495,000. Switching to the high-markup policy raises import duties to $180,000 and simultaneously lowers affiliate B's income taxes by half that amount, or $90,000. Total taxes plus tariffs rise to $450,000. The high-markup policy is still desirable, but its benefit has been reduced by $15,000 to $45,000. In general, the higher the ad valorem tariff relative to the income tax differential, the more likely it is that a low transfer price is desirable.

There are some costs associated with using transfer prices for tax reduction. If the price is too high, tax authorities in the purchaser's (affiliate B's) country will see revenues foregone; if the price is too low, both governments might intervene. Affiliate A's government may view low transfer prices as tax evasion at the same time that the tariff commission in affiliate B's country sees dumping and/or revenue foregone. These costs must be paid for in the form of legal fees, executive time, and penalties.

Exhibit 15.3 Tax-Plus-Tariff-Effect of High Versus Low Transfer Price ($ Thousands)

	Affiliate A	Affiliate B	Affiliates A + B
Low-Markup Policy			
Revenue	1,500	2,200	2,200
Cost of goods solds	1,000	1,500	1,000
Import duty (10%)	—	150	150
Gross profit	500	550	1,050
Other expenses	100	100	200
Income before taxes	400	450	850
Taxes (30%/50%)	120	225	345
Net income	280	225	505
High-Markup Policy			
Revenue	1,800	2,200	2,200
Cost of goods sold	1,000	1,800	1,000
Import duty	—	180	180
Gross profit	800	220	1,020
Other expenses	100	100	200
Income before taxes	700	120	820
Taxes (30%/50%)	210	60	270
Net income	490	60	550

Most countries have specific regulations governing transfer prices. For instance, *Section 482* of the U.S. Revenue Code calls for *arm's-length prices*—that is, prices at which a willing buyer and a willing unrelated seller would freely agree to transact.

In light of Section 482, and the U.S. government's willingness to use it, and similar authority by most other nations, current practice by MNCs appears to be setting standard prices for standardized products. However, the innovative nature of the typical multinational ensures a continual stream of new products for which no market equivalent exists. Hence, some leeway is possible on transfer pricing. In addition, although finished products do get traded among affiliates, trade between related parties increasingly is in high-tech, custom-made components and subassemblies (for example, automobile transmissions and circuit boards) where there are no comparable sales to unrelated buyers. Firms also have a great deal of latitude in setting prices on rejects, scrap, and returned goods.

> Most governments regulate the transfer prices MNCs can use.

ILLUSTRATION: *President Clinton Seeks $45 Billion from Foreign Companies*

One of the linchpins of President Clinton's economic revival plan is a proposal to extract billions from foreign companies doing business in the United States. By closing loopholes and instituting more vigorous enforcement, Clinton has said he believes that the federal government can raise $45 billion over four years from foreign companies, which take in nearly $1 trillion in U.S. revenue annually. Clinton's contention is based on a view prevalent in the IRS that foreign multinationals are manipulating their transfer prices on goods they sell to their U.S. subsidiaries so as to avoid paying U.S. tax. However, many analysts are skeptical that there is all that much to be gained by tougher enforcement of Section 482. For example, one government study reportedly found that the IRS had only limited success in recovering additional taxes in transfer pricing cases involving foreign MNCS. From 1987 through 1989, the IRS got only 26.5% of the $757 million it sought.

In addition, the circumstantial evidence the IRS relied on to support its case is suspect. For example, in 1990, the IRS cited as evidence of transfer pricing manipulation the fact that, over a 10-year period, foreign-controlled companies' (1) gross income had more than doubled while (2) the taxes paid by these companies had hardly changed. However, this argument makes no sense since on U.S. tax returns, "gross income" is "sales" less "cost of sales"; and thus transfer price manipulation, if any, would reduce "gross income" (by raising the cost of goods sold). Therefore, a doubling of "gross income" cannot indicate transfer price manipulation.

Exchange Controls. Another important use of transfer pricing is to avoid currency controls. For example, in the absence of offsetting foreign tax credits, a U.S. parent will wind up with $0.66Q_0 after tax for each dollar increase in the price at

Transfer pricing can be used to avoid currency controls.

which it sells Q_0 units of a product to an affiliate with blocked funds (based on a U.S. corporate tax rate of 34%). Hence, a transfer price change from P_0 to P_1 will lead to a shift of $0.66(P_1 - P_0)Q_0$ dollars to the parent. The subsidiary, of course, will show a corresponding reduction in its cash balances and taxes, due to its higher expenses.

In fact, bypassing currency restrictions appears to explain the seeming anomaly whereby subsidiaries operating in less-developed countries (LDCs) with low tax rates are sold overpriced goods by other units. In effect, companies appear to be willing to pay a tax penalty to access otherwise unavailable funds.

MNCs can use transfer pricing to increase their share of profits from joint ventures.

Joint Ventures. Conflicts over transfer pricing often arise when one of the affiliates involved is owned jointly by one or more other partners. The outside partners are often suspicious that transfer pricing is being used to shift profits from the joint venture, where they must be shared, to a wholly owned subsidiary. Although there is no pat answer to this problem, the determination of fair transfer prices should be resolved before the establishment of a joint venture. Continuing disputes may still arise, however, over the pricing of new products introduced to an existing venture.

Disguising Profitability. Many LDCs erect high tariff barriers in order to develop import-substituting industries. However, because they are aware of the potential for abuse, many host governments simultaneously attempt to regulate the profits of firms operating in such a protected environment. When confronted by a situation where profits depend on government regulations, the MNC can use transfer pricing (buying goods from sister affiliates at a higher price) to disguise the true profitability of its local affiliate, enabling it to justify higher local prices. Lower reported profits may also improve a subsidiary's bargaining position in wage negotiations. It is probably for this reason that several international unions have called for fuller disclosure by multinationals of their worldwide accounting data.

Evaluation and Control. Transfer price adjustments will distort the profits of reporting units and create potential difficulties in evaluating managerial performance. In addition, managers evaluated on the basis of these reported profits may have an incentive to behave in ways that are suboptimal for the corporation as a whole.

Fees and Royalties

Management services such as headquarters advice, allocated overhead, patents, and trademarks are often unique and, therefore, are without a reference market price. The consequent difficulty in pricing these corporate resources makes them suitable for use as additional routes for international fund flows by varying the *fees* or *royalties* charged for using these intangible factors of production.

Transfer prices for services or intangible assets have the same tax and exchange control effects as those for transfer prices on goods. However, host governments often look with more favor on payments for industrial know-how than for profit remittances. Where restrictions do exist, they are more likely to be modified to permit a fee for technical knowledge than to allow for dividends.

For MNCs, these charges have assumed a somewhat more important role as a conduit for funneling remittances from foreign affiliates. To a certain extent, this trend reflects the fact that many of these payments are tied to overseas sales or assets that grew very rapidly during the 1960s and early 1970s, as well as the growing importance of tax considerations and exchange controls. For example, by setting low transfer prices on intangibles to manufacturing subsidiaries in low-tax locations like Puerto Rico or Singapore, multinationals can receive profits essentially tax free.

In recognition of this possibility, the United States in 1986 amended Section 482 to provide that the transfer price of an intangible must be "commensurate with the income" the intangible generates. This means in practice that the IRS will not consider a related-party transfer price for an intangible arm's length unless it produces a split in profits between transferor and transferee that falls within the range of profits that unrelated parties realize (1) on similar intangibles (2) in similar circumstances. Armed with this amendment, the IRS now carefully scrutinizes the pricing of intangibles.

The most common approach to setting fee and royalty charges is for the parent to decide on a desired amount of total fee remittances from the overseas operations, usually based on an allocation of corporate expenses, and then to apportion these charges according to subsidiary sales or assets. This method, which sometimes involves establishing identical licensing agreements with all units, gives these charges the appearance of a legitimate and necessary business expense, thereby aiding in overcoming currency restrictions.

Governments typically prefer prior agreements and steady and predictable payment flows; a sudden change in licensing and service charges is likely to be looked at with suspicion. For this reason, firms try to avoid abrupt changes in their remittance policies. However, where exchange controls exist or are likely, or if there are significant tax advantages, many firms will initially set a higher level of fee and royalty payments while still maintaining a stable remittance policy.

Special problems exist with joint ventures because the parent company will have to obtain permission from its partner(s) to be able to levy charges for its services and licensing contributions. These payments ensure the parent of receiving at least some compensation for the resources it has invested in the joint venture, perhaps in lieu of dividends over which it may have little or no control.

Fees and royalties are often a more convenient way of accessing subsidiary profits.

MNCs tend to follow a stable remittance policy for fees and royalties.

Leading and Lagging

A highly favored means of shifting liquidity among affiliates is an acceleration (*leading*) or delay (*lagging*) in the payment of interaffiliate accounts by modifying the credit terms extended by one unit to another. For example, suppose affiliate A sells goods worth $1 million monthly to affiliate B on 90-day credit terms. Then, on average, affiliate A has $3 million of accounts receivable from affiliate B and is,

Exhibit 15.4 Fund-Transfer Effects of Leading and Lagging

Affiliate A Sells $1 Million in Goods Monthly to Affiliate B

	Credit Terms		
Balance-Sheet Accounts	*Normal (90 days)*	*Leading (30 days)*	*Lagging (180 days)*
Affiliate A Accounts receivable from B	$3,000,000	$1,000,000	$6,000,000
Affiliate B Accounts payable to A	$3,000,000	$1,000,000	$6,000,000
Net Cash Transfers From B to A	—	$2,000,000	
From A to B	—		$3,000,000

Leading and lagging of interaffiliate payments is a common method of shifting money from one unit to another.

in effect, financing $3 million of working capital for affiliate B. If the terms are changed to 180 days, there will be a one-time shift of an additional $3 million to affiliate B. Conversely, reducing credit terms to 30 days will create a flow of $2 million from affiliate B to affiliate A, as shown in Exhibit 15.4.

Shifting Liquidity.   The value of leading and lagging depends on the opportunity cost of funds to both the paying unit and the recipient. When an affiliate already in a surplus position receives payment, it can invest the additional funds at the prevailing local lending rate; if it requires working capital, the payment received can be used to reduce its borrowings at the borrowing rate. If the paying unit has excess funds, it loses cash that it would have invested at the lending rate; if it is in a deficit position, it has to borrow at the borrowing rate. To assess the benefits of shifting liquidity among affiliates, these borrowing and lending rates must be calculated on an after-tax dollar (HC) basis.

Suppose, for example, that a multinational company faces the following effective, after-tax dollar borrowing and lending rates in Germany and the United States:

	Borrowing Rate (%)	*Lending Rate (%)*
United States	3.8	2.9
Germany	3.6	2.7

Both the U.S. and German units can have either a surplus (+) or deficit (−) of funds. The four possibilities, along with the domestic interest rates (U.S./German) and interest differentials (U.S. rate − German rate) associated with each state, are as follows:

		Germany	
		+	−
United States	+	2.9%/2.7% (0.2%)	2.9%/3.6% (−0.7%)
	−	3.8%/2.7% (1.1%)	3.8%/3.6% (0.2%)

For example, if both units have excess funds, then the relevant opportunity costs of funds are the U.S. and German lending rates of 2.9% and 2.7%, respectively, and the associated interest differential (in parentheses) is 0.2%. Similarly, if the U.S. unit requires funds while the German affiliate has a cash surplus, then the relevant rates are the respective U.S. borrowing and German lending rates of 3.8% and 2.7% and the interest differential is 1.1%.

If the interest rate differential is positive, the corporation as a whole—by moving funds to the United States—will either pay less on its borrowing or earn more interest on its investments. This move can be made by leading payments to the United States and lagging payments to Germany. Shifting money to Germany—by leading payments to Germany and lagging them to the United States—will be worthwhile if the interest differential is negative.

The value of leading and lagging depends on the opportunity cost of funds to both the paying unit and the recipient.

Based on the interest differentials in this example, all borrowings should be done in Germany, and surplus funds should be invested in the United States. Only if the U.S. unit has excess cash and the German unit requires funds should money flow into Germany.

For example, suppose the German unit owes $2 million to the U.S. unit. The timing of this payment can be changed by up to 90 days in either direction. Assume the U.S. unit is borrowing funds, and the German unit has excess cash available. According to the prevailing interest differential of 1.1%, given the current liquidity status of each affiliate, the German unit should speed up, or lead, its payment to the U.S. unit. The net effect of these adjustments is that the U.S. firm can reduce its borrowing by $2 million, and the German unit has $2 million less in cash—all for 90 days. Borrowing costs for the U.S. unit are pared by $19,000 ($2,000,000 × 0.038 × 90/360), and the German unit's interest income is reduced by $13,500 ($2,000,000 × 0.027 × 90/360). There is a net savings of $5,500. The savings could be computed more directly by using the relevant interest differential of 1.1% as follows: $2,000,000 × 0.011 × 90/360 = $5,500.

Advantages. Leading and lagging has several advantages over direct intercompany loans.

1. No formal note of indebtedness is needed, and the amount of credit can be adjusted up or down by shortening or lengthening the terms on the accounts. Governments do not always allow such freedom on loans.
2. Governments are less likely to interfere with payments on intercompany accounts than on direct loans.
3. Section 482 allows intercompany accounts up to six months to be interest free. In contrast, interest must be charged on all intercompany loans. The ability to

set a zero interest rate is valuable if the host government does not allow interest payments on parent company loans to be tax deductible or if there are withholding taxes on interest payments.

Government Restrictions.   As with all other transfer mechanisms, government controls on intercompany credit terms are often tight and given to abrupt changes. While appearing straightforward on the surface, these rules are subject to different degrees of government interpretation and sanction. For example, in theory Japan permits firms to employ leads and lags. However, in reality leading and lagging is very difficult because regulations require that all settlements be made in accordance with the original trade documents unless a very good reason exists for an exception. On the other hand, Sweden, which prohibits import leads, will often lift this restriction for imports of capital goods.

Intercompany Loans

A principal means of financing foreign operations and moving funds internationally is to engage in intercompany lending activities. The making and repaying of *intercompany loans* is often the only legitimate transfer mechanism available to the MNC.

Intercompany loans add value to the MNC if credit rationing, currency controls, or differences in national tax rates exist.

Intercompany loans are more valuable to the firm than arm's-length transactions only if at least one of the following market distortions exist: (1) credit rationing (due to a ceiling on local interest rates), (2) currency controls, or (3) differential tax rates among countries. This list is not particularly restrictive because it is the rare MNC that faces none of these situations in its international operations.

Although a variety of types of intercompany loans exist, the most important methods at present are direct loans, back-to-back financing, and parallel loans. *Direct loans* are straight extensions of credit from the parent to an affiliate or from one affiliate to another. The other types of intercompany loans typically involve an intermediary.

Back-to-Back Loans.   *Back-to-back loans*, also called *fronting loans* or *link financing*, are often employed to finance affiliates located in nations with high interest rates or restricted capital markets, especially when there is a danger of currency controls or when different rates of withholding tax are applied to loans from a financial institution. In the typical arrangement, the parent company deposits funds with a bank in country A that in turn lends the money to a subsidiary in country B. These transactions are shown in Exhibit 15.5. By contrasting these transactions with a direct intercompany loan, the figure reveals that, in effect, a back-to-back loan is an intercompany loan channeled through a bank. From the bank's point of view, the loan is risk free because the parent's deposit fully collateralizes it. The bank simply acts as an intermediary or a front; compensation is provided by the margin between the interest received from the borrowing unit and the rate paid on the parent's deposit.

A back-to-back loan may offer several potential advantages when compared with a direct intercompany loan. Two of the most important advantages are as follows:

Exhibit 15.5 Structure of a Back-to-Back Loan

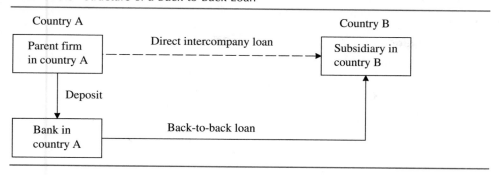

1. Certain countries apply different withholding-tax rates to interest paid to a foreign parent and interest paid to a financial institution. A cost saving in the form of lower taxes may be available with a back-to-back loan.
2. If currency controls are imposed, the government will usually permit the local subsidiary to honor the amortization schedule of a loan from a major multinational bank; to stop payment would hurt the nation's credit rating. Conversely, local monetary authorities would have far fewer reservations about not authorizing the repayment of an intercompany loan. In general, back-to-back financing provides better protection than does a parent loan against expropriation and/or exchange controls.

Back-to-back arrangements can also be used to access blocked currency funds without physically transferring them. Suppose Xerox wishes to use the excess funds being generated by its Brazilian operation to finance a needed plant expansion in Colombia, where long-term money is virtually unobtainable. Xerox prefers not to invest additional dollars in Colombia because of the high probability of a Colombian peso devaluation. Because of stringent Brazilian exchange controls, though, this movement of cruzeiros cannot take place directly. However, Xerox may be able to use the worldwide branching facilities of an international bank as a substitute for an internal transfer. For example, suppose the Brazilian branch of Chase Manhattan Bank needs cruzeiro deposits to continue funding its loans in a restrictive credit environment. Chase may be willing to lend Xerox long-term pesos through its branch in Colombia in return for a cruzeiro deposit of equivalent maturity in Brazil.

Back-to-back loans can be used to avoid currency controls and reduce taxes.

In this way, Xerox gets the use of its funds in Brazil and at the same time receives locally denominated funds in Colombia. Protection is provided against a peso devaluation, although the firm's cruzeiro funds are, of course, still exposed. The value of this arrangement is based on the relative interest rates involved, anticipated currency changes, and the opportunity cost of the funds being utilized. Given the exchange and credit restrictions and other market imperfections that exist, it is quite possible that both the bank and its client can benefit from this type of arrangement. Negotiation between the two parties will determine how these benefits are to be shared.

A parallel loan consists of two related but separate borrowings, usually involving four parties in two different countries.

Parallel Loans. A *parallel loan* is a method of effectively repatriating blocked funds (at least for the term of the arrangement), circumventing exchange control restrictions, avoiding a premium exchange rate for investments abroad, financing foreign affiliates without incurring additional exchange risk, or obtaining foreign currency financing at attractive rates. As shown in Exhibit 15.6, it consists of two related but separate—that is, parallel—borrowings and usually involves four parties in at least two different countries. In Exhibit 15.6a, a U.S. parent firm wishing to invest in Spain lends dollars to the U.S. affiliate of a Spanish firm that wants to invest in the United States. In return, the Spanish parent lends pesetas in Spain to the U.S. firm's Spanish subsidiary. Drawdowns, payments of interest, and repayments of principal are made simultaneously. The differential between the rates of interest on the two loans is determined, in theory, by the cost of money in each country and anticipated changes in currency values.

Exhibit 15.6b shows how a parallel loan can be used to access blocked funds. In this instance, the Brazilian affiliate of ITT is generating cruzeiros that it is unable to repatriate. It lends this money to the local affiliate of Dow Chemical; in turn, Dow lends dollars to ITT in the United States. Hence, ITT would have the use of dollars in the United States while Dow would obtain cruzeiros in Brazil. In

Exhibit 15.6 Structure of a Parallel Loan

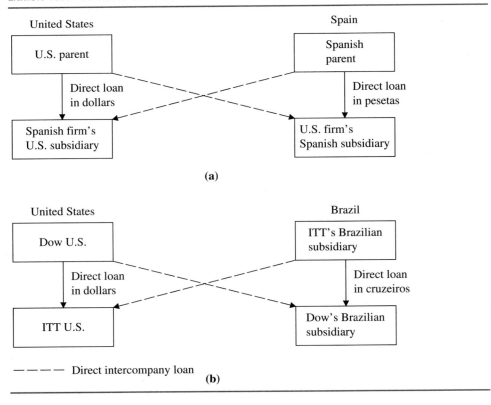

(a)

(b)

– – – – – Direct intercompany loan

both cases, the parallel transactions are the functional equivalent of direct inter-company loans.

Fees to banks brokering these arrangements usually run from 0.25% to 0.5% of the principal for each side. (Chapter 22 discusses currency swaps, which are an outgrowth of parallel loans.)

Dividends

Dividends are by far the most important means of transferring funds from foreign affiliates to the parent company, typically accounting for over 50% of all remittances to U.S. firms. Among the various factors that MNCs consider when deciding on dividend payments by their affiliates are taxes, financial statement effects, exchange risk, currency controls, financing requirements, availability and cost of funds, and the parent's dividend payout ratio. Firms differ, though, in the relative importance they place on these variables, as well as in how systematically the variables are incorporated in an overall remittance policy. The parent company's *dividend payout ratio* often plays an important role in determining the dividends to be received from abroad. Some firms require the same payout percentage as the parent's rate for each of their subsidiaries; others set a target payout rate as a percentage of overall foreign-source earnings without attempting to receive the same percentage from each subsidiary. The rationale for focusing on the parent's payout ratio is that the subsidiaries should contribute their share of the dividends paid to the stockholders. Thus, if the parent's payout rate is 60%, then foreign operations should contribute 60% of their earnings toward meeting this goal. Establishing a uniform percentage for each unit, rather than an overall target, is explained as an attempt to persuade foreign governments, particularly those of less-developed countries, that these payments are necessary rather than arbitrary.

> Dividends are the most important means of transferring funds from foreign affiliates to the parent company.

Tax Effects. A major consideration behind the dividend decision is the effective tax rate on payments from different affiliates. By varying payout ratios among its foreign subsidiaries, the corporation can reduce its total tax burden.

Once a firm has decided on the amount of dividends to remit from overseas, it can then reduce its tax bill by withdrawing funds from those locations with the lowest transfer costs. To take a highly simplified example, suppose a U.S. company, International Products, wishes to withdraw $1 million from abroad in the form of dividends. Its three foreign subsidiaries—located in Germany, the Republic of Ireland, and France—have each earned $2 million before tax this year and, hence, are all capable of providing the funds. The problem for International Products is to decide on the dividend strategy that will minimize the firm's total tax bill.

> By varying dividend payout rates among its foreign units, the MNC can reduce its total taxes.

The German subsidiary is subject to a split corporate tax rate of 50% on retained earnings and 36% on dividends as well as a dividend withholding tax of 10%. As an export incentive, the Republic of Ireland grants a 15-year tax holiday on all export profits. Since the Irish unit receives all its profits from exports, it pays no taxes. There are no dividend withholding taxes. The French affiliate is taxed at a rate of 45% and must also pay a 10% withholding tax on its dividend remittances. It is assumed there are no excess foreign tax credits available and that any credits generated cannot be used elsewhere. Exhibit 15.7 summarizes the relevant tax consequences of remitting $1 million from each affiliate in turn.

These calculations indicate that it would be cheapest to remit dividends from Germany. In fact, by paying this $1 million dividend with its associated tax cost of $1.86 million, International Products is actually reducing its worldwide tax costs by $40,000—compared with its total tax bill of $1.9 million in the absence of any dividend. This result is due to the tax penalty that the German government imposes on retained earnings.

Financing Requirements. In addition to their tax consequences, dividend payments lead to liquidity shifts. The value of moving these funds depends on the different opportunity costs of money among the various units of the corporation. For instance, an affiliate that must borrow funds will usually have a higher opportunity cost than a unit with excess cash available. Moreover, some subsidi-

Exhibit 15.7 Tax Effects of Dividend Remittances from Abroad

Location of Foreign Affiliate	Dividend Amount	Host Country Income Tax If Dividend Paid	Host Country Withholding Tax	U.S. Income Tax	Total Taxes If Dividend Paid	Host Country Income Tax If No Dividend Paid	Worldwide Tax Liability If Dividend Paid*
Germany	$1,000,000	$360,000 500,000 $860,000	$100,000	0[1]	$ 960,000	$1,000,000	$1,860,000
Republic of Ireland	$1,000,000	0	0	$340,000	$ 340,000	0	$2,240,000
France	$1,000,000	$900,000	$100,000	0	$1,000,000	$900,000	$2,000,000

[1]Computation of U.S. tax owed

		Included in U.S. income:	
Profit before tax	$2,000,000		
Tax = $1,000,000 × 0.50 + $1,000,000 × 0.36 =	860,000	Gross dividend received	$1,000,000
Profit after tax	1,140,000	Foreign indirect tax deemed paid	842,105
Dividend paid to U.S. parent company	1,000,000	U.S. gross dividend included	$1,842,105
Less withholding tax @ 10%	100,000	U.S. tax @ 34%	626,316
Net dividend received in United States	$ 900,000	Less foreign tax credit[2]	942,105
		Net U.S. tax cost (credit)	$(315,789)
		U.S. tax payable	0

[2]Foreign tax credit
(a) Direct credit for withholding tax   100,000
(b) Indirect foreign tax credit

$$\frac{\text{Dividend paid}}{\text{Profit after tax}} \times \text{Foreign tax} = \frac{1,000,000}{1,140,000} \times 960,000 = 842,105$$

Total tax credit $942,105

*Worldwide tax liability if dividend paid equals tax liability for foreign affiliate paying the dividend plus tax liabilities of non-dividend-paying affiliates plus any U.S. taxes owed.

aries will have access to low-cost financing sources, while others have no recourse but to borrow at a relatively high interest rate.

All else being equal, a parent can increase its value by exploiting yield differences among its affiliates—that is, setting a high dividend payout rate for subsidiaries with relatively low opportunity costs of funds while requiring smaller dividend payments from those units facing high borrowing costs or having favorable investment opportunities.

Exchange Controls. Exchange controls are another major factor in the dividend decision. Nations with balance-of-payments problems are apt to restrict the payment of dividends to foreign companies. These controls vary by country, but in general they limit the size of dividend remittances, either in absolute terms or as a percentage of earnings, equity, or registered capital.

Many firms try to reduce the danger of such interference by maintaining a record of consistent dividends. The record is designed to show that these payments are part of an established financial program, rather than an act of speculation against the host country's currency. Dividends are paid every year, whether they are justified by financial and tax considerations or not, just to demonstrate a continuing policy to the local government and central bank. Even when they cannot be remitted, dividends are sometimes declared for the same reason, namely, to establish grounds for making future payments when these controls are lifted or modified.

A record of consistent dividend payments reduces the threat of government interference with these payments.

Some companies even set a uniform dividend payout ratio throughout the corporate system to set a global pattern and maintain the principle that affiliates have an obligation to pay dividends to their stockholders. If challenged, the firm can then prove that its French or Brazilian or Italian subsidiaries must pay an equivalent percentage dividend. MNCs are often willing to accept higher tax costs to maintain the principle that dividends are a necessary and legitimate business expense. Many executives believe that a record of paying dividends consistently (or at least declaring them) helps in getting approval for further dividend disbursements.

Joint Ventures. The presence of local stockholders may constrain an MNC's ability to adjust its dividend policy in accordance with global factors. In addition, to the extent that multinationals have a longer-term perspective than their local partners, conflicts might arise with local investors demanding a shorter payback period and the MNC insisting on a higher earnings retention rate.

Equity Versus Debt

Corporate funds invested overseas, whether they are called debt or equity, require the same rate of return, namely, the firm's marginal cost of capital. Nonetheless, MNCs generally prefer to invest in the form of loans rather than equity for several reasons.

First, a firm typically has wider latitude to repatriate funds in the form of interest and loan repayments than as dividends or reductions in equity because the latter fund flows are usually more closely controlled by governments. In

MNCs can realize several advantages by investing overseas in the form of debt rather than equity.

addition, a reduction in equity may be frowned on by the host government and is likely to pose a real problem for a firm trying to repatriate funds in excess of earnings. Withdrawing these funds by way of dividend payments will reduce the affiliate's capital stock, whereas applying this money toward repayment of a loan will not affect the unit's equity account. Moreover, if the firm ever desired to increase its equity investment, it can relatively easily convert the loan into equity.

A second reason for the use of intercompany loans over equity investments is the possibility of reducing taxes. The likelihood of a tax benefit is due to two factors: (1) Interest paid on a loan is ordinarily tax-deductible in the host nation, whereas dividend payments are not; and (2) unlike dividends, loan repayments do not normally constitute taxable income to the parent company.

Firms do not have complete latitude in choosing their debt-to-equity ratios abroad, though. This subject is frequently open for negotiation with the host governments. In addition, dividends and local borrowings are often restricted to a fixed percentage of equity. A small equity base can also lead to a high return on equity, exposing a company to charges of exploitation.

Another obstacle to taking complete advantage of parent company loans is the U.S. government. The IRS may treat loan repayments as constructive dividends and tax them if it believes the subsidiary is too thinly capitalized. Many executives and tax attorneys feel that the IRS is satisfied as long as the debt-to-equity ratio does not exceed four to one.

Firms normally use guidelines such as 50% of total assets or fixed assets in determining the amount of equity to provide their subsidiaries. These guidelines usually lead to an equity position greater than that required by law, causing MNCs to sacrifice flexibility and pay higher taxes than necessary.

15.3   DESIGNING A GLOBAL REMITTANCE POLICY

The task facing international financial executives is to coordinate the use of the various financial linkages in a manner consistent with value maximization for the firm as a whole. This task requires the following four interrelated decisions: (1) how much money (if any) to remit; (2) when to do so; (3) where to transmit these funds; and (4) which transfer method(s) to use.

In order to take proper advantage of its internal financial system, the firm must conduct a systematic and comprehensive analysis of the available remittance options and their associated costs and benefits. It must also compare the value of deploying funds in affiliates other than just the remitting subsidiary and the parent. For example, rather than just deciding whether to keep earnings in Germany or remit them to the U.S. parent, corporate headquarters must consider the possibility and desirability of moving those funds to, say, Italy or France via leading and lagging or transfer price adjustments. In other words, the key question to be answered is, Where and how in the world can available funds be deployed most profitably? Most multinationals, however, make their dividend remittance decision independently of, say, their royalty or leading and lagging decision, rather than considering what mix of transfer mechanisms would be best for the company overall.

In part, the decision to "satisfice" rather than optimize is due to the complex nature of the financial linkages in a typical multinational corporation. For instance, if there are ten financial links connecting each pair of units in a multinational enterprise, then a firm consisting of a parent and two subsidiaries will have 30 intercompany links, three times as many as a parent with just one affiliate. A parent with three subsidiaries will have 60 links; a company with n units will have $10n(n + 1)/2$ financial linkages.

Most MNCs satisfice rather than optimize the use of their internal financial transfer system.

Since a real-life firm will have many more than three affiliates, the exponential growth of potential intercompany relationships means that unless the options are severely limited, system optimization will be impossible. It is not surprising, therefore, that surveys by Zenoff and by Robbins and Stobaugh found that few firms seemed to think in terms of a worldwide pool of funds to be allocated in accordance with global profit maximization.[2] Instead, most parents allowed their affiliates to keep just enough cash on hand to meet their fund requirements, with the rest sent back home.

This limited approach to managing international financial transactions is understandable in view of the tangled web of interaffiliate connections that has already been depicted. Still, compromising with complexity ought not to mean ignoring the system's profit potential. A hands-off policy is not the only alternative to system optimization. Instead, the MNC should search for relatively high-yield uses of its internal financial system. This task is often made easier by choices that are generally more limited in practice than in theory.

First of all, many of the potential links will be impossible to use because of government regulations and the specifics of the firm's situation. For example, two affiliates may not trade with each other, eliminating the transfer pricing link. Other channels will be severely restricted by government controls.

Furthermore, in many situations, it is not necessary to develop an elaborate mathematical model to figure out the appropriate policy. For example, where a currency is blocked and investment opportunities are lacking or local tax rates are quite high, it will normally be in the company's best interest to shift its funds and profits elsewhere. Where credit rationing exists, a simple decision rule usually suffices: Maximize local borrowing. Moreover, most MNCs already have large staffs for data collection and planning, as well as some form of computerized accounting system. These elements can form the basis for a more complete overseas planning effort.

The more limited, although still numerous, real-life options facing a firm and the existing nucleus of a planning system can significantly reduce the costs of centralizing the management of a firm's intercompany transactions. In addition, for most multinationals, fewer than ten affiliates account for an overwhelming majority of intercompany fund flows. Recognizing this situation, several firms

[2]David B. Zenoff, "Remitting Funds from Foreign Affiliates," *Financial Executive,* March 1968, pp. 46–63; and Sidney M. Robbins and Robert B. Stobaugh, *Money in the Multinational Enterprise* (New York: Basic Books, 1973), p. 86.

have developed systems to optimize flows among this limited number of units. The lack of global optimization (interactions with other affiliates are taken as given, rather than treated as decision variables) is not particularly costly because most of the major fund flows are already included. Realistically, the objective of such an effort should be profit improvement rather than system optimization.

Prerequisites

The value of an MNC's internal financial system depends on the number of financial links and the volume of intercompany transactions.

A number of factors strongly impact on an MNC's ability to benefit from its internal financial transfer system. These include (1) the number of financial links, (2) the volume of interaffiliate transactions, (3) the foreign affiliate ownership pattern, (4) the degree of product and service standardization, and (5) the government regulations.

Because each channel has different costs and benefits associated with its use, the wider the range of choice, the greater a firm's ability to achieve specific goals. For example, some links are best suited to avoiding exchange controls, while others are most efficiently employed in reducing taxes. In this vein, a two-way flow of funds will give a firm greater flexibility in deploying its money than if all links are only in one direction. Of course, the larger the volume of flows through these financial arteries, the more funds that can be moved by a given adjustment in intercompany terms. A 1% change in the transfer price on goods flowing between two affiliates will have a 10 times greater absolute effect if annual sales are $10 million rather than just $1 million. Similarly, altering credit terms by 30 days will become a more effective means of transferring funds as the volume of intercompany payables and receivables grows.

A large volume of intercompany transactions is usually associated with the worldwide dispersal and rationalization of production activities. As plants specialize in different components and stages of production, interaffiliate trade increases, as do the accompanying financial flows. Clearly, 100% ownership of all foreign affiliates removes a major impediment to the efficient allocation of funds worldwide. The existence of joint ventures is likely to confine a firm's transfer activities to a set of mutually agreed-upon rules, eliminating its ability to react swiftly to changed circumstances.

Government regulations simultaneously motivate and constrain the use of intercompany financial maneuvers by MNCs.

Also, the more standardized are its products and services, the less latitude an MNC has to adjust its transfer prices and fees and royalties. Conversely, a high-technology input, strong product differentiation, and short product life cycle enhance a company's ability to make use of its mechanisms for transfer pricing and fee adjustments. Because the latter situation is more typical of the MNC, it is not surprising that the issue of transfer pricing is a bone of contention between multinationals and governments.

Last, and most importantly, government regulations exert a continuing influence on international financial transactions. It is interesting to consider that government tax, credit allocation, and exchange control policies provide the principal incentives for firms to engage in international fund maneuvers at the same time that government regulations most impede these flows.

Information Requirements

In order to take full advantage of its global financial system, a multinational firm needs detailed information on affiliate financing requirements, sources and costs of external credit, local investment yields, available financial channels, the volume of interaffiliate transactions, all relevant tax factors, and government restrictions and regulations on fund flows.

Without belaboring the points already made, it is clear that the costs and benefits of operating an integrated financial system depend on the funds and transfer options available, as well as on the opportunity costs of money for different affiliates and the tax effects associated with these various transfer mechanisms. Hence, the implementation of centralized decision making requires information concerning all these factors.

Behavioral Consequences

Manipulating transfer prices on goods and services, adjusting dividend payments, and leading and lagging remittances lead to a reallocation of profits and liquidity among a firm's various affiliates. Although the aim of this corporate intervention is to boost after-tax global profits, the actual result may be to destroy incentive systems based on profit centers and to cause confusion and computational chaos. Subsidiaries may rebel when asked to undertake actions that will benefit the corporation as a whole, but will adversely affect their own performance evaluations. To counter this reaction, the rules must be clearly spelled out, and profit center results adjusted to reflect true affiliate earnings rather than the distorted remnants of a global profit-maximizing exercise.

Companies that shift profits and cash among their various affiliates must consider the behavioral consequences.

15.4 ILLUSTRATION: TRANSFER PRICING AND TAX EVASION

On September 19, 1983, the Swiss-based commodities trading firm Marc Rich & Co. AG, its U.S. unit, and its two principal officers, Marc Rich and Pincus Green, were indicted by the U.S. government for allegedly evading over $100 million in U.S. taxes, making it the biggest tax-evasion case in history. The U.S. government charged that Marc Rich, his companies, and Pincus Green had the U.S. unit transfer profit to the Swiss parent by having the U.S. affiliate pay the Swiss company artificially high prices for oil.

In 1982, the United States subpoenaed from the Swiss parent documents that it thought would buttress its case—and that would make public a great deal of information about the company. Despite its size—annual revenue exceeding $10 billion—Marc Rich & Co. has a penchant for secrecy. Because of its refusal to give the documents to a grand jury, Marc Rich was cited in contempt of court and subject to a $50,000-a-day fine while it appealed a federal judge's refusal to vacate the contempt order. In September 1983, Marc Rich's internal documents were seized by the Swiss government on the ground that releasing them to U.S. authorities would violate Swiss secrecy laws.

Marc Rich settled with the U.S. government in October 1984. The back taxes plus interest, penalties, fines, and seized assets made the settlement worth almost $200 million—the most ever recovered in a criminal tax-evasion case.

But except for its magnitude, the Rich case isn't unique. Since the late 1960s, the Department of Justice has been cracking down on the use of transfer pricing to evade U.S. taxes. One case was U.S. Gypsum Co. Strange things were happening to the price of gypsum rock that the company mined in Canada and shipped to the United States. The rock was sold by the company's Canadian unit at a low price, keeping Canadian profit and taxes down, and was resold to the U.S. unit at a high price, keeping U.S. profit and taxes down. The profit was siphoned into another U.S. Gypsum subsidiary that owned the rock only while it fell through the air from the Canadian conveyor belt down to the hold of a U.S. ship. This intermediate subsidiary was a paper company and was in a low tax bracket. The Department of Justice challenged this arrangement in court and won in a civil case.

In June 1983, the American sales subsidiary of Toyota Motor Co. was ordered by a federal judge to turn over to the Internal Revenue Service information about the prices its parent firm charged its car dealers in Japan. The IRS maintained that the Japanese data were necessary for it to determine whether the transfer prices it charged Toyota Motor Sales U.S.A. for Toyota products in the United States were being used to reduce its U.S. tax liability. The IRS claimed that the U.S. sales unit of Toyota trimmed its taxable U.S. income by paying its Japanese parent higher than reasonable prices for the vehicles sold in the United States. This case and a similar one brought against Nissan Motor Co. were settled in late 1987 when the U.S. sales units of both companies paid undisclosed amounts of additional income taxes to the IRS. Reportedly, the combined payments exceeded $600 million. These taxes were offset by tax refunds of an equivalent (though lesser) amount received from Japan's national tax agency for taxes paid on the income previously recorded in Japan but now reallocated to the United States. Currently, the IRS has cases pending against a number of Japanese and South Korean companies, including Hitachi, Mitsubishi Electric, Tokai Bank, and Daewoo.

Sometimes it is not the U.S. government that feels cheated. Amway of Canada and its U.S. parent, Amway Corp., were fined $25 million in November 1983 after pleading guilty in Ontario Supreme Court to using a complex transfer pricing scheme to undervalue goods they were exporting to Canada, defrauding the Canadian government of more than $28 million in customs duties and sales tax.

15.5 SUMMARY AND CONCLUSIONS

This chapter examined a variety of different fund-shifting mechanisms. Corporate objectives associated with the use of these techniques include financing foreign operations, reducing interest costs, reducing tax costs, and removing blocked funds.

It is apparent after examining these goals that there are trade-offs involved. For instance, removing blocked funds from a low-tax nation is likely to raise the firm's worldwide tax bill. Similarly, reducing exchange risk often results in higher interest expenses and adds to the financing needs of affiliates in soft-currency nations. The realistic weight that should be assigned to each of these goals depends on the individual impact of each goal on corporate profitability. Focusing on just one or two of these goals, such as avoiding exchange risk or minimizing taxes, to the exclusion of all others will probably lead to suboptimal decisions.

The recommended global approach to managing fund transfers is best illustrated by the creative use of financial linkages, whereby one unit becomes a conduit for the movement of funds elsewhere. For example, requiring affiliate A to remit dividends to its parent while financing this withdrawal by lowering transfer prices on goods sold to affiliate A by affiliate B will reduce income taxes and/or customs duties in the process. Or cash can be shifted from A to B through leading and lagging, with these same funds moved on to affiliate C by adjusting royalties or repaying a loan. Taking advantage of being multinational means remitting funds to the parent and other affiliates via royalties and licensing fees from some countries, dividend payments from other nations, and loan repayments from still others; all these maneuvers are to be coordinated with an eye toward maximizing corporate benefits.

It is apparent that the major benefit expected from engaging in these various maneuvers comes from government actions that distort the risk-return trade-offs associated with borrowing or lending in different currencies or that alter after-tax returns because of tax asymmetries. The fact that a particular action is legal and profitable, however, does not necessarily mean it should be undertaken. When devising currency, credit, and tax regulations, governments obviously have other goals in mind besides creating profitable arbitrage opportunities for multinational firms. A company that consistently attempts to apply a "sharp pencil" and take maximum advantage of these arbitrage opportunities may optimize short-run profits, but this "penciling" is likely to be done at the expense of long-run profits.

The notion of being a good corporate citizen may be an amorphous concept, but firms that are perceived as being short-run profit oriented may face questions regarding their legitimacy. More and more, multinationals are dependent on the good will of home and host governments, and actions that undermine this key factor may reduce the viability of their foreign operations.

Thus, it may well be worthwhile to pass up opportunities to make higher profits today if these profits are gained at the expense of the corporation's long-run international existence. As in all business decisions, of course, it is important to evaluate the costs and benefits associated with particular actions, which has been the goal of this chapter in the area of intercompany fund flows.

QUESTIONS

1. Where does the value of an MNC's multinational financial system reside?

2. California, like several other states, applies the unitary method of taxation to firms doing business within the state. Under the unitary method a state determines the tax on a company's worldwide profit through a formula based on the share of the company's sales, assets, and payroll falling within the state. In California's case, the share of worldwide profit taxed is calculated as the average of these three factors.

    a. What are the predictable corporate responses to the unitary tax?

    b. What economic motives might help explain why Oregon, Florida, and several other states have eliminated their unitary tax schemes?

3. Under what circumstances is leading and lagging likely to be of most value?

4. What are the principal advantages of investing in foreign affiliates in the form of debt instead of equity?

5. When comparing a multinational firm's reported foreign profits with domestic profits, caution must be exercised. This same caution must also be applied when analyzing the reported profits of the firm's various subsidiaries. Only coincidentally will these reported profits correspond to actual profits.

    a. Describe five different means that MNCs use to manipulate reported profitability among their various units.

    b. What adjustments to its reported figures would be required to compute the true profitability of a firm's foreign operations so as to account for these distortions?

    c. Describe at least three reasons that might explain some of these manipulations.

6. In 1987, the most recent year for which aggregate information is available, U.S.-controlled companies earned an average 2.09% return on assets, nearly four times their foreign-controlled counterparts. A number of American politicians have used these figures to argue that there is widespread tax cheating by foreign-owned multinationals.

    a. What are some economically plausible reasons (other than tax evasion) that would explain the low rates of return earned by foreign-owned companies in the United States? Consider the consequences of the debt-financed U.S.-investment binge that foreign companies went on during the 1980s and the dramatic depreciation of the U.S. dollar beginning in 1985.

    b. What are some of the mechanisms that foreign-owned companies can use to reduce their tax burden in the United States?

    c. The corporate tax rate in Japan is 60%, whereas it is 34% in the United States. Are these figures consistent with the argument that big Japanese companies are overcharging their U.S. subsidiaries in order to avoid taxes? Explain.

PROBLEMS

1. Suppose Navistar's Canadian subsidiary sells 1,500 trucks monthly to the French affiliate at a transfer price of $27,000 per unit. Assume the Canadian and French marginal tax rates on corporate income equal 45% and 50%, respectively.

    a. Suppose the transfer price can be set at any level between $25,000 and $30,000. At what transfer price will corporate taxes paid be minimized? Explain.

    b. Suppose the French government imposes an ad valorem tariff of 15% on imported tractors. How would this affect the optimal transfer pricing strategy?

    c. If the transfer price of $27,000 is set in French francs and the French franc revalues by 5%, what will happen to the firm's overall tax bill? Consider the tax consequences both with and without the 15% tariff.

    d. Suppose the transfer price is increased from $27,000 to $30,000 while credit terms are extended from 90 days to 180 days. What are the fund-flow implications of these adjustments?

2. Suppose a U.S. parent owes $5 million to its English affiliate. The timing of this payment can be changed by up to 90 days in either direction; assume the following effective annualized after-tax dollar borrowing and lending rates in England and the United States.

	Lending (%)	Borrowing (%)
United States	3.2	4.0
England	3.0	3.6

a. If the U.S. parent is borrowing funds while the English affiliate has excess funds, should the parent speed up or slow down its payment to England?

b. What is the net effect of the optimal payment activities in terms of changing the units' borrowing costs and/or interest income?

3. Suppose that covered after-tax lending and borrowing rates for three units of Eastman Kodak—located in the United States, France, and Germany—are

	Lending (%)	Borrowing (%)
United States	3.1	3.9
France	3.0	4.2
Germany	3.2	4.4

Currently, the French and German units owe $2 million and $3 million, respectively, to their U.S. parent. The German unit also has $1 million in payables outstanding to its French affiliate. The timing of these payments can be changed by up to 90 days in either direction. Assume that Kodak U.S. is borrowing funds while both the French and German subsidiaries have excess cash available.

a. What is Kodak's optimal leading and lagging strategy?

b. What is the net profit impact of these adjustments?

c. How would Kodak's optimal strategy and associated benefits change if the U.S. parent has excess cash available?

4. Suppose that in the section on dividends, International Products has $500,000 in excess foreign tax credits available. How will this situation affect its dividend remittance decision?

5. Suppose affiliate A sells 10,000 chips monthly to affiliate B at a unit price of $15. Affiliate A's tax rate is 45%, and affiliate B's tax rate is 55%. In addition, affiliate B must pay an ad valorem tariff of 12% on its imports. If the transfer price on chips can be set anywhere between $11 and $18, how much can the total monthly cash flow of A and B be increased by switching to the optimal transfer price?

6. Suppose GM France sells goods worth $2 million monthly to GM Denmark on 60-day credit terms. A switch in credit terms to 90 days will involve a one-time shift of how much money between the two affiliates?

7. Suppose that DMR SA, located in Switzerland, sells $1 million worth of goods monthly to its affiliate DMR Gmbh, located in Germany. These sales are based on a unit transfer price of $100. Suppose the transfer price is raised to $130 at the same time that credit terms are lengthened from the current 30 days to 60 days.

a. What is the net impact on cash flow for the first 90 days? Assume that the new credit terms apply only to new sales already booked but uncollected.

b. Assume the tax rate is 25% in Switzerland and 50% in Germany and that revenues are taxed and costs deducted upon sale or purchase of goods, not upon collection. What is the impact on after-tax cash flows for the first 90 days?

8. Suppose a firm earns $1 million before tax in Spain. It pays Spanish tax of $0.52 million and remits the remaining $0.48 million as a dividend to its U.S. parent. Under current U.S. tax law, how much U.S. tax will the parent owe on this dividend?

9. Suppose a French affiliate repatriates as dividends all the after-tax profits it earns. If the French income tax rate is 50% and the dividend withholding tax is 10%, what is the effective tax rate on the French affiliate's before-tax profits, from the standpoint of its U.S. parent?

10.* Merck Mexicana SA, the wholly owned affiliate of the U.S. pharmaceutical firm, is considering alternative financing packages for its increased working capital needs resulting from growing market penetration. Ps 250 million are needed over the next six months and can be financed as follows:

—From the Mexican banking system at the semiannual rate of 50%.
—From the U.S. parent company at the semiannual rate of 6%.

The parent company loan would be denominated in dollars and would have to be repaid through the floating-exchange-rate tier of the Mexican exchange market. The exchange loss would, thus, be fully incurred by the Mexican subsidiary. The exchange rate as of March 1, 1984, was Ps 250 = $1 and widely expected to depreciate further.

a. If interest payments can be made through the stabilized tier of the Mexican exchange market where the dollar is worth Ps 125, what is the break-even exchange rate on the floating tier that would make Merck Mexicana indifferent between dollar and peso financing?

b. Merck Mexicana imports from its U.S. parent $500,000 worth of chemical compounds monthly, payable on a 90-day basis. Suppose that the parent adjusts its transfer prices so that Merck Mexicana must now pay $700,000 monthly for its chemical supplies. All payments for imports of chemicals involved in the manufacture of pharmaceuticals are transacted through the stabilized tier of the exchange market. At the current exchange rate of Ps 250 = $1, what is the net before-tax annual benefit to Merck of this transfer price increase?

BIBLIOGRAPHY

Arpan, Jeffrey S. *International Intracorporate Pricing*. New York: Praeger, 1972.

Lessard, Donald R. "Transfer Prices, Taxes, and Financial Markets: Implications of International Financial Transfers within the Multinational Firm." In *The Economic Effects of Multinational Corporations,* Robert G. Hawkins, ed. Greenwich, Conn.: JAI Press, 1979.

Obersteiner, Erich. "Should the Foreign Affiliate Remit Dividends or Reinvest?" *Financial Management*, Spring 1973, pp. 88–93.

Robbins, Sidney M., and Robert B. Stobaugh. *Money in the Multinational Enterprise*. New York: Basic Books, 1973.

Rutenberg, David P. "Maneuvering Liquid Assets in a Multinational Company." *Management Science*, June 1970, pp. B–671–684.

Zenoff, David B. "Remitting Funds from Foreign Affiliates." *Financial Executive*, March 1968, pp. 46–63.

*Contributed by Laurent Jacque.

Foreign Investment Analysis

International Portfolio Investment

16

Capital now flows at the speed of light across national borders and into markets once deemed impregnable.

Citicorp Annual Report

CHAPTER LEARNING OBJECTIVES

- To calculate the return associated with investing in securities issued in different markets and denominated in various currencies
- To describe the advantages of international investing
- To explain how international investing can allow investors to achieve a better risk-return trade-off than by investing solely in U.S. securities
- To identify the barriers to investing overseas
- To describe the various ways in which U.S. investors can diversify into foreign securities
- To explain why investing in foreign stocks and bonds provides a better risk-return trade-off than investing in either foreign stocks or bonds alone

There was a time when investors treated national boundaries as impregnable barriers, limiting their reach and financial options to predominantly domestic and regional markets. Times have changed. Just as companies and consumers are going global, so are increasing numbers of investors. American investors are buying foreign stocks and bonds and foreign investors are purchasing U.S. securities. The purpose of this chapter is to examine the nature and consequences of international portfolio investing. Although the chapter focuses on international investing from an American perspective, its lessons are applicable to investors from around the world.

16.1 MEASURING THE TOTAL RETURN FROM FOREIGN PORTFOLIO INVESTING

The total dollar return on a foreign investment consists of dividend/interest income, capital gains, and currency gains.

Before proceeding further, it is necessary to determine how we are going to measure the return associated with investing in securities issued in different markets and denominated in a variety of currencies. In general, the *total dollar return* on an investment can be decomposed into three separate elements: dividend/interest income, capital gains (losses), and currency gains (losses).

Bonds

The one-period total dollar return on a foreign bond investment $R_\$$ can be calculated as follows:

$$\frac{\text{Dollar}}{\text{return}} = \frac{\text{Foreign currency}}{\text{return}} \times \frac{\text{Currency}}{\text{gain (loss)}}$$

$$1 + R_\$ = \left[1 + \frac{B(1) - B(0) + C}{B(0)}\right](1 + g) \tag{16.1}$$

where $B(t)$ = foreign currency (FC) bond price at time t
C = foreign currency coupon income
g = percent change in dollar value of the foreign currency

For example, suppose the initial bond price is FC 95, the coupon income is FC 8, the end-of-period bond price is FC 97, and the foreign currency appreciates by 3% against the dollar during the period. Then, according to Equation 16.1, the total dollar return is 13.8%:

$$R_\$ = [1 + (97 - 95 + 8)/95](1 + 0.03) - 1$$
$$= (1.105)(1.03) - 1$$
$$= 13.8\%$$

Note that the currency gain applies to both the foreign currency principal and to the foreign currency return.

Stocks

Using the same terminology, the one-period total dollar return on a foreign stock investment $R_\$$ can be calculated as follows:

$$\frac{\text{Dollar}}{\text{return}} = \frac{\text{Foreign currency}}{\text{return}} \times \frac{\text{Currency}}{\text{gain (loss)}}$$

$$1 + R_\$ = \left[1 + \frac{P(1) - P(0) + \text{DIV}}{P(0)}\right](1 + g) \tag{16.2}$$

where $P(t)$ = foreign currency stock price at time t
DIV = foreign currency dividend income

For example, suppose the beginning stock price is FC 50, the dividend income is FC 1, the end-of-period stock price is FC 48, and the foreign currency depreciates by 5% against the dollar during the period. Then according to Equation 16.2, the total dollar return is –6.9%:

$$R_\$ = [1 + (48 - 50 + 1)/50](1 - 0.05) - 1$$
$$= (0.98)(0.95) - 1$$
$$= -6.9\%$$

In this case, the investor suffered both a capital loss on the FC principal and a currency loss on the investment's dollar value.

16.2 THE BENEFITS OF INTERNATIONAL EQUITY INVESTING

The advantages of *international investing* are several. For one thing, an international focus offers far more opportunity. About 60% of the world's stock market capitalization is in non-U.S. companies and this fraction has generally increased over time (see Exhibit 16.1). In fact, if you want to invest in certain products with huge global markets, you'll find that most of the big, highly profitable manufacturers are overseas. For example, videotape recorders are the world's best-selling consumer electronics product, and 95% of them are made in Japan, over 80% of all cars are made abroad, 85% of all stereo systems, and 99% of all 35mm cameras. The Japanese dominance of these and other consumer product markets helps explain why in recent years Japanese market capitalization actually exceeded that of the United States. The 60% plunge in the Tokyo Stock Exchange between 1990 and 1993 has evened up market capitalizations.

International Diversification

The expanded universe of securities available internationally suggests the possibility of achieving a better *risk-return trade-off* than by investing solely in U.S. securities: That is, expanding the universe of assets available for investment should lead to higher returns for the same level of risk or less risk for the same

International investing yields a better risk/return trade-off.

Exhibit 16.1 Stock Market Capitalizations as Percent of World Total (20 Main Markets)

	March 1966	December 1970	December 1980	November 1990	November 1991
Japan	3%	5%	15%	32%	32%
United States	71	66	53	32	36
Europe	19	20	20	31	31
Rest of world	7	9	12	5	5

SOURCE: *Morgan Stanley Capital International*, various issues.

level of expected return. This follows from the basic rule of portfolio diversification: *The broader the diversification, the more stable the returns and the more diffuse the risks.*

Domestic diversification reduces risk, but the degree of risk reduction is limited.

Prudent investors know that diversifying across industries leads to a lower level of risk for a given level of expected return. For example, a fully diversified U.S. portfolio is only about 27% as risky as a typical individual stock. Put another way, about 73% of the risk associated with investing in the average stock can be eliminated in a fully diversified U.S. portfolio. Ultimately, though, the advantages of such diversification are limited because all companies in a country are more or less subject to the same cyclical economic fluctuations. Through *international diversification*—that is, by diversifying across nations whose economic cycles are not perfectly in phase—investors should be able to reduce still further the variability of their returns. In other words, risk that is systematic in the context of the U.S. economy may be unsystematic in the context of the global economy. For example, an oil price shock that hurts the U.S. economy helps the economies of oil-exporting nations, and vice versa. Thus, just as movements in different stocks partially offset one another in an all-U.S. portfolio, so also movements in U.S. and non-U.S. stock portfolios cancel out each other somewhat.

The possibility of achieving a better risk-return trade-off by investing internationally is supported by Exhibit 16.2, which shows the annualized returns and

Exhibit 16.2 Ten-Year Annualized Returns and Standard Deviation of Returns, 1981–1990

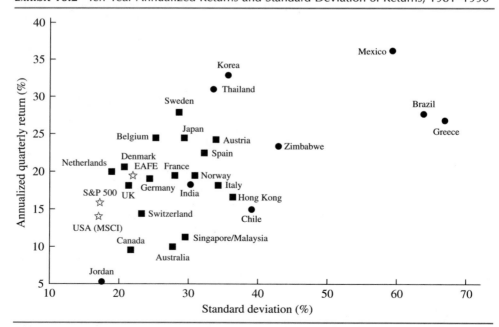

SOURCE: Lawrence S. Speidell and Ross Sappenfield, "Global Diversification in a Shrinking World," *Journal of Porftolio Management*, Fall 1992, p. 58.

standard deviations of returns for a variety of developed and emerging stock markets over the 10-year period 1981–1990. Exhibit 16.2 illustrates three points:

1. Historically, national stock markets have wide differences in returns and risk (as measured by the standard deviation of annual returns).
2. *Emerging markets* (shown as circles)—a term that encompasses all of South and Central America; all of the Far East with the exception of Japan, Australia, and New Zealand; all of Africa; and parts of Southern Europe, as well as Eastern Europe and countries of the former Soviet Union—have had higher risk and return than the developed markets (shown as squares).
3. The *Morgan Stanley Capital International Europe, Australia, Far East (EAFE) Index* (which reflects all major stock markets outside of North America) has had lower risk than most of its individual country components.

Empirical research bears out the significant benefits from international equity diversification suggested by Exhibit 16.2. Bruno Solnik and Donald Lessard, among others, have both presented evidence that national factors have a strong impact on security returns relative to that of any common world factor.[1] They also found that returns from the different national equity markets have relatively low correlations with one another.

> The value of international equity diversification appears to be substantial.

Exhibit 16.3 contains some data on correlations between the U.S. and non-U.S. stock markets. *Foreign market betas*, which are a measure of market risk derived from the capital asset pricing model (see Chapter 19), are calculated relative to the U.S. market in the same way that individual asset betas are calculated:

$$\frac{\text{Foreign market}}{\text{beta}} = \frac{\text{Correlation with}}{\text{U.S. market}} \times \frac{\text{Standard deviation of foreign market}}{\text{Standard deviation of U.S. market}}$$

For example, the Canadian market beta is 0.60 x 21.9/18.2 = 0.72.

Measured for the 10-year period 1974–1983, foreign markets in developed (EAFE) countries correlated with the U.S. market from a high of 0.60 for Canada and the Netherlands to a low of 0.06 for Spain. The relatively high correlations for Canada and the Netherlands reveal that these markets tracked the U.S. market's ups and downs. Spain's low correlation, on the other hand, indicates that the Spanish and U.S. markets have tended to move largely independently of each other.

Notice also that the investment risks associated with these different markets can be quite different—with the Hong Kong market showing the highest level and the Austrian market the lowest. Indeed, all but the Austrian market had a higher level of risk, as measured by the standard deviation of returns, than the U.S. market. Yet the internationally diversified *Morgan Stanley Capital International World Index* had the next-lowest level of risk—lower even than the U.S. market.

> Much of the risk associated with individual markets is unsystematic and so can be diversified away.

[1]Bruno H. Solnik, "Why Not Diversify Internationally Rather Than Domestically?" *Financial Analysts Journal*, July–August 1974, pp. 48–54; and Donald R. Lessard, "World, Country, and Industry Relationships in Equity Returns: Implications for Risk Reduction Through International Diversification," *Financial Analysts Journal*, January–February 1976, pp. 32–38.

Exhibit 16.3 How Foreign Markets Correlate with the U.S. Market, 1974–1983

Country	Correlation with U.S. Market	Standard Deviation of Returns (%)	Market Risk (Beta) from U.S. Perspective
United States	1.00	18.2	1.00
Canada	0.60	21.9	0.72
United Kingdom	0.33	34.4	0.62
France	0.25	28.8	0.40
West Germany	0.31	19.4	0.33
Switzerland	0.46	23.5	0.59
Italy	0.19	31.5	0.33
Netherlands	0.60	22.6	0.75
Belgium	0.36	22.0	0.44
Austria	0.21	15.0	0.17
Spain	0.06	20.9	0.07
Sweden	0.30	21.7	0.36
Norway	0.25	35.5	0.49
Japan	0.38	20.5	0.43
Hong Kong	0.34	45.5	0.85
Singapore	0.39	41.1	0.88
Australia	0.43	29.3	0.69
EAFE Index[1]	0.47	17.2	0.44
World Index[2]	0.91	17.1	0.86

[1]The Morgan Stanley Capital International Europe, Australia, Far East (EAFE) Index is the non-American part of the world index and consists of stock markets from these parts of the world.

[2]The Morgan Stanley Capital International World Index has a combined market value of $2.1 trillion, covers 19 countries including the United States, and includes about 1600 of the largest companies worldwide.

SOURCE: Based on data appearing in *Morgan Stanley Capital International*, various issues.

The reason, of course, is that much of the risk associated with markets in individual countries is unsystematic and so can be eliminated by diversification, as indicated by the relatively low betas of these markets.

These results imply that international diversification may significantly reduce the risk of portfolio returns. In fact, the standard deviation of an internationally diversified portfolio appears to be as little as 11.7% of that of individual securities. In addition, as shown in Exhibit 16.4, the benefits from international diversification are significantly greater than those that can be achieved solely by adding more domestic stocks to a portfolio. Specifically, an internationally diversified portfolio appears to be less than half as risky as a fully diversified U.S. portfolio.

Foreign investing has been more profitable than investing in the U.S. in recent decades.

Moreover, from 1961 through 1990, the compound annual return for the EAFE Index was 13.7% compared with 9.6% for the U.S. market. Further, the EAFE Index outpaced the U.S. market 19 times during the 30-year period 1961–1990. Just between 1980 and 1991, the cumulative return for the EAFE Index was about 550%, in comparison to about 450% for the S&P 500 (see Exhibit 16.5). Even more

Exhibit 16.4 The Potential Gains from International Diversification

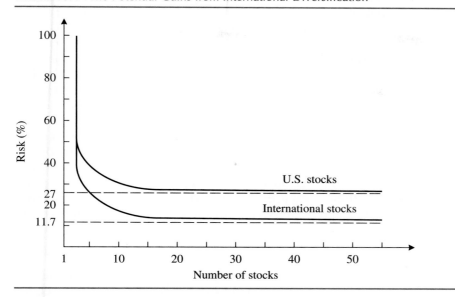

SOURCE: Bruno H. Solnik, "Why Not Diversify Internationally Rather Than Domestically?" *Financial Analysts Journal*, July–August 1974, p. 51. Reprinted by permission of the publisher.

Exhibit 16.5 Cumulative Returns on S&P 500 and EAFE Indexes, 1980–1991

SOURCE: Lawrence S. Speidell and Ross Sapenfield, "Global Diversification in a Shrinking World," *Journal of Portfolio Management*, Fall 1992, p. 58.

astounding, from 1949 to 1990, the Japanese market soared an incredible 25,000%. Even with the recent plunge in the Tokyo Stock Exchange, an investor in the Japanese stock market would still be way ahead.

International diversification pushes out the efficient frontier.

The obvious conclusion is that international diversification pushes out the *efficient frontier*—the set of portfolios that has the smallest possible standard deviation for its level of expected return and has the maximum expected return for a given level of risk—allowing investors simultaneously to reduce their risk and increase their expected return. The effect of international diversification on the efficient frontier is illustrated by Exhibit 16.6.

One way to estimate the benefits of international diversification is to consider the expected return and standard deviation of return for a portfolio consisting of a fraction a invested in U.S. stocks and the remaining fraction, $1 - a$, invested in foreign stocks. Define r_{us} and r_{rw} to be the expected returns on the U.S. and rest-of-world stock portfolios, respectively. Similarly, let σ_{us} and σ_{rw} be the standard deviations of the U.S. and rest-of-world portfolios. The expected return r_p can be calculated as

$$r_p = ar_{us} + (1 + a)r_{rw} \tag{16.3}$$

To calculate the standard deviation of this portfolio, it helps to know that the general formula for the standard deviation of a two-asset portfolio with weights w_1 and w_2 ($w_1 + w_2 = 1$) is

$$\text{Portfolio standard deviation} = (w_1^2\sigma_1^2 + w_2^2\sigma_2^2 + 2w_1w_2r_{12}\sigma_1\sigma_2)^{1/2} \tag{16.4}$$

where σ_1^2 and σ_2^2 are the respective variances of the two assets, σ_1 and σ_2 are their standard deviations, and r_{12} is their correlation. We can apply Equation 16.4 to our internationally diversified portfolio by treating the domestic and foreign portfolios as separate assets. This yields a portfolio standard deviation σ_p equal to

Exhibit 16.6 International Diversification Pushes Out the Efficient Frontier

Relative to portfolio A:
1. Portfolio B has the same expected return but less risk.
2. Portfolio C has the same risk but higher expected return.
3. Portfolio D has higher expected return *and* less risk.

$$\sigma_p = [a^2\sigma_{us}^2 + (1-a)^2\sigma_{rw}^2 + 2a(1-a)\sigma_{us}\sigma_{rw}r_{us,\,rw}]^{1/2} \qquad \textbf{(16.5)}$$

where $r_{us,rw}$ is the correlation between the returns on the U.S. and foreign stock portfolios.

To see the benefits of international diversification, assume that the portfolio is equally invested in U.S. and foreign stocks, where the EAFE Index represents the foreign stock portfolio. Using data from Exhibit 16.3, we see that $\sigma_{us} = 18.2\%$, $\sigma_{rw} = 17.1\%$, and $r_{us,rw} = 0.47$. According to Equation 16.5, these figures imply that the standard deviation of the internationally diversified portfolio is

$$\sigma_p = [0.5^2(18.2)^2 + 0.5^2(17.1)^2 + 0.5^2 \times 2 \times 18.2 \times 17.1 \times 0.47]^{1/2}$$

$$= 0.5(912.57)^{1/2} = 15.1\%$$

Here the risk of an internationally diversified portfolio is considerably below the risk of the U.S. portfolio. As indicated earlier, the expected return is higher as well.

The correlations among the countries shown in Exhibit 16.2 have generally increased during the 1980s. In addition, as shown in Exhibit 16.5, the U.S. market has generally outperformed the Japanese and European markets in recent years, reducing the expected return on the EAFE Index relative to the S&P 500 Index. Taken together, these changes have diminished the risk-return benefits of international investing. Nonetheless, these benefits still exist.

Exhibit 16.7 calculates the standard deviations and annualized returns of different mixes of the S&P 500 and the EAFE Index using quarterly data for the

An internationally diversified portfolio is less risky than a diversified U.S. stock portfolio.

Exhibit 16.7 Ten-Year Average Returns and Standard Deviation of Returns Through 1990

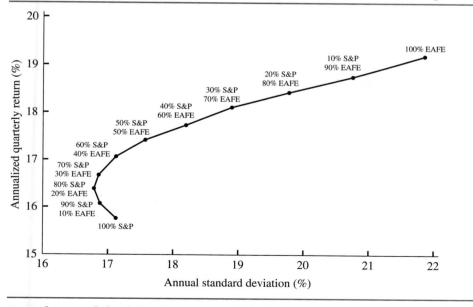

SOURCE: Lawrence S. Speidell and Ross Sappenfield, "Global Diversification in a Shrinking World," *Journal of Portfolio Management*, Fall 1992, p. 58.

10-year period 1981–1990. By shifting from a portfolio invested 100% in the S&P 500 to one that contains up to 20% invested in the EAFE Index, risk is reduced at the same time that return is increased. As the percentage invested in the EAFE Index is increased past 20%, both portfolio risk and return rise.

Investing in Emerging Markets

Emerging markets present attractive investment opportunities.

We have already seen in Exhibit 16.2 some of the high risks and rewards historically associated with investing in emerging markets. So it should come as less of a surprise that often these countries, with volatile economic and political prospects, offer the greatest degree of diversification and the highest expected returns.[2] Exhibit 16.8 shows how some of these "emerging markets" performed over the five-year period ending June 30, 1991. The relative capitalization for each market (the dollar value of all stocks trading in that market) is indicated by the area of its circle. As can be seen, historically, no other stock markets so lavishly rewarded investors. Gains of 50% to 70% and more a year were not unusual.

Exhibit 16.8 Risk and Return for Emerging Markets, July 1986 Through June 1991

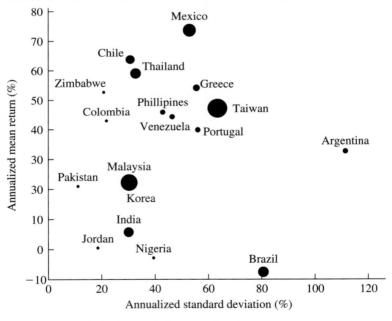

NOTE: Circle size is relative to market size.

SOURCE: Data from *IFC Quarterly Review of Emerging Markets* in Jarrod W. Wilcox, "Taming Frontier Markets," *Journal of Portfolio Management*, Fall 1992, p. 52.

[2]See, for example, Vihang R. Errunza, "Gains from Portfolio Diversification into Less Developed Countries," *Journal of International Business Studies*, Fall–Winter 1977, pp. 83–99; and Warren Bailey and Rene M. Stulz, "Measuring the Benefits from International Diversification with Daily Data: The Case of Pacific Basin Stock Markets," working paper, Ohio State University, April 1990.

But the high returns possible in emerging markets are matched by some breathtaking risks. To begin, these are small markets, representing in the aggregate less than 10% of the world's stock market capitalization. Hence, they are subject to the usual volatility and lack of liquidity associated with small markets. But they face some unique risks as well: relatively unstable governments, the risk of nationalization of businesses, less protection of property rights, and the threat of abrupt price movements. For example, in February 1990, when the newly elected Brazilian president froze most personal bank accounts, the Sao Paulo exchange plummeted 70% in a few days. Similarly, Taiwan's market rose more than 1,000% from January 1987 to its peak in February 1990. It then gave back most of these gains, falling nearly 80% by October 1990. Despite their high investment risks, however, emerging markets can reduce portfolio risk because of their low correlations with returns elsewhere. That is, most of their high total risk is unsystematic in nature.

The fact that most of the emerging markets as a group as well as individually have low correlations with the U.S. market and the *Financial Times (FT) World Index* indicates the potential for significant diversification benefits. Exhibit 16.9 shows the risk and return of a global portfolio that combines in varying proportions the FT-World Index with the *IFC Emerging Markets Index,* published by the International Finance Corporation (an international lending organization discussed in Chapter 21).

Emerging markets tend to have low correlations with the U.S. market.

We see that by shifting from a portfolio invested 100% in the FT-World Index to one that contains up to 20% invested in the IFC Emerging Markets Index, risk is reduced at the same time that expected return is increased. Beyond that point, the higher volatility of the Emerging Markets Index more than offsets the benefits of diversification. Thus, even if one did not expect the emerging markets to outperform the developed country markets, risk reduction alone would dictate an investment of up to 20% in the emerging markets. Since the emerging markets

Despite their high individual risks, emerging markets can reduce portfolio risk.

Exhibit 16.9 Risk and Return for Various Mixes of FT-World and IFC Emerging Markets Indices, February 1986 Through March 1991

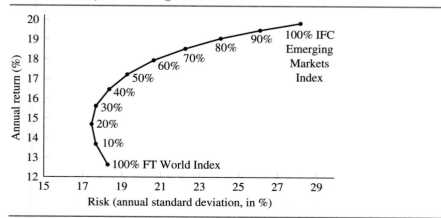

SOURCE: Arjun B. Divecha, Jaime Drach, and Dan Stefek, "Emerging Markets: A Quantitative Perspective," *Journal of Portfolio Management,* Fall 1992, p. 49.

substantially outperformed the developed country markets during this period, a 20% investment in the IFC Index would have reduced the annual standard deviation by 0.81% and increased the annual return by 2.1% as well.

ILLUSTRATION: *Latin American Stocks Are Hotter Than Salsa*

A conversion to free-market economics in much of Latin America has done wonders for their stock markets. Investors are expecting that tighter monetary policies, lower tax rates, significantly lower budget deficits, and the sale of money-losing state enterprises will go a long way to cure the sickly Latin economies. These expectations, in turn, have helped stock markets to soar in recent years in all the countries shown in Exhibit 16.10 except Brazil—the one country that has backslid on instituting serious market-oriented reforms. Overall, from 1988 through 1992, Latin American stock markets have risen almost 500%, far exceeding the returns available in any other region of the world.

Barriers to International Diversification

The benefits to international diversification will be limited, however, to the extent that there are barriers to investing overseas. Such barriers do exist. They include

Exhibit 16.10 Latin American Stock Markets Take Off, 1989–1992

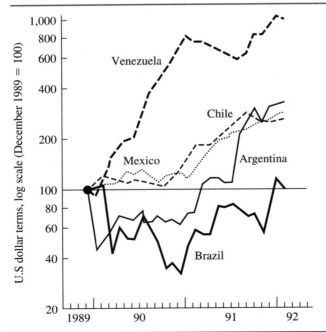

SOURCE: Data from IFC as reported in *The Economist*, February 15, 1992, p. 120. © 1992 The Economist Newspaper Group, Inc. Reprinted with permission.

legal, informational, and economic impediments that serve to segment national capital markets, deterring investors seeking to invest abroad. The lack of *liquidity*—the ability to buy and sell securities efficiently—is a major obstacle on some overseas exchanges. Other barriers include currency controls, specific tax regulations, relatively less-developed capital markets abroad, exchange risk, and the lack of readily accessible and comparable information on potential foreign security acquisitions. The lack of adequate information can significantly increase the perceived riskiness of foreign securities, giving investors an added incentive to keep their money at home.

Some of these barriers are apparently being eroded. Money invested abroad by both large institutions and individuals is growing dramatically. For the world as a whole, a recent study by the investment bank Salomon Brothers estimated that *cross-border equity trading*—investors in one country buying stocks in another—was about $1.4 trillion in 1989.[3] Salomon also estimated that at year end 1988, investors worldwide held about $640 billion in foreign stocks, or 6.7% of global equity markets.

Barriers to investing overseas are being eroded.

Despite this growth in the level of foreign investing, however, these holdings still represent a relatively minor degree of international diversification (for example, about 4% of U.S. pension fund assets are invested in foreign equities), certainly when compared to MNCs with over half of their earnings coming from overseas. Nonetheless, discussions with U.S. institutional investors indicate that many intend to have 20%–25% of their funds invested overseas by the year 2000.[4]

There are several ways in which U.S. investors can diversify into foreign securities. A small number of foreign firms—fewer than 100—have listed their securities on the New York Stock Exchange (NYSE) or the American Stock Exchange. Historically, a major barrier to foreign listing has been the NYSE requirements for substantial disclosure and audited financial statements. For firms that wished to sell securities in the United States, the U.S. Securities and Exchange Commission's (SEC) disclosure regulations have also been a major obstruction. However, the gap between acceptable NYSE and SEC accounting and disclosure standards and those acceptable to European multinationals has narrowed substantially. Moreover, Japanese and European multinationals that raise funds in international capital markets have been forced to conform to stricter standards. This change may encourage other foreign firms to list their securities and gain access to the U.S. capital market.

U.S. investors have several ways to diversify into foreign securities.

Investors can always buy foreign securities in their home markets. One problem with buying stocks listed on foreign exchanges is that it can be expensive, primarily because of steep brokerage commissions. Owners of foreign stocks also face the complications of foreign tax laws and the nuisance of converting dividend payments into dollars.

Instead of buying foreign stocks overseas, investors can buy foreign equities traded in the United States in the form of

[3]Salomon's study was reported by Michael R. Sesit, "Foreign Investing Makes a Comeback," *The Wall Street Journal*, September 1, 1989, pp. C1 and C14.

[4]These discussions were reported by Michael R. Sesit, "Foreign Investing Makes a Comeback."

1. *American Depository Receipts* (ADRs). These receipts are certificates of ownership issued by a U.S. bank as a convenience to investors in lieu of the underlying shares it holds in custody. The investors in ADRs absorb the handling costs through transfer and handling charges. ADRs for over 1,000 companies from 33 foreign countries are currently traded on U.S. exchanges.
2. *American shares.* These shares are securities certificates issued in the United States by a transfer agent acting on behalf of the foreign issuer. The foreign issuer absorbs part or all of the handling expenses involved.

Internationally diversified mutual funds provide a low-cost vehicle for international investing.

The easiest approach to investing abroad is to buy shares in an internationally diversified mutual fund, of which a growing number are available. There are four basic categories of mutual fund that invest abroad:

1. *Global funds* can invest anywhere in the world, including the United States.
2. *International funds* invest only outside the United States.
3. *Regional funds* focus on specific geographic areas overseas, such as Asia or Europe.
4. *Single-country funds* invest in individual countries, such as Germany or Taiwan.

The greater diversification of the global and international funds reduces the risk for investors, but it also lessens the chances of a high return if one region (for example, Asia) or country (for example, Germany) suddenly gets hot. The problem with this approach is that forecasting returns is essentially impossible in an efficient market. This suggests that most investors would be better off buying an internationally diversified mutual fund. Of course, it is possible to construct one's own internationally diversified portfolio by buying shares in several different regional or country funds.

16.3 INTERNATIONAL BOND INVESTING

The benefits of international diversification extend to bond portfolios as well. Barnett and Rosenberg started with a portfolio fully invested in U.S. bonds and then replaced them, in increments of 10%, with a mixture of foreign bonds from seven markets.[5] They then calculated for the period 1973–1983 the risk and return of the 10 portfolios they created. Their conclusions, which can be seen in Exhibit 16.11, were as follows:

1. As the proportion of U.S. bonds fell, the portfolio return rose. This result reflects the fact that foreign bonds outperformed U.S. bonds over this 10-year period.
2. As the proportion of U.S. bonds fell from 100% to 70%, the volatility of the portfolio fell. This fact reflects the low correlation between U.S. and foreign bond returns.
3. By investing up to 60% of their funds in foreign bonds, U.S. investors could have raised their return substantially while not increasing risk above the level associated with holding only U.S. bonds.

Internationally diversified bond portfolios offer superior investment performance.

[5]G. Barnett and M. Rosenberg, "International Diversification in Bonds," *Prudential International Fixed Income Investment Strategy,* Second Quarter 1983.

Exhibit 16.11 Risk-Return Trade-Off of an Internationally Diversified Bond Portfolio, January 1973 to March 1983

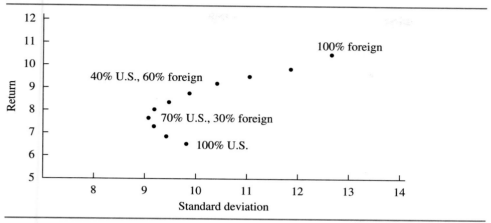

SOURCE: G. Barnett and M. Rosenberg, "International Diversification in Bonds," *Prudential International Fixed Income Investment Strategy,* Second Quarter 1983. Reprinted by permission.

Other studies examining different time periods and markets have similarly found that an internationally diversified bond portfolio delivers superior performance.

16.4 OPTIMAL INTERNATIONAL ASSET ALLOCATION

The evidence clearly indicates that both international stock diversification and international bond diversification pays off. Not surprisingly, expanding the investment set to include stock and bonds, both domestic and foreign, similarly pays off in terms of an improved risk-return trade-off.

The most detailed study to date of the advantages of international stock and bond diversification is by Solnik and Noetzlin.[6] They compared the performances of various investment strategies over the period 1970–1980. Exhibit 16.12 shows the outcome of their analysis. The right-hand curve is the efficient frontier when investments are restricted to stocks only. The left-hand curve is the efficient frontier when investors can buy both stocks and bonds. All returns are calculated in U.S. dollars.

The conclusions of their study were as follows:

1. International stock diversification yields a substantially better risk-return trade-off.
2. International diversification combining stock and bond investments results in substantially less risk than international stock diversification alone.

International stock and bond diversification together offer a better risk/return trade-off than either alone.

[6]Bruno H. Solnik and Bernard Noetzlin, "Optimal International Asset Allocation," *Journal of Portfolio Management,* Fall 1982, pp. 12–21.

Exhibit 16.12 Efficient Frontiers, December 1970 to December 1980

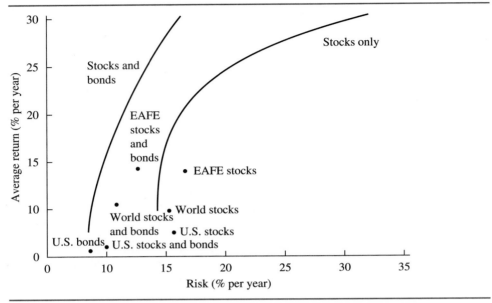

SOURCE: Bruno H. Solnik and Bernard Noetzlin, "Optimal International Asset Allocation," *Journal of Portfolio Management*, Fall 1982. Reprinted by permission.

3. A substantial improvement in the risk-return trade-off can be realized by investing in internationally diversified stock and bond portfolios whose weights don't conform to relative market capitalizations. In other words, the various market indexes used to measure world stock and bond portfolios (e.g., EAFE Index and World Index) don't lie on the efficient frontier.

As indicated by Exhibit 16.12, optimal *international asset allocation* makes it possible to double or even triple the return from investing in an index fund without taking on more risk. Although Solnik and Noetzlin had the advantage of hindsight in constructing their efficient frontier, they concluded that the opportunities for increased risk-adjusted returns are sizable and that the performance gap between optimal international asset allocations and passive investing in simple index funds is potentially quite large.

16.5 SUMMARY AND CONCLUSIONS

As the barriers to international capital flows come down and improved communications and data processing technology provide low-cost information about foreign securities, investors are starting to realize the enormous potential in international investing. We saw in this chapter that international stock and bond diversification can provide substantially higher returns with less risk than investment in a single market. A major reason is that international investment offers a much broader range of opportunities than domestic investment alone, even in a market as large as the United States. An investor restricted to the U.S. stock market, for example, is cut off, in effect, from over two-thirds of the available investment opportunities.

Even though a passive international portfolio—one invested in an index fund based on market capitalization weights—improves risk-adjusted performance, an active strategy can do substantially better. The latter strategy bases the portfolio proportions of domestic and foreign investments on their expected returns and their correlations with the overall portfolio.

QUESTIONS

1. As seen in Exhibit 16.3, Hong Kong stocks are about 2.5 times more volatile than U.S. stocks. Does that mean that risk-averse American investors should avoid Hong Kong equities? Explain.

2. What characteristics of foreign securities lead to diversification benefits for American investors?

3. Will increasing integration of national capital markets reduce the benefits of international diversifications?

4. Studies show that the correlations between domestic stocks are greater than the correlations between domestic and foreign stocks. Explain why this is likely to be the case. What implications does this fact have for international investing?

5. An alternative to investing in foreign stocks is to invest in the shares of domestic multinationals. Are multinationals likely to provide a reasonable substitute for international portfolio investment?

6. Who is likely to gain more from investing overseas, a resident of the United States or of Mexico? Explain.

7. Why have Latin American stocks performed so well in recent years? Is this performance likely to continue? Explain.

8. Would you expect emerging markets on average to outperform developed country markets in the future? Explain.

9. Mexican bonds are currently yielding over 100% annually. Does this make them suitable for American investors looking to raise the return on their portfolios? Explain.

10. The Brazilian stock market rose by 165% during 1988. Are American investors likely to be pleased with that performance? Explain.

11. Comment on the following statement: "On October 19, 1987, the U.S. stock market crashed. As the globe turned the following day, the devastation spread from New York to Tokyo, Hong Kong, Sydney, and Singapore, and on to Frankfurt, Paris, and London, then back to New York. The domino-style spread of the crash from one market to the next accelerated as international investors attempted to outrun the wave of panic selling from Tokyo to London and back to New York. It is difficult to imagine that some investors thought they had been able to diversify their investment risks by spreading their money across different stock markets around the world, when in fact their downside risks were actually multiplying as one market followed another into decline."

12. Persian Gulf countries receive virtually all their income from oil revenues denominated in dollars. At the same time, they buy substantial amounts of goods and services from Japan and Western Europe. Their investment portfolios are heavily weighted towards short-term U.S. Treasury bills and other dollar-denominated money market instruments. Comment on their asset allocation.

13. According to one investment advisor, "I feel more comfortable investing in Western Europe or Canada. I would not invest in South America or other regions with a record of debt defaults and restructurings. The underwriters of large new issues of ADRs of companies from these areas assure us that things are different now. Maybe, but who can say that a government that has defaulted on debt won't change the rules again?" Comment on this statement.

14. Investors should avoid Hong Kong, given its problematic outlook after Britain surrenders the colony to China in 1997. Comment.

15. In deciding where to invest your money, you read that Germany looks like it's well positioned to capitalize on the opening of Eastern Europe. But Britain is troubled by weak growth and high inflation and interest rates. Which of these countries would it make sense to invest in? Explain.

16. As noted in the chapter, from 1949 to 1990, the Japanese market rose 25,000%.
   a. Given these returns, does it make sense for Japanese investors to diversify internationally?
   b. What arguments would you use to persuade a Japanese investor to invest overseas?
   c. Why might Japanese (and other) investors still prefer to invest in domestic securities despite the potential gains from international diversification?

PROBLEMS

1. During the year the price of British gilts (government bonds) went from £102 to £106, while paying a coupon of £9. At the same time, the exchange rate went from £1:$1.76 to £1:$1.62. What was the total dollar return, in percent, on gilts for the year?

2. During the first half of 1990, Swiss government bonds yielded a local-currency return of –1.6%. However, the Swiss franc rose by 8% against the dollar over this six-month period. Corresponding figures for France were 1.8% and 2.6%. Which bond earned the higher U.S. dollar return? What was the return?

3. During the year Toyota Motor Company shares went from ¥9,000 to ¥11,200, while paying a dividend of ¥60. At the same time, the exchange rate went from $1 = ¥145 to $1 = ¥120. What was the total dollar return, in percent, on Toyota stock for the year?

4. During 1989, the Mexican stock market climbed 112% in peso terms while the peso depreciated by 28.6% against the U.S. dollar. What was the dollar return on the Mexican stock market during the year?

5. Here are data on stock market returns and exchange rate changes during 1988 for some of the world's stock markets. Determine the dollar return on each of these markets.

| Country | Return in Local Currency (%) | Current Units Per Dollar | |
		12/31/87	12/31/88
Australia	14.5	1.41	1.17
Belgium	56.3	35.10	38.80
Canada	10.9	1.29	1.20
France	56.8	5.65	6.31
West Germany	27.9	1.68	1.85
Holland	42.8	1.88	2.09
Italy	26.2	1230.00	1357.00
Japan	44.8	129.00	128.00
Spain	25.0	114.00	116.00
Sweden	60.5	6.03	6.30
Switzerland	31.9	1.37	1.58
United Kingdom	9.1	0.56	0.57

6. Suppose that the dollar is now worth DM 1.6372. If one-year German bunds are yielding 9.8% and one-year U.S. Treasury bonds are yielding 6.5%, at what end-of-year exchange rate will the dollar returns on the two bonds be equal? What amount of DM appreciation or depreciation does this equilibrating exchange rate represent?

7. Suppose that over a ten-year period the annualized peseta return of a Spanish bond has been 12.1%. If a comparable dollar bond has yielded an annualized return of 8.3%, what cumulative devaluation of the peseta over this period would be necessary for the return on the dollar bond to exceed the dollar return on the Spanish bond?

8. A portfolio manager is considering the benefits of increasing his diversification by investing overseas. He can purchase shares in individual country funds with the following characteristics:

	United States (%)	United Kingdom (%)	Spain (%)
Expected return	15	12	5
Standard deviation of return	10	9	4
Correlation with the United States	1.0	0.33	0.06

    a. What is the expected return and standard deviation of return of a portfolio with 25% invested in the United Kingdom and 75% in the United States?

    b. What is the expected return and standard deviation of return of a portfolio with 25% invested in Spain and 75% in the United States?

    c. Calculate the expected return and standard deviation of return of a portfolio with 50% invested in the United States and 50% in the United Kingdom. With 50% invested in the United States and 50% invested in Spain.

    d. Calculate the expected return and standard deviation of return of a portfolio with 25% invested in the United States and 75% in the United Kingdom. With 25% invested in the United States and 75% invested in Spain.

    e. Plot these two sets of risk-return combinations, (a) through (d), as in Exhibit 16.5. Which leads to a better set of risk-return choices, Spain or the United Kingdom?

    f. How can you achieve an even better risk-return combination?

9. Suppose that the standard deviations of the British and U.S. stock markets haver risen to 38% and 22%, respectively, while the correlation between the U.S. and British markets has risen to 0.67. What is the new beta of the British market from a U.S. perspective?

BIBLIOGRAPHY

Bailey, Warren and Rene M. Stulz, "Benefits of International Diversification: The Case of Pacific Basin Stock Markets," *Journal of Portfolio Management*, Summer 1990, pp. 57–62.

Errunza, Vihang R., "Gains from Portfolio Diversification into Less Developed Countries," *Journal of International Business Studies*, Fall–Winter 1977, pp. 83–99.

Ibbotson, Roger C., Richard C. Carr, and Anthony W. Robinson. "International Equity and Bond Returns." *Financial Analysts Journal*, July–August 1982, pp. 61–83.

Lessard, Donald R. "World, Country, and Industry Relationships in Equity Returns: Implications for Risk Reduction Through International Diversification." *Financial Analysts Journal*, January–February 1976, pp. 32–38.

Solnik, Bruno H. "Why Not Diversify Internationally Rather Than Domestically?" *Financial Analysts Journal*, July–August 1974, pp. 48–54.

———. *International Investments*. Reading, Mass.: Addison-Wesley, 1988.

———, and Bernard Noetzlin. "Optimal International Asset Allocation." *Journal of Portfolio Management*, Fall 1982, pp. 11–21.

Corporate Strategy and Foreign Direct Investment

17

Luck. There isn't any. Just winners and losers.
                                    The Silver Fox

CHAPTER LEARNING OBJECTIVES

- To identify the fundamental motives for companies to invest abroad in order to determine those foreign investments that are most likely to be successful
- To identify the competitive advantages that a firm must have to be a successful multinational
- To describe the strategies followed by MNCs in defending and exploiting barriers to entry created by product and factor market imperfections
- To identify the factors that help determine whether a firm will export its output, license foreign companies to manufacture its products, or set up its own production or service facilities abroad
- To explain why for many firms becoming multinational is not a matter of choice but, rather, one of survival
- To assess the nature of global competition and be able to identify the key factors leading to globalization of markets and competition
- To specify a five-step approach to designing a global expansion strategy
- To describe the Japanese strategy for penetrating world markets
- To describe the characteristics of a firm and its products that might lead it to prefer 100% ownership of all of its overseas subsidiaries versus the characteristics of a firm and its products that might lead it to prefer joint ventures overseas
- To explore the competitive implications of Europe 1992 for multinationals

KEY TERMS

competitive advantage
corporate international
   diversification
cross investment
economic rent
economies of scale
economies of scope
Europe 1992
foreign direct investment
   (FDI)
global-scanning capability
horizontal direct
   investment
industrial organization (IO)
intangible capital
internalization
international portfolio
   investment
learning curve
market imperfections
net present value (NPV)
rationalization
total quality control (TQC)
vertical integration
world-scale

Although investors are buying an increasing amount of foreign stocks and bonds, most still invest overseas indirectly, by holding shares of multinational corporations. MNCs create value for their shareholders by investing overseas in projects that have positive *net present values* (NPVs)—returns in excess of those required by shareholders. To continue to earn excess returns on foreign projects, multinationals must be able to transfer abroad their sources of domestic competitive advantage. This chapter discusses how firms create, preserve, and transfer overseas their competitive strengths.

The focus here on competitive analysis and value creation stems from the view that generating projects that are likely to yield *economic rent*—excess returns that lead to positive net present values—is a critical part of the capital budgeting process. This is the essence of corporate strategy—creating and then taking best advantage of imperfections in product and factor markets that are the precondition for the existence of economic rent.

The purpose of this chapter is to examine the phenomenon of *foreign direct investment* (FDI)—the acquisition abroad of plant and equipment—and identify those market imperfections that lead firms to become multinational. Only if these imperfections are well understood can a firm determine which foreign investments are likely ex ante to have positive NPVs. The chapter also analyzes corporate strategies for international expansion and presents a normative approach to global strategic planning and foreign investment analysis.

17.1 THEORY OF THE MULTINATIONAL CORPORATION

It has long been recognized that all MNCs are oligopolists (although the converse is not true), but it is only recently that oligopoly and multinationality have been explicitly linked via the notion of *market imperfections.* These imperfections can be related to product and factor markets or to financial markets.

Product and Factor Market Imperfections

Multinationals owe their existence to product and factor market imperfections.

The most promising explanation for the existence of multinationals relies on the theory of *industrial organization* (IO), which focuses on imperfect product and/or factor markets. IO theory points to certain general circumstances under which each approach—exporting, licensing, or local production—will be the preferred alternative for exploiting foreign markets.

According to this theory, multinationals have *intangible capital* in the form of trademarks, patents, general marketing skills, and other organizational abilities.[1] If this intangible capital can be embodied in the form of products without adaptation, then exporting will generally be the preferred mode of market penetration. Where the firm's knowledge takes the form of specific product or process technologies that can be written down and transmitted objectively, then foreign expansion will usually take the licensing route.

Often, however, this intangible capital takes the form of organizational skills that are inseparable from the firm itself. A basic skill involves knowing how best to service a market through new-product development and adaptation, quality control, advertising, distribution, after-sales service, and the general ability to

[1]Richard E. Caves, "International Corporations: The Industrial Economics of Foreign Investment," *Economica*, February 1971, pp. 1–27.

read changing market desires and translate them into salable products. Because it would be difficult, if not impossible, to unbundle these services and sell them apart from the firm, this form of market imperfection often leads to corporate attempts to exert control directly via the establishment of foreign affiliates. But internalizing the market for an intangible asset by setting up foreign affiliates makes economic sense if—and only if—the benefits from circumventing market imperfections outweigh the administrative and other costs of central control.

A useful means to judge whether a foreign investment is desirable is to consider the type of imperfection that the investment is designed to overcome.[2] *Internalization,* and hence FDI, is most likely to be economically viable in those settings where the possibility of contractual difficulties make it especially costly to coordinate economic activities via arm's-length transactions in the marketplace.

> Foreign direct investment is most likely where contractual difficulties make it costly to deal with unrelated foreign companies.

Such "market failure" imperfections lead to both vertical and horizontal direct investment. *Vertical integration*—direct investment across industries that relate to different stages of production of a particular good—enables the MNC to substitute internal production and distribution systems for inefficient markets. For instance, vertical integration might allow a firm to install specialized cost-saving equipment in two locations without the worry and risk that facilities may be idled by disagreements with unrelated enterprises. *Horizontal direct investment*— investment that is cross-border but within an industry—enables the MNC to utilize an advantage such as know-how or technology and avoid the contractual difficulties of dealing with unrelated parties. Examples of contractual difficulties are the MNC's inability to price know-how or to write, monitor, and enforce use restrictions governing technology transfer arrangements. Thus, foreign direct investment makes most sense when a firm possesses a valuable asset and is better off directly controlling use of the asset rather than selling or licensing it.

Yet the existence of market failure is not sufficient to justify FDI. Because local firms have an inherent cost advantage over foreign investors (who must bear, for example, the costs of operating in an unfamiliar, and possibly hostile, environment), multinationals can succeed abroad only if the production or marketing edge that they possess cannot be purchased or duplicated by local competitors. Eventually, though, all barriers to entry erode, and the firm must find new sources of *competitive advantage* or be driven back to its home country. Thus, to survive as multinational enterprises, firms must create and preserve effective barriers to direct competition in product and factor markets worldwide.

Financial Market Imperfections

An alternative, though not necessarily competing, hypothesis for explaining foreign direct investment relies on the existence of financial market imperfections. We have already seen in Chapter 15 that the ability to reduce taxes and circumvent currency controls may lead to greater project cash flows and a lower cost of funds for the MNC than for a purely domestic firm.

---

[2]These considerations are discussed by William Kahley, "Direct Investment Activity of Foreign Firms," *Economic Review,* Federal Reserve Bank of Atlanta, Summer 1987, pp. 36–51.

An even more important financial motivation for foreign direct investment is likely to be the desire to reduce risks through international diversification. This motivation may be somewhat surprising because the inherent riskiness of the multinational corporation is usually taken for granted. Exchange rate changes, currency controls, expropriation, and other forms of government intervention are some of the risks that are rarely, if ever, encountered by purely domestic firms. Thus, the greater a firm's international investment, the riskier its operations should be.

Being multinational can reduce the riskiness of a firm.

Yet, there is good reason to believe that being multinational may actually reduce the riskiness of a firm. Much of the systematic or general market risk affecting a company is related to the cyclical nature of the national economy in which the company is domiciled. Hence, the diversification effect due to operating in a number of countries whose economic cycles are not perfectly in phase should reduce the variability of MNC earnings. Several studies indicate that this result, in fact, is the case.[3] Thus, since foreign cash flows are generally not perfectly correlated with those of domestic investments, the greater riskiness of individual projects overseas can well be offset by beneficial portfolio effects. Furthermore, because most of the economic and political risks specific to the multinational corporation are unsystematic, they can be eliminated through diversification.

The value of international diversification was made clear in Chapter 16. Thus, the ability of multinationals to supply an indirect means of international diversification should be advantageous to investors. But this *corporate international diversification* will prove beneficial to shareholders only if there are barriers to direct *international portfolio investment* by individual investors. These barriers do exist and were described in Chapter 16. However, we also saw that many of these barriers are eroding.

Our present state of knowledge does not allow us to make definite statements about the relative importance of financial and nonfinancial market imperfections in stimulating foreign direct investment. Most researchers who have studied this issue, however, would probably agree that the latter market imperfections are much more important than the former ones. In the remainder of this chapter, therefore, we will concentrate on the effects of nonfinancial market imperfections on overseas investment.

17.2 THE STRATEGY OF MULTINATIONAL ENTERPRISE

An understanding of the strategies followed by MNCs in defending and exploiting those barriers to entry created by product and factor market imperfections is crucial to any systematic evaluation of investment opportunities. For one thing, such an understanding would suggest those projects that are most compatible

---

[3]See, for example, Benjamin I. Cohen, *Multinational Firms and Asian Exports* (New Haven, Conn.: Yale University Press, 1975); and Alan Rugman, "Risk Reduction by International Diversification," *Journal of International Business Studies*, Fall 1976, pp. 75–80.

with a firm's international expansion. This ranking is useful because time and money constraints limit the investment alternatives that a firm is likely to consider. More importantly, a good understanding of multinational strategies should help to uncover new and potentially profitable projects; only in theory is a firm fortunate enough to be presented, with no effort or expense on its part, with every available investment opportunity. This creative use of knowledge about global corporate strategies is as important an element of rational investment decision making as is the quantitative analysis of existing project possibilities.

Some MNCs rely on product innovation, others on product differentiation, and still others on cartels and collusion to protect themselves from competitive threats. We will now examine three broad categories of multinationals and their associated strategies.[4]

Innovation-Based Multinationals

Firms such as 3M (United States), N. V. Philips (Netherlands), and Sony (Japan) create barriers to entry by continually introducing new products and differentiating existing ones, both domestically and internationally. Firms in this category spend large amounts of money on R&D and have a high ratio of technical to factory personnel. Their products are typically designed to fill a need perceived locally that often exists abroad as well.

MNCs often create barriers to entry through product innovation and differentiation.

But technological leads have a habit of eroding. In addition, even the innovative multinationals retain a substantial proportion of standardized product lines. As the industry matures, other factors must replace technology as a barrier to entry; otherwise, local competitors may succeed in replacing foreign multinationals in their domestic markets.

The Mature Multinationals

What strategies have enabled the automobile, petroleum, paper and pulp, and packaged foods industries, among others, to maintain viable international operations long after their innovative leads have disappeared and their products have become standardized? Simply put, these industries have maintained international viability by erecting the same barriers to entry internationally as those that allowed them to remain domestic oligopolists. A principal barrier is the presence of *economies of scale*, which exist whenever a given increase in the scale of production, marketing, or distribution results in a less-than-proportional increase in cost. The existence of scale economies means that there are inherent cost advantages to being large. The more significant these scale economies are, therefore, the greater will be the cost disadvantage faced by a new entrant to the market.

As an industry matures, economies of scale and scope often replace technology as a barrier to entry.

Some companies, such as Coca-Cola and Procter & Gamble, take advantage of enormous advertising expenditures and highly developed marketing skills to differentiate their products and keep out potential competitors that are wary of the high marketing costs of new product introduction. By selling in foreign

[4]These categories are described by Raymond Vernon, *Storm Over the Multinationals* (Cambridge, Mass.: Harvard University Press, 1977); and Ian H. Giddy, "The Demise of the Product Cycle in International Business Theory," *Columbia Journal of World Business*, Spring 1978, p. 93.

markets, these firms can exploit the premium associated with their strong brand names. Other firms, such as Alcan and Exxon, fend off new market entrants by exploiting economies of scale in production and transportation.

Economies of scale also explain why so many firms invested in Western Europe in preparation for *Europe 1992,* when cross-border barriers to the movement of goods, services, labor, and capital were removed. Their basic rationale was that once Europe becomes a single market, the opportunities to exploit economies of scale will be greatly expanded. Companies that were not well positioned in the key European markets feared that they would be at a cost disadvantage relative to multinational rivals that were better able to exploit these scale economies.

Still other firms take advantage of economies of scope. *Economies of scope* exist whenever the same investment can support multiple profitable activities less expensively in combination than separately. Examples abound of the cost advantages to producing and selling multiple products related by a common technology, set of production facilities, or distribution network. For example, Honda has leveraged its investment in small-engine technology in the automobile, motorcycle, lawn mower, marine engine, chain saw, and generator businesses. Similarly, Matsushita has leveraged its investment in advertising and distribution of Panasonic products in a number of consumer and industrial markets, ranging from personal computers to VCRs. Each dollar invested in the Panasonic name or distribution system aids sales of dozens of different products.

Production economies of scope are becoming more prevalent as flexible manufacturing systems allow the same equipment to produce a variety of products more cheaply in combination than separately. The ability to manufacture a wide variety of products—with little cost penalty relative to large-scale manufacture of a single product—opens up new markets, customers, channels of distribution, and with them, new routes to competitive advantage.

Many MNCs take advantage of the learning curve to cut costs and drive out competitors.

A strategy that is followed by Texas Instruments, Sony, and others, is to take advantage of the *learning curve* in order to reduce costs and drive out actual and potential competitors. This latter concept is based on the old dictum that you improve with practice. As production experience accumulates, costs can be expected to decrease because of improved production methods, product redesign and standardization, and the substitution of cheaper materials or practices. Thus, there is a competitive payoff from rapid growth. By acquiring a larger share of the world market, a firm can lower its production costs and gain a competitive advantage over its rivals.

The consequences of disregarding these economic realities are illustrated by U.S. television manufacturers, which (to their sorrow) ignored the growing market for color TVs in Japan in the early 1960s. The failure of the U.S. manufacturers to preempt Japanese color-TV development spawned a host of Japanese competitors—such as Sony, Matsushita, and Hitachi—that not only came to dominate their own market but eventually took most of the U.S. market. The moral seems to be that to remain competitive at home, it is often necessary to attack potential rivals in their local markets.

To counter the danger that a foreign multinational will use high home-country prices to subsidize a battle for market share overseas, firms will often invest in one another's domestic markets. This strategy is known as *cross investment*. The implied threat is that "if you undercut me in my home market, I'll do the same in your home market." Firms with high domestic market share, and minimal sales overseas, are especially vulnerable to the strategic dilemma illustrated by the example of Fiat.

> Cross investment can discourage rivals from launching price wars in foreign markets.

ILLUSTRATION: Fiat's Strategic Dilemma

Suppose Toyota, the Japanese auto company, cuts prices in order to gain market share in Italy. If Fiat, the dominant Italian producer with minimal foreign sales, responds with its own price cuts, it will lose profit on most of its sales. In contrast, only a small fraction of Toyota's sales and profits are exposed. Fiat is effectively boxed in: If it responds to the competitive intrusion with a price cut of its own, the response will damage it more than Toyota.

The correct competitive response is for the local firm (Fiat) to cut price in the intruder's (Toyota's) domestic market (Japan). Having such a capability will deter foreign competitors from using high home-country prices to subsidize marginal cost pricing overseas. But this necessitates investing in the domestic markets of potential competitors. The level of market share needed to pose a credible retaliatory threat depends on access to distribution networks and the importance of the market to the competitor's profitability. The easier distribution access is and the more important the market is to competitor profitability, the smaller the necessary market share.[5]

The Senescent Multinationals

Eventually, product standardization is far enough advanced or organizational and technological skills sufficiently dispersed that all barriers to entry erode. What strategies do large multinationals follow when the competitive advantages in their product lines or markets become dissipated?

One possibility is to enter new markets where little competition currently exists. For example, Crown Cork & Seal, the Philadelphia-based maker of bottle tops and cans, reacted to slowing growth and heightened competition in its U.S. business by expanding overseas. It set up subsidiaries in such countries as Thailand, Malaysia, Zambia, Peru, and Ecuador, guessing—correctly, as it turned out—that in those developing and urbanizing societies, people would eventually switch from home-grown produce to food in cans and drinks in bottles. However, local firms are soon capable of providing stiff competition for those

---

[5]The notion of undercutting competitors in their home market is explored in Gary Hamel and C. K. Prahalad, "Do You Really Have a Global Strategy?" *Harvard Business Review*, July–August 1985, pp. 139–148.

foreign multinationals that are not actively developing new sources of differential advantage.

One strategy often followed when senescence sets in is to use the firm's *global-scanning capability* to seek out lower cost production sites. Costs can then be minimized by combining production shifts with *rationalization* and *integration* of the firm's manufacturing facilities worldwide. This strategy usually involves plants specializing in different stages of production—for example, in assembly or fabrication as well as in particular components or products. Yet the relative absence of market imperfections confers a multinational production network with little, if any, advantage over production by purely local enterprises. For example, many U.S. electronics and textile firms shifted production facilities to Asian locations, such as Taiwan and Hong Kong, to take advantage of lower labor costs there. However, as more firms took advantage of this cost-reduction opportunity, competition in U.S. consumer electronics and textile markets—increasingly from Asian firms—intensified, causing domestic prices to drop and excess profits to be dissipated.

In general, the excess profits due to processing new information are temporary. Once new market or cost-reduction opportunities are recognized by other companies, the profit rate declines to its normal level. Hence, few firms rely solely on cost minimization or entering new markets to maintain competitiveness.

The more common choice is to drop old products and turn corporate skills to new products. Companies that follow this strategy of continuous product rollover are likely to survive as multinationals. Those who are unable to transfer their original competitive advantages to new products or industries must plan on divesting their international operations and returning home. But firms that withdraw from overseas operations because of a loss of competitive advantage should not count on a very profitable homecoming.

ILLUSTRATION: *The U.S. Tire Industry Gets Run Over*

The U.S. tire industry illustrates the troubles faced by multinational firms that have lost their source of differential advantage. Although Europe had once been a profitable market for the Big Four U.S. tiremakers—Goodyear, Firestone, Goodrich, and Uniroyal—each of these firms has, by now, partially or completely eliminated its European manufacturing operations. The reason is the extraordinary price competition resulting from a lack of unique products or production processes and the consequent ease of entry into the market by new firms. Moreover, these firms then faced well-financed challenges in the U.S. market by, among others, the French tiremaker Michelin, the developer of the radial tire and its related production technology. Uniroyal responded by selling off its European tire-manufacturing operation and reinvesting its money in businesses that were less competitive there (and, hence, more profitable) than the tire industry. This reinvestment includes its chemical, plastics, and industrial products businesses in Europe. Similarly, Goodrich stopped producing tires for new cars and expanded its operations in polyvinyl chloride resin and specialty chemicals. In 1986, Uniroyal and Goodrich merged their tire units to become Uniroyal Goodrich Tire, selling only in North America. Late in 1989, its future in doubt, Uniroyal Goodrich sold out to Michelin. The previous year, in early 1988, Firestone sold out to the Japanese tiremaker Bridgestone.

Foreign Direct Investment and Survival

Thus far we have seen how firms are capable of becoming and remaining multi-nationals. However, for many of these firms, becoming multinational is not a matter of choice but, rather, one of survival.

For many firms, becoming multinational is not a matter of choice but one of survival.

Cost Reduction. It is apparent, of course, that if competitors gain access to lower-cost sources of production abroad, following them overseas may be a prerequisite for domestic survival. One strategy that is often followed by firms for which cost is the key consideration is to develop a global-scanning capability to seek out lower-cost production sites or production technologies worldwide. In fact, firms in competitive industries have to continually seize new nonproprietary cost reduction opportunities, not to earn excess returns but to make normal profits and survive.

Economies of Scale. A somewhat less-obvious factor motivating foreign investment is the effect of economies of scale. In a competitive market, prices will be forced close to marginal costs of production. Hence, firms in industries characterized by high fixed costs relative to variable costs must engage in volume selling just to break even. A new term describes the size that is required in certain industries to compete effectively in the global marketplace: *world-scale*. These large volumes may be forthcoming only if the firms expand overseas. For example, companies manufacturing products such as computers that require huge R&D expenditures often need a larger customer base than that provided by even a market as large as the United States in order to recapture their investment in knowledge. Similarly, firms in capital-intensive industries with enormous production economies of scale may also be forced to sell overseas in order to spread their overhead over a larger quantity of sales.

L. M. Ericsson, the highly successful Swedish manufacturer of telecommunications equipment, is an extreme case. The manufacturer is forced to think internationally when designing new products because its domestic market is too small to absorb the enormous R&D expenditures involved and to reap the full benefit of production scale economies. Thus, when Ericsson developed its revolutionary AXE digital switching system, it geared its design to achieve global market penetration.

These firms may find a foreign market presence necessary in order to continue selling overseas. Local production can expand sales by providing customers with tangible evidence of the company's commitment to service the market. It also increases sales by improving a company's ability to service its local customers. Domestic retrenchment can thus involve not only the loss of foreign profits but also an inability to price competitively in the home market because it no longer can take advantage of economies of scale.

ILLUSTRATION: U.S. Chipmakers Produce in Japan

Many U.S. chipmakers have set up production facilities in Japan. One reason is that the chipmakers have discovered they can't expect to increase Japanese sales from halfway around the world. It can take weeks for a company without testing facilities in Japan to respond to customer complaints. A customer must send a faulty chip back to the maker for analysis. That can take up to three weeks if the maker's facilities are in the United States. In the meantime, the customer will have to shut down its assembly line, or part of it. With testing facilities in Japan, however, the wait can be cut to a few days.

But a testing operation alone would be inefficient; testing machines cost millions of dollars. Because an assembly plant needs the testing machines, a company usually moves in an entire assembly operation. Having the testing and assembly operations also reassures procurement officials about quality: They can touch, feel, and see tangible evidence of the company's commitment to service the market.

Multiple plants may provide multinationals with valuable options to reduce currency and political risks.

Multiple Sourcing. Once a firm has decided to produce abroad, it must determine where to do so. Although cost minimization will often dictate concentrating production in one or two plants, fear of strikes and political risks usually lead firms to follow a policy of multiple sourcing. For example, a series of strikes against British Ford in the late 1960s and early 1970s caused Ford to give lower priority to rationalization of supplies. It went for safety instead, by instituting a policy of double sourcing. Ford has since modified this policy, but many other firms still opt for several smaller plants in different countries instead of one large plant that can take advantage of scale economies but that would be vulnerable to disruptions.

The costs of multiple sourcing are obvious; the benefits, less apparent. One benefit is the potential leverage that can be exerted against unions and governments by threatening to shift production elsewhere. For example, to reach settlement in the previously mentioned strikes against British Ford, Henry Ford II used the threat of withholding investments from England and placing them in Germany. Another, more obvious, benefit is the additional safety achieved by having several plants capable of supplying the same product.

Multiple facilities also give the firm the option of switching production from one location to another to take advantage of transient unit cost differences arising from, say, real exchange rate changes or new labor contracts. This option is enhanced, albeit at a price, by building excess capacity into the plants.

Knowledge Seeking. Some firms enter foreign markets for the purpose of gaining information and experience that is expected to prove useful elsewhere. For instance, Beecham, an English firm (now SmithKline Beecham), deliberately set out to learn from its U.S. operations how to be more competitive, first in the area of consumer products and, later, in pharmaceuticals. This knowledge proved highly valuable in competing with American and other firms in its European markets.

Similarly, in late 1992, the South Korean conglomerate Hyundai moved its PC division to the United States in order to keep up with the rapidly evolving personal computer market, whose direction was set by the U.S. market.

The flow of ideas is not all one way, however. As Americans have demanded better-built, better-handling, and more fuel-efficient small cars, Ford of Europe has become an important source of design and engineering ideas and management talent for its U.S. parent, including the hugely successful Taurus.

In industries characterized by rapid product innovation and technical breakthroughs by foreign competitors, it is imperative to track overseas developments constantly. Japanese firms excel here, systematically and effectively collecting information on foreign innovation and disseminating it within their own research and development, marketing, and production groups. The analysis of new foreign products as soon as they reach the market is an especially long-lived Japanese technique. One of the jobs of Japanese researchers is to tear down a new foreign product and analyze how it works as a base on which to develop a product of their own that will outperform the original. In a bit of a switch, Data General's Japanese operation is giving the company a close look at Japanese technology, enabling it to quickly pick up and transfer back to the United States new information on Japanese innovations in the areas of computer design and manufacturing.

More firms are building labs in Japan and hiring its scientists and engineers to absorb Japan's latest technologies. For example, Texas Instruments works out production of new chips in Japan first because, an official says, "production technology is more advanced and Japanese workers think more about quality control."[6] A firm that remains at home can be "blind sided" by current or future competitors with new products, manufacturing processes, or marketing procedures.

Tough competition in a foreign market is a valuable experience in itself. For many industries, a competitive home marketplace has proved to be as much of a competitive advantage as cheap raw materials or technical talent. Fierce domestic competition is one reason the U.S. telecommunications industry has not lost its lead in technology, R&D, design, software, quality, and cost. Japanese and European firms are at a disadvantage in this business because they don't have enough competition in their home markets. U.S. companies have been able to engineer a great leap forward because they saw firsthand what the competition could do. Thus, for telecommunications firms like Germany's Siemens, Japan's NEC, and France's Alcatel, a position in the U.S. market has become mandatory.

Similarly, it is slowly dawning on consumer electronics firms that to compete effectively elsewhere, they must first compete in the toughest market of all: Japan. What they learn in the process—from meeting the extraordinarily demanding standards of Japanese consumers and battling a dozen relentless Japanese rivals—is invaluable and will possibly make the difference between survival and extinction.

Although it may be stating the obvious to note that operating in a competitive marketplace is an important source of competitive advantage, this viewpoint

Margin notes:

MNCs can use foreign markets to gain information and experience that will prove useful elsewhere.

A competitive home marketplace often provides a valuable competitive advantage.

---

[6]*The Wall Street Journal*, August 1, 1986, p. 6.

appears to be a minority one today. Many companies prepared for Europe 1992 by seeking mergers, alliances, and collaboration with competitors. Some went further and petitioned their governments for protection from foreign rivals and assistance in R&D. But to the extent companies succeed in sheltering themselves from competition, they endanger the basis of true competitive advantage: dynamic improvement, which derives from continuous effort to enhance existing skills and learn new ones.

Companies often follow their domestic customers overseas to provide uninterrupted service.

Keeping Domestic Customers.   Suppliers of goods or services to multinationals will often follow their customers abroad in order to guarantee them a continuing product flow. Otherwise, the threat of a potential disruption to an overseas supply line—for example, a dock strike or the imposition of trade barriers—can lead the customer to select a local supplier, which may be a domestic competitor with international operations. Hence, comes the dilemma: Follow your customers abroad or face the loss of not only their foreign but also their domestic business. A similar threat to domestic market share has led many banks, advertising agencies, and accounting, law, and consulting firms to set up foreign practices in the wake of their multinational clients' overseas expansion.

ILLUSTRATION: Bridgestone Buys Firestone

As noted earlier, in March 1988, Bridgestone, the largest Japanese tiremaker, bought Firestone and its worldwide tire operations. Like other Japanese companies that preceded it to the United States, Bridgestone was motivated by a desire to circumvent potential trade barriers and soften the impact of the strong yen. The move also greatly expanded Bridgestone's customer base, allowing it to sell its own tires directly to U.S. automakers, and strengthened its product line. Bridgestone excelled in truck and heavy-duty-vehicle tires, while Firestone's strength was in passenger-car tires. But beyond these facts, a key consideration was Bridgestone's wish to reinforce ties with Japanese auto companies that had set up production facilities in the United States. By1992, these companies, either directly or in joint ventures with U.S. firms, had the capacity to produce about 2 million vehicles annually in the United States. Firestone also contributed plants in Spain, France, Italy, Portugal, Argentina, Brazil, and Venezuela. Thus, Bridgestone's purchase of Firestone has firmly established the company not only in North America, but in Europe and South America as well. Formerly, it had been primarily an Asian firm, but had come to acknowledge the need to service Japanese automakers globally by operating closer to their customers' production facilities. The increasing globalization of the automobile market has prompted vehicle producers and tiremakers alike to set up production facilities in each of the three main markets: North America, Western Europe, and Japan.

Two main factors have been responsible for this trend toward globalization: transport costs are high for tires and, as a result, exporting has ceased to be a viable long-term strategy for supplying distant markets. For another, shifting manufacturing overseas was the only way for the tire companies to meet the logistic challenges posed by the adoption of "just-in-time" manufacturing and inventory systems by automakers.

A series of combinations in the tire industry—including Sumitomo Rubber's purchase of Dunlop Tire's European and U.S. operations, Pirelli's acquisition of Armstrong Tire and Rubber, and Continental AG's acquisition of General Tire and Rubber and its subsequent joint venture with two Japanese tiremakers—practically forced Bridgestone to have a major presence in the important American market if it were to remain a key player in the United States and worldwide. Absent such a move, its Japanese competitors may have taken Bridgestone's share of the business of Japanese firms producing in the United States and Europe. This result would have affected its competitive stance in Japan as well.

A similar desire to increase its presence in the vital North American market was behind Michelin's 1989 acquisition of Uniroyal Goodrich. For Michelin, the addition of Uniroyal Goodrich provided entry into private-label and associate-label tire markets from which it had been absent, as well as added sales to U.S. automakers.

By now it should be apparent that a foreign investment may be motivated by considerations other than profit maximization and that its benefits may accrue to an affiliate far removed from the scene. Moreover, these benefits may take the form of a reduction in risk or an increase in cash flow, either directly or indirectly. Direct cash flows would include those based on a gain in revenues or a cost savings. Indirect flows include those resulting from a competitor's setback or the firm's increased leverage to extract concessions from various governments or unions (for example, by having the flexibility to shift production to another location). In computing these indirect effects, a firm must consider, of course, what would have been the company's worldwide cash flows in the absence of the investment.

The benefits of a foreign investment may accrue elsewhere in the organization.

17.3 DESIGNING A GLOBAL EXPANSION STRATEGY

Although a strong competitive advantage today in, say, technology or marketing skills may give a company some breathing space, these competitive advantages will eventually erode, leaving the firm susceptible to increased competition both at home and abroad. The emphasis must be on systematically pursuing policies and investments congruent with worldwide survival and growth. This approach involves five interrelated elements.

1. It requires an awareness of those investments that are likely to be most profitable. As we have previously seen, these investments are ones that capitalize on and enhance the differential advantage possessed by the firm; that is, an investment strategy should focus explicitly on building competitive advantage. This strategy could be geared to building volume where economies of scale are all important or to broadening the product scope where economies of scope are

An investment strategy should be geared toward building competitive advantage.

critical to success. Such a strategy is likely to encompass a sequence of tactical projects; several may yield low returns when considered in isolation, but together they may either create valuable future investment opportunities or allow the firm to continue earning excess returns on existing investments. To properly evaluate a sequence of tactical projects designed to achieve competitive advantage, the projects must be analyzed jointly, rather than incrementally.

For example, if the key to competitive advantage is high volume, the initial entry into a market should be assessed on the basis of its ability to create future opportunities to build market share and the associated benefits thereof. Alternatively, market entry overseas may be judged according to its ability to deter a foreign competitor from launching a market-share battle by posing a credible retaliatory threat to the competitor's profit base. By reducing the likelihood of a competitive intrusion, foreign market entry may lead to higher future profits in the home market.

In designing and valuing a strategic investment program, a firm must be careful to consider the ways in which the investments interact. For example, where scale economies exist, investment in large-scale manufacturing facilities may only be justified if the firm has made supporting investments in foreign distribution and brand awareness. Investments in a global distribution system and a global brand franchise, in turn, are often economical only if the firm has a range of products (and facilities to supply them) that can exploit the same distribution system and brand name.

Developing a broad product line usually requires and facilitates (by enhancing economies of scope) investment in critical technologies that cut across products and businesses. Investments in R&D also yield a steady stream of new products that raises the return on the investment in distribution. At the same time, a global distribution capability may be critical in exploiting new technology.

The return to an investment in R&D is largely determined by the size of the market in which the firm can exploit its innovation and the durability of its technological advantage. As the technology imitation lag shortens, a company's ability to fully exploit a technological advantage may depend on its being able to quickly push products embodying that technology through distribution networks in each of the world's critical national markets.

Individually or in pairs, investments in large-scale production facilities, worldwide distribution, a global brand franchise, and new technology are likely to be negative net present value projects. Together, however, they may yield a highly positive NPV by forming a mutually supportive framework for achieving global competitive advantage.

2. This global approach to investment planning necessitates a systematic evaluation of individual entry strategies in foreign markets, a comparison of the alternatives, and selection of the optimal mode of entry. For example, in the absence of strong brand names or distribution capabilities but with a labor-cost advantage, Japanese television manufacturers entered the U.S. market by selling low-cost, private-label, black-and-white TVs.

3. A key element is a continual audit of the effectiveness of current entry modes, bearing in mind that a market's sales potential is at least partially a function of the entry strategy. As knowledge about a foreign market increases or sales potential grows, the optimal market penetration strategy will likely change. By the late 1960s, for example, the Japanese television manufacturers had built a large volume base by selling private-label TVs. Using this volume base, they invested in new process and product technologies, from which came the advantages of scale and quality. Recognizing the transient nature of a competitive advantage built on labor and scale advantages, Japanese companies, such as Matsushita and Sony, strengthened their competitive position in the U.S. market by investing throughout the 1970s to build strong brand franchises and distribution capabilities. The new-product positioning was facilitated by large-scale investments in R&D. By the 1980s, the Japanese competitive advantage in TVs and other consumer electronics had switched from being cost based to one based on quality, features, strong brand names, and distribution systems.[7]

Over time, the optimal foreign market penetration strategy will likely change.

4. A systematic investment analysis requires the use of appropriate evaluation criteria. Nevertheless, despite the complex interactions between investments or corporate policies and the difficulties in evaluating proposals (or perhaps because of them), most firms still use simple rules of thumb in selecting projects to undertake. Analytical techniques are used only as a rough screening device or as a final checkoff before project approval. While simple rules of thumb are obviously easier and cheaper to implement, there is a danger of obsolescence and consequent misuse as the fundamental assumptions underlying their applicability change. On the other hand, the use of the theoretically sound and recommended present value analysis is anything but straightforward. The strategic rationale underlying many investment proposals can be translated into traditional capital budgeting criteria, but it is necessary to look beyond the returns associated with the project itself to determine its true impact on corporate cash flows and riskiness. For example, an investment made to save a market threatened by competition or trade barriers must be judged on the basis of the sales that would otherwise have been lost. Also, export creation and direct investment often go hand in hand. In the case of ICI, the British chemical company, its exports to Europe were enhanced by its strong market position there in other product lines, a position due mainly to ICI's local manufacturing facilities.

We saw earlier that some foreign investments are designed to improve the company's competitive posture elsewhere. For example, Air Liquide, the world's largest industrial-gas maker, opened a facility in Japan because Japanese factories make high demands of their gas suppliers and keeping pace with them ensures that the French company will stay competitive elsewhere. In the words of the Japanese unit's president, "We want to develop ourselves to be strong wherever our com-

---

[7]For an excellent discussion of Japanese strategy in the U.S. TV market and elsewhere, see Hamel and Prahalad, "Do You Really Have a Global Strategy?"

petitors are."[8] Similarly, a spokesperson says that Air Liquide has expanded its U.S. presence because the United States is "the perfect marketing observatory."[9] U.S. electronics companies and papermakers have found new uses for the company's gases, and Air Liquide has brought back the ideas to European customers.

Investments should be evaluated based on their underlying strategic rationale.

Applying this concept of evaluating an investment on the basis of its global impact will force companies to answer tough questions: How much is it worth to protect our reputation for prompt and reliable delivery? What effect will establishing an operation here have on our present and potential competitors or on our ability to supply competitive products, and what will be the profit impact of this action? One possible approach is to determine the incremental costs associated with, say, a defensive action such as building multiple plants (as compared with several larger ones) and then use that number as a benchmark against which to judge how large the present value of the associated benefits (e.g., greater bargaining leverage vis-à-vis host governments) must be to justify the investment.

5. The firm must estimate the longevity of its particular form of competitive advantage. If this advantage is easily replicated, both local and foreign competitors will not take long to apply the same concept, process, or organizational structure to their operations. The resulting competition will erode profits to a point where the MNC can no longer justify its existence in the market. For this reason, the firm's competitive advantage should be constantly monitored and maintained to ensure the existence of an effective barrier to entry into the market. Should these entry barriers break down, the firm must be able to react quickly and either reconstruct them or build new ones. But no barrier to entry can be maintained indefinitely; to remain multinational, firms must continually invest in developing new competitive advantages that are transferable overseas and that are not easily replicated by the competition.

17.4 ILLUSTRATION: THE JAPANESE STRATEGY FOR GLOBAL EXPANSION

In 1945, Japan was a bombed-out wreck of a nation, humiliated and forced into unconditional surrender. All through the 1950s, Japanese exports were hampered by a low-quality image. Yet less than 20 years later, Japanese companies such as Sony, Hitachi, Seiko, Canon, and Toyota had established worldwide reputations equal to those of Zenith, Kodak, Ford, Philips, and General Electric.

Here are some lessons about international strategy to be learned from the Japanese, who arguably are the most successful global expansionists in history. To begin, it should be pointed out that the Japanese have invested a great deal of money and effort in quality, ever since quality gurus W. Edwards Deming and J. M. Juran crossed the Pacific in the 1950s to teach them how to manage for quality—an approach often called *Total Quality Control* (TQC). Few U.S. compa-

---

[8]*The Wall Street Journal,* November 12, 1987, p. 32.

[9]*The Wall Street Journal,* February 23, 1988, p. 20.

nies paid much heed to Deming or Juran and TQC, but the Japanese avidly embraced their ideas. In fact, the Deming Prize is now Japan's most prestigious award for industrial quality control.

Beyond quality, the Japanese have followed a simple strategy—repeated time and again—for penetrating world markets. Whether in cars, TVs, motorcycles, or photocopiers, the Japanese have started at the low end of the market. In each case, this market segment had been largely ignored by U.S. firms focusing on higher margin products. At the same time, the Japanese firms invested money in process technologies and simpler product design to cut costs and expand market share. Japan's lower-cost products sold in high volume, giving the manufacturers production economies of scale that other contenders could not match.

U.S. companies retreated to the high-end segment of each market, believing that the Japanese could not challenge them there. The incumbents' willingness to surrender the low end of the market was not entirely irrational. In each case, the incumbents had successful, established products that would be cannibalized by a vigorous response. General Motors, for example, believed that if it came up with high-quality smaller cars, sales of these cars would come at the expense of its bigger, higher-margin cars. So, it chose to hold back in responding to competitive attacks by the Japanese.

> Japanese companies start at the low end of a market, build up production volume and global brand franchises, and move up-market.

But the Japanese weren't content to remain in the low-end segment of the market. Over time, they invested in new-product development, built strong brand franchises and global distribution networks, and moved up-market. They amortized the costs of these investments by rapid expansion across contiguous product segments and by acceleration of the product life cycle. Here, *contiguous* refers to products that share a common technology, brand name, or distribution system. In this way, the Japanese managed to take full advantage of the economies of scope inherent in core technologies, brand franchises, and distribution networks. Simultaneously, global expansion allowed them to build up production volume and garner available scale economies.

ILLUSTRATION: *Canon Doesn't Copy Xerox*

The tribulations of Xerox illustrate the dynamic nature of Japanese competitive advantage.[10] Xerox dominates the U.S. market for large copiers. Its competitive strengths—a large direct sales force that constitutes a unique distribution channel, a national service network, a wide range of machines using custom-made components, and a large installed base of leased machines—have defeated attempts by IBM and Kodak to replicate its success by creating matching sales and service networks. Canon's strategy, by contrast, was simply to sidestep these barriers to entry by (1) creating low-end copiers that it sold through office-product dealers, thereby avoiding the need to set up a national sales force; (2) designing reliability and serviceability into its machines, so users or nonspecialist dealers could serv-

---

[10]This example appears in Gary Hamel and C. K. Prahalad, "Strategic Intent," *Harvard Business Review,* May–June 1989, pp. 63–76.

ice them; (3) using commodity components and standardizing its machines to lower costs and prices and boost sales volume; and (4) selling rather than leasing its copiers. By 1986, Canon and other Japanese firms had over 90% of copier sales worldwide. And having ceded the low end of the market to the Japanese, Xerox soon found those same competitors flooding into its stronghold sector in the middle and upper ends of the market.

Canon's strategy points out an important distinction between *barriers to entry* and *barriers to imitation*.[11] Competitors like IBM that tried to imitate Xerox's strategy had to pay a matching entry fee. Through competitive innovation, Canon avoided these costs and, in fact, stymied Xerox's response. Xerox realized that the quicker it responded—by downsizing its copiers, improving reliability, and developing new distribution channels—the quicker it would erode the value of its leased machines and cannibalize its existing high-end product line and service revenues. Hence, what were barriers to entry for imitators became barriers to retaliation for Xerox.

U.S. companies dominate many high technology industries.

Despite the challenge posed by Japanese and other foreign competitors, many U.S. companies that rely on scientific and technical research are growing in strength. U.S. companies dominate such high-technology industries as aerospace, computers and computer peripherals, communications, chemicals, pharmaceuticals, biotechnology, and software. And U.S. companies excel in some former Japanese strongholds: Hewlett-Packard is the world leader in computer printers; AT&T dominates the cordless phone market; Motorola leads the world in cellular phones and pagers; and Motorola and Intel dominate the huge global market for microprocessors.

The American companies that have managed to succeed against their foreign competitors are those that focused on their competitive strengths and were willing to stick with markets even when profitability declined. Many of these competitive strengths are readily apparent: America's overwhelming lead in software and microprocessors, the two most profitable areas of the computer industry; the benefits of telecommunications deregulation, which spurred growth in wireless telephony; the U.S. skill in meshing software and hardware; and the strong links between American universities and American industry, which have enabled U.S. companies to dominate the pharmaceuticals and biotechnology industries.

Winners in global markets closely link R&D to market realities.

Successful companies have also learned that, as product cycles shorten, the key to profitability is not innovation by itself but innovation that is quickly embodied in new products. New products typically command a price premium based on their de facto monopoly status. At the same time, as product cycles shorten, speed to market is becoming an economic necessity, not a luxury. Indeed, without those early new product price premiums, the company may not be able to recoup its development costs.

---

[11]This distinction is emphasized by Hamel and Prahalad, "Strategic Intent."

ILLUSTRATION: America Regains the Lead in Semiconductors

In 1992, U.S. chipmakers reclaimed the global top spot from the Japanese who grabbed it in 1986. The United States, which first commercialized the memory chip and the microprocessor in the 1960s, controlled the business well into the 1970s. Then the Japanese came on strong, targeting the highest-volume chip—the dynamic random access memory, or DRAM—and slashing prices to gain market share. By the mid-1980s, six Japanese companies dominated the DRAM market.

U.S. chipmakers got American politicians to implement a trade pact in 1986 that forced the Japanese to open their market to American chips and raise prices on their own memory chips (which increased the profitability of U.S. DRAM manufacturers). Higher prices also encouraged Korean companies to enter the field, raising capacity and eventually forcing down DRAM prices and the profitability of Japanese chipmakers.

But what really hurt the Japanese was the fact that DRAMs became a commodity product, with commodity profit margins. In contrast, U.S. chipmakers began focusing their efforts on developing, and getting to market quickly, higher value-added, higher-margin innovative products, such as microprocessors and custom-made circuits, which exploited American strengths in software and design. The result—an American revival in an industry that many thought was lost to the United States forever.

Japanese companies still dominate those industries, like autos and television manufacturing, where incremental improvements in production technology is the critical value driver. However, Japanese companies have generally proved less adept at dealing with markets where the way ahead is ambiguous. For example, for years the focus of big Japanese computer makers like Hitachi and Fujitsu was to beat IBM. But just when they seemed ready to catch up with IBM, IBM itself was bypassed—not by a Japanese company but by smaller and more nimble U.S. competitors, who have redefined the computer market. These companies—like Compaq, Dell, Apple, and Sun—have humbled both IBM and its Japanese competitors. It remains to be seen how many Japanese companies will be as successful at charting new paths as have been Sony and Nintendo.

Japanese companies excel in industries that require incremental product improvement.

17.5 SUMMARY AND CONCLUSIONS

For many firms, becoming multinational was the end result of an apparently haphazard process of overseas expansion. But, as international operations provide a more important source of profit and as competitive pressures increase, these firms are trying to develop global strategies that will enable them to maintain their competitive edge both at home and abroad.

The key to the development of a successful strategy is to understand and then capitalize on those factors that led to success in the past. In this chapter, we saw that the rise of the multinational firm can be attributed to a variety of market imperfections that prevent the completely free flow of goods and capital internationally. These imperfections include government regulations and controls, such as tariffs and capital controls, that impose barriers to free trade and private portfolio investment. More significant as a spawner of multinationals are market failures in the areas of firm-specific skills and information. There are various transaction, contracting, and coordinating costs involved in trying to sell a firm's managerial skills and knowledge apart from the goods it produces. To overcome these costs, many firms have created an internal market, one in which these firm-specific advantages can be embodied in the services and products they sell.

Searching for and utilizing those sources of differential advantage that have led to prior success is clearly a difficult process. This chapter sketched some of the key factors involved in conducting an appropriate global investment analysis. Essentially, such an analysis requires the establishment of corporate objectives and policies that are congruent with each other and with the firm's resources and that lead to the continual development of new sources of differential advantage as the older ones obsolescence.

Clearly, such a comprehensive investment approach requires large amounts of time, effort, and money; yet, competitive pressures and increasing turbulence in the international environment are forcing firms in this direction. Fortunately, the supply of managers qualified to deal with such complex multinational issues is rising to meet the demand for their services.

QUESTIONS

1. Why do firms from each category below become multinational? Identify the competitive advantages that a firm in each category must have to be a successful multinational.
  a. Raw-materials seekers
  b. Market seekers
  c. Cost minimizers

2. What factors help determine whether a firm will export its output, license foreign companies to manufacture its products, or set up its own production or service facilities abroad? Identify the competitive advantages that lead companies to prefer one mode of international expansion over another.

3. Warner Brothers is trying to decide whether to license foreign companies to produce its films and records or to set up foreign sales affiliates to sell its products directly. What factors might determine whether it expands abroad via licensing or by investing in its own sales force and distribution network?

4. What are the important advantages of going multinational? Consider the nature of global competition.

5. Given the added political and economic risks that appear to exist overseas, are multinational firms more or less risky than purely domestic firms in the same industry? Consider whether a firm that decides not to operate abroad is insulated from the effects of economic events that occur outside the home country.

6. How does the nature of IBM's competitive advantages relate to its becoming a multinational firm?

7. Goodyear Tire and Rubber Company, the world's number-one tire producer before Michelin's acquisition of Uniroyal Goodrich, is competing in a global tire industry. To maintain its leadership, Goodyear has invested over $1 billion to build the most automated tire-making facilities in the world and is aggressively expanding its chain of wholly owned tire stores to maintain its position as the largest retailer of tires in the United States. It has also invested heavily in R&D to produce tires that are recognized as being at the cutting edge of world-class performance. Based on product innovation and high advertising expenditures, Goodyear dominates the high-performance segment of the tire market; it has captured nearly 90% of the market for high-performance tires sold as original equipment on American cars and is well represented on sporty imports. Geography has given Goodyear and other American tire manufacturers a giant assist in the U.S. market. Heavy and bulky, tires are expensive to ship overseas.

a. What barriers to entry has Goodyear created or taken advantage of?

b. Goodyear has production facilities throughout the world. What competitive advantages might global production provide Goodyear?

c. How do tire-manufacturing facilities in Japan fit in with Goodyear's strategy to create shareholder value?

d. How will Bridgestone's acquisition of Firestone affect Goodyear? How might Goodyear respond to this move by Bridgestone?

8. Black & Decker, the maker of small, hand-held power tools, finds that when it builds a plant in a foreign country, sales of both its locally manufactured products and its exports to that country grow. What could account for this boost in sales? Consider the likely reactions of customers, distributors, and retailers to the fact that Black & Decker is producing there.

9. OPEC nations have obviously preferred portfolio investments abroad to direct foreign investment. How does the theory of market imperfections explain this preference?

10. What was the Japanese strategy for penetrating the TV market? What similarities are there between it and the Japanese strategy for entering the U.S. car market? The photocopier market?

11. What are the benefits of having a global distribution capability?

12. How sustainable is a competitive advantage based on technology? On low-cost labor? On economies of scale? Explain.

13. The value of a particular foreign subsidiary to its parent company may bear little relationship to the subsidiary's profit-and-loss statement. In addition to the manipulations described in Chapter 15, the strategic purpose or nature of a foreign unit may dictate that some of the value of the unit will show up in the form of higher profits in other affiliates.

a. Describe three ways, aside from profit manipulations, in which the incremental cash flows associated with a foreign unit can diverge from its actual cash flows.

b. Describe two strategic rationales for establishing and maintaining a foreign subsidiary that will lead to higher profits elsewhere in the corporation, but will not be reflected in the subsidiary's profit-and-loss statement.

14. Politicians, business executives, and the media lament the sale of corporate America to foreign buyers. Recent foreign acquisitions include Firestone Tire, Pillsbury, and CBS Records. A persistent theme sounded by executives and the business press is that the depreciated dollar offers a significant financial advantage to foreign bidders for American companies. According to this argument, if the dollar has depreciated relative to, say, the yen, a Japanese company can buy a U.S. company at a discount. Evaluate this argument.

15. In 1989, the British company Beecham Group merged with the U.S. company SmithKline Beckman. What economic advantages might the two drug companies be expecting from their marriage? More generally, what economic forces underlie the ongoing process of consolidation and globalization in the world pharmaceutical industry? Consider the merger's impact in the areas of R&D, marketing, and production.

PROBLEMS

1.   Suppose the worldwide profit breakdown for General Motors is 85% in the United States, 3% in Japan, and 12% in the rest of the world. Its principal Japanese competitors earn 40% of their profits in Japan, 25% in the United States, and 35% in the rest of the world. Suppose further that through diligent attention to productivity and substitution of enormous quantities of capital for labor (for example, Project Saturn), GM manages to get its automobile production costs down to the level of the Japanese.

a. Who is likely to have the global competitive advantage? Consider, for example, the ability of GM to respond to a Japanese attempt to gain U.S. market share through a sharp price cut.

b. How might GM respond to the Japanese challenge?

c. Which competitive response would you recommend to GM's CEO?

2.   More and more Japanese companies are moving in on what once was an exclusive U.S. preserve: making and selling the complex equipment that makes semiconductors. World sales are between $3 billion and $5 billion annually. The U.S. equipment makers already have seen their share of the Japanese market fall to 30% recently from a dominant 70% in the late 1970s. Because sales in Japan are expanding as rapidly as 50% a year, Japanese concerns have barely begun attacking the U.S. market. But U.S. experts consider it only a matter of time.

a. What are the possible competitive responses of U.S. firms?

b. Which one(s) would you recommend to the head of a U.S. firm? Why?

3.   Airbus Industrie, the European consortium of aircraft manufacturers, buys jet engines from U.S. companies. According to a recent story in *The Wall Street Journal*, "as a result of the weaker dollar, the cost of a major component (jet engines) is declining for Boeing's biggest competitor." The implication is that the lower price of engines for Airbus gives it a competitive advantage over Boeing. Will Airbus now be more competitive relative to Boeing? Explain.

4.   Nordson Co. of Amherst, Ohio, a maker of painting and glue equipment, exports nearly half its output. Customers value its reliability as a supplier. Because of an especially sharp run-up in the value of the dollar against the French franc, Nordson is reconsidering its decision to continue supplying the French market. What factors are relevant in reaching a decision?

5.   Tandem Computer, a U.S. maker of fault-tolerant computers, is thinking of shifting virtually all the labor-intensive portion of its production to Mexico. What risks is Tandem likely to face if it goes ahead with this move?

6.   Germany's $28 billion electronics giant, Siemens AG, sells medical and telecommunications equipment, power plants, automotive products, and computers. Siemens has been operating in the United States since 1952, but its U.S. revenues account for only about 10% of worldwide revenues. It intends to expand further in the U.S. market.

a. According to the head of its U.S. operation, "The United States is a real testing ground. If you make it here, you establish your credentials for the rest of the world." What does this statement mean? How would you measure the benefits flowing from this rationale for investing in the United States?

b. What other advantages might Siemens realize from a larger American presence?

7. Kao Corporation is a highly innovative and efficient Japanese company that has managed to take on and beat Proctor & Gamble in Japan. Two of Kao's revolutionary innovations include disposable diapers with greatly enhanced absorption capabilities and concentrated laundry detergent. However, Kao has had difficulty in establishing the kind of market-sensitive foreign subsidiaries that P&G has built.

a. What competitive advantages might P&G derive from its global network of market-sensitive subsidiaries?

b. What competitive disadvantages does Kao face if it is unable to replicate P&G's global network of subsidiaries?

BIBLIOGRAPHY

Caves, Richard E. "International Corporations: The Industrial Economics of Foreign Investment." *Economica,* February 1971, pp. 1–27.

Hamel, Gary, and C. K. Prahalad. "Do You Really Have a Global Strategy?" *Harvard Business Review,* July–August 1985, pp. 139–148.

———. "Strategic Intent," *Harvard Business Review,* May–June 1989, pp. 63–76.

Rugman, Alan M. "Motives for Foreign Investment: The Market Imperfections and Risk Diversification Hypothesis." *Journal of World Trade Law,* September–October 1975, pp. 567–573.

Shapiro, Alan C. "Capital Budgeting and Corporate Strategy." *Midland Corporate Finance Journal,* Spring 1985, pp. 22–36.

———. "Economic Import of Europe 1992." *Journal of Applied Corporate Finance,* Winter 1991, pp. 25–36.

18 Capital Budgeting for the Multinational Corporation

Nobody can really guarantee the future. The best we can do is size up the chances, calculate the risks involved, estimate our ability to deal with them, and then make our plans with confidence.

Henry Ford II

CHAPTER LEARNING OBJECTIVES

- To assess the profitability of foreign investments by identifying the incremental cash flows generated by these investments
- To explain the various ways in which incremental cash flow can differ from total project cash flow
- To contrast the net present value approach using a weighted cost of capital with the adjusted present value approach for valuing foreign projects and explain when each method is most appropriate
- To identify the differences between foreign project and parent cash flows and describe a three-stage approach to account for these differences in a capital-budgeting analysis
- To describe the three main methods for incorporating political and economic risks into foreign investment analysis and determine the circumstances (if any) under which each of these methods is most appropriate
- To describe a two-step procedure for incorporating exchange rate changes and inflation into a foreign investment analysis
- To show how foreign project cash-flow adjustments can be carried out
- To explain what growth options are, why they are of great importance to multinational firms, what factors affect their value, and how to incorporate them in a capital-budgeting analysis

Multinational corporations evaluating foreign investments find their analyses complicated by a variety of problems that are rarely, if ever, encountered by domestic firms. This chapter examines several such problems, including differences between project and parent company cash flows, foreign tax regulations, expropriation, blocked funds, exchange rate changes and inflation, project-specific financing, and differences between the basic business risks of foreign and domestic projects. The purpose of this chapter is to develop a framework that allows measuring, and reducing to a common denominator, the consequences of these complex factors on the desirability of the foreign investment opportunities under review. In this way, projects can be compared and evaluated on a uniform basis. The major principle behind methods proposed to cope with these complications is to maximize the use of available information while reducing arbitrary cash flow and cost of capital adjustments.

18.1 BASICS OF CAPITAL BUDGETING

Once a firm has compiled a list of prospective investments, it must then select from among them that combination of projects that maximizes the company's value to its shareholders. This selection requires a set of rules and decision criteria that enables managers to determine, given an investment opportunity, whether to accept or reject it. It is generally agreed that the criterion of net present value is the most appropriate one to use since its consistent application will lead the company to select the same investments the shareholders would make themselves, if they had the opportunity.

The net present value criterion is the most appropriate one to use in selecting foreign investments.

Net Present Value

The *net present value* (NPV) is defined as the present value of future cash flows discounted at an appropriate rate minus the initial net cash outlay for the project. Projects with a positive NPV should be accepted; negative NPV projects should be rejected. If two projects are mutually exclusive, the one with the higher NPV should be accepted. The discount rate, known as the *cost of capital,* is the expected rate of return on projects of similar risk. For now, we take its value as given. Chapter 19 discusses its derivation in detail.

In mathematical terms, the formula for net present value is

$$\text{NPV} = -I_0 + \sum_{t=1}^{n} \frac{X_t}{(1+k)^t} \tag{18.1}$$

where
I_0 = the initial cash investment
X_t = the net cash flow in period t
k = the project's cost of capital
n = the investment horizon

To illustrate the NPV method, consider a plant expansion project with the following stream of cash flows and their present values:

Year	Cash Flow	×	Present Value Factor (10%)	=	Present Value	Cumulative Present Value
0	−$4,000,000		1.00000		−$4,000,000	−$4,000,000
1	1,200,000		0.9091		1,091,000	− 2,909,000
2	2,700,000		0.8264		2,231,000	− 678,000
3	2,700,000		0.7513		2,029,000	1,351,000

Assuming a 10% cost of capital, the project is acceptable.

The most desirable property of the NPV criterion is that it evaluates investments in the same way the company's shareholders do; the NPV method properly focuses on cash rather than on accounting profits and emphasizes the opportunity cost of the money invested. Thus, it is consistent with shareholder wealth maximization.

Another desirable property of the NPV criterion is that it obeys the *value additivity principle.* That is, the NPV of a set of independent projects is just the sum of the NPVs of the individual projects. This property means that managers can consider each project on its own. It also means that when a firm undertakes several investments, its value increases by an amount equal to the sum of the NPVs of the accepted projects. Thus, if the firm invests in the previously described plant expansion, its value should increase by $1,351,000, the NPV of the project.

Incremental Cash Flows

The most important and also the most difficult part of an investment analysis is to calculate the cash flows associated with the project: the cost of funding the project; the cash inflows during the life of the project; and the terminal, or ending value, of the project. Shareholders are interested in how many additional dollars they will receive in the future for the dollars they lay out today. Hence, what matters is not the project's total cash flow per period, but the *incremental cash flows* generated by the project.

The distinction between a project's total and incremental cash flows is a crucial one.

The distinction between total and incremental cash flows is a crucial one. Incremental cash flow can differ from total cash flow for a variety of reasons. We now examine some of these reasons.

Cannibalization. When Honda introduced its Acura line of cars, some customers switched their purchases from the Honda Accord to the new models. This example illustrates the phenomenon known as *cannibalization,* a new product taking sales away from the firm's existing products. Cannibalization also occurs when a firm builds a plant overseas and winds up substituting foreign production for parent company exports. To the extent that sales of a new product or plant just replace other corporate sales, the new project's estimated profits must be reduced by the earnings on the lost sales.

The previous examples notwithstanding, it is often difficult to assess the true magnitude of cannibalization because of the need to determine what would have happened to sales in the absence of the new product or plant. Consider the case of Motorola building a plant in Japan to supply chips to the Japanese market previously supplied via exports. In the past, Motorola got Japanese business whether it manufactured in Japan or not. But now Japan is a chip-making dynamo whose buyers no longer have to depend on U.S. suppliers. If Motorola had not invested in Japan, it might have lost export sales anyway. But instead of losing these sales to local production, it would have lost them to one of its rivals. The incremental effect of cannibalization—which is the relevant measure for capital-budgeting purposes—equals the lost profit on lost sales that would not have been lost had the new project not been undertaken. Those sales that would have been lost anyway should not be counted a casualty of cannibalization.

Sales Creation.   Black & Decker, the U.S. power tool company, significantly expanded its exports to Europe after investing in European production facilities that gave it a strong local market position in several product lines. Similarly, GM's auto plants in England use parts made by its U.S. plants, parts that would not otherwise be sold if GM's English plants disappeared.

In both cases, an investment either created or was expected to create additional sales for existing products. Thus, *sales creation* is the opposite of cannibalization. In calculating the project's cash flows, the additional sales and associated incremental cash flows should be attributed to the project.

Opportunity Cost.   Suppose IBM decides to build a new office building in Sao Paulo on some land it bought ten years ago. IBM must include the cost of the land in calculating the value of undertaking the project. Also, this cost must be based on the current market value of the land, not the price it paid ten years ago.

This example demonstrates a more general rule. Project costs must include the true economic cost of any resource required for the project, regardless of whether the firm already owns the resource or has to go out and acquire it. This true cost is the *opportunity cost*, the cash the asset could generate for the firm should it be sold or put to some other productive use. It would be foolish for a firm that acquired oil at \$3/barrel and converted it into petrochemicals to sell those petrochemicals based on \$3/barrel oil if the price of oil has risen to \$30/barrel. So, too, it would be foolish to value an asset used in a project at other than its opportunity cost, regardless of how much cash changes hands.

Transfer Pricing.   By raising the price at which a proposed Ford plant in Dearborn will sell engines to its English subsidiary, Ford can increase the apparent profitability of the new plant, but at the expense of its English affiliate. Similarly, if Matsushita lowers the price at which its Panasonic division buys microprocessors from its microelectronics division, the latter's new semiconductor plant will show a decline in profitability.

It is evident from these examples that the transfer prices at which goods and services are traded internally can significantly distort the profitability of a proposed investment. Where possible, the prices used to evaluate project inputs or outputs should be market prices. If no market exists for the product, then the firm must evaluate the project based on the cost savings or additional profits to the corporation of going ahead with the project. For example, when Atari decided to switch most of its production to Asia, its decision was based solely on the cost savings it expected to realize. This approach was the correct one to use because the stated revenues generated by the project were meaningless, an artifact of the transfer prices used in selling its output back to Atari in the United States.

Fees and Royalties.   Often companies will charge projects for various items such as legal counsel, power, lighting, heat, rent, research and development, headquarters staff, management costs, and the like. These charges appear in the form of fees and royalties. They are costs to the project, but are a benefit from the stand-

> Foreign production facilities may cannibalize existing sales or create additional sales for existing products.

> Transfer prices can distort the true profitability of a proposed investment.

point of the parent firm. From an economic standpoint, the project should be charged only for the additional expenditures that are attributable to the project; those overhead expenses that are unaffected by the project should not be included when estimating project cash flows.

In general, incremental cash flows associated with an investment can be found only by subtracting worldwide corporate cash flows without the investment from postinvestment corporate cash flows. In performing this incremental analysis, the key question that managers must ask is, What will happen if we *don't* make this investment? Failure to heed this question led General Motors during the 1970s to slight investment in small cars despite the Japanese challenge; small cars looked less profitable than GM's then-current mix of cars. As a result, Toyota, Nissan, and the other Japanese automakers were able to expand and eventually threaten GM's base business. Similarly, many U.S. companies that thought overseas expansion too risky today find their worldwide competitive positions eroding. They didn't adequately consider the consequences of *not* building a strong global position.

> In performing an incremental analysis, managers must ask, What will happen if we don't make this investment?

ILLUSTRATION: *Investing in Memory Chips*

Since 1984, the intense competition from Japanese firms has caused most U.S. semiconductor manufacturers to lose money in the memory chip business. As we saw in Chapter 17, the only profitable part of the chip business for them is in making microprocessors and other specialized chips. Why did they continue investing in facilities to produce memory chips (the DRAMs) despite their losses in this business?

Historically, U.S. companies cared so much about memory chips because of their importance in fine-tuning the manufacturing process. Memory chips are manufactured in huge quantities and are fairly simple to test for defects, which makes them ideal vehicles for refining new production processes. Having worked out the bugs by making memories, chip companies apply an improved process to hundreds of more complex products. Until recently, without manufacturing some sort of memory chip, it was very difficult to keep production technology competitive. Thus, making profitable investments elsewhere in the chip business was contingent on producing memory chips. As manufacturing technology has changed, diminishing the importance of memory chips as process technology drivers, U.S. chipmakers like Intel have stopped producing DRAMs.

Clearly, although the principle of incremental analysis is a simple one to state, its rigorous application is a tortuous undertaking. However, this rule at least points executives responsible for estimating cash flows in the right direction. Moreover, when estimation shortcuts or simplifications are made, it provides those responsible with some idea of what they are doing and how far they are straying from a thorough analysis.

Alternative Capital-Budgeting Frameworks

As we have just seen, the standard capital-budgeting analysis involves first calculating the expected after-tax values of all cash flows associated with a prospective investment, and then discounting those cash flows back to the present, using an appropriate discount rate. Typically, the discount rate used is the *weighted average cost of capital* (WACC), where the weights are based on the proportion of the firm's capital structure accounted for by each source of capital.

An Adjusted Present Value Approach. The weighted cost of capital is simple in concept and easy to apply. A single rate is appropriate, however, only if the financial structures and commercial risks are similar for all investments undertaken. Projects with different risks are likely to possess differing debt capacities with each project, therefore necessitating a separate financial structure. Moreover, the financial package for a foreign investment often includes project-specific loans at concessionary rates or higher-cost foreign funds due to home country exchange controls, leading to different component costs of capital.

> Project risks and financial structures often vary by country, production stage, and position in the product life cycle.

The weighted cost of capital figure can be modified, of course, to reflect these deviations from the firm's typical investment. But for some companies, such as those in extractive industries, there is no norm. Project risks and financial structure vary by country, raw material, production stage, and position in the life cycle of the project. An alternative approach is to discount cash flows at a rate that reflects only the business risks of the project and abstracts from the effects of financing. This rate, called the *all-equity rate,* would apply directly if the project were financed entirely by equity. The all-equity rate k^* can be used in capital budgeting by viewing the value of a project as being equal to the sum of the following components: (1) the present value of project cash flows after taxes but before financing costs, discounted at k^*; (2) the present value of the tax savings on debt financing, which is also known as the *interest tax shield*; and (3) the present value of any savings (penalties) on interest costs associated with project-specific financing.[1] This latter differential would generally be due to government regulations and/or subsidies that caused interest rates on restricted funds to diverge from domestic interest payable on unsubsidized, arm's-length borrowing. The *adjusted present value* (APV) with this approach is

$$
\begin{array}{cccc}
\text{Present value} & \text{Present value} & \text{Present value} & \text{Present value} \\
\text{APV} = \text{of investment} + \text{of operating} + \text{of interest} + \text{of interest} \\
\text{outlay} & \text{cash flows} & \text{tax shield} & \text{subsidies}
\end{array}
$$

$$
\text{APV} = -I_0 + \sum_{t=1}^{n} \frac{X_t}{(1+k^*)^t} + \sum_{t=1}^{n} \frac{T_t}{(1+k_d)^t} + \sum_{t=1}^{n} \frac{S_t}{(1+k_d)^t} \tag{18.2}
$$

where T_t = tax savings in year t due to the specific financing package

> The adjusted present value framework incorporates the effects of financing subsidies and interest tax shields in separate terms.

[1]This material is based on Donald R. Lessard, "Evaluating Foreign Projects: An Adjusted Present Value Approach," in Donald R. Lessard, ed., *International Financial Management,* 2nd ed. (Boston: Warren, Gorham & Lamont, 1985).

S_t = before-tax dollar (home currency) value of interest subsidies (penalties) in year t due to project-specific financing

k_d = before-tax cost of dollar (home currency) debt

The last two terms in Equation 18.2 are discounted at the before-tax cost of dollar debt to reflect the relatively certain value of the cash flows due to tax shields and interest savings (penalties). The interest tax shield in period t, T_t, equals $\tau k_d D_t$, where τ is the corporate tax rate and D_t is the incremental debt supported by the project in period t.

It should be emphasized that the all-equity cost of capital equals the required rate of return on a specific project—that is, the riskless rate of interest plus an appropriate risk premium based on the project's particular risk). Thus, k^* varies by project as project risks vary.

According to the capital asset pricing model (CAPM), the market prices only *systematic risk* relative to the market rather than total corporate risk. In other words, only interactions of project returns with overall market returns are relevant in determining project riskiness; interactions of project returns with total corporate returns can be ignored. Thus, each project has its own required return and can be evaluated without regard to the firm's other investments. If a project-specific approach is not used, the primary advantage of the CAPM is lost—the concept of value additivity, which allows projects to be considered independently.

18.2 ISSUES IN FOREIGN INVESTMENT ANALYSIS

The analysis of a foreign project raises two additional issues other than those dealing with the interaction between the investment and financing decisions. The two issues are

1. Should cash flows be measured from the viewpoint of the project or the parent?
2. Should the additional economic and political risks that are uniquely foreign be reflected in cash-flow or discount rate adjustments?

Parent Versus Project Cash Flows

Parent and project cash flows can diverge significantly because of tax regulations, currency controls, and other factors.

A substantial difference can exist between the cash flow of a project and the amount that is remitted to the parent firm because of tax regulations and exchange controls. In addition, project expenses such as management fees and royalties are returns to the parent company. Furthermore, the incremental revenue contributed to the parent MNC by a project can differ from total project revenues if, for example, the project involves substituting local production for parent company exports or if transfer price adjustments shift profits elsewhere in the system.

Given the differences that are likely to exist between parent and project cash flows, the question arises as to the relevant cash flows to use in project evaluation. Economic theory has the answer to this question. According to economic theory, the value of a project is determined by the net present value of future cash flows back to the investor. Thus, the parent MNC should value only those cash flows that are, or can be, repatriated net of any transfer costs (such as taxes) because only accessible funds can be used for the payment of dividends and interest, for amortization of the firm's debt, and for reinvestment.

A Three-Stage Approach. To simplify project evaluation, a three-stage analysis is recommended. In the first stage, project cash flows are computed from the subsidiary's standpoint, exactly as if the subsidiary were a separate national corporation. The perspective then shifts to the parent company. This second stage of analysis requires specific forecasts concerning the amounts, timing, and form of transfers to headquarters, as well as information about what taxes and other expenses will be incurred in the transfer process. Finally, the firm must take into account the indirect benefits and costs that this investment confers on the rest of the system, such as an increase or decrease in export sales by another affiliate.

Estimating Incremental Project Cash Flows. Essentially, the company must estimate a project's true profitability. *True profitability* is an amorphous concept, but basically it involves determining the marginal revenue and marginal costs associated with the project. In general, as mentioned earlier, incremental cash flows to the parent can be found only by subtracting worldwide parent company cash flows (without the investment) from postinvestment parent company cash flows. This estimating entails the following:

Estimating a project's true profitability requires various adjustments to the project's cash flows.

1. Adjust for the effects of transfer pricing and fees and royalties.
   — Use market costs/prices for goods, services, and capital transferred internally
   — Add back fees and royalties to project cash flows since they are benefits to the parent
   — Remove the fixed portions of such costs as corporate overhead
2. Adjust for global costs/benefits that are not reflected in the project's financial statements. These costs/benefits include
   — Cannibalization of sales of other units
   — Creation of incremental sales by other units
   — Additional taxes owed when repatriating profits
   — Foreign tax credits usable elsewhere
   — Diversification of production facilities
   — Market diversification
   — Provision of a key link in a global service network

The second set of adjustments involves incorporating the project's strategic purpose and its impact on other units. These strategic considerations embody the factors that were discussed in Chapter 17.

A foreign investment analysis should incorporate the project's strategic purpose and its impact on other units.

Although the principle of valuing and adjusting incremental cash flows is itself simple, it can be complicated to apply. Its application is illustrated in the case of taxes.

Tax Factors. Because only after-tax cash flows are relevant, it is necessary to determine when and what taxes must be paid on foreign-source profits. To illustrate the calculation of the incremental tax owed on foreign-source earning, suppose an affiliate will remit after-tax earnings of $150,000 to its U.S. parent in the form of a dividend. Assume the foreign tax rate is 25%, the withholding tax on dividends is 4%, and excess foreign tax credits are unavailable. The marginal rate of additional taxation is found by adding the withholding tax that must be paid locally to the U.S. tax owed on the dividend. Withholding tax equals $6,000 (150,000 × 0.04), while U.S. tax owed equals $12,000. This latter tax is calculated as follows. With a before-tax local income of $200,000 (200,000 × 0.75 = 150,000), the U.S. tax owed would equal $200,000 × 0.34, or $68,000. The firm then receives foreign tax credits equal to $56,000—the $50,000 in local tax paid and the $6,000 dividend withholding tax—leaving a net of $12,000 owed the IRS. This calculation yields a marginal tax rate of 12% on remitted profits, as follows:

$$\frac{6,000 + 12,000}{150,000} = 0.12$$

If excess foreign tax credits are available, then the marginal tax rate on remittances is just the dividend withholding tax rate of 4%.

Political and Economic Risk Analysis

All else being equal, firms prefer to invest in countries with stable currencies, healthy economies, and minimal political risks, such as expropriation. But all else is usually not equal, so firms must assess the consequences of various political and economic risks for the viability of potential investments.

There are three main methods for incorporating political and economic risks into a foreign investment analysis.

The three main methods for incorporating the additional political and economic risks, such as the risks of currency fluctuation and expropriation, into foreign investment analysis are (1) shortening the minimum payback period, (2) raising the required rate of return of the investment, and (3) adjusting cash flows to reflect the specific impact of a given risk.

Adjusting the Discount Rate or Payback Period. The additional risks confronted abroad are usually described in general terms instead of being related to their impact on specific investments. This rather vague view of risk probably explains the prevalence among multinationals of two unsystematic approaches to account for the added political and economic risks of overseas operations. One is to use a higher discount rate for foreign operations; another, to require a shorter payback period. For instance, if exchange restrictions are anticipated, a normal required return of 15% might be raised to 20%, or a five-year payback period may be shortened to three years.

Neither of the aforementioned approaches, however, lends itself to a careful evaluation of the actual impact of a particular risk on investment returns. Thorough risk analysis requires an assessment of the magnitude and timing of risks and their implications for the projected cash flows. For example, an expropriation five years hence is likely to be much less threatening than one expected next year, even though the probability of it occurring later may be higher. Thus, using a uniformly higher discount rate just distorts the meaning of the present value of a project by penalizing future cash flows relatively more heavily than current ones, without obviating the necessity for a careful risk evaluation. Furthermore, the choice of a risk premium is an arbitrary one, whether it is 2% or 10%. Instead, adjusting cash flows makes it possible to fully incorporate all available information about the impact of a specific risk on the future returns from an investment.

Adjusting the discount rate for the added risks abroad can distort the meaning of a project's NPV.

Adjusting Expected Values. The recommended approach is to adjust the cash flows of a project to reflect the specific impact of a given risk, primarily because there is normally more and better information on the specific impact of a given risk on a project's cash flows than on its required return. The cash-flow adjustments presented in this chapter employ only expected values; that is, the analysis reflects only the first moment of the probability distribution of the impact of a given risk. While this procedure does not assume that shareholders are risk neutral, it does assume either that risks such as expropriation, currency controls, inflation, and exchange rate changes are unsystematic or that foreign investments tend to lower a firm's systematic risk. In the latter case, adjusting only the expected values of future cash flows will yield a lower bound on the value of the investment to the firm.

Although the suggestion that cash flows from politically risky areas should be discounted at a rate that ignores those risks is contrary to current practice, the difference is more apparent than real: Most firms evaluating foreign investments discount most likely (modal) rather than expected (mean) cash flows at a risk-adjusted rate. If an expropriation or currency blockage is anticipated, then the mean value of the probability distribution of future cash flows will be significantly below its mode. From a theoretical standpoint, of course, cash flows should always be adjusted to reflect the change in expected values caused by a particular risk; however, only if the risk is systematic should these cash flows be further discounted.

Exchange Rate Changes and Inflation

The present value of future cash flows from a foreign project can be calculated using a two-stage procedure: (1) Convert nominal foreign currency cash flows into nominal home currency terms, and (2) discount those nominal cash flows at the nominal domestic required rate of return. In order to properly assess the effect of exchange rate changes on expected cash flows from a foreign project, one must first remove the effect of offsetting inflation and exchange rate changes. It is worthwhile to analyze each effect separately because different cash flows may be differentially affected by inflation. For example, the *depreciation tax shield* will not rise with inflation, while revenues and variable costs are likely to rise in line with inflation. Or local price controls may not permit internal price adjustments. In practice, correcting for these effects means first adjusting the foreign currency cash flows for inflation and then converting the projected cash flows back into dollars using the forecast exchange rate.

Exchange rate changes and inflation can be analyzed separately when estimating a foreign project's cash flows.

ILLUSTRATION: Factoring in Currency Depreciation and Inflation

Suppose that with no inflation the cash flow in year 2 of a new project in France is expected to be FF 1 million, and the exchange rate is expected to remain at its current value of FF 1 = $0.20. Converted into dollars, the FF 1 million cash flow yields a projected cash flow of $200,000. Now suppose that French inflation is expected to be 6% annually, but project cash flows are expected to rise only 4% annually because the depreciation tax shield will remain constant. At the same time, because of purchasing power parity, the franc is expected to devalue at the rate of 6% annually—giving rise to a forecast exchange rate in year 2 of $0.20 \times (1 - 0.06)^2 = \$0.1767$. Then the forecast cash flow in year 2 becomes FF $1,000,000 \times 1.04^2 = $ FF 1,081,600, with a forecast dollar value of $191,119 ($0.1767 \times 1,081,600$).

18.3 FOREIGN PROJECT APPRAISAL: THE CASE OF INTERNATIONAL DIESEL CORPORATION

This section illustrates how to deal with some of the complexities involved in foreign project analysis by considering the case of a U.S. firm with an investment opportunity in England. International Diesel Corporation (IDC-U.S.), a U.S.-based multinational firm, is trying to decide whether to establish a diesel manufacturing plant in the United Kingdom (IDC-U.K.). IDC-U.S. expects to significantly boost its European sales of small diesel engines (40–160 hp) from the 20,000 it is currently exporting there. At the moment, IDC-U.S. is unable to increase exports because its domestic plants are producing to capacity. The 20,000 diesel engines it is currently shipping to Europe are the residual output that it is not selling domestically.

IDC-U.S. has made a strategic decision to significantly increase its presence and sales overseas. A logical first target of this international expansion is the European Community (EC). Market growth seems assured by recent large increases in fuel costs, and the advent of Europe 1992. IDC-U.S. executives believe that manufacturing in England will give the firm a key advantage with customers both in England and throughout the rest of the EC.

England is the most likely production location because IDC-U.S. can acquire a 1.4-million-square-foot plant in Manchester from BL, which used it to assemble gasoline engines before its recent closing. As an inducement to locate in this vacant plant and, thereby, ease unemployment among auto workers in Manchester, the National Enterprise Board (NEB) will provide a five-year loan of £5 million ($10 million) at 3% interest, with interest paid annually at the end of each year and the principal to be repaid in a lump sum at the end of the fifth year. Total acquisition, equipment, and retooling costs for this plant are estimated to equal $50 million.

Full-scale production can begin six months from the date of acquisition because IDC-U.S. is reasonably certain it can hire BL's plant manager and about 100 other former employees. In addition, conversion of the plant from producing gasoline engines to producing diesel engines should be relatively simple.

The parent will charge IDC-U.K. licensing and overhead allocation fees equal to 7% of sales in pounds sterling. In addition, IDC-U.S. will sell its English affiliate valves, piston rings, and other components that account for approximately 30% of the total amount of materials used in the manufacturing process. IDC-U.K. will be billed in dollars at the current market price for this material. The remainder will be purchased locally. IDC-U.S. estimates that its all-equity nominal required rate of return for the project will equal 12%, based on an anticipated 3% U.S. rate of inflation and the business risks associated with this venture. The debt capacity of such a project is judged to be about 20%—that is, a debt/equity ratio for this project of about 1:4 is considered reasonable.

To simplify its investment analysis, IDC-U.S. uses a five-year capital budgeting horizon and then calculates a terminal value for the remaining life of the project. If the project has a positive net present value for the first five years, there is no need to engage in costly and uncertain estimates of future cash flows. If the initial net present value is negative, then IDC-U.S. can calculate a break-even terminal value at which the net present value will just be positive. This break-even value is then used as a bench mark against which to measure projected cash flows beyond the first five years.

We now apply the three-stage investment analysis outlined in Section 18.2: (1) Estimate project cash flows; (2) forecast the amounts and timing of cash flows to the parent; and (3) add to, or subtract from, these parent cash flows the indirect benefits or costs that this project provides the remainder of the multinational firm.

Estimation of Project Cash Flows

A principal cash outflow associated with the project is the initial investment outlay, consisting of the plant purchase, equipment expenditures, and working-capital requirements. Other cash outflows include operating expenses, later additions to working capital as sales expand, and taxes paid on its net income.

IDC-U.K. has cash inflows from its sales in England and other EC countries. It also has cash inflows from three other sources:

— The tax shield provided by depreciation and interest charges
— Interest subsidies
— The terminal value of its investment, net of any capital gains taxes owed upon liquidation

Recapture of working capital is not assumed until eventual liquidation because this working capital is necessary to maintain an ongoing operation after the fifth year.

Initial Investment Outlay. Total plant acquisition, conversion, and equipment costs for IDC-U.K. were previously estimated at $50 million. The plant and equipment will be depreciated on a straight-line basis over a five-year period, with a zero salvage value.

Of the $50 million in net plant and equipment costs, $10 million will be financed by NEB's loan of £5 million at 3%. The remaining $40 million will be supplied by the parent in the form of equity capital.

Working-capital requirements—comprising cash, accounts receivable, and inventory—are estimated at 30% of sales, but this amount will be partially offset by accounts payable to local firms, which are expected to average 10% of sales. Therefore, net investment in working capital will equal approximately 20% of sales. The transfer price on the material sold to IDC-U.K. by its parent includes a 25% contribution to IDC-U.S.'s profit and overhead. That is, the variable cost of production equals 75% of the transfer price. Lloyds Bank is providing an initial working-capital loan of £1.5 million ($3 million). All future working-capital needs will be financed out of internal cash flow. Exhibit 18.1 summarizes the initial investment.

Financing IDC-U.K. Based on the information just provided, IDC-U.K.'s initial balance sheet, both in pounds and dollars, is presented in Exhibit 18.2. The debt ratio (debt/total assets) for IDC-U.K. is 5/25, or 20%. Note that this debt ratio could vary all the way up to 100%, if the parent provided all of its $40 million investment for plant and equipment as debt. In other words, an affiliate's capital structure is not independent; rather, it is a function of its parent's investment policies. (Chapter 23 elaborates on subsidiary capital structure.)

As discussed in the previous section (see Equation 18.2), the tax shield benefits of interest write-offs are represented separately. Assume that IDC-U.K. contributes $10.6 million to its parent's debt capacity (0.2 × $53 million), the dollar market rate of interest for IDC-U.K. is 8%, and the U.K. tax rate is 40%. This calculation translates into a cash flow in the first and subsequent years equal to $10,600,000 × 0.08 × 0.40, or $339,000. Discounted at 8%, this cash flow provides a benefit equal to $1.4 million over the next five years.

Interest Subsidies. Based on a 5% anticipated rate of inflation in England and on an expected annual 2% depreciation of the pound relative to the dollar, the market rate on the pound loan to IDC-U.K. would equal about 10%. Thus, the 3% interest rate on the loan by the National Enterprise Board represents a 7% subsidy to IDC-U.K. The cash value of this subsidy equals £350,000 (£5,000,000 × 0.07), or approximately $700,000 annually for the next five years, with a present value of $2.6 million.[2]

Exhibit 18.1 Initial Investment Outlay in IDC-U.K. (£1 = $2)

	£ (Millions)	$ (Millions)
Plant purchase and retooling expense	17.5	35
Equipment	7.5	15
Working capital	1.5	3
Total initial investment	£26.5	$53

[2]The exact present value of this subsidy is given by the difference between the present value of debt service on the 3% loan discounted at 10% and the face value of the loan.

Exhibit 18.2 Initial Balance Sheet of IDC-U.K. (£1 = $2)

	£ (Millions)	$ (Millions)
Assets		
Current assets	1.5	3
Plant and equipment	25	50
Total assets	26.5	53
Liabilities		
Loan payable (to Lloyds)	1.5	3
Total current liabilities	1.5	3
Loan payable (to NEB)	5	10
Total liabilities	6.5	13
Equity	20	40
Total liabilities plus equity	£26.5	$53

Sales and Revenue Forecasts.   At a profit-maximizing price of £250 per unit in the first year ($490 at the projected year 1 exchange rate), demand for diesel engines in England and the other Common Market countries is expected to increase by 10% annually, from 60,000 units in the first year to 88,000 units in the fifth year. It is assumed here that purchasing power parity holds with no lag and that real prices remain constant in both absolute and relative terms. Hence, the sequences of nominal pound prices and exchange rates, reflecting anticipated annual rates of inflation equaling 5% and 3% for the pound and dollar, respectively, are

			Year			
	0	*1*	*2*	*3*	*4*	*5*
Price (pounds)	—	250	278	308	342	380
Exchange rate (dollars)	2.00	1.96	1.92	1.89	1.85	1.82

It is also assumed here that purchasing power parity holds with respect to the currencies of the various EC countries to which IDC-U.K. exports. These exports account for about 60% of total IDC-U.K. sales. Disequilibrium conditions in the currency markets or relative price changes can be dealt with using an approach similar to that taken in the exposure measurement example (Spectrum Manufacturing) in Chapter 10.

In the first year, although demand is at 60,000 units, IDC-U.K. can produce and supply the market with only 30,000 units (due to the six-month start-up period). Another 20,000 units are exported by IDC-U.S. to its English affiliate at a unit transfer price of £250, leading to no profit for IDC-U.K. Since these units would have been exported anyway, IDC-U.K. is not credited from a capital budgeting standpoint with any profits on these sales. IDC-U.S. ceases its exports of finished products to England and the EC after the first year. From year 2 on, IDC-U.S. is counting on an expanding U.S. market to absorb the 20,000 units. Based on these assumptions, IDC-U.K.'s projected sales revenues are shown in Exhibit 18.3, line C.

Exhibit 18.3 Present Value of IDC-U.K.: Project Viewpoint

				Year			
	0	*1*	*2*	*3*	*4*	*5*	*5+*
A. Sales (units)		30,000	66,000	73,000	80,000	88,000	
B. Price per unit (£)		250.0	263.0	276.0	289.0	304.0	
C. Sales revenue (£ millions)		7.5	17.3	20.1	23.2	26.7	
D. Variable cost per unit (£)		140.0	147.0	154.0	162.0	170.0	
E. Total variable cost (£ millions)		4.2	9.7	11.3	13.0	15.0	
F. Licensing fees and royalties ($0.07 \times$ line C, in £ millions)		0.5	1.2	1.4	1.6	1.9	
G. Overhead expenses		0.6*	1.2	1.3	1.4	1.5	
H. Depreciation (£ millions)		5.0	5.0	5.0	5.0	5.0	
I. Total expenses (E + F + G + H, in £ millions)		10.3	17.1	19.0	21.0	23.3	
J. Profit before tax (C – I, in £ millions)		(2.8)	0.2	1.2	2.2	3.4	
K. U.K. corporate income taxes @ 40% = $0.40 \times$ J**		0.0	0.0	0.0	0.3	1.4	
L. Net profit after tax (J – K, in £ millions)		(2.8)	0.2	1.2	1.9	2.0	
M. Terminal value for IDC-U.K. [$3 \times$ (L + H), for year 5, in £ millions)							21.1
N. Initial investment, including working capital (£ millions)	(26.5)						
O. Working capital investment at 20% of revenue ($0.2 \times$ C, in £ millions)		1.5	3.5	4.0	4.6	5.3	
P. Required addition to working capital (line O for year t – line O for year t –1; $t = 2,...,5$, in £ millions)		0.0	2.0	0.6	0.6	0.7	
Q. IDC-U.K. net cash flow (L + H + M – N – P, in £ millions)	(26.5)	2.2	3.3	5.6	6.3	6.3	21.1
R. £ exchange rate ($)	$2.00	$1.96	$1.92	$1.89	$1.85	$1.82	$1.82
S. IDC-U.K. cash flow (Q $\times$ R, in $ millions)	(53.0)	4.3	6.3	10.6	11.6	11.5	38.4
T. Present value factor at 12%	1.0	0.8929	0.7972	0.7118	0.6255	0.5674	0.5066
U. Present value (S $\times$ T, in $ millions)	(53.0)	3.8	5.0	7.5	7.4	6.5	19.4
V. Cumulative present value ($ millions)	$(53.0)	$(49.2)	$(44.2)	$(36.7)	$(29.3)	$(22.8)	$(3.4)

*Represents overhead for less than one full year.
**Loss carryforward from year 1 of £2.8 eliminates tax for years 2 and 3 and reduces tax for year 4.

In nominal terms, IDC-U.K.'s pound sales revenues are projected to rise at a rate of 15.5% annually, based on a combination of the 10% annual increase in unit demand and the 5% annual increase in unit price (1.10 × 1.05 = 1.155). Dollar revenues will increase at about 13% annually, due to the anticipated 2% annual pound devaluation.

Production Cost Estimates. Based on the assumption of constant relative prices and purchasing power parity holding continually, variable costs of production, stated in real terms, are expected to remain constant, whether denominated in pounds or dollars. Hence, the pound prices of both labor and material sourced in England and components imported from the United States are assumed to increase by 11% annually. Unit variable costs in the first year are expected to equal £140, including £30 ($60) in components purchased from IDC-U.S.

In addition, the license fees and overhead allocations, which are set at 7% of sales, will rise at an annual rate of 15.5% because pound revenues are rising at that rate. With a full year of operation, initial overhead expenses would be expected to equal £1,100,000. Actual overhead expenses incurred, however, are only £600,000 because the plant does not begin operation until midyear. Since these expenses are partially fixed, their rate of increase should be about 8% annually.

The plant and equipment, valued at £25 million, can be written off over five years, yielding an annual depreciation charge against income of £5 million. The cash flow associated with this tax shield remains constant in nominal pound terms but declines in nominal dollar value by 2% annually. With a 3% rate of U.S. inflation, its real value is, therefore, reduced by 5% annually, the same as its loss in real pound terms.

Annual production costs for IDC-U.K. are estimated in Exhibit 18.3., lines D–I. It should be realized, of course, that some of these expenses are, like depreciation, a noncash charge or, like licensing fees, a benefit to the overall corporation.

Total production costs rise less rapidly each year than the 15.5% annual increase in nominal revenue. This situation is due both to the fixed depreciation charge and to the semifixed nature of overhead expenses. Thus, the profit margin should increase over time.

Projected Net Income. Net income for years 1 through 5 is estimated on line L of Exhibit 18.3. The effective tax rate on corporate income faced by IDC-U.K. in England is estimated to be 40%. The £2.8 million loss in the first year is applied against income in years 2, 3, and 4, reducing corporate taxes owed in these years.

Additions to Working Capital. One of the major outlays for any new project is the investment in working capital. IDC-U.K. begins with an initial investment in working capital of £1.5 million ($3 million). Working-capital requirements are projected at a constant 20% of sales. Thus, the necessary investment in working capital will increase by 15.5% annually, the rate of increase in pound sales revenue. These calculations are shown on lines O and P of Exhibit 18.3.

Terminal Value. Calculating a terminal value is a complex undertaking, given the various possible ways to treat this issue. Three different approaches are pointed out. One approach is to assume the investment will be liquidated after the end of the planning horizon and to use this value. However, this approach just takes the question one step further: What would a prospective buyer be willing to pay for this project? The second approach is to estimate the market value of the project, assuming that it is the present value of remaining cash flows. Again, though, the value of the project to an outside buyer may differ from its value to the parent firm, due to parent profits on sales to its affiliate, for instance. The third approach is to calculate a break-even terminal value at which the project is just acceptable to the parent, and then use that as a bench mark against which to judge the likelihood of the present value of future cash flows exceeding that value.

Most firms try to be quite conservative in estimating terminal values. IDC-U.K. calculates a terminal value based on the assumption that the market value of the project will be three times the net cash flow in year 5 (net income plus depreciation), or £21.1 million.

Estimated Project Present Value. We are now ready to estimate the net present value of IDC-U.K. from the viewpoint of the project. As shown in Exhibit 18.3, line V, the NPV of project cash flows equals –$3.4 million. Adding to this amount the $2.6 million value of interest subsidies and the $1.4 million present value of the tax shield on interest payments yields an overall positive project net present value of $0.6 million. The estimated value of the interest tax shield would be correspondingly greater if this analysis were to incorporate benefits derived over the full ten-year assumed life of the project, rather than including benefits from the first five years only. Over ten years, the present value of the tax shield would equal $2.4 million, bringing the overall project net present value to $1.6 million. The latter approach is the conceptually correct one.

Despite the favorable net present value for IDC-U.K., it is unlikely a firm would undertake an investment that had a positive value only because of interest subsidies or the interest tax shield provided by the debt capacity of the project. However, this is exactly what most firms do if they accept a marginal project, using a weighted cost of capital. Based on the debt capacity of the project and its subsidized financing, IDC-U.K. would have a weighted cost of capital of approximately 10%. At this discount rate, IDC-U.K. would be marginally profitable.

It would be misleading, however, to conclude the analysis at this point without recognizing and accounting for differences between project and parent cash flows and their impact on the worth of investing in IDC-U.K. Ultimately, shareholders in IDC-U.S. will benefit from this investment only to the extent that it generates cash flows that are, or can be, transferred out of England. The value of this investment is now calculated from the viewpoint of IDC-U.S.

Estimation of Parent Cash Flows

From the parent's perspective, additional cash outflows are recorded for any taxes paid to England or the United States on remitted funds. IDC-U.S. has additional cash inflows as well. It receives licensing and overhead allocation fees each year for which it incurs no additional expenses. If it did, the expenses would have to be charged against the fees. IDC-U.S. also profits from exports to its English affiliate.

Loan Payments. IDC-U.K. will first make all necessary loan repayments before paying dividends. Specifically, IDC-U.K. will repay the £1.5 million working-capital loan from Lloyds at the end of year 2 and NEB's loan of £5 million at the end of the fifth year. Their dollar repayment costs are estimated at $2.9 million and $9.3 million, respectively, based on the forecasted exchange rates. These latter two loan repayments are counted as parent cash inflows because they reduce the parent's outstanding consolidated debt burden and increase the value of its equity by an equivalent amount. Assuming that the parent would repay these loans regardless, having IDC-U.K. borrow and repay funds is equivalent to IDC-U.S. borrowing the money, investing it in IDC-U.K., and then using IDC-U.K.'s higher cash flows (because it no longer has British loans to service) to repay IDC-U.S.'s debts.

Remittances to IDC-U.S. IDC-U.K. is projected to pay dividends equal to 100% of its remaining net cash flows after making all necessary loan repayments. It also pays licensing and overhead allocation fees equal, in total, to 7% of gross sales. On both these forms of transfer, the English government will collect a 10% withholding tax. These remittances are shown in Exhibit 18.4. IDC-U.S., however, will not owe any further tax to the IRS because the company is assumed to have excess foreign tax credits. Otherwise, IDC-U.S. would have to pay U.S. corporate income taxes on the dividends and fees it receives, less any credits for foreign income and withholding taxes already paid. In this case, IDC-U.K. losses in the first year, combined with the higher British corporate tax rate will assure that IDC-U.S.

Exhibit 18.4 Dividends and Fees and Royalties Received by IDC-U.S. (U.S.$ Millions)

	Year					
	1	2	3	4	5	5+
A. Net cash flow to IDC-U.K. (from Exhibit 18.3, line S)	$4.3	6.3	10.6	11.6	11.5	38.4
B. Loan repayments by IDC-U.K.		2.9			9.3	
C. Dividend paid to IDC-U.S. (A – B)	4.3	3.3	10.6	11.6	2.2	38.4
D. Fees and royalties (Exhibit 18.3, line F × line G)	1.0	2.3	2.7	3.0	3.4	15.5*
E. Witholding tax paid to England @ 10% = .10 × (C + D)	0.5	0.6	1.3	1.5	0.6	5.4
F. Net income received by IDC-U.S. (C + D – E, in $ millions)	$4.8	$5.1	$11.9	$13.1	$5.1	$48.5
G. Exchange rate	$1.96	$1.92	$1.89	$ 1.85	$1.82	$1.82

*Estimated present value of future fees and royalties. These were not incorporated in the terminal value figure of $38.4 million.

would owe minimal taxes to the IRS even if it did not have any excess foreign tax credits.

Earnings on Exports to IDC-U.K. With a 25% margin on its exports, and assuming it has sufficient spare-parts manufacturing capacity, IDC-U.S. has incremental earnings on sales to IDC-U.K. equaling 25% of the value of these shipments. After U.S. corporate tax of 34%, IDC-U.S. generates cash flows valued at 16.5% (25% × 66%) of its exports to IDC-U.K. These cash flows are presented in Exhibit 18.5.

Estimated Present Value of Project to IDC-U.S. In Exhibit 18.6, all the various cash flows are added up, net of tax and interest subsidies on debt; and their present value is calculated at $7.3 million. Adding the $4 million in debt-related subsidies ($1.4 million for the interest tax shield and $2.6 million for the NEB loan subsidy) brings this value up to $11.3 million. It is apparent that, despite the additional taxes that must be paid to England and the United States, IDC-U.K. is more valuable to its parent than it would be to another owner on a stand-alone basis. This situation is primarily due to the various licensing and overhead allocation fees received and the incremental earnings on exports to IDC-U.K.

Lost Sales. There is a circumstance, however, that can reverse this conclusion. This discussion has assumed that IDC-U.S. is now producing at capacity and that the 20,000 diesels currently being exported to the EC can be sold in the United States, starting in year 2. Should this assumption not be the case (that is, should 20,000 units of IDC-U.K. sales just replace 20,000 units of IDC-U.S. sales), then the project would have to be charged with the incremental cash flow that IDC-U.S. would have earned on these lost exports. We now see how to incorporate this effect in a capital-budgeting analysis.

Suppose the incremental after-tax cash flow per unit to IDC-U.S. on its exports to the EC equals $180 at present and that this contribution is expected to

Exhibit 18.5 Net Cash Flows from Exports to IDC-U.K.

		Year				
	1	*2*	*3*	*4*	*5*	*5+*
A. Sales (units)	30,000	66,000	73,000	80,000	88,000	88,000
B. Components purchased from IDC-U.S.						
1. Unit price	60	61.8	63.7	65.6	67.5	67.5
2. Total export revenue (A × B1 in $ millions)	1.8	4.1	4.6	5.2	5.9	5.9
C. After-tax cash flow (0.165 × B2 in $ millions)	$0.3	$0.7	$0.8	$0.9	$1.0	$1.0

Exhibit 18.6 Present Value of IDC-U.K.: Parent Viewpoint ($ Millions)

				Year			
	0	1	2	3	4	5	5+
A. Cash inflows							
1. Loan repayments (from (Exhibit 18.4, line B)			2.9			9.3	
2. Dividends paid to IDC-U.S. (from Exhibit 18.4, line C)		4.3	3.3	10.6	11.6	2.2	38.4
3. Fees and royalties paid to IDC-U.S. (from Exhibit 18.4, line D)		1.0	2.3	2.7	3.0	3.4	15.5
4. Net cash flows from exports (from Exhibit 18.5, line C)		0.3	0.7	0.8	0.9	1.0	4.1*
5. Total cash inflows		5.6	6.3	14.0	15.4	6.6	58.0
B. Cash outflows							
1. Plant and equipment	50						
2. Working capital	3						
3. Withholding tax paid to U.K. (from Exhibit 18.4, line E)		0.5	0.6	1.3	1.5	0.6	5.4
4. Total cash outflows	53	0.5	0.6	1.3	1.5	0.6	5.4
C. Net cash flow (A5 − B4)	53	5.1	5.8	12.7	14.0	6.0	52.6
D. Present value factor at 12%	1.0	0.8929	0.7972	0.7118	0.6355	0.5674	0.5674
E. Present value (C × D)	$(53)	4.5	4.6	9.0	8.9	3.4	29.8
F. Cumulative present value $ millions	$(53)	$(48.5)	$(43.9)	$(34.9)	$(26.0)	$(22.5)	$7.3

*Estimated present value of future earnings on export sales to IDC-U.K.

maintain its value in current dollar terms over time. Then, in nominal dollar terms, this margin grows by 8% annually. Assuming lost sales of 20,000 units per year, beginning in year 2 and extending through year 10, and a discount rate of 12%, the present value associated with these lost sales equals $19.5 million. The calculations are presented in Exhibit 18.7. Subtracting the present value of lost sales from the previously calculated present value of $11.3 million yields a net present value of IDC-U.K. to its parent equal to –$8.2 million (–$12.2 million ignoring the interest tax shield and subsidy).

This example points up the importance of looking at incremental cash flows generated by a foreign project, rather than total cash flows. An investment that would be marginally profitable on its own, and quite profitable when integrated with parent activities, becomes unprofitable when taking into account earnings on lost sales.

Exhibit 18.7 Value of Lost Export Sales

	Year								
	2	3	4	5	6	7	8	9	10
A. Lost unit sales	20,000	20,000	20,000	20,000	20,000	20,000	20,000	20,000	20,000
B. Cash flow per unit*	185.4	191.0	196.7	202.6	208.7	214.9	221.4	228.0	234.9
C. Total cash flow from exports (A × B)	3.7	3.8	3.9	4.1	4.2	4.3	4.4	4.6	4.7
D. Present value factor at 12%	0.7972	0.7118	0.6355	0.5674	0.5066	0.4523	0.4039	0.3606	0.3220
E. Present value (C × D)	3.0	2.7	2.5	2.5	2.1	1.9	1.8	1.6	1.5
F. Cumulative present value	$ 3.0	$ 5.7	$ 8.2	$ 8.2	$12.6	$14.5	$16.3	$18.0	$19.5

*The figures in this row grow by 3% each year. So, 185.4 = 180(1.03), and so on.

18.4 POLITICAL RISK ANALYSIS

It is apparent from the figures in Exhibit 18.5 that IDC-U.S.'s English investment is quite sensitive to the potential political risks of currency controls and expropriation. The net present value of the project does not turn positive until well after its fifth year of operation (assuming there are no lost sales). Should expropriation occur or exchange controls be imposed at some point during the first five years, it is unlikely that the project will ever be viable from the parent's standpoint. Only if compensation is sufficiently great in the event of expropriation, or if unremitted funds can earn a return reflecting their opportunity cost to IDC-U.S. with eventual repatriation in the event of exchange controls, can this project still be viable in the face of these risks.

Political risks can be incorporated into an NPV analysis by adjusting expected project cash flows to reflect these risks.

The general approach recommended previously for incorporating political risk in an investment analysis usually involves adjusting the cash flows of the project (rather than its required rate of return) to reflect the impact of a particular political event on the present value of the project to the parent. This section shows how these cash flow adjustments can be made for the cases of expropriation and exchange controls.

Expropriation

The extreme form of political risk is *expropriation*. Expropriation is an obvious case where project and parent company cash flows diverge. The approach suggested here examines directly the impact of expropriation on the present value of the project to the parent. In this section, we examine the technique of adjusting expected cash flows to show how expropriation and currency controls affect the value of specific projects.

ILLUSTRATION: United Fruit Company Calculates the Consequences of Expropriation

Suppose that United Fruit Company (UFC) is worried that its banana plantation in Honduras will be expropriated during the next 12 months.[3] The Honduran government has promised, however, that compensation of $100 million will be paid at the year's end if the plantation is expropriated. UFC believes that this promise would be kept. If expropriation does not occur this year, it will not occur anytime in the foreseeable future. The plantation is expected to be worth $300 million at the end of the year. A wealthy Honduran has just offered UFC $128 million for the plantation. If UFC's risk-adjusted discount rate is 22%, what is the probability of expropriation at which UFC is just indifferent between selling now or holding onto its plantation?

Exhibit 18.8 displays UFC's two choices and their consequences. If UFC sells out now, it will receive $128 million today. Alternatively, if it chooses to hold onto the plantation, its property will be worth $300 million if expropriation doesn't occur and worth only $100 million in the event the Honduran government expropriates its plantation and compensates UFC. If the probability of expropriation is p, then the expected end-of-year value of the plantation to UFC (in millions of dollars) is $100p + 300(1 - p) = 300 - 200p$. The present value of the amount, using UFC's discount rate of 22%, is $(300 - 200p)/1.22$. Setting this equal to the $128 million offer by the wealthy Honduran yields a value of $p = 72\%$. In other words, if the probability of expropriation is at least 72%, UFC should sell out now for $128 million. If the probability of expropriation is less than 72%, it would be more worthwhile for UFC to hold on to its plantation.

Blocked Funds

The same method of adjusting expected cash flows can be used to analyze the effects of various exchange controls. In discussing *blocked funds*, it must be pointed out that if all funds are expected to be blocked in perpetuity, then the value of the project is zero.

Exhibit 18.8 United Fruit Company's Choices (U.S. $ Millions)

	Expropriation	*No Expropriation*	*Expected Present Value*
Sell out now	128	128	128
Wait	100	300	$[100p + 300(1 - p)]/1.22$

[3]Illustration suggested by Richard Roll.

ILLUSTRATION: *Brascan Calculates the Consequences of Currency Controls*

On January 1, 1981, the Indonesian electrical authority expropriated a power-generating station owned by Brascan, Inc., a Canadian operator of foreign electric facilities.[4] In compensation, a perpetuity of C$50 million will be paid annually at the end of each year. Brascan believes, however, that the Indonesian Central Bank may block currency repatriations during the calendar year 1983, allowing only 75% of each year's payment to be repatriated (and no repatriation of reinvestments from the other 25%). Assuming a cost of capital of 20% and a probability of currency blockage of 40%, what is the current value (on January 1, 1981) of Indonesia's compensation?

Exhibit 18.9 displays the two possibilities and their consequences for the cash flows Brascan expects to receive. If currency controls are not imposed, Brascan will receive C$50 million annually, with the first payment due December 31, 1981. The present value of this stream of cash equals C$250 million (50/0.2). Alternatively, if controls are imposed, Brascan will receive C$50 million at the end of the first two years and C$37.5 million (50 × 0.75) on each December 31 thereafter. The present value of these cash flows is C$206.6 million $[50/1.2 + 50/(1.2)^2 + (37.5/0.2)/(1.2)^2]$.[5] Weighting these present values by the probability that each will come to pass yields an expected present value (in millions of Canadian dollars) of 0.6 × 250 + 0.4 × 206.6 = C$232.6 million.

18.5 GROWTH OPTIONS AND PROJECT EVALUATION

The discounted cash flow (DCF) analysis presented so far treats a project's expected cash flows as given at the outset. This approach presupposes a static approach to investment decision making: It assumes that all operating decisions are set in advance. In reality, though, the opportunity to make decisions contin-

Exhibit 18.9 Cash Flows to Brascan (C$ Millions)

	Cash Flow at Year End		
	1981	*1982*	*1983 and On*
Currency controls	50.0	50.0	37.5
No currency controls	50.0	50.0	50.0

[4]Illustration suggested by Richard Roll.

[5]As of the end of year 2 the $37.5 million annuity beginning in year 3 has a present value equal to 37.5/0.2. The present value of this annuity as of today equals $[37.5/0.2]/(1.2)^2$.

gent on information to become available in the future is an essential feature of many investment decisions.

Consider the decision of whether to reopen a gold mine. The cost of doing so is expected to be $1 million. There are an estimated 40,000 ounces of gold remaining in the mine. If the mine is reopened, the gold can be removed in one year at a variable cost of $390 per ounce. Assuming an expected gold price in one year of $400/ounce, the expected profit per ounce mined is $10. Clearly, the expected cash inflow (ignoring taxes) of $400,000 next year ($10 × 40,000) is far below that necessary to recoup the $1 million investment in reopening the mine, much less to pay the 15% yield required on such a risky investment. But intuition—which suggests a highly negative project NPV of −$652,174 (−$1,000,000 + 400,000/1.15)—is wrong in this case. The reason is that the cash flow projections underlying the classical DCF analysis ignore the option *not* to produce gold if it is unprofitable to do so.

Here is a simple example that demonstrates the fallacy of always using expected cash flows to judge an investment's merits. Suppose there are only two possible gold prices next year: $300/ounce and $500/ounce, each with probability 0.5. The expected gold price is $400/ounce, but this expected price is irrelevant to the optimal mining decision rule: Mine gold if, and only if, the price of gold at year's end is $500/ounce. Exhibit 18.10 shows the cash flow consequences of that decision rule. Closure costs are assumed to be zero.

Incorporating the mine owner's option *not* to mine gold when the price falls below the cost of extraction reveals a positive net present value of $913,043 for the decision to reopen the gold mine:

$$\frac{\text{NPV of gold mine}}{\text{investment}} = \$1,000,000 + \frac{\$2,200,000}{1.15} = \$913,043$$

As the example of the gold mine demonstrates, the ability to alter decisions in response to new information may contribute significantly to the value of a

Ignoring the options associated with an investment will understate the NPV of that investment.

Exhibit 18.10 The Gold Mine Operating Decision

project. Such investments bear the characteristics of options on securities and should be valued accordingly. As we saw in the case of foreign exchange, a call option gives the holder the right, but not the obligation, to buy a security at a fixed, predetermined price (called the exercise price) on or before some fixed future date. By way of analogy, the opportunities a firm may have to invest capital to increase the profitability of its existing product lines and benefit from expanding into new products or markets may be thought of as *growth options*.[6] Similarly, a firm's ability to capitalize on its managerial talent, experience in a particular product line, its brand name, technology, or its other resources may provide valuable but uncertain future prospects.

Growth options are of great importance to multinational firms and require an expanded NPV rule.

Growth options are of great importance to multinational firms. Consider the value of IDC-U.K.'s production and market positions at the end of its planning horizon. IDC-U.S. may increase or decrease the diesel plant's output depending on current market conditions, expectations of future demand, and relative cost changes, such as those due to currency movements. The plant can be expanded; it can be shut down, then reopened when production and market conditions are more favorable; or it can be abandoned permanently. Each decision is an option from the viewpoint of IDC-U.S. The value of these options, in turn, affects the value of the investment in IDC-U.K.

Moreover, by producing locally, IDC-U.S. will have an enhanced market position in the EC that may enable the company to expand its product offerings at a later date. The ability to exploit this market position depends on the results of IDC-U.S.'s R&D efforts and the shifting pattern of demand for its products. In all these cases, the optimal operating policy depends on outcomes that are not known at the project's inception.

Similarly, the investments that many Western firms are now considering in Eastern Europe can also be thought of as growth options. Some view investments there as a way to gain entre into a potentially large market. Others see Eastern Europe as an underdeveloped area with educated and skilled workers but low wages and view such investments as a low-cost backdoor to Western European markets. In either case, companies who invest there are buying an option that will pay off in the event that Eastern European markets boom or that Eastern European workers turn out to be much more productive with the right technology and incentives than they have been under communism. By failing to take into account the benefits of operating flexibility and potentially valuable add-on projects, the traditional DCF will tend to understate project values.

The problem of undervaluing investment projects using the standard DCF analysis is particularly acute for strategic investments. Many strategically important investments, such as investments in R&D, factory automation, a brand name, or a distribution network, provide growth opportunities because they are often but the first link in a chain of subsequent investment decisions.

Valuing investments that embody discretionary follow-up projects requires an expanded net present value rule that considers the attendant options. More

---

[6]A good discussion of growth options is contained in W. Carl Kester, "Today's Options for Tomorrow's Growth," *Harvard Business Review*, March–April 1984, pp. 153–160.

specifically, the value of an option to undertake a follow-up project equals the expected project NPV using the conventional discounted cash-flow analysis plus the value of the discretion associated with undertaking the project. This relation is shown in Exhibit 18.11. Based on the discussion of currency options in Chapter 6, the latter element of value (the discretion to invest or not invest in a project) depends on the following.

1. *The length of time the project can be deferred*: The ability to defer a project gives the firm more time to examine the course of future events and to avoid costly errors if unfavorable developments occur. A longer time interval also raises the odds that a positive turn of events will dramatically boost the project's profitability and turn even a negative NPV project into a positive one.

2. *The risk of the project*: Surprisingly, the riskier the investment, the more valuable is an option on it. The reason is the asymmetry between gains and losses. A large gain is possible if the project's NPV becomes highly positive, whereas losses are limited by the option not to exercise when the project NPV is negative. The riskier the project, the greater the odds of a large gain without a corresponding increase in the size of the potential loss. Thus, growth options are likely to be especially valuable for MNCs because of the large potential variation in costs and the competitive environment.

Options on riskier projects are more valuable.

3. *The level of interest rates*: Although a high discount rate lowers the present value of a project's future cash flows, it also reduces the present value of the cash

Exhibit 18.11 Valuing a Growth Option to Undertake a Follow-Up Project

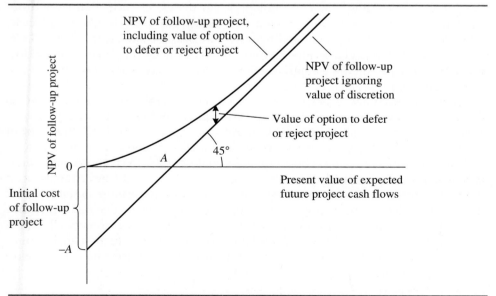

outlay needed to exercise an option. The net effect is that high interest rates generally raise the value of projects that contain growth options.

4. *The proprietary nature of the option*: An exclusively owned option is clearly more valuable than one that is shared with others. The latter might include the chance to enter a new market or to invest in a new production process. Shared options are less valuable because competitors can replicate the investments and drive down returns. For the multinational firm, though, most growth options arise out of its intangible assets. These assets, which take the form of skills, knowledge, brand names, and the like, are difficult to replicate and so are likely to be more valuable.

ILLUSTRATION: *Ford Gives Up on Small Car Development*

In late 1986, Ford gave up on small-car development in the United States and handed over the job to Japan's Mazda. Although seemingly cost effective in the short run (Ford should save about $500 million in development costs for one car model alone), such a move—which removed a critical mass from Ford's own engineering efforts—could prove dangerous in the longer term. Overcoming engineering obstacles unique to subcompact cars—for example, the challenges of miniaturization—enhances engineers' skills and allows them to apply innovations to all classes of vehicles. By eroding its technological base, Ford may have yielded the option of generating ideas that can be applied elsewhere in its business. Moreover, the cost of re-entering the business of in-house design can be substantial. The abandonment option is not one to be exercised lightly.

Some American consumer-electronics companies, for example, are learning the penalties of ceding major technologies and the experiences that come from working with these technologies on a day-to-day basis. Westinghouse Electric, after quitting the development and manufacture of color television tubes in 1976, recently decided to get back into the color-video business. But, because it had lost touch with the product, Westinghouse has been able to re-enter only by way of a joint venture with Japan's Toshiba.

Similarly, RCA and other U.S. manufacturers several years ago conceded to the Japanese development of videocassette recorders and laser video disk players. Each technology has since spawned entirely new, popular product lines—from video cameras to compact disk players—in which U.S. companies are left with nothing to do beyond marketing Japanese-made goods. Even those companies that merely turn to outside partners for technical help could nevertheless find their skills atrophying over the years as their partners handle more of the complex designing and manufacturing. Such companies range from Boeing, which has enlisted three Japanese firms to help engineer a new plane, to Honeywell, which is getting big computers from NEC. The corresponding reduction in in-house technological skills decreases the value of the option these firms have to develop and apply new technologies in novel product areas.

18.6 SUMMARY AND CONCLUSIONS

Capital budgeting for the multinational corporation presents many elements that rarely, if ever, exist in domestic capital budgeting. The primary thrust of this chapter has been to adjust project cash flows instead of the discount rate to reflect the key political and economic risks that MNCs face abroad. Tax factors are also incorporated via cash-flow adjustments. Cash-flow adjustments are preferred on the pragmatic grounds that there is available more and better information on the effect of such risks on future cash flows than on the required discount rate. Furthermore, adjusting the required rate of return of a project to reflect incremental risk does not usually allow for adequate consideration of the time pattern and magnitude of the risk being evaluated. Using a uniformly higher discount rate to reflect additional risk involves penalizing future cash flows relatively more heavily than present ones.

This chapter showed how these cash-flow adjustments can be carried out by presenting a lengthy numerical example. It also discussed the significant differences that can exist between project and parent cash flows and showed how these differences can be accounted for when estimating the value to the parent firm of a foreign investment. The chapter also pointed out that failure to take into account the options available to managers to adjust the scope of a project will lead to a downward bias in estimating project cash flows. These options include the possibility of expanding or contracting the project or abandoning it, the chance to employ radical new process technologies by utilizing skills developed from implementing the project, and the possibility of entering the new lines of business to which a project may lead.

QUESTIONS

1. A foreign project that is profitable when valued on its own will always be profitable from the parent firm's standpoint. True or false. Explain.

2. What are the principal cash outflows associated with the IDC-U.K. project?

3. What are the principal cash inflows associated with the IDC-U.K. project?

4. In what ways do parent and project cash flows differ on the IDC-U.K. project? Why?

5. Suppose the real value of the pound declines. How would this decline likely affect the economics of the IDC-U.K. project?

6. Describe the alternative ways to treat the interest subsidy provided by the British government.

7. Suppose England raised its corporate tax rate by one percentage point. How would this affect the economics of the IDC-U.K. project?

8. Why are IDC-U.S. earnings on exports to IDC-U.K. credited to the project?

9. Why are loan repayments by IDC-U.K. to Lloyds and NEB treated as a cash inflow to the parent company?

10. Under what circumstances should IDC-U.S. earnings on lost export sales to the United Kingdom and the rest of the EC countries be treated as a cost of the project?

11. Under what circumstances should these lost export earnings be ignored when evaluating the project?

12. How sensitive is the value of the project to the threat of currency controls and expropriation? How can the financing be structured so as to make the project less sensitive to these political risks?

13. What options does investment in the new British diesel plant provide to IDC-U.S.? How can these options be accounted for in the traditional capital budgeting analysis?

14. Early results on the Lexus, Toyota's upscale car, showed it was taking the most business from customers changing from either BMW (15%), Mercedes (14%), Toyota (14%), General Motors' Cadillac (12%), and Ford's Lincoln (6%). With what in the auto business is considered a high percentage of sales coming from its own customers, how badly is Toyota hurting itself with the Lexus?

15. Comment on the following statement that appeared in *The Economist* (August 20, 1988, p. 60): "Those oil producers that have snapped up overseas refineries—Kuwait, Venezuela, Libya and, most recently, Saudi Arabia—can feed the flabbiest of them with dollar-a-barrel crude and make a profit. . . . The majority of OPEC's existing overseas refineries would be scrapped without its own cheap oil to feed them. Both Western European refineries fed by Libyan oil (in West Germany and Italy) and Kuwait's two overseas refineries (in Holland and Denmark) would almost certainly be idle without it."

16. Some economists have stated that too many companies aren't calculating the cost of *not* investing in new technology, world-class manufacturing facilities, or market position overseas. What are some of these costs? How do these costs relate to the notion of growth options discussed in the chapter?

17. In December 1989, General Electric spent $150 million to buy a controlling interest in Tungsram, the Hungarian state-owned light bulb maker. Even in its best year, Tungsram earned less than a 4% return on equity (based on the price GE paid).

    a. What might account for GE's decision to spend so much money to acquire such a dilapidated, inefficient manufacturer?

    b. A Hungarian lighting worker earns about $170 a month in Hungary, compared with about $1,700 a month in the United States. Do these figures indicate that Tungsram will be a low-cost producer?

PROBLEMS

1. Suppose a firm projects a $5 million perpetuity from an investment of $20 million in Spain. If the required return on this investment is 20%, how large does the probability of expropriation in year 4 have to be before the investment has a negative NPV? Assume that all cash inflows occur at the end of each year and that the expropriation, if it occurs, will occur just prior to the year-4 cash inflow or not at all. There is no compensation in the event of expropriation.

2. Suppose a firm has just made an investment in France that will generate $2 million annually in depreciation, converted at today's spot rate. Projected annual rates of inflation in France and in the United States are 7% and 4%, respectively. If the real exchange rate is expected to remain constant and the French tax rate is 50%, what is the expected real value (in terms of today's dollars) of the depreciation charge in year 5, assuming that the tax write-off is taken at the end of the year?

3. Jim Toreson, chairman and CEO of Xebec Corporation, a Sunnyvale, California, manufacturer of disk-drive controllers, is trying to decide whether to switch to offshore production. Given Xebec's well-developed engineering and marketing capabilities, Toreson could use offshore manufacturing to ramp up production, taking full advantage of both low-wage labor and a grab bag of tax holidays, low-interest loans, and other government largess. Most of his competitors seem to be doing it. The faster he follows suit, the better off Xebec would be according to the conventional discounted cash-flow analysis, which showed that switching production offshore was clearly a positive NPV investment. However, Toreson is concerned that such a move would entail the loss of certain intangible strategic benefits associated with domestic production.

a. What might be some strategic benefits of domestic manufacturing for Xebec? Consider the fact that its customers are all U.S. firms and that manufacturing technology—particularly automation skills—is key to survival in this business.

b. What analytic framework can be used to factor these intangible strategic benefits of domestic manufacturing (which are intangible costs of offshore production) into the factory location decision?

c. How would the possibility of radical shifts in manufacturing technology affect the production location decision?

d. Xebec is considering producing more-sophisticated drives that require substantial customization. How does this possibility affect its production decision?

e. Suppose the Taiwan government is willing to provide a loan of $10 million at 5% to Xebec to build a factory there. The loan would be paid off in equal annual installments over a five-year period. If the market interest rate for such an investment is 14%, what is the before-tax value of the interest subsidy?

f. Projected before-tax income from the Taiwan plant is $1 million annually, beginning at the end of the first year. Taiwan's corporate tax rate is 25%, and there is a 20% dividend withholding tax. However, Taiwan will exempt the plant's income from corporate tax (but not withholding tax) for the first five years. If Xebec plans to remit all income as dividends back to the United States, how much is the tax holiday worth?

g. An alternative sourcing option is to shut down all domestic production and contract to have Xebec's products built for it by a foreign supplier in a country such as Japan. What are some of the potential advantages and disadvantages of foreign contracting vis-à-vis manufacturing in a wholly owned foreign subsidiary?

BIBLIOGRAPHY

Lessard, Donald R. "Evaluating Foreign Projects: An Adjusted Present Value Approach." In *International Financial Management*, 2nd. ed. Donald R. Lessard, ed. New York: John Wiley & Sons, 1985.

Shapiro, Alan C. "Capital Budgeting for the Multinational Corporation." *Financial Management*, Spring 1978, pp. 7–16.

———. "International Capital Budgeting." *Midland Journal of Corporate Finance*, Spring 1983, pp. 26–45.

19

The Cost of Capital for Foreign Investments

Traders and other undertakers may, no doubt, with great propriety, carry on a very considerable part of their projects with borrowed money. In justice to their creditors, however, their own capital ought to be, in this case, sufficient to ensure, if I may say so, the capital of those creditors; or to render it extremely improbable that those creditors should incur any loss, even though the success of the project should fall very short of the expectations of the projectors.

Adam Smith (1776)

CHAPTER LEARNING OBJECTIVES

- To determine the cost of capital for foreign investments and identify those circumstances under which that cost should be higher, lower, or the same as that for comparable domestic projects
- To identify the factors that determine the relevant market portfolio against which to estimate the foreign project beta
- To assess whether Japanese companies have a cost of capital advantage vis-à-vis U.S. companies

A central question for the multinational corporation is whether the required rate of return on foreign projects should be higher, lower, or the same as that for domestic projects. To answer this question, we must examine the issue of cost of capital for multinational firms, one of the most complex in international financial management. Yet, it is an issue that must be addressed because the foreign investment decision cannot be made properly without knowledge of the appropriate cost of capital.

In this chapter we will seek to determine the cost-of-capital figure(s) that should be used in appraising the profitability of foreign investments. By definition, the *cost of capital* for a given investment is the minimum risk-adjusted return required by shareholders of the firm for undertaking that investment. As such, it is the basic measure of financial performance.

Unless the investment generates sufficient funds to repay suppliers of capital, the firm's value will suffer. This return requirement is met only if the net present value of future project cash flows, using the project's cost of capital as the discount rate, is positive.

The development of appropriate cost-of-capital measures for multinational firms is closely bound up with how those measures will be used. Since they are to be used as discount rates to aid in the global resource allocation process, the rates must reflect the value to firms of engaging in specific activities. Thus, the emphasis here is on the cost of capital or required rate of return for a specific foreign project rather than for the firm as a whole. Unless the financial structures and commercial risks are similar for all projects engaged in, the use of a single overall cost of capital for project evaluation is incorrect. Different discount rates should be used to value projects that are expected to change the risk complexion of the firm.

19.1 THE COST OF EQUITY CAPITAL

The *cost of equity capital* for a firm is the minimum rate of return necessary to induce investors to buy or hold the firm's stock. This required return equals a basic yield covering the time value of money plus a premium for risk. Because owners of common stock have only a residual claim on corporate income, their risk is the greatest, and so also are the returns they demand.

Alternatively, the cost of equity capital is the rate used to capitalize total corporate cash flows. As such, it is just the weighted average of the required rates of return on the firm's individual activities. From this perspective, the corporation is a mutual fund of specified projects, selling a compound security to capital markets. According to the principle of value additivity, the value of this compound security equals the sum of the individual values of the projects.

Although both definitions are equivalent, the latter view is preferred from a conceptual standpoint because it focuses attention on the most important feature of the cost of equity capital; namely, that this cost is not an attribute of the firm per se, but is a function of the riskiness of the activities it engages in. Thus, the cost of equity capital for the firm as a whole can be used to value the stream of future equity cash flows—that is, to set a price on equity shares in the firm. It cannot be used as a measure of the required return on equity investments in future projects unless these projects are of a similar nature to the average of those already being undertaken by the firm.

A company's cost of equity capital varies with the riskiness of its activities.

One approach to determining the project-specific required return on equity is based on modern capital market theory. According to this theory, an equilibrium relationship exists between an asset's required return and its associated risk, which can be represented by the *capital asset pricing model* (CAPM):

$$r_i = r_f + \beta_i(r_m - r_f) \tag{19.1}$$

where r_i = equilibrium expected return for asset i

r_f = rate of return on a risk-free asset, usually measured as the yield on a 30-day U.S. government Treasury bill

r_m = expected return on the market portfolio consisting of all risky assets

$\beta_i = \text{cov}(r_i, r_m)/\sigma^2(r_m)$, where $\text{cov}(r_i, r_m)$ refers to the covariance between returns on security i and the market portfolio and $\sigma^2(r_m)$ is the variance of returns on the market portfolio

The capital asset pricing model is a widely used method for estimating a company's cost of capital.

The CAPM is based on the notion that intelligent risk-averse shareholders will seek to diversify their risks, and as a consequence, the only risk that will be rewarded with a risk premium will be systematic risk. As can be seen from Equation 19.1, the risk premium associated with a particular asset i is assumed to equal $\beta_i(r_m - r_f)$, where β_i is the *systematic* or *nondiversifiable* risk of the asset. In effect, measures the correlation between returns on a particular asset and returns on the market portfolio. The term $r_m - r_f$ is known as the *market risk premium*.

Where the returns and financial structure of an investment are expected to be similar to those of the firm's typical investment, the corporate-wide cost of equity capital may serve as a reasonable proxy for the required return on equity of the project. In this case, estimates of the value of the project's β can be found either by direct computation using the CAPM or through professional investment companies that keep track of company βs.

One check on the required return derived from the CAPM is to compare it with the cost of equity capital obtained from the dividend valuation model. According to this model,

$$P_0 = \frac{\text{DIV}_1}{k_e - g} \tag{19.2}$$

where k_e = company's cost of equity capital

DIV_1 = expected dividend in year 1

P_0 = current stock price

g = average expected annual dividend growth rate

From Equation 19.2, we can estimate the cost of equity capital as

$$k_e = \frac{\text{DIV}_1}{P_0} + g \tag{19.3}$$

The cost of capital for a project depends on the risk of that project.

It should be emphasized again that estimates of the required return on equity capital, using either of these methods, apply only at the corporate level or to investments with financial characteristics typical of the "pool" of projects represented by the corporation. These cost of equity capital estimates are useless in calculating project-specific required returns on equity when the characteristics of the project diverge from the corporate norm.

19.2 THE WEIGHTED COST OF CAPITAL FOR FOREIGN PROJECTS

As commonly used, the required return on equity for a particular investment assumes that the financial structure and risk of the project is similar to that for the firm as a whole. This cost of equity capital, k_e, is then combined with the after-tax cost of debt, $k_d(1 - t)$, to yield a *weighted cost of capital* (WACC) for the parent and the project, k_0, computed as

$$k_0 = (1 - L)k_e + Lk_d(1 - t) \tag{19.4}$$

The weighted average cost of capital is appropriate only if the financial structures and commercial risks are similar for all new investments.

where L is the parent's debt ratio (debt/total assets). This cost of capital is then used as the discount rate in evaluating the specific foreign investment. It should be stressed that k_e is the required return on the firm's stock given the particular debt ratio selected.

Two caveats in employing the weighted average cost of capital are appropriate here. First, the weights must be based on the proportion of the firm's capital structure accounted for by each source of capital using *market*, not *book*, values. Second, in calculating the WACC, the firm's historical debt-equity mix is not relevant. Rather, the weights must be marginal weights that reflect the firm's *target capital structure*, that is, the proportions of debt and equity the firm plans to use in the future.

ILLUSTRATION: *Estimating the Weighted Average Cost of Capital*

Suppose a company is financed with 60% common stock, 30% debt, and 10% preferred stock, with respective after-tax costs of 20%, 6%, and 14%. Based on the financing proportions and the after-tax costs of the various capital components, and employing Equation 19.4, the WACC for this firm is calculated as 15.2% (0.6 × 0.20 + 0.3 × 0.06 + 0.1 × 0.14). If the net present value of those cash flows—discounted at the weighted average cost of capital—is positive, the investment should be undertaken; if negative, the investment should be rejected.

19.3 THE ALL-EQUITY COST OF CAPITAL FOR FOREIGN PROJECTS

The various adjustments needed to go from the weighted average cost of capital for the firm to the weighted average cost of capital for the project makes it a somewhat awkward technique to use at times. An alternative (suggested in Chapter 18) is the use of an *all-equity discount rate*, k^*, that abstracts from the project's financial structure and that is based solely on the riskiness of the project's anticipated cash flows.

To calculate the all-equity rate, we rely on the CAPM introduced earlier in Equation 19.1:

$$k^* = r_f + \beta^*(r_m - r_f) \tag{19.5}$$

where β^* is the *all-equity beta*—that is, the beta associated with the unleveraged cash flows.

ILLUSTRATION: *Estimating a Foreign Project's Cost of Capital*

Suppose that a foreign project has a beta of 1.15, the risk-free return is 13%, and the required return on the market is estimated at 21%. Then based on Equation 19.7, the project's cost of capital is

$$k^* = 0.13 + 1.15(0.21 - 0.13) = 22.2\%$$

In reality, of course, the firm will not be able to estimate β^* with the degree of precision implied here. Instead, it will have to use guesswork based on theory. The considerations involved in the estimation process are discussed in the following section.

If the project is of similar risk to the average project selected by the firm, it is possible to estimate β^* by reference to the firm's stock price beta, β_e. In other words, β_e is the beta that appears in the estimate of the firm's cost of equity capital, k_e.

To transform β_e into β^*, we must separate out the effects of debt financing. This is known as *unlevering*, or converting a levered equity beta to its unlevered or all-equity value. Unlevering can be accomplished by using the following approximation:

$$\beta^* = \frac{\beta_e}{1 + (1 - t)D/E} \tag{19.6}$$

where t is the firm's marginal tax rate, and D/E is its current debt/equity ratio. Thus, for example, if a firm has a stock price beta of 1.1, a debt/equity ratio of 0.6, and a marginal tax rate of 34%, Equation 19.6 estimates its all-equity beta as 0.79 $[1.1/(1 + 0.66 \times 0.6)]$.

19.4 DISCOUNT RATES FOR FOREIGN INVESTMENTS

The importance of the CAPM for the international firm is that the relevant component of risk in pricing a firm's stock is its systematic risk—that is, that portion of return variability that cannot be eliminated through diversification. Evidence suggests that most of the economic and political risk faced by MNCs is unsystematic risk, which therefore can be eliminated through diversification on the level of the individual investor. While these risks may be quite large, they should not affect the discount rate to be used in valuing foreign projects.

On the other hand, much of the systematic or general market risk affecting a company, at least as measured using a domestic stock index such as the Standard and Poor's 500 or the New York Stock Exchange index, is related to the cyclical nature of the national economy in which the company is domiciled. Consequently, the returns on a project located in a foreign country whose economy is not perfectly synchronous with the home country's economy should be less highly correlated with domestic market returns than the returns on a comparable domestic project. If this is the case, then the systematic risk of a foreign project actually could be lower than the systematic risk of its domestic counterpart.

The relevant component of risk in estimating a foreign project's cost of capital is its systematic risk.

Paradoxically, it is the less developed countries (LDCs), where political risks are greatest, that are likely to provide the greatest diversification benefits. This is because the economies of LDCs are less closely tied to the United States, or to any other Western economy. By contrast, the correlation among the economic cycles of developed countries is considerably stronger, so the diversification benefits from investing in industrialized countries, from the standpoint of a Western investor are proportionately less.

It should be noted, however, that the systematic risk of projects even in relatively isolated LDCs is unlikely to be far below the average for all projects because these countries are still tied into the world economy. The important point about projects in LDCs, then, is that their ratio of systematic to total risk generally is quite low; their systematic risk, while perhaps slightly lower, is probably not significantly less than that of similar projects located in industrialized countries.

Even if a nation's economy is not closely linked to the world economy, the systematic risk of a project located in that country might still be rather large. For example, a foreign copper mining venture probably will face systematic risk very similar to that faced by an identical extractive project in the United States, whether the foreign project is located in Canada, Chile, or Zaire. The reason is that the major element of systematic risk in any extractive project is related to variations in the price of the mineral being extracted, which is set in a world market. The world market price in turn depends on worldwide demand, which itself is systematically related to the state of the world economy. By contrast, a market-oriented project in an LDC, whose risk depends largely on the evolution of the domestic market in that country, is likely to have a systematic risk that is small both in relative and absolute terms.

An example of the latter would be a Ford plant in Brazil whose profitability is closely linked to the state of the Brazilian economy. The systematic risk of the project, therefore, largely depends on the correlation between the Brazilian economy and the U.S. economy. While positive, this correlation is much less than one.

Thus, *corporate international diversification* should prove beneficial to shareholders, particularly where there are barriers to *international portfolio diversification*. To the extent that multinational firms are uniquely able to supply low-cost international diversification, investors may be willing to accept a lower rate of return on shares of MNCs than on shares of single-country firms. By extension, the risk premium applied to foreign projects may be lower than the risk premium for

Corporate international diversification should prove beneficial to shareholders.

domestic ones; that is, the required return on foreign projects may be less than the required return on comparable domestic projects. The net effect may be to enable MNCs to undertake overseas projects that would otherwise be unattractive.

But if international portfolio diversification can be accomplished as easily and as cheaply by individual investors, then although required rates of return on MNC securities would be lower to reflect the reduced covariability of MNC returns caused by international diversification, the discount rate would not be reduced further to reflect investors' willingness to pay a premium for the indirect diversification provided by the shares of MNCs. In fact, though, we saw in Chapter 16 that American investors actually undertake very little foreign portfolio investment. The lack of widespread international portfolio diversification has an important implication for estimating the beta coefficient.

Estimating Project Betas

A major issue when selecting a discount rate for foreign investments is the relevant market portfolio for estimating a project's beta coefficient. Is the relevant base portfolio against which beta is measured the domestic portfolio of the investor or the world market portfolio? Selecting the appropriate portfolio matters because a risk that is systematic in the context of the home country market portfolio may well be diversifiable in the context of the world portfolio. If this is the case, using the domestic market portfolio to calculate beta will result in a higher required return—and a less desirable project—than if beta were calculated using the world market portfolio.

The relevant market portfolio for estimating a project's beta is currently unknown.

The appropriate market portfolio to use in measuring a *project beta* depends on one's view of world capital markets. More precisely, it depends on whether or not capital markets are globally integrated. If they are, then the world portfolio is the correct choice; if they are not, the correct choice is the domestic portfolio. The test of capital market integration depends on whether these assets are priced in a common context; that is, capital markets are integrated to the extent that security prices offer all investors worldwide the same trade-off between systematic risk and real expected return.

The truth probably lies somewhere in between. Capital markets are now integrated to a great extent, and they can be expected to become ever more so with time.[1] However, because of various government regulations and other market imperfections, that integration is not complete. Unfortunately, it is not currently within our power, if indeed it ever will be, to empirically determine the relevant market portfolio and, hence, the correct beta to use in project evaluation. (This problem also arises domestically as well as internationally.)

---

[1]Evidence on the integration of national capital markets is supplied by K. C. Chan, G. Andrew Karolyi, and Rene M. Stulz, "Global Financial Markets and the Risk Premium on U.S. Equity," *Journal of Financial Economics*, October 1992, pp. 137–167; Chinhyung D. Cho, Cheol S. Eun, and Lemma W. Senbet, "International Arbitrage Pricing Theory: An Empirical Investigation," *Journal of Finance*, June 1986, pp. 313–330. Campbell R. Harvey, "The World Price of Covariance Risk," *Journal of Finance*, March 1991, pp. 111–157; and Simon Wheatley, "Some Tests of International Equity Integration" *Journal of Financial Economics* 21 (1988), pp. 177–212.

A pragmatic recommendation to American managers is to measure the betas of international projects against the U.S. market portfolio. This recommendation is based on the following two reasons:

1. It ensures comparability of foreign with domestic projects, which are evaluated using betas that are calculated relative to a U.S. market index.
2. The relatively minor amount of international diversification attempted (as yet) by American investors suggests that the relevant portfolio from their standpoint is the U.S. market portfolio.

This reasoning suggests that the required return on a foreign project may well be lower, and is unlikely to be higher, than the required return on a comparable domestic project. Thus, applying the same discount rate to an overseas project as to a similar domestic project probably will yield a conservative estimate of the relative systematic riskiness of the project.

A foreign project's systematic risk, and hence its cost of capital, is unlikely to be higher than that of a comparable domestic project.

Using the domestic cost of capital to evaluate overseas investments also is likely to understate the benefits that stem from the ability of foreign activities to reduce the firm's total risk. As we saw in Chapter 1, reducing total risk can increase a firm's cash flows. By confining itself to its domestic market, a firm would be sensitive to periodic downturns associated with the domestic business cycle and other industry-specific factors. By operating in a number of countries, the MNC can trade off negative swings in some countries against positive ones in others. This option is especially valuable for non-American firms, whose local markets are small relative to the efficient scale of operation.

Despite the apparent benefits of corporate international diversification for shareholders, however, research by Jacquillat and Solnik concluded that although multinational firms do provide some diversification for investors, they are poor substitutes for international portfolio diversification.[2] Their results indicate that an internationally diversified portfolio leads to a much greater reduction in variance than does one comprised of firms with internationally diversified activities. Thus, the advantages of international portfolio diversification remain.

19.5 COMPARING THE COST OF CAPITAL IN THE UNITED STATES AND JAPAN

According to conventional wisdom, U.S. companies have a much higher cost of capital than Japanese companies, up to twice as high. Many economists and business executives often cite these differences in the cost of capital to explain why Japanese companies outspend their U.S. competitors in plant modernization and research and development.[3] The argument is that capital in the United States is too expensive to justify huge investments in automated equipment, new facto-

[2]Bertrand Jacquillat and Bruno H. Solnik, "Multinationals Are Poor Tools for Diversification," *Journal of Portfolio Management,* Winter 1978, pp. 8–12.

[3]See, for example, the comments in Louis S. Richman, "How Capital Costs Are Crippling America," *Fortune,* August 14, 1989, pp. 50–54.

Japanese companies are said to have a lower cost of capital than their U.S. competitors.

ries, and cutting-edge research with longer-term payoffs. Conversely, Japanese companies with their lower cost of capital logically focus less on short-term profits and emphasize investments, even riskier ones, that are designed to promote the creation of dominant positions in the marketplace.

The evidence to support these contentions includes the historically higher U.S. interest rates, high debt ratios in Japan that allow Japanese companies to substitute cheap debt for equity, and sky-high Japanese price/earnings (P/E) ratios. However, there may be less here than meets the eye.

High U.S. Interest Rates

Although interest rates have historically been higher in the United States than in Japan, this difference is deceptive since it is based on nominal and not real interest rates. The differential largely disappears once allowance is made for inflation and taxes. One cost of capital study found that during the second half of the 1980s, real after-tax debt costs were virtually identical for the United States (1.85%), Japan (1.82%), and Britain (1.82%).[4] Exhibit 19.1 shows the convergence of real U.S. and Japanese interest rates over the period 1973-1989.

Exhibit 19.1 Japanese and U.S Government Bond Yields, 1973–1989

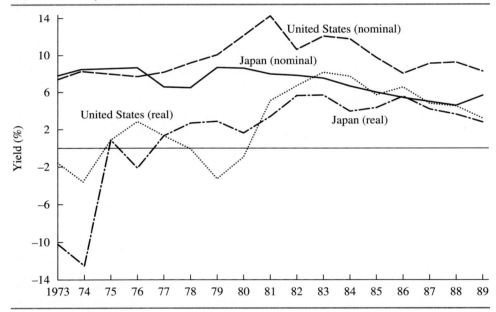

SOURCE: Based on Niso Abuaf and Kathleen Carmody, "The Cost of Capital in Japan and the United States: A Tale of Two Markets," Salamon Brothers, July 1990, p. 4.

[4]Robert N. McCauley and Steven A. Zimmer, "Explaining International Differences in the Cost of Capital," *FRBNY Quarterly Review,* Summer 1989, pp. 7–27.

The evidence provided by Exhibit 19.1 is consistent with the behavior of Japanese companies during the 1980s, when they raised over $125 billion overseas—behavior that would be inexplicable if more attractive terms were available at home. And, if yen debt was really less expensive than dollar debt, why would U.S. companies not borrow yen? Indeed, taking into account currency changes, dollars have been much less expensive to borrow than yen during the 1980s.

High Japanese Leverage

Many observers point to high Japanese leverage as another source of their capital cost advantage. Because the tax deductibility of interest makes debt cheaper than equity, Japanese companies are said to have a lower weighted average cost of capital. However, this conclusion suffers from three basic problems. First, the measurement of debt/equity (D/E) ratios is usually done with book values, instead of market values. Book values are especially tricky things to use for cross-country comparisons. Different accounting conventions and other practices distort them. For example, Japanese companies value land on their balance sheet at cost. The phenomenal rise in Tokyo property prices in recent years can mean that the market value is up to 100 times the book value, seriously understating the debt-to-equity ratios of Japanese companies on a replacement cost basis.

Japanese leverage is not as high as is often assumed.

Using market value weights, Japanese leverage has systematically fallen and U.S. leverage systematically risen during the past decade. Exhibit 19.2 illustrates this phenomenon with aggregate data for the period 1971-1989. By 1989, the U.S. D/E ratio had surpassed the Japanese ratio. Even though the plunge in the Tokyo Stock Exchange that began in 1990 has raised Japanese leverage on a market value basis, the trend is clearly moving in the opposite direction.[5]

Second, the measurement of leverage must adjust for the excess cash that many Japanese firms hold. According to Michael Jensen, "Many of Japan's public companies are flooded with free cash flow far in excess of their opportunities to invest in profitable internal growth. In 1987, more than 40% of Japan's large public companies had no net bank borrowings—that is, cash balances larger than their short- and long-term borrowings."[6] In addition, Japanese firms give banks "compensating balances" in the form of deposits in order to borrow from them. On average, a Japanese firm wanting to borrow ¥100 will have to borrow ¥160 and place ¥60 on deposit with its bank. This practice boosts the Japanese corporate sector's measured debt ratio while leaving unchanged its actual degree of financial risk.

Third, as pointed out earlier, the appropriate weights in the WACC must reflect the target capital structure, not historical figures. As Exhibit 19.2 shows,

---

[5]Two studies found that Japanese firms are no more highly levered than American firms when equity is valued at market instead of book. See Allen Michel and Israel Shaked, "Japanese Leverage: Myth or Reality," *Financial Analysts Journal,* Winter 1985, pp. 61–67; and Carl W. Kester, "Capital and Ownership Structure: A Comparison of United States and Japanese Manufacturing Corporations," *Financial management,* Spring 1986, pp. 17–24.

[6]Michael C. Jensen, "Eclipse of the Public Corporation," *Harvard Business Review,* September–October 1989, p. 73.

Exhibit 19.2 Japanese and U.S. Debt-to-Equity Ratios, 1971–1989

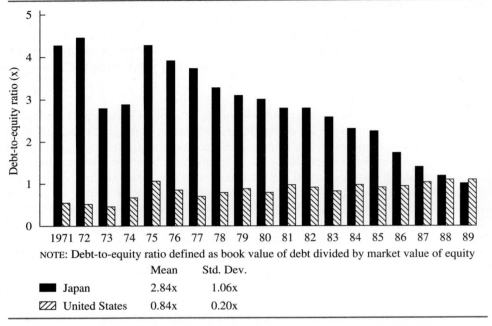

NOTE: Debt-to-equity ratio defined as book value of debt divided by market value of equity

	Mean	Std. Dev.
■ Japan	2.84x	1.06x
▨ United States	0.84x	0.20x

SOURCE: Niso Abauf and Kathleen Carmody, "The Cost of Capital in Japan and the United States: A Tale of Two Markets," Salomon Brothers, July 1990, p. 7.

since the late 1970s, U.S. companies have taken on more and more debt whereas Japanese firms have been deleveraging. It appears that target weights for debt are now lower for Japanese firms than for American firms.

Keiretsu ties provide Japanese companies with a safety net.

To the extent that large Japanese firms do have a leverage advantage, it stems in part from the vast mutual-aid networks that most of them can tap into. These are the fabled *keiretsu*, the large industrial groupings—often with a major bank at the center—that form the backbone of corporate Japan. Keiretsu ties comprise a complex web of tradition, cross-shareholdings, trading relationships, management, cooperative projects, and information swapping. The keiretsu provide financial backing, management advice, and favorable contracts to their members. A key mission of the keiretsu is to provide a safety net when corporate relatives get in trouble.

Partly because of the difference in industrial structures in the two countries, U.S. and Japanese firms relate to the banking system in a different way. Almost all big Japanese companies have one main bank—usually the bank around which the keiretsu is formed—that is their primary source of long-term loans. The main bank will have access to information about the company and have a say in its management that in most other countries would be unacceptable. Moreover, Japanese banks, unlike their U.S. counterparts, can hold industrial shares. So, the main bank often holds a sizable amount of the equity of its borrowers. For example, until recently, Japanese banks owned nearly 40% of the outstanding stock of Japanese manufacturing companies. Thus, for Japanese companies, the strong relation with one main bank—along with close ties to the other members of their keiretsu—is their main method of minimizing the risk of financial distress. In the United States, where corporate bank relations are less intimate, companies rely primarily on equity as a shock absorber.

ILLUSTRATION: *Toyo Kogyo and Chrysler Experience Financial Distress*

The contrasting experiences of Toyo Kogyo (producer of Mazda cars) and Chrysler during recent periods of financial distress illustrate the unusual features of the Japanese financial system. In 1973, Toyo Kogyo (TK) was a successful producer of light and medium-sized cars. The energy crisis of 1974 precipitated a crisis at TK because of the high energy consumption of its rotary-engine Mazda models. Worldwide sales plunged 19%. To weather the storm, TK required a massive infusion of funds to develop new product offerings. Sumitomo Bank, its main bank, had the resources to rescue TK. Based on its thorough knowledge of TK's operations, Sumitomo decided that the company could be profitable with new product offerings and massive cost cutting. But because it lacked confidence in TK's senior management, Sumitomo replaced them. With its own hand-picked executives in place, Sumitomo then financed the simultaneous development of three new models and the overhaul of TK's production system. The new models were highly successful and labor productivity grew by 118% over the next seven years.

In contrast to the situation at TK, Chrysler was able to persist with poor performance for over two decades because its investors had no effective remedies. Chrysler could ignore the need to restructure its operations due to its continued ability to borrow money (because it still had a substantial, though dwindling, amount of shareholders' equity to support these loans). Despite the activities of some dissident shareholders, Chrysler continued under a self-perpetuating management until the crisis of 1979. Although Chrysler faced bankruptcy, its banks refused to lend it more money. In contrast to TK's Japanese banks, Chrysler's banks had an incomplete understanding of its plight and no way to obtain all the essential information. Even if they had, they could not have sent in the same type of rescue team that Sumitomo sent into TK. In the end, Chrysler was rescued by the U.S. government, which offered loan guarantees sufficient for the company's survival at about half its former size.

The price that Japanese and German companies pay for their heavy reliance on bank debt is less freedom of action. As the cost of accessing the capital markets directly has dropped, the main-bank relationship has gradually eroded in Japan and Germany, and Japanese and German companies have looked more to the equity market as their cushion against financial distress. The pace of change was accelerated in Japan because of a new law that forced Japanese banks to reduce their shareholdings in individual companies to 5% or less by December 1987.

High Japanese Price/Earnings Ratios

Japanese P/E ratios are higher than those for American companies.

Finally, the high Japanese P/E ratios shown in Exhibit 19.3. are said to "prove" that Japanese firms have a lower cost of equity capital. Having peaked at over 60 times, Japanese P/E multiples in the mid-30s are still much higher than those in other major countries despite the sharp decline in the Japanese market since 1990.

Assuming a zero growth rate in profits, and a 100% dividend payout rate, Equation 19.3 shows that a P/E ratio of 40 implies a 2.5% cost of equity capital, while a P/E ratio of 12 (the average for U.S. firms) implies that $k_e = 8.33\%$. Taken at face value, therefore, the high Japanese P/E ratios do suggest a low cost of equity capital. But this conclusion ignores the role of growth in pricing stocks. To the extent that the profits of Japanese firms are expected to grow more rapidly than those of U.S. companies, Japanese companies should have higher P/E ratios even with an identical cost of equity capital. But even after adjusting for higher Japanese earnings growth, Japanese companies still appear to have a lower cost of equity capital.

Exhibit 19.3 Price-to-Earnings Ratios, January 1973–April 1990

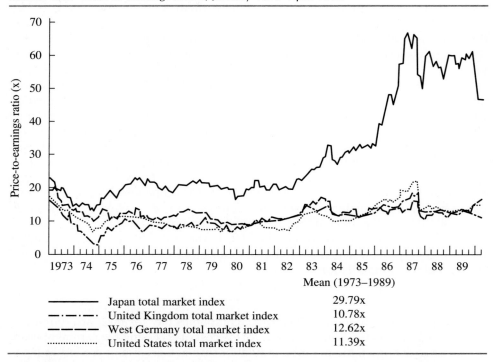

	Mean (1973–1989)
———— Japan total market index	29.79x
—·—·—· United Kingdom total market index	10.78x
——— West Germany total market index	12.62x
·········· United States total market index	11.39x

SOURCE: Niso Abuaf and Kathleen Carmody, "The Cost of Capital in Japan and the United States: A Tale of Two Markets," Salomon Brothers, July 1990, p. 8.

The use of unadjusted P/E ratios also fails to take into account the extensive crossholding—ownership by affiliated companies—of Japanese shares and consequent understatement of corporate earnings. This understatement arises because a Japanese firm that owns less than a 20% share of another company does not include the latter company's retained earnings in its own reported earnings.

An alternative approach to estimating the Japanese cost of equity capital is based on modern finance theory, which relies on the CAPM and observed returns. The observed returns, taken over a 15- to 20-year period are assumed to approximate expected returns, and so can be used to infer the market risk premium that enters the CAPM. Based on the high returns historically from investing in the Japanese market, the estimated equity risk premium is substantially higher for Japan than for the United States. After deleveraging the Japanese market to put it on a comparable basis with the U.S. market (using the formula provided in Equation 19.6), one study found that the equity risk premiums appear to be about the same in both markets (3.44% in Japan versus 3.45% in the United States).[7] With U.S. and Japanese real interest rates approximately the same, this should give Japanese and U.S. companies the same cost of capital.

Where does that leave us? Three separate studies that made various combinations of these adjustments all concluded that Japanese companies have a cost of capital advantage on the order of 1.5% to 3%.[8] They also concluded that this gap is closing. That is not surprising, considering that it would be foolish for Japanese investors to continue investing in Japanese securities expected to earn several percentage points less than U.S. securities when they can easily invest in the United States. More broadly, capital markets around the world are increasingly integrated. Investors, armed with round-the-clock computerized trading systems, can shift billions from one country to another, eliminating any persistent disparities in real returns.

> Researchers estimate that Japanese companies have historically had a 1.5% to 3% cost of capital advantage.

A recent study, by Carl Kester and Timothy Luehrman, argues that in fact U.S. firms have *never* faced a significantly higher average cost of capital than their Japanese competitors.[9] According to Kester and Luehrman, most of the studies that found the average cost of capital to be lower in Japan than in America failed to take into account differences in the riskiness of the companies. Once you take these differences into account, they say, then the cost of capital for comparable firms of similar risk was the same in both countries during the 1980s. In their research, they treat the cost of capital as it should be treated in such a study—as the sum of a real risk-free rate plus a risk premium. Based on this approach, their

---

[7]See Niso Abuaf and Kathleen Carmody, "The Cost of Capital in Japan and the United States: A Tale of Two Markets," Salomon Brothers, Financial Strategy Group, July 1990.

[8]These studies include McCauley and Zimmer, "Explaining International Differences in the Cost of Capital"; Abouf and Carmody, "The Cost of Capital in Japan and the United States: A Tale of Two Markets"; and Ronald K. Langford, "The Cost of Capital in the U.S. and Japan: Comparisons and Implications," *Commentary*, Marakon Associates, Fall 1989, pp. 11–20.

[9]Their findings are summarized in W. Carl Kester and Timothy A. Luehrman, "The Myth of Japan's Low-Cost Capital," *Harvard Business Review*, May–June 1992, pp. 130–138.

data show that differences in capital costs between the United States and Japan have been isolated and temporary, not broad and persistent.

The Japanese cost of capital advantage has disappeared by now.

Despite these contrasting findings, there appears to be common ground among researchers today. Even those who argued that the Japanese did have a cost of capital advantage in the past now believe that the stunning collapse of the Japanese stock market combined with the sharp decline in U.S. interest rates has virtually eliminated the cost of capital difference between the two countries. Indeed, a number of financial analysts now argue that, if anything, the U.S. currently has a cost of capital *advantage*. For example, a recent study by J.P. Morgan estimates that by early 1992 the cost of equity capital in the United States had fallen below that in Japan (see Exhibit 19.4).

Coping with a Cost of Capital Disadvantage

To the extent that American companies face a higher cost of capital, such a gap, even if it is a small one, can have a large strategic impact in certain situations. A cost of capital disadvantage is most harmful in capital intensive industries where companies compete primarily on price. For example, a cost of capital differential is much more important in the capital intensive auto industry than in the know-

Exhibit 19.4 Comparing the Cost of Equity Capital in Japan and the United States

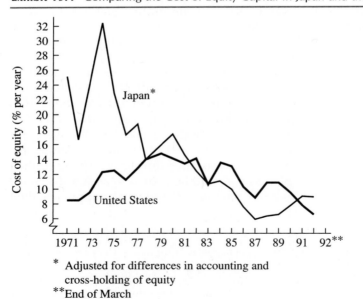

* Adjusted for differences in accounting and cross-holding of equity

**End of March

SOURCE: Data from J. P. Morgan as reported in *The Economist*, May 23, 1992, p. 71. © 1992 The Economist Newspaper Group, Inc. Reprinted with permission.

ledge-intensive software business. Moreover, capital cost differences are more important for the economy car segment of the market than for the luxury car segment.

Companies have several ways to deal with a cost of capital disadvantage. First, companies can attempt to reduce the capital intensity of the business. This can often be accomplished by reducing working capital and changing the production process. For example, studies of the auto industry indicate that the Japanese cost advantage is not due primarily to lower capital costs in Japan but to the fact that Japanese producers seem to require much less plant and equipment per vehicle produced and to have much lower work in-process inventories than American producers. Second, as with currency risk management, companies can attempt to increase product differentiation and, thereby, reduce the price sensitivity of its output.

Companies can cope with a cost of capital disadvantage in several ways.

Perhaps the most important advice to U.S. companies is to recognize both the costs of *not* undertaking investments in factory modernization and new technology as well as the growth options that these investments often create. Many financial economists now believe that undervaluing such growth options is a major reason why U.S. companies often underinvest in new products and processes. As we saw in Chapter 18, such follow-up projects, which create options on investments in other products, markets, or production processes, are sometimes referred to as *growth options* and may be an important component of firm value. For example, an auto company may give up on ceramic engines because they seem technically infeasible. Meanwhile, a Japanese rival who makes ordinary ceramic parts with the aim of one day using that knowledge to build a ceramic engine can quickly change the competitive balance.

19.6 ILLUSTRATION: INTERNATIONALIZING THE COST OF CAPITAL OF NOVO INDUSTRI

Capital market segmentation implies that the same firm raising debt or equity funds in different national capital markets may face a different cost of capital as a result of diverging investor perceptions between domestic and foreign shareholders or of asymmetry in tax policies, exchange controls, and political risks. Indeed, a firm based in a fully segmented capital market is likely to have a higher cost of capital due to a relatively depressed price for its stock than if it had access to fully integrated capital markets. A good illustration of how a company can overcome such segmentation barriers in order to effectively reduce its cost of capital is provided by Novo Industri, the Danish multinational firm that is a recognized industry leader in the manufacturing of industrial enzymes and pharmaceuticals (mostly insulin) in Western Europe.[10]

---

[10]Adapted from *Internationalizing the Cost of Capital in Theory and Practice: The Novo Experience and National Policy Implications* by Arthur I. Stonehill and Kare B. Dullum (London: Wiley, 1983) by Laurent L. Jacque and Alan C. Shapiro.

Novo perceived it had a high cost of capital relative to its foreign competitors for several reasons. First, Danish investors were prohibited from investing in foreign stocks. Since Danish stock price movements are closely correlated with each other, Danish investors bore a great deal of systematic risk, raising their required returns. Second, Denmark taxed capital gains on stocks at prohibitive rates, reducing stock turnover and hence liquidity. These effects combined to greatly increase the pre-tax return required by Danish investors. Finally, foreign investors were quite unfamiliar with the Danish market, thereby reducing their incentive to arbitrage away the high returns available on Danish stocks.

Novo internationalized its cost of capital to improve its competitiveness.

In 1977, Novo embarked on an ambitious strategy aimed at internationalizing its cost of capital in order to be in a position to better compete with its major multinational rivals such as Eli Lilly (United States), Miles Laboratory (United States-based but a subsidiary of the giant chemical conglomerate Bayer, headquartered in West Germany), and Gist Brocades (the Netherlands). The first step was for Novo to float a $20 million convertible Eurobond issue (1978). In connection with this offering, it listed its shares on the London Stock Exchange (1979) to facilitate conversion and to gain visibility among foreign investors. Next, Novo decided to capitalize on the emerging interest among U.S. investors for biotechnology companies. It ran a seminar in New York (1980) and then sponsored an American Depository Receipts system and listed its shares on the U.S. over-the-counter market (NASDAQ, in 1981).

Having gained significant visibility among both the London and New York investment communities, Novo was ready to take the final and most difficult step—floating an equity issue on the New York Stock Exchange. Under the guidance of Goldman Sachs, a prospectus was prepared for SEC registration of a U.S. stock offering and eventual listing on the NYSE. On July 8, 1981, Novo became the first Scandinavian firm to successfully sell stock through a public issue in the United States.

Exhibit 19.5 illustrates how the price of Novo's B shares increased dramatically between the issue of the convertible Eurobond (1978) and the equity issue on the New York Stock Exchange (1981). This gain in share price correlates highly with, and is probably a result of, steady foreign buying. Indeed by July 1981, foreign ownership of Novo's B shares exceeded 50% as Danish investors were more than willing to sell a stock that many considered to be grossly and increasingly overvalued; at the same time, foreign investors-mostly from the United States—were ready to step up their investment in a stock that they considered to be either grossly undervalued or a suitable vehicle for international diversification. As its P/E ratio had more than tripled from 9 to 31, Novo was successful in sourcing much needed capital to better compete with its foreign rivals.[11]

---

[11]This is, of course, an illustration, not a proof, of how selling securities to foreign investors can affect the cost of capital for a firm.

Exhibit 19.5 Novo's B Share Prices Compared to Stock Market Indexes, 1977–1982

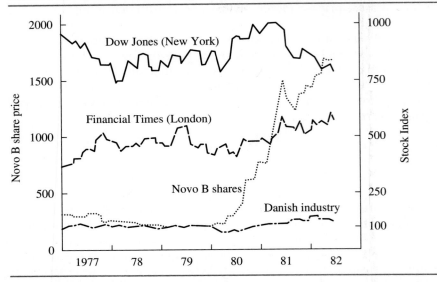

SOURCE: A. Stonehill and K. Dullum, *Internationalizing the Cost of Capital in Theory and Practice: The Novo Experience and National Policy Implications* (London: Wiley, 1983). Copyright © 1983. Reproduced by permisison of John Wiley & Sons, Limited.

19.7 SUMMARY AND CONCLUSIONS

Analysis of the available evidence on the impact of foreign operations on firm riskiness suggests that if there is an effect, that effect is generally to reduce both actual and perceived riskiness. These results indicate that corporations should continue investing abroad as long as there are profitable opportunities there. Retrenching because it is believed that investors desire smaller international operations is likely to lead to the forgoing of profitable foreign investments that would be rewarded, instead of penalized, by the firm's shareholders. At the very least, executives of multinational firms should seriously question the use of a risk premium to account for the added political and economic risks of overseas operations, when evaluating prospective foreign investments.

The use of any risk premium ignores the fact that the risk of an overseas investment in the context of the firm's other investments, domestic as well as foreign, will be less than the project's total risk. How much less depends on how highly correlated are the outcomes of the firm's different investments. Thus, the automatic inclusion of a premium for risk when evaluating a foreign project is not a necessary element of conservatism; rather, it is a management short cut that is unlikely to benefit the firm's shareholders. Some investments, however, are more risk-prone than are others, and these risks must be accounted for. Chapter 18, on capital budgeting, presented a method for conducting the necessary risk analysis for foreign investments when the foreign risks were unsystematic. This chapter

showed how the necessary adjustments in project discount rates can be made, using the capital asset pricing model, when those additional foreign risks are systematic in nature.

With regard to the oft-cited Japanese cost of capital advantage, such an advantage may have been largely illusory in the past and by now appears to be nonexistent for most practical purposes. We saw that much of the apparent difference in estimated costs of capital between the United States and Japan was likely due to problems in measuring relative risks and failure to distinguish real from nominal interest rates.

QUESTIONS

1.   Should the cost of capital for the IDC-U.K. project presented in Chapter 18 be higher, lower, or the same as the cost of capital for a similar project to manufacture and sell diesel engines in the United States? Explain.

2.   Comment on the following statement: "There is a curious contradiction in corporate finance theory: Since equity is more expensive than debt, highly leveraged subsidiaries should be assigned a low hurdle rate. But when the highly leveraged subsidiaries are in risky nations, country risk dictates just the opposite: a high hurdle rate."

3.   Comment on the following statement: "Our conglomerate recognizes that foreign investments have a very low covariance with our domestic operations and, thus, are a good source of diversification. We do not 'penalize' potential foreign investments with a high discount rate but, rather, use a discount rate just 3% above the prevailing riskless rate."

4.   According to a recent article in *Forbes*, "American companies can and are raising capital in Japan at relatively low rates of interest. Dow Chemical, for instance, has raised $500 million in yen. That cost the company over 50% less than it would have at home." Comment on this statement.

5.   In early 1990, major Tokyo Stock Exchange issues sold for an average 60 times earnings, more than four times the 13.8 price-earnings ratio for the S&P 500 at that time. According to *Business Week* (February 12, 1990, p. 76), "Since p-e ratios are a guide to a company's cost of equity capital, this valuation gap implies that raising new equity costs Japanese companies less than 2% a year, vs. an average 7% for the U.S." Comment on this statement.

PROBLEMS

1.   A firm with a corporate-wide debt/equity ratio of 1:2, an after-tax cost of debt of 7%, and a cost of equity capital of 15% is interested in pursuing a foreign project. The debt capacity of the project is the same as for the company as a whole, but its systematic risk is such that the required return on equity is estimated to be about 12%. The after-tax cost of debt is expected to remain at 7%.

a. What is the project's weighted average cost of capital? How does it compare with the parent's WACC?

b. If the project's equity beta is 1.21, what is its unlevered beta?

2. Suppose that a foreign project has a beta of 0.85, the risk-free rate is 12%, and the required return on the market is estimated at 19%. What is the project's cost of capital?

BIBLIOGRAPHY

Adler, Michael, and Bernard Dumas. "International Portfolio Choice and Corporation Finance: A Synthesis." *Journal of Finance*, June 1983, pp. 925–984.

Agmon, Tamir, and Donald R. Lessard, "Investor Recognition of Corporate International Diversification." *Journal of Finance*, September 1977, pp. 1049–1056.

Black, Fischer. "International Capital Market Equilibrium with Investment Barriers." *Journal of Financial Economics*, December 1974, pp. 337–352.

Chan, K.C., G. Andrew Karolyi, and Rene M. Stulz. "Global Financial Markets and the Risk Premium on U.S. Equity." *Journal of Financial Economics*, October 1992, pp. 137–167.

Cho, Chinhyung D., Cheol S. Eun, and Lemma W. Senbet, "International Arbitrage Pricing Theory: An Empirical Investigation," *Journal of Finance*, June 1986, pp. 313–330.

Grauer, Frederick L. A., Robert H. Litzenberger, and Richard E. Stehle. "Sharing Rules and Equilibrium in an International Capital Market Under Uncertainty." *Journal of Financial Economics*, June 1976, pp. 233–257.

Harvey, Campbell R. "The World Price of Covariance Risk." *Journal of Finance*, March 1991, pp. 111–157.

Kester, W. Carl, and Timothy A. Luehrman, "The Myth of Japan's Low-Cost Capital," *Harvard Business Review*, May–June 1992, pp. 130–138.

Shapiro, Alan C. "Financial Structure and the Cost of Capital in the Multinational Corporation." *Journal of Financial and Quantitative Analysis*, June 1978, pp. 211–226.

Solnik, Bruno H. "Testing International Asset Pricing: Some Pessimistic Views." *Journal of Finance*, May 1977, pp. 503–512.

Stonehill, Arthur I. and Kare B. Dullum. *Internationalizing the Cost of Capital in Theory and Practice: The Novo Experience and National Policy Implications.* London: Wiley, 1983.

Stulz, Rene M. "A Model of International Asset Pricing." *Journal of Financial Economics*, December 1981, pp. 383–406.

Wheatley, Simon. "Some Tests of International Equity Integration." *Journal of Financial Economics*, 21 (1988), pp. 177–212.

20 The Measurement and Management of Political Risk

People say they want clarification of the rules of the game, but I think it isn't very clear what isn't clear to them.

> Adolfo Hegewisch Fernandez,
> Mexico's Former Subsecretary for Foreign Investment

Potential investors don't want flexibility, they want fixed rules of the game.

> John Gavin, Former U.S. Ambassador to Mexico

CHAPTER LEARNING OBJECTIVES

- To define what political risk means from the standpoint of an MNC
- To describe the social, cultural, political, and economic factors that affect the general level of political risk in a country and identify key indicators of political risk
- To assess the implications of various forms of political risk for corporate operations
- To describe the specific operating and financial characteristics of a company and its foreign investments that help determine its susceptibility to political risk
- To describe how a firm can structure its foreign investments to minimize political risk
- To describe the different operating policies that firms can use to manage their political risk
- To explain how firms can respond to confiscation of its property by a foreign government
- To describe what we can learn about economic development from the contrasting experiences of a variety of countries

In recent years, there has been a significant increase in developing and developed countries alike in the types and magnitudes of political risks that multinational companies have historically faced. Currency controls, expropriation, changes in tax laws, and requirements for additional local production are just some of the more visible forms of political risk. The common denominator of such risks, however, is not hard to identify:

government intervention into the workings of the economy that affects, for good or ill, the value of the firm. While the consequences are usually adverse, changes in the political environment can provide opportunities. The imposition of quotas on autos from Japan, for example, was undoubtedly beneficial to U.S. automobile manufacturers.

The purpose of this chapter is to provide a framework that can facilitate a formal assessment of political risk and its implications for corporate decision making. Both international banks and nonbank multinationals analyze political risk, but from different perspectives. This chapter takes the perspective of nonbank MNCs, who analyze political risk in order to determine the investment climate in various countries. Political risk assessments may be used in investment analyses to screen out countries that are excessively risky or to monitor countries in which the firm is currently doing business to determine whether new policies are called for.

The basic approach to managing political risk presented here involves three steps: (1) identifying political risk and its likely consequences; (2) developing policies in advance to cope with the possibility of political risk; and (3) in the event of the extreme form of political risk, *expropriation*, developing measures to maximize compensation. The experiences in Chile of Kennecott and of Anaconda, detailed in Section 20.5, illustrate this approach.

20.1 MEASURING POLITICAL RISK

Despite the near-universal recognition among multinational corporations, political scientists, and economists of the existence of *political risk*, there is no unanimity yet as to what constitutes that risk and how to measure it. The two basic approaches to viewing political risk are from a country-specific perspective and a firm-specific perspective. The former perspective depends on *country risk analysis*, whereas the latter depends on a more micro approach.

Political risk is a tricky concept and is difficult to estimate.

A number of commercial and academic political risk forecasting models are available today. These models normally supply country risk indexes that attempt to quantify the level of political risk in each nation. Most of these indexes rely on some measure(s) of the stability of the local political regime.

Political Stability

Measures of political stability may include the frequency of changes of government, the level of violence in the country (for example, violent deaths per 100,000 population), number of armed insurrections, conflicts with other states, and so on. The basic function of these stability indicators is to determine how long the current regime will be in power and whether that regime also will be willing and able to enforce its foreign investment guarantees. Most companies believe that greater political stability means a safer investment environment.

A basic problem in many Third World countries is that the local actors have all the external trappings of genuine nation-states—United Nations-endorsed borders, armies, foreign ministries, flags, currencies, national airlines. But they are nothing of the kind. They lack social cohesion, political legitimacy, and the institutional infrastructures that are necessary for economic growth.

ILLUSTRATION: Threats to the Nation-State

From Canada to Czechoslovakia, from India to Ireland, and from South Africa to the former Soviet Union, political movements centered around ethnicity, national identity, and religion are reemerging to contest some of the most fundamental premises of the modern nation-state. In the process, they are reintroducing ancient sources of conflict so deeply submerged by the Cold War that they seemed almost to have vanished from history's equation.

The implications of this resurgence of national, ethnic, and religious passions are profound.

— A host of modern nation-states—from Canada to Lebanon to Iraq—are beginning to crumble, while others—like Yugoslavia, Czechoslovakia, and Somalia—have already disintegrated, because the concept of the "melting pot," the idea that diverse and even historically hostile peoples could readily be assimilated under larger political umbrellas in the name of modernization and progress, has failed them. Even in the strongest nations, including the United States, the task of such assimilation has proved difficult and the prognosis is for even greater tension in the years ahead.

— After 70 years on the road to nowhere, the Soviet Union disappeared in 1991. Now, turmoil in the states making up the former Soviet Union and parts of China threaten to blow apart the last remnants of an imperial age that began more than 500 years ago. The turbulent dismantling of 19th Century European empires after World War II may be matched by new waves of disintegration within the former Soviet and Chinese Communist empires, with incalculable consequences for the rest of the world. Stretching from the Gulf of Finland to the mountains of Tibet and beyond, the sheer scale of the potential instability would tax the world's capacity to respond. Ethnic unrest could spill into neighboring countries, old border disputes could reignite and, if the central governments tried to impose order with force, civil wars could erupt within two of the world's largest nuclear powers.

— Around the world, fundamentalist religious movements have entered the political arena in a direct challenge to one of the basic principles of the modern age: that governments and other civic institutions should be predominantly secular and religion confined to the private lives of individuals and groups. Since the end of the Middle Ages, when religion dominated not just government but every aspect of society, the pervasive trend in the past 500 years has been to separate church and state. Now, in many parts of the world, powerful movements—reacting against the secular quality of modern public culture and the tendency of traditional values to be swept aside in periods of rapid change—are insisting on a return to God-centered government. One consequence of this trend is to make dealings between states and groups more volatile. As the United States learned with the Arab-Israeli conflict, the Iranian revolution, and the Persian Gulf war, disputes are far harder to manage when governments root their positions in religious principle.

Paradoxically, at the same time that many states and societies are fragmenting over religion, ethnicity, and national culture, their people nourish hopes of achieving economic progress by allying themselves to one or another of the new trade blocs—Europe, North America, Pacific Rim—now taking shape. Yet in many cases such dreams will not materialize. Civil strife and dogmatic politics hold little allure for foreign investors; bankers lend money to people whose first priority is money, not religion or ethnic identity. The challenge for business is to create profitable opportunities in a world that is simultaneously globalizing and localizing.

Economic Factors

Other frequently used indicators of political risk include various economic factors, such as inflation, balance-of-payments deficits or surpluses, and the growth rate of per capita GNP. The intention behind these measures is to determine whether the economy is in good shape or requires a quick fix, such as expropriation to increase government revenues or currency inconvertibility to improve the balance of payments. In general, the better a country's economic outlook, the less likely it is to face political and social turmoil that will inevitably harm foreign companies.

Political risk models include both objective economic factors and subjective indicators of attitudes toward property rights.

Subjective Factors

More subjective measures of political risk are based on a general perception of the country's attitude toward private enterprise: whether private enterprise is considered a necessary evil to be eliminated as soon as possible or is actively welcomed. The attitude toward multinationals is particularly relevant and may differ from the feeling regarding local private ownership. Consider, for example, the Soviet Union and other Eastern European countries that have actively sought products, technology, and even joint ventures with Western firms while refusing to tolerate (until recently) domestic free enterprise. In general, most countries probably view foreign direct investment in terms of a cost/benefit trade-off and are not either for or against it in principle.

An index that tries to incorporate all these various economic, social, and political factors into an overall measure of the business climate, including the political environment, is the Business Environment Risk Index (BERI), shown in Exhibit 20.1. The scores of countries listed on the BERI scale are based on an aggregation of the subjective assessments of a panel of experts.

Exhibit 20.1   BERI Rankings, 1993

Low Risk	*Category**	*High Risk*	*Category**
Switzerland	82	Italy	48
Taiwan (R.O.C.)	80	Colombia	46
Japan	78	Mexico	46
Singapore	78	South Africa	46
Germany	74	Indonesia	43
Netherlands	74	Iran	43
Austria	73	Kazakhstan	43
United States	71	Venezuela	43
Norway	70	Belarus	42
		Poland	42
Medium Risk		Philippines	41
Belgium	67	Argentina	40
France	62		
Ireland	62	*Prohibitive Risk*	
Spain	62	Egypt	39
Sweden	62	India	39
Portugal	61	Pakistan	39
United Kingdom	61	Ukraine	39
Korea (South)	59	Greece	38
China (P.R.C.)	58	Ecuador	35
Denmark	58	Russia	35
Malaysia	58	Brazil	34
Australia	57	Nigeria	32
Saudi Arabia	55	Peru	29
Canada	54		
Czech Republic	54		
Chile	52		
Thailand	52		
Hungary	51		
Turkey	51		

*BERI Categories:

100	Perfect country
99–70	Unusually stable and superior business environment for the foreign investor.
69–60	Typical for an industrialized economy. Any tendency toward nationalism is offset in varying degrees by the country's efficiency, market opportunities, financial entities, etc.
59–50	Moderate-risk countries with complications in day-to-day operations. Usually the political structure is sufficiently stable to permit business without serious disruption.
49–40	High risk for foreign-owned businesses. Only special situations should be considered (e.g., scarce raw materials).
Below 39	Unacceptable business conditions.

SOURCE: Business Environment Risk Information, BERI S.A., Washington, D.C., 1993.

Political Risk and Uncertain Property Rights. Models such as BERI are useful insofar as they provide an indication of the general level of political risk in a country. From an economic standpoint, political risk refers to uncertainty over *property rights*. If the government can expropriate either legal title to property or the stream of income it generates, then political risk exists. Political risk also exists if property owners may be constrained in the way they use their property. This definition of political risk encompasses government actions ranging from outright expropriation to a change in the tax law that alters the government's share of corporate income to laws that change the rights of private companies to compete against state-owned companies. Each action affects corporate cash flows and hence the value of the firm.

ILLUSTRATION: Political Risk in Venezuela

According to *The Wall Street Journal* (December 31, 1980, p. 10), when Venezuela's oil income quadrupled in 1973, a high government official declared, "Now we have so much money that we won't need any new foreign investment." President Carlos Perez calculated that the country was rich enough to buy machinery from abroad and set up factories without any foreign participation. He overlooked the fact that Venezuela didn't have enough skilled technicians to run and maintain sophisticated equipment. Despite an orgy of buying foreign-made machinery, economic growth stalled as companies were left with equipment they couldn't operate.

By 1980, President Luis Herrera, who succeeded Perez, recognized the mistake and invited foreigners back. But once shunned, foreigners didn't rush back, particularly since the Herrera administration sent out such mixed signals that investors couldn't be certain how sincere the welcome was or how long it would last.

Consider the uncertainty faced by a foreign investor trying to decipher government policy from the following statements. On the one hand, the Superintendent of Foreign Investment insisted that the government had had "a change of heart" and declared that the country needed "new capital and new technology in manufacturing, agro-industry, and construction of low-cost housing." On the other hand, the head of the powerful Venezuelan Investment Fund, which invests much of the country's oil income, was downright hostile to foreign investors. He said, "Foreign investment is generally unfavorable to Venezuela. Foreign investors think Venezuela is one big grab bag, where they can come and pick out whatever goodies they want." Still another official, the president of the Foreign Trade Institute, said, "It is a grave error to think that foreign investment can contribute to the transfer of technology, capital formation, the development of managerial capacity, and equilibrium in the balance of payments."

Capital Flight. One good indicator of the degree of political risk is the seriousness of capital flight. *Capital flight* refers to the export of savings by a nation's citizens

One good indicator of political risk is capital flight.

because of fears about the safety of their capital. By its nature, capital flight is difficult to measure accurately because it is not directly observed in most cases. Nevertheless, one can usually infer the capital outflows, using balance-of-payments figures—particularly the entry labeled "errors and omissions." These estimates indicate that capital flight represents an enormous outflow of funds from developing countries. For example, as of the end of 1988, Morgan Guaranty estimated that Latin Americans held $243 billion in assets abroad, far exceeding the amount of loans to the region held by U.S. banks. And this excludes assets taken abroad before 1977. Exhibit 20.2 shows the breakdown of the $243 billion figure by country.

Capital flight occurs for several reasons, most of which have to do with inappropriate economic policies. These reasons include government regulations, controls, and taxes that lower the return on domestic investments. In countries where inflation is high and domestic inflation hedging is difficult or impossible, investors may hedge by shifting their savings to foreign currencies deemed less likely to depreciate. They may also make the shift when domestic interest rates are artificially held down by their governments, or when they expect a devaluation of an overvalued currency.

Perhaps the most powerful motive for capital flight is political risk. In unstable political regimes (and in some stable ones) wealth is not secure from government seizure, especially when changes in regime occur. Savings may be shifted overseas to protect them. For example, the citizens of Hong Kong, which will be turned over to communist China in 1997, have responded to the anticipated change in regime by sending large sums of money abroad.

Common sense dictates that if a nation's own citizens don't trust the government, then investment there is unsafe. After all, residents presumably have a better feel for conditions and governmental intentions than do outsiders. Thus,

Exhibit 20.2 Latin American Flight Capital: Estimated Assets Held Abroad at Year-End, 1988

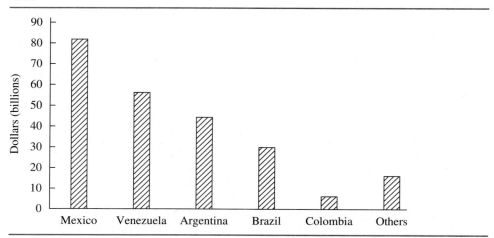

when analyzing investment or lending opportunities, multinational firms and international banks must bear in mind the apparent unwillingness of the nation's citizens to invest and lend in their own country.

What's needed to halt capital flight are tough-minded economic policies—the kind of policies that make investors want to put their money to work instead of taking it out. As we shall see in the next section, these policies include cutting budget deficits and taxes, removing barriers to investment by foreigners, selling off state-owned enterprises, allowing for freer trade, and avoiding currency overvaluations that virtually invite people to ship their money elsewhere before the official exchange rate falls.

Sound economic policies will reverse capital flight.

Such policies are now being employed in Latin America, with predictable results. As seen in Exhibit 20.3, beginning in 1990, capital flight has been reversed, with private capital flooding back into Latin America. These capital inflows have helped fuel the extraordinary performance of the Latin American stock markets that we saw in Chapter 16.

The Micro Approach

Despite the increased sophistication of political risk models such as BERI, however, their usefulness remains problematic. For one thing, political instability by itself does not necessarily contribute to political risk. Changes of government in Latin America, for example, are quite frequent; yet most multinationals continue to go about their business undisturbed.

The most important weakness of these indices, however, lies in their assumption that each firm in a country is facing the same degree of political risk. This is

Exhibit 20.3 Private Capital Returns to Latin America

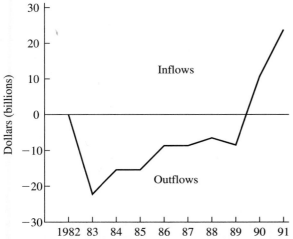

SOURCE: Data from Inter-American Development Bank as reported in *The Economist*, October 31, 1992, p. 86. © 1992 The Economist Newspaper Group, Inc. Reprinted with permission.

manifestly untrue, as is indicated by the empirical evidence on the post-World War II experiences of American and British MNCs. The data clearly show that except in those countries that went communist, companies differ in their susceptibilities to political risk depending on their industry, size, composition of ownership, level of technology, and degree of vertical integration with other affiliates.[1] For example, expropriation or creeping expropriation is more likely to occur in the extractive, utility, and financial service sectors of an economy than in the manufacturing sector. Exhibit 20.4 shows corporate susceptibility to expropriation by industry. Moreover, some firms may benefit from the same event that harms other firms. For instance, a company that relies on imports will be hurt by trade restrictions, whereas an import-competing firm may well be helped.

Corporate susceptibility toward political risk depends on the company's operating and financial characteristics.

Because political risk has a different meaning for, and impact on, each firm, it is doubtful that any index of generalized political risk will be of much value to a company selected at random. The specific operating and financial characteristics of a company will largely determine its susceptibility to political risk and, hence, the effects of that risk on the value of its foreign investment.

In general, the greater the perceived benefits to the host economy and the more expensive its replacement by a purely local operation, the smaller the degree of risk to the MNC. This selectivity suggests that firms can take actions to control their exposure to political risk.

Exhibit 20.4 Expropriation by Industry Group, 1960–1974

Industry	Number of Expropriations	Percent of Total
Oil	84	12.0
Extraction	38	18.0
Utilities and transportation	17	4.0
Insurance and banking	33	4.0
Manufacturing	30	1.2
Agriculture	19	*
Sales and service	16	*
Land, property, and construction	23	*

*Data unavailable

SOURCE: David Bradley, "Managing Against Expropriation," *Harvard Business Review,* July–August 1977, p. 79. Reprinted by permission of the *Harvard Business Review,* Copyright © 1977 by the President and Fellows of Harvard College; all rights reserved.

[1]See, for example, studies by J. Frederick Truitt, "Expropriation of Foreign Investment: Summary of the Post–World War II Experience of American and British Investors in Less Developed Countries," *Journal of International Business Studies,* Fall 1970, pp. 21–34; Robert G. Hawkins, Norman Mintz, and Michael Provissiero, "Government Takeovers of U.S. Foreign Affiliates," *Journal of International Business Studies,* Spring 1976, pp. 3–15; and David Bradley, "Managing Against Expropriation," *Harvard Business Review,* July–August, 1977, pp. 75–83.

20.2 COUNTRY RISK ANALYSIS

We now examine in more detail some of the economic and social factors that contribute to the general level of risk in the country as a whole—termed *country risk*. The primary focus here is on how well the country is doing economically. As noted earlier, the better a nation's economic performance, the lower the likelihood that its government will take actions that adversely affect the value of companies operating there.

Fiscal Irresponsibility

To begin, fiscal irresponsibility is one sign of a country likely to be politically risky since it will probably have an insatiable appetite for money. Thus, one country risk indicator is the government deficit as a percentage of gross national product. The higher this figure, the more the government is promising to its citizens relative to the resources it is extracting in payment. This gap lowers the possibility that the government can meet its promises without resorting to expropriations of property.

Controlled Exchange Rate System

The economic problems presented by a fiscally irresponsible government are compounded by having a *controlled exchange rate system*, where the government uses currency controls to fix the exchange rate. A controlled rate system goes hand in hand with an overvalued local currency, which is the equivalent of taxing exports and subsidizing imports. The risk of tighter currency controls and the ever-present threat of a devaluation encourage capital flight. Similarly, multinational firms will try to repatriate their local affiliates' profits rather than reinvest them. A controlled rate system also leaves the economy with little flexibility to respond to changing relative prices and wealth positions, exacerbating any unfavorable trend in the nation's terms of trade.

A key country risk indicator is an overvalued currency

Wasteful Government Spending

Another indicator of potential political risk is the amount of unproductive spending in the economy. To the extent that capital from abroad is used to subsidize consumption or is wasted on showcase projects, the government will have less wealth to draw on to repay the nation's foreign debts and is more likely to resort to exchange controls, higher taxes, and the like. Additionally, funds diverted to the purchase of assets abroad (capital flight) will not add to the economy's dollar-generating capacity unless investors feel safe in repatriating their overseas earnings.

Resource Base

The resource base of a country consists of its natural, human, and financial resources. Others things equal, a nation with substantial natural resources, such as oil or copper, is a better economic risk than is one without those resources. But typically, all is not equal. Hence, nations such as South Korea or Taiwan turn out to be better risks than resource-rich Argentina or Brazil. The reason has to do with the quality of human resources and the degree to which these resources are allowed to be put to their most efficient use.

Political stability and free markets promote economic growth.

A nation with highly skilled and productive workers, a large pool of scientists and engineers, and ample management talent will have many of the essential ingredients needed to pursue a course of steady growth and development. Two further factors are necessary: (1) a stable political system that encourages hard work and risk taking by allowing entrepreneurs to reap the rewards (and bear the losses) from their activities, and (2) a free-market system that ensures that the prices people respond to correctly signal the relative desirability of engaging in different activities. In this way, the nation's human and natural resources will be put to their most efficient uses. The evidence by now is overwhelming that free markets bring wealth, and that endless state meddling brings waste. The reason is simple: Unlike a government-controlled economy, free markets do not tolerate and perpetuate mistakes.

Country Risk and Adjustment to External Shocks

Recent history shows that the impact of external shocks is likely to vary from nation to nation, however, with some countries dealing successfully with these shocks and others succumbing to them. The evidence suggests that domestic policies play a critical role in determining how effectively a particular nation will deal with external shocks. Asian nations, for example, successfully coped with falling commodity prices, rising real interest rates, and rising exchange rates because their policies promoted timely internal and external adjustment, as is manifest in relatively low inflation rates and small current-account deficits.

Statist policies that downgraded the role of market forces underlie Latin America's economic problems.

The opposite happened in Latin America where most countries accepted the then-prevalent ideology that growth is best promoted by an *import-substitution development strategy* characterized by extensive state ownership, controls, and policies to encourage import substitution. Many of these countries took over failing private businesses, nationalized the banks, protected domestic companies against imports, ran up large foreign debts, and heavily regulated the private sector. Whereas the "East Asian Tigers"—Hong Kong, South Korea, Taiwan, and Singapore—tested their ability to imitate and innovate in the international marketplace, Latin American producers were content with the exploitation of the internal market, charging prices that were typically several times the international price for their goods. The lack of foreign competition has contributed to long-term inefficiency among Latin American manufacturers.

In addition, by raising the cost of imported materials and products used by the export sector, the Latin American import-substitution development strategies worsened their international competitive position, leaving the share of exports in GNP far below that of other LDCs. Moreover, state expenditures on massive capital projects diverted resources from the private sector and exports. Much of the investment went to inefficient state enterprises, leading to wasted resources and large debts.

The decline in commodity prices and the simultaneous rise in real interest rates should have led to reduced domestic consumption. But fearing that spending cuts would threaten social stability, the Latin American governments delayed cutting back on projects and social expenditures. The difference between consumption and production was made up by borrowing overseas, thereby enabling their societies to temporarily enjoy artificially high standards of living.

Latin American governments also tried to stimulate their economies by increasing state spending, fueled by high rates of monetary expansion. This response exacerbated their difficulties because the resulting high rates of inflation combined with their fixed exchange rates to boost real exchange rates substantially and resulted in higher imports and lower exports. Moreover, the overvalued exchange rates, interest rate controls, and political uncertainties triggered massive capital flight from the region—estimated at up to $100 billion during the two-year period of 1981 and 1982. The result was larger balance-of-payments deficits that necessitated more foreign borrowing and higher debt service requirements. Moreover, in an attempt to control inflation, the Latin American governments imposed price controls and interest rate controls. These controls led to further capital flight and price rigidity. Distorted prices gave the wrong signals to the residents, sending consumption soaring and production plummeting.

The centralization of economic power in much of the Third World turned the state into a huge patronage machine and spawned a swollen and corrupt bureaucracy to administer the all-encompassing rules and regulations. Avaricious elites, accountable to no one, used the labyrinthine controls and regulations to enrich themselves and further the interests of their own ethnic groups or professional class at the expense of national economic health and well-being.

Many of these countries are finally rejecting earlier policies and trying to stimulate the private sector and individual initiative. The experience in countries that are reforming their economies—including the former Soviet Union, China, and India, as well as much of Latin America—illustrates that it is far easier to regulate and extend the state's reach than to deregulate and retrench. When the state becomes heavily involved in the economy, many special interests from the state bureaucracy, business, labor, and consumer groups come to rely on state benefits. Of course, they actively oppose reforms that curtail their subsidies.

Third World nations are promoting the private sector and individual initiative in an attempt to stimulate economic growth.

The process of reform is greatly complicated by egalitarian ideologies that deprecate private success while justifying public privilege and by the pervasiveness of the state, which distorts the reward pattern and makes it easier to get rich by politics than by industry, by connections than by performance. These ideologies tend to take investment and the provision of productive capacity for granted, while being generally more concerned with redistributing the benefits and mitigating the costs of economic progress than with protecting its foundations.

The message is clear. In evaluating a nation's riskiness, it is not sufficient to identify factors—such as real interest shocks or world recession—that would systematically affect the economies of all foreign countries to one extent or another. It is necessary also to determine the susceptibility of the various nations to these shocks. This determination requires a focus on the financial policies and development strategies pursued by the different nations.

Based on the preceding discussion, some of the common characteristics of country risk include the following:

— A large government deficit relative to GNP
— A high rate of money expansion, especially if it is combined with a relatively fixed exchange rate
— Substantial government expenditures yielding low rates of return
— Price controls, interest rate ceilings, trade restrictions, and other government-imposed barriers to the smooth adjustment of the economy to changing relative prices
— Vast state-owned firms run for the benefit of their managers and workers
— A citizenry that demands, and a political system that accepts, government responsibility for maintaining and expanding the nation's standard of living through public sector spending and regulations (The less stable the political system, the more important this factor will likely be.)

Market-oriented policies improve a nation's economic health and its creditworthiness.

Alternatively, indicators of a nation's long-run economic health include the following:

— *A structure of incentives that rewards risk taking in productive ventures*: People have clearly demonstrated that they respond rationally to the incentives they face, given the information and resources available to them. This statement is true whether we are talking about shopkeepers in Nairobi or bankers in New York. A necessary precondition for productive investment to take place is secure legal rights to own and sell at least some forms of property.
— *A legal structure that stimulates the development of free markets*: The resulting price signals are most likely to contain the data that are essential to making efficient use of the nation's resources.
— *Minimal regulations and economic distortions*: Complex regulations are costly to implement and waste management time and other resources.
— *Clear incentives to save and invest*: In general, when there are such incentives, when the economic rules of the game are straightforward and stable, when property rights are secure, and when there is political stability, a nation's chances of developing are maximized.
— *An open economy*: Not only does free trade increase competition and permit the realization of comparative advantage, it also constrains government policies and makes them conform more closely to those conducive to increases in living standards and rapid economic growth.

The sorry economic state of Eastern Europe dramatically illustrates the consequences of pursuing policies that are the exact opposite of those recommended. Thus, the ability of the Eastern European countries to share in the prosperity of the Western world depends critically on their reversing the policies they have followed under communist rule.

Realism demands that nations—especially those in the Third World and Eastern Europe—come to terms with their need to rely more on self-help. The most successful economies, such as South Korea and Taiwan, demonstrate the importance of aligning domestic incentives with world market conditions. Like it or not, nations must make their way in an increasingly competitive world economy that puts a premium on self-help and has little time for the inefficiency and pretension of *statism*—that is, the substitution of state-owned or state-guided enterprises for the private sector—as the road to economic success. This recognition—that they cannot realize the benefits of capitalism without the institutions of capitalism—is dawning in even the most socialist countries of Europe, Asia, and Latin America. For example, in 1989, Vietnamese families were given the right to work their own land and sell their output at market prices. Within a year, rice production rose so dramatically that Vietnam went from the edge of famine to the world's third-largest rice exporter.

The hard fact is that the LDCs must rely on self-help to cope with their problems.

Market-oriented reform of Eastern European and LDC economic policies lies at the heart of any credible undertaking to secure these nations' economic and financial rehabilitation. The first and most critical step is to cut government spending. In practical terms, cutting government spending means reducing the bloated public sectors that permeate most Latin American and communist countries.

Reform of the public sector has probably gone the furthest in Latin America, where, shocked by the severe miseries of the 1980s (known in Latin America as the *Lost Decade*), many of these countries abandoned the statism, populism, and protectionism that have crippled their economies since colonial times. Chile and Colombia have embarked on fairly comprehensive reform programs, and despite some backsliding, Mexico has made surprisingly good headway (see Exhibit 20.5 for a summary of the changes in Mexico's economic policies). We saw also in Chapter 2 that Argentina has begun radical reform of its economy, highlighted by *privatizing*—returning to the private sector from the public sector—major activities and galvanizing the private sector by deregulation and the elimination of protectionism. And Poland has instituted a radical set of market reforms.

Yet in the best of circumstances, structural reform meets formidable political obstacles: labor unions facing job and benefit losses, bureaucrats fearful of diminished power and influence (not to mention their jobs), and local industrialists concerned about increased competition and reduced profitability. All are well

Structural reform is necessary, but politically unpopular.

Exhibit 20.5 Mexico's Economic Policies: Then and Now

Old Mexican Model	New Mexican Model
Large budget deficits	Fiscal restraint
Rapid expansion of money supply	Monetary discipline
Nationalization	Privatizations
Restrict foreign direct investment	Attract FDI
High tax rates	Tax reform
Import substitution	Trade liberalization
Controlled currency	End currency controls
Price and interest rate controls	Prices and interest rates set by market
Government dominates economy	Reduced size and scope of government

aware that the benefits of restructuring are diffuse and materialize only gradually, while they must bear the costs immediately.

Despite these obstacles, reducing state subsidies on consumer goods and to inefficient industries, removing trade barriers and price controls, and freeing interest rates and the exchange rate to move to market levels is probably the most straightforward and workable solution to economic stagnation. These actions, if implemented, can increase output by making the economy more efficient, can reduce consumption, and, thereby, can increase the quantity of goods available for export. They will also discourage capital flight and stimulate domestic savings and investment.

ILLUSTRATION: Strategies for Eastern European Economic Success

Eastern Europe has the basic ingredients for successful development: an educated work force, low wages, and proximity to large markets. However, the key to creating a dynamic market economy is to mobilize the energies and savings of the populace on the broadest possible scale, without whose support any reform package is doomed to failure. Unfortunately, under communism, people had no incentive to take risks, and, thus, took no initiative. State-owned firms were focused on the bureaucrats who gave them orders rather than the customers who bought from them, towards output rather than profit, towards the social welfare of their employees rather than efficiency. Market signals became even more muffled because the state banking system continued to finance loss-makers, no matter how hopeless, so that jobs were not jeopardized. The result was no innovation, an insatiable demand for investment capital, no concern with profitability, no consumer orientation, and low quality merchandise. Based on these considerations, here is a thumbnail sketch of the factors that will influence its chances of economic success.

— *Prerequisites*: Privatization of bloated state enterprises to force efficiency and customer responsiveness; market prices to signal relative scarcity and opportunity cost; private property, to provide incentives; and a complete revamping of the legal, financial, and administrative institutions that govern economic activity to permit enforceable contracts and property rights.

— *Economic reforms*: Decontrolling prices; eliminating subsidies and restrictions on international trade; creating strong, convertible currencies, so that people can receive something for their efforts; permitting bankruptcy, so that assets and people can be redeployed; doing away with regulations of small businesses; introducing a free capital market; and demonopolizing state enterprises through privatization to introduce competition.

These are not mere details. Completing such tasks will embroil the region in all the wrangles about wealth distribution and the size and role of the state that

Western countries have spent generations trying to resolve. And there's another complicating factor. For those born since 1945, the habits that constitute the tradition of private property, markets, and creativity have been blotted out. Two generations in Eastern Europe have never experienced private property, free contracts, markets, or inventive enterprise; the skills are gone. Whether and how fast these skills and habits can be resurrected remains an open question. Nonetheless, given the prerequisites and reforms outlined above, here are four strategies aimed at getting Eastern Europe off to a fast start.

1. *Deregulating agriculture* (especially farmers' access to markets, ownership of land, and decontrol of prices) offers the best hope for quickly easing food shortages and for containing food price increases as subsidies are eliminated. Communal ownership of land stifles initiative. Raising efficiency in agriculture is critical to successful development. Vietnam provides a good example of the potential gains from freeing up farmers.

2. *Privatizing small businesses*, on the broadest possible scale, is desperately needed in order to create new job opportunities for workers displaced by the inevitable restructuring of heavy industry. Small businesses have the greatest potential for harnessing individual initiative and creating new jobs quickly and are an indispensable part of the infrastructure of any dynamic market economy.

3. *Manufacturing low-technology goods* plays a key role in increasing skill levels and in disseminating technology throughout the economy. The region's current comparative advantage lies in low-technology manufactured goods. East Europeans cannot be expected immediately to produce cars, computers, and consumer electronics of sufficient quality to compete with the West; moving up the ladder to more sophisticated products will take considerable time and lots of Western investment and expertise.

4. *Direct investment in local production* is a preferred strategy since none of the countries in the region can afford a huge influx of imports. Western companies should target relatively cheap, everyday products of less than premium quality. Living standards in Eastern Europe and the Soviet Union are too low to warrant mass purchases of anything but the most basic Western goods.

20.3 MANAGING POLITICAL RISK

Once the firm has analyzed the political environment of a country and assessed its implications for corporate operations, it must then decide whether to invest there and, if so, how to structure its investment to minimize political risk. The key point remains that political risk is not independent of the firm's activities; the configuration of the firm's investments will, in large measure, determine its susceptibility to changing government policies.

Preinvestment Planning

Given the recognition of political risk, an MNC has at least four separate, though not necessarily mutually exclusive, policies that it can follow: (1) avoidance, (2) insurance, (3) negotiating the environment, and (4) structuring the investment.

Avoidance. The easiest way to manage political risk is to avoid it, and many firms do so by screening out investments in politically uncertain countries. However, inasmuch as all governments make decisions that influence the profitability of business, all investments, including those made in the United States, face some degree of political risk. For example, U.S. steel companies have had to cope with stricter environmental regulations requiring the expenditure of billions of dollars for new pollution control devices, while U.S. oil companies have been beleaguered by so-called windfall profit taxes, price controls, and mandatory allocations. Thus, risk avoidance is impossible.

The real issue is the degree of political risk a company is willing to tolerate and the return required to bear it. A policy of staying away from countries considered to be politically unstable ignores the potentially high returns available and the extent to which a firm can control these risks. After all, companies are in business to take risks, provided these risks are recognized, intelligently managed, and provide compensation.

The Overseas Private Investment Corporation provides low-cost political risk insurance subsidized by the U.S. government.

Insurance. An alternative to risk avoidance is insurance. By insuring assets in politically risky areas, firms can concentrate on managing their businesses and forget about political risk—or so it appears. Most developed countries sell *political risk insurance* to cover the foreign assets of domestic companies. The coverage provided by the U.S. government through the *Overseas Private Investment Corporation* (OPIC) is typical. Although its future has been in doubt several times—some U.S. citizens believe it is an instrument of U.S. imperialism, and others feel the government has no right to subsidize a service that would otherwise be provided by private enterprise—OPIC has managed to survive because of the general belief that this program, by encouraging U.S. direct investment in less-developed countries, helps these countries to develop.

The OPIC program provides U.S. investors with insurance against loss due to the specific political risks of expropriation, currency inconvertibility, and political violence—that is, war, revolution, or insurrection. To qualify, the investment must be a new one or a substantial expansion of an existing facility and must be approved by the host government. Coverage is restricted to 90% of equity participation. For very large investments or for projects deemed especially risky, OPIC coverage may be limited to less than 90%. The only exception is institutional loans to unrelated third parties, which may be insured for the full amount of principal and interest.

Similar OPIC political risk protection is provided for leases. OPIC's insurance provides lessors with coverage against loss due to various political risks, including the inability to convert into dollars local currency received as lease payments.

OPIC also provides business income coverage (BIC), which protects a U.S. investor's income flow if political violence causes damage that interrupts operation of the foreign enterprise. For example, an overseas facility could be bombed and partially or totally destroyed. It may take weeks or months to rebuild the plant. But during the rebuilding process the company still must meet its interest and other contractual payments and pay skilled workers in order to retain their services pending the reopening of the business. BIC allows a business to meet its continuing expenses and to make a normal profit during the period its operations are suspended. This is similar to the business interruption insurance available from private insurers for interruptions caused by nonpolitical events.

Another special program run by OPIC provides coverage for U.S. exporters of goods and services. OPIC insures against arbitrary drawings by a government buyer of bid, performance, advance payment and other guaranties (usually issued in the form of standby letters of credit). An arbitrary drawing is one not justified by the terms of the contract. OPIC will also insure a contractor's assets against loss due to political violence or confiscation. Protection in the event of contractual disputes is offered as well.

Premiums are computed for each type of coverage on the basis of a contractually stipulated maximum insured amount and a current insured amount that may, within the limits of the contract, be elected by the investor on a yearly basis. The current insured amount represents the insurance actually in force during any contract year.

The difference between the current insured amount and maximum insured amount for each coverage is called the standby amount. The major portion of the premium is based on the current insured amount, with a reduced premium rate being applicable to the standby amount. For expropriation and war coverage, the insured must maintain current coverage at a level equal to the amount of investment at risk.

The cost of the coverage varies by industry and risk insured. These costs, which are listed in Exhibit 20.6, are not based solely on objective criteria; they also reflect subsidies geared to achieving certain political aims, such as fostering development of additional energy supplies.

The only private insurer of consequence against expropriation risks is Lloyd's of London. There are several possible reasons why a large-scale private market for expropriation insurance has failed to develop. One major barrier to entry is the magnitude of the potential expropriation losses. A $1 billion claim may bankrupt a private insurer, unless that loss is only a small percentage of its total operations. However, the large loss factor can be dealt with by reinsuring most of the risks with other insurance firms and private investors. This reinsuring is routinely done in the insurance field.

Other possible obstacles to private insurers contemplating the sale of expropriation insurance are the problems of adverse selection and adverse incentives. *Adverse selection* refers to the possibility that only high-risk multinationals will seek insurance. This problem can be dealt with in several ways. The ways include adjusting premiums in accord with the perceived risks, screening out certain high-risk applicants, and providing premium reductions for firms engaged in activities that are likely to reduce expropriation risks.

The cost of OPIC insurance varies by industry and risk insured.

Exhibit 20.6 OPIC Insurance Fees: Annual Base Rates per $100 of Coverage

Coverage	Manufacturing/ Services Projects		Natural Resource Projects Other Than Oil and Gas		Oil and Gas Projects		Institutional Loans/Leases		Contractors and Exporters Guaranty Coverage	
	Current	(Standby)[1]	Current	(Standby)[1]	Exploration	Production	Current	(Unused Commitment)	Current	(Standby)
Inconvertibility	$0.30	$(0.25)	$0.30	$(0.25)	$0.30	$0.30	$0.50[2]	$(0.20)	$0.30	$(0.25)
Expropriation	0.60	(0.25)	0.90	(0.25)	0.40	1.50	0.40–0.90	(0.20)	0.60	(0.25)
Political violence	—	(0.25)	—	(0.25)	—	—	0.40–0.70	(0.20)	0.60	(0.25)
Business income	0.45	(0.25)	0.45	(0.25)	0.75	0.75	—	—	—	—
Assets	0.60	(0.25)	0.60	(0.25)	0.40	0.40	—	—	—	—
Interference with operations	—	—	—	—	—	—	—	—	—	—
Bid bonds	—	—	—	—	—	—	—	—	0.50	(0.25)
Performance, advance payment, and other guaranties	—	—	—	—	—	—	—	—	0.60	(0.25)
Disputes	—	—	—	—	—	—	—	—	0.70	(0.25)

[1]Does not apply to most equity investments.
[2]Incovertibility base rate for leases is $0.45.

SOURCE: "OPIC Investment Insurance Rates," Overseas Private Investment Corporation, August 1992.

The problem of *adverse incentives* is that by reducing the riskiness of certain activities, insurance may prompt firms to engage in activities with a higher probability of expropriation. Firms may undertake investments that were previously too risky and neglect certain policies responsive to the host country's needs. If the local affiliate is in financial difficulty, the parent can also take actions that would increase the possibility of expropriation or else collude with the host government to expropriate the affiliate—in much the same way that the owner of a failing business might commit arson to collect on the fire insurance. In effect, purchasing political risk insurance is equivalent to purchasing a put option on the project. The MNC will seek to exercise this put option—which effectively involves selling its foreign project to the insurance company for the amount of coverage—whenever the market value of the project falls below the insurance claim.

The problem of adverse incentives can be coped with to a certain extent by *coinsurance*—forcing the purchaser to self-insure part of the losses—and by refusing to pay off on a claim if it can be shown that the insured firm caused the expropriation. While these are not ideal solutions, the problems of adverse selection and adverse incentives should not pose major deterrents to the establishment of a viable market for expropriation insurance.

> Political risk insurers must cope with the problems of adverse selection and adverse incentives.

The most important barrier preventing private competition with Lloyd's is likely to be the existence of OPIC and other government-operated expropriation schemes. By offering subsidized insurance, these government plans have made private expropriation insurance unprofitable. As in other instances of market distortion, it is in the MNC's best interest to buy insurance when it is priced at a below-market rate. Since the rate is uniform across countries (for example, 0.6% for manufacturing operations), it clearly pays to insure in risky nations (mostly LDCs) and not insure in low-risk nations. Thus, government plans are faced with the aforementioned problem of adverse selection.

Even with subsidized rates, there are two fundamental problems with relying on insurance as a protection from political risk. First, there is an asymmetry involved. If an investment proves unprofitable, it is unlikely to be expropriated. Since business risk is not covered, any losses must be borne by the firm itself. On the other hand, if the investment proves successful and is then expropriated, the firm is compensated only for the value of its assets. This result relates to the second problem: Whereas the economic value of an investment is the present value of its future cash flows, only the capital investment in assets is covered by insurance. Thus, although insurance can provide partial protection from political risk, it falls far short of being a comprehensive solution.

Negotiating the Environment. In addition to insurance, therefore, some firms try to reach an understanding with the host government before undertaking the investment, defining rights and responsibilities of both parties. Also known as a *concession agreement*, such an understanding specifies precisely the rules under which the firm can operate locally.

These concession agreements were quite popular among firms investing in less-developed countries, especially in colonies of the home country. They often were negotiated with weak governments. In time, many of these countries became independent or their governments were overthrown. Invariably, the new rulers repudiated these old concession agreements, arguing that they were a form of exploitation.

Concession agreements are still being negotiated today, but they seem to carry little weight among Third World countries. Their high rate of obsolescence has led many firms to pursue a more active policy of political risk management.

Companies can structure their foreign investments to minimize political risk.

Structuring the Investment. Once a firm has decided to invest in a country, it can then try to minimize its exposure to political risk by increasing the host government's cost of interfering with company operations. This action involves adjusting the operating policies (in the areas of production, logistics, exporting, and technology transfer) and the financial policies so as to closely link the value of the foreign project to the multinational firm's continued control. In effect, the MNC is trying to raise the cost to the host government of exercising its ever-present option to expropriate or otherwise reduce the local affiliate's value to its parent.[2]

One key element of such a strategy is keeping the local affiliate dependent on sister companies for markets and/or supplies. Chrysler, for example, managed to hold on to its Peruvian assembly plant even though other foreign property was being nationalized. Peru ruled out expropriation because of Chrysler's stranglehold on the supply of essential components. Only 50% of the auto and truck parts were manufactured in Peru. The remainder—including engines, transmissions, sheet metal, and most accessories—were supplied from Chrysler plants in Argentina, Brazil, and Detroit. In a similar instance of vertical integration, Ford's Brazilian engine plant generates substantial exports, but only to other units of Ford. Not surprisingly, the data reveal no expropriations of factories that sell more than 10% of their output to the parent company.[3]

MNCs can minimize political risk by closely linking the value of their foreign operations to the parent's continued control.

Similarly, by concentrating R&D facilities and proprietary technology, or at least key components thereof, in the home country, a firm can raise the cost of nationalization. To be effective, it is necessary that other multinationals with licensing agreements not be permitted to service the nationalized affiliate. Another element of this strategy is establishing a single, global trademark that cannot be legally duplicated by a government. In this way, an expropriated consumer products company would sustain significant losses by being forced to operate without its recognized brand name.

Control of transportation—including shipping, pipelines, and railroads—has also been used at one time or another by the United Fruit Company and other multinationals to gain leverage over governments. Likewise, sourcing production in multiple plants reduces the government's ability to hurt the worldwide firm by seizing a single plant and, thereby, changes the balance of power between government and firm.

---

[2]Arvind Mahajan, "Pricing Expropriation Risk," *Financial Management*, Winter 1990, pp. 77–86, points out that when a multinational firm invests in a country, it is effectively writing a call option to the government on its property. The aim of political risk management is to reduce the value to the government of exercising this option.

[3]Bradley, "Managing Against Expropriation," pp. 75–83.

Another defensive ploy is to develop external financial stakeholders in the venture's success. This defense involves raising capital for a venture from the host and other governments, international financial institutions, and customers (with payment to be provided out of production) rather than employing funds supplied or guaranteed by the parent company. In addition to spreading risks, this strategy will elicit an international response to any expropriation move or other adverse action by a host government. A last approach, particularly for extractive projects, is to obtain unconditional host government guarantees for the amount of the investment that will enable creditors to initiate legal action in foreign courts against any commercial transactions between the host country and third parties if a subsequent government repudiates the nation's obligations. Such guarantees provide investors with potential sanctions against a foreign government, without having to rely on the uncertain support of their home governments.

One means of reducing political risk is to develop external stakeholders in the venture's success.

Operating Policies

Once the multinational has invested in a project, its ability to further influence its susceptibility to political risk is greatly diminished but not ended. It still has at least five different policies that it can pursue with varying chances of success: (1) planned divestment, (2) short-term profit maximization, (3) changing the benefit/cost ratio of expropriation, (4) developing local stakeholders, and (5) adaptation.

Planned Divestment. Several influential authors, notably Raul Prebisch and Albert Hirschman, have suggested that multinational firms phase out their ownership of foreign investments over a fixed time period by selling all or a majority of their equity interest to local investors.[4] Such *planned divestment*, however, may be difficult to conclude to the satisfaction of all parties involved. If the buyout price were set in advance and the investment is unprofitable, the government would probably not honor the purchase commitment. Moreover, with the constant threat of expropriation present during the bargaining, it is unlikely a fair price can be negotiated.

Short-Term Profit Maximization. Confronted with the need to divest itself wholly or partially of an equity position, the multinational corporation may respond by attempting to withdraw the maximum amount of cash from the local operation. By deferring maintenance expenditures, cutting investment to the minimum necessary to sustain the desired level of production, curtailing marketing expenditures, producing lower-quality merchandise, setting higher prices, and eliminating training programs, cash generation will be maximized for the short term, regardless of the effects of such actions on longer-run profitability and viability. This policy, which almost guarantees that the company will not be in business locally for long, is a response of desperation. Of course, the behavior is

MNCs threatened with political risk may engage in short-term profit maximization.

[4]Raul Prebisch, "The Role of Foreign Private Investment in the Development of Latin America," Sixth Annual Meeting of the IA-ECOSOC, June 1969; and Albert O. Hirschman, "How to Divest in Latin America, and Why," *Essays in International Finance*, No. 76, Princeton University, November 1969.

likely to accelerate expropriation if such was the government's intention—perhaps even if it were not the government's intention originally.

Hence, the firm must select its time horizon for augmenting cash outflow and consider how this behavior will affect government relations and actions. Surprisingly, most politicians do not seem to appreciate how strongly their rhetoric affects corporate decisions. In effect, government rhetoric about the evils of multinationals becomes a self-fulfilling prophecy because these threats induce more and more myopic corporate behavior.

Short-term profit maximization may have undesirable side effects.

The secondary implications of the short-term profit maximization strategy must be evaluated as well. The unfriendly government can be replaced by one more receptive to foreign investment (as occurred in Chile), or the multinational firm may want to supply the local market from affiliates in other countries. In either case, an aggressive tactic of withdrawing as much as possible from the threatened affiliate will probably be considered a hostile act and will vitiate all future dealings between the MNC and the country. Moreover, it is unlikely that a firm can get away with this behavior for long. Other governments will be put on notice and begin taking closer and more skeptical looks at the company's actions in their countries.

One alternative to this indirect form of divestment is to do nothing and hope that even though the local regime can take over an affiliate (with minor cost), it will choose not to do so. This wish is not necessarily in vain because it rests on the premise that the country needs foreign direct investment and will be unlikely to receive it if existing operations are expropriated without fair and full compensation. However, this strategy is essentially passive, resting on a belief that other multinationals will hurt the country (by withholding potential investments) if the country nationalizes local affiliates. Whether or not this passive approach will succeed is a function of how dependent the country is on foreign investment to realize its own development plans and the degree to which economic growth will be sacrificed for philosophical or political reasons.

ILLUSTRATION: Beijing Jeep

After the United States restored diplomatic relations with China in 1979, Western businesses rushed in to take advantage of the world's largest undeveloped market. Among them was American Motors Corporation (AMC). In 1983, AMC and Beijing Automotive Works formed a joint venture called the Beijing Jeep Company to build and sell jeeps in China.[5] The aim of Beijing Jeep was to first modernize the old Chinese jeep, the BJ212, and then replace it with a "new, second-generation vehicle" for sale domestically and overseas. Because it was one of the earliest attempts to combine Chinese and foreign forces in heavy manufacturing, Beijing Jeep became the "flagship" project other U.S. firms watched to asses the business environment in China. Hopes were high.

---

[5]This example is adapted from Jim Mann, *Beijing Jeep: The Short, Unhappy Romance of American Business in China* (New York: Simon and Shuster, 1989).

AMC viewed this as a golden opportunity: Build jeeps with cheap labor and sell them in China and the rest of the Far East. The Chinese government wanted to learn modern automotive technology and earn foreign exchange. Most importantly, the People's Liberation Army wanted a convertible-top, four-door jeep, so that Chinese soldiers could jump in and out and open fire from inside the car.

That the army had none of these military vehicles when they entered Tienanmen Square in 1989 has to do with the fact that this jeep could not be made from any of AMC's existing jeeps. But in signing the initial contracts, the two sides glossed over this critical point. They also ignored the realities of China's economy. For managers and workers, productivity was much lower than anybody at AMC had ever imagined. Equipment maintenance was minimal. Aside from windshield solvents, spare-tire covers, and a few other minor parts, no parts could be manufactured in China. The joint venture, thus, had little choice but to turn the new Beijing jeep into the Cherokee Jeep, using parts kits imported from the United States. The Chinese were angry and humiliated not to be able to manufacture any major jeep components locally.

They got even madder when Beijing Jeep tried to force its Chinese buyers to pay half of the Cherokee's $19,000 sticker price in U.S. dollars. With foreign exchange in short supply, the Chinese government ordered its state agencies, the only potential customers, not to buy any more Cherokees and refused to pay the $2 million that various agencies owed on 200 Cherokees already purchased.

The joint venture would have collapsed right then had Beijing Jeep not been such an important symbol of the government's modernization program. After deciding it could not let the venture fail, China's leadership arranged a bailout. The Chinese abandoned their hopes of making a new military jeep. And AMC gained the right to convert renminbi (the Chinese currency) into dollars at the official (and vastly overvalued) exchange rate. With this right, AMC realized it could make more money by replacing the Cherokee with the old, and much cheaper to build, BJ212s. The BJ212s were sold in China for renminbi and these profits were converted into dollars.

It was the ultimate irony: An American company that originally expected to make huge profits by introducing modern technology to China and by selling its superior products to the Chinese found itself surviving, indeed thriving, by selling the Chinese established Chinese products. AMC succeeded because its venture attracted enough attention to turn the future of Beijing Jeep into a test of China's open-door policy.

A more active strategy is based on the premise that expropriation is basically a rational process—that governments generally seize property when the economic benefits outweigh the costs. This premise suggests two maneuvers characteristic of active political risk management: Increase the benefits to the government if it does not nationalize a firm's affiliate, and increase the costs if it does.

Changing the Benefit/Cost Ratio.   If the government's objectives in an expropriation are rational—that is, based on the belief that economic benefits will more

A political risk management strategy should raise the cost of expropriation to the host government.

than compensate for the costs—the multinational firm can initiate a number of programs to reduce the perceived advantages of local ownership and, thereby, diminish the incentive to expel foreigners. These steps include establishing local R&D facilities, developing export markets for the affiliate's output, training local workers and managers, expanding production facilities, and manufacturing a wider range of products locally as substitutes for imports. It should be recognized that many of the foregoing actions lower the cost of expropriation and, consequently, reduce the penalty for the government. A delicate balance must be observed.

Realistically, however, it appears that those countries most liable to expropriation view the benefits—real, imagined, or both—of local ownership as more important than the cost of replacing the foreign investor. Although the value of a subsidiary to the local economy can be important, its worth may not be sufficient to protect it from political risk. Thus, one aspect of a protective strategy must be to engage in actions that raise the cost of expropriation by increasing the negative sanctions it would involve. These actions include control over export markets, transportation, technology, trademarks and brand names, and components manufactured in other nations. Some of these tactics may not be available once the investment has been made, but others may still be implemented. However, an exclusive focus on providing negative sanctions may well be self-defeating by exacerbating the feelings of dependence and loss of control that often lead to expropriation in the first place. Where expropriation appears inevitable, with negative sanctions only buying more time, it may be more productive to prepare for negotiations to establish a future contractual-based relationship.

Satisfied local stakeholders can provide protection against political risk.

Developing Local Stakeholders. A more positive strategy is to cultivate local individuals and groups who have a stake in the affiliate's continued existence as a unit of the parent MNC. Potential stakeholders include consumers, suppliers, the subsidiary's local employees, local bankers, and joint-venture partners.

Consumers worried about a change in product quality or suppliers concerned about a disruption in their production schedules (or even a switch to other suppliers) brought about by a government takeover may have an incentive to protest. Similarly, well-treated local employees may lobby against expropriation.[6] Local borrowing could help give local bankers a stake in the health of the MNC's operations if any government action threatened the affiliate's cash flows and, thereby, jeopardized loan repayments.

Having local private investors as partners seems to provide protection. One study finds that joint ventures with local partners have historically suffered only a 0.2% rate of nationalization, presumably because this arrangement establishes a powerful local voice with a vested interest in opposing government seizure.[7]

---

[6]French workers at U.S.-owned plants, satisfied with their employers' treatment of them, generally stayed on the job during the May 1968 student-worker riots in France, even though most French firms were struck.

[7]Bradley, "Managing Against Expropriation," pp. 75–83.

The shield provided by local investors may be of limited value to the MNC, however. The partners will be deemed to be tainted by association with the multinational. A government probably would not be deterred from expropriation or enacting discriminatory laws because of the existence of local shareholders. Moreover, the action can be directed solely against the foreign investor. And the local partners can be the genesis of a move to expropriate to enable them to acquire the whole of a business at a low or no cost.

Adaptation. Today, some firms are trying a more radical approach to political risk management. Their policy entails adapting to the inevitability of potential expropriation and trying to earn profits on the firm's resources by entering into licensing and management agreements. For example, oil companies whose properties were nationalized by the Venezuelan government received management contracts to continue their exploration, refining, and marketing operations. These firms have recognized that it is not necessary to own or control an asset such as an oil well to earn profits. This form of arrangement may be more common in the future as countries develop greater management abilities and decide to purchase from foreign firms only those skills that remain in short supply at home. Those firms that are unable to surrender control of their foreign operations due to the integration of these operations in a worldwide production planning system or some other form of global strategy are also those least likely to be troubled by the threat of property seizure, as was pointed out in the aforementioned Chrysler example.

> It is not necessary to own or control an asset to profit from it.

20.4 ILLUSTRATION: KENNECOTT AND ANACONDA IN CHILE

Most raw material seekers active in the Third World have found themselves under considerable pressure either to divest or to enter into minority joint ventures in order to avoid outright expropriation by host governments submerged by the tidal wave of economic nationalism. The tale of the involvement of two U.S. copper MNCs in Chile illustrates how political risk can be managed ex ante through a policy of multilateral entrapment.[8]

Both Kennecott and Anaconda had long held and operated substantial copper mines in Chile, but had radically different outlooks on Chile's future. Kennecott relied on the giant mine of El Teniente for 30% of its world output, but invested minimally above depreciation to keep production slightly increasing. Between 1945 and 1965 it did not attempt to develop any new mining sites. But in 1964, under pressure from President Frei to expand and modernize its operation at El Teniente, Kennecott initiated an ambitious capital expenditures plan aimed at increasing copper production from 180,000 metric tons to 280,000 metric tons per year. The expansion plan was to be financed by selling a 51%

---

[8]Adapted from Theodore H. Moran, *The Politics of Dependence: Copper in Chile* (Princeton, N.J.: Princeton University Press, 1974), by Laurent L. Jacque and Alan C. Shapiro.

Kennecott protected itself in Chile by developing a multinational web of stakeholders in the project.

interest in the mine for $80 million to the Chilean government in exchange for a ten-year management contract. In addition, further financing was sourced from the U.S. Eximbank ($110 million to be paid back over a period of 10–15 years) and the Chilean Copper Corporation ($24 million). In exchange for agreeing to a minority position in the newly created joint venture, Kennecott obtained a special reassessment of the book value of the El Teniente property (from $69 million to $286 million) and a dramatic reduction in taxes from 80% to 44% on its share of the profits.

Not only did Kennecott not commit one cent to the new mine, but it also developed a multinational web of stakeholders in the project. Kennecott began by insuring its equity sale to the Chilean government (reinvested in the mine) with the U.S. Agency for International Development (AID) and ensured that the Eximbank loan be unconditionally guaranteed by the Chilean state. In addition, any disputes between Kennecott and Chile would be submitted to the law of the state of New York. Kennecott also raised $45 million for the new joint venture by writing long-term contracts for the future output (literally mortgaging copper still in the ground) with European and Asian customers. Finally, collection rights on these contracts were sold to a consortium of European banks ($30 million) and Mitsui & Co., the Japanese trading company ($15 million).

Anaconda, which trusted in the Chilean government's good will, saw its mines expropriated without compensation.

Anaconda, by contrast, had been bullish on Chile all along. Having invested heavily in its own name from 1945 to 1965 in new mines and the modernization of old ones, it refused voluntary divestiture and was eventually forced to sell 51% of its Chilean holdings to the state in 1969. Although it had partial coverage of its holdings with AID prior to its forced divestiture, Anaconda had allowed the policy to lapse after 1969.

The real test of these different strategies came in 1971, when the defiant new Marxist government of President Allende assumed power. Both firms shortly fell prey to Chilean vengeance as Allende fulfilled his pledge to expropriate without compensation the foreign interests in Chilean copper. Kennecott received compensation from OPIC (the successor organization to AID) of $80 million plus interest—an amount that surpassed the book value of its pre-1964 holdings and that was eventually reimbursed to the U.S. government by Chile as a condition for rolling over the Chilean debt. Kennecott, on its own, was using the unconditional guarantee initially extracted from the Frei government for the original sale amount to obtain a writ of attachment in the U.S. federal courts against all Chilean property within the courts' jurisdiction, including the jets of Lanchile when they landed in New York. Faced with these actions, the Allende government assumed all debt obligations that the joint venture had contracted with Eximbank and the consortium of European banks and Mitsui. In effect, Kennecott had been freed from any further international obligations, financial and otherwise.

Anaconda was expropriated without compensation from either the Chilean government—because it had no leverage being the sole investor—or from OPIC—because it had failed to insure against political risk. The only recourse left to Anaconda's board of directors was to fire its entire management—which the board did.

20.5 SUMMARY AND CONCLUSIONS

Country risk analysis is the assessment of factors that influence the likelihood that a country will have a healthy investment climate. To summarize, a favorable political risk environment depends on the existence of a stable political and economic system in which entrepreneurship is encouraged and free markets predominate. Under such a system, resources are most likely to be allocated to their highest valued uses and people will have the greatest incentive to take risks in productive ventures.

Regardless of whether a nation has a high or low country risk rating, however, individual foreign investments are typically subject to differing degrees of political risk, based on their time pattern of benefits. The major benefits to a host country from a foreign investment usually appear at the beginning. Over time, the added benefits become smaller and the costs more apparent. Unless the firm is continually renewing these benefits—by introducing more products, say, or by expanding output and developing export markets—it is likely to be subject to increasing political risks. The common attitude of government is to ignore the past and ask what a firm will do for it in the future. In a situation where the firm's future contributions are unlikely to evoke a favorable government reaction, the firm had best concentrate on protecting its foreign investments by raising the costs of nationalization.

QUESTIONS

1. When investing in a copper mine in Peru, how can a U.S. mining firm such as Kennecott reduce its political risk?

2. Generally speaking, what is the most appropriate means of managing expropriation risk?

3. Can avoiding politically risky countries eliminate a company's political risk? Explain.

4. What factors affect the degree of political risk faced by a firm operating in a foreign country?

5. How might a government budget deficit lead to inflation?

6. What political realities underlie a government budget deficit?

7. What are some indicators of country risk? Of country health?

8. What obstacles do Third World countries such as Argentina, Brazil, and Ghana face in becoming developed nations with strong economies?

9. What can we learn about economic development and political risk from the contrasting experiences of East and West Germany, North and South Korea, and communist China and Taiwan, Hong Kong and Singapore?

10. What role do property rights and the price system play in national development and economic efficiency?

11. What indicators would you look for in assessing the political riskiness of an investment in Eastern Europe?

12. Exhibit 20.5 describes some economic changes that have been instituted by Mexico in recent years.

    a. What are the likely consequences of those changes?

    b. Who are the winners and the losers from these economic changes?

13. What is the link between a controlled exchange rate system and political risk?

14. Milton Friedman has suggested that public sector firms in Latin American countries should simply be given away, possibly to their employees. How do you think workers would feel about being given (for free) ownership of the public sector firms that employ them? Why?

PROBLEMS

1. Comment on the following statement discussing Mexico's recent privatization. "Mexican state companies are owned in the name of the people, but are run and now privatized to benefit Mexico's ruling class."

2. Between 1981 and 1987, direct foreign investment in the Third World plunged by over 50%. The World Bank is concerned about this decline and wants to correct it by improving the investment climate in Third World countries. Its solution: Create a Multilateral Investment Guarantee Agency (MIGA) that will guarantee foreign investments against expropriation at rates to be subsidized by Western governments.

    a. Assess the likely consequences of MIGA on both the volume of Western capital flows to Third World nations and the efficiency of international capital allocation.

    b. How will MIGA affect the probability of expropriation and respect for property rights in Third World countries?

    c. Is MIGA likely to improve the investment climate in Third World nations?

    d. According to a senior World Bank official (*The Wall Street Journal*, December 22, 1987, p. 20), "There is vastly more demand for political risk coverage than the sum total available." Is this a valid economic argument for setting up MIGA? Explain.

    e. Assess the following argument made on behalf of MIGA by a State Department memo: "We should avoid penalizing a good project [by not providing subsidized insurance] for bad government policies over which they have limited influence... Restrictions on eligible countries [receiving insurance subsidies because of their doubtful investment policies] will decrease MIGA's volume of business and spread of risk, making it harder to be self-sustaining." (Quoted in *The Wall Street Journal*, December 22, 1987, p. 20.)

3. You have been asked to head up a special presidential commission on the Russian economy. Your first assignment is to assess the economic consequences of the following seven policies and suggest alternative policies that may have more favorable consequences.

    a. Under the current Russian system, any profits realized by a state enterprise are turned over to the state to be used as the state sees fit. At the same time, shortfalls of money don't constrain enterprises from consuming resources. Instead, the state bank automatically advances needy enterprises credit, at a zero interest rate, to buy the inputs they need to fulfill the state plan and to make any necessary investments.

    b. The Russian fiscal deficit has risen to an estimated 13.1% of GNP. This deficit has been financed almost exclusively by printing rubles. At the same time, prices are controlled for most goods and services.

c. Russian enterprises are allocated foreign exchange to buy goods and services necessary to accomplish the state plan. Any foreign exchange earned must be turned over to the state bank.

d. In an effort to introduce a more market-oriented system, some Russian enterprises have been allowed to set their own prices on goods and services. However, other features of the system have not been changed: Each enterprise is still held accountable for meeting a certain profit target; only one state enterprise can produce each type of good or service; and individuals are not permitted to compete against state enterprises.

e. Given the disastrous state of Russian agriculture, the Russian government has permitted some private plots on which anything grown can be sold at unregulated prices in open-air markets. Because of their success, the government has recently expanded this program, giving Russian farmers access to much more acreage. At the same time, a number of Western nations are organizing massive food shipments to Russia to cope with the current food shortages.

f. The United States and other Western nations are considering instituting a Marshall Plan for Eastern Europe that would involve massive loans to Russia and other Eastern European nations in order to prop up the reform governments.

4. The president of Mexico has asked you to advise him on the likely economic consequences of the following five policies designed to improve Mexico's economic environment. Describe the consequences of each policy, and evaluate the extent to which these proposed policies will achieve their intended objective.

a. Expand the money supply to drive down interest rates and stimulate economic activity.

b. Increase the minimum wage so as to raise the incomes of poor workers.

c. Impose import restrictions on most products so as to preserve the domestic market for local manufacturers and, thereby, increase national income.

d. Raise corporate and personal tax rates from 50% to 70% to boost tax revenues and reduce the Mexican government deficit.

e. Fix the nominal exchange rate at its current level in order to hold down the cost to Mexican consumers of imported necessities (assume that inflation is currently 100% annually in Mexico).

BIBLIOGRAPHY

Bradley, David. "Managing Against Expropriation." *Harvard Business Review*, July–August 1977, pp. 75–83.

Kobrin, Stephen J. "Political Risk: A Review and Reconsideration." *Journal of International Business Studies*, Spring–Summer 1979, pp. 67–80.

Krueger, Anne O. "Asian Trade and Growth Lessons." *American Economic Review*, May 1990, pp. 108–112.

Landes, David S. "Why Are We So Rich and They So Poor?" *American Economic Review*, May 1990, pp. 1–13.

Shapiro, Alan C. "The Management of Political Risk." *Columbia Journal of World Business*, Fall 1981, pp. 45–56.

Stobaugh, Robert B. "How to Analyze Foreign Investment Climates." *Harvard Business Review*, September–October 1969, pp. 100–108.

Van Agtamael, A.W. "How Business Has Dealt with Political Risk." *Financial Executive*, January 1976, pp. 26–30.

Case IV.1 EURO DISNEYLAND

In 1987, in a muddy sugar-beet field 20 miles east of Paris, Walt Disney Co. was creating Euro Disneyland. By the time of its scheduled opening in 1992, Euro Disneyland (EDL) was expected to cost FF 15 billion ($2.5 billion based on an exchange rate of FF 6 = $1). Most signs pointed to the park's success. Two million Europeans already visit its American parks every year. And Paris demographics looked great: In two hours, 17 million people could drive to the park and 310 million people could fly to the park.

Disney's risk appears modest. It has invested $350 million in planning the park but has put up just $145 million for 49% of EDL's equity. Public investors will pay $1 billion for the other 51% in a stock offering in October 1989. The public company, through its traded shares, will give Europeans a chance to participate in the success of the project once the gates open in 1992. When the stock begins trading on the Paris Bourse in October 1989, Disney's stake is valued at $1 billion—an $800 million gain in value.

Even if profits are weak, Disney will rake in fat management fees. And it could clean up just on the land: It has rights to buy 4,800 acres from the government at just $7,500 an acre—compared to $750,000 an acre for similar land in the area. Disney can resell chunks to other developers for any price it can get. The acreage should jump in value once high-speed rail lines from Paris and London (via the Chunnel, the tunnel under the English Channel) are in place.

But there is risk nonetheless. The most critical variable is attendance. Many experts think surprises may await Disney. They doubt that attendance will meet Disney's expectations. Others think the crowds will come but spend less than Disney projects. Disney faces other unknowns as well. MCA/Universal, which will be bought by Matsushita in 1990, is thinking of building a park in London, which would cannibalize Euro Disneyland's attendance. There's also the grim winter weather, which prompts European parks to close until spring. Then there's the challenge of training 12,000 Europeans, half of them French, to be Disney "cast members." Bowing to French individualism, Disney will relax its personal grooming code a bit. Disney may also decide to change its ban on booze if customers call loudly enough for wine and beer. Disney claims that its experience with Tokyo Disneyland, its last major development project, shows that it can deal with non-American culture and bad weather. Tokyo Disneyland was completed on time and within 1% of budget. It has also been a huge commercial success.

FINANCING

In March 1987, Disney and the French government signed a "Master Agreement" for Euro Disneyland. In accordance with that agreement, Disney formed a holding company to control development of the entire site. It paid $145 million for 49% of the holding company's shares and sold 51% of EDL to European investors for a little over $1 billion; of the latter shares, around half were sold to the French.

The holding company is set up as an SCA (*Societe Commanditee par Actions*), a unique French corporate form that is very similar to an American limited partnership. Disney is the *gerant*, or general partner. The SCA structure allows Disney to control management, even with a minority shareholding. Thus, even though the holding company owns EDL, Disney will manage it and collect an estimated $35 million a year in royalties on sales of admission tickets, food, and souvenirs.

The master agreement was basically an inducement for Disney to bring Euro Disneyland to Paris rather than to Spain's Mediterranean coast. The inducements included the following:

— Loans of up to FF 4.8 billion were available from a French government agency. The loans carried a fixed interest rate of 7.85%, in contrast to a normal commercial rate of 9.25%.

— EDL could use accelerated depreciation to write off the construction costs of its extravaganza over a 10-year period.

— The French government would invest $350 million in park-related infrastructure. This included sewer and telephone trunk lines, subway and road links to Paris, and a new line of its 156-mile-per-hour *train a grande vitesse* (TGV) that would link EDL to the Chunnel (and thence to London), Brussels, and Lyons.

— Disney was allowed to buy 4,800 acres of land at 1971 prices. The average cost of FF 11.1 per square meter compared with FF 1,000 per square meter for development land in the Paris suburbs.

— The French government agreed to cut the value-added tax (VAT) on ticket sales to just 7% instead of the usual 18.5%.

Disney will structure the $2.5 billion Euro Disneyland project so that the operating losses created during construction can be used, along with the accelerated depreciation benefits, as tax shelters. These tax benefits will be sold to a group of French companies for $200 million. Equity contributions include the $1.15 billion stock sale plus Disney's $350 million investment in project planning. The remaining $800 million of project financing will come from French government-subsidized loans. The repayment schedule on these loans is as follows (in FF millions):

1992–1996	1997	1998	1999	2000	2001
0	FF 960	FF 960	FF 960	FF 960	FF 960

Euro Disneyland will also require about $115 million in working capital initially and this amount is expected to grow at the rate of sales revenue. The working capital will be financed by French franc bank loans carrying an interest rate expected to average about 9.5% annually.

FINANCIAL PROJECTIONS

Disney's projections assume a minimum 1992 attendance range at Euro Disneyland of 11 million visitor days and a maximum of 16 million. These numbers compare with 1988 attendance at the domestic U.S. parks of 25.1 million for Orlando's DisneyWorld and 13 million for Anaheim's Disneyland. In projecting future years, a conservative 3% annual growth rate is reasonable. The range of EDL attendance figures based on these assumptions appears in Exhibit IV.1.1.

The next step is to forecast individual expenditures at the park on a daily basis, for admission as well as for food and merchandise. Disney's projections assume that each visitor spends FF 78.6 on merchandise, FF 59.5 on food and beverages, and FF 5.5 on parking and other items (e.g., stroller rentals). Admission fees are estimated at FF 144.4 apiece.

These estimates are based on 1989 francs. French inflation is expected to increase these figures by 5% each year. As of late 1989, the French franc:dollar exchange rate was about FF 6 = $1, but this rate could obviously vary considerably. For example, U.S. inflation is expected to average about 4% annually, about 1% below the expected French inflation rate.

Euro Disneyland will also collect "participation fees" from various corporate sponsors, such as Kodak and Renault. These fees are payment for the privilege of sponsoring specific attractions in return for promotional considerations (e.g., Kraft's "The Land") and are expected to approximate $35 million in 1992.

EDL's pre-tax operating margin is expected to be about 35%. That money will not all flow into the hands of EDL shareholders. EDL must pay interest on its debt and French

Exhibit IV.1.1   Projected Number of Visitor Days at Euro Disneyland (Millions)

1992	1993	1994	1995	1996
11	11.3	11.7	12.0	12.4
12	12.4	12.7	13.1	13.5
13	13.4	13.8	14.2	14.6
14	14.4	14.9	15.3	15.8
15	15.5	15.9	16.4	16.9
16	16.5	17.0	17.5	18.0

SOURCE: Liz Buyer, "EuroDisney: As Close to Risk Free as a Deal Can Get," *The Journal of European Business,* March/April 1992, p. 27.

tax. The effective tax rate is estimated at 55%. In addition, EDL must pay Disney royalties, a base management fee, and an incentive-based bonus fee. Under the master agreement, Disney will collect 10% of the revenues generated by ticket sales and 5% of all expenditures on food, beverage, and merchandise. Disney also can collect significantly higher fees from EDL if the park exceeds certain operating cash flow (OCF) targets. Specifically, Disney collects 30% of the park's OCF in the range of FF 1.4–2.1 billion; 40% of all OCF between FF 2.1–2.8 billion; and 50% of all OCF above FF 2.8 billion. Disney receives no incentive fee if the park's OCF is less than FF 1.4 billion. In this case, the operating cash flow equals operating income since Disney has sold its depreciation tax benefits.

In November 1989, Walt Disney Co. announced plans to add a movie studio theme park as the second gated attraction to Euro Disneyland. The park is expected to open in 1996. In addition to strengthening Disney's film production capabilities in Europe (where the movement to enforce geographic quotas continues to gain momentum), the second attraction could add as much as FF 3.3 billion to 1996 operating revenues.

QUESTIONS

1. These questions relate to the $800 million (FF 4.8 billion at FF 6 = $1) in French government-subsidized loans.

    a. What is the value to Disney of the French government's loan subsidies?

    b. What exchange risk is this project subject to from the standpoint of Disney? How can financing be used to mitigate this exchange risk?

    c. Suppose it turns out that having $800 million in franc financing acutally adds to Disney's economic exposure. How could this affect Disney's willingness to accept the full amount of financing offered by the French government?

2. Based on purchasing power parity, project the dollar:franc exchange rate from 1989 through 1996.

3. What is the range of projected dollar net income for Euro Disneyland for the years 1992-1996?

4. Suppose the terminal value at the end of 1996 is estimated at seven times net income for 1996. Using a 15% cost of capital, what is the range of net present values of Euro Disneyland as a standalone project?

5. Using the same 15% cost of capital, what is the range of net present values of Walt Disney's investment in Euro Disneyland?

6. Should Walt Disney go ahead with this project? What other factors might you consider in estimating the value of Euro Disneyland to Walt Disney?

Part **V**

Financing Foreign Operations

International Financing and International Financial Markets

21

Money, like wine, must always be scarce with those who have neither where-withal to buy it nor credit to borrow it.

Adam Smith (1776)

CHAPTER LEARNING OBJECTIVES

- To describe trends and differences in corporate financing patterns around the world
- To define securitization and explain the forces that underlie it and how it has affected the financing policies of MNCs
- To explain why bank lending is on the decline worldwide and how banks have responded to their loss of market share
- To explain what is meant by the globalization of financial markets and identify the factors that have affected the process of globalization
- To describe the external medium- and long-term financing options available to the multinational corporation
- To identify the functions and consequences of financial markets
- To describe the links between national and international capital markets
- To explain why firms may choose to raise capital overseas
- To describe the Eurocurrency market and explain why it exists
- To describe the characteristics of Eurocurrency loans
- To describe the Eurobond market and explain why it exists
- To describe the characteristics of Eurobonds
- To describe the types, roles, and consequences of development banks

The growing internationalization of capital markets and the increased sophistication of companies means that the search for capital no longer stops at the water's edge. This reality is particularly true for multinational corporations. A distinctive feature of the financial strategy

509

of MNCs is the wide range of external sources of funds that they use on an ongoing basis. General Motors packages car loans as securities and sells them in Europe and Japan. British Telecommunications offers stock in London, New York, and Tokyo, while Beneficial Corporation issues Euroyen notes that may not be sold in either the United States or Japan. Swiss Bank Corporation—aided by Italian, Belgian, Canadian, and German banks, as well as other Swiss banks—helps RJR Nabisco sell Swiss franc bonds in Europe and then swap the proceeds back into U.S. dollars.

This chapter explores the MNC's external medium- and long-term financing alternatives. While many of the sources are internal to the countries in which the MNCs operate, more of their funds are coming from offshore markets, particularly the Eurocurrency and Eurobond markets. We will, therefore, study both national and international capital markets in this chapter and the links between the two. We begin by discussing trends in corporate financing patterns.

21.1 CORPORATE SOURCES AND USES OF FUNDS

Firms can raise funds internally or externally.

Firms have three general sources of funds available: internally generated cash, short-term external funds, and long-term external funds. External finance can come from investors or lenders. Investors give a company money by buying the securities it issues in the financial markets. These securities, which are generally *negotiable* (tradeable), usually take the form of debt or equity.

The main alternative to issuing public debt securities directly in the open market is to obtain a loan from a specialized financial intermediary that issues securities (or deposits) of its own in the market. These alternative debt instruments usually are commercial bank loans—for short-term and medium-term credit—or privately placed bonds—for longer-term credit. Unlike *publicly issued bonds, privately placed bonds* are sold directly to only a limited number of sophisticated investors, usually life insurance companies and pension funds. Moreover, privately placed bonds are generally nonnegotiable and have complex, customized loan agreements—called *covenants.* The restrictions in the covenants range from limits on dividend payments to prohibitions on asset sales and new debt issues. They provide a series of checkpoints that permit the lender to review actions by the borrower that have the potential to impair the lender's position. These agreements have to be regularly renegotiated prior to maturity. As a result, privately placed bonds are much more like loans than publicly issued and traded securities.

National Financing Patterns

Companies in different countries have different financial appetites. British companies get an average of about 50% of their funds from external suppliers, whereas German companies get about 75% of their funds from internal sources. In Japan, where their profitability has been low, companies have relied heavily on external finance, getting almost 70% of their money from outside sources. The shortfall of funds reflects the Japanese strategy of making huge industrial investments and pursuing market share at the expense of profit margins. As Japanese firms emphasize profits over sales growth, they will probably rely more heavily on internal sources of funds.

In contrast to Japan, in Europe and the United States internal finance has consistently supplied the lion's share of financial requirements. The percentage of external finance fluctuates more or less in line with the business cycle: When profits are high, firms are even less reliant on external finance. Moreover, the predominance of internal financing is not accidental. After all, companies could pay out internal cash flow as dividends and issue additional securities to cover their investment needs. The preference for internal finance is explicit in Gordon Donaldson's 1961 study of the financing practices of large American firms. He observed that "management strongly favored internal generation as a source of new funds even to the exclusion of external funds except for occasional unavoidable 'bulges' in the need for funds."[1]

Another empirical regularity about financing behavior relates to the composition of external finance. Regardless of the country studied, debt accounts for the overwhelming share of external funds. By contrast, new stock issues play a relatively small and declining role in financing investment.

Financial Markets Versus Financial Intermediaries

Industry's sources of external finance also differ widely from country to country. German and French companies rely heavily on bank borrowing (as have Japanese companies, until recently) whereas U.S. and British industry raise much more money directly from financial markets by the sale of securities. In all these countries, however, bank borrowing is on the decline. There is a growing tendency for corporate borrowing to take the form of negotiable securities issued in the public capital markets rather than in the form of nonmarketable loans provided by financial intermediaries.

This process, termed *securitization*, is most pronounced among the Japanese companies. Securitization largely reflects a reduction in the cost of using financial markets at the same time that the cost of bank borrowing has risen. Until recently, various regulatory restrictions enabled banks to attract low-cost funds from depositors. With *financial deregulation*, which began in the United States in 1981 and in Japan in 1986, banks must now compete for funds with a wide range of institutions at market rates. In addition, regulatory demands for a stronger capital base have forced U.S. banks to use more equity financing, raising their cost of funds. Inevitably, these changes have pushed up the price of bank loans. Any top-flight company can now get money more cheaply by issuing commercial paper than it can from its banks. As a result, banks now have a smaller share of the short-term business credit market.

Companies in different countries exhibit different financing patterns.

Securitization, which involves replacing loans from banks with securities issued in the public markets, is increasing everywhere.

[1]Gordon Donaldson, *Corporate Debt Capacity: A Study of Corporate Debt Policy and the Determination of Corporate Debt Capacity* (Boston: Division of Research, Harvard Graduate School of Business Administration, 1961), p. 67.

Securitization is replacing financial intermediation as the costs of gathering information on foreign firms declines.

At the same time, the cost of accessing the public markets is coming down, especially for smaller and less well known companies. Historically, these companies found it more economical simply to obtain a loan from a bank or to place a private bond issue with a life insurance company. These *private placements* proved cheaper because banks and life insurance companies specialize in credit analysis and assume a large amount of a borrower's debt. Consequently, they could realize important cost savings in several functions, such as gathering information about the condition of debtor firms, monitoring their actions, and renegotiating loan agreements.

Recent technological improvements in such areas as data manipulation and telecommunications have greatly reduced the costs of obtaining and processing information about the conditions that affect the creditworthiness of potential borrowers. Any analyst now has computerized access to a wealth of economic and financial information at a relatively low cost, along with programs to store and manipulate this information. Thus, investors are now more likely to find it cost-effective to lend directly to companies, rather than indirectly through *financial intermediaries*, such as commercial banks.

Globalization of Financial Markets

The globalization of financial markets stems from advances in communications and technology combined with financial deregulation.

These same advances in communications and technology, together with financial deregulation abroad—the lifting of regulatory structures that inhibit competition and protect domestic markets—have blurred the distinction between domestic and foreign financial markets. As the necessary electronic technology has been developed and the cost of transactions has plummeted, the world has become one vast, interconnected market. Markets for U.S. government securities and certain stocks, foreign exchange trading, interbank borrowing and lending—to cite a few examples—operate continuously around the clock and around the world and in enormous size. The *globalization of financial markets* has brought about an unprecedented degree of competition among key financial centers and financial institutions that has further reduced the costs of issuing new securities.

Growing competition has also led to increasing deregulation of financial markets worldwide. Deregulation is hastened by the process of *regulatory arbitrage*, whereby the users of capital markets issue and trade securities in financial centers with the lowest regulatory standards and, hence, the lowest costs. In order to win back business, financial centers around the world are throwing off obsolete and costly regulations. Deregulation is little more than an acknowledgement that the rules do not—and cannot—work.

ILLUSTRATION: Capital Markets Compete for Business

In mid-1989, Germany abolished its 10% withholding tax on interest income, less than six months after it took effect. The tax led to record capital flight from Germany, putting downward pressure on the Deutsche mark. Upon announcement of the repeal, German bonds jumped in value.

Similarly, in early 1990, Sweden announced that it would scrap a turnover tax on bond trading and halve a similar tax on trading in equities that had driven most international trading of Swedish shares abroad. The taxes had been imposed one year earlier as political concessions to powerful Swedish unions, who resented the large amounts of money being made in Swedish financial markets. Almost everyone else vehemently opposed the levies. The dire consequences predicted by critics were borne out in decimated trading volumes. For example, the tax on bond trading slashed average daily trading volume of Swedish government securities by 78% from the year before. At the same time, volume on the Stockholm Stock Exchange plunged by 20% even though the market rose 119% in the period. The final straw was a study by the Finance Ministry that showed the various levies actually resulted in a net reduction in tax collections for Sweden as trades shifted abroad. On the day the tax cuts were announced, stocks of the largest Swedish companies rose almost 2.5%.

The combination of freer markets with widely available information has laid the foundation for global growth. Cross-border securities trading was estimated in 1990 to be $12 trillion.[2] Fund raising is also global now as well. In 1992, an estimated $450 billion was raised in international capital markets. Treasurers are not confined to domestic markets as their source of funding and are now quick to exploit any attractive opportunity that occurs anywhere in the world.

Whereas competition drives the international financial system, innovation is its fuel. *Financial innovation* segments, transfers, and diversifies risk. It also enables companies to tap previously inaccessible markets and permits investors and issuers alike to take advantage of tax loopholes. Because of financial innovation, international capital mobility has increased dramatically.

Financial innovation segments, transfers, and diversifies risk.

As in the domestic case, cross-border financial transfers can take place through international securitization or international financial intermediation. The hypothetical case depicted in Exhibit 21.1 illustrates the distinction between these two mechanisms for international fund flows. A Belgian corporation with surplus funds seeks an investment outlet, while a Japanese corporation requires additional funds. International securitization might involve the Japanese firm issuing new bonds and selling them directly to the Belgian firm.

Alternatively, the Belgian firm's surplus funds could be transferred to the Japanese firm through international financial intermediation. This intermediation could involve three (or more) stages. First, the Belgian firm deposits its funds with a local Belgian bank. Second, the Belgian bank redeposits the money with an international money center bank in London that turns around and lends those funds to a Japanese bank. In stage three, the Japanese bank lends those funds to the Japanese corporation.

Whether international fund flows take place through financial intermediation or securitization depends on the relative costs and risks of the two mechanisms.

---

[2]This figure was cited in "A Survey of the International Capital Markets," *The Economist,* July 21, 1990, p. 7.

Exhibit 21.1 Securitization Versus Intermediation

SOURCE: Anthony Saunders, "The Eurocurrency Interbank Market: Potential for International Crises?" *Business Review,* Federal Reserve Bank of Philadelphia, January/February 1988, p. 19. Used with permission.

The key determinant here is the cost of gathering information on foreign firms. As these costs continue to come down, international securitization should become increasingly more cost-effective.

21.2 NATIONAL CAPITAL MARKETS AS INTERNATIONAL FINANCIAL CENTERS

Well-functioning financial markets lead to more and better projects being financed.

The principal functions of a financial market are to transfer current purchasing power (in the form of money) from savers to borrowers in exchange for the promise of greater future purchasing power and to allocate those funds among the potential users on the basis of risk-adjusted returns. The consequences of well-functioning financial markets is that more and better projects get financed, and individuals are able to select their preferred time pattern of consumption. Not surprisingly, most of the major financial markets attract both investors and fund raisers from abroad. That is, these markets are also *international financial markets* where foreigners can both borrow and lend money.

International Financial Markets

International financial markets can develop anywhere, provided that local regulations permit the market and that the potential users are attracted to it. The most important international financial centers are London, Tokyo, and New York. All the other major industrial countries have important domestic financial markets as well but only some, such as Germany and—recently—France, are also important international financial centers. On the other hand, some countries that have relatively unimportant domestic financial markets are important world financial centers. The markets of those countries—which include Switzerland, Luxembourg, Singapore, Hong Kong, the Bahamas, and Bahrain—serve as financial *entrepots*, or channels through which foreign funds pass. That is, these markets serve as financial intermediaries between nonresident suppliers of funds and nonresident users of funds.

Political stability and minimal government intervention are prerequisites for becoming and remaining an important international financial center, especially an entrepot center. Historically, London's preeminence as an entrepot for international finance comes from its being a lightly regulated offshore market in a world of financial rigidities. That is why it became home to the Euromarkets some 30 years ago. As financial markets deregulate, London's strength has shifted to its central location and financial infrastructure—its access to information by dint of its position astride huge international capital flows, its pool of financial talent, its well-developed legal system, and its telecommunications links.

Foreign Access to Domestic Markets

Despite the increasing liberalization of financial markets, governments are usually unwilling to rely completely on the market to perform the functions of gathering and allocating funds. Foreigners particularly are often hampered in their ability to gain access to domestic capital markets because of government-imposed or government-suggested restrictions relating to the maturities and amounts of money that they can raise. They are hampered as well by the government-legislated extra costs, such as special taxes (for example, the U.S. interest equalization tax (INT) that was in effect from 1963 to 1974) that they must bear on those funds that they can raise. Nonetheless, the financial markets of many countries are open wide enough to permit foreigners to borrow or invest.

> Foreigners are often hampered in their ability to access domestic capital markets because of government regulations.

As a citizen of many nations, the multinational firm has greater leeway in tapping a variety of local money markets than does a purely domestic firm, but it too is often the target of restrictive legislation aimed at reserving local capital for indigenous companies or the local government. The capital that can be raised is frequently limited to local uses through the imposition of exchange controls. As we have seen previously, however, multinationals are potentially capable of transferring funds, even in the presence of currency controls, by using a variety of financial channels. To the extent, therefore, that local credits substitute for parent- or affiliate-supplied financing, the additional monies are available for removal.

The Foreign Bond Market. The *foreign bond market* is an important part of the international financial markets. It is simply that portion of the domestic bond market that represents issues floated by foreign companies or governments. As such, foreign bonds are subject to local laws and must be denominated in the local currency. At times, these issues face additional restrictions as well. For example, foreign bonds floated in Switzerland, Germany, and the Netherlands are subject to a queuing system, where they must wait for their turn in line.

> The foreign bond market is that portion of the domestic bond market that represents issues floated by foreigners.

The United States and Switzerland contain the most important foreign bond markets. Major foreign bond markets are also located in Japan and Luxembourg. Data on the amounts of foreign bond issues are presented in Exhibit 21.2.

The Foreign Bank Market. The *foreign bank market* represents that portion of domestic bank loans supplied to foreigners for use abroad. As in the case of foreign bond issues, governments often restrict the amounts of bank funds destined for foreign purposes.

Foreign banks are an increasingly important source of funding.

The growing importance of foreign banks, particularly Japanese banks, as a funding source for U.S. corporations is obvious from Exhibit 21.3, which shows that commercial and industrial loans to U.S. businesses by foreign banks rose from $86 billion in 1983 to $348 billion by the end of 1991. The net effect of this rapid growth in foreign bank loans is that the foreign bank share of the U.S. commercial and industrial (C&I) loan market increased to 45% by the end of 1991, from 18% in 1983.

Another indication of the importance of foreign banks, and particularly Japanese banks, is the fact that of the world's 25 largest banks ranked by assets as of December 31, 1991, 16 are Japanese. The highest ranked U.S. bank, Citicorp, was 26th in size. (Of the world's 100 largest banks, only 7 are American; 27 are Japanese.) The minimal representation by American banks among the world's largest owes primarily to prohibitions on interstate banking in the United States, as well as the high Japanese savings rate.

Exhibit 21.2 Foreign Bond Market (U.S.$ Millions)

Market	1987	(%)	1988	(%)	1989	(%)	1990	(%)	1991	(%)	1992*	(%)
Austria	99	(0.2)	—		319	(0.7)	496	(1.0)	380	(0.8)	624	(1.2)
Belgium	672	(1.7)	114	(0.2)	106	(0.2)	192	(0.4)	233	(0.5)	310	(0.6)
France	674	(1.7)	578	(1.2)	729	(1.7)	366	(0.7)	689	(1.4)	357	(0.7)
Germany	—		—		754	(1.7)	—		—		—	
Italy	147	(0.4)	340	(0.7)	146	(0.3)	160	(0.3)	335	(0.7)	—	
Japan	4071	(10.2)	6720	(14.1)	8156	(18.7)	7880	(15.9)	5171	(10.5)	6605	(12.3)
Luxembourg	1380	(3.4)	1774	(3.7)	1674	(3.8)	4419	(8.9)	5555	(11.3)	5191	(9.7)
Netherlands	1008	(2.5)	750	(1.6)	274	(0.6)	644	(1.3)	219	(0.4)	112	(0.2)
Portugal	—		35	(0.1)	62	(0.1)	274	(0.6)	690	(1.4)	297	(0.6)
Spain	240	(0.6)	728	(1.5)	2225	(5.1)	1681	(3.4)	2590	(5.3)	1645	(3.1)
Switzerland	24301	(60.7)	26318	(55.1)	18624	(42.7)	23187	(46.9)	20183	(41.1)	16028	(29.8)
United Kingdom	—		355	(0.7)	1155	(2.6)	252	(0.5)	84	(0.2)	—	
United States	7416	(18.5)	10051	(21.0)	9440	(21.6)	9900	(20.0)	12933	(26.4)	22531	(42.0)
Total	40008	(100.0)	47763	(100.0)	43664	(100.0)	49451	(100.0)	49062	(100.0)	53700	(100.0)

*1992 data through November annualized

SOURCE: OECD Financial Statistics Monthly, various issues.

Exhibit 21.3 Foreign Funding of U.S. Corporate Loans

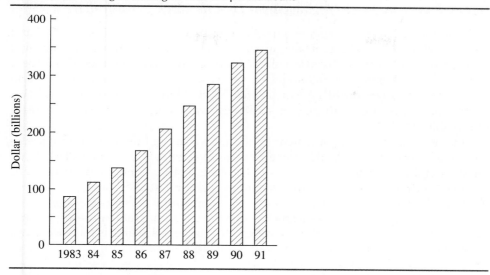

SOURCE: Data from Robert N. McCauley and Rama Seth, "Foreign Bank Credit to U.S. Corporations: The Implications of Offshore Loans," *FRBNY Quarterly Review,* Federal Reserve Bank of New York, Spring 1991, p. 54.

The Foreign Equity Market. The idea of placing stock in foreign markets has long attracted corporate finance managers. One attraction of the *foreign equity market* is the diversification of equity funding risk: A pool of funds from a diversified shareholder base insulates a company from the vagaries of a single national market. Some issues are too large to be taken up only by investors in the national stock market. For large companies located in small countries, foreign sales may be a necessity. When KLM, the Dutch airline, issued 50 million shares in 1986 to raise $304 million, it placed 7 million shares in Europe, 7 million in the United States, and 1 million in Japan. According to a spokesman for the company, "The domestic market is too small for such an operation."[3]

Selling stock overseas also increases the potential demand for the company's shares, and hence its price, by attracting new shareholders. In addition, for a firm that wants to project an international presence, an international stock offering can spread the firm's name in local markets. In the words of a London investment banker, "If you are a company with a brand name, it's a way of making your product known and your presence known in the financial markets, which can have a knock-off effect on your overall business. A marketing exercise is done; it's just like selling soap."[4]

Equity issues are increasingly being sold abroad.

[3]"International Equities: The New Game in Town," *Business International Money Report,* September 29, 1987, p. 306.

[4]"International Equities: The New Game in Town."

ILLUSTRATION: Waste Management Lists Its Stock in Australia

Chicago-based Waste Management has been operating in Australia since 1984 and has gained a leading share of the garbage collection market through expansion and acquisition. In 1986, the firm issued shares in Australia and then listed these shares on the Australian exchanges. A principal reason for the listing was to enhance its corporate profile. According to a Waste Management spokesman, "We view Australia as a growth market, and what we really wanted was to increase our visibility."[5]

Listing gets Waste Management better known in the financial community as well. This visibility in turn aids the expansion program, which hinges largely on mergers and acquisitions, by increasing contacts with potential joint venture or acquisition candidates. Listing also facilitates stock-for-stock swaps.

An Australian listing also enhances the local profit-sharing package. Waste Management uses an employee stock program as an integral feature of its compensation. By listing locally, the prominence of the firm's shares is increased, and the program becomes more attractive to employees.

Rule 144a has improved foreign access to the U.S. equity market.

To capture some of these potential benefits, more companies are selling stock issues overseas (see Exhibit 21.4 for the announcement of a $512 million *international equity offering* by Hong Kong Telecommunications). For example, the largest common stock offering in the United States in 1991 was a $1.2 billion issue by Telephonos de Mexico (Telmex), part of a $2.2 billion global offering. In all, *Yankee stock issues*—stock sold by foreign companies to U.S. investors—totaled over $5.8 billion in 1991. And that number increased in 1992. For example, in October 1992, Roche Holding Ltd., the Swiss pharmaceutical giant, announced that it had completed a U..S private placement of $275 million worth of stock. The move reflected Roche's desire to tap into the world's largest capital market because its rapid growth had "left Roche simply too big for the Swiss market."[6]

An important new avenue for foreign equity issuers, ranging from France's Rhone-Poulenc to Korea's Pohang Iron & Steel, to gain access to the U.S. market was opened up in 1990 when the Securities and Exchange Commission (SEC) adopted *Rule 144A*, which allows qualified institutional investors to trade in unregistered private placements, making them a closer substitute for public issues. This greatly increases the liquidity of the private placement market and makes it more attractive to foreign companies, who are frequently deterred from entering the U.S. market by the SEC's stringent disclosure and reporting requirements.

The desire to build a global shareholder base is also inducing many American companies—which until recently issued stock almost exclusively in the United

---

[5]"Waste Management Who? Why One U.S. Giant Is Now Listed Down Under," *Business International Money Report*, December 22, 1986, p. 403.

[6]Quoted in "Roche Sells 100,000 Shares in U.S. Market," *Wall Street Journal*, October 2, 1992, p. A7.

Exhibit 21.4 The International Equity Offering by Hong Kong Telecommunications

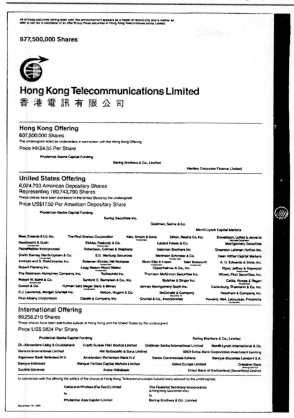

SOURCE: Used by permission.

States—to now sell part of their issues overseas. For example, in May 1992, General Motors raised $2.1 billion by selling 40 million shares in the United States, 6 million in Britain, 4.5 million in Europe, and 4.5 million in the Far East. Exhibit 21.5 shows the announcement of that issue. As usual, the benefits of expanded ownership must be traded off against the added costs of inducing more investors to become shareholders.

Most major stock exchanges permit sales of foreign issues provided the issue satisfies all the listing requirements of the local market. Some of the major stock markets list large numbers of foreign stocks. For example, Union Carbide, Black & Decker, Caterpillar, and General Motors are among the more than 200 foreign stocks listed on the German stock exchanges. Similarly, over 500 foreign stocks—including ITT, Hoover and Woolworth—are listed on the British exchanges. More companies are also seeking to be listed on the Tokyo Stock Exchange. Exhibit 21.6 announces Bell Atlantic's listing on the Tokyo exchange.

Exhibit 21.5   General Motors' Global Equity Issue

SOURCE: Morgan Stanley & Company, Inc. Used with permission.

Exhibit 21.6   Announcement of Bell Atlantic's Listing on the Tokyo Stock Exchange

Today, Bell Atlantic's shares will be listed on the Tokyo Stock Exchange. This step is in recognition of the internationalization of capital markets and of Japan's increasingly important role in international trade.

Bell Atlantic™ is currently listed on the following stock exchanges:
New York, Boston, Mid-West, Pacific, Philadelphia, London, Zurich, Geneva, Basel.

SOURCE: Used with permission of Bell Atlantic Network Services, Inc.

21.3 THE EUROMARKETS

This section discusses the Eurocurrency and Eurobond markets. It describes the functioning of these markets and then shows how each can be used to meet the multinational firm's financing requirements.

The Eurocurrency Market

A *Eurocurrency* is a dollar or other freely convertible currency deposited in a bank outside its country of origin. Thus, U.S. dollars on deposit in London become *Eurodollars*. These deposits can be placed in a foreign bank or in the foreign branch of a domestic U.S. bank.[7] The *Eurocurrency market* then consists of those banks—called *Eurobanks*—that accept deposits and make loans in foreign currencies.

The Eurobond and Eurocurrency markets are often confused with each other, but there is a fundamental distinction between the two. In the *Eurobond market*, *Eurobonds,* which are bonds sold outside the countries in whose currencies they are denominated, are issued directly by the final borrowers; whereas the Eurocurrency market enables investors to hold short-term claims on commercial banks, which then act as intermediaries to transform these deposits into long-term claims on final borrowers. However, banks do play an important role in placing these bonds with the final investors.

The dominant Eurocurrency is the U.S. dollar. But the importance of the Eurodollar waxes and wanes with the strength of the U.S. dollar. With dollar weakness in the latter parts of both the 1970s and 1980s, other currencies—particularly the Deutsche mark and the Swiss franc—increased in importance.

Modern Origins. The origin of the post–World War II Eurodollar market is often traced to the fear of Soviet Bloc countries that their dollar deposits in U.S. banks might be attached by U.S. citizens with claims against Communist governments. Therefore, they left their dollar balances with banks in France and England.

Whatever its postwar beginnings, the Eurocurrency market has thrived for one reason: government regulation. By operating in Eurocurrencies, banks and suppliers of funds are able to avoid certain regulatory costs that would otherwise be imposed. The following series of U.S. government policies provided a major impetus for the rapid development of the Eurodollar market.

1. Regulation Q set interest rate ceilings on deposits in the United States. These ceilings imposed by the Federal Reserve allowed overseas banks to attract dollar deposits whenever equilibrium rates rose above the Regulation Q limit.
2. Federal Reserve Regulation M in the United States mandated fractional reserves on dollar deposits taken in, whereas Eurobanks were not required to maintain reserves against the dollar deposits.

> The Eurocurrency market consists of banks that accept deposits and make loans in foreign currencies.

> The Eurocurrency market thrives because of various government regulations.

---

[7]The term foreign is relative to the operation unit's location, not to its nationality.

3. The interest equalization tax (INT) introduced in 1963 taxed interest on foreign debt sold in the United States, thereby raising significantly the cost of borrowing in U.S. capital markets by non-U.S. corporations and governments. Borrowers had to look outside the United States for funds, often turning to the Eurodollar market.
4. Regulations in 1968 from the U.S. Office of Foreign Direct Investment (OFDI) restricted U.S. companies in their use of domestic dollars overseas. Future expansion had to be financed overseas, greatly increasing the demand for external dollars, or Eurodollars.

Continuing government regulations and taxes provide opportunities to engage in Eurocurrency transactions.

Although the INT and OFDI regulations and Regulation Q have been abolished, the Eurodollar market still exists. In 1992, for example, approximately $114 billion in Eurocurrency loans were made, about the same as in 1991 and down from $122 billion in 1990. Despite its ups and downs, it will continue to exist as long as there are profitable opportunities to engage in offshore financial transactions. These opportunities persist because of continuing government regulations and taxes that raise costs and lower returns on domestic transactions.

Eurodollar Creation. The creation of Eurodollars can be illustrated by using a series of T-accounts to trace the movement of dollars into and through the Eurodollar market.

First, suppose that Leksell AB, a Swedish firm, sells medical diagnostic equipment worth $1 million to a U.S. hospital. It receives a check payable in dollars drawn on Citibank in New York. Initially, Leksell AB deposits this check in its Citibank checking account for dollar-working-capital purposes. This transaction would be represented on the firm's and Citibank's accounts as follows:

Citibank		Leksell AB	
	Demand deposit due Leksell AB +$1M	Demand deposit in Citibank +$1M	

In order to earn a higher rate of interest on the $1 million account (U.S. banks cannot pay interest on corporate checking accounts), Leksell decides to place the funds in a time deposit with Barclays Bank in London. This transaction is recorded as follows:

Citibank		Barclays	
	Demand deposit due Leksell AB −$1M Demand deposit due Barclays +$1M	Demand deposit in Citibank +$1M	Time deposit owed Leksell +$1M

Leksell AB

Demand deposit in Citibank −$1M	
Demand deposit in Barclays +$1M	

One million Eurodollars have just been created by substituting a dollar account in a London bank for a dollar account held in New York. Notice that no dollars have left New York, although ownership of the U.S. deposit has shifted from a foreign corporation to a foreign bank.

Barclays can leave those funds idle in its account in New York, but the opportunity cost would be too great. If it cannot immediately loan those funds to a government or commercial borrower, Barclays will place the $1 million in the London interbank market. This involves loaning the funds to another bank active in the Eurodollar market. The interest rate at which such interbank loans are made is called the *London interbank offer rate* (LIBOR). In this case, however, Barclays chooses to loan these funds to Ronningen SA, a Norwegian importer of fine wines. The loan is recorded as follows:

The interest rate on interbank loans is called the London interbank offer rate or LIBOR.

Citibank

Demand deposit due Barclays −$1M	
Demand deposit due Ronningen SA +$1M	

Barclays

Demand deposit in Citibank +$1M	Time deposit owed Leksell +$1M
Loan to Ronningen SA +$1M	

Ronningen AB

Demand deposit in Citibank +$1M	Eurodollar loan from Barclays +$1M

We can see from this example that the Eurocurrency market involves a chain of deposits and a chain of borrowers and lenders, not buyers and sellers. One does not buy or sell Eurocurrencies. Ordinarily, an owner of dollars will place them in a time-deposit or demand-deposit account in a U.S. bank, and the owner of a French franc deposit will keep it in an account with a French bank. Until the dollar (or franc) deposit is withdrawn, control over its use resides with the U.S. (or French) bank. In fact, the majority of Eurocurrency transactions involve transferring control of deposits from one Eurobank to another Eurobank. Loans to nonEurobanks account for fewer than half of all Eurocurrency loans. The net market size (subtracting off interEurobank liabilities) is much smaller than the gross market size; in 1987, for example, the gross market size was about $4.4 trillion, while the net market size was about $2.4 trillion.

The example and data presented indicate that Eurocurrency operations differ from the structure of domestic banking operations in two ways:

1. There is a *chain of ownership* between the original dollar depositor and the U.S. bank.
2. There is a *changing control over the deposit* and the use to which the money is put.

It should be noted, however, that despite the chain of transactions, the total amount of foreign dollar deposits in the United States remains the same. Moreover, on the most fundamental level—taking in deposits and allocating funds—the Eurocurrency market operates much as does any other financial market, except for the absence of government regulations on loans that can be made and interest rates that can be charged. This section now examines some of the particular characteristics of Eurocurrency lending.

Eurocurrency Loans.   The most important characteristic of the Eurocurrency market is that loans are made on a floating-rate basis. Interest rates on loans to governments and their agencies, corporations, and nonprime banks are set at a fixed margin above LIBOR for the given period and currency chosen. At the end of each period, the interest for the next period is calculated at the same fixed margin over the new LIBOR. For example, if the margin is 0.75% and the current LIBOR is 13%, then the borrower is charged 13.75% for the upcoming period. The period normally chosen is six months, but shorter periods such as one month or three months are possible. The LIBOR used corresponds to the maturity of the rollover period.

> *Eurocurrency loans are made on a floating-rate basis.*

The *margin*, or spread between the lending bank's cost of funds and the interest charged the borrower, varies a good deal among borrowers and is based on the borrower's perceived riskiness. Typically, such spreads have ranged from slightly below 0.5% to over 3%, with the median being somewhere between 1% and 2%.

The *maturity* of a loan can vary from approximately three to 10 years. Maturities have tended to lengthen over time, from a norm of about five years originally to a norm of eight to 10 years these days for prime borrowers. Lenders in this market are almost exclusively banks. In any single loan, there will normally be a number of participating banks that form a syndicate. The bank originating the loan will usually manage the syndicate. This bank, in turn, may invite one or two other banks to comanage the loan. The managers charge the borrower a once-and-for-all fee of 0.25% to 1% of the loan value, depending on the size and type of the loan. Part of this fee is kept by the managers, and the rest is divided up among all the participating banks (including the managing banks) according to the amount of funds each bank supplies.

The *drawdown*—the period over which the borrower may take down the loan—and the repayment period vary in accordance with the borrower's needs. A commitment fee of about 0.5% per annum is paid on the unused balance, and prepayments in advance of the agreed-upon schedule are permitted but are sometimes subject to a penalty fee.

Multicurrency Clauses. Borrowing can be done in many different currencies, although the dollar is still the dominant currency. Increasingly, Eurodollars have a multicurrency clause. This clause gives the borrower the right (subject to availability) to switch from one currency to another on any rollover date. The multicurrency option enables the borrower to match currencies on cash inflows and outflows (a potentially valuable exposure management technique as we saw in Chapter 9). Equally important, the option allows a firm to take advantage of its own expectations regarding currency changes (if they differ from the market's expectations) and shop around for those funds with the lowest effective cost.

An example of a typical multicurrency loan is a $100 million, 10-year revolving credit arranged by the Dutch firm Thyssen Bornemisza NV with nine Dutch, German, U.S., and Swiss banks, led by Amsterdam-Rotterdam Bank. Rates are fixed, at the company's discretion, at three-month, six-month, or 12-month intervals. At each rollover date, the firm can choose from any freely available Eurocurrency except Eurosterling, but only four different Eurocurrencies may be outstanding at any one time.

Relationship Between Domestic and Eurocurrency Money Markets. The presence of arbitrage activities ensures a close relationship between interest rates in national and international (Eurocurrency) money markets. Interest rates in the U.S. and Eurodollar markets, for example, can differ only to the extent that there are additional costs, controls, or risks associated with moving dollars between, say, New York and London. Otherwise, arbitrageurs would borrow in the low-cost market and lend in the high-return market, quickly eliminating any interest differential between the two.

> Interest rates in national and Euro-currency market are closely linked through arbitrage.

Since the cost of shifting funds is relatively insignificant, we must look to currency controls or risk to explain any substantial differences between domestic and external rates. To the extent that exchange controls are effective, the national money market can be isolated or segmented from its international counterpart. In fact, the difference between internal and external interest rates can be taken as a measure of the effectiveness of the monetary authorities' exchange controls.

Interest differentials can also exist if there is a danger of future controls. The possibility that at some future time either the lender or borrower will not be able to transfer funds across a border—also known as sovereign risk—can help sustain persistent differences between domestic and external money market rates.

In general, Eurocurrency spreads (a spread is the margin between lending and deposit rates) are narrower than in domestic money markets. Lending rates can be lower for the following reasons:

1. The lack of reserve requirements increases a bank's earning asset base (that is, a larger percentage of deposits can be lent out).
2. Regulatory expenses, such as the requirement to pay Federal Deposit Insurance Corporation fees, are lower or nonexistent.
3. Eurobanks are not forced to lend money to certain borrowers at concessionary rates, thereby raising the return on their assets.
4. Most borrowers are well known, reducing the cost of information gathering and credit analysis.

5. Eurocurrency lending is characterized by high volumes, allowing for lower margins; transactions costs are reduced because most of the loan arrangements are standardized and conducted by telephone or telex.
6. Eurocurrency lending can and does take place out of tax-haven countries, providing for higher after-tax returns.

Eurocurrency deposit rates are higher than domestic rates for the following reasons:

1. They must be higher to attract domestic deposits.
2. Eurobanks can afford to pay higher rates based on their lower regulatory costs.
3. Eurobanks are able to pay depositors higher interest rates because they are not subject to the interest rate ceilings that prevail in many countries.
4. A larger percentage of deposits can be lent out.

Euromarket Trends. In recent years, the London interbank offer rate has started to fade as a benchmark for lending money in the Eurocurrency market, in much the same way that the prime rate is no longer the all-important benchmark in the U.S. bank loan market. In a trend that shows no sign of abating, a growing number of creditworthy borrowers—including Denmark, Sweden, several major corporations, and some banks—are obtaining financing in the Euromarkets at interest rates well below LIBOR.

This trend largely reflects the fact that because many international bank loans soured in the early 1980s, banks lost much of their appeal to investors. As a result, banks' ability to impose themselves as the credit yardstick by which all other international borrowers are measured has faltered drastically. What the Euromarket is saying in effect is that borrowers such as Denmark are considered better credit risks than are most banks.

Moreover, investor preferences for an alternative to bank Eurodollar certificates of deposit (whereby banks substitute their credit risk for their borrowers') have enabled investment banks to transform usual bank syndicated lending into securities offerings, such as floating-rate notes (FRNs). This preference for the ultimate borrower's credit risk, rather than the bank's credit risk, has led to rapid growth in the Eurobond market, particularly in its floating-rate segment.

Eurobonds

Eurobonds are bonds sold outside the country in whose currency they are denominated.

Eurobonds are similar in many respects to the public debt sold in domestic capital markets. Unlike domestic bond markets, however, the Eurobond market is almost entirely free of official regulation, but instead is self-regulated by the Association of International Bond Dealers. The prefix Euro indicates that the bonds are sold outside the countries in whose currencies they are denominated. For example, the General Motors issue shown in Exhibit 21.7 is a Eurobond. You can tell that because the tombstone says, "These securities have not been registered under the United States Securities Act of 1933 and may not be offered or sold in the United States or to United States persons as part of the distribution."

Exhibit 21.7 Announcement of a GMAC Eurobond Issue

These securities have not been registered under the United States Securities Act of 1933 and may not be offered or sold in the United States or to United States persons as part of the distribution.

General Motors Acceptance Corporation

(Incorporated in the State of New York, United States of America)

U.S.$200,000,000

7⅝ per cent. Notes due September 3, 1991

Swiss Bank Corporation International Limited

Credit Suisse First Boston Limited	Deutsche Bank Capital Markets Limited
Merrill Lynch Capital Markets	Morgan Stanley International
Nomura International Limited	Salomon Brothers International Limited

Union Bank of Switzerland (Securities) Limited

Algemene Bank Nederland N.V.	BankAmerica Capital Markets Group
Bankers Trust International Limited	Banque Bruxelles Lambert S.A.
Banque Générale du Luxembourg S.A.	Banque Nationale de Paris
Banque Paribas Capital Markets Limited	Commerzbank Aktiengesellschaft
Crédit Lyonnais	Creditanstalt-Bankverein
Daiwa Europe Limited	IBJ International Limited
Leu Securities Limited	The Nikko Securities Co., (Europe) Ltd.
Shearson Lehman Brothers International	Société Générale
Sumitomo Trust International Limited	Swiss Volksbank
S.G. Warburg Securities	Wood Gundy Inc.

Yamaichi International (Europe) Limited

New Issue   This announcement appears as a matter of record only.   September 1986

SOURCE: Used with permission of General Motors Acceptance Corporation.

Until recently, the Eurobond market has been substantially smaller than the Eurocurrency market. Borrowers in the Eurobond market must be well known and must have impeccable credit ratings (for example, developed countries, international institutions, and large multinational corporations). Even then the amounts raised in the Eurobond market have historically been far less than those in the Eurocurrency market.

As can be seen in Exhibit 21.8, however, the Eurobond market has grown dramatically over the past decade and its size now rivals that of the Eurocurrency market. But Exhibit 21.8 also shows that the Eurobond market has had its ups and downs.

The Eurobond market grew dramatically during the 1980s.

Swaps. The major catalyst for growth in the Eurobond market over the last few years has been the emergence of a technique known as the *swap*, a financial transaction in which two counterparties agree to exchange streams of payments over time. It is now estimated that 70% of Eurobond issues are "swap-driven." Swaps allow borrowers to raise money in one market and to swap one interest

Exhibit 21.8 Eurobond New Issues, 1979–1992

rate structure for another (for example, from fixed to floating), or to go further and to swap principal and interest from one currency to another. These swaps allow borrowers to arbitrage their relative access to different currency markets; a borrower whose paper is much in demand in one currency can obtain a cost saving in another currency by raising money in the former and swapping the funds into the latter currency. Chapter 22 discusses swaps in detail.

Arbitrage ensures close links between the Euro-bond and domestic bond markets.

Links Between the Domestic and Eurobond Markets. The growing presence of sophisticated investors willing to arbitrage between the domestic dollar and Eurodollar bond markets—in part because the United States no longer imposes withholding taxes on foreign investors—has eliminated much of the interest disparity that used to exist between Eurobonds and domestic bonds. Despite the closer alignment of the two markets, though, the Eurobond issuer may at any given time take advantage of Eurobond "windows" when a combination of domestic regulations, tax laws, and expectations of international investors enable the issuer to achieve a lower all-in financing cost—often involving currency and interest swaps—than is available in domestic markets.[8] In addition to the possibility of reduced borrowing costs, the Eurobond issuer may diversify its investor base and funding sources by having access to the international Eurocapital markets of Western Europe, North America, and the Far East.

Placement. Issues are arranged through an underwriting group, often with a hundred or more underwriting banks involved for an issue as small as $25

[8]The existence of such windows is documented by Yong-Cal Kim and Rene M. Stulz in "The Eurobond Market and Corporate Financial Policy: A Test of the Clientele Hypothesis," *Journal of Financial Economics*, 22 (1988), pp. 189–205, and "Is There Still a Global Market for Convertible Bonds?" working paper, Ohio State University, April 1990.

million. A growing volume of Eurobonds is being placed privately because of the simplicity, speed, and privacy with which private placements can be arranged.

Currency Denomination. Historically, about 75% of Eurobonds have been dollar denominated. During the late 1970s, however, when the dollar was in a downward spiral, other currencies (particularly the Deutsche mark) became more important in the Eurobond market. The sharp increase in the share of dollar-denominated Eurobonds in the period up to mid-1985, shown in Exhibit 21.8, largely reflects the surging value of the dollar. The subsequent drop in the dollar's value again led to a rise in nondollar issues, particularly yen and Deutsche mark issues. The absence of Swiss franc Eurobonds is due to the Swiss Central Bank's ban on using the Swiss franc for Eurobond issues.

As an alternative to issuing dollar, Deutsche-mark, or other single-currency-denominated Eurobonds, several borrowers in recent years have offered bonds whose value is a weighted average or "basket" of several currencies. The most successful of these currency "cocktails" is the European Currency Unit (ECU). From 1983 through 1992, corporations and government agencies sold about $120 billion of ECU bonds.

ECU bonds offer advantages to both investors and borrowers, including the following:

1. *Access to markets that might not otherwise be available*: The markets for some individual European currencies are not very liquid and certain European capital markets—such as the Belgian franc, French franc, Italian lira, and Danish krone bond markets—are difficult to tap directly for funds because of remaining capital controls. Using the ECU lowers transaction costs, enables indirect access to currencies otherwise unavailable, and allows wider market diversification.

2. *Diversification of currency risk, especially for investors and borrowers within the European Monetary System*: The effect of weakening currencies will—to some degree—be offset by strengthening currencies within the basket. Although the currency percentage contained in an ECU bond is probably suboptimal in terms of its risk-return trade-off, investors and borrowers dealing in ECUs may face lower transaction costs than if they were to tailor their own currency baskets.

3. *A hedge against the dollar*: Because the ECU basket excludes the dollar, the value of the ECU in terms of any of its component currencies is generally unaffected by changes in the dollar's value.

Investors snapped up ECU bonds on the assumption that monetary union would force the inflation and interest rates of all European countries into line with those of Germany. ECU yields were expected to fall towards those of German bonds, the lowest in Europe. That would mean the price of ECU bonds would soar. However, following the events of September 1992—which put an end to those speculations—investor demand for new ECU issues dried up, trading activity all but disappeared, and prices fell sharply.

Eurobond Secondary Market. Historically, there has been a lack of depth in the Eurobond *secondary market* (the market where investors trade securities already

> Most Eurobonds are denominated in dollars but other currencies and the ECU are becoming more important.

bought). However, the growing number of institutions carrying large portfolios of Eurobonds for trading purposes has increased the depth and sophistication of this market, making it second only to the U.S. domestic bond market in liquidity—where liquidity refers to the ease of trading securities at close to their quoted price. Until recently, the liquidity of Eurobonds has not mattered because investors were usually willing to purchase and lock such issues away. But because of heightened volatility in bond and currency markets, investors increasingly want assurance that they can sell Eurobonds before maturity at bid-ask spreads (the difference between the buy and the sell rate, which is a major determinant of liquidity) comparable to those in other capital markets.

One problem is that there is no central trading floor where dealers post prices. Hence, buyers sometimes have difficulty getting price quotes on Eurobonds. However, many commercial banks, investment banks, and securities trading firms act as *market makers* in a wide range of issues by quoting two-way prices (buy and sell) and being prepared to deal at those prices. Another factor adding liquidity to the market is the presence of bond brokers. They act as middlemen, taking no positions themselves but transacting orders when a counterparty is found to match a buy or sell instruction. Brokers deal only with market makers and never with the ultimate investor.

Eurobond Retirement. Sinking funds or purchase funds are usually required if a Eurobond is of more than seven years' maturity. A *sinking fund* requires the borrower to retire a fixed amount of bonds yearly after a specific number of years. By contrast, a *purchase fund* often starts in the first year, and bonds are retired only if the market price is below the issue price. The purpose of these funds is to support the market price of the bonds as well as reduce bondholder risk by assuring that not all the firm's debt will come due at once.

The desire for price support is reinforced by the fact that, historically there has been a lack of depth in the secondary market. However, the growing number of institutions carrying large portfolios of Eurobonds for trading purposes has increased the depth and sophistication of this market, thereby enhancing liquidity.

Most Eurobond issues carry *call provisions,* giving the borrower the option of retiring the bonds prior to maturity should interest rates decline sufficiently in the future. As with domestic bonds, Eurobonds with call provisions require both a call premium and higher interest rates relative to bonds without call provisions.

Rationale for Existence of Eurobond Market. The Eurobond market survives and thrives because, unlike any other major capital market, it remains largely unregulated and untaxed. Thus, big borrowers, such as Texaco, IBM, and Sears Roebuck, can raise money more quickly and more flexibly than they can at home. And because the interest investors receive is tax free, these companies have historically been able to borrow at a rate that is below the rate at which the U.S. Treasury could borrow.

The Eurobond market exists because it enables issuers and investors to avoid government regulations and taxes.

The tax-free aspect of Eurobonds relates to the notice in the tombstone for the GMAC Eurobond issue that it may not be offered to the U.S. public. U.S. tax law requires that for interest and principal to be payable in the United States, bonds must be in registered form. Eurobonds, however, are issued in bearer form, meaning they are unregistered, with no record to identify the owners. (Money can be considered to be a zero-coupon bearer bond.) This feature allows investors to collect interest in complete anonymity and, thereby, evade taxes. Although U.S. law discourages the sale of such bonds to U.S. citizens or residents, bonds issued in bearer form are common overseas. As expected, investors are willing to accept lower yields on bearer bonds than on nonbearer bonds of similar risk.

Highly rated American firms have long taken advantage of this opportunity to reduce their cost of funds by selling overseas Eurobonds in bearer form. Often corporations could borrow abroad below the cost at which the U.S. government could borrow at home. Exxon's issue of zero-coupon Eurobonds shows how companies were able to exploit the arbitrage possibilities inherent in such a situation. Zero-coupon bonds pay no interest until maturity. Instead, they are sold at a deep discount from their par value.

ILLUSTRATION: Exxon Engages in International Tax Arbitrage

In the fall of 1984, Exxon sold \$1.8 billion principal amount of zero-coupon Eurobonds due November 2004 at an annual compounded yield of 11.65%, realizing net proceeds of about \$199 million:

$$\text{Bond value} = \$1,800,000,000/(1.1165)^{20} = \$199,000,000$$

It then used part of the proceeds to buy \$1.8 billion principal amount of U.S. Treasury bonds maturing in November 2004 from which the coupons had been removed and sold separately. The yield on these "stripped" Treasurys, which are effectively zero-coupon Treasury bonds, was around 12.20%.[9] At this yield, it would have cost Exxon \$180 million to purchase the \$1.8 billion in stripped Treasury bonds:

$$\text{Bond value} = \$1,800,000,000/(1.1220)^{20} = \$180,000,000$$

At this price, Exxon earned the difference of about \$19 million.

A peculiar quirk in Japanese law is largely responsible for the big difference in yield between zero-coupon Eurobonds and stripped Treasurys: Japanese investors—who were the principal buyers of the Eurobonds—did not have to pay tax on a zero-coupon bond's accrued interest if they sold the bond prior to maturity. Because of this tax advantage, they were willing to pay a premium price for zeros (relative to coupon-bearing bonds). Although in principle the Japanese would have preferred to purchase the higher-yielding (and safer) stripped U.S. Treasury bonds, they are prohibited by Japanese law from doing so. The threatened taxation of the accrued interest on zeros in Japan has eliminated this arbitrage opportunity.

---

[9]This case is discussed at greater length in John D. Finnerty, "Zero Coupon Bond Arbitrage: An Illustration of the Regulatory Dialectic at Work," *Financial Management*, Winter 1985, pp. 13–17.

It is apparent that the Eurobond market, like the Eurocurrency market, exists because it enables borrowers and lenders alike to avoid a variety of monetary authority regulations and controls, as well as providing them with an opportunity to escape the payment of some taxes. As long as governments attempt to regulate domestic financial markets but allow a (relatively) free flow of capital among countries, the various external financial markets will survive. If tax and regulatory costs rise, these markets will grow in importance.

Recent years have seen a reversal of some of these tax and regulatory costs. In 1984, the United States repealed its withholding tax on interest paid to foreign bondholders. That made domestic bonds, particularly U.S. Treasurys, more attractive to foreign investors. Whereas yields on top-rated Eurodollar bonds were about 40 basis points *below* similar-maturing Treasurys in 1984, the same Eurobonds in 1988 yielded about 70 basis points more than did Treasurys (see Exhibit 21.9).

At the same time, the United States began permitting well-known companies—precisely the ones that would otherwise have used the Eurobond market—to bypass complex securities laws when issuing new securities by using the *shelf registration* procedure. By lowering the cost of issuing bonds in the United States and dramatically speeding up the issuing process, shelf registration improved the competitive position of the U.S. capital market relative to the Eurobond market. More recently, the SEC's adoption of Rule 144A now enables companies to issue bonds simultaneously in Europe and the United States, further blurring the distinction between the U.S. bond market and its Eurobond equivalent. Other nations, such as Japan and England, are also deregulating their financial markets.

With repeal of the withholding tax and financial market deregulation in the United States and elsewhere, the Eurobond market lost some of the cost advan-

Financial deregulation and the repeal of U.S. withholding tax on interest paid to foreigners is reducing the Eurobond market's appeal.

Exhibit 21.9   Eurodollar Bond Yields Relative to Ten-Year U.S. Treasury Bond Yields

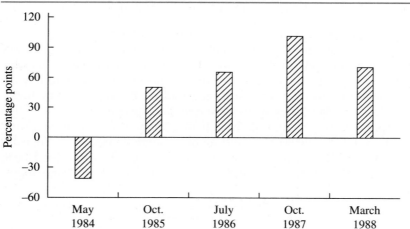

tage that lured corporate borrowers in the first place. Nonetheless, as long as Eurobond issuance entails low regulatory and registration costs relative to domestic bond issuance, the Eurobond market will continue to attract investors and borrowers from all over the world.

Despite several forecasts of imminent death, the Eurobond market has survived, largely because its participants are so fleet of foot. As demand for one type of bond declines, quick-witted investment bankers seem to find other opportunities to create value for their customers. When the demand for fixed-rate Eurobonds fell, the Eurobond market led the boom in floating-rate note issues. When the FRN market collapsed in 1986, this business was replaced by issues of Japanese corporate bonds with equity warrants attached. *Equity warrants* confer on their holder the option to buy a given issuer's shares at a specified price over a set period. In return for what is in effect a long-dated call option on the issuer's stock, the investor accepts a lower interest rate on the Eurobond to which the equity warrant is attached.

The Eurobond survives because of its adaptability.

Demand for such issues soared as investors used the warrants to play Japan's rising stock market. In turn, Japanese companies found the Eurobond market easier and cheaper to use than the regulated domestic-yen market. However, the Tokyo stock market's plunge in 1990 triggered a 71.5% drop in the Japanese equity-warrant issue market and a 14.4% fall in the Eurobond market overall.

The financial infrastructure in place in London should ensure the Eurobond market's survival. However, tax harmonization, financial deregulation, and the widespread loosening of capital controls mean that issuers have less incentive to borrow money offshore, and so are returning to their domestic markets to raise capital. If these trends persist, the Eurobond market may never regain its preeminence. But it can still preserve its basic role—as the nimblest intermediary for international capital flows between domestic markets.

Eurobonds Versus Eurocurrency Loans

Both Eurocurrency and Eurobond financing have their advantages and disadvantages. Although many of these factors are reflected in the relative borrowing costs, not all factors are so reflected. For a given firm, therefore, and for a specific set of circumstances, one method of financing may be preferred to the other. The differences are categorized in five ways.

1. *Cost of borrowing*: Eurobonds are issued in both fixed-rate and floating-rate forms. Fixed-rate bonds are an attractive exposure management tool since known long-term currency inflows can be offset with known long-term outflows in the same currency. By contrast, the interest rate on a Eurocurrency loan is variable, which makes Eurocurrency loans better hedges for noncontractual currency exposures. The variable interest rate benefits borrowers when rates decline but hurts them when rates rise. Arbitrage between Eurobonds and Eurocurrencies, however, should not provide a certain cost advantage to one or the other form of borrowing.

2. *Maturity*: While the period of borrowing in the Eurocurrency market has tended to lengthen over time, Eurobonds still have longer maturities.

3. *Size of issue*: Historically, the amount of loanable funds available at any one time has been much greater in the interbank market than in the bond market. In 1983, for the first time, the volume of Eurobond offerings exceeded voluntary global bank lending (those loans not forced by debt reschedulings). In many instances, borrowers have discovered that the Eurobond market can easily accommodate financings of a size and at a price not previously thought possible. When Digital Equipment, Texas Instruments, International Paper, and Illinois Power brought out $475 million worth of Eurodollar bonds over two days in February 1984, they saved as much as 0.45% on the cost of issuing debt in the United States. This translates into millions of dollars of interest savings. Moreover, although in the past the flotation costs of a Eurocurrency loan have been much lower than on a Eurobond (about 0.5% of the loan amount versus about 2.25% of the face value of a Eurobond issue), competition has led to lower Eurobond flotation costs.

Eurocurrency loans tend to be more flexible than Eurobonds.

4. *Flexibility*: In the case of a Eurobond issue, the funds must be drawn down in one sum on a fixed date and repaid according to a fixed schedule unless the borrower pays an often substantial prepayment penalty. By contrast, the drawdown in a floating-rate loan can be staggered to suit the borrower's needs with a fee of about 0.5% per annum paid on the unused portion (normally much cheaper than drawing down and redepositing) and can be prepaid in whole or in part at any time, often without penalty. Moreover, a Eurocurrency loan with a multicurrency clause enables the borrower to switch currencies on any rollover date, whereas switching the denomination of a Eurobond from currency A to currency B would require a costly combined refunding and reissuing operation. A much cheaper and comparable alternative, however, would be to sell forward for currency B an amount of currency A equal to the value of the Eurobond issue still outstanding. There is a rapidly growing market in such currency swaps that enable the proceeds from bonds issued in one currency to be converted into money in another currency.

5. *Speed*: Internationally known borrowers can raise funds in the Eurocurrency market very quickly, often within two to three weeks of first request. A Eurobond financing generally takes more time to put together, although here again the difference is becoming less significant.

Note Issuance Facilities

Eurobanks have responded to the competition from the Eurobond market by creating a new instrument: the *note issuance facility* (NIF). The NIF, which is a low-cost substitute for syndicated credits, allows borrowers to issue their own short-term notes that are then placed or distributed by the financial institutions providing the NIF. NIFs—sometimes also called *short-term note issuance facilities* or *SNIFs*—have some features of the U.S. commercial paper market and some features of U.S. commercial lines of credit. Like commercial paper, notes under NIFs are unsecured short-term debt generally issued by large corporations with excellent credit ratings. Indeed, NIFs are sometimes referred to as Euro-commercial paper. Like loan commitments in the United States, NIFs generally include a market-based interest rate and one or more fees known as participation, facility, and underwriting fees. Participation fees are paid when the contract is formalized and are generally about 10 basis points (100 basis points equals 1%) times the facility size. Other fees are paid annually and are sometimes based on the full size of the facility, sometimes on the unused portions thereof.

Many NIFs also include underwriting services as part of the arrangements. When they are included, the arrangement generally takes the form of a *revolving underwriting facility* (RUF). The RUF gives borrowers long-term continuous access to short-term money underwritten by banks at a fixed margin.

NIFs are more flexible than floating-rate notes and usually cheaper than syndicated loans. Banks eager to beef up their earnings without fattening their loan portfolios (which would then require them to add expensive equity capital) made NIFs an important new segment of the Euromarket. As in the case of FRNs, the popularity of NIFs benefits from the market's current preference for lending to high-grade borrowers through securities rather than bank loans.

Here's how the basic facility works (although alternate methods exist in abundance in the marketplace). A syndicate of banks underwrites an amount—usually about $50–200 million—for a specified period, typically for five to seven years. A LIBOR-based underwriting margin is set, determined by the credit rating of the borrower, the size of the issue, and market conditions. When the borrower decides to draw on the facility, the borrower can choose to issue promissory notes, called Euronotes, with one-month, three-month, six-month, or 12-month maturities. A tender panel of banks is then established, whose members submit competitive bids. Any bids above the agreed underwriting margin are not accepted but are automatically purchased by the underwriters at the agreed-upon margin over LIBOR.

In effect, NIFs are put options. They give borrowers the right to sell their paper to the bank syndicate at a price that yields the prearranged spread over LIBOR. Borrowers will exercise this right only if they cannot place their notes at a better rate elsewhere, a plight most likely to occur if their creditworthiness deteriorates. The primary risk to the banks, therefore, is that they might someday have to make good on their pledge to buy paper at a spread that is too low for the credit risks involved. Although Euronote issuers generally are firms with sound credit standing, a NIF may oblige the banks to keep rolling the notes over for five to 10 years—time enough for even the best credit risk to turn into a nightmare.

Note issuance facilities are basically put options.

Most Euronotes are denominated in U.S. dollars and are issued with high face values (often $500,000 or more). They are intended for professional or institutional investors rather than private individuals.

Note Issuance Facilities Versus Eurobonds

In addition to their lower direct costs, NIFs offer several other benefits to the issuer relative to floating rate notes, their most direct competitor.

1. *Drawdown flexibility*: Note issuers can usually opt to draw down all or part of their total credit whenever their need arises, and they can roll over portions at will. This option is especially valuable for borrowers with seasonal or cyclical needs.

2. *Timing flexibility*: With FRNs, the borrower must live with the prevailing rate for the period's duration. By contrast, a Euronote borrower who thinks rates are going to fall can wait a month or so to issue. However, unless the financial director is better able to forecast interest rates, this option to wait is a dubious advantage.

3. *Choice of maturities*: FRN issuers are generally locked into one maturity setting—three months or six months—over the life of the deal. NIFs, on the other hand, give borrowers the choice of issuing notes with different maturities whenever they choose to draw down new debt or roll over old.

4. *Secondary market*: The secondary market for Euronotes is relatively undeveloped compared to the market for FRNs. This condition makes Euronotes less liquid, limiting Euronote investors to those who want to hold them to maturity.

The Asiacurrency Market

Although dwarfed by its European counterpart, the Asiacurrency (or Asiadollar) market has been growing rapidly in terms of both size (an average of 20% a year between 1985 and 1990) and range of services provided. Asiadollar assets totaled $355 billion in assets as of the end of 1992. Located in Singapore, because of the lack of restrictive financial controls and taxes there, the Asiadollar market was founded in 1968 as a satellite market to channel to and from the Eurodollar market the large pool of offshore funds, mainly U.S. dollars, circulating in Asia. Its primary economic functions these days are to channel investment dollars to a number of rapidly growing Southeast Asian countries and to provide deposit facilities for those investors with excess funds.

21.4 DEVELOPMENT BANKS

Development banks help finance projects that would not otherwise be funded by private capital.

To help provide the huge financial resources required to promote the development of economically backward areas, the United States and other countries have established a variety of *development banks* whose lending is directed to investments that would not otherwise be funded by private capital. These investments include dams, roads, communication systems, and other infrastructure projects whose economic benefits cannot be completely captured by private investors, as well as projects such as a steel mill or chemical plant whose value lies in perceived political and social advantages to the nation (or at least to its leaders). Development bank loans generally are medium-term to long-term and carry concessionary rates. Even though most lending is done directly to a government, this type of financing has two implications for the private sector. First, the projects require goods and services, which corporations can provide. Second, by establishing an infrastructure, new investment opportunities become available for multinational corporations.

There are three different types of development banks: the World Bank Group, regional development banks, and national development banks.

The World Bank Group

The *World Bank Group* is a multinational financial institution established at the end of World War II to help provide long-term capital for the reconstruction and development of member countries. It comprises three related financial institutions: the *International Bank for Reconstruction and Development* (IBRD), also known as the *World Bank*; the *International Development Association* (IDA); and the *International Finance Corporation* (IFC). The Group is important to multinational corporations because it provides much of the planning and financing for economic development projects involving billions of dollars for which private businesses can act as contractors and as suppliers of goods and engineering-related services.

The most important development bank is the World Bank Group, which consists of the IBRD, the IFC, and the IDA.

IBRD. The IBRD, or World Bank, makes loans at nearly conventional terms for projects of high economic priority. To qualify for financing, a project must have costs and revenues that can be estimated with reasonable accuracy. A government guarantee is a necessity for World Bank funding. The bank's main emphasis has been on large infrastructure projects such as roads, dams, power plants, education, and agriculture. However, in recent years the bank more and more has emphasized quick loans to help borrower countries alleviate their balance-of-payments problems. These loans are tied to the willingness of the debtor nations to adopt economic policies that will spur growth: freer trade, more open investment, and a more vigorous private sector. Besides its members' subscriptions, the World Bank raises funds by issuing bonds to private sources.

IFC. The purpose of the IFC is to finance various projects in the private sector through loans and equity participations. In contrast to the World Bank, the IFC does not require government guarantees; it emphasizes providing risk capital for manufacturing firms that have a reasonable chance of earning the investors' required rate of return and that will provide economic benefits to the nation.

IDA. The World Bank concentrates on projects that have a high probability of being profitable; consequently, many of the poorest of the less-developed countries (LDCs) were unable to access its funds. IDA was founded in 1960 to remedy this shortcoming. As distinguished from the World Bank, IDA is authorized to make soft (highly concessionary) loans (for example, 50-year maturity with no interest). It does require a government guarantee, however. The establishment of IDA illustrates a major unresolved issue for the World Bank Group: Should its emphasis be on making sound loans to developing countries, or should it concentrate on investing in those projects most likely to be of benefit to the host country? These goals are not necessarily in conflict, although many of a project's benefits may not be captured by the project itself but instead will appear elsewhere in the economy (for example, the benefits of an educational system).

Regional and National Development Banks

The past two decades have seen a proliferation of development banks. The functions of a development bank are to provide debt and equity financing to aid in the economic development of underdeveloped areas. This financing includes extending intermediate-term to long-term capital directly, strengthening local capital markets, and supplying management consulting services to new companies. The professional guidance helps to safeguard, and thereby encourage, investments in a firm.

Regional development banks finance industrial, agricultural, and infrastructure projects considered important to development.

Regional Development Banks. Regional development banks provide funds for the financing of manufacturing, mining, agricultural, and infrastructure projects considered important to development. They tend to support projects that promote regional cooperation and economic integration. Repayment terms for the loans, in most cases, are over a five-year to 15-year period at favorable interest rates. Some of the leading regional development banks include the following.

1. *European Investment Bank* (EIB): The EIB offers funds for certain public and private projects in European and other nations associated with the Common Market. It emphasizes loans to the lesser-developed regions in Europe and to associated members in Africa.
2. *Inter-American Development Bank* (IADB): The IADB is one of the key sources of long-term capital in Latin America. It lends to joint ventures, both minority and majority foreign-owned.
3. *Atlantic Development Group for Latin America* (ADELA): ADELA is an international private investment company dedicated to the socioeconomic development of Latin America. Its objective is to strengthen private enterprise by providing capital and entrepreneurial and technical services.
4. *Asian Development Bank* (ADB): The ADB guarantees or makes direct loans to private ventures in Asian/Pacific countries and helps to develop local capital markets by underwriting securities issued by private enterprises.
5. *African Development Bank* (ADB): The bank makes or guarantees loans and provides technical assistance to member states for various development projects. Beneficiaries of ADB loans and activities are normally governments or government-related agencies.
6. *Arab Fund for Economic and Social Development* (AFESD): The AFESD is a multilateral Arab fund that actively searches for projects (restricted to Arab League countries) and then assumes responsibility for project implementation by conducting feasibility studies, contracting, controlling quality, and supervising the work schedule.
7. *European Bank for Reconstruction and Development* (EBRD). The EBRD, which was founded in 1990 with an initial capital of about $13 billion, is supposed to finance the privatization of Eastern Europe. Many are skeptical of its chances, however, since the person appointed to head it is a French socialist who masterminded the most sweeping program of nationalizations in French history. The EBRD's reputation was not helped when it was revealed in 1993 that in its first two years of operation, it had spent over twice as much on its building, staff, and overhead (over $300 million) as it had disbursed in loans (about $150 million) to its 25 client countries.

National Development Banks. Some national development banks concentrate on a particular industry or region; others are multipurpose. Although most are public institutions, there are several privately controlled development banks as well. The characteristics for success, however, are the same: They must attract capable, investment-oriented management; and they must have a large enough supply of economically viable projects to enable management to select a reasonable portfolio of investments.

The Proper Role of Development Banks

Critics of development banks claim that they tend to perpetuate economic stagnation by financing statist solutions, rather than free-market solutions. By giving money to governments, rather than providing capital to private firms, these banks support bureaucratic planning over private enterprise. This support builds up the public sector at the expense of the private sector. In the absence of funds from development banks, governments might have to grant more freedom to the private sector. Since the marketplace is a far more efficient mechanism for supplying goods and services, any policy that hampers the private sector will retard economic growth.

> Development banks may hamper economic growth because they build up the public sector at the expense of the private sector.

ILLUSTRATION: The World Bank's Role in Africa's Agricultural Failure

The decline of African agriculture throughout the 1970s and 1980s is now widely understood to be due primarily to African governments' penchant for state marketing boards. These set the "official" and only price at which farmers may sell, and the government is frequently the sole legal buyer. To guarantee cheap food to urban populations—the politically important constituency—the rule of the African marketing boards has been: Buy low, sell low (or lower). Most have run up large deficits for decades. Price conscious farmers responded by selling their produce in black markets, smuggling it across the border, reverting to subsistence agriculture, or leaving the land entirely to join the urban swell. At the same time, low food prices led to increased demand and shortages.

The World Bank had a pivotal role in this. From 1974 to 1986 the bank channeled $5.5 billion into African agriculture—an eightfold increase in the lending rate over the previous period. Much of this money was used to set up and finance—that is, subsidize—state marketing boards.

During its 30-year history, the IDB has lent more than $35 billion, much of it to underwrite a development strategy that concentrated investment decisions in the hands of hugely unsuccessful parastatal companies. In short, the IDB has financed inefficient state monopolies at the expense of private, competitive development.

Because they are government-owned and government-controlled institutions doing business with other governments, it is perhaps not surprising that development banks have been hostile in general to enforcing stringent free-market principles as conditions for receiving loans. Thus, they have been unable—and unwilling—to foster the prime conditions for development: sound economic policies and stable political environments. Economic success stories such as the United States, post–World War II Japan and West Germany, modern Taiwan, South Korea, Hong Kong, and Singapore all have a common factor: reliance on private enterprise to organize most economic activity.

If one accepts the view that a vigorous private sector is key to economic growth, then development banks could play an important role in LDC development if they would condition their loans on the elimination in Third World economies of price controls, nationalized industries, high tax rates, government subsidies, state monopolies, trade restrictions, and impediments to private capital flows.

The Baker Plan calls for development aid only if borrowers pursue free-market policies.

The Reagan administration recognized this role and tried to turn these banks into positive forces for LDC development. In 1985, Treasury Secretary James Baker outlined the so-called Baker Plan. The *Baker Plan* called for parceling out development aid only if borrowers pursue free-market reforms to encourage private enterprise. For example, the United States vetoed a concessional IADB loan to Guyana, which wanted a subsidized loan to aid its ailing rice farmers. The U.S. Treasury pointed out that rice farmers would be better served by eliminating Guyana's government price controls, a major cause of the poor rice production.

But the Baker Plan and others like it face hostility from less market-oriented major members such as France, Canada, and Japan. Moreover, many of the banks' staffs are hostile to marketplace solutions and tend to emphasize capital flows from their banks as the key factor in development.

21.5 SUMMARY AND CONCLUSIONS

Although there are significant differences among countries in their methods and sources of finance, corporate practice appears to be converging. Most significantly, more firms are bypassing financial intermediaries, mainly commercial banks, and going directly to the financial markets for funds. The convergence of corporate financing practice largely reflects the globalization of financial markets, the inextricable linkage—through arbitrage—of financial markets worldwide. In line with this trend, firms are finding that it pays to seek capital on a global basis, rather than restricting their search to any one nation or capital market.

We saw that the growth of the international capital markets, specifically the Eurocurrency and Eurobond markets, is largely a response to the various restrictions and regulations that governments impose on domestic financial transactions. At the same time, capital flows between the international capital markets and domestic markets have linked domestic markets in a manner that increasingly makes such government intervention irrelevant.

We also saw that while some sources of funds are readily accessible (for example, the Eurocurrency market), others (such as government-subsidized export credits) are strictly limited in terms of availability. It is, of course, just this latter type of financing that is so appealing to corporate financial executives.

QUESTIONS

1. What are some basic differences between the financing patterns of U.S. and Japanese firms? What might account for some of these differences?

2. How and why has the Japanese pattern of finance changed over time?

3. What is securitization? What forces underlie it and how has it affected the financing policies of multinational corporations?

4. Why is bank lending on the decline worldwide? How have banks responded to their loss of market share?

5. What is meant by the globalization of financial markets? How has technology affected the process of globalization?

6. How has globalization affected government regulation of national capital markets?

7. Many financial commentators believe that bond owners and traders today have an enormous collective influence over a nation's economic policies. Explain why this might be.

8. Why are large multinational corporations located in small countries such as Sweden, Holland, and Switzerland interested in developing a global investor base?

9. What is the difference between a Eurocurrency loan and a Eurobond?

10. What is the difference between a foreign bond and a Eurobond?

11. Why might investors and borrowers be attracted to an ECU bond?

12. What is the basic reason for the existence of the Eurodollar market? What factors have accounted for its growth over time?

13. Suppose the French government imposes an interest rate ceiling on French bank deposits. What is the likely effect on Eurofranc interest rates of this regulation?

14. List some reasons why a U.S.-based corporation might issue debt denominated in a foreign currency.

15. What factors account for the rise and recent decline of the Eurobond market as a source of financing for American companies?

16. In Section 21.3, it was stated that if other European interest rates converged toward German rates, ECU bonds would soar in value. Explain why this would be so.

17. a. What factors account for the growth of note issuance facilities?
    b. In what sense is the NIF part of the process of securitization?
    c. Why is the NIF described as a put option?

PROBLEMS

1. Suppose that the current 180-day interbank Eurodollar rate is 9% (all rates are stated on an annualized basis). If next period's rate is 9.5%, what will a Eurocurrency loan priced at LIBOR plus 1% cost?

2. Refer to the example of Exxon's zero-coupon Eurobond issue in Section 21.3.

a. How much would Exxon have earned if the yield on the stripped Treasurys had been 12.10%? 12.25%?

b. Suppose the Japanese government taxed the accretion in the value of zero-coupon bonds at a rate of 15%. Assuming the same 11.65% after-tax required yield, how would this tax have affected the price Japanese investors were willing to pay for Exxon's Eurobond issue? What would the pre-tax yield be at this new price? Would any arbitrage incentive still exist for Exxon?

c. Suppose Exxon had sold its zero-coupon Eurobonds to yield 11.5% and bought stripped Treasury bonds yielding 12.30% to meet the required payment of $1.8 billion. How much would Exxon have earned through its arbitrage transaction?

3. A European company issues common shares that pay taxable dividends and bearer shares that pay an identical dividend but offer an opportunity to evade taxes. (Bearer shares come with a large supply of coupons that can be redeemed anonymously at banks for the current value of the dividend.)

a. Suppose taxable dividends are taxed at the rate of 10%. What is the ratio between market prices of taxable and bearer shares? If a new issue is planned, should taxable or bearer shares be sold?

b. Suppose, in addition, that it costs 10% of proceeds to issue a taxable dividend, whereas it costs 20% of the proceeds to issue bearer stocks because of the expense of distribution and coupon printing. What type of share will the corporation prefer to issue?

c. Suppose now that individuals pay 10% taxes on dividends, and corporations pay no taxes, but bear an administrative cost of 10% of the value of any bearer dividends. Can you determine the relative market prices for the two types of shares?

BIBLIOGRAPHY

Dufey, Gunter, and Ian H. Giddy. *The International Money Market.* Englewood Cliffs, N.J.: Prentice-Hall, 1978.

———. "Innovation in the International Financial Markets." *Journal of International Business Studies,* Fall 1981, pp. 35–51.

Financing Foreign Operations. Business International Corporation, various issues.

George, Abraham M., and Ian H. Giddy, eds. *International Finance Handbook.* New York: John Wiley & Sons, 1983.

Grabbe, Oren J. *International Financial Markets.* New York: Elsevier, 1986.

Kim, Yong-Cheol, and Rene M. Stulz. "The Eurobond Market and Corporate Financial Policy: A Test of the Clientele Hypothesis." *Journal of Financial Economics,* vol. 22 (1988), pp. 189–205.

———. "Is There Still a Global Market for Convertible Bonds?" working paper, Ohio State University, April 1990.

Solnik, Bruno H. *International Investments.* Reading, Mass.: Addison-Wesley, 1987.

Swaps

22

Man is not the creature of circumstances, circumstances are the creatures of men.

Benjamin Disraeli

CHAPTER LEARNING OBJECTIVES

- To describe interest rate and currency swaps and explain how they can be used to reduce financing costs and risk
- To calculate the appropriate payments and receipts associated with a given interest rate or currency swap
- To identify the factors that underlie the economic benefits of swaps
- To describe LDC debt-equity swaps and explain how these transactions can be used to reduce financing costs and risk
- To explain how a typical LDC debt-equity swap works

T he purpose of this chapter is to examine two special financing vehicles that multinational corporations can use to fund their foreign investments. These vehicles include interest rate and currency swaps and bank loan swaps. Each of them presents opportunities to the multinational firm to reduce financing costs and/or risk.

22.1 INTEREST RATE AND CURRENCY SWAPS

Corporate financial managers can use swaps to arrange complex, innovative financings that reduce borrowing costs and increase control over interest rate risk and foreign currency exposure. As a result of the deregulation and integration of national capital markets and extreme interest rate and currency volatility, the relatively new swaps market has experienced explosive growth, with outstanding swaps in early 1991 in excess of $2 trillion. In fact, few Eurobonds are issued without at least one swap behind them to give the borrower cheaper or in some way more desirable funds.

This section discusses the structure and mechanics of the two basic types of swaps—interest rate swaps and currency swaps—and shows how swaps can be used to achieve diverse goals. Swaps have had a major impact on the treasury function, permitting firms to tap new capital markets and to take further advantage of innovative products without an increase in risk. Through the swap, they can trade a perceived risk in one market or currency for a liability in another. The swap has led to a refinement of risk-management techniques, which in turn has facilitated corporate involvement in international capital markets.

Interest Rate Swaps

An *interest rate swap* is an agreement between two parties to exchange U.S. dollar interest payments for a specific maturity on an agreed upon notional amount. The term *notional* refers to the theoretical principal underlying the swap. Thus, the *notional principal* is simply a reference amount against which the interest is calculated. No principal ever changes hands. Maturities range from under a year to over 15 years; however, most transactions fall within a two-year to ten-year period. The two main types are coupon swaps and basis swaps. In a *coupon swap*, one party pays a *fixed rate* calculated at the time of trade as a spread to a particular Treasury bond, while the other side pays a *floating rate* that resets periodically throughout the life of the deal against a designated index. In a *basis swap*, two parties exchange floating interest payments based on different reference rates. Basically, using this relatively straightforward mechanism, interest rate swaps transform debt issues, assets, liabilities, or any cash flow from type to type and—with some variation in the transaction structure—from currency to currency.

The Classic Swap Transaction. Counterparty A in Exhibit 22.1 is an institution that invests in fixed-rate mortgages yielding 13.25%. Counterparty A is not an investment-grade credit. It is funding its assets through a floating-rate loan from a group of banks that is charging A the six-month London Interbank Offer Rate (LIBOR) plus 50 basis points (a basis point equals 0.01%). A's profitability depends on the actual level of the floating interest rate that is paid over the long run. Thus, a large upward swing in interest rates will burden A with large debt service expenses. And A will actually lose money whenever LIBOR exceeds 12.75% (13.25 − 0.50) on any reset date. Concerned that this risk may threaten the profitability and even solvency of the firm, the risk manager seeks a way to reduce it.

Exhibit 22.1 Situations Confronting Counterparties A and B Before the Swap

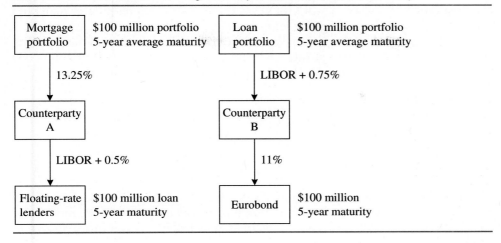

Suppose that a second firm, counterparty B in Exhibit 22.1, has also borrowed $100 million for five years, but at a fixed rate. B is a AAA-rated bank and is funding its loan portfolio with funds generated by a Eurobond carrying an 11% coupon. B's loan portfolio is yielding LIBOR plus 75 basis points. The profitability of B depends on the actual floating interest rate that is received on its loan portfolio. Whenever LIBOR is less than 10.25% (11 − 0.75) on any reset date, B is losing money.

In order to eliminate its interest rate risk, A enters into the following interest rate swap with BigBank, as diagrammed in Exhibit 22.2. A agrees that it will pay BigBank 11.35% for five years, with payments calculated by multiplying that rate

Interest rate swaps can reduce interest rate risk.

Exhibit 22.2 Counterparty A's Interest Rate Swap Agreement with BigBank

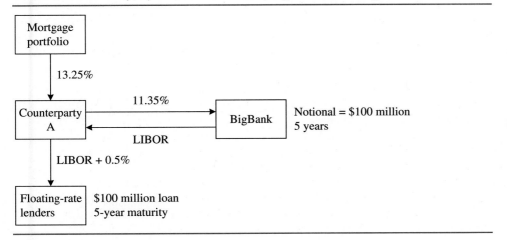

by the $100 million notional principal amount. In return for this payment, Big-Bank agrees to pay A six-month LIBOR over five years, with reset dates matching the reset dates on its floating rate loan.

Counterparty A, through the swap with BigBank, has eliminated the volatility in its earnings due to interest rate fluctuations over the five-year horizon of the swap and should now earn a locked-in spread of 1.4% on its loan portfolio:

Receive on portfolio	13.25%
Pay BigBank	(11.35%)
Receive from BigBank	LIBOR
Pay on loan	(LIBOR + 0.50%)
Cost of funds	(11.85%)
Locked-in spread	1.40%

In a similar fashion, B enters into a swap with BigBank where it agrees to pay six-month LIBOR to BigBank on a notional principal amount of $100 million for five years in exchange for receiving payments of 11.25%. This swap is shown in Exhibit 22.3.

The net result to B is as follows:

Receive on portfolio	LIBOR + 0.75%
Pay BigBank	LIBOR
Receive from BigBank	11.25
Pay on Eurobond	(11.00%)
Cost of funds	(LIBOR − 0.25%)
Locked-in spread	1.00%

Once the effect of the swap is netted against the payments on the Eurobond, it is clear that B has reduced its cost of funds to LIBOR less 25 basis points, resulting in a locked-in spread on its portfolio of 100 basis points.

Exhibit 22.3 Counterparty B's Interest Rate Swap Agreement with BigBank

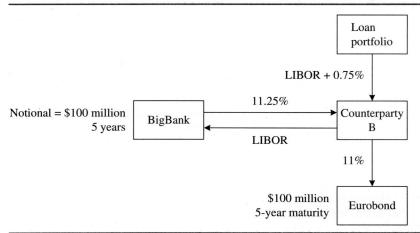

Why would BigBank or any financial intermediary enter into such transactions? The net result in each of these transactions is that the risk of loss due to interest rate fluctuations has been transferred from the counterparty to BigBank. The reason BigBank is willing to enter into such contracts is more evident when looking at the transaction in its entirety. This classic swap structure is shown in Exhibit 22.4.

As a financial intermediary, BigBank puts together both transactions. The risks net out, and BigBank is left with a spread of 10 basis points:

Receive	11.35%
Pay	(11.25%)
Receive	LIBOR
Pay	(LIBOR)
Net	10 basis points

BigBank thus receives compensation equal to $100,000 annually for the next five years on the $100 million swap transaction:

$$\text{Swap profit to BigBank} = 0.001 \times \$100,000,000 = \$100,000$$

Cost Savings Associated with Swaps. The example just discussed shows the risk-reducing potential of interest rate swaps. However, swaps may also be used to reduce costs. Their ability to do so depends on a difference in perceived credit quality across financial markets. In essence, interest rate swaps exploit the comparative advantages—if they exist—enjoyed by different borrowers in different markets, thereby increasing the options available to both borrower and investor.

Returning to the previous example, suppose that A is a company with a BBB rating, while B is a AAA-rated bank. Although A has good access to banks or other sources of floating-rate funds for its operations, it may have difficulty raising fixed-rate funds from bond issues in the capital markets at a price it finds attrac-

Swaps can reduce costs for both parties if there is a difference in perceived credit quality across financial markets.

Exhibit 22.4 Classic Swap Structure

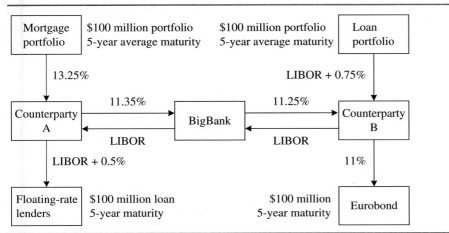

tive. By contrast, B can borrow at the finest rates in either market. Exhibit 22.5 outlines the cost to each party of accessing either the fixed-rate or the floating-rate market for a new five-year debt issue.

The basic point noted in Exhibit 22.5 is that there is an anomaly between the two markets: One judges that the difference in credit quality between a AAA-rated firm and a BBB-rated firm is worth 150 basis points; the other determines that this difference is worth only 50 basis points. Since both markets cannot simultaneously be correct, at least one of these markets is mispricing different quality credits. The bottom line is that there is a difference of 100 basis points that the interest rate swap has permitted the parties to share among themselves as follows:

Party	Normal Funding Cost (%)	Cost After Swap (%)	Difference (%)
Counterparty A	12.50	11.85	0.65
Counterparty B	LIBOR	LIBOR – 0.25	0.25
BigBank	—	—	0.10
		Total	1.00

In this example, A lowers its fixed-rate costs by 65 basis points, B lowers its floating-rate costs by 25 basis points, and BigBank receives 10 basis points for arranging the transaction and bearing the credit risk of the counterparties.

You might expect that the process of financial arbitrage would soon eliminate any such cost savings opportunities associated with a mispricing of credit quality. Despite this efficient markets view, many players in the swaps market believe that such anomalies in perceived credit risk continue to exist. The explosive growth in the swaps market supports this belief. It may also indicate the presence of other factors, such as differences in information and risk aversion of lenders across markets, that are more likely to persist.

Currency Swaps

Interest rate swaps can be arranged across currencies.

Swap contracts can also be arranged across currencies. Such contracts are known as currency swaps and can help manage both interest rate and exchange rate risk. Many financial institutions count the arranging of swaps, both domestic and foreign currency, as an important line of business.

Exhibit 22.5 Credit Costs in the Fixed-Rate and Floating-Rate Markets

Borrower	Fixed Rate (%)	Floating Rate (%)
Counterparty A = BBB-rated	12.50	LIBOR + 0.50
Counterparty B = AAA-rated	11.00	LIBOR
Difference	1.50	0.50
	Spread differential = 100 basis points	

Technically, a *currency swap* is an exchange of debt service obligations denominated in one currency for the service on an agreed upon principal amount of debt denominated in another currency. By swapping their future cash flow obligations, the counterparties are able to replace cash flows denominated in one currency with cash flows in a more desired currency. In this way, a corporation that has borrowed, say, Japanese yen at a fixed interest rate can transform its yen debt into a fully-hedged dollar liability. In effect, a U..S. firm engaged in a currency swap has borrowed foreign currency and converted its proceeds into dollars, while simultaneously arranging for a counterparty to make the requisite foreign currency payment in each period. In return for this foreign currency payment, the firm pays an agreed-upon amount of dollars to the counterparty.

The counterparties to a currency swap will be concerned about their *all-in cost*—that is, the effective interest rate on the money they have raised. This interest rate is calculated as the discount rate that equates the present value of the future interest and principal payments to the net proceeds received by the issuer.

Currency swaps achieve an economic purpose similar to the parallel loan arrangements discussed in Chapter 15. They have effectively displaced the use of parallel loans, however, because they solve two potential problems associated with parallel loans: (1) If there is no right of offset, default by one party does not release the other from making its contractually obligated payments; and (2) parallel loans remain on the balance sheet, even though they effectively cancel one another. With a currency swap, the *right of offset*, which gives each party the right to offset any nonpayment of principal or interest with a comparable nonpayment, is more firmly established. Moreover, because a currency swap is not a loan, it does not appear as a liability on the parties' balance sheets.

Although the structure of currency swaps differs from interest rate swaps in a variety of ways, the major difference is that with a currency swap, there is always an exchange of principal amounts at maturity at a predetermined exchange rate. Thus, the swap contract behaves like a long-dated forward foreign exchange contract, where the forward rate is the current spot rate.

The reason that there is always an exchange of principal amounts at maturity can be explained as follows. Assume the prevailing coupon rate is 8% in one currency and 5% in the other currency. What would convince an investor to pay 8% and receive 300 basis points less? The answer lies in the spot and long-term forward exchange rates and how currency swaps adjust to compensate for the differentials. According to interest rate parity theory, forward rates are a direct function of the interest rate differential for the two currencies involved. As a result, a currency with a lower interest rate has a correspondingly higher forward exchange value. It follows that future exchange of currencies at the present spot exchange rate would offset the current difference in interest rates. This *exchange of principals* is what occurs in every currency swap at maturity based on the original amounts of each currency and, by implication, done at the original spot exchange rate.

The following example illustrates an *interest rate/currency swap*. This swap is designed to convert a liability in one currency with a stipulated type of interest payment into one denominated in another currency with a different type of interest payment.

> The exchange of principals at maturity in a currency swap offsets the interest differential between the currencies.

Kodak's Zero-Coupon Australian Dollar Interest Rate/Currency Swap

In late March 1987, Eastman Kodak Company, a AAA-rated firm, indicated to Merrill Lynch that it needed to raise U.S.$400 million.[1] Kodak's preference was to fund through nontraditional structures, obtaining U.S.$200 million for both five and 10 years. Kodak stated that it would spend up to two weeks evaluating nondollar financing opportunities for the five-year tranche, targeting a minimum size of U.S.$75 million and an all-in cost of U.S. Treasurys plus 35 basis points. In contrast, a domestic bond issue by Kodak would have to be priced to yield an all-in cost equal to about 50 basis points above the rate on U.S. Treasurys. At the end of the two-week period, the remaining balance was to be funded with a competitive bid.

After reviewing a number of potential transactions, the Capital Markets group at Merrill Lynch decided that investor interest in nondollar issues was much stronger in Europe than in the United States and that Merrill Lynch should focus on a nondollar Euroissue for Kodak. The London Syndicate Desk informed the Capital Markets Desk that it was a co-lead manager of an aggressively priced five-year, Australian dollar (A$) zero-coupon issue that was selling very well in Europe. The London Syndicate believed it could successfully underwrite a similar five-year A$ zero-coupon issue for Kodak. It was determined that Merrill Lynch could meet Kodak's funding target if an attractively priced A$ zero-coupon swap could be found.

To meet Kodak's minimum issue size of U.S.$75 million, an A$200 million zero-coupon issue would be necessary, which was the largest A$ zero-coupon issue ever underwritten. Merrill Lynch then received a firm mandate on a five-year A$130 million zero-coupon swap with Australian Bank B at a semiannual interest rate of 13.39%. The remaining A$70 million was arranged through a long-dated forward foreign exchange contract with Australian Bank A at a forward rate of A$1 = U.S.$0.5286.

With the currency swap mandate and the long-dated forward contract, Merrill Lynch received final approval by Kodak for the transaction, and the five-year A$200 million zero-coupon issue was launched in Europe at a net price of 54 1/8%, with a gross spread of 1 1/8%. Net proceeds to Kodak were 53% of A$200 million, or A$106 million. Kodak converted this principal into U.S.$75 million at the spot rate of U.S.$0.7059. Simultaneously, Merrill Lynch entered into a currency swap with Kodak to convert the Australian dollar cash flows into U.S. dollar cash flows at 7.35% paid semiannually, or U.S. Treasurys plus 35 basis points (since five-year Treasury bonds were then yielding approximately 7%). That is, Kodak's all-in cost was 7.35%. As part of this swap, Merrill Lynch agreed to make semiannual interest payments of LIBOR less 40 basis points to Australian Bank B. Merrill Lynch then arranged an interest rate swap to convert a portion of the fixed-rate payments from Kodak into floating-rate payments to Bank B. Exhibit 22.6 con-

---

[1]This example was supplied by Grant Kvalheim of Merrill Lynch, whose help is greatly appreciated. The actual interest rates and spot and forward rates have been disguised.

Exhibit 22.6 Kodak's A$200 Million Zero-Coupon Eurobond and Currency Swap

[a]Investors receive a single payment of A$200 million on 5/12/92, which represents both principal and interest.

[b]The bonds are priced at 54 1/8% less 1 1/8% gross spread. Net proceeds to Kodak at settlement on 5/12/87 are A$106 million.

[c]Kodak exchanges A$106 million with Merrill Lynch and receives U.S. $75 million at a fixed semiannual interest rate of 7.35%.

[d]Australian Bank B provides a 5-year A$130 million zero-coupon swap at a semiannual rate of 13.39%. In the currency swap's initial exchange on 5/12/87, Merrill Lynch pays Australian Bank B A$68 million (A$130,000,000 × [1/(1 + (13.39%/2))^{10}]) and receives U.S. $48 million (A$68,000,000 × .7059) based on a spot exchange rate of U.S. $0.7059/A$1.

[e]Merrill Lynch sells the remaining A$38 million (A$106,000,000 – A$68,000,000) to Australian Bank A on 5/12/87 at a spot rate of U.S.$.7105/A$1, and receives U.S. $27 million.

[f]Kodak makes seminannual fixed-rate interest payments of U.S.$2,756,250 to Merrill Lynch ((7.35%/2) × U.S. $75,000,000).

[g]Merrill Lynch makes semiannual floating-rate interest payments of LIBOR less 40 basis points on a notional principal amount of U.S.$48 million to Australian Bank B.

[h]Merrill Lynch makes semiannual interest payments of U.S. $1,884,000 based on a notional principal amount of U.S. $48 million and fixed interest rate of 7.85% and receives semiannual floating-rate interest payments of LIBOR flat in a fixed-floating rate swap with its book.

[i]Merrill Lynch receives A$130 million and pays U.S.$48 million in the Australian Bank B currency swap's final exchange on 5/12/92.

[j]In a long-dated forward foreign exchange transaction with Australian Bank A, Merrill Lynch purchases A$70 million on 5/12/92 for U.S.$37 million based on a forward exchange rate of U.S.$0.5286/A$1.

[k]On 5/12/92, Kodak pays U.S.$75 million to Merrill Lynch, receives A$200 million in return, and Kodak then pays the A$200 million to its zero-coupon bondholders.

tains an annotated schematic diagram of the currency and interest rate swaps and the long-dated foreign exchange purchase that appeared in a Merrill Lynch ad. Exhibit 22.7 summarizes the period-by-period cash flows associated with these transactions.

Exhibit 22.7 MLCS Cash Flows E astman Kodak Transaction

Date	Cash-Flow Type	Kodak Currency Swap A$	Kodak Currency Swap U.S.$	Austalian Bank B Currency Swap A$	Austalian Bank B Currency Swap U.S.$	Foreign Exchange Market A$	Foreign Exchange Market U.S.$	Fixed/Floating U.S.$ Swap Fixed	Fixed/Floating U.S.$ Swap Floating	Net U.S.$ Flows
12 May 87	Initial exchange	106,000,000	(75,000,000)[1]	(68,000,000)	48,000,000	38,000,000	27,000,000	—	—	968,250[3]
12 Nov. 87	Interest	—	2,756,250	—	(LIBOR – 40BPS)	—	—	(1,884,000)[2]	LIBOR	968,250
12 May 88	Interest	—	2,756,250	—	(LIBOR – 40BPS)	—	—	(1,884,000)	LIBOR	968,250
12 Nov. 88	Interest	—	2,756,250	—	(LIBOR – 40BPS)	—	—	(1,884,000)	LIBOR	968,250
12 May 89	Interest	—	2,756,250	—	(LIBOR – 40BPS)	—	—	(1,884,000)	LIBOR	968,250
12 Nov. 89	Interest	—	2,756,250	—	(LIBOR – 40BPS)	—	—	(1,884,000)	LIBOR	968,250
12 May 90	Interest	—	2,756,250	—	(LIBOR – 40BPS)	—	—	(1,884,000)	LIBOR	968,250
12 Nov. 90	Interest	—	2,756,250	—	(LIBOR – 40BPS)	—	—	(1,884,000)	LIBOR	968,250
12 May 91	Interest	—	2,756,250	—	(LIBOR – 40BPS)	—	—	(1,884,000)	LIBOR	968,250
12 Nov. 91	Interest	—	2,756,250	—	(LIBOR – 40BPS)	—	—	(1,884,000)	LIBOR	968,250
12 May 92	Interest	—	2,756,250	—	(LIBOR – 40BPS)	—	—	(1,884,000)	LIBOR	968,250
12 May 92	Final exchange	(200,000,000)	75,000,000	130,000,000	(48,000,000)	70,000,000	(37,000,000)			(10,000,000)

[1] (U.S.$75,000,000) × (0.0735) × (180 days/360 days)

[2] (U.S.$48,000,000) × (0.0785) × (180 days/360 days)

[3] U.S.$2,756,250 – U.S.$1,884,000 + [U.S.$48,000,000 × 0.004 × (180 days/360 days)]

The final column of Exhibit 22.7 presents the net cash flows to Merrill Lynch from these transactions. The net present value of these flows discounted at $r\%$ compounded semiannually is

$$NPV = \sum_{t=1}^{10} \frac{\$968,250}{(1 + r/2)^2} - \frac{\$10,000,000}{(1 + r/2)^{10}}$$

Discounted at the then risk-free, five-year Treasury bond rate of 7% compounded semiannually, the NPV of these flows is $963,365. Using a higher discount rate, say 7.5%, to reflect the various risks associated with these transactions results in a net present value to Merrill Lynch of $1,031,826. The actual NPV of these cash flows falls somewhere in between these two extremes.

By combining a nondollar issue with a currency swap and interest rate swap, Merrill Lynch was able to construct an innovative, lower-cost source of funds for Kodak. The entire package involved close teamwork and a complex set of transactions on three continents. In turn, through its willingness to consider nontraditional financing methods, Kodak was able to lower its cost of funds by about 15 basis points, yielding an annual savings of approximately $112,500 (0.0015 × $75,000,000). The present value of this savings discounted at 7.5% compounded semiannually (or 3.75% every six months) is

$$\sum_{t=1}^{10} \frac{\$56,250}{(1.0375)^t} = \$461,969$$

Dual Currency Bond Swaps

Another variant on the currency swap theme is a currency swap involving a *dual currency bond*—one that has the issue's proceeds and interest payments stated in foreign currency and the principal repayment stated in dollars. An example of a dual currency bond swap is the one involving the Federal National Mortgage Association (FNMA, or Fannie Mae). On October 1, 1985, FNMA agreed to issue 10-year, 8% coupon debentures in the amount of 50 billion (with net proceeds of ¥49,687,500,000) and to swap these yen for approximately $209 million. In return, Fannie Mae agreed to pay interest averaging about $21 million annually and to redeem these bonds at the end of 10 years at a cost of $240,400,000. Exhibit 22.8 shows the detailed yen and dollar cash flows associated with this currency swap. The net effect of this swap was to give Fannie Mae an all-in dollar cost of 10.67% annually. In other words, regardless of what happened to the yen/dollar exchange rate in the future, Fannie Mae's dollar cost on its yen bond issue would remain at 10.67%. The 10.67% figure is the interest rate that just equates the dollar figures in column 3 to zero.

To illustrate the mechanics of this swap, note that at the end of the first year, FNMA is obligated to pay its bondholders ¥4 billion in interest (an 8% coupon payment on a ¥50 billion face value debenture). To satisfy this obligation, FNMA pays $18,811,795 to Nomura, which in turn makes the ¥4 billion interest payment. As the last column of Exhibit 22.8 shows, FNMA has effectively contracted with

A dual currency bond has the principal repayment stated in one currency and the interest payments in another.

Exhibit 22.8 Cash Flows Associated with Yen Debenture Currency Swap

Payment Date	Payment on Dual Currency Debenture	Dollar Payment Under Swap	Yen:Dollar Exchange Rate
October 1, 1985	− ¥49,687,500,000[1]	−$209,168,297[2]	¥237.3777/$1
October 1, 1986	¥ 4,000,000,000	18,811,795	212.6325/ 1
October 1, 1987	¥ 4,000,000,000	19,124,383	209.1571/ 1
October 1, 1988	¥ 4,000,000,000	19,464,369	205.5037/ 1
October 1, 1989	¥ 4,000,000,000	19,854,510	201.4656/ 1
October 1, 1990	¥ 4,000,000,000	20,304,260	197.0030/ 1
October 1, 1991	¥ 4,000,000,000	20,942,380	191.0003/ 1
October 1, 1992	¥ 4,000,000,000	21,499,717	186.0490/ 1
October 1, 1993	¥ 4,000,000,000	22,723,857	180.8574/ 1
October 1, 1994	¥ 4,000,000,000	22,723,857	176.0265/ 1
October 1, 1995	¥ 4,000,000,000	23,665,098	169.0253/ 1
October 1, 1995	$ 240,400,000	240,400,000	207.9867/ 1

[1]This figure is the ¥50 billion face amount net of issue expenses.
[2]Net proceeds received after reimbursing underwriters for expenses of $150,000.

Nomura to buy ¥4 billion forward for delivery in one year at a forward rate of ¥212.6325.

Similarly, FNMA satisfies its remaining yen obligations (shown in column 2) by paying a series of dollar amounts (shown in column 3) to Nomura, which in turn makes the required yen payments. The exchange of fixed dollar payments in the future for fixed yen payments in the future is equivalent to a sequence of forward contracts entered into at the forward exchange rates shown in the fourth column. Since the actual spot rate at the time the swap was entered into (August 29, 1985) was about ¥240/$1, the implicit forward rates on these forward contracts reveal that the yen was selling at a forward premium relative to the dollar; that is, it cost fewer yen to buy a dollar in the forward market than in the spot market. The reason the yen was selling at a forward premium was the same reason that Fannie Mae was borrowing yen: At this time, the interest rate on yen was below the interest rate on dollars.

Since this particular issue was a dual currency bond, with the issue's proceeds and interest payments stated in yen and the principal repayment stated in dollars, the final payment is stated in dollars only. However, it should be noted that by agreeing to a principal repayment of $240,400,000, instead of ¥50 billion, Fannie Mae was actually entering into the equivalent of a long-dated forward contract at an implicit forward rate of ¥207.9867/$1 (¥50,000,000,000/$240,400,000).

Economic Advantages of Swaps

Swaps provide economic benefits to both parties when barriers to arbitrage exist.

For swaps to provide a real economic benefit to both parties, a barrier generally must exist to prevent arbitrage from functioning fully. This impediment must take the form of legal restrictions on spot and forward foreign exchange transactions, different perceptions by investors of risk and creditworthiness of the two parties, appeal or acceptability of one borrower to a certain class of investor, tax differentials, and so forth.[2]

Swaps also allow firms to lower their cost of foreign exchange risk management. A U.S. corporation, for example, may want to secure fixed-rate funds in Deutsche marks in order to reduce its DM exposure, but is hampered in doing so because it is a relatively unknown credit in the German financial market. In contrast, a German company that is well established in its own country may desire floating-rate dollar financing, but is relatively unknown in the U.S. financial market.

In such a case, a bank intermediary familiar with the funding needs and "comparative advantages" in borrowing of both parties may arrange a currency swap. The U.S. company borrows floating-rate dollars, and the German company borrows fixed-rate DM. The two companies then swap both principal and interest payments. When the term of the swap matures, say, in five years, the principal amounts revert to the original holder. Both parties receive a cost savings because they borrow initially in the market where they have a comparative advantage and then swap for their preferred liability.

Currency swaps, thus, are often used to provide long-term financing in foreign currencies. This function is important because in many foreign countries, long-term capital and forward foreign exchange markets are notably absent or not well developed. Swaps are one type of vehicle providing liquidity to these markets.

In effect, swaps allow the transacting parties to engage in some form of tax, regulatory system, or financial market arbitrage. If the world capital market were fully integrated, the incentive to swap would be reduced because fewer arbitrage opportunities would exist. As noted above, however, even in the United States, where financial markets function freely, interest rate swaps are extremely popular and are credited with cost savings.

22.2 LDC DEBT-EQUITY SWAPS

In recent years, a market has developed that enables investors to purchase the external debt of less-developed countries (LDCs) to acquire equity or domestic currency in those same countries. The market for *LDC debt-equity swaps*, as the transactions are called, has grown rapidly over the past few years. Between 1985, when swapping began, and 1988, about $15 billion worth of LDC loans were swapped. Although the rate at which debt swaps are occurring is still small in relation to the $437 billion that the 15 most-troubled debtor nations owe the world's commercial banks, there are indications that the debt swaps market is poised for faster growth. Six major debtor nations—Chile, Brazil, Mexico, Venezuela, Argentina, and the Philippines—have initiated debt swaps programs, and more will likely follow.

The market for LDC debt-equity swaps has grown rapidly in recent years.

[2]This explanation is provided in Clifford W. Smith, Jr., Charles W. Smithson, and Lee M. Wakeman, "The Evolvling Market for Swaps," *Midland Corporate Finance Journal*, Winter 1986, pp. 20–32.

Types of Debt Swaps and Their Rationale

Swaps can be quite complex, but the basics are fairly simple. For several years, European and regional U.S. commercial banks have been selling troubled LDC loans in the so-called secondary market—an informal network of large banks, big multinational corporations, and some Wall Street investment banks that trade loans of troubled debtor nations over the telephone and by telex. The trading, centered in New York, has grown steadily since the international debt crisis broke in 1982. Traders estimate that $15 billion or more in LDC debt changed hands in this market in 1988.

LDC loans often trade at deep discounts to their face value, reflecting their substantial risk.

The loans trade at deep discounts to their face value, reflecting the market's opinion that they will not be repaid in full. For example, in mid-1987, Chilean debt sold at about 70% of its face value, or 70 cents on the dollar. Mexican loans traded at about 60% of par, Brazilian loans at 40%, and Bolivian debt at a mere 10%.

Usually, discount market quotations are cast in terms of bids and offers, not single market-clearing transaction prices. Exhibit 22.9 contains a set of bid-offer quotations for six Latin American countries from July 1985 to January 1989. The spread between bid and offered prices is frequently rather wide—one indication of a thin market—although it seems to have narrowed over time.

Regarding the level of prices quoted, it is clear that substantial variation can occur across countries. During January 1986, for example, average prices ranged from Venezuela at about 80 cents per dollar to Peru at about 20 cents. There has also been a tendency for prices to drift down over this time period, as the dimensions of the debt problem became clearer (see Exhibit 22.10). Prices bottomed in 1989 and then began to move up as Latin American countries began to restructure their economies. Chile, which has generally followed sound economic policies, and bought back substantial amounts of its debt, has seen the greatest appreciation in the price of its debt.

In a typical deal, a multinational that wants to invest in, say, Chile hires an intermediary (usually a bank) to buy Chilean loans in the secondary market. The

Exhibit 22.9 Bid-Offer Quotations in the Secondary Market for Developing Country Debt (Percent of Face Value of Loans)

	Argentina	Brazil	Chile	Mexico	Peru	Venezuela
July 1985	60–65%	75–81%	65–69%	80–82%	45–50%	81–83%
January 1986	62–66	75–81	65–69	69–73	25–30	80–82
January 1987	62–65	74–76.5	65–68	54–57	16–19	72–74
January 1988	30–33	44–47	60–63	50–52	2–7	55–57
January 12, 1989	21–22	38–40	58–60	40–41	5–8	38–39
January 20, 1989	18–19	34–35	60–61	38–39	5–8	37–38

SOURCE: Leroy O. Laney, "The Secondary Market in Developing Country Debt," *Economic Review*, Federal Reserve Bank of Dallas, July 1987, p. 2. Data for 1988 and 1989 from Shearson Lehman Hutton, Inc.

Exhibit 22.10 Secondary Market Debt Prices (As Percent of Face Value)

SOURCE: Salomon Brothers

company (again through a middleman) presents the loans, denominated in dollars, to the Chilean central bank, which redeems them for pesos. The central banks pay less than face value, but more than the loans trade for in the secondary market. Chile pays about 92 cents on the dollar, and Mexico an average of 88 cents.

Thus, a company that wants to expand in Chile can pick up $100 million of loans in the secondary market for $70 million and swap them for $92 million in pesos. Chile gets $100 million of debt off its books and doesn't have to part with precious dollars. The company gets $92 million of investment for $70 million, which amounts to a 24% subsidy (22/92).

ILLUSTRATION: Citicorp Structures a Debt Swap for Nissan

In 1986, Citicorp learned that Nissan Motors wanted to invest the equivalent of $54 million to expand its truck factory in Mexico. When Citicorp offered to get them the $54 million in pesos for much less than $54 million through a debt-equity swap, Nissan liked the idea.

Citicorp went to the Mexican government and got their approval for the swap. The Mexican government agreed to pay $54 million in pesos for approximately $60 million of their external debt, a 10% discount. Citicorp went out and bought the $60 million in Mexican bank debt for about $38 million. Nissan wound up with the peso equivalent of $54 million at a price of only $40 million. Mexico retired about $60 million in bank debt. And Citicorp was paid about $2 million for structuring the deal and assuming the risk.

The variations on this theme are endless. Chrysler has used some of the pesos it got in swaps to pay off local debt owed by its Mexican subsidiary. Kodak and Unisys have used swaps to expand their operations in Chile. Club Med is building a new beach resort in Mexico. Big U.S. banks usually act only as intermediaries in these deals, but a few have swapped for themselves, trading their LDC loans for equity in Latin businesses. In 1988, Manufacturers Hanover used a debt-equity swap to exchange some of its $2 billion in Brazilian debt for a 10% equity stake in Companhia Suzano de Papel e Celulose, a Brazilian paper and pulp company (see Exhibit 22.11 for details).

In addition to debt-equity swaps, there are also "debt-peso" swaps. *Debt-peso swaps* enable residents of a debtor country to purchase their country's foreign debt at a discount and to convert this debt into domestic currency. To finance these purchases, residents use funds held abroad or hard currency acquired from international trade or in the exchange market.

Swaps enable investors to obtain domestic currency assets at a discount.

By arrangement with the debt country, domestic currency assets obtained via debt swaps are acquired at closer to the original face value of the debt. For example, in 1986, a purchaser who acquired Mexican debt for 57 cents on the dollar could obtain equity worth 82 cents. Even after accounting for fees and redemption discounts applied by debtor countries to convert the debt into domestic currency, debt-swaps allow investors to acquire the domestic currency of debtor countries much more cheaply than do official exchange markets. In effect, investors resorting to the debt swap market enjoy a preferential exchange rate.

Because the debt swap market offers a more favorable exchange rate than do official exchange markets, it creates an incentive for arbitrage. For example, a resident of a debtor country may exchange 100 pesos in domestic currency in the

Exhibit 22.11 How a Debt-Equity Swap Works

Manufacturers Hanover takes $115 million in Brazilian government loans to Multplic, a Sao Paulo broker.	The broker takes the loans to the Brazilian central bank's monthly debt auction, where they are valued at an average of 86¢ on the dollar.
With its cruzados, Manufacturers Hanover buys 10% of Companhia Suzano de Papel e Celulose's stock, and Suzano uses the bank's cash to expand production and exports.	Through the broker, Manufacturers Hanover exchanges the loans at the central bank for $100 million worth of Brazilian cruzados.* It pays the broker a $150,000 commission. The central bank retires the loans.

* At the time of this transaction, the cruzado was the Brazilian currency.

official exchange market to acquire a dollar. The resident may then use this dollar to acquire, via the debt swap market, 125 pesos in domestic currency and thus gain a 25 peso profit. Exchange controls will not necessarily be effective in preventing this "round trip" process because domestic residents may elude exchange controls in a number of ways (for example, by overstating imports or understating exports).

Typically, access to swap programs involves wading through a lot of government red tape. For example, rules for foreign investors to participate in Mexico's swap program are outlined, in sometimes indecipherable language, in a 44-page *Manual Operativo*. Mexico also tailors its swap program to promote industrial policy goals. It does that by redeeming loans at different prices, depending on how the proceeds will be used. If a foreign investor wants to buy shares in a nationalized company that the government is trying to privatize, the central bank redeems loans at full face value. It pays as much as 95 cents on the dollar if the pesos will be invested in tourism and other businesses that help the trade balance. However, it pays only 75 cents on the dollar on deals that create no jobs, no exports, and no new technology.

Debt Swaps and Inflation

One problem with debt swaps is that there is no free lunch. All too frequently, governments finance their purchases of bank debt by simply printing more currency. Consider Brazil. Suppose it buys back $100 million of its debt during a particular month. If the government isn't running a surplus, which it rarely is, it must print money to pay for the debt. The net result is fewer dollars of foreign debt outstanding but higher inflation. In effect, the country has taxed its citizens (by means of the inflation tax) and turned over the proceeds to banks, which then use them to acquire local assets.

Debt swaps may cause higher inflation in the LDC debtor.

22.3 SUMMARY AND CONCLUSIONS

Multinational corporations can use creative financing to achieve various objectives. These include reducing their cost of funds, cutting taxes, and reducing political risk. This chapter focused on two such techniques—interest and currency swaps and LDC loan swaps.

Interest and currency swaps involve a financial transaction in which two counterparties agree to exchange streams of payments over time. In an interest rate swap, no actual principal is exchanged either initially or at maturity, but interest payment streams are exchanged according to predetermined rules and based on an underlying notional amount. The two main types are coupon swaps (or fixed rate to floating rate) and basis swaps (from floating rate against one reference rate to floating rate with another reference rate).

Currency swap refers to a transaction in which two counterparties exchange specific amounts of two currencies at the outset and repay over time according to a predetermined rule that reflects both interest payments and amortization of principal. A cross-currency interest rate swap involves swapping fixed-rate flows in one currency to floating-rate flows in another.

Under a debt-equity program, a firm buys a country's dollar debt on the secondary loan market at a discount and swaps it into local equity. Although such programs are still in their infancy, debt-equity swaps can provide cheap financing for expanding plant and for retiring local debt in hard-pressed LDCs. However, debt swaps are not an unmixed blessing for the participating countries, since they tend to exacerbate already high rates of inflation.

QUESTIONS

1. What is the difference between a basis swap and a coupon swap?

2. What is a currency swap?

3. What factors underlie the economic benefits of swaps?

4. Comment on the following statement. "In order for one party to a swap to benefit, the other party must lose."

5. As noted in Chapter 21, the Swiss Central Bank bans the use of Swiss franc for Eurobond issues. Explain how currency swaps can be used to enable foreign borrowers who want to raise Swiss francs through a bond issue outside of Switzerland to get around this ban.

6. Comment on the following statement. "During the period 1987–1989, Japanese companies issued some $115 billion of bonds with warrants attached. Nearly all were issued in dollars. The dollar bonds usually carried coupons of 4% or less; by the time the Japanese companies swapped that exposure into yen (whose interest rate was as much as five percentage points lower than the dollar's), their cost of capital was zero or negative."

7. In May 1988, Walt Disney Productions sold to Japanese investors a 20-year stream of projected yen royalties from Tokyo Disneyland. The present value of that stream of royalties, discounted at 6% (the return required by the Japanese investors), was 93 billion. Disney took the yen proceeds from the sale, converted them to dollars, and invested the dollars in bonds yielding 10%. According to Disney's chief financial officer, Gary Wilson, "In effect, we got money at a 6% discount rate, reinvested it at 10%, and hedged our royalty stream against yen fluctuations—all in one transaction."

   a. At the time of the sale, the exchange rate was 124 = $1. What dollar amount did Disney realize from the sale of its yen proceeds?

   b. Demonstrate the equivalence between Walt Disney's transaction and a currency swap. (*Hint*: A diagram would help.)

   c. Comment on Gary Wilson's statement. Did Disney achieve the equivalent of a free lunch through its transaction?

8. Explain the benefits of a debt-equity swap program to
   a. A multinational firm seeking to expand its investment in the country.
   b. The host government.
   c. The bank that sells its LDC debt in the secondary market.

9. How can debt swaps cause inflation?

10. Jose Angel Gurria, Mexico's chief debt negotiator and the architect of its swap program, questions the gain to Mexico from its swap program: "The latest restructuring

package on our debt gives us 20 years to repay principal, with no principal payments for seven years. So why are we giving money away? Why pay 88 cents for debt that is worth only 60 cents?" Comment on Seor Gurria's statement.

PROBLEMS

1. Company A, a low-rated firm, desires a fixed-rate, long-term loan. A presently has access to floating interest rate funds at a margin of 1.5% over LIBOR. Its direct borrowing cost is 13% in the fixed-rate bond market. In contrast, company B, which prefers a floating-rate loan, has access to fixed-rate funds in the Eurodollar bond market at 11% and floating-rate funds at LIBOR + 1/2%.
　a. How can A and B use a swap to advantage?
　b. Suppose they split the cost savings. How much would A pay for its fixed-rate funds? How much would B pay for its floating-rate funds?

2. Square Corp. has not tapped the Swiss franc public debt market because of concern about a likely appreciation of that currency and only wishes to be a floating-rate dollar borrower, which it can be at LIBOR + 3/8%. Circle Corp. has a strong preference for fixed-rate Swiss franc debt, but it must pay 1/2 of 1% more than the 5 1/4% coupon that Square Corp.'s notes would carry. Circle Corp., however, can obtain Eurodollars at LIBOR flat (a zero margin). What is the range of possible cost savings to Square from engaging in a currency swap with Circle?

3. In the Kodak Australian dollar swap example, suppose Merrill Lynch had been able to arrange a forward contract for the A$70 million at a rate of A$1 = U.S.$0.49.
　a. If Merrill Lynch retained full benefits from the better forward rate, what would have been the present value of its profit on the deal?
　b. If Merrill Lynch had passed these savings on to Kodak, what would have been Kodak's annualized all-in rate on the swap? (*Hint*: Take the internal rate of return on all of Kodak's cash flows.)
　c. Suppose the interest rate swap with Australian bank B had been at LIBOR − 20 basis points. If Merrill Lynch passed this higher cost along to Kodak, what would Kodak's all-in cost have been?

4. Chrysler has decided to make a $100 million investment in Mexico via a debt-equity swap. Of that $100 million, $20 million will go to pay off high-interest peso loans in Mexico. The remaining $80 million will go for new capital investment. The government will pay 86 cents on the dollar for debt used to pay off peso loans and 92 cents on the dollar for debt used to finance new investment. If Chrysler can buy Mexican debt in the secondary market for 60 cents on the dollar, how much will it cost Chrysler to make its $100 million investment?

BIBLIOGRAPHY

Fierman, Jaclyn. "Fast Bucks in Latin Loan Swaps." *Fortune*, August 3, 1987, pp. 91–99.
Moreno, Ramon. "LDC Debt Swaps." *FRBSF Weekly Letter*, Federal Reserve Bank of San Francisco, September 4, 1987.
Smith, Clifford W., Jr., Charles W. Smithson, and Lee M. Wakeman. "The Evolving Market for Swaps." *Midland Corporate Finance Journal*, Winter 1986, pp. 20–32.

23 Designing a Global Financing Strategy

Let us all be happy and live within our means, even if we have to borrow money to do it with.

Artemus Ward

CHAPTER LEARNING OBJECTIVES

- To identify the key elements and objectives involved in the design of a company's global financing strategy
- To describe a three-stage hierarchical framework for financing worldwide operations
- To calculate how much a particular below-market financing option is worth
- To describe the various market imperfections that an MNC may be able to take advantage of to reduce its financing costs
- To describe how a firm can use financing to reduce economic and political risks
- To identify the relevant factors and trade-offs in establishing a company's worldwide debt ratio

In selecting an appropriate strategy for financing its worldwide operations, the multinational corporation (MNC) must consider the availability of different sources of funds and the relative cost and effects of these sources on the firm's operating risks. Some of the key variables in the evaluation include the firm's capital structure (debt-equity mix), taxes, exchange risk, diversification of fund sources, the freedom to move funds across borders, and a variety of government credit and capital controls and subsidies. The eventual funding strategy selected must reconcile a variety of potentially conflicting objectives, such as minimizing expected financing costs, reducing economic exposure, providing protection from currency controls and other forms of political risk, and ensuring availability of funds in times of tight credit.

The choice of trade-offs to be made in establishing a worldwide financial policy requires an explicit analytical framework. The approach taken in this chapter separates the financing of international operations into three largely separable objectives:

1. Minimize expected after-tax financing costs.
2. Arrange financing to reduce the riskiness of operating cash flows.
3. Achieve an appropriate worldwide financial structure.[1]

23.1 MINIMIZING EXPECTED AFTER-TAX FINANCING COSTS

Sharp-eyed firms are always on the lookout for financing choices that are "bargains"—that is, financing options priced at below-market rates. The value of arranging *below-market financing* can be illustrated by examining a case involving Sonat, the energy and energy services company based in Birmingham, Alabama. In late 1984, Sonat ordered from Daewoo Shipbuilding, a South Korean shipyard, six drilling rigs that can be partly submerged. Daewoo agreed to finance the $425 million purchase price with an 8.5-year loan at an annual interest rate of 9% paid semiannually. The loan is repayable in 17 equal semiannual installments. How much is this loan worth to Sonat? That is, what is its net present value?

> Firms can create value by arranging below-market financing.

At 9% interest paid semiannually, Sonat must pay interest equal to 4.5% of the loan balance plus $25 million in principal repayment every six months for the next 8.5 years. In return, Sonat receives $425 million today. Given these cash inflows and outflows, we can calculate the loan's NPV just as we would for any project analysis. Note, however, that unlike the typical capital-budgeting problem we looked at, the cash inflow occurs immediately and the cash outflows later. But the principle is the same. All we need now is the required return on this deal and Sonat's marginal tax rate.

The required return is based on the opportunity cost of the funds provided, that is, the rate that Sonat would have to pay to borrow $425 million in the capital market. At the time the loan was arranged, in late 1984, the market interest rate on such a loan would have been about 16%. If the marginal tax rate at which the interest payments are written off is 50% (the federal plus state corporate tax rate at that time), then the after-tax semiannual required return is 4% (8% annually), and the after-tax semiannual interest payments are $0.0225 \times P_t$, where P_t is the loan balance in period t and 2.25% is the after-tax interest rate ($0.5 \times 4.5\%$). Now we can calculate the NPV of Sonat's financing bargain:

$$NPV = \$425{,}000{,}000 - \sum_{t=1}^{17} 0.0225P/(1.04)^t - \sum_{t=1}^{17} \$25{,}000{,}000/(1.04)^t$$

$$= \$425{,}000{,}000 - \$372{,}210{,}000$$

$$= \$52{,}790{,}000$$

These calculations are shown in Exhibit 23.1. You don't need a degree in financial economics to realize that borrowing money at 9% when the market rate

---

[1]This chapter is based in part on Donald R. Lessard and Alan C. Shapiro, "Guidelines for Global Financing Choices," *Midland Corporate Finance Journal*, Winter 1984, pp. 68–80; and Alan C. Shapiro, *Modern Corporate Finance* (New York: Macmillan, 1990), especially Chapter 16.

Exhibit 23.1 Calculating the Value of Sonat's Low-Cost Loan Arrangement (U.S.$ Millions)

Period	Principal Balance (1)	Interest (1) × 0.0225 = (2) +	Principal Repayment (3) =	Total Payment (4) ×	PV Factor @ 4% (5) =	Present Value (6)
1	$425	$9.56	$25	$34.56	0.962	$ 33.25
2	400	9.00	25	34.00	0.925	31.45
3	375	8.44	25	33.44	0.889	29.73
4	350	7.88	25	32.88	0.855	28.11
5	325	7.31	25	32.31	0.822	26.56
6	300	6.75	25	31.75	0.790	25.08
7	275	6.19	25	31.19	0.760	23.70
8	250	5.63	25	30.63	0.731	22.39
9	225	5.06	25	30.06	0.703	21.13
10	200	4.50	25	29.50	0.676	19.94
11	175	3.94	25	28.94	0.650	18.81
12	150	3.38	25	28.38	0.625	17.73
13	125	2.81	25	27.81	0.601	16.71
14	100	2.25	25	27.25	0.578	15.75
15	75	1.69	25	26.69	0.555	14.81
16	50	1.13	25	26.13	0.534	13.95
17	25	0.56	25	25.56	0.513	13.11
					Sum	$372.21

is 16% is a good deal. But what the NPV calculations tell you is just how much a particular below-market financing option is worth.

Below-market financing typically stems from government-induced financial market distortions.

Raising funds at a below-market rate is easier said than done, however. A company selling securities is competing for funds on a global basis, not only with other firms in its industry but with all firms, foreign and domestic, and with numerous government units and private individuals as well. The fierce competition for funds makes it much less likely that the firm can find bargain-priced funds. But, as we shall see, the task is not impossible. *Financial market distortions* arising from taxes, *government credit and capital controls*, and *government subsidies and incentives* sometimes enable firms to raise funds at below-market rates. Companies may also be able to raise low-cost money by devising securities for which specific investors are willing to pay a higher price.

Taxes

The asymmetrical tax treatment of various components of financial cost—such as dividend payments versus interest expenses and exchange losses versus exchange gains—often means that equality of before-tax costs will lead to inequality in after-tax costs. This asymmetry holds out the possibility of reducing after-tax costs by judicious selection of securities. Yet, everything is not always what it seems.

For example, many firms consider debt financing to be less expensive than equity financing because interest expense is tax-deductible, whereas dividends are paid out of after-tax income. But this comparison is too limited. In the absence of any restrictions, the supply of corporate debt can be expected to rise. Yields will also have to rise in order to attract investors in higher and higher tax brackets. Companies will continue to issue debt up to the point at which the marginal investor tax rate will equal the marginal corporate tax rate.[2] At this point, the necessary yield would be such that there would no longer be a tax incentive for issuing more debt.

The tax advantage of debt can be preserved only if the firm can take advantage of some tax distortion, issue tax-exempt debt, or sell debt to investors in marginal tax brackets below 34%. The example of zero-coupon bonds illustrates all of these categories.

Tax asymmetries can lead to bargain financing for MNCs.

Zero-Coupon Bonds. In 1982, PepsiCo issued the first long-term *zero-coupon bond*. Although they have since become a staple of corporate finance, zero-coupon bonds initially were a startling innovation. They don't pay interest, but are sold at a deep discount to their face value. For example, the price on PepsiCo's 30-year bonds was around $60 for each $1,000 face amount of the bonds. Investors gain from the difference between the discounted price and the amount they receive at redemption.

Between 1982 and 1985, investors paid $4 billion for $18.9 billion worth of zero-coupon bonds, about half of which were purchased by Japanese investors. The offerings were attractive in Japan because the government doesn't tax the capital gain on bonds sold prior to maturity. Catering to this tax break, a number of companies—including Exxon (see the illustration in Chapter 21) and IBM—were able to obtain inexpensive financing by targeting Japanese investors for zero-coupon bonds offered on international markets.

The ability to take advantage quickly of such tax windows is evident considering subsequent developments in Japan. Japan's Finance Ministry, embarrassed at this tax break, has effectively ended the tax exemption for zero-coupon bond gains; Japanese investors have accordingly demanded higher yields to compensate for their anticipated tax liability. The reaction by the Japanese government to the proliferation of zero-coupon debt illustrates a key point: If one devises a legal way to engage in unlimited tax arbitrage through the financial markets, the government will change the law.

This example also points out that even though the world's capital markets are highly integrated, companies can still profit from tax differentials and government restrictions on capital flows between countries. But the benefits go to those who are organized to quickly take advantage of such windows of opportunity.

Debt versus Equity Financing. Interest payments on debt extended by either the parent or a financial institution generally are tax-deductible by an affiliate, but dividends are not. In addition, principal repatriation is tax free, whereas dividend

[2]This insight first appeared in Merton Miller, "Debt and Taxes," *Journal of Finance*, May 1977, pp. 261–276.

payments may lead to further taxation. Thus, parent company financing of foreign affiliates in the form of debt rather than equity has certain tax advantages. These and other factors are discussed in Section 23.3.

Government Credit and Capital Controls

Governments intervene in their financial markets for a number of reasons: to restrain the growth of lendable funds, to make certain types of borrowing more or less expensive, and to direct funds to certain favored economic activities. In addition, corporate borrowing is often restricted in order to hold down interest rates (thereby providing the finance ministry with lower-cost funds to meet a budget deficit). When access to local funds markets is limited, interest rates in them are usually below the risk-adjusted equilibrium level. There is often an incentive to borrow as much as possible where nonprice credit rationing is used.

Restraints on, or incentives to promote, overseas borrowing are often employed as well. There are numerous examples of restraints and incentives affecting overseas borrowing. Certain countries have limited the amount of local financing the subsidiary of a multinational firm can obtain to that required for working-capital purposes; any additional needs will have to be satisfied from abroad. A prerequisite condition for obtaining official approval for a new investment or acquisition often is a commitment to inject external funds. Capital-exporting nations may attempt to control balance-of-payments deficits by restricting overseas investment flows—as the United States did from 1968 to 1974 under the Office of Foreign Direct Investment (OFDI) regulations.

Conversely, when a nation is concerned about excess capital inflows, a portion of any new foreign borrowing might have to be placed on deposit with the government, thereby raising the effective cost of external debt. Ironically, the effect of many of these government credit allocation and control schemes has been to hasten the development of the external financial markets—the Eurocurrency and Eurobond markets—further reducing government ability to regulate domestic financial markets.

Government credit and capital controls lead to financial distortions that multinationals can take advantage of.

The multinational firm with access to a variety of sources and types of funds and the ability to shift capital with its internal transfer system has more opportunities to secure the lowest risk-adjusted cost money and to circumvent credit restraints. These attributes should give it a substantial advantage over a purely domestic company.

Government Subsidies and Incentives

Despite the often hostile rhetoric directed against the multinational firm, many governments offer a growing list of incentives to MNCs to influence their production and export sourcing decisions. Direct investment incentives include interest rate subsidies, loans with long maturities, official repatriation guarantees, grants related to project size, favorable prices for land, and favorable terms for the building of plants. For example, new investments located in the Mezzogiorno region of Italy can qualify for cash grants that cover up to 40% of the cost of plant and equipment, in addition to low interest rate loans.

Governments sometimes will make the infrastructure investments as well by building the transportation, communication, and other links to support a new industrial project. Some indirect incentives include corporate income tax holidays, accelerated depreciation, and a reduction or elimination of the payment of other business taxes and import duties on capital equipment and raw materials.

In addition, all governments of developed nations have some form of export financing agency whose purpose is to boost local exports by providing loans with long repayment periods at interest rates below the market level and with low-cost political and economic risk insurance. These export credit programs can often be employed advantageously by multinationals. The use will depend on whether the firm is seeking to export or import goods or services, but the basic strategy remains the same: Shop around among the various export credit agencies for the best possible financing arrangement.

Multinationals can take advantage of export financing to lower their cost of funds.

ILLUSTRATION: *Texas Instruments Searches for Low-Cost Capital*

Texas Instruments (TI) is seeking to finance an aggressive capital spending program through a series of joint ventures and other cooperative arrangements with foreign governments and corporations. In Italy, TI received a package of development grants and low-cost loans from the government which will offset more than half of TI's investment in a state-of-the-art semiconductor plant there—an investment expected to total more than $1 billion over a multiyear period. TI was able to negotiate the incentive package because the Italian government was seeking to improve its technological infrastructure in the area selected by TI for the new plant.

In Taiwan, TI and a Taiwanese customer, Acer Computer Company, established a joint venture in which Acer's majority stake is financed with Taiwanese equity capital that would be unavailable to a U.S. company acting alone. In Japan, TI entered into a joint venture with Kobe Steel, a company seeking diversification. Here, too, TI relies on its foreign partner to supply a majority of the equity. In both Asian joint ventures, however, TI has an option to convert its initial minority stake into a majority holding.

Export Financing Strategy. Massey-Ferguson (now Varity Corp.), the multinational Canadian farm-equipment manufacturer, illustrates how MNCs are able to generate business for their foreign subsidiaries at minimum expense and risk by playing off various national export credit programs against each other.

The key to this *export financing strategy* is to view the foreign countries in which the MNC has plants not only as markets, but also as potential sources of financing for exports to third countries. For example, in early 1978, Massey-Ferguson was looking to ship 7200 tractors (worth $53 million) to Turkey, but it was unwilling to assume the risk of currency inconvertibility.[3] Turkey at that time

---

[3]"Massey-Ferguson's No-Risk Tractor Deal," *Business International Money Report*, February 3, 1978, pp. 35–36.

already owed $2 billion to various foreign creditors, and it was uncertain whether it would be able to come up with dollars to pay off its debts (especially since its reserves were at about zero).

Massey solved this problem by manufacturing the tractors at its Brazilian subsidiary, Massey-Ferguson of Brazil, and selling them to Brazil's Interbras—the trading-company arm of Petrobras, the Brazilian national oil corporation. Interbras, in turn, arranged to sell the tractors to Turkey and pay Massey in cruzeiros. The cruzeiro financing for Interbras came from Cacex, the Banco do Brazil department that is in charge of foreign trade. Cacex underwrote all the political, commercial, and exchange risks as part of the Brazilian government's intense export promotion drive. Before choosing Brazil as a supply point, Massey made a point of shopping around to get the best export credit deal available.

Importers may be able to access to low-cost financing of their purchases.

Import Financing Strategy. Firms engaged in projects that have sizable import requirements may be able to finance these purchases on attractive terms. A number of countries, including the United States, make credit available to foreign purchasers at low (below-market) interest rates and with long repayment periods. These loans are almost always tied to procurement in the agency's country; thus, the firm must compile a list of goods and services required for the project and relate them to potential sources by country. Where there is overlap among the potential suppliers, the purchasing firm may have leverage to extract more favorable financing terms from the various export credit agencies involved.

Perhaps the best-known application of this *import financing strategy* in recent years is the financing of the Soviet gas pipeline to Western Europe. The Soviet Union played off various European and Japanese suppliers and export financing agencies against each other and managed to get extraordinarily favorable credit and pricing terms.

Regional and International Development Banks. Organizations such as the World Bank and Inter-American Development Bank (which were discussed in Chapter 21) are potential sources of low-cost, long-term, fixed-rate funds for certain types of ventures. The time-consuming nature of arranging financing from them, however—in part due to their insistence on conducting their own in-house feasibility studies—usually leaves them as a secondary source of funds. Their participation may be indispensable, however, for projects that require heavy infrastructure investments such as roads, power plants, schools, communications facilities, and housing for employees. These infrastructure investments are the most difficult part of a project to arrange financing for because they generate no cash flow of their own. Thus, loans or grants from an international or regional development bank are often essential to fill a gap in the project financing plan.

Financial Innovation

The dizzying pace of securities innovation in recent years has created an overwhelming abundance of financing alternatives. To a person schooled in marketing, the reasons for such variety are obvious. The vast array of securities in the marketplace exists for the same reasons that M&Ms come in more than one color and that Fords, Chevrolets, and Volkswagens coexist with one another and with Mercedes-Benzes and Rolls-Royces. People have different tastes, preferences, and wealth levels. And whether the market is for cars or financial securities, the better designed the product is and the more closely it is tailored to the particular needs and desires of its potential customers, the higher the price it can command. Moreover, as the environment changes, whether in the form of higher oil prices, new tax laws, or more uncertain inflation, opportunities arise for astute managers to design new cars or securities that fit the new needs of the marketplace.

Furthermore, as Baskin-Robbins has successfully demonstrated, even though plain vanilla may be the most popular ice cream flavor, there's also a market out there for peanut butter ice cream. This suggests a potential source of value creation: To the extent that the firm can design a security that appeals to a special niche in the capital market, it can attract funds at a cost that is less than the market's required return on securities of comparable risk.

Financial innovation can reduce the cost of capital.

But as we saw in the case of zeros, such a rewarding situation is likely to be temporary, because the demand for a security that fits a particular niche in the market is not unlimited. On the other hand, the supply of securities designed to tap that niche is likely to increase dramatically once the niche is recognized. However, even though financial innovation may not be a sustainable form of value creation, it can nonetheless enable the initial issuers to raise money at a below-market rate.

ILLUSTRATION: *The Swedish Export Credit Corporation Innovates*

The Swedish Export Credit Corporation (SEK) borrows about $2 billion annually. To keep its funding costs low, SEK relies heavily on financial innovation. For example, SEK recently issued a straight bond, stripped it down to its two components—an annuity consisting of the interest payments and a zero-coupon bond consisting of the principal repayment at maturity—and sold the pieces to different investors. The annuity cash flow was tailored to meet the demands of a Japanese insurance company that was looking for an interest-only security, while the zero-coupon portion appealed to European investors who desired earnings taxed as capital gains rather than interest income. By unbundling the bond issue into separate parts that appealed to distinct groups of investors, SEK created a financial transaction whose parts were more valuable than the whole.

23.2 REDUCING OPERATING RISKS

After taking advantage of the opportunities available to it to lower its risk-adjusted financing costs, the firm should then arrange its additional financing in such a way that the risk exposures of the company are kept at manageable levels. The profitability, and thus the market value, of any company depends to a large extent on its ability to compete. A key element of corporate competitiveness is the

Firms should arrange their financing to reduce risk if the cost of doing so is not too great.

firm's ability to inspire sufficient trust and confidence such that customers, employees, and other stakeholders are willing to develop relationships with the firm. One prerequisite for such confidence is that the firm be seen as financially sound and viable over the long run.

Clearly, excessive risk taking—with a corresponding decrease in the firm's survival odds—could adversely affect the firm's relationships with its noninvestor stakeholders, thereby jeopardizing the firm-specific capital that has been accumulated over time. The result is that higher total risk can lead to a reduction in a company's operating cash flows by decreasing sales or increasing operating costs.[4]

Thus, to the extent that a particular element of risk contributes materially to the firm's total risk, management will want to lay off that risk as long as the cost of doing so is not too great. The risks and their relationship to financing arrangements that we examine here arise from four sources: currency fluctuations, political instability, sales uncertainty, and changing access to funds.

Since the political and economic changes that bring about these risks are impossible to predict—otherwise there would be no risk—the firm cannot expect to profit from financial arrangements that lay such risks off to others. Otherwise, arbitrage opportunities would present themselves, a condition inconsistent with financial market efficiency. Rather, these financial arrangements should be viewed as insurance against corporate risk.

Excessive risk-taking can adversely affect a firm's relations with its noninvestor stakeholders.

Exchange Risk

We saw in Chapter 11 that if financing opportunities in various currencies are fairly priced, firms can structure their liabilities so as to reduce their exposure to foreign exchange risk at no added cost to shareholders. In the case of contractual items—those fixed in nominal terms—this structuring simply involves matching net positive positions (ones with net cash inflows) in each currency with borrowings of similar maturity. The goal here is to offset unanticipated changes in the dollar value of its cash flows with identical changes in the dollar cost of servicing its liabilities.

With noncontractual operating cash flows—those from future revenues and costs—the same financing principle applies: Finance assets that generate foreign currency cash flows with liabilities denominated in those same foreign currencies. Although it is impossible to perfectly hedge operating cash flows in this manner due to the many uncertainties concerning the effects of currency changes on operating flows, the hedging objective at least provides a clear-cut goal for firms to strive for.

Political Risk

The use of financing to reduce political risks typically involves mechanisms to avoid or at least reduce the impact of certain risks, such as those of exchange

---

[4]This point is elaborated on in Alan C. Shapiro and Sheridan Titman, "An Integrated Approach to Corporate Risk Management," *Midland Corporate Finance Journal*, Summer 1985, pp. 41–56.

controls. It may also involve financing mechanisms that actually change the risk itself, as in the case of expropriation or other direct political acts.

Firms can sometimes reduce the risk of currency inconvertibility by appropriately arranging their affiliates' financing. Strategies include investing parent funds as debt rather than equity, arranging back-to-back and parallel loans, and using local financing to the maximum extent possible. Of course, such arrangements will be most valuable when the banks or local investors face significantly fewer restrictions or smaller risks—especially if the risk in question involves possible discrimination against direct foreign investors. While local investors may often have an advantage in this regard, this advantage cannot be taken as a general rule. Even if a particular political risk cannot be modified by shifting it from one firm or investor to another, a firm with substantial exposure will benefit by laying off such risks to investors with less exposure.

Another approach used by multinational firms, especially those in the expropriation-prone extractive industries, is to finance their foreign investments with funds from the host and other governments, international development agencies, overseas banks, and from customers—with payment to be provided out of production—rather than supplying their own capital. Because repayment is tied to the project's success, the firm(s) sponsoring the project can create an international network of banks, government agencies, and customers with a vested interest in the faithful fulfillment of the host government's contract with the sponsoring firm(s). Any expropriation threat is likely to upset relations with customers, banks, and governments worldwide. As we saw in Chapter 20, this strategy was employed successfully by Kennecott to finance a major copper mine expansion in Chile. Despite the subsequent rise to power of Salvador Allende—a politician who promised to expropriate all foreign holdings in Chile with "ni un centavo" in compensation—Chile was forced to honor all prior government commitments to Kennecott.

International leasing is another financing technique that may help multinationals to reduce their political risk. In particular, international leasing allows multinationals to limit the ownership of assets by subsidiaries in politically unstable countries and to more easily extract cash from affiliates located in countries where there are exchange controls.

> MNCs can reduce their political risk by financing projects with funds from various governments, development banks, and customers.

Product Market Risk

Some firms sell their project's or plant's expected output in advance to their customers on the basis of mutual advantage. The purchaser benefits from these so-called *"take-or-pay"* contracts by having a stable source of supply, usually at a discount from the market price. The seller also benefits by having an assured outlet for its product—which protects the firm against, *product market risk*, the risk of demand fluctuations—and a contract that it can then discount with a consortium of banks. That is, it sells collection rights on these contracts to the banks. As noted earlier, this technique, which is similar to factoring but on a far grander scale, was used to help finance Kennecott's Chilean copper mine expansion and the Soviet Union's natural gas pipeline to Western Europe. Similarly, Texas Instruments seeks to lower its risk by establishing long-term supply agreements in which customers make advance payments for purchases of semiconductors.

Securing Access to Funds

A multinational firm's operational flexibility is dependent in part on its ability to secure continual access to funds at a reasonable cost and without onerous restrictions. In this way, the firm can meet temporary shortfalls of cash and also take advantage of profitable investment opportunities without having to sell off assets or otherwise disrupt operations. The fear is that during some future period of monetary stringency, the quantity of credit available to them might be limited, while their competitors retain access to funds in a broader range of markets. In such conditions of uneven credit allocation, the market shares of their own business would be at risk because the scale of their operations would be limited by the scale of available finance. This potential problem creates demand among firms for access to an expanded range of credit sources.

The MNC's operating flexibility and ability to respond to competitive intrusions depends on assuring access to funds.

The ability to marshal substantial financial resources also signals competitors, actual and potential, that the firm will not be an easy target. Consider the alternative: a firm that is highly leveraged with no excess lines of credit or cash reserves. A competitor can move into the firm's market and gain market share with less fear of retaliation. In order to retaliate—by cutting price, say, or by increasing advertising expenditures—the firm will need more money. Since it has no spare cash and can't issue additional debt at a reasonable price, it will have to go to the equity market. But firms issuing new equity are suspect because of the asymmetric information relationship between investors and management (Is the firm selling equity now because it knows the stock is overpriced?). The problem of *information asymmetry* will be particularly acute when the firm is trying to fend off a competitive attack. Thus, a firm that lacks financial reserves faces a Hobson's choice: Acquiesce in the competitive attack or raise funds on unattractive terms.

To ensure adequate financial reserves, an MNC can maintain substantial unused debt capacity and liquid assets. It can also diversify its fund sources and indirectly buy insurance through excess borrowing. Having these extra financial resources signals competitors, as well as customers and other stakeholders, that the firm is financially healthy and has staying power; temporary setbacks will not become permanent ones.

Diversification of Fund Sources. A key element of any MNC's global financial strategy should be to gain access to a broad range of fund sources to lessen its dependence on any one financial market. An ancillary benefit to *diversification of fund sources* is that the firm broadens its sources of economic and financial information, providing a useful supplement to its domestic information sources and aiding in its financial decision-making process.

For example, in January 1985, Signal Cos. issued $125 million of Eurodollar bonds, even though it had $1.2 billion in cash and very little debt at the time. According to the chief financial officer, Signal "wanted access to a large capital market that's separate from the U.S. Next time, we may come to this market for

$500 million and we'll know we can do a major offering at a substantial savings [to a comparable U.S. financing]."[5]

The added benefit of dealing with several financial institutions at once has been described by Richard K. Goeltz, Vice President Finance of Joseph E. Seagram & Sons, Inc., as follows:

> [B]y being a major client at a number of high quality firms rather than only one, we are able to avail ourselves of the knowledge, ingenuity and expertise of different groups of skilled professionals. No one bank is omniscient and omnipotent; we must be able to draw on the resources of many organizations.[6]

The threat of domestic credit controls has accelerated the trend toward global diversification of financing sources. For example, after the Federal Reserve Board tightened credit in October 1979 and proposed a voluntary ceiling on loan growth in March 1980, many anxious corporate treasurers feared that mandatory credit controls might be close at hand. So, large numbers of them arranged to borrow abroad, far from the Fed's reach.

A key element of global financing strategy is to diversify financing sources internationally.

Monsanto, for example, negotiated a short-term credit line of nearly $200 million with eight European banks. Dow Chemical had about $1 billion in unused credit lines with foreign banks. Ford Motor opened a $1 billion credit line with a group of banks, including some European banks. In the event that the United States imposed formal controls, these firms planned to tap their foreign credit lines and repatriate the funds back home. According to John Rolls, Monsanto's treasurer, "To us, this credit line is insurance. We probably won't need it, but it's a good idea to have it."[7]

Similarly, Japanese firms are issuing securities in the United States. By familiarizing American investors with their names, they can more easily raise funds in the United States in the future as a safeguard against one of the periodic credit controls imposed by the Bank of Japan, the Japanese central bank.

Excess Borrowing. Most firms have lines of credit with a number of banks that give them the right to borrow up to an agreed-upon credit limit. Unused balances carry a commitment fee, normally on the order of 0.5% per annum. In order not to tie up funds unnecessarily, most banks periodically review each credit limit to see whether the customer's account activity level justifies that credit line. Some firms are willing to borrow funds that they do not require (and then place them on deposit) in order to maintain their credit limit in the event of a tight money situation. In effect, they are buying insurance against the possibility of being squeezed out of the money market. One measure of the cost of this policy is the difference between the borrowing rate and the deposit rate, multiplied by the average amount of borrowed funds placed on deposit.

---

[5]*The Wall Street Journal,* January 23, 1985, p. 38.

[6]Richard Karl Goeltz, "Citibank Treasurers' Conference," June 28, 1984, p. 5. This is the text of a speech by Mr. Goeltz.

[7]Anthony Ramirez, "Dodging the Fed," *The Wall Street Journal,* April 17, 1980, p. 44.

23.3 ESTABLISHING A WORLDWIDE CAPITAL STRUCTURE

In the two previous sections, we examined various motivations for using particular types of financing. However, while knowledge of the costs and benefits of each individual source of funds is helpful, it is not sufficient to establish an optimal global financial plan. This plan requires consideration not only of the component costs of capital, but also of how the use of one source affects the cost and availability of other sources. A firm that uses too much debt might find the cost of equity (and new-debt) financing prohibitive. The capital structure problem for the multinational enterprise, therefore, is to determine the mix of debt and equity for the parent entity and for all consolidated and unconsolidated subsidiaries that maximizes shareholder wealth.

In establishing an MNC's capital structure, the focus must be on the MNC's consolidated worldwide financial structure.

The focus is on the consolidated, *worldwide capital structure* because suppliers of capital to a multinational firm are assumed to associate the risk of default with the MNC's worldwide debt ratio. This association stems from the view that bankruptcy or other forms of financial distress in an overseas subsidiary can seriously impair the parent company's ability to operate domestically. Any deviations from the MNC's target capital structure will cause adjustments in the mix of debt and equity used to finance future investments.

Another factor that may be relevant in establishing a worldwide debt ratio is the empirical evidence that earnings variability appears to be a decreasing function of foreign-source earnings. Because the risk of bankruptcy for a firm is dependent on its total earnings variability, the earnings diversification provided by its foreign operations may enable the multinational firm to leverage itself more highly than can a purely domestic corporation, without increasing its default risk.

Foreign Subsidiary Capital Structure

Once a decision has been made regarding the appropriate mix of debt and equity for the entire corporation, questions about individual operations can be raised. How should MNCs arrange the capital structures of their foreign affiliates? And what factors are relevant in making this decision? Specifically, the problem is whether *foreign subsidiary capital structures should*

— Conform to the capital structure of the parent company
— Reflect the capitalization norms in each foreign country
— Vary to take advantage of opportunities to minimize the MNC's cost of capital

Disregarding public and government relations and legal requirements for the moment, the parent company could finance its foreign affiliates by raising funds in its own country and investing these funds as equity. The overseas operations would then have a zero debt ratio (debt/total assets). Alternatively, the parent could hold only one dollar of share capital in each affiliate and require all to borrow on their own, with or without guarantees; in this case, affiliate debt ratios would approach 100%. Or the parent can itself borrow and relend the monies as intracorporate advances. Here again, the affiliates' debt ratios would be close to

Exhibit 23.2 Subsidiary Capital Structure

I.	100% Parent Financed		II.	100% Parent Financed	
	$100	D = $50		$100	D = $100
		E = 50			E = 0
	D/E = 1:1			D/E = Infinity	
III.	100% Parent Financed		IV.	100% Bank Financed	
	$100	D = $ 0		$100	D = $100
		E = 100			E = 0
	D/E = 0			D/E = Infinity	

100%. In all these cases, the total amount of borrowing and the debt/equity mix of the consolidated corporation are identical. Thus, the question of an optimal capital structure for a foreign affiliate is completely distinct from the corporation's overall debt/equity ratio.

Moreover, any accounting rendition of a separate capital structure for the subsidiary is wholly illusory *unless* the parent is willing to allow its affiliate to default on its debt.[8] As long as the rest of the MNC group has a legal or moral obligation or sound business reasons for preventing the affiliate from defaulting, the individual unit has no independent capital structure. Rather, its true debt/equity ratio is equal to that of the consolidated group. Exhibits 23.2 and 23.3 show

An individual subsidiary has no independent capital structure, unless the parent will allow its subsidiary to default.

Exhibit 23.3 Consolidated Parent Balance Sheet

Before Foreign Investment

	$1,000	D = $300
		E = 700
	D/E = 3:7	

After Foreign Investment

Cases I, II, and III Parent Financed with 100% Bank Debt			Case IV Subsidiary Financed with 100% Bank Debt		
Domestic	$1,000	D = $400	Domestic	$1000	D = $400
Foreign	100	E = 700	Foreign	100	E = 700
	D/E = 4:7			D/E = 4:7	

[8]See, for example, Michael Adler, "The Cost of Capital and Valuation of a Two-Country Firm," *Journal of Finance*, March 1974, pp. 119–132; and Alan C. Shapiro, "Financial Structure and Cost of Capital in the Multinational Corporation," *Journal of Financial and Quantitative Analysis*, June 1978, pp. 211–226.

the stated and the true debt-to-equity ratios for a subsidiary and its parent for four separate cases. In cases I, II, and III, the parent borrows $100 to invest in a foreign subsidiary, in varying portions of debt and equity. In case IV, the subsidiary borrows the $100 directly from the bank. Depending on what the parent calls its investment, the subsidiary's debt-to-equity ratio can vary from zero to infinity. Despite this variation, the consolidated balance sheet shows a debt-to-equity ratio following the foreign investment of 4:7 regardless of how the investment is financed and what it is called.

Exhibit 23.4 shows that the financing mechanism does affect the pattern of returns, whether they are called dividends or interest and principal payments. It also determines the initial recipient of the cash flows. Are the cash flows from the foreign unit paid directly to the outside investor (the bank) or are they first paid to the parent, which then turns around and repays the bank?

The point of this exercise is to show that unlike the case for the corporation as a whole, an affiliate's degree of leverage does not determine its financial risk. Therefore, the first two options—having affiliate financial structures conform to parent or local norms—are unrelated to shareholder wealth maximization.

The irrelevance of subsidiary capital structure is recognized by many multinationals.

The irrelevance of subsidiary financial structures seems to be recognized by multinationals. In a 1979 survey by Business International of eight U.S.-based MNCs, most of the firms expressed little concern with the debt/equity mixes of their foreign affiliates.[9] (Admittedly, for most of the firms interviewed, the debt ratios of affiliates had not significantly raised the MNCs' consolidated indebtedness.) Their primary focus was on the worldwide, rather than individual, capital structure. The third option of varying affiliate financial structures to take advan-

Exhibit 23.4 Subsidiary Capital Structure Depends on What Its Funds Are Called

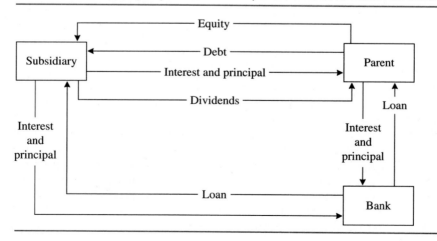

[9]"Policies of MNCs on Debt/Equity Mix," *Business International Money Report,* September 21, 1979, pp. 319–320.

tage of local financing opportunities appears to be the appropriate choice. Thus, within the constraints set by foreign statutory or minimum equity requirements, the need to appear to be a responsible and good guest, and the requirements of a worldwide financial structure, a multinational corporation should finance its affiliates to minimize its incremental average cost of capital.

A subsidiary with a capital structure similar to its parent may forgo profitable opportunities to lower its cost of funds. For example, rigid adherence to a fixed debt/equity ratio may not allow a subsidiary to take advantage of government-subsidized debt or low-cost loans from international agencies. Furthermore, it may be worthwhile to raise funds locally if the country is politically risky. In the event the affiliate is expropriated, for instance, it would default on all loans from local financial institutions. Similarly, borrowing funds locally will decrease the company's vulnerability to exchange controls. Local currency (LC) profits can be used to service its LC debt. On the other hand, forcing a subsidiary to borrow funds locally to meet parent norms may be quite expensive in a country with a high-cost capital market or if the subsidiary is in a tax-loss-carryforward position. In the latter case, since the subsidiary can't realize the tax benefits of the interest write-off, the parent should make an equity injection financed by borrowed funds. In this way, the interest deduction need not be sacrificed.

Leverage and the Tax Reform Act of 1986. The choice of where to borrow to finance foreign operations has become more complicated with passage of the Tax Reform Act of 1986 because the distribution of debt between U.S. parents and their foreign subsidiaries affects the use of foreign tax credits. Moreover, the Tax Reform Act has put many U.S.-based MNCs in a position of excess foreign tax credits. One way to use up these FTCs is to push expenses overseas—and thus lower overseas profits—by increasing the leverage of foreign subsidiaries. In the aforementioned example, the U.S. parent may have one of its taxpaying foreign units borrow funds and use them to pay a dividend to the parent. The parent can then turn around and invest these funds as equity in the nontaxpaying subsidiary. In this way, the worldwide corporation can reduce its taxes without being subject to the constraints imposed by the Tax Reform Act.

The Tax Reform Act of 1986 has complicated the financing decision for MNCs.

Leasing and the Tax Reform Act of 1986. As an alternative to increasing the debt of foreign subsidiaries, U.S. multinationals could expand their use of leasing in the United States. Although leasing an asset is economically equivalent to using borrowed funds to purchase the asset, the international tax consequences differ. Prior to 1986, U.S. multinationals counted virtually all their interest expense as a fully deductible U.S. expense. Under the new law, firms must allocate interest expense on general borrowings to match the location of their assets, even if all the interest is paid in the United States. This allocation has the effect of reducing the amount of interest expense that can be written off against U.S. income. Rental expense, on the other hand, can be allocated to the location of the leased property. Lease payments on equipment located in the United States, therefore, can be fully deducted.

At the same time, leasing equipment to be used in the United States, instead of borrowing to finance it, increases reported foreign income (since there is less interest expense to allocate against foreign income). The effect of leasing, therefore, is to increase the allowable foreign tax credit to offset U.S. taxes owed on foreign source income, thereby providing another tax advantage of leasing for firms that owe U.S. tax on their foreign source income.

Cost Minimizing Approach to Global Capital Structure. The cost-minimizing approach to determining foreign affiliate capital structures would be to allow subsidiaries with access to low-cost capital markets to exceed the parent company capitalization norm, while subsidiaries in higher-capital-cost nations would have lower target debt ratios. These costs must be figured on an after-tax basis, taking into account the company's worldwide tax position.

Some companies require their foreign units to be financially independent to motivate them.

The basic hypothesis proposed in this section is that a subsidiary's capital structure is relevant only insofar as it affects the parent's consolidated worldwide debt ratio. Nonetheless, some companies have a general policy of "every tub on its own bottom." Foreign units are expected to be financially independent following the parent's initial investment. The rationale for this policy is to "avoid giving management a crutch." By forcing foreign affiliates to stand on their own feet, affiliate managers will presumably be working harder to improve local operations, thereby generating the internal cash flow that will help replace parent financing. Moreover, the local financial institutions will have a greater incentive to monitor the local subsidiary's performance because they can no longer look to the parent company to bail them out if their loans go sour.

But companies that expect their subsidiaries to borrow locally had better be prepared to provide enough initial equity capital or subordinated loans. In addition, local suppliers and customers are likely to shy away from a new subsidiary operating on a shoestring if that subsidiary is not receiving financial backing from its parent. The foreign subsidiary may have to show its balance sheet to local trade creditors, distributors, and other stakeholders. Having a balance sheet that shows more equity demonstrates that the unit has greater staying power.

It also takes more staff time to manage a highly leveraged subsidiary in countries like Brazil and Mexico where government controls and high inflation make local funds scarce. One treasury manager complained, "We spend 75–80% of management's time trying to figure out how to finance the company. Running around chasing our tails instead of attending to our basic business—getting production costs lower, sales up, and making the product better."[10]

Joint Ventures

Because many MNCs participate in joint ventures, either by choice or necessity, establishing an appropriate financing mix for this form of investment is an important consideration. The previous assumption that affiliate debt is equivalent to parent debt in terms of its impact on perceived default risk may no longer be valid. In countries such as Japan and Germany, increased leverage will not necessarily lead to increased financial risks, due to the close relationship between the

[10]"Determining Overseas Debt/Equity Ratios," *Business International Money Report,* January 27, 1986, p. 26.

local banks and corporations. Thus, debt raised by a joint venture in Japan, for example, may not be equivalent to parent-raised debt in terms of its impact on default risk. The assessment of the effects of leverage in a joint venture requires a qualitative analysis of the partner's ties with the local financial community, particularly with the local banks.

Unless the joint venture can be isolated from its partners' operations, there are likely to be some significant conflicts associated with this form of ownership. Transfer pricing, setting royalty and licensing fees, and allocating production and markets among plants are just some of the areas in which each owner has an incentive to engage in activities that will harm its partners. These conflicts explain why bringing in outside equity investors is generally such an unstable form of external financing.

> Joint ventures complicate the financing decision.

Because of their lack of complete control over a joint venture's decisions and its profits, most MNCs will, at most, guarantee joint venture loans in proportion to their share of ownership. But where the MNC is substantially stronger financially than its partner, the MNC may wind up implicitly guaranteeing its weaker partner's share of any joint-venture borrowings, as well as its own share. In this case, it makes sense to push for as large an equity base as possible; the weaker partner's share of the borrowings is then supported by its larger equity investment.

23.4 ILLUSTRATION: NESTLE

Nestle, the $17 billion Swiss foods conglomerate, is about as multinational as a company can be. About 98% of its sales take place overseas, and the group's diversified operations span 150 countries. Nestle's numerous (and generally wholly owned) subsidiaries are operationally decentralized. However, finances are centralized in Vevey, Switzerland. Staffed by just 12 people, the finance department makes all subsidiary funding decisions, manages the resulting currency exposures, determines subsidiary dividend amounts, sets the worldwide debt/equity structure, and evaluates subsidiary performance.

Nestle's centralized finance function plays the pivotal role in the firm's intricate web of subsidiary-to-headquarters profit remittances and headquarters-to-subsidiary investment flows. Profits and excess cash are collected by the treasury department in Vevey and then channeled back to overseas subsidiaries in the form of equity and debt investments. Nestle considers this approach to be the best possible investment for the group's wealth.

When a subsidiary is first established, its fixed assets—which form about half of the total investment—are financed by the Nestle group, generally with equity. Later on, the group may supply long-term debt as needed to support operations. The local subsidiary manager handles all the marketing and production decisions, but decisions regarding long-term debt and equity funding are managed solely by Vevey headquarters.

The other half of the investment—working capital—is then acquired locally, usually via bank credit or commercial paper. However, Nestle varies this general approach to suit each country. In certain countries—those that permit free transfers of funds—Nestle finances part of the working capital from Vevey instead of using local bank credits.

Central control over affiliate capital structures is facilitated by the policy of forcing local managers to dividend out almost 100% of their profits to Switzerland. The particular capital structure chosen for an affiliate depends on various considerations, including taxes, political risk, and currency risk.

To ensure that it borrows at the lowest possible cost, Nestle takes considerable care to structure its capital base to keep a top credit rating. The desire for a low-risk capital structure is also consistent with Nestle's business strategy. According to Senior Vice President, Finance, Daniel Regolatti, "Our basic strategy is that we are an industrial company. We have a lot of risks in a lot of countries, so we should not add high financial risks."[11]

23.5 SUMMARY AND CONCLUSIONS

This chapter has attempted to provide a framework for multinational firms to use in arranging their global financing. The primary emphasis is on taking advantage of distortions resulting from government intervention in financial markets or from differential national tax laws, either of which may cause differences to exist in the risk-adjusted after-tax costs of different sources and types of funds. Secondarily, this framework includes the possibility of reducing various operating risks resulting from political or economic factors. Last, it seeks to determine appropriate parent, affiliate, and worldwide capital structures—taking into account the unique attributes of being a multinational corporation.

QUESTIONS

1. What are the likely effects of the Japanese government's relaxing its restrictions on the ability of Japanese firms to raise funds in the Euromarkets on
   a. Japanese firms?
   b. Their foreign competitors?
   c. Japanese investors who can now purchase Eurosecurities?
2. Low-cost export financing is often a bad sign. Explain.
3. Why do governments provide subsidized financing for some investments?
4. How can reducing operating risks increase corporate profitability?
5. Why have Eurobonds traditionally yielded less than comparable domestic issues?
6. What are some of the advantages and disadvantages of having highly leveraged foreign subsidiaries?
7. How has the Tax Reform Act of 1986 affected the capital structure choice for foreign subsidiaries?

[11]"The Nestle Approach to Capital Markets and Innovation," *Business International Money Report,* October 27, 1986, p. 337.

8. What financing problems might be associated with joint ventures?

9. Under what circumstances does it make sense for a company to not guarantee the debt of its foreign affiliates?

10. How does government intervention in financial markets affect the choice of financing?

11. How can financial strategy be used to reduce political risk?

12. In order to develop large agricultural estates, the Republic of Coconutland offers the following financing deal: If an investor agrees to purchase a plantation and put up half the cost in U.S. dollars, the government will make a 20-year, zero-interest loan of U.S. dollars to cover the other half.
    a. What risks does the scheme entail?
    b. How can an investor use financing to reduce these risks?

13. Comment on the following statement. "Interest costs affect your ability to price competitively. If you're competing against a German or Japanese company that's paying 4% locally, and you're paying 9%, that's as if you had expensive labor. You can't be a low-cost producer that way."

PROBLEMS

1. Suppose that the cost of borrowing restricted French francs is 7% annually, whereas the market rate for these funds is 12%. If a firm can borrow FF 10 million of restricted funds, how much will it save annually in before-tax franc interest expense?

2. Suppose that one of the inducements provided by Taiwan to woo Xidex into setting up a local production facility is a 10-year, $12.5 million loan at 8% interest. The principal is to be repaid at the end of the tenth year. The market interest rate on such a loan is about 15%. With a marginal tax rate of 40%, how much is this loan worth to Xidex?

3. Compania Troquelados ARDA is a medium-sized Mexico City auto parts maker. It is trying to decide whether to borrow dollars at 9% or Mexican pesos at 75%. What advice would you give it? What information would you need before you gave the advice?

4. Boeing Commercial Airplane Co. manufactures all its planes in the United States and prices them in dollars, even the 50% of its sales destined for overseas markets. What financing strategy would you recommend for Boeing? What data do you need?

5. All-Nippon Airways, a Japanese airline, flies exclusively within Japan. It is looking to finance a recent purchase of Boeing 737s. The director of finance for All-Nippon is attracted to dollar financing because he expects the yen to keep appreciating against the dollar. What is your advice to him?

6. United Airlines recently inaugurated service to Japan and now wants to finance the purchase of Boeing 747s to service that route. The CFO for United is attracted to yen financing because the interest rate on yen is 300 basis points lower than the dollar interest rate. Although he doesn't expect this interest differential to be offset by yen appreciation over the 10-year life of the loan, he would like an independent opinion before issuing yen debt.
    a. What are the key questions you would ask in responding to UAL's CFO?
    b. Can you think of any other reason for using yen debt?
    c. What would you advise him to do, given his likely responses to your questions and your answer to part b?

7. The CFO of Eastman Kodak is thinking of borrowing Japanese yen because of their low interest rate, currently at 4.5%. The current interest rate on U.S. dollars is 9%. What is your advice to the CFO?

8. Rohm & Haas, a Philadelphia-based specialty chemicals company, traditionally finances its Brazilian operations from outside that country because it's "too expensive" to borrow local currency in Brazil. Brazilian interest rates vary from 50% to over 100%. Rohm & Haas is now thinking of switching to cruzeiro financing because of a pending cruzeiro devaluation. Assess Rohm & Haas's financing strategy.

9. Nord Resources's Ramu River property in Papua New Guinea contains one of the world's largest deposits of cobalt and chrome outside of the Soviet Union and South Africa. The cost of developing a mine on this property is estimated to be around $150 million.
   a. Describe three major risks in undertaking this project.
   b. How can Nord structure its financing so as to reduce these risks?
   c. How can Nord use financing to add value to this project?

10. United Carbon wants to take advantage of the current low interest rate, 9.5%, that the Japanese investment banks are offering on Eurodollar bonds. United would like to finance its $150 million borrowing needs with them rather than in the United States, where its borrowing rate is 12%. However, the company can borrow only at a 10-year maturity in the Eurodollar market, whereas the money is needed for 20 years. Thus, if United accepts the Japanese offer, in 10 years it will have to roll over its borrowing for another 10 years. Should United Carbon issue the Eurobonds? Assume that all principal payments are made at maturity. Ignore taxes. (*Hint:* What interest rate on a 10-year loan would have to prevail at the end of 10 years in order to make the Japanese deal unattractive? How likely is it that interest rates will reach that level?)

BIBLIOGRAPHY

Adler, Michael. "The Cost of Capital and Valuation of a Two-Country Firm." *Journal of Finance*, March 1974, pp. 119–132.

Cornell, Bradford, and Alan C. Shapiro. "Corporate Stakeholders and Corporate Finance." *Financial Management*, Spring 1987, pp. 5–14.

Goeltz, Richard Karl. "The Corporate Borrower and the International Capital Markets." Manuscript dated March 6, 1984, p. 5.

Hodder, James E., and Lemma W. Senbet. "International Capital Structure Equilibrium." *Journal of Finance*, December 1990, pp. 1495–1516.

Lessard, Donald R., and Alan C. Shapiro. "Guidelines for Global Financing Choices." *Midland Corporate Finance Journal*, Winter 1984, pp. 68–80.

Shapiro, Alan C. "Financial Structure and Cost of Capital in the Multinational Corporation." *Journal of Financial and Quantitative Analysis*, June 1978, pp. 211–226.

Stobaugh, Robert B. "Financing Foreign Subsidiaries of U.S.-Controlled Multinational Enterprises," *Journal of International Business Studies*, Summer 1970, pp. 43–64.

Case V.1   MULTINATIONAL MANUFACTURING, INC.

PART I

Multinational Manufacturing, Inc. (MMI) is a large manufacturing firm engaged in the production and sale of a widely diversified group of products in a number of countries throughout the world. Some product lines enjoy outstanding success in new fields developed on the basis of an active research and development program; other product lines, whose innovative leads have disappeared, face very severe competition.

Each domestic product line and foreign affiliate is a separate profit center. Headquarters influences these centers primarily by evaluating their managers on the basis of certain financial criteria, including return on investment, return on sales, and growth in earnings.

Division and affiliate executives are held responsible for planning and evaluating possible new projects. Each project is expected to yield at least 15%. Projects requiring an investment below $250,000 (about one-third of the projects) are approved at the division or affiliate level without formal review by headquarters management. The present cutoff rate was established three years ago as part of a formal review of capital budgeting procedures. The conclusion at that time was that the company's weighted average cost of capital was 15%, and it should be applied when calculating net present values of proposed projects. In announcing the policy, Mr. Thomas Black, Vice President-Finance, said, "It's about time that we introduced some modern management techniques in allocating our capital resources."

Now Mr. Black is concerned that the policy introduced three years ago is having some unintended consequences. Specifically, top management gets to review only obvious investment candidates. Low-risk, low-return projects and high-risk, high-return projects seem to be systematically screened out along the way. The basis for this screening is not entirely clear, but it appears to be related to the way in which managerial performance is evaluated. Local executives seem to be concerned that low-potential projects will hurt their performance appraisal, while high-potential projects can turn out poorly. The president of one foreign affiliate said privately when asked why he never submitted projects at the extremes of risk and return, "Why should I take any chances? When headquarters says it wants 15%, it means 15% and nothing less. My crystal ball isn't good enough to allow me to accurately estimate sales and costs in this country, especially when I never know what the government is going to do."

QUESTIONS: PART I

1. Should MMI lower the hurdle rate in order to encourage the submission of more proposals, or should it drop the hurdle rate concept completely?

2. Should MMI invest in lower-return projects that are less risky and/or in high-risk projects that appear promising? What is the relevant measure of risk?

3. How should MMI factor in the additional political and economic risks it faces overseas in conducting these project analyses?

4. Why are projects at the extremes of risk and return not reaching top management for review?

5. What actions, if any, should Mr. Black take to correct the situation?

PART II

In line with this current review of capital budgeting procedures, Mr. Black is also reconsidering certain financial policies that he recently recommended to MMI's board of directors. These policies include the maintenance of a debt/total assets ratio of 35% and a dividend payout rate equal to 60% of consolidated earnings. In order to achieve these ratios for the firm overall, each affiliate has been directed to use these ratios as guidelines in planning its own capital structure and payout rate.

This directive has been controversial. The executives of several foreign affiliates have raised questions about the appropriateness of applying these guidelines at the local level. The general managers of some of the largest affiliates have been particularly vocal in their objections, stating that it simply was not possible for overall policies relative to capital structure proportions to be given much consideration in financial planning at the local level. They pointed out that differences in the economic and political environment in which the various affiliates operate are far too great to force them into a financial straitjacket designed by headquarters. In their view, they must be left free to respond to their own unique set of circumstances.

The executives of the Brazilian affiliate, for example, felt that their financing should not follow the same pattern as that of the overall firm because inflationary conditions made local borrowing especially advantageous in Brazil. Executives of other foreign affiliates stressed the need for varying capital structures in order to cope with the exchange risks posed by currency fluctuations. The general manager of the Mexican affiliate, which is owned on a 50–50 basis with local investors, has argued forcefully that, despite effective headquarters control over the policies of this operation, joint ventures such as his cannot and should not be financed in the same manner as firms wholly owned by MMI. In addition, the tax manager of MMI has expressed his concern that implementing a rigid policy of repatriating 60% of each affiliate's earnings in the form of dividends will impose substantial tax costs on MMI. Moreover, Mr. Black recently attended a seminar at which it was pointed out that overseas affiliates can sometimes be financed in such a way that their susceptibility to political and economic risks is diminished.

QUESTIONS: PART II

1. What are the pros and cons of using the following sources of funds to finance the operations of the foreign affiliates: equity funds versus loans from MMI, retained earnings of the affiliates, and outside borrowings? Consider cost, political and economic risks, and tax consequences in your answer.

2. Given these considerations, under what circumstances, if any, should the capital structure of foreign affiliates include more or less debt than the 35% considered desirable for the firm as a whole?

3. How will the resultant capital structures affect the required rates of return on affiliate projects? The actual rates of return?

4. How should MMI's dividend policy be implemented at the affiliate level?

International Banking

Part VI

International Banking

International Banking Trends and Strategies

24

Whether we like it or not, the globalization of financial markets and institutions is a reality.

E. Gerald Corrigan
President, Federal Reserve
Bank of New York

CHAPTER LEARNING OBJECTIVES

- To describe recent trends in international banking activities
- To identify the organizational forms used by banks to expand overseas and the advantages and disadvantages of each form
- To explain why banks have expanded their international operations and loan portfolios in the post–World War II period
- To examine new regulatory initiatives designed to reduce the risks associated with banking

KEY TERMS

Bank for International
  Settlements (BIS)
Basel agreement
correspondent bank
Edge Act and Agreement
  corporations
foreign bank branch
international banking
  facilities (IBFs)
lender of last resort
OPEC
"petrodollar" recycling
regulatory arbitrage
representative office
risk-based capital
  standards

The growth and increasing integration of the world economy since the end of World War II has been paralleled by expansion of global banking activities. Banks followed their customers overseas and lent to governments presiding over promising national economies. One indication of the worldwide scope of banking today is suggested by the fact that international bank loans extended by commercial banks located in major financial centers around the world have increased year after year over the past decade, reaching a total of $4.8 trillion outstanding by September 1987. Underneath the facade of unbroken growth, however, lie many divergent trends that have been profoundly influencing the direction of international banking activities over the past dozen years.

This chapter provides an overview of international banking. It focuses on recent trends in the expansion of international banking activities and the organizational forms and strategies associated with overseas bank expansion.

24.1 RECENT PATTERNS OF INTERNATIONAL BANKING ACTIVITIES

International banking has grown notably in both complexity and risk over the past two decades. Until recently, international banking was confined largely to providing foreign exchange and to financing specific export and import transactions through letters of credit and acceptances. This limitation is no longer the case.

International banking has grown steadily throughout the post–World War II period. Expansion of international trade in the 1950s and the effective emergence of the MNC in the 1960s sharply increased the demand for international financial services. Banks located in the traditional financial centers responded by extending loans and developing new, highly innovative financial techniques (such as the Eurocurrency markets) that laid the foundation for totally new approaches to the provision of international banking services. For many of these banks, their initial ventures overseas were defensive in nature, designed to retain the domestic business of customers who invested abroad by expanding and improving the scope of their activities abroad. In the words of an economist at Deutsche Bank, "In a global market, if you can't serve your multinational customers in all the major cities of the world, they won't need you even in their home country."[1] But it was the onset of the "energy crisis" that launched international banks into a period of phenomenal growth.

The Era of Growth

International banks grew rapidly during the 1970s by recycling petrodollars.

The energy crisis, brought about by the quadrupling of oil prices in late 1973, created a great need for global financial intermediation—for recycling *OPEC's* (Organization of Petroleum Exporting Countries) surplus revenues back to deficit-plagued oil-importing countries. Without such *"petrodollar" recycling*, the balance-of-payments deficits of the oil-importing countries would not have been financed, threatening dire consequences for the entire world economy. The alternative would have entailed massive economic dislocation to speedily adapt to the changing relative price of oil.

International banks were able to recycle funds from oil-exporting to oil-importing nations because (1) they had broad experience in international lending, backed by capable staffs and worldwide facilities; and (2) they were the recipients of large shares of OPEC's surplus revenues in the form of deposits placed with them by OPEC's central bankers. These deposits rose from $16 billion in 1973 to $117 billion in 1979.

Flush with OPEC money, the banks embarked upon a rapid lending expansion, often with the active encouragement of their governments. The net claims outstanding of banks in the reporting area of the *Bank for International Settlements* (BIS)—which acts as the central bank for the industrial countries' central banks—

---

[1]Quoted in *Fortune*, February 26, 1990, p. 95.

increased from $155 billion at year-end 1973 to $665 billion at year-end 1979—a more than fourfold increase in loans to final borrowers in just six years.

Of this amount, $157 billion (24%) were loans to less-developed countries (LDCs) and $60 billion (9%) were loans to Communist countries. Thus, about one-third of these loans, aggregating $217 billion, were to nations that turned out to be very risky credits.

Banks located in major financial centers throughout the world participated in this expansion of international lending. The largest share of the total was booked by banks located in major European centers, particularly in London, where foreign branches of major banks throughout the world (including U.S. banks) were operating.

Most of the loans being extended were denominated in U.S. dollars. The BIS data show over 82% of the total bank loans outstanding at the end of 1979 were loans denominated in dollars. DM-denominated loans represented the second largest category, at 12%.

Loans to the less-developed countries were the fastest growing category of international bank loans during the 1970s. A combination of sharply increased oil import bills and a recession in the industrial countries that cut into the LDCs' export earnings—compounded by unrealistic exchange rate policies (see the discussion in Chapter 20)—sharply raised these countries' aggregate balance-of-payments deficits from an annual average of about $7 billion in the 1970–1973 period to $21 billion in 1974 and $31 billion in 1975. The banks, replete with funds and faced with declining domestic loan demand, were willing and able to provide financing in the forms of direct government loans and development financing.

> Loans to LDCs were the fastest growing category of international bank loans during the 1970s.

The International Banking Crisis of 1982

Bank lending to LDCs continued to grow rapidly during the early 1980s. In the summer of 1982, however, the international financial markets were shaken when a number of developing countries found themselves unable to meet payments to major banks around the world on debt amounting to several hundred billion dollars. With the onset of the debt crisis, lending to LDCs quickly dried up.

Confronted with interruptions in inflows of funds due to repayment problems on their past loans, with the drying up of new sources, and with the growing uncertainties as to the capacity of their borrowers to service their debt, the international banks pulled back sharply on their lending to LDCs. This pattern is evident in the data presented in Exhibits 24.1 and 24.2. New loans to the LDCs dropped from about $40 billion in 1981 to $20 billion in 1982 and to $12 billion in 1983. The pullback was actually much sharper than the figures indicate. A great majority of the new loans represented "involuntary" lending—loans made by banks to facilitate both rescheduling of past loans and payment of interest by their creditors. Banks actually reduced their Latin loans starting in 1985.

The Climate During the 1980s

By late 1983, the intensity of the international debt crisis began to ease as the world's economic activities picked up—boosting the LDCs' export earnings—and

Exhibit 24.1 Total International Bank Lending, 1973–1983

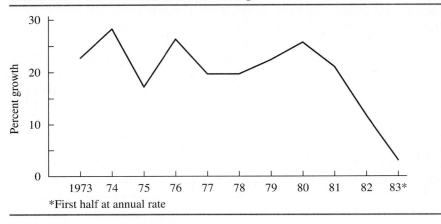

*First half at annual rate

SOURCE: *International Letter*, Federal Reserve Bank of Chicago, December 16, 1983, p. 1.

International lending activity slowed down during the 1980s.

as the orderly rescheduling of many overdue international loans was completed. However, although lending by international banks has picked up, it continues to be depressed compared to the high-growth period of the late 1970s. The major reason for the slowdown in international lending activity through the 1980s has been the inability of the LDC debtor nations to achieve sustained economic growth. Moreover, even those LDCs that are experiencing strong economic growth again—particularly the nations of Latin America that privatized and reformed their economies—are looking more for equity capital than new bank lending.

International Bank Regulation

As the world's financial markets globalize, bank regulators are increasingly concerned about establishing a well-defined official framework that sets ground rules for safe operation of all banks. The fear is that bank failures in one nation could spill across borders and affect the world banking system. Up to now, however, the standards applied by the various national authorities have differed considerably, artificially creating competitive advantages—and competitive disadvantages—between international banks. One concern is that banks will taken advantage of the different degrees of regulatory scrutiny by engaging in *regulatory arbitrage*—transferring activities across borders to those nations that impose the laxest standards. Two additional and related issues that arise in regulating internationally active banks are determining who is responsible for (1) guaranteeing the safety of these banks—that is, who is the *lender of last resort* if they get in trouble—and (2) who is responsible for monitoring these banks: Is the responsible party regulators in their home market or regulators in the foreign markets that they operate in? The danger is that without an overarching supervisory structure some banks could fall between the cracks of the regulatory system.

Exhibit 24.2 International Loans Extended by Banks in the Major Industrial Countries

NOTE: Loans are new lending minus repayment of loans to residents of countries other than in the major industrial countries and offshore banking centers. Areas below the line indicate net repayment.

- ▨ Other developed countries
- ▥ Eastern Europe
- ■ Non-OPEC developing countries
- ☐ OPEC

SOURCE: *International Letter,* Federal Reserve Bank of Chicago, December 16, 1983, p. 2.

To some extent, this is the problem that arose in the case of the Bank of Credit and Commerce International (BCCI), a fraud-ridden Pakistani bank, also known as the Bank of Crooks and Criminals International, that operated on a global scale. A small group within BCCI stole billions of dollars from the institution, laundered drug money, faked loans, and hid losses under the noses of regulators for years. To some extent, each of the different national regulators thought that someone else was supervising BCCI.

Some banks, such as BCCI, have taken advantage of regulatory arbitrage.

However, the problems of BCCI are just the tip of the iceberg. The major national banking systems in the 1980s experienced a decade of hasty deregulation, globalization, and innovation, which ended with a long list of sins, scandals, and financial excesses. Bankers around the world bet the bank on ever-increasing asset values—real estate, oil, stocks—but instead they have been hit with asset deflation—a decline in the value of the assets that secure their loans or constitute bank capital. In response to possibilities like BCCI, as well as reckless lending practices of banks worldwide, bank supervisors are now trying to work together more systematically to reduce the risks to the international banking system. One outcome is new *risk-based capital standards.*

International Risk-Based Capital Standards. One of the most important factors currently affecting international bank expansion is the new capital requirements

The BIS has set risk-based capital standards for the world's banks.

set down by the Basel Committee under the auspices of the Bank for International Settlements in Basel, Switzerland, and which took effect in 1993. In late 1987, the Basel Committee developed a risk-based framework for measuring the adequacy of *bank capital*—the equity capital and other reserves available to protect depositors against credit losses. Its objective was to strengthen the international banking system and to reduce competitive inequalities arising from differences in capital requirements across nations. In part, the Basel Committee's requirements were aimed at Japanese banks, since their reserves were so much smaller than those required by most Western central banks. Under the *Basel agreement*, by the end of 1992 banks had to achieve a minimum 8% risk-based ratio of capital to assets.

There was disagreement in Basel on how to define bank capital, with a political compromise eventually producing a two-tier system. Core or Tier 1 capital consists of shareholders' funds and retained earnings. Supplemental or Tier 2 capital consists of internationally accepted noncommon equity items—such as hidden reserves, preferred shares, and subordinated debt—to add to core capital. However, Tier 2 capital can make up only 50% of a bank's capital. Thus, core capital must amount to at least 4% of risk-weighted assets.

To meet the capital standards, banks are focusing more on profits and less on growth. This is especially true for Japanese banks.

Japanese International Bank Expansion

Japanese banks have aggressively expanded overseas.

Perhaps the most significant phenomenon in recent years has been the aggressive international expansion of Japanese banks. Since the mid-1980s, Japanese banks—flush with the proceeds of Japan's trading surpluses—set out to gain market share worldwide through low-cost loans.[2] With more cash than caution, Japanese banks tripled their overseas loan portfolio by 1990, accounting for 38% of international banking assets and over 12% of total lending in the United States.

However, financial adversity at home is now changing the way Japanese banks do business abroad. No longer can they push for market share at the expense of profits. Instead, Japanese banks are making fewer overseas loans, and on those fewer loans they are demanding higher returns. In part, this change is a response to financial market deregulation in Japan, which combined with the recent jump in Japanese interest rates, raised the cost of funds to the banks. The new focus on profit is also affected by the Basel capital requirements.

Like all banks, Japanese banks are trying to meet the new Basel standards. But the Tokyo stock market's collapse during 1990 has made that harder in two ways. For Japanese banks, Tier 2 capital consisted mainly of 45% of the unrealized gains on their huge equity stakes in other companies. The sharp drop in Japanese equity values means that the value of these "hidden reserves" has plunged.

The stock market fall also hurt the ability of Japanese banks to issue equity-linked securities. These issues have been crucial sources of capital, providing

---

[2]One indication of the Japanese drive for market share is reflected in the fact that overseas assets account for nearly half of the major bank's total assets, but the margins on these assets are less than one-tenth of those achieved in Japan.

Japanese banks with ¥6 trillion ($40 billion) of fresh money between 1987 and 1989.

Moreover, the sharp rise in Japanese interest rates inflicted huge losses on the banks' bond portfolios and lowered their capital ratios still further. By the end of 1990, all the large Japanese banks had slipped below the 8% capital adequacy ratio that they were to meet by 1993. To meet this standard, banks must either reduce lending growth, which reduces the amount of equity capital they must hold, or boost profits, which adds to equity. The plunge in Japanese real estate prices put further pressure on Japanese banks to shrink their lending, given their enormous real estate exposure. According to some estimates, Japanese banks in 1992 had over $500 billion in problem loans to contend with.

Not all of these problem loans are in Japan. Between 1986 and 1990, Japanese banks boosted their share of property lending in California from 10% to 20%, lending when property values were at their peak. Prices have since then fallen sharply. Their problems are most evident in downtown Los Angeles, where virtually every new office project in the late 1980s was financed by the Japanese. With a vacancy rate in 1993 exceeding 22% in prime buildings, Japanese banks are stuck with billions in nonperforming loans on L.A. real estate alone.

Japanese banks have suffered huge losses on their foreign loans and are now pulling back.

In response to these pressures, Japanese banks are pulling back from "commodity" lending, the business of lending large volumes of money at low margins that fueled their expansion during the 1980s. In so doing, Japanese banks are no longer as dominant a force in international finance. For example, the number of Japanese banks leading syndicated loans in the low-margin Eurocurrency market dropped to just four out of the top 20 in the first six months of 1990. In 1989, they led seven of the top 20 syndicates. After accounting for a peak of 39.4% of all cross-border bank transactions by March 1989, Japanese banks' market share shrank in 1990 for the first time since 1984 to 36%. That compares with 12% for U.S. banks and 9.6% for German banks. The days of lending money at cheap rates just to grab market share are gone for Japanese banks.

24.2 ORGANIZATIONAL FORMS AND STRATEGIES IN BANK EXPANSION OVERSEAS

Decisions by banks as to how to approach foreign markets are influenced by a number of variables, such as overall financial resources, level of experience with the markets, knowledge of the markets, volume of international business, and the strategic plans of the bank—as well as the banking structure of the foreign countries in which business is done. Possible entry strategies include branching, local bank acquisitions, and representative offices. However, until the volume of business in another country is substantial, most banks will choose to rely on correspondent banking relationships to handle their needs in that country. U.S. banks also make use of domestic organizational forms for carrying on international banking activities, including Edge Act and Agreement corporations and international banking facilities. Each of these forms and strategies is described in more detail in this section.

Banks have several possible foreign market entry strategies.

Correspondent Banking

A *correspondent bank* is a bank located elsewhere that provides a service for another bank. U.S. banks without branches abroad have relied on their foreign correspondents to help finance their multinational corporate clients' local foreign subsidiaries that need local currency funding. Foreign correspondents can also provide other services, such as foreign exchange conversions and letters of credit.

Advantages. The major advantage of taking the correspondent route is that the cost of market entry is minimal and can be adjusted to the scale of service required in a given locale; no investment in staff or facilities is required. Yet the bank can still enjoy the benefits derived from having multiple sources of business given and received, as well as referrals of local banking opportunities. Moreover, correspondents' local knowledge and contacts may be extensive and highly useful in rendering services to the bank's clients doing business in that country.

Disadvantages. One problem with relying on correspondent banks to provide all necessary services is that correspondents may assign low priority to the needs of the U.S. bank's customers. In addition, due to legal restrictions on traditional banking policies, certain types of credits may be difficult to arrange. Correspondents may also be reluctant to provide credits on a more regular and extensive basis.

Representative Offices

Correspondent banking and representative offices provide low-cost entry to foreign markets.

Representative offices are small offices opened up to provide advisory services to banks and customers and to expedite the services of correspondent banks. They also serve as foreign loan production offices able to negotiate various business transactions. Representative offices are not authorized to obtain and transfer deposits and do not provide on-site operating services. The assets and liabilities attributable to a representative office are booked elsewhere in the parent bank's system.

Such offices are regarded as excellent sources of economic and political intelligence on the host country and the local market. They also provide financial contacts with local institutions, commercial contacts for the bank's domestic customers, and assistance to customers in obtaining government approvals or understanding government regulations. Representative offices are especially appropriate when the expected business volume in a market is too small to justify the investment required to establish a branch, or local opportunities are uncertain, and the bank wants to learn more about the market at minimal cost before deciding whether further expansion is warranted.

Advantages. As with exporting, representative offices provide a low-cost means of scouting out the local market. They can deliver certain services more efficiently than can a branch, especially if the required volume is small. They can help the bank attract additional business or prevent the loss of current business.

Disadvantages. Taking the analogy to exporting further, the benefits may at times be outweighed by the inability to effect more substantial market penetration. And despite the fact that they are not capital intensive when compared with branches or local acquisitions, representative offices can be expensive nonetheless. Moreover, it is more difficult to attract qualified personnel to work in a representative office overseas than in a foreign branch.

Foreign Branches

The principal service offered by *foreign bank branches,* as with commercial banking anywhere, is the extension of credit, primarily in the form of lending money. The major portion of the lending done by branches in important international money centers such as London and Singapore involves cross-border loans, primarily because these locations are the major trading and booking centers for the Eurocurrency and Asiacurrency markets. These branches also serve as deposit-taking institutions.

Despite government regulations that have held down bank branching in foreign markets, the phenomenal growth of international banking over the past 25 years has been paralleled by an explosive expansion in overseas branching. Prior to 1960, only seven U.S. banks maintained a total of 132 branches abroad. By the end of 1979, those numbers had grown to 130 banks with just under 800 foreign branches. Major banks from Canada, Japan, and the Western European countries have also jumped on the branching bandwagon.

There are several reasons for this massive proliferation of overseas branching. First, there is the "follow the customer" rationale. Unless domestic customers that expand abroad are serviced overseas, the bank is likely to lose its clients' domestic, as well as foreign, business. Yet, it turns out that only a minor share of foreign branch business is with head-office customers. Increasingly, the business of overseas branches is with purely local, indigenous enterprises.

Foreign branches are much more expensive but provide greater access to local markets.

This trend relates to the second reason for having foreign branches: the direct contribution to bank earnings that the branches provide, quite aside from any indirect contribution associated with protecting the domestic customer base. Specifically, business with local companies has turned out to be profitable on a stand-alone basis. Moreover, foreign earnings help to diversify the bank's earnings base, thereby moderating swings in domestic earnings.

The third reason for establishing foreign branches is the access these branches provide to overseas money markets. Large international banks have a need for branches located in international money markets abroad, such as London and Singapore, to fund their international assets. At the same time, these international money markets often offer opportunities to invest funds at more attractive rates than can be done in a bank's own domestic money markets.

Advantages. In addition to the above-mentioned advantages, a bank can exert maximum control over its foreign operations through a branch. For one thing, operating and credit policies can be closely integrated. More importantly, a foreign branch network allows the parent to offer its customers—both domestic and foreign—direct and integrated service, such as the rapid collection and transfer of funds internationally in a number of countries on a consistent policy basis. Thus, Citibank may require a branch in France as much to accommodate Siemens and

Sony as Coca-Cola. Foreign branches also allow a bank to better manage its customer relationships, providing services to a customer based on the value of its worldwide relationship rather than its relationship in a specific country.

Disadvantages. The cost of establishing a branch can be quite high, running to several hundred thousand dollars annually for a typical European branch, plus the fixed cost of remodeling the new facilities. An indirect cost is the possibility of alienating correspondent banks when a new branch is opened. Developing and training management to staff these branches is also difficult and expensive. On the plus side, having foreign branches offers the chance for junior officers to gain valuable overseas experience, as well as making it easier to attract good personnel eager for that type of experience.

Acquisitions

The alternative to expanding by opening new branches is to grow through acquisitions. This approach is followed by most foreign banks trying to penetrate the U.S. market.

Acquiring a local bank provides immediate access to the local market, but most acquirers tend to overpay.

Advantages. Acquiring a local bank has two main advantages. First, buying an existing retail bank will afford immediate access to the local deposit market, eliminating the problem of funding local loans. Second, the existing management will have an established network of local contacts and clients that would be difficult (if not impossible) to duplicate.

Disadvantages. Despite these advantages, the history of bank acquisitions abroad is littered with examples of ill-fated investments—particularly in the United States. The acquisition by Britain's Midland Bank of a 57% interest in Crocker National, a California bank, must rank as one of the most expensive entrance tickets to a market; Midland's stake, which cost it $820 million in 1981, was worth about $300 million in early 1985. At that time, Midland agreed to buy the remaining 43% of Crocker for about $250 million. In the interim, however, Crocker's continued troubles (it lost $325 million in 1984 alone) forced Midland to invest an additional $250 million in Crocker at the end of 1983 and to lend it $125 million more. In 1986, Midland sold Crocker to Wells Fargo. The other big British banks (National Westminster, Lloyds, and Barclays) have also had their share of troubles in the United States.

These troubles are not confined to British banks entering the U.S. market. In August 1983, Bank of America paid $147 million for Banco Internacional in Argentina—just before the Argentine peso dropped through the floor and the country's seemingly intractable debt problems blew up. France's Credit Lyonnais has been obliged to pump large amounts of fresh capital into its Dutch subsidiary. Sweden's Skandinaviska Enskilda Banken's 24% stake in Banque Scandinaive of Switzerland was followed by two years of large losses.

The basic problem with these troubled investments seems to be that the acquiring banks spent too much energy on making the deal, often to the exclusion of developing future strategy. The usual rationale for the acquisition—

synergy—is overworked. In the case of its acquisition of Crocker, for example, Midland brought little more to the deal than new money. The absence of any other contribution by the acquirer is usually a warning sign, for if the business being acquired is healthy apart from needing more capital, why is it choosing to sacrifice its independence rather than to go to the capital markets for additional funds?

The message seems to be that banking acquisitions are expensive, highly risky, and difficult to make work effectively, especially if all the acquirer brings to the deal is money. Unfortunately, most acquirers don't bring more than money to the deal. Not surprisingly, acquirers typically lose in such deals.

Edge Act and Agreement Corporations

Edge Act and Agreement corporations are subsidiaries of U.S. banks that are permitted to carry on international banking and investment activities. The practical effect of the various restrictions they operate under is to limit Edge Act institutions to handling foreign customers and to handling the international business of domestic customers. The list of permissible international activities for an Edge Act corporation includes deposit taking from outside the United States, lending money to international businesses, and making equity investments in foreign corporations, a power denied to its U.S. parent. An Agreement corporation is functionally similar to an Edge Act corporation. Usually it is a state-chartered corporation that enters into an agreement with the Federal Reserve to limit its activities to those of an Edge Act corporation.

> Edge Act and Agreement Corporations are U.S. bank subsidiaries that can carry on international banking and investment activities.

Edge Act corporations are physically located in the United States, usually in a state other than where the head office is located to get around the prohibition on interstate branch banking. For example, a California bank can set up an Edge Act subsidiary in New York City to compete with New York banks for corporate business related to international activities—foreign exchange trading, export and import financing, accepting deposits associated with such operations, international fund remittances, and buying and selling domestic securities for foreign customers or foreign securities for domestic customers. Since June 1979, when the Federal Reserve permitted interstate branching by Edge Act corporations, these corporations have rivaled loan production offices in giving money-center banks and major regional banks on-site access to otherwise restricted markets.

A growing share of Edge Act business involves maintaining individual accounts for U.S. citizens living abroad and foreign citizens wanting their deposits in New York, Miami, Los Angeles, or some other U.S. city. Although they don't openly acknowledge the fact, an important source of relatively low cost deposits for Edge Act corporations is in the form of "flight capital" from wealthy Central and South American depositors concerned with the lack of political stability in their own countries.

International Banking Facilities

As we saw in Chapter 21, because of the unfavorable regulatory and tax environment in the United States, many domestic banks conduct their international operations through offshore branches. Frequently, these offices are simply "shell" operations used solely for booking purposes. By using foreign offices, banks are able to avoid state and local taxes on their foreign business profits, as well as costly reserve requirements and interest rate ceilings that would apply if the deposits were placed in the United States.

International banking facilities can conduct international banking activities exempt from U.S. regulation.

As a result of these advantages, London became the center of international banking activities. In addition, the number of branches in such places as the Cayman Islands and the Bahamas has grown significantly. Late in 1981, in an attempt to attract Eurodollar business back to the United States from these offshore locations, the Federal Reserve authorized U.S. financial institutions, including U.S. branches and agencies of foreign banks, to establish *international banking facilities* (IBFs). IBFs are permitted to conduct international banking business (such as receiving foreign deposits and making foreign loans) largely exempt from domestic regulatory constraints.

IBFs are merely bookkeeping entities that represent a separate set of asset and liability accounts of their establishing offices. The only requirement to establish an IBF is that the establishing institution must give the Federal Reserve two weeks' notice. The major activities of an IBF are deposit taking and lending to statutorily defined foreign persons, subject to certain restrictions. The major restrictions are (1) engaging only in foreign deposit taking and lending, (2) a minimum transaction size of $100,000, and (3) prohibition from issuing negotiable instruments, such as certificates of deposit (CDs).

Despite these restrictions, IBFs are popular because they are accorded most of the advantages of offshore banking without the need to be physically offshore. Most important is waiver of the regulation requiring that banks keep a percentage of their deposits in noninterest-earning accounts at the Federal Reserve. In addition, deposits in IBFs are not subject to interest rate ceilings or deposit insurance assessment.

IBFs are located mainly in the major financial centers; almost half of the nearly 500 IBFs are in New York, with the remainder being primarily in California, Florida, and Illinois. Although the geographical distribution of IBFs largely reflects the preexisting distribution of international banking business, differences in tax treatment has had some effect on the location decision. Florida, for example, exempts IBFs from state taxes and also ranks first in the number of Edge Act IBFs and second (next to New York) in the number of IBFs set up by U.S.-chartered banks.

IBFs appear to have a very high proportion of both assets and liabilities due to other banking institutions. This interbank activity reinforces the belief that IBFs are now an integral part of the Eurodollar market. As we saw in Chapter 22, a high proportion of interbank business is one of the characteristics of the Eurocurrency markets since there may be several interbank transactions between ultimate borrowers and ultimate lenders. Thus far, IBFs seem to have had the intended effect of shifting international banking business from offshore locations back to the United States; they have not expanded the total volume of international banking business.

Foreign Banks in the United States

Foreign bank activity in the United States has grown dramatically in recent years. This expansion reflects several key factors, including (1) the rapid growth of U.S. international trade, (2) the size and importance of U.S. financial markets, (3) the growth of foreign direct investment in the United States, and (4) the role of the U.S. dollar as an international medium of exchange.

Foreign banks operating in the U.S. market typically concentrate their activities heavily on the wholesale market; they are generally not major factors in retail banking markets. In addition, most of the foreign banks that have a sizable presence in the United States are affiliated with well-known major banks abroad (for example, Barclays, Mitsubishi Bank, Swiss Bank Corporation, and Bank of Montreal).

As of year-end 1990, there were more than 250 foreign banks that had some kind of presence in the United States. In the aggregate, the assets of such foreign banks equaled an estimated $868 billion at year-end 1990 and constituted nearly 22% of total U.S. banking assets (see Exhibit 24.3). Foreign banks also account for more than 21% of all commercial and industrial loans outstanding to U.S. companies. Most of the foreign-bank expansion in the United States has been by Japanese banks (as Exhibit 24.3 shows, other foreign banks actually lost U.S. market share), which now account for almost half of the total assets and commercial loans outstanding at foreign banks in the United States. Japanese-owned banks now control about 25% of the banking market in California, largely owing to pricing so razor-thin that American banks have formally ceded certain types of lending. In certain markets, such as standby letters of credit associated with municipal bond offerings, Japanese banks now account for up to 70% of the total U.S. market.

Foreign banks have greatly expanded their U.S. activities in recent years.

Exhibit 24.3 Foreign-Owned Bank Market Share in the United States

SOURCE: Gary C. Zimmerman, "Slower Growth for Foreign Banks?" *FRBSF Weekly Letter,* Federal Reserve Bank of San Francisco, January 25, 1991, p. 1.

All this is changing, however, as the push for growth over profits appears to be at an end. More stringent international capital standards and risk-based capital requirements are constraining the growth prospects of foreign and domestic banks alike. These tightened standards, added to the reduction in the value of Japanese banks' "hidden reserves," mean that Japanese banks no longer make cheap loans to corporate borrowers to build market share. And they no longer seek to issue every letter of credit written in America. These developments signal slower growth ahead for foreign banks in the United States.

Implications of Europe 1992 for Banks

With the completion of a single European market by the end of 1992, banks can now branch throughout the European Community while providing a greater range of financial services.[3] The single license should enable all banks in Europe to realize a number of cost benefits, primarily by being able to operate throughout the EC using common distribution networks, managers, and support systems. A single banking license should also lower bank costs in Europe by eliminating overlapping or conflicting standards and regulatory procedures.

> With the completion of Europe 1992, banks can now branch throughout the European Community.

Despite the potential cost advantages of establishing an EC-wide bank network, however, the empirical evidence suggests that the scope for economies of scale in banking is rather limited. Indeed, the correlation between size and profitability for the largest EC banks is either negative or minimal. Economies of scale in banking appear limited to instances where the bank's strategy involves common customers, information systems, skills, or processing facilities. One such business is credit cards, which benefits from economies of scale in issuance, centralized data processing, and design standardization.

Absent these commonalities, it appears unlikely that cross-border mergers between large institutions will create value: The cost of merging operations will probably exceed any economies of scale or scope they might achieve. Moreover, the ever-present danger is that as entry barriers start falling, new entrants might overpay in trying to get established and gain market share. Value-creating mergers are most likely to be between relatively small local banks in countries characterized by relatively low concentration ratios.

Banks seeking to benefit from Europe 1992 should focus on pursuing businesses in which they have a sustainable competitive advantage rather than competing directly against dominant local banks that have strongly entrenched positions in delivering basic banking services.

ILLUSTRATION: Citicorp's Strategy for Europe 1992

Citicorp's EC strategy has been to utilize a cadre of experienced professionals, with expertise in a number of product categories and management techniques, to develop and deliver products in multiple markets. Although each market pre-

---

[3]This section is based on Alan C. Shapiro, "Economic Import of Europe 1992," *Journal of Applied Corporate Finance*, Winter 1991, pp. 25–36.

sents a unique set of challenges, Citicorp employees have already experienced most, if not all, of these situations elsewhere in the world and, thus, have ideas and procedures for dealing with them. Citicorp's large EC credit-card operation, for example, relies heavily on its extensive U.S. experience. It has also employed its experience in circumventing U.S. restrictions on interstate banking to build a 700-branch network throughout Europe.

24.3 VALUE CREATION IN INTERNATIONAL BANKING

This section examines some of the strategies that international banks can use to create value in their marketplace. It also examines the likely shape of future international banking competition.

Capital Adequacy

Banks with a large capital base can gain competitive advantage in underwriting securities and reducing the cost of funding loans. They can also develop more profitable business relations since companies today are paying added attention to the financial strength of the banks they deal with. Given the protracted investment of time and money in building a relationship with a bank, many chief financial officers will only deal with well-capitalized banks, whom they naturally regard as being more reliable financial partners. Such banks can also serve as a credible counterparty where customers assume bank counterparty risk, including L/Cs, swaps, and forwards.

> Well-capitalized banks have an easier time developing customer relationships.

Human Resources and the Banking Organization

International banking is a fiercely competitive business. A corollary is that it contains no obvious, unexploited profitable niches. Any new insight in developing competitive advantage, such as a novel product or service, is quickly imitated and the extra profits competed away. The real source of competitive advantage is having the organization that can exploit information to learn and to innovate more quickly than competitors. Unfortunately, the advice to be continually innovative and creative is easier said than done.

For a bank to be a successful innovator, its front line people must have—in addition to the necessary information and skills—the authority, accountability, and motivation to use their minds to exploit that information. That means that career systems—promotions, reward, and development—have to be geared to creating and sustaining a learning environment. In the competitive world of international banking, the returns will come not by lending money but by selling companies on the belief that the bank knows how to solve their corporate finance problems and can do so quickly. That is, CFOs expect their bankers to do more than evaluate loan requests. They expect bankers to create tailor-made solutions to corporate financial problems. The demand by large companies for their banks to serve as consultants and problem solvers offers banks the opportunity to perform higher margin, fee-generating services. A bank will succeed in this world

> Successful international banks are innovative organizations.

only if the people meeting the customers can identify their problems and willingly share that information with others who can develop profitable solutions to those problems.

Bank officers require a lot of training in order to offer such high quality service. This training must emphasize recognizing market opportunities, understanding the corporate environment, and clearly communicating to customers the often complex options available to solve problems.

This view of value creation in international banking suggests that bank strategies should not rely on hardware or expensive acquisitions. Rather, banks should invest in preparing and enabling people to recognize and respond to customer problems. This process is ongoing because today's creative solution to a problem—such as currency swaps—is tomorrow's commodity product. Banks must also invest in the information technology necessary to identify customer problems and create new services and products to solve them.

Information Systems

International banks must make major investments in information technology.

Perhaps the most pervasive challenge facing the banker in the international market is the requirement for investment in technology. The value of good information is as important today as it was in Baron Rothschild's day when he used carrier pigeons to bring him the news that Wellington had triumphed at Waterloo. Rothschild made his fortune on state-of-the-art communications. Today, bankers rely on computers and telecommunications, not carrier pigeons, but the quest is much the same—seeking tools to carry out banking faster and better than the competition.

Thus, merely to compete in complex global markets requires substantial investment in information systems. A bank can gain by being a purveyor of information transfer systems, either because it has better information to influence business decisions or because it is able to sell information to others. However, the scale of investment in technology to fully exploit the benefits of information acquisition and transfer is bound to be so great that only those banks with a firm commitment to the concept of providing a global service are likely to undertake it.

Transaction Processing Services

Companies that are globalizing their operations are demanding seamless service around the world, including a transfer agent who can pull together all transactions on a global, integrated basis. Thus, transaction processing services, such as funds movement, foreign exchange, international cash management, lockboxes, disbursements, and global custody can be very profitable bank services. However, banks must invest huge amounts of money in a state-of-the-art information system to be a credible player in these businesses. Given the significant economies of scale, market share is critical.

Instead of trying to provide global cash management services, a bank could focus on particular niches. An example would be PC-based treasury workstations that integrated foreign exchange, funds movements, and cash management, instead of mainframe-based bank systems with dumb terminals. Banks are starting to sell the same cross-border payments services to smaller companies that larger companies are now using. With an increasing number of smaller companies doing international business, this is a growing market.

Global Competition in International Banking

The 1990s promises to be an era of intensified global competition in international banking. Already, big banks are battling each other on many fronts: lending, underwriting, leasing, financial advice and risk-management services, currency and securities trading, insurance, money management, and consumer banking. Some experts predict that of some 40 to 50 banks now aspiring to be global banking powerhouses, only six to 10 will actually make the grade by the end of the 1990s. Survival will demand an ability to serve the financing and risk-management needs of corporations, big and small, anywhere in the world. They must also be able to intermediate a large share of the growing cross-border flow of capital and be flexible enough to shift resources quickly to fast-growing areas and high-return businesses. At the same time, they must cope with deregulation and the industry's over capacity—too many banks chasing too few customers.

The major competitors include European, Japanese, and American banks. Each has important competitive strengths and weaknesses.

European, Japanese, and U.S. banks all have important strengths and weaknesses.

European Banks. Some of the strongest contenders for global dominance are European banks. Their strengths include solid capital bases, strong balance sheets, and dominant shares of home markets expected to grow quickly with the advent of Europe 1992. But they have little experience with head-to-head competition. Moreover, European banking's profit sanctuaries—local markets protected from price-cutting competition by collusive arrangements—will be invaded in the post-1992 world. The resulting shakeout could leave the strongest European banks—Germany's Deutsche Bank, Union Bank of Switzerland, Credit Suisse, Swiss Bank Corporation, and England's Barclays—stronger than ever. Domestic market dominance will enable them to subsidize forays abroad, but as we saw earlier they will be able to capitalize on their financial strength only if they can bring more to the table than money. So far they have not demonstrated transferable skills that will confer on them a competitive advantage abroad.

Japanese Banks. The giant Japanese banks, historically backed by a strong economy, diligent savers, and powerful corporate customers, are rich in assets. But they are poor in capital and innovativeness and are learning that size does not necessarily translate into competitive advantage. Now, as noted earlier, Japanese banks are under unprecedented financial stress as financial deregulation narrows their spreads between borrowing and lending money and huge losses on real estate and other loans deplete their capital. Even the main bank relationship that has historically locked customers to their primary bank is threatened under the strain of capital shortages and competition.

U.S. Banks. Most large American banks are plagued with weak capital bases and the threat of huge write-downs on their loans to LDCs, real estate developers, and leveraged buyouts. But after two decades of competing domestically and internationally against each other, as well as against insurers, investment banks, and money managers, U.S. banks have developed superior creative skills. By investing heavily in computers, information systems, and personnel training, banks such as Citicorp, Bankers Trust, and J.P. Morgan have effectively managed to institutionalize the process of innovation. Their innovativeness and advanced technology give them the edge in currency and securities trading and in designing and distributing myriad new products—capabilities widely expected to enable them to seize profitable opportunities in the deregulating European and Japanese markets.

24.4 SUMMARY AND CONCLUSIONS

This chapter has examined the various means and reasons whereby banks have expanded their international operations and loan portfolios in the post–World War II period. Banks have several options in their overseas expansion, including foreign branches, correspondent banking, representative offices, acquisitions of local banks, Edge Act and Agreement corporations, and international banking facilities. We have explored the advantages and disadvantages of each of these vehicles for international expansion. In general, those banks that only brought money to the international marketplace have not earned sufficient profits to justify their presence there.

The pattern of bank lending overseas has been one of rapid expansion, beginning in the early 1960s and sharply accelerating after the first OPEC oil price shock in late 1973. This expansion has been followed by a sharp contraction in international bank lending on the heels of the great debt crisis of 1982. More recently, Japanese banks greatly expanded their overseas loan portfolios but are now in the process of retrenching. One reason for this pull-back is the new international agreement setting minimum risk-based capital standards for banks that became effective in 1993. Marginal banks will find international lending to be uneconomical under these standards.

QUESTIONS

1. What are the relative advantages and disadvantages of expanding overseas via
   a. Foreign branches?
   b. Representative offices?
   c. Acquisitions?
   d. Correspondent banking?

2. What impact will the new capital requirements have on international bank expansion? on the Eurocurrency market?

3. Japanese banks' share of total bank assets in Los Angeles jumped from 11% to 24% between 1983 and 1988.
   a. What factors might account for the large increase in Japanese bank activity in Southern California?

b. How will the new capital requirements likely affect Japanese bank expansion in the United States?

4. According to John Reed, Citicorp's chairman, money is "information on the move." Explain what Mr. Reed might mean by this statement.

5. Why have international bank mergers generally been failures?

6. Assess the competitive strengths and weaknesses of European, U.S., and Japanese banks. How is financial deregulation in Japan and Europe likely to affect the competitive balance in international banking?

BIBLIOGRAPHY

Baughn, William H., and Donald R. Mandich, eds. *The International Banking Handbook.* Homewood, Ill.: Dow Jones-Irwin, 1983.

Chrystal, K. Alec. "International Banking Facilities." *Federal Reserve Bank of St. Louis Review,* April 1984, pp. 5–11.

International Letter. Federal Reserve Bank of Chicago, various issues.

Maidment, Paul. "A Survey of International Banking." *The Economist,* April 7, 1990, special report.

Unger, Brooke. "A Survey of World Banking." *The Economist,* May 2, 1992, special report.

25 The International Debt Crisis and Country Risk Analysis

In 1555, the French government issued the "Grand Parti," a ten-year loan consolidating outstanding loans plus a certain amount of new money at a relatively high 16 percent; the large number of individuals who rushed to participate in the loan were disappointed when the loan defaulted two years later.

Steven I. Davies

CHAPTER LEARNING OBJECTIVES

- To describe the economic and political factors that determine a country's ability and willingness to repay its foreign debts
- To describe how banks structure the international loans they make to improve their collectibility
- To identify the key factors contributing to the international debt crisis that began in 1982
- To describe plans to resolve the international debt crisis and the results of these plans up to now
- To identify the link between government policies and the international debt crisis
- To describe some key causes and indicators of country risk and country health
- To identify the role and consequences of debt renegotiations and debt relief in coping with the international debt crisis
- To describe the market-oriented reforms that are necessary for the economic and political rehabilitation of the troubled debtor nations

The big money-center banks, as well as many regional banks, rechanneled hundreds of billions of petrodollars during the 1970s and early 1980s to less-developed countries and Communist countries. Major banks earned fat fees for arranging loans to Poland, Mexico, Brazil, and other such borrowers. The regional banks earned the spreads between what they borrowed Eurodollars at and the rates at which these loans were syndicated. These spreads were minimal, usually on the order of 0.5% to 0.75%.

Most of the money was squandered on all sorts of extravagant and profitless projects, from Amazon highways to highly automated steel mills in Africa. All this made sense, however, only as long as banks and their depositors were willing to suspend their disbelief about the risks of international lending. By now, the risks are big and obvious. The purpose of this chapter is to explore some of the factors that led to the *international debt crisis* and that, more generally, determine a country's ability to repay its foreign debts. This is the subject called *country risk analysis*—clearly not a new phenomenon, according to this chapter's opening observation.

The focus here is on *country risk* from a bank's standpoint, the possibility that borrowers in a country will be unable to service or repay their debts to foreign lenders in a timely manner. The essence of country risk analysis at commercial banks, therefore, is an assessment of factors that affect the likelihood that a country, such as Mexico, will be able to generate sufficient dollars to repay foreign debts as these debts come due.

We saw in Chapter 20 that these factors are both economic and political. Among economic factors are the quality and effectiveness of a country's economic and financial management policies, the country's resource base, and the country's external financial position. Political factors include the degree of political stability of a country and the extent to which a foreign entity, such as the United States, is willing to implicitly stand behind the country's external obligations. Lending to a private-sector borrower also exposes a bank to commercial risks, in addition to country risk. Because these commercial risks are generally similar to those encountered in domestic lending, they are not treated separately.

25.1 THE INTERNATIONAL BANKING CRISIS OF 1982

The events that culminated in the *international banking crisis of 1982* began to gather force in 1979. Several developments set the stage. One of these was the growing trend in overseas lending to set interest rates on a floating basis—that is, at a rate that would be periodically adjusted based on the rates prevailing in the market. Floating-rate loans made borrowers vulnerable to increases in real interest rates as well as to increases in the real value of the dollar because most of these loans were in dollars. Because of high U.S. inflation and a declining dollar during most of the 1970s, borrowers were not concerned with these possibilities. Borrowers seemed to believe that inflation would bail them out by reducing the real cost of loan repayment. (Note the inconsistency of this belief with the Fisher effect.) A second development was the second jump in oil prices, in 1979. In the absence of policies that promoted rapid adjustment to this new shock, the LDCs' balance-of-payments deficits soared to $62 billion in 1980 and $67 billion in 1981 and increased the LDCs' need for external financing; the banks responded by increasing the flow of loans to LDCs to $39 billion in 1980 (from $22 billion in 1978 and $35 billion in 1979) and to $40 billion in 1981.

> Floating-rate loans made borrowers vulnerable to increases in real interest rates.

The catalyst of the crisis was provided by the economic policies pursued by the industrial countries in general, and by the United States in particular, in their efforts to deal with rising domestic inflation. The combination of an expansionary fiscal policy and tight monetary policy led to sharply rising real interest rates in the United States—and in the Euromarkets where the banks funded most of their international loans. The variable rate feature of the loans combined with rising indebtedness boosted the LDCs' net interest payments to banks from $11 billion in 1978 to $44 billion in 1982. Furthermore, the dollar's sharp rise in the early 1980s increased the real cost to the borrowers of meeting their debt payments.

The final element setting the stage for the crisis was the onset of a recession in industrial countries. The recession reduced the demand for the LDCs' products and, thus, the export earnings needed to service their bank debt. The interest payments/export ratio reached 50% for some of these countries in 1982. This ratio meant that more than half of these countries' exports were needed to maintain up-to-date interest payments, leaving less than half of the export earnings to finance essential imports and to repay principal on their bank loans. These trends made the LDCs highly vulnerable.

Onset of the Crisis

With the onset of the international debt crisis in 1982, banks pulled back sharply on their international lending.

The first major blow to the international banking system came in August 1982, when Mexico announced that it was unable to meet its regularly scheduled payments to international creditors. Shortly thereafter, Brazil and Argentina—the second- and third-largest debtor nations—found themselves in a similar situation. By the spring of 1983, about 25 LDCs—accounting for two-thirds of the international banks' claims on this group of countries—were unable to meet their debt payments as scheduled and had entered into loan-rescheduling negotiations with the creditor banks.

Compounding the problems for the international banks was a sudden drying up of funds from OPEC. A worldwide recession that reduced the demand for oil put downward pressure on oil prices and on OPEC's revenues. In 1980, OPEC contributed about $42 billion to the loanable funds of the BIS-reporting banks. By 1982, the flow had reversed, as OPEC nations became a net drain of $26 billion in funds. At the same time, banks cut back sharply on their lending to LDCs.

The Baker Plan

The Baker Plan called on LDCs to undertake growth-oriented structural reforms.

In October 1985, U.S. Treasury Secretary James Baker called on 15 principal middle-income debtor LDCs—the *"Baker 15 countries"*—to undertake growth-oriented structural reforms that would be supported by increased financing from the World Bank, continued modest lending from commercial banks, and a pledge by industrial nations to open their markets to LDC exports. The goal of the *Baker Plan* was to buttress LDC economic growth, making these countries more desirable borrowers and restoring their access to international capital markets.

Achievement fell far short of these objectives. Most of the Baker 15 lagged in delivering on promised policy changes and economic performance. Instead of getting their economic house in order, many of the LDCs—feeling they had the big banks on the hook—sought to force the banks to make more and more lending concessions. The implied threat was that the banks would otherwise be forced to take large write-offs on their existing loans.

In May 1987, Citicorp's new chairman, John Reed, threw down the gauntlet to big debtor countries by adding $3 billion to the bank's loan-loss reserves. Citicorp's action was quickly followed by large additions to loss reserves by most other big U.S. and British banks. The banks who boosted their loan-loss reserves have become tougher negotiators, arguing against easing further the terms for developing countries' debt settlements. The decisions of these banks to boost their reserves—plus the announcement by some of their intention, one way or another, to dispose of a portion of their existing LDC loans—precipitated fresh questioning of the LDC debt strategy, in particular of the Baker initiative. The problem, however, was not with the Baker initiative, but rather with its implementation. By adding to their loan-loss reserves, Citicorp and the other banks that followed suit put themselves in a stronger position to demand reforms in countries to which they lend—a key feature of the Baker Plan.

The Brady Plan

Faced with the Baker Plan's failure to resolve the ongoing debt crisis, Nicholas Brady, James Baker's successor as U.S. Treasury Secretary, put forth a new plan in 1989 that emphasized debt relief through *forgiveness* instead of new lending. Under the *Brady Plan*, banks have a choice: They either could make new loans or they could write off portions of their existing loans in exchange for new government securities whose interest payments were backed with money from the International Monetary Fund. The problem with the Brady Plan was that for it to work commercial banks would have to do both: make new loans at the same time that they were writing off existing loans. Instead, many banks used the Brady Plan as an opportunity to exit the LDC debt market. They added billions to their loan-loss reserves to absorb the necessary loan writedowns, virtually guaranteeing that they would slash new LDC lending to the bone. In the aggregate, banks had to say goodbye to $26 billion of their LDC loans.

> The Brady Plan emphasized debt relief through forgiveness.

ILLUSTRATION: Mexico Implements the Brady Plan

Mexico's Brady Plan agreement in February 1990 offered three options to the banks: (1) convert their loans into salable bonds with guarantees attached, but worth only 65% of the face value of the old debt; (2) convert their debt into new guaranteed bonds whose yield was just 6.5%; or (3) keep their old loans but provide new money worth 25% of their exposure's value. Only 10% of the banks risked the new money option, while 41% agreed to debt reduction and 49% chose a lower interest rate. This agreement saved Mexico $3.8 billion a year in debt-servicing costs, but it is unlikely to receive new money in the foreseeable future.

As part of this restructuring, the U.S. government agreed to sell Mexico 30-year, zero-coupon Treasury bonds in a face amount of $33 billion. Mexico bought the zeros to serve as collateral for the bonds it planned to issue as a substitute for the bank loans. When the Mexican deal was struck, 30-year Treasury zeros were selling in the open market to yield 7.75%. But the U.S. Treasury priced the zeros it sold to Mexico to yield 8.05%, reflecting the price not of zeros but of conventional 30-year Treasury bonds. The Treasury also charged Mexico a service fee of 0.125% per annum, as is customary in such special Treasury sales. As a result, Mexico received an effective annual interest yield of 7.925% (8.05% − 0.125%).

The sale of zero-coupon bonds to Mexico at a cut-rate price brought criticism from Congress and Wall Street. Many argued that any U.S. aid to Mexico ought to flow through normal channels, and not be done in a back-door financing scheme. Without taking sides in this dispute, what is the value of the subsidy the Treasury provided to Mexico?

Solution. If the Treasury had priced the zeros to yield 7.75% less the 0.125% service fee, or 7.625%, the $33 billion face value of bonds would have cost Mexico

$$\$33 \text{ billion}/(1.07925)^{30} = \$3.64 \text{ billion}$$

By pricing the bonds to yield 7.925%, the Treasury sold the bonds to Mexico at a price of

$$\$33 \text{ billion}/(1.07925)^{30} = \$3.35 \text{ billion}$$

The result is a savings to Mexico of about $290 million.

The international debt crisis led to a deterioration in the creditworthiness of large U.S. money-center banks.

The market clearly recognized the deteriorating condition of the LDC debt held by the large U.S. money-center banks. This recognition is reflected in the bond market's increasingly grim view during this period of the creditworthiness of these banks. Yields on money-center bank debt securities approached the levels associated with junk bonds (see Exhibit 25.1). Banks responded to the decline in the market values of their portfolios by raising additional capital and curtailing asset growth in general and LDC loan growth in particular. The Brady Plan only hastened their move out of LDC lending.

The pressure from the financial marketplace made it more difficult for banks to lend money to Brazil and other LDCs. Indeed, the flow of capital went in the opposite direction: As of February 1990, U.S. bank claims on the 15 most heavily indebted LDCs totaled about $59 billion, down 34% from $90 billion in June 1982. Although much of that reduction is accounted for by loan sales and write-offs, the total bank credit available to the LDCs also dropped. Simply put, the banks washed their hands of the LDC debt mess. They were saying, in effect, that there are few good loans to be made in Latin America or Africa, because the politics and systems are so bad that no loan would be good even if the old debts were all canceled.

As we saw in Chapter 20, bold reforms in Latin America have reversed the flow of capital there. And this new capital will not create another debt crisis because most of it is equity, not debt. In contrast to the floating-rate loans of the

Exhibit 25.1   Deterioration in Creditworthiness of Major U.S. Banks

NOTE: Yield margin of 10-year notes rated single-A over Treasury notes
due in 10 years; margins in basis points (1/100th of a percentage point)

SOURCE: *The Wall Street Journal,* February 2, 1988, p. 7. Reprinted with permission of *The Wall Street Journal,* © Dow Jones & Company, Inc. 1988. All rights reserved worldwide.

1970s and early 1980s, much of the new capital flowing into Latin America comes from investors buying shares in local companies and direct investment by multinational firms.

Overall, the share of commercial bank lending in total financial flows to developing countries has fallen from 33% in 1982 to 13% in 1990, while the share of foreign direct investment has more than doubled, from 11% to 23%. At the same time, the share of official grants and loans has risen from 38% to 55%.

Debt Renegotiations

The decade of the 1980s was characterized by a seemingly endless series of *debt renegotiations.* Underlying these debt renegotiations was some hard arithmetic. In order to grow, the LDCs required capital formation. But servicing their foreign debts required the use of scarce capital, thereby constraining growth. Thus, the debtor LDCs were determined to reduce their net financial transfers—by limiting interest payments and increasing net capital inflows—to levels consistent with desired economic growth. In short, they wanted more money from their banks. However, the banks first wanted to see economic reforms that would improve the odds that the LDCs would be able to service their debts. The principal hindrance to bank willingness to supply more funds was skepticism about the ability and willingness of the debtor nations to make sound economic policy.

The predicament facing the LDCs can best be understood by dividing the current-account surplus into two components: the noninterest surplus and interest payments. In order to service their debts without added funding, the LDCs must run a noninterest surplus large enough to pay interest expenses as well as

The 1980s saw a seemingly endless series of debt renegotiations.

any principal payments that come due. Without economic growth—there was virtually none during the 1980s—either consumption must contract to boost savings or investment must fall. The object is to increase net savings so as to finance the added capital outflow.

Exhibit 25.2 shows how the Latin American debtor nations financed their debt service charges. For the period from 1977 through 1982, these countries ran a noninterest deficit. Consequently, debts increased to finance the noninterest deficit, to finance interest payments, and to finance the flight of capital. The rise in external debt led to an increase in the fraction of gross domestic product (GDP) required to service interest payments. In the period between 1983 and 1985, the noninterest deficit turned into a large surplus, around 5% of GDP. Because the noninterest surplus was almost equal to the interest payments due, very little new money was needed to finance interest payments. The bottom line, however, shows that rather than interest payments coming out of consumption, they were financed by a dramatic cut in domestic investment. That is, the 5.5% turnaround in the noninterest surplus (4.7 + 0.8) was matched by a 5.8% drop in net investment (calculated as a percent of GDP).

One response to this hard arithmetic is seen in Peru's unilateral limit on debt service payments, in effect since 1985. The result was no new money for Peru. Virtually cut off from credit, Peru conducted some of its external trade by barter. Further, Peru has experienced foreign-direct-investment withdrawals and capital flight.

Another approach is *debt relief*—that is, reducing the principal and/or interest payments on loans. Yet, the middle-income debtor nations addressed by the Baker and Brady Plans are neither very poor nor insolvent. They possess considerable human and natural resources, reasonably well developed infrastructures and productive capacities, and the potential for substantial growth in output and exports given sound economic policies. In addition, many of these countries possess considerable wealth—much of it invested abroad.

Although debt burdens exacerbated the economic problems faced by these countries, all too often the underlying causes were to be found in bloated bureaucracies, overvalued currencies, massive corruption, and politically motivated government investments in money-losing ventures. The Baker countries also

Exhibit 25.2 Latin America's Adjustment to the International Debt Crisis (Percent of GDP)

	1977–1982	1983–1985
External debt	34.3	47.2
Interest payments	3.2	5.6
Noninterest surplus	−0.8	4.7
Net investment	11.3	5.5

SOURCE: Rudiger Dornbusch, "International Debt and Economic Instability," *Economic Review*, Federal Reserve Bank of Kansas City, January 1987, p. 19. The original data are from the IMF.

suffered from markets distorted by import protection for inefficient domestic producers and government favors for politically influential groups. For these countries, debt relief was at best an ineffectual substitute for sound macro-economic policy and major structural reform; relief would have only weakened discipline over economic policy and undermined support for structural reform.

LDC debtors must rely on self-help rather than debt relief to cope with their problems.

Ten years after it began, the decade-long Latin American debt crisis ended in July 1992, with the signing of an agreement with Brazil to restructure the $44 billion it owed foreign banks. In the end, however, it was not negotiation that cut the Gordian knot of Latin American debt—no new money until Latin America showed economic growth and no growth without new money—but genuine economic reforms, forced on unwilling governments by the unrelenting pressures of the debt crisis. Mexico and Chile, hopelessly mired in debt, so thoroughly reformed their economies, spurring economic growth in the process, that they were able to raise new money from the international capital markets. These economic reforms included opening their markets to imports, tearing down barriers to foreign investment, selling off state-owned companies, instituting tight money policies, and cutting government deficits. The examples of Mexico and Chile led others, like Argentina and Venezuela, to change their policies as well.

The experiences of Mexico, Chile, and Argentina—countries that appear to have successfully implemented economic reform programs—shows that they all met the following criteria:[1]

Chile, Mexico, and Argentina have successfully implemented economic reform programs.

— A head of state who demonstrates strong will and political leadership
— A viable and comprehensive economic plan that is implemented in a proper sequence
— A motivated and competent economic team working in harmony
— Belief in the plan from the head of state, his cabinet, and other senior officials
— An integrated program to sell the plan to all levels of society through the media

These criteria are applicable not just to Latin America, but to all LDCs anywhere in the world. Even with the best of intentions, however, economic reform is painful and difficult to make stick unless all levels of society are convinced that instituting free market policies will bring the long-term benefits of sustained growth.

25.2 COUNTRY RISK ANALYSIS IN INTERNATIONAL BANKING

It is worthwhile to note some differences between international loans and domestic loans because these difference have a lot to do with the nature of country risk. Ordinarily banks can control borrowers by means of loan covenants on their

[1]These criteria appear in William R. Rhodes, "Third World Debt: The Disaster That Didn't Happen," *The Economist*, September 12, 1992, pp. 21–23.

dividend and financing decisions. Quite often, however, the borrowers in international loan agreements are sovereign states, or their ability to repay depends on the actions of a sovereign state. The unique characteristics of a sovereign borrower render irrelevant many of the loan covenants—such as dividend or merger restrictions—normally imposed on borrowers. Moreover, sovereign states ordinarily refuse to accept economic or financial policy restrictions imposed by foreign banks.

> Banks have great difficulty in enforcing their international loan contracts.

The key issue posed by international loans, therefore, is how do banks ensure the enforceability of these debt contracts? What keeps borrowers from incurring debts and then defaulting voluntarily? In general, seizure of assets is not useful unless the debtor has substantial external assets, as in the case of Iran. Ordinarily, though, the borrower has few external assets.

One answer to the question of enforceability is that it is difficult for borrowers that repudiate their debts to reenter private capital markets.[2] That is, banks find it in their best interest, ex post, to deny further credit to a borrower that defaults on its bank loans. If the bank fails to adhere to its announced policy of denying credit to its defaulters, some of its other borrowers may now decide to default on their debts because they realize that default carries no penalty. Having a reputation for being a tough bank is a valuable commodity in a hard world that has no love for moneylenders.

> Countries that default on their foreign debts may be frozen out of the capital markets.

The presence of *loan syndications*—in which several banks share a loan—and *cross-default clauses*—which ensure that a default to one bank is a default to all banks—means that if the borrower repudiates its debt to one bank, it must repudiate its debt to *all* the banks. This constraint makes the penalty for repudiation much stiffer because a large number of banks will now deny credit to the borrower in the future. After a few defaults, the borrower will exhaust most of the potential sources of credit in the international financial markets. For many borrowers, this penalty is severe enough that they do not voluntarily default on their bank loans. Thus, countries will sometimes go to extraordinary lengths to continue servicing their debts. Bank country risk analysis can, therefore, focus largely on ability to repay rather than willingness to repay.

Notice, however, that the threat to cut off credit to borrowers who default is meaningful only so long as the banks have sufficient resources to reward with further credit those who do not default. But if several countries default simultaneously, then the banks' promise to provide further credit to borrowers who repay their debts is no longer credible; the erosion in their capital bases caused by the defaults will force the banks to curtail their loans. Under these circumstances, even those borrowers who did not default on their loans will suffer a reduction of credit. The lesser penalty for defaulting may induce borrowers to default en masse. The possibility of mass defaults is the real *international debt crisis*.

---

[2]The discussion of debt repudiation and the nature of international loans comes from Bhagwan Chowdry, "What Is Different About International Lending?" working paper, University of Chicago, November 1987.

Country Risk and the Terms of Trade

What ultimately determines a nation's ability to repay foreign loans is that nation's ability to generate foreign exchange. This ability, in turn, is based on the nation's *terms of trade*, the weighted average of the nation's export prices relative to its import prices—that is, the exchange rate between exports and imports. Most economists would agree that these terms of trade are largely independent of the nominal exchange rate, unless the observed exchange rate has been affected by government intervention in the foreign exchange market.

In general, if its terms of trade increase, a nation will be a better credit risk. Alternatively, if its terms of trade decrease, a nation will be a poorer credit risk. This *terms-of-trade risk*, however, can be exacerbated by political decisions. When a nation's terms of trade improve, foreign goods become relatively less expensive, the nation's standard of living rises, and consumers and businesses become more dependent on imports. But since there is a large element of unpredictability to relative price changes, shifts in the terms of trade will also be unpredictable. When the nation's terms of trade decline, as must inevitably happen when prices fluctuate randomly, the government will face political pressure to maintain the nation's standard of living.

> Default risk on a country's debts partly depends on how the government responds to a change in its terms of trade.

As we saw in Chapter 20, a typical response is for the government to fix the exchange rate at its former (and now overvalued) level—that is, to subsidize the price of dollars. Loans made when the terms of trade improved are now doubly risky: first, because the terms of trade have declined and, second, because the government is maintaining an *overvalued currency*, further reducing the nation's net inflow of dollars. The deterioration in the trade balance usually results in added government borrowing. This was the response of the Baker 15 countries to the sharp decline in their terms of trade shown in Exhibit 25.3. Capital flight

Exhibit 25.3   Decline in Terms of Trade in Baker 15 Countries

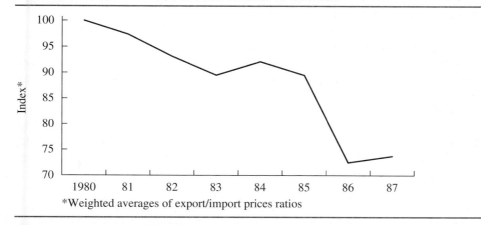

*Weighted averages of export/import prices ratios

SOURCE: Data from OECD, IMF, and Federal Reserve Bank of New York.

exacerbates this problem, as residents recognize the country's deteriorating economic situation.

To summarize, a terms-of-trade risk can be exacerbated if the government tries to avoid the necessary drop in the standard of living when the terms of trade decline by maintaining the old and now overvalued exchange rate. In reality, of course, this element of country risk is a political risk. The government is attempting by political means to hold off the necessary economic adjustments to the country's changed wealth position.

A key issue, therefore, in assessing country risk is the speed with which a country adjusts to its new wealth position. In other words, how fast will the necessary austerity policy be implemented? The speed of adjustment will be determined in part by the government's perception of the costs and benefits associated with austerity versus default.

Capital flight has exacerbated the debt crisis.

The Government's Cost/Benefit Calculus

The cost of austerity is determined primarily by the nation's external debts relative to its wealth, as measured by its gross national product (GNP). The lower this ratio, the lower the relative amount of consumption that must be sacrificed to meet a nation's foreign debts.

The cost of default is the likelihood of being cut off from international credit. This possibility brings with it its own form of austerity. Most nations will follow this path only as a last resort, preferring to stall for time in the hope that something will happen in the interim. That something could be a bailout by the IMF, the Bank for International Settlements, the Federal Reserve, or some other major central bank. The bailout decision is largely a political decision. It depends on the willingness of citizens of another nation, usually the United States, to tax themselves on behalf of the country involved.[3] This willingness is a function of two factors: (1) the nation's geopolitical importance to the United States and (2) the probability that the necessary economic adjustments will result in unacceptable political turmoil.

Highly variable terms of trade and an unstable political system magnify country risk.

The more a nation's terms of trade fluctuate and the less stable its political system, the greater the odds the government will face a situation that will tempt it to hold off on the necessary adjustments. Terms-of-trade variability will probably be inversely correlated with the degree of product diversification in the nation's trade flows. With limited diversification—for example, dependence on the export of one or two primary products or on imports heavily weighted toward a few commodities—the nation's terms of trade are likely to be highly variable. This characterizes the situation facing many Third World countries. It also describes, in part, the situation of those OECD (Organization for Economic Cooperation and Development) nations heavily dependent on oil imports.

[3]See Tamir Agmon and J. K. Dietrich, "International Lending and Income Redistribution: An Alternative View of Country Risk," *Journal of Banking and Finance*, December 1983, pp. 483–495, for a discussion of this point.

Exhibit 25.4   Debt Service/Exports Ratios for Selected Countries as of Year-End 1982 and Year-End 1990

Country	1982	1990
Mexico	0.70	0.20
Brazil	0.56	0.30
Chile	0.54	0.18
Argentina	0.41	0.39
Venezuela	0.32	0.15
Philippines	0.25	0.18
Baker 15	0.35	0.22

SOURCE: Data from Robert E. Weintraub, *International Debt: Crisis and Challenge* (Fairfax, Va: George Mason University, Department of Economics monograph, April 1983), p. 17; and Brian O'Reilly, "Cooling Down the Debt Bomb," *Fortune,* May 20, 1991, p. 123.

Debt Service Measures

Two measures of the risk associated with a nation's debt burden are the debt service/exports and debt service/GNP ratios, where debt service includes both interest charges and loan repayments. Exhibit 25.4 contains 1982 and 1990 year-end statistics on the debt service/exports ratio for several individual countries and for the Baker 15. To put these figures in perspective, most bankers consider a debt service/exports ratio of 0.25 or higher to be dangerous. The figures indicate the debt woes these countries faced in 1982, but they also record a dramatic improvement in recent years.

Ex ante what matters is not just the *coverage ratio* but also the variability of the difference between export revenues, X, and import costs, M, relative to the nation's debt-service requirements (i.e., c.v.$[(X - M)/D]$ where c.v. is the coefficient of variation and D is the debt service requirement). In calculating this measure of risk, it is important to recognize that export volume is likely to be positively correlated—and import volume negatively correlated—with price. In addition, import expenditures are usually positively related to export revenues.

25.3 SUMMARY AND CONCLUSIONS

The end of "let's pretend" in international banking has led to a new emphasis on country risk analysis. From the bank's standpoint, country risk—the credit risk on loans to a nation—is largely determined by the real cost of repaying the loan versus the real wealth that the country has to draw on. These parameters, in turn, depend on the variability of the nation's terms of trade and the government's willingness to allow the nation's standard of living to adjust rapidly to changing economic fortunes.

The experience of those countries that have made it through the international debt crisis suggests that others in a similar situation can only get out if they institute broad systemic reforms. Their problems are caused by governments spending too much money they don't have to meet promises they should not make. They create public sector jobs for people to do things they shouldn't do and subsidize companies to produce high priced goods and services. These countries need less government and fewer bureaucratic rules. Debt forgiveness or further capital inflows would just tempt these nations to postpone economic adjustment further.

QUESTIONS

1.   What were the key contributing factors to the international debt crisis that began in 1982?

2.   What economic and political factors account for the fact that the foreign loans of major banks are in such bad shape?

3.   How are U.S. international banking practices likely to be influenced by the belief that the Federal Reserve would not permit a major U.S. bank to fail?

4.   Prior to 1983, U.S. banks did not have to, and generally did not, provide data to the public on the geographical distribution of their loan portfolios. If the stock market is strongly efficient, how would you predict it responded to the public release of information in early 1983 that concerned the extent of bank loans to various Latin American countries? Recall that the international debt crisis struck in mid-1982.

5.   Why is it crucial for banks to prevent several defaults at once?

6.   What incentive do borrowers have to form a debtors' cartel and simultaneously default? Who would choose not to belong to such a cartel?

7.   In the week following Citicorp's $3 billion write down of its Latin American debt, its stock price rose by 10%. What might explain this rise in Citicorp's stock price?

8.   How does capital flight contribute to the international debt crisis?

PROBLEMS

1.   In the Mexican debt restructuring discussed in the chapter, suppose that when the deal was struck 30-year Treasury zeros were selling in the open market at a yield of about 7.62%. But the U.S. Treasury priced the zeros that it sold to Mexico to yield 8.15%. The Treasury also charged Mexico its customary service fee of 0.125% per annum, giving Mexico an effective annual interest yield of 8.025%.

    a. Under these circumstances, what would have been the amount of the subsidy provided by the Treasury (relative to the cost to Mexico of buying the zeros to yield 7.62% less 0.125%)?

    b. What does this complicated deal accomplish? Who benefits? Who loses?

2.   In early 1988, the Mexican government sought to swap about $15 billion of its outstanding bank debt for $10 billion in bonds. The principal amount of the Mexican bonds would be secured by 20-year, zero-coupon U.S. Treasury bonds having a face value of $10 billion. Because of doubts about Mexico's creditworthiness, Mexican bank debt was then valued by the market at about 50 cents on the dollar.

a. How should Mexico's offer be evaluated?

b. Suppose the bond interest payments are more certain than bank debt payments. Before the bond swap is worthwhile, how much would a Mexican promise to pay $1 in bond interest have to be worth relative to a Mexican promise to pay $1 in bank debt?

BIBLIOGRAPHY

Lessard, Donald R. "North-South: The Implications for Multinational Banking." *Journal of Banking and Finance*, 7(1983), pp. 521–536.

———, and John Williamson, eds. *Capital Flight and Third World Debt*. Washington, D.C.: Institute for International Economics, 1987.

Shapiro, Alan C. "Risk in International Banking." *Journal of Financial and Quantitative Analysis*, December 1982, pp. 727–739.

———. "Currency Risk and Country Risk in International Banking." *Journal of Finance*, July 1985, pp. 881–891.

———. "Risk in International Banking." *Journal of Financial and Quantitative Analysis*, December 1982, pp. 727–739.

Wihlborg, Clas. "Currency Risks in International Financial Markets," *Princeton Studies in International Finance No. 44*, December 1978.

Case VI.1   PLANO CRUZADO

On February 28, 1986, President Jose Sarnay of Brazil announced the Plano Cruzado. At the time, Brazilian inflation was running at an annualized rate of more than 400%. The Plan slashed inflation by freezing prices and wages. The purpose of the Plan was to impose "shock treatment" on the economy and break the cycle of "inertial inflation" caused by high inflationary expectations. However, in a move that foreshadowed the splits that bedeviled the Plan, workers were granted pay hikes of 8% and 15%, just before the freeze. At the same time, government spending went largely unchecked, and the public-sector deficit—financed largely by printing more cruzados—grew to 4.5% of gross national product.

In November, the Plan achieved its first incontrovertible success: Government parties swept the congressional and gubernatorial races. Price controls were eased just after the election. However, the government found it politically impossible to remove subsidies to state industries because these industries formed the base for political power. Instead, large price hikes for state companies were granted by imposing huge increases in indirect taxes and tariffs on their products, and an attempt was made to disguise the effect of these increases on inflation by altering the basket of goods on which inflation was calculated. "They wanted me to tamper with inflation—simple as that," commented the head of the National Statistics Office, who immediately resigned.

QUESTIONS

1. What were the likely consequences for Brazil of controlling prices while gunning the money supply? Consider the effect on production and the availability of products in the stores.

2. How did the Plano Cruzado affect Brazil's huge trade surplus?

3. What would be your forecast of the Plan's effect on Brazil's ability to service its foreign debts?

4. President Sarnay terminated Plano Cruzado in February 1987, one year after it began. What impact do you think the Plan had in reducing inflation and inflation expectations? How would you go about measuring the effect of the Plan on inflation expectations?

5. What was the likely price response to the removal of price controls?

6. If you were a banker, how would seeing such a Plan put into effect affect your willingness to lend money to Brazil? Explain.

SOURCE: Based on a report in *The Wall Street Journal*, February 13, 1987, p. 27.

GLOSSARY

KEY WORDS AND TERMS IN INTERNATIONAL FINANCE

Accounting exposure The change in the value of a firm's foreign-currency-denominated accounts due to a change in exchange rates.

Act of state doctrine This doctrine says that a nation is sovereign within its own borders and its domestic actions may not be questioned in the courts of another nation.

Adjusted present value The net present value of a project using the all-equity rate as a discount rate. The effects of financing are incorporated in separate terms.

Administrative pricing rule IRS rules used to allocate income on export sales to a foreign sales corporation

Agency costs Costs that stem from conflicts between managers and stockholders and between stockholders and bondholders.

All-equity rate The discount rate that reflects only the business risks of a project and abstracts from the effects of financing.

American Depository Receipt (ADR) A certificate of ownership issued by a U.S. bank as a convenience to investors in lieu of the underlying foreign corporate shares it holds in custody.

American shares Securities certificates issued in the United States by a transfer agent acting on behalf of the foreign issuer. The certificates represent claims to foreign equities.

Appreciation *See* Revaluation.

Arbitrage Purchase of securities or commodities on one market for immediate resale on another in order to profit from a price discrepancy.

Arm's-length price Price at which a willing buyer and a willing unrelated seller would freely agree to transact (i.e., a market price).

Back-to-back financing An intercompany loan channeled through a bank.

Baker plan A plan by U.S. Treasury Secretary James Baker under which 15 principal middle-income debtor countries (the "Baker countries") would undertake growth-oriented structural reforms, to be supported by increased financing from the World Bank and continued lending from commercial banks.

Balance of Payments Net value of all economic transactions—including trade in goods and services, transfer payments, loans, and investments—between residents of the same country and those of all other countries.

Balance of trade New flow of goods (exports minus imports) between countries.

Balance-sheet exposure *See* Accounting exposure.

Bank draft A draft addressed to a bank; *See* Draft.

Banker's acceptance Draft accepted by a bank; *See* Draft.

Bank loan swap *See* Debt swap.

Bearer securities Securities that are unregistered.

Beta A measure of the systematic risk faced by an asset or project. Beta is calculated as the covariance between returns on the asset and returns on the market portfolio divided by the variance of returns on the market portfolio.

Bill of exchange *See* Bank draft.

Bill of lading A contract between a carrier and an exporter in which the former agrees to carry the latter's goods from port of shipment to port of destination. It is also the exporter's receipt for the goods.

Black market An illegal market that often arises when price controls or official rationing lead to shortages of goods, services, or assets.

Blocked currency A currency that is not freely convertible to other currencies due to exchange controls.

Brady Plan A plan by Nicholas Brady, James Baker's successor as U.S. Treasury Secretary, that emphasized debt relief through forgiveness, instead of new lending. Under this plan, banks have a choice: They either could make new loans or they could write off portions of their existing loans in exchange for government securities whose interest payments were backed with money from the International Monetary Fund.

Branch A foreign operation incorporated in the home country.

Bretton Woods Agreement An agreement, implemented in 1946, whereby each member government pledged to maintain a fixed, or pegged, exchange rate for its currency vis-à-vis the dollar or gold. These fixed exchange rates were supposed to reduce the riskiness of international transactions, thus promoting growth in world trade.

Capital account Net results of public and private international investment and lending activities.

Capital asset pricing model (CAPM) A model for pricing risk. The CAPM assumes that investors must be compensated for the time value of money plus systematic risk, as measured by an asset's beta.

Capital flight The transfer of capital abroad in response to fears of political risk.

Cash pooling *See* Pooling.

CHIPS *See* Clearing House Interbank Payments System.

Clean float *See* Free float.

Clearing House Interbank Payments System (CHIPS) A computerized network for transfer of international dollar payments, linking about 140 depository institutions that have offices or affiliates in New York City.

Concession agreement An understanding between a company and the host government that specifies the rules under which the company can operate locally.

Controlled foreign corporation (CFC) A foreign corporation whose voting stock is more than 50% owned by U.S. stockholders, each of who owns at least 10% of the voting power.

Correspondent bank A bank located in any other city, state, or country that provides a service for another bank.

Countertrade A sophisticated form of barter in which the exporting firm is required to take the countervalue of its sale in local goods or services instead of in cash.

Country risk General level of political and economic uncertainty in a country affecting the value of loans or investments in that country.

Covered-interest arbitrage Movement of short-term funds between two currencies to take advantage of interest differentials with exchange risk eliminated by means of forward contracts.

Cross-default clauses Clause in a loan agreement that says that a default by a borrower to one lender is a default to all lenders.

Cross rate The exchange rate between two currencies, neither of which is the U.S. dollar, calculated by using the dollar rates for both currencies.

Currency arbitrate Taking advantage of divergencies in exchange rates in different money markets by buying a currency in one market and selling it in another.

Currency call option A financial contract that gives the buyer the right, but not the obligation, to buy a specified number of units of foreign currency from the option seller at a fixed dollar price, up to the option's expiration date.

Currency futures contract Contract for future delivery of a specific quantity of a given currency, with the exchange rate fixed at the time the contract is entered. Futures contracts are similar to forward contracts except that they are traded on organized futures exchanges and the gains and losses on the contracts are settled each day.

Currency of denomination Currency in which a transaction is stated.

Currency of determination Currency whose value determines a given price.

Currency put option A financial contract that gives the buyer the right, but not the obligation, to sell a specified number of foreign currency units to the option seller at a fixed dollar price, up to the option's expiration date.

Currency risk sharing An agreement by the parties to a transaction to share the currency risk associated with the transaction. The arrangement involves a customized hedge contract imbedded in the underlying transaction.

Currency swap A simultaneous borrowing and lending operation whereby two parties exchange specific amounts of two currencies at the outset at the spot rate. They also exchange interest rate payments in the two currencies. The parties undertake to reverse the exchange after a fixed term at a fixed exchange rate.

Current account Net flow of goods, services, and unilateral transactions (gifts) between countries.

Debt relief Reducing the principal and/or interest payments on LDC loans.

Debt swap A set of transactions (also called a debt-equity swap) in which a firm buys a country's dollar bank debt at a discount and swaps this debt with the central bank for local currency that it can use to acquire local equity.

Depreciation *See* Devaluation.

Depreciation tax shield The value of the tax write-off on depreciation of plant and equipment.

Devaluation A decrease in the spot value of a currency.

"Dirty" float *See* Managed float.

Doctrine of sovereign immunity Doctrine that says a nation may not be tried in the courts of another country without its consent.

Domestic International Sales Corporation (DISC) A domestic U.S. corporation that receives a tax incentive for export activities.

Double dip lease A cross-border lease in which the disparate rules of the lessor's and lessee's countries let both parties be treated as the owner of the leased equipment for tax purposes.

Draft An unconditional order in writing—signed by a person, usually the exporter, and addressed to the importer—ordering the importer or the importer's agent to pay, on demand (sight draft) or at a fixed future date (time draft), the amount specified on its face.

Dual syndicate equity offering An international equity placement where the offering is split into two tranches—domestic and foreign—and each tranche is handled by a separate lead manager.

EAFE Index The Morgan Stanley Capital International Europe, Australia, Far East Index, which reflects the performance of all major stock markets outside of North America.

Economic exposure The extend to which the value of the firm will change due to an exchange rate change.

Economies of scale Situation in which increasing production leads to a less-than-proportionate increase in cost.

Economies of scope Scope economies exist whenever the same investment can support multiple profitable activities less expensively in combination than separately.

Edge Act corporation A subsidiary, located in the United States, of a U.S. bank that is permitted to carry on international banking and investment activities.

Efficient market A market in which new information is readily incorporated into the prices of traded securities.

Eurobond A bond sold outside the country in whose currency it is denominated.

Euro-commercial paper (Euro-CP) Euronotes that are not underwritten.

Eurocurrency A currency deposited in a bank outside the country of its origin.

Euroequity issue A syndicated equity offering placed throughout Europe and handled by one lead manager.

Euronote A short-term note issued outside the country of the currency it is denominated in.

European Community A group of 11 European nations whose purpose is to reduce trade barriers among member states.

European Currency Unit (ECU) A composite currency, consisting of fixed amounts of 10 European currencies.

European Monetary System (EMS) Monetary system formed by the major European countries under which the members agree to maintain their exchange rates within a specific margin around agreed-upon, fixed central exchange rates. These central exchange rates are denominated in currency units per ECU.

Europe 1992 An agreement among the members of the European Community to create a single European market for goods and services by December 1992. The objective of Europe 1992 is to tear down barriers to trade and commerce within Europe so that European nations can achieve economic prosperity.

Exchange-rate mechanism (ERM) A process whereby each member of the European Monetary System determines a mutually agreed upon central exchange rate for its currency; each rate is denominated in currency units per ECU.

Exchange risk The variability of a firm's value that is due to uncertain exchange rate changes.

Export-Import Bank (Eximbank) U.S. government agency dedicated to facilitating U.S. exports, primarily through subsidized export financing.

Exposure netting Offsetting exposures in one currency with exposures in the same or another currency, where exchange rates are expected to move in such a way that losses (gains) on the first exposed position should be offset by gains (losses) on the second currency exposure.

Factor Specialized buyer, at a discount, of company receivables.

FASB No. 8 *See* Statement of Financial Accounting Standards no. 8.

FASB No. 52 *See* Statement of Financial Accounting Standards no. 52.

Fiat money Nonconvertible paper money.

Fisher effect States that the nominal interest differential between two countries should equal the inflation differential between those countries.

Fixed exchange rate An exchange rate whose value is fixed by the governments involved.

Floating exchange rate An exchange rate whose value is fixed by the governments involved.

Foreign banking market That portion of domestic bank loans supplied to foreigners for use abroad.

Foreign bond market That portion of the domestic bond market that represents issues floated by foreign companies or governments.

Foreign direct investment The acquisition abroad of physical assets such as plant and equipment, with operating control residing in the parent corporation.

Foreign equity market That portion of the domestic equity market that represents issues floated by foreign companies.

Foreign market beta A measure of foreign market risk that is designed to provide a tax incentive for exporting U.S.-produced goods.

Foreign Sales Corporation (FSC) A special type of corporation created by the Tax Reform Act of 1984 that is designed to provide a tax incentive for exporting U.S.-produced goods.

Foreign tax credit Home country credit against domestic income tax for foreign taxes already paid on foreign-source earnings.

Forward differential Annualized percentage difference between spot and forward rates.

Forward rate The rate quoted today for delivery at a fixed future date of a specified amount of one currency against dollar payment.

Free float An exchange rate system characterized by the absence of government intervention. Also known as a clean float.

Functional currency As defined in FASB No. 52, an affiliate's functional currency is the currency of the primary economic environment in which the affiliate generates and expends cash.

G-5 nations A group of five large nations—the United States, France, Japan, Great Britain, and Germany—that meets periodically to coordinate economic policies. Also known as the Group of Five.

G-7 nations The G-5 plus Canada and Italy. Also known as the Group of Seven.

Global fund A mutual fund that can invest anywhere in the world, including the United States.

Gold standard A system of setting currency values whereby the participating countries commit to fix the prices of their domestic currencies in terms of a specified amount of gold.

Growth options The opportunities a company may have to invest capital so as to increase the profitability of its existing product lines and benefit from expanding into new products or markets.

Hedge To enter into a forward contract in order to protect the home currency value of foreign-currency-denominated assets or liabilities.

Import-substitution development strategy A development strategy followed by many Latin American countries and other LDCs that emphasized import substitution—accomplished through protectionism—as the route to economic growth.

Intercompany loan Loan made by one unit of a corporation to another unit of the same corporation.

Intercompany transaction Transaction carried out between two units of the same corporation.

Interest rate parity A condition where the interest differential is (approximately) equal to the forward differential between two currencies.

Interest rate swap An agreement between two parties to exchange interest payments for a specific maturity on an agreed upon principal amount.

The most common interest rate swap involves exchanging fixed interest payments for floating interest payments.

Interest tax shield The value of the tax write-off on interest payments (analogous to the depreciation tax shield).

International Bank for Reconstruction and Development (IBRD) Also known as the World Bank, the IBRD is owned by its member nations and makes loans at nearly conventional terms to countries for projects of high economic priority.

International Banking Facility (IBF) A bookkeeping entity of a U.S. financial institution that is permitted to conduct international banking business (such as receiving foreign deposits and making foreign loans) largely exempt from domestic regulatory constraints.

International diversification The attempt to reduce risk by investing in more than one nation. By diversifying across nations whose economic cycles are not perfectly in phase, investors can typically reduce the variability of their returns.

International finance subsidiary A subsidiary incorporated in the United States (usually in Delaware) whose sole purpose was to issue debentures overseas and invest the proceeds in foreign operations, with the interest paid to foreign bondholders not subject to U.S. withholding tax. The elimination of the corporate withholding tax has ended the need for this type of subsidiary.

International Fisher effect States that the interest differential between two countries should be an unbiased predictor of the future change in the spot rate.

International fund A mutual fund that can invest only outside the United States.

International Monetary Fund (IMF) International organization created at Bretton Woods, N.H., in 1944 to promote exchange rate stability, including the provision of temporary assistance to member nations trying to defend their currencies against transitory phenomena.

International monetary system The set of policies, institutions, practices, regulations, and mechanisms that determine the rate at which one currency is exchanged for another.

J-curve theory Theory that says a country's trade deficit will initially worsen after its currency depreciates because higher prices on foreign imports will more than offset the reduced volume of imports in the short run.

Law of one price The theory that exchange-adjusted prices for identical tradeable goods and financial assets must be within transaction costs of equality worldwide.

LDC debt swap *See* Debt swap.

Leading and lagging Accelerating (leading) and delaying (lagging) international payments by modifying credit terms, normally on trade between affiliates.

Letter of credit A letter addressed to the seller, written and signed by a bank acting on behalf of the buyer, in which the bank promised to honor drafts drawn on itself if the seller conforms to the specific conditions contained in the letter.

Link financing *See* Back-to-back financing.

Loan syndication Group of banks sharing a loan.

London interbank offer rate (LIBOR) The deposit rate on interbank transactions in the Eurocurrency market.

Look-thru A method for calculating U.S. taxes owed on income from controlled foreign corporations that was introduced by the Tax Reform Act of 1986.

Louvre Accord An agreement, named for the Paris landmark where it was negotiated, that called for the G-7 nations to support the falling dollar by pegging exchange rates within a narrow, undisclosed range, while they also moved to bring their economic policies into line.

Managed float Also known as a "dirty" float, this is a system of floating exchange rates with central bank intervention to reduce currency fluctuations.

Monetary union Agreement among several economic units to establish one central bank with the sole power to issue a single currency. The European Community is currently talking about monetary union.

Money market hedge The use of borrowing and lending transactions in foreign currencies to lock in the home currency value of a foreign currency transaction.

Multicurrency clause This clause gives a Eurocurrency borrower the right to switch from one currency to another when the loan is rolled over.

Netting *See* Exposure netting or Payments netting.

Nominal exchange rate Actual spot rate.

Note issuance facility (NIF) A facility provided by a syndicate of banks that allows borrowers to issue short-term notes, which are then placed by the syndicate providing the NIF. Borrowers usually have the right to sell their notes to the bank syndicate at a price that yields a prearranged spread over LIBOR.

Official reserves Holdings of gold and foreign currencies by official monetary institutions.

Offshore finance subsidiary A wholly owned affiliate incorporated overseas, usually in a tax-haven country, whose function is to issue securities abroad for use in either the parent's domestic or foreign business.

Open-market operation Purchase or sale of government securities by the monetary authorities to increase or decrease the domestic money supply.

Operating exposure Degree to which an exchange rate change, in combination with price changes, will alter a company's future operating cash flows.

Optimum currency area The largest economic unit that should have the same currency. This is the area that trades off the benefits of a single currency (reduced risk and lower transactions costs) against its costs (loss of pricing flexibility).

Outright rate Actual forward rate expressed in dollars per currency unit, or vice versa.

Outsourcing The practice of purchasing a significant percentage of intermediate components from outside suppliers.

Parallel loan Simultaneous borrowing and lending operation usually involving four related parties in two different countries.

Payments netting Reducing fund transfers between affiliates to only a netted amount. Netting can be done on a bilateral basis (between pairs of affiliates) or on a multilateral basis (taking all affiliates together).

Plaza Agreement A program launched in September 1985 by the G-5 nations that was designed to force down the dollar against other major currencies and, thereby, improve American competitiveness.

Political risk Uncertain government action that affects the value of a firm.

Pooling Transfer of excess affiliate cash into a central account (pool), usually located in a low-tax nation, where all corporate funds are managed by corporate staff.

Possession Corporation A U.S. corporation operating in a U.S. possession. Such companies are entitled to certain tax breaks.

Price-specie-flow mechanism An automatic balance-of-payments adjustment mechanism under the classical gold standard whereby disturbances in the price level in one country would be wholly or partly offset by the flow of gold coins (also called specie).

Private Export Funding Corporation (PEFCO) Company that mobilized private capital for financing the export of big-ticket items by U.S. firms by purchasing at fixed interest rates the medium-to-long-term debt obligations of importers of U.S. products.

Privatization The act of returning state-owned or state-run companies back to the private sector, usually by selling them off.

Product cycle The time it takes to bring new and improved products to market. Japanese companies have excelled in compressing product cycles.

Property rights Rights of individuals and companies to own and utilize property as they see fit and to receive the stream of income that their property generates.

Protectionism Protecting domestic industry from import competition by means of tariffs, quotas, and other trade barriers.

Purchasing power parity The notion that the ratio between domestic and foreign price levels should equal the equilibrium exchange rate between domestic and foreign currencies.

Rational expectations The idea that people rationally anticipate the future and respond to what they see ahead.

Real exchange rate The spot rate adjusted for relative price level changes since a base period.

Regional fund A mutual fund that invests in a specific geographic area overseas, such as Asia or Europe.

Reinvoicing center A subsidiary that takes title to all goods sold by one corporate unit to another affiliate or to a third-party customer. The center pays the seller and in turn is paid by the buyer.

Reporting currency The currency in which the parent firm prepares its own financial statements; that is, U.S. dollars for a U.S. company.

Revaluation An increase in the spot value of a currency.

Section 482 United States Department of Treasury regulations governing transfer prices.

Securitization The matching up of borrowers and lenders wholly or partly by way of the financial markets. This process usually refers to the replacement of nonmarketable loans provided by financial intermediaries with negotiable securities issued in the public capital markets.

Single-country fund A mutual fund that invests in individual countries outside the United States, such as Germany or Thailand.

Society for Worldwide Interbank Financial Telecommunications (SWIFT) A dedicated computer network to support funds transfer messages internationally between over 900 member banks worldwide.

Sovereign risk The risk that the country or origin of a currency a bank is buying or selling will impose foreign exchange regulations that will reduce or negate the value of the contract; also refers to the risk of government default on a loan made to it or guaranteed by it.

Special Drawing Rights (SDR) A new form of international reserve assets, created by the IMF in 1967, whose value is based on a portfolio of widely used currencies.

Spot rate The price at which foreign exchange can be bought or sold with payment set for the same day.

Statement of Financial Accounting Standards No. 8 This is the currency translation standard previously in use by U.S. firms.

Statement of Financial Accounting Standards No. 52 This is the currency translation currently in use by U.S. firms.

Sterilized intervention Foreign exchange market intervention in which the monetary authorities have insulated their domestic money supplies from the foreign exchange transactions with offsetting sales or purchases or domestic assets.

Subpart F Special category of foreign-source "unearned" income that is currently taxed by the IRS whether or not it is remitted back to the United States.

Subsidiary A foreign-based affiliate that is a separately incorporated entity under the host country's law.

Swap rate The different between spot and forward rates expressed in points (e.g., $.0001 per pound sterling or DM .0001 per dollar).

SWIFT *See* Society for Worldwide Interbank Financial Telecommunications.

Systematic risk That element of an asset's risk that cannot be eliminated no matter how diversified an investor's portfolio.

Target-zone arrangement A monetary system under which countries pledge to maintain their exchange rates within a specific margin around agreed-upon, fixed central exchange rates.

Tax haven A nation with a moderate level of taxation and/or liberal tax incentives for undertaking specific activities such as exporting.

Tax Reform Act of 1986 A 1986 law involving a major overhaul of the U.S. tax system.

Terms of trade The weighted average of a nation's export prices relative to its import prices.

Total dollar return The dollar return on a nondollar investment, which includes the sum of an dividend/interest income, capital gains (losses), and currency gains (losses) on the investment.

Trade acceptance A draft accepted by a commercial enterprise; *see* Draft.

Trade draft A draft addressed to a commercial enterprise; *see* Draft.

Transaction exposure The extent to which a given exchange rate change will change the value of foreign-currency-denominated transactions already entered into.

Transfer price The price at which one unit of a firm sells goods or services to an affiliated unit.

Translation exposure *See* Accounting exposure.

Two-tier foreign exchange market This arrangement involves an official market (at the official rate) for certain transaction and a free market for remaining transaction.

Unsterilized intervention Foreign exchange market intervention in which the monetary authorities have not insulated their domestic money supplies from the foreign exchange transactions.

Value-added tax Method of indirect taxation whereby a tax is levied at each stage of production on the value added at that specific stage.

Value additivity principle The principle that the net present value of a set of independent projects is just the sum of the NPVs of the individual projects.

Value-dating Refers to when value (credit) is given for funds transferred between banks.

World Bank *See* International Bank for Reconstruction and Development.

APPENDIX A

THE EUROPEAN EXCHANGE RATE MECHANISM IS ABANDONED IN AUGUST 1993

The currency crisis of August 1993 was touched off on July 29, 1993, when the Bundesbank left its key lending rate, the discount rate, unchanged. Traders and investors had been expecting the Bundesbank to cut the discount rate to relieve the pressure on the French franc and other weak currencies within the ERM. As had happened the year before, however, the Bundesbank largely disregarded the pleas of its ERM partners and concentrated on reining in 4.3% German inflation and its fast-growing money supply, both of which stem from the spiraling cost of bailing out the former East Germany. Given the way the ERM works, and the central role played by the Deutsche mark, other countries could not both lower interest rates and keep their currencies within their ERM bands unless Germany did so.

The French franc was the main focus of the ERM struggle. With high real interest rates, recession, and unemployment running at a post–World War II high of 11.6%, speculators doubted that France had the will power to stay with the Bundesbank's tight monetary policy and allow its interest rates to decline only gradually in line with German rates. The initial onslaught against the franc was triggered in early July by news of France's (and Europe's) gloomier economic prospects. Against this background, investors had grave doubts about whether the French government would be willing to keep interest rates high, much less raise them to defend the franc. Speculators reacted logically: They dumped the French franc and other European currencies and bought DM, gambling that economic pressures, such as rising unemployment and deepening recession, would prevent these countries from keeping their interest rates well above those in Germany.

The speculators smelled blood on Friday, July 30, following the Bundesbank's refusal to help out its ERM partners. Despite heavy foreign exchange market intervention (the Bundesbank alone spent $35 billion trying to prop up the franc), the devastating assault by speculators on the ERM forced the franc to its ERM floor of DM 0.29150. Other European central banks also intervened heavily to support the Danish krone, Spanish peseta, Portuguese escudo, and Belgian franc, which came under heavy attack as well.

It was all to no avail, however. Without capital controls, or a credible commitment to move to a single currency in the near future, speculators could easily take advantage of a one-sided bet. The result was massive capital flows that overwhelmed the central banks to stabilize exchange rates. Over the weekend of July 31–August 1, the EC finance ministers agreed to essentially abandon the defense of each other's currencies. Under the new plan, announced on August 2, seven of the nine currencies could trade within a band of 15% above or below their central rates. The band for the peseta and the escudo was set at ±6%, while Germany and the Netherlands agreed to maintain the old 2.25% flunctuation range between their currencies. The immediate effect of the radically wider bands on the DM:FF exchange rate was a sharp drop in the DM value of the French franc. Because the new trading bands are so wide, the European Monetary System has become a floating-rate system in all but name only. Its preservation in form, but not substance, provides a fig leaf for politicians to say the system is still in place.

In response to the crack-up of the ERM, and investors' belief that decoupling their economies from Germany would allow France and its neighbors to lower interest rates, bond markets in France, Denmark, Spain, Italy, Belgium, and Sweden rallied. U.S. and European stock markets also rose on the belief that falling interest rates and cheaper currencies would bring with them stronger European economic growth. In effect, investors appeared to accept the conventional wisdom that abandoning the ERM would liberate these nations from the recessionary straitjacket of tight German monetary policy and its resulting high interest rates. That, in fact, is what happened after Britain pulled out of the ERM in September 1992 and let the pound fall against other European currencies (in effect, a competitive devaluation). While continental Europe remained mired in recession, Britain's economy began growing. A risk is that other nations will also be tempted to engage in competitive devaluations, an old habit that the ERM was supposed to do away with. An even bigger risk is that the monetary disarray will further erode Europeans' interest in pursuing economic integration.

Although the events of August 2, 1993, bear a striking resemblance to the currency crisis of September 1992, there is one big difference: The August crisis was not triggered by differences in current economic fundamentals. Rather, it was generated by the belief that the Bundesbank would not reduce its interest rates sufficiently to permit cuts in interest rates in countries—particularly France and Denmark—where unemployment was high and inflation low. In other words, the French franc and Danish krone were not considered to be overvalued, given their higher interest rates, lower inflation rates (the French inflation rate at 1.9% was less than half that of Germany), and relatively sounder economies than Germany. Nonetheless, based on the historical behavior of their central banks, it was commonly believed that France and other ERM nations would likely reflate their economies (by priming the monetary pump) to cope with recession (whereas Germany would maintain its tight money policy), thereby making current exchange rates unrealistic. This is a powerful example of the role of expectations in driving exchange rates. Of course, if France had an independent central bank (it doesn't) that had historically demonstrated its commitment to price stability (it hasn't), it could have had both low interest rates *and* a strong currency.

At the same time, the currency turmoil showed once again that a genuinely stable European Monetary System, and eventually a single currency, requires the political will to direct fiscal and monetary policies at that European goal and not at purely national ones. In showing that they lacked that will, European governments proved once again that allowing words to run ahead of actions is a recipe for failure.

The events of August 1993 also demonstrated that any currency system that becomes too rigid—unless it is a single currency system—will eventually come apart. In the case of the ERM, its rigidity precluded it from adjusting to economic shocks. And, no shock could have been bigger than German unification and the huge budget deficits that flowed from it. By not permitting the DM to appreciate against other ERM currencies right after reunification, the stage was set for a future blowout, which was bigger than it would have been if the currency realignment had been made three years earlier.

INDEX

Frequently Used Symbols and Acronyms

a_h	Expected real return on home currency loan
a_f	Expected real return on a foreign currency loan
ADR	American Depository Receipt
APV	Adjusted present value
B/L	Bill of lading
β	Beta coefficient, a measure of an asset's riskiness
$\beta*$	All-equity beta
β_e	Levered β
C_t	Local currency cash flows in period t
C	Cost
d	Amount of currency devaluation
D	Forward discount
D_f	Amount of foreign currency debt
e_t	Nominal exchange rate at time t
e_t'	Real exchange rate at time t
E	Amount of equity
E_f	Foreign subsidiary retained earnings
f_t	t-period forward exchange rate
HC	Home currency
i_d	Before-tax cost of domestic debt
i_f	(a) Expected foreign inflation rate or (b) Before-tax cost of foreign debt
i_h	Expected home country inflation rate
I_0	Initial investment
IRPT	Interest rate parity theorem
k	Cost of capital
k_0	Weighted cost of capital
k_e	Cost of equity capital given the firm's degree of leverage